HISTORY OF THE LABOR MOVEMENT
IN THE UNITED STATES
VOLUME III

BY PHILIP S. FONER

History of the Labor Movement in the United States VOLUME I: *From Colonial Times to the Founding of the American Federation of Labor* VOLUME II: *From the Founding of the American Federation of Labor to the Emergence of American Imperialism*

A History of Cuba and Its Relations with the United States (2 vols.)
The Life and Writings of Frederick Douglass (4 vols.)
The Complete Writings of Thomas Paine (2 vols.)
Business and Slavery: The New York Merchants and the Irrepressible Conflict
The Fur and Leather Workers Union
Jack London: American Rebel
Mark Twain: Social Critic
The Jews in American History: 1654–1865
The Basic Writings of Thomas Jefferson
The Selected Writings of George Washington
The Selected Writings of Abraham Lincoln
The Selected Writings of Franklin D. Roosevelt

HISTORY OF
THE LABOR MOVEMENT
IN THE UNITED STATES

— V, 3 —

VOLUME III: The Policies and Practices
of the American Federation of Labor,
1900–1909

BY PHILIP S. FONER

INTERNATIONAL PUBLISHERS, *NEW YORK*

© *copyright by* INTERNATIONAL PUBLISHERS CO., INC., 1964

Fourth Printing 1981

For this edition the author has added the footnotes on pages 135 and 412

ISBN 0-7178-0093-8 (cloth); 0-7178-0389-9 (paperback)

Library of Congress Catalog Card Number: 47-19381

MANUFACTURED IN THE UNITED STATES OF AMERICA

CONTENTS

PREFACE

The period from 1900 to America's entrance into the World War in April 1917 is one of the most important in the entire history of the American labor movement. During these years, the fundamental policies and practices of the American Federation of Labor were shaped. It was during this period, too, that the opposition to these policies and practices emerged most sharply. This period, moreover, saw the greatest growth of the Socialist Party and its greatest influence within the American labor movement.

Because of the significance of the period and the vast body of sources to which I had access, three volumes will be devoted to this era. The present volume covers the policies and practices of the A.F. of L. in the years 1900–1909. The next volume will cover the history of the Industrial Workers of the World from its formation in 1905 to America's entrance into World War I, the period of the greatest activity of the I.W.W. The third volume will deal with the A.F. of L., the Railroad Brotherhoods, and the Socialists, 1909–1917.

I have referred above to the vast body of sources available to me in studying the period 1900 to 1917. Unfortunately, the most important of these sources is no longer fully available to scholars. This is the incoming correspondence of the American Federation of Labor, once a rich treasure-house of the letters of A.F. of L. officials, international and local unions, and of leaflets and pamphlets, often the only copies in existence. For many years, I was privileged to be able to study this vast collection housed in the basement of the old A.F. of L. building in Washington, D.C. Unfortunately, most of the material was destroyed prior to the A.F. of L.'s move to new headquarters. A small fraction has been preserved on microfilm—mainly manuscripts and records of routine interest—and a small collection was transferred to the Wisconsin State Historical Society. But of the many crates, letter boxes and file drawers in the basement of the old A.F. of L. building, only a tiny portion has survived, and much of this is of only marginal value. (*See,* in this connection, Edward T. James, "Where Are the A.F. of L. Papers," *Labor Historians' Bulletin,* Spring, 1959, pp. 1–5.) This is a tragic loss, not only for scholars but also for the labor movement itself.

Apart from the incoming correspondence of the A.F. of L. and the Letter-Books of Samuel Gompers, in preparing the present volume I have had access to collections of manuscripts, newspapers, pamphlets, and unpublished and published studies in numerous libraries and historical societies. I wish to thank the staffs of the Chicago Historical Society, Chicago

Public Library, Historical Society of Montana, Lewiston (Maine) Public Library, Library of the Department of Labor, Washington D.C., Library of Congress, Library of the London School of Economics, Milwaukee County Historical Commission, National Archives, New York Public Library, Rockland (Maine) Public Library, Tamiment Institute Library, Wisconsin State Historical Society, and the libraries of the following colleges and universities: Robert Brookings School of Economics and Government, Catholic University of America, Chicago, California, Columbia, Cornell, Hartford Seminary Foundation, Harvard, Indiana, Iowa, Michigan, New School for Social Research, University of London, New York, Northwestern, Notre Dame, Princeton, Radcliffe, Rochester, Southern California, Stanford, Stevens Institute of Technology, Teachers College (Columbia University), Wisconsin, Vanderbilt, and Yale. I wish to thank Dr. Bernard Mandel for the opportunity to read his definitive biography of Samuel Gompers in manuscript prior to its publication. I wish also to thank Mrs. Louise Heinze, Director of the Tamiment Institute Library, for valuable assistance in obtaining material through interlibrary loan. Finally, I wish to express my gratitude to the Louis M. Rabinowitz Foundation for a grant which made publication of the present volume possible.

PHILIP S. FONER

Croton-on-Hudson, New York
March 1964

ABBREVIATIONS USED IN FOOTNOTES AND REFERENCE NOTES

AFL Corr.—American Federation of Labor Correspondence, American Federation of Labor Archives, American Federation of Labor Building, Washington, D.C.

GLB.—Samuel Gompers Letter-Books, American Federation of Labor Building. Washington, D.C.

JFP.—John P. Frey Papers, Library of Congress, Washington, D.C.

JMP.—John Mitchell Papers, Mullen Library of the Catholic University of America, Washington, D.C.

NCFA.—National Civic Federation Archives, New York Public Library

TIL.—Tamiment Institute Library, New York City

TRP.—Theodore Roosevelt Papers, Library of Congress, Washington, D.C.

WSHS.—Wisconsin State Historical Society, Madison, Wisconsin

CHAPTER I

Labor Moves into a New Century

American capitalism entered the 20th century in a joyful mood. The economic crisis of the 'nineties had gradually receded, and once again "prosperity" had dawned. By the turn of the century, the ground lost during the depression years which began in 1893 had more than been regained, and business men were entering an era of high profits. "There are going to be more great fortunes in this country," the *New York Times* prophesied on January 3, 1900. "Millionaires will be commonplace and the country will be the better for them, better for their wealth, better for the good they will do in giving employment to labor in the industries which produce their fortunes."

CAPITAL REJOICES

Frederick Winslow Taylor had already written the first of a steady stream of books and articles expounding his new doctrine of "scientific management" which—by speeding up the work, timing the worker's task by stop watch, and gearing his wage to the time of performance—promised augmented profits in the new century.[1]

American capitalists pointed with pride to the fact that during the last decade of the 19th century, despite the depression, the United States had emerged as the world's foremost industrial power. In 1890 the United States had taken over world leadership in the production of iron and steel. In 1899 the United States had become the world's largest producer of coal. In the late 'nineties, American banking made its first important ventures into the field of foreign finance. Between 1896 and 1900, $100,-000,000 of American capital was exported to Canada, and in 1900 and 1901, American financiers furnished one-fifth of the funds for the Boer War.[2]

Especially for big business the new century promised unparalleled profits. Vast numbers of small concerns were being swept up and gathered into a few enormous enterprises, capitalized at huge sums and often possessing monopoly or near-monopoly control over the business of their respective fields. During the years from 1898 to 1903, the period of most intensive consolidation, some 276 new combinations were organized and the first billion-dollar corporation, U.S. Steel, established in 1901, had been created. The steel combine, organized by the House of Morgan with a capital of $1,400,000,000, welded together 11 big steel, mining and shipping companies into one economic empire with practical control of most of the heavy industries concerned with metal, fuel, and transport, from the Atlantic Coast to the iron and copper, lead, zinc and gold mines of the Rocky Mountains and California.

By 1904, according to John Moody, noted financial expert and editor, "about 445 active trusts" had been formed, with a total capitalization of $20,379,162,551—almost one-seventh the national wealth at the time. Moody classified the following industries as controlled by the "greater industrial trusts": copper, smelting, sugar, tobacco, marine (or shipping), oil, and steel. Three of these trusts were "dominated" by Standard Oil (the Rockefellers) and two of them by the Morgan interests. But there was a high degree of mutual interest existing between the two financial titans. The Rockefeller group held a minority position on the board of Morgan's U.S. Steel. On the other hand, Robert Baker, a Morgan man, served on the board of Rockefeller's Amalgamated Copper Co.[3] Industrial and banking capital were thus combined and on the way to establishing a secure hold over American economic life.

The United States was now a world power. A new American empire had come into being as a result of the Spanish-American War. The Philippines and Puerto Rico were American possessions; Cuba was an American protectorate, and along with Guam and Hawaii, these areas furnished new opportunities for investment abroad.

The political scene at the turn of the century gave American capitalists additional cause to rejoice. A pro-imperialist, Republican administration, openly operating as an agency of big business, was in the saddle, and every sign pointed to its continuation in office for years to come. In January 1901, Isaac Cowen, the general organizer of the American branches of the British Engineers' Union, wrote to London: "America has the advantage of the skill and ingenuity of men from all nations of the world who have come here to seek a home. . . . As a rule, the Rockefellers, Morgans, Vanderbilts, Carnegies and other trust magnates have captured these benefits for themselves, either through prostrated courts, bribed legislators, or using the gatling gun wherever organized labor demanded a small portion of their product."

A leading capitalist told the American press in January 1903: "We have good reason for rejoicing. We have done more business and sold more goods, both at home and abroad, than ever before. Prices of agricultural products and manufactured articles have gone upward. . . . Manufacturing concerns have extended their operations enormously and Business Men have sold more goods and at a better price than they anticipated."[4]

PROSPERITY FOR WHOM?

Labor, however, had no great cause for rejoicing. The economic crisis of the 1890's had taken a severe toll in the workers' living standards, and they enjoyed few of the fruits of the so-called "unprecedented prosperity." Testimony before the Industrial Commission of 1900, a federal agency, revealed that wages, on the average, were 10 per cent lower than they were before the panic of 1893. Carroll D. Wright, U.S. Commissioner of Labor, testified that there had been a constant decrease in wages since 1893, and that only a few skilled trades had recuperated the losses sustained during the crisis years. Prof. T. S. Adams calculated that in 1900 only 16.2 per cent of the workers received $15 or more per week; that the median wage was about $10.05 a week, and that the average yearly earnings were something like $480. Professor Adams was quick to add that this average annual wage applied only to workers who were fully employed. Yet, according to the Census of 1900, nearly six and one-half million workers were unemployed during some part of the year, and of these, nearly two million were idle four to six months out of the twelve.[5] The seasonal aspect of so many trades, together with numerous other reasons for unemployment, were an important factor in reducing total yearly earnings. The truth is that most workers never knew when unemployment and long periods of idleness would rap at their doors.

In 1900, Andrew Carnegie made $23,000,000 with no income tax to pay. That same year a government investigation of conditions in the anthracite regions disclosed that the miners' wages averaged $240 a year—about $4.60 a week. Small wonder workers laughed bitterly when they read the headlines in the press: "Coal a Barometer of Prosperity!"[6]

Noting that women workers in New York's clothing industry earned 30 cents a day in 1900, Frederick Lewis Allen observed in 1952: "Try translating that into terms of today: even after you have multiplied it by three to take into account the tripled cost of living, you arrive at the noble sum of 90 cents a day, which is $5.40 a week, which is $280.00 for a full working year!"[7] Try translating, too, the wages of women who as late as 1910 were working in Chicago's cigar factories from five A.M. until six P.M. for $2.40 a week, averaging 40 cents a day.[8]

Wages for most skilled workers advanced in the years following the depression of the 'nineties, but for some skilled and for the vast majority of the unorganized unskilled workers, wages advanced only slightly or were nearly stationary. Meanwhile, the prices of commodities rose earlier and went higher than the wages of labor. A contemporary study disclosed that the cost of food to the average working-class family increased 16 per cent between 1896 and 1903. The same study revealed that the cost of such commodities as coal and coal oil had increased 40 per cent and of rent 20 per cent. "In view of these facts," the study concluded, "the working man may well ask what has become of his share of the great prosperity of the country."[9]

In 1914 the cost of living was 39 per cent higher than it had been in the 1890's. At the same time earnings in terms of purchasing power (real wages) did not show any increase, and, in fact, were precisely the same as they had been in the decade 1890–1899.[10]

American workers, Socialist Congressman Victor L. Berger declared in August 1911, in supporting his old-age pension plan in the Congress (the first straight pension plan ever introduced in that body), had an average income of not over $400 annually, received a small part of what they produced, and spent it all merely to survive.* From the turn of the century until 1914 a living wage was the exception not the rule for one-half to two-thirds of American wage earners. Indeed, two leading authorities on labor economics estimated that during this period, three-fourths of the adult male wage earners did not earn sufficient incomes to provide standard families with a minimum level of health and decency, while many did not even earn enough to maintain their families above the poverty level. This estimate included families in which members other than the husband were contributing to the total earnings. In a book simply named *Poverty,* Robert Hunter in 1904 revealed that of the total population of 80,000,000 some 10,000,000 lived in poverty, "underfed, under-clothed, and poorly housed," with 4,000,000 of them public paupers. In 1905, Rev. Henry Van Dyke, addressing the Interchurch Conference on Federation, asked: "What shall we say of the modern industrial order, in which one man in ten is doomed to hopeless poverty, and the right to live is made impossible for many? . . . The right to be happy is blotted out for thousands of families, each herded in a single room and hungering for daily bread."[11]

The *World Almanac* of 1902 listed 4,000 American millionaires! The extremes of wealth and poverty were as great as those in the Old World.

On one page of the August 24, 1902, issue of the Baltimore *Sun* there appeared a huge picture of President Theodore Roosevelt telling a group of people of "the great prosperity of the American workingman to-day." On the other side of the same sheet there was the following extract from a report of Mr. J. G. Schonfarber of the Maryland Board of Statistics

---

* On January 13, 1912, Berger stated in Congress that the average income of American workers was $476 and the amount produced was worth $1,150, giving the "capitalist exploiter" a surplus value or profit of $674. (*Cong. Record,* 62nd Cong., 2nd Sess., p. 930.)

who had been investigating wages and cost of living in the city of Baltimore:

"Only two of twenty typical Baltimore workingmen's families own their own homes, and only two of them are able to save anything from their earnings. Eight of the twenty have a total income of less three hundred dollars. The average number in each family is eight persons. The average earnings per family, in many instances being the total from three to five persons, is but a trifle more than six hundred dollars per annum. When distributed among this average family of eight, the amount upon which a person is compelled to subsist and meet all expenditures of life is less than eighty dollars per capita per year, or about $1.50 each week. Ten of these twenty families consumed their income, but did not run into debt. Eight of them, however, were in debt at the end of the year at amounts ranging from $30 to $200. Some of this deficit was due to the misfortune of illness, but more of it was due to the necessarily idle time and the small amount of wages paid when at work."

The wages of coal miners were so small in 1902, declared Rev. James V. Hussie, pastor of St. Gabriel's Church, Hazleton, Pennsylvania, that the miners' families could not meet the necessary expenses. He asked several of his flock—90 per cent of his parishioners were miners—about funeral expenses, especially one German because "I consider the German very frugal. . . . He told me that it took him six years to pay the funeral expenses of $200.00."[12]

PLIGHT OF THE CHILDREN

The following description was given by an investigator for the Chicago Board of Education in 1908:

"Five thousand children who attend the public schools of Chicago are habitually hungry. . . .

"I further report that 10,000 other children in the city—while in not such extreme cases as the aforesaid—do not have sufficient nourishing food. . . .

"There are several thousand more children under six who are also underfed, and who are too young to attend school.

"The question of food is not the only question to be considered. Many of the children lack shoes and clothing. Many have no beds to sleep in. They cuddle together on hard floors. The majority of the indigent children live in damp, unclean or overcrowded homes, that lack proper ventilation and sanitation."[13]

Most of the children described above went to school. But in 1900, 284,-000 children between the ages of 10 and 15 spent their days in mills, factories, mines, and shops. In 1903 children strikers who worked in Philadelphia's textile mills for 60 hours a week carried signs which read:

WE WANT TO GO TO SCHOOL!
MORE SCHOOLS LESS HOSPITALS!
PROSPERITY! WHERE IS OUR SHARE?
55 HOURS OR NOTHING![14]

What of the children in Chicago's stockyards? Here is the state factory inspector's description of what these children, most of them below the age of 14, had to endure: "Some of these boys act as butchers, sticking sheep, lambs and swine; others cut the hide from the quivering flesh of freshly stunned cattle; still others sort entrails, pack meat and make the tin cans in which the goods are shipped. In several places a boy has been found at work at a dangerous machine. *Because his father had been disabled by it,* and his keeping the place depended upon the boy's doing the work during the father's absence."[15]

In Chicago's stamping works and canning factories, reported Prof. William O. Krohn, "not a day passes but some child is made a helpless cripple. These accidents occur after three o'clock in the afternoon. The child that has begun his work in the morning with a reasonable degree of vigor, after working under constant pressure for several hours, at about three o'clock becomes so wearied, beyond the point of recovery, that he can no longer direct the tired fingers and aching arms with any degree of accuracy. He thus becomes the prey of the great cutting knives, or of the jaws of the tin-stamping machine."[16]

In New York's canning factories, a State Factory Investigating Commission reported, the children became "little machines with their fingers tied up in rags," for their wrists and fingers were sore from snipping beans or husking corn all day. Many boys and girls under 14 worked from four in the morning until nine or ten at night. Mary Chamberlain, one of the investigators for the Factory Commission, testified as follows on the hours of labor of a girl named Milly, aged 10:

"On August 15th [1912], she worked from 11 A.M. until 6:45 P.M.—7 and ¾ hours, and ate only a peach for lunch. On August 17th, she worked from 7:30 A.M. until 10:30 A.M., picking; 10:30 A.M. to 3 P.M. snipping, and a little bread and butter for lunch—total 7 and ½ hours. August 20th, she worked from 4:30 A.M. until 7:30 A.M. snipping; 11 A.M. until 12:30 P.M. snipping; 1 P.M. until 6 P.M. snipping; 6:30 P.M. until 9:30 P.M. snipping—Total 12 and ½ hours."

"Q: That child went to work that day at what hour? A: 4:30 in the morning."

"Q: And she stopped work at what time? A: 9:30 P.M."

This grinding routine without enough sleep combined with carrying heavy crates, weighing from 40 to 60 pounds, produced terribly exhausted children.[17]

Factory laws in many states prohibited the employment of children under 14, but it was common knowledge that thousands upon thousands of children worked who were far below that age. Concealment was easy. Pauline Newman recalls that in all her years on the job in New York's garment trades she remembers only one visit by a factory inspector and on that occasion, "the event was made known to us when we youngsters were hidden in wooden cases covered with shirt waists and told not to move lest the inspectors discover us." The New York State Factory Investigating Commission reported cases where "children were put in the elevators, which were lowered so they were between the floors and could not be seen" by factory inspectors.[18]

The law of Pennsylvania prescribed that no children under the age of 14 should be employed inside the mine and none under the age of 12 outside the mine. This law was a dead letter. Some of the operators demanded a sworn statement from the parents that their boys were of legal age before they would employ them. This statement was often given falsely by the parents on account of their poverty. Other operators did not even demand such a statement. As a result thousands of boys below the legal age worked every day the collieries operated. Their job was to pick impurities from the coal as it passed through the chutes and screens. Inhaling dust-laden air, they sat all day in a cramped position on a board over the chute. For this work they received 27, 33 or 39 cents for a 10-hour day.[19]

Throughout the United States—in Philadelphia, New York, New Orleans, everywhere, from one end of the country to the other—children were being denied the right of childhood. They grew up with bodies and minds stunted from being forced to work at a tender age in textile mills, glass factories, coal mines, cigar factories, slaughter houses, and in tenement house sweatshops.[20]

"Just think of it," Dr. William H. Maxwell, Superintendent of Public Schools of New York City, told an audience of educators in 1903. "Think of today in these great United States, children five and six years old, working from 6 in the morning until 6 in the evening, and at the hardest and most trying kind of labor. These children are being ruined by thousands by manufacturers." If the manufacturers and their spokesmen thought of it at all, they justified this tragic state of affairs with such arguments as "boys are better off at work than loafing around saloons. Our substantial citizens are men who as boys worked in the factories."

The program of the National Child Labor Committee was denounced by mill owners as socialistic, un-Christian, and meddling with parental authority over children. Asa G. Candler of Atlanta, the founder of Coca-Cola, declared: "The most beautiful sight that we see is the child at labor; as early as he may get at labor the more beautiful, the most useful does his life get to be." Indeed, it was "an element of strength not only of national strength in a commercial sense, but strength of a municipality as well, that it has factories in which unemployed child labor may be employed."[21] It was evidently not a measure of a nation's strength that its children were in schools!

WAGES AND HOURS

An independent survey made in 1909 estimated that $800 was the lowest possible annual income with which a family could maintain the minimum requirements of health, working efficiency, and social decency. Six years later, the New York State Factory Commission estimated that $876 was the yearly income necessary to sustain a family of 3.3 consuming units. In February 1914 the New York Association for Improving the Condition of the Poor estimated that a family of five must have a minimum annual income of $1,058 "for the family to live in such a way as to preserve health, mind, character, self-respect and proper conditions of family life." Yet in an investigation of 109,481 workers employed by 693 firms, conducted by the New York State Factory Commission, it was brought out that one-half of all the wage earners received less than $8 a week, one-eighth less than $5, one-third less than $10 and only one-sixth were paid $15 or more. The Commission discovered that in a whole series of industries—paper box, confectionery, shirt, and millinery—the average wages were frequently below the estimated required living wage. In the millinery industry, for example, the median salary was between $8 and $9 a week, while 20 per cent of those investigated reported earnings of less than $5. More than half earned below $9, and only nine per cent of the workers received $15 a week or more. In the garment industries, more than half the workers received a wage of from $10 to $12 a week, and 15 to 30 per cent of the working force, classified as learners, received $3 to $6 a week. The seasonal nature of work in this field reduced average wages to even lower figures, as did fines imposed by employers because of lateness, breakage and mistakes, and in some factories, because of charges for the use of sewing machines, needle and thread. The average yearly income of New York dock workers fluctuated between $520 and $624 a year.[22]

In 1905 the average weekly wage of women in all industries was $5.25. But many worked for less. Of 473 women workers interviewed, 28 per cent earned less than $300 yearly, 53 per cent between $300 and $500 and only 7 per cent $600 or more. The position of these workers was best expressed by a woman who earned $6.00 a week: "I didn't live. I simply existed. I couldn't live what you would call living. I certainly had to deprive myself of lots of things I should have had. It took me months and months to save up money to buy a dress or a suit or a pair of shoes. . . . I had the hardest struggle I ever had in my life."[23]

Employers discriminated against women by paying them less for the same work than they paid men. The clothing industry paid women 68.5 per cent of the salary given to men employees. The hourly rate for women 16 and over was .148 cents; that for men .216 cents. In the packing plants, if a man received $1.75 a day for a certain job, a woman would receive $1.25 for performing the same task.[24]

All over the United States long working hours were the rule. Men worked 12 or 14 hours a day. In the steel industry workers put in 12 hours a day, seven days a week, and won a Sunday of rest every other week only by working the dreaded "long turn" of 24 hours on the alternate Sunday. An investigation of the steel industry disclosed that some men worked as long as "thirty-six hours at a stretch." In the transit systems, carmen worked seven days a week with no provision for a day off. The basic working day was 10 hours time actually spent on a car run, but it frequently took 14 or 15 hours on the job to receive 10 hours pay. Transit employers made no provision for additional overtime wages.

Women toiled long hours at night as well as day. Indeed, night work for women was a general practice. Many women worked night shifts in book binderies and laundries, in candy, paper box, and garment factories. Work usually started after supper and lasted until the early hours of the morning or even to dawn. Many women with a home and children to care for slept only four hours a day. Investigators described these women as "worn looking," "pale, with drawn white faces, and stooping gait."[25]

"Standing outside the door of a factory where twine is manufactured," wrote one investigator, "we watched the women come out. Pale, narrow-chested, from head to foot, they were covered with fibrous dust. . . . They were types of factory workers—pale, haggard feeders of machines —like those described in the days of a century past in England. The fibre . . . must rest heavily in the lungs of women who bend over rushing, whirring machines ten hours a day without fresh air and exercise."

The same writer also told of girls in the binding industry who worked 13 hours a day, 78 hours a week and were discharged if they refused unpaid overtime.[26]

Mrs. Florence Kelley, at one time a factory inspector in Illinois, observed: "In Chicago the laundries maintain hours which are regularly irregular. Monday being a short day and Friday and Saturday having neither beginning nor ending except as work is completed. It is no rare thing for girls to faint at their work. Girls have been removed from the laundry to the hospital suffering exhaustion after working sixteen, eighteen and even twenty hours in heat and dampness in ill-ventilated laundries."[27]

Women in New York canneries frequently worked 15, 16 or 17 hours a day for as little as 10 cents an hour. It was common for women to work 70 hours a week continuously for many weeks. Before and after their grueling work in the cannery, most of these women did their own housekeeping—they cooked, made beds, washed, and took care of the children. One investigator testified that the floors of these canneries were "concrete and covered with water; the room was hot and full of steam; the noise of the machinery was deafening, and the combination was more than I could stand."[28] Yet thousands of women had to face the drudgery, week in and out, of standing at work in such factories all day and part of the night.

Under such conditions the "Promise of American Life" became an illusion. There was little more to life than an endless routine of work, eat, sleep, and work. The end, if one escaped death or crippling injury, was old age at forty.

ACCIDENTS AND HEALTH HAZARDS

Not too many workers, however, escaped. The absence of standards of safety was typical throughout most of American industry. In the single year 1901, one out of every 399 railroad employees was killed, and one out of every 26 was injured. Among engineers, conductors, brakemen, trainmen, the figures for that single year showed that one out of every 137 was killed. Colorado mines took an average of 6.2 lives for every one thousand employed in 1901; the average rose in 1905 to 8.15.[29]

In one year it was found that over 50,000 accidents had taken place in New York factories alone, in which 167 workers had been killed. Safety experts concluded that this cruel and unnecessary toll of human life and limb could have been reduced by two-thirds if simple and inexpensive precautions had been taken. Such things as guards on saws, halls that were lighted, passenger elevators that were enclosed, and fire escapes that worked could have cut the number of accidents by at least one-half.[30]

In the testimony to the State Factory Investigating Commission given by the Fire Commission of New York City, the factory buildings were described as simply filled with rubbish piled in all corners without thought of systematic disposal of refuse. Such factories were terrible fire hazards. The Fire Commissioner of New York City testified: "I think that a great many of the fire escapes in buildings to-day are only put up to be called a fire escape. They are absolutely inadequate and absolutely useless."[31]

How inadequate and useless was indelibly etched in the public mind on Saturday, March 25, 1911. At 10 minutes to five, just before closing, the fire alarm sounded in the Triangle Waist Co. shop at Washington Place and Greene Street in New York City. The company occupied the three upper stories of a 10-story building which had no outside fire escapes. A fire escape in the light shaft was to prove a death trap. The door to one of the stairways was locked. The other one was blocked by fire. The only way out was through the elevators. Panic soon gripped the girls, most of whom were Italian and Jewish immigrants. The fire spread quickly. Many workers were burned to death; many were crushed when they tried to jump to safety. Others were impaled on a fence in the light shaft. The fire escape did not reach to the ground, and those in front were pushed off onto iron spokes beneath by those crowding behind them. In all, 145 of the 500 workers, predominantly young girls, lost their lives—victims of a system that showed more concern for improved machinery than for improved working conditions. All of the conditions in the loft that made the tragedy inevitable—floors littered with flammable materials; narrow staircases in draughty, vertical wells; doors at the landings that opened inward if they opened at all (and one did not); the absence of sprinklers—had been called to the attention of the owners and employers many times. But nothing was done.* On the contrary, a Fire Department suggestion for the use of sprinklers had been rejected by a property owners' association on the ground that the cost amounted to "confiscation."[32]

In 1904 a corps of expert statisticians compiled figures showing the mortality in trades and occupations commonly classed as dangerous. Of the 19,659,440 workers in various parts of the country whose records were examined, the mortality due to conditions on the job in manufacturing industries, was 15,136, and in the transportation and agricultural industries, 12,005. Of these workers, also, 643.07 hat and cap makers per 100,000 succumbed to pulmonary and respiratory diseases; cigar and tobacco workers, 454.45, and marble and stone workers, 398.73. Other occupations in which the mortality was very high were those of quarrymen, masons, carpenters (one carpenter in every 1,212 was killed in the single year 1903), bricklayers, railroad workers, glass polishers, bottlers, garment workers, iron workers, painters, dyers, printers, enamelers, miners—in short, a pretty fair cross section of the American working class.

In the pottery factories where the air was filled all day with choking dust clouds asthma took a huge toll; in the glass factories, lead poisoning produced a large mortality year after year (the carriage builder, the plumber, the painter, the dyer, and the enameler were also prey to it); in the lithographic printing trades, arsenic poisoning claimed its annual victims; in the bottling establishments, serious injuries were caused by the explosion of bottles of aerated water, and many an eye was blown out; in the sweatshops of New York, where hundreds of thousands of garment workers were huddled together in a few filthy East Side

---

* The Triangle Fire led to the appointment of the New York State Factory Investigating Commission.

garrets, the mortality rate from a wide variety of diseases was incredibly high. "It is an undeniable fact," the report concluded, "that several millions of men and women in the United States are to-day engaged in occupations that yearly take their toll of human life and health as inevitably, as inexorably as the seasons roll in their grooves."[33]

The Cleveland *Citizen* put it more tersely when it called the United States "the industrial slaughter house."[34]

The Coroner's jury had the usual explanation for the death of a worker in a mine, mill or factory: "That deceased met death due to his negligence." Or: "The deceased came to his death by an accident that was unavoidable." In general, nothing was said of the absence of safety devices; of the refusal of the corporations to abide by the state codes or recommendations by inspection officials, or of the failure of these officials to enforce their recommendations; of incredible speed-up on the job; of the fact that workers who complained about dangerous conditions or refused to work in dangerous factories and mines were discharged and blacklisted. But the reports of the state Bureaus of Labor Statistics tell a long tale of human destruction caused by negligence and greed on the part of corporations too much concerned with maximum production at minimum cost to provide adequate safeguards for their workers.[35]

The heavy accident rate in American industry was even more appalling considering the absence of workmen's compensation. The surviving widow and children were left to wage a hopeless struggle against poverty and insecurity. The following dialogue in 1913 between a U.S. government investigator and the President of the Victor-American Fuel Co. of Colorado, a Rockefeller-controlled corporation, could have been duplicated in every state during the opening decade of the 20th century:

"*Commissioner Weinstock:* 'How do you deal with injured workers? How are they compensated, if at all, during the existing conditions?'

"*Mr. Osgood:* 'We have no system; we have no regular plan of compensation; we have no compensation law in this state.'

"*Mr. Weinstock:* 'If a worker loses his life, are his dependents compensated in any way?'

"*Mr. Osgood:* 'Not necessarily. In some cases they are and in some cases not.'

"*Mr. Weinstock:* 'If he is crippled for life is there any compensation?'

"*Mr. Osgood:* 'No sir; there is none.'

"*Mr. Weinstock:* 'The question is suggested as to whether their pay goes on if they are injured during the period of their injury?'

"*Mr. Osgood:* 'It does not.'

"*Mr. Weinstock:* 'Then the whole burden is thrown directly upon their shoulders?'

"*Mr. Osgood:* 'Yes, sir.'

"*Mr. Weinstock:* 'The industry bears none of it?'

"*Mr. Osgood:* 'No; the industry bears none of it.' "[36]

The first workmen's compensation acts were passed in Germany in 1884 and in England in 1897. But in 1896, 12 years after Germany under Bismarck had evolved the idea of workmen's accident compensation, a labor law text published in New York made no reference to employers' liability, and none to workmen's compensation.[37]

The first American workmen's compensation law was passed by Maryland in 1902, but it was declared unconstitutional. The compensation laws of Montana (1909) and New York (1910) were also declared unconstitutional on the grounds that they deprived employers of their property without due process of law. Judge William E. Warner, speaking for the New York Court in the decision handed down on March 24, 1911, noted: "The statute [the Workmen's Compensation Law] judged by our common-law standards, is plainly revolutionary."[38]

The basic principle of the common law is that: "The employer is liable only in case he is at fault; that is, he must have been negligent in some respect and this negligence must have been the proximate and sole cause of the accident." The common law thus prevented the workman from obtaining relief unless he could show that the employer was solely to blame, and that rarely could be proven, for many accidents were not the result of anybody's "fault or wrong" but the consequence of the inevitable risks of a trade. A study of 1,500 serious factory accidents in New York State during 1909 revealed "that the average machine stamp will once in so many thousand times crush and mangle a finger, that each revolving belting will in so many thousand revolutions tear away a worker's arm, and that the ratio is as exact and remorseless as the ratio of deaths that go to make up a mortality table of the life insurance companies." The report emphasized that the appalling ratio of maimed and crippled was "a constant accompaniment of the use of machinery, no matter what preventive devices were used, and the great burden of the loss fell upon those [the workers] least able to bear it."[39]

Despite this, the courts in general held that the workman knew the risks that he must run when he accepted the job, even if safety devices had not been provided, and that he had voluntarily accepted the risks. Even when Employers' Liability Laws were enacted,* the position of the injured workman was not much improved. "To recover he had to go to the courts and had to meet the strong opposition of insurance companies or of his employer. . . . Of every $100 paid by employers in premiums,

---

* New York enacted an Employers' Liability Law in 1902, but it left the common law essentially unaltered. Thus an injured workman had to prove decisively that the accident was not due to contributory negligence on his part or carelessness on the part of another employee. Workers had little chance under these restrictions of recovering any damages for any of the injuries that they had suffered. (*See* New York State Commission on Employers' Liability, *First Report to the Legislature, Mar. 19, 1910,* Albany, 1910, pp. 11–15.)

only $28 reached the workmen [due to exorbitant fees for legal counsel] and the amount only after a long legal action in many instances. In certain leading industrial states it was found that it required on the average two to six years to reach final judgment in a fatal accident case under employers' liability."[40]

Add to these difficulties the likelihood that the employee would lose his job after suing the employer, and the obstacles for the injured worker became almost insurmountable. Workers looked forward to the day when

The workman shall enjoy the fruit of his labor;
That his mother shall have the comfort of his arm in her old age;
That his wife shall not be untimely a widow;
That his children shall have a father, and
That cripples and hopeless wrecks who were once strong men
Shall no longer be a by-product of industry.[41]

WORKERS' HOUSING AND HOMEWORK

The vast majority of American workers were doomed to pass their off-the-job hours in small, dingy, and unventilated dwellings. A single block in New York's East Side included 39 tenements, containing 605 separate apartments for 2,871 persons. There was not one bath in the entire block and only 40 of the apartments were supplied with hot water. Of the rooms, 441 were dark (no more than closets), having no direct ventilation or illumination except that derived from other rooms; 635 rooms obtained their sole light and air from dark, narrow air-shafts, commonly called "germ tubes." For these miserable accommodations the owners derived yearly rentals amounting to $113,964. In another block, 1,238 people were found living in 121 rooms, an average of 10 people to a room. There was not a bathtub in the whole block and only one family had hot water arrangements.[42]

These conditions could be duplicated in Chicago, Philadelphia, Pittsburgh, Fall River, Lawrence—in every industrial center. Small wonder one of the new immigrants wrote: "This was the boasted American freedom and opportunity—the freedom for respectable citizens to sell cabbages from hideous carts, the opportunity to live in those monstrous, dirty caves that shut out the sunshine." Small wonder, too, that investigating committees reported that mortality rates were much higher in the working class districts than in other parts of the country.[43]

Frequently the bleak tenement flat doubled as a home and as a manufacturing establishment. The terrifying pressure of poverty forced the immigrant worker to bring work home. The institution of homework increased at a rapid pace. As of November 1911, there were 13,268 licensed tenements in New York City compared to 2,604 in 1904. Each of the licensed tenements had from three to 50 separate apartments in which manufacturing might be carried on. In these the manufacture of 41 articles specified in the State law was permitted. But at least 60 other articles were produced without license; indeed, even though State licenses were easily obtainable and licensed houses went largely unsupervised, much work was done in unlicensed places.

In these dingy rooms in the tenement the whole family, including very young children, wrapped cigars or worked hard sewing, packaging, and sorting other products. One investigation made in New York in 1912 by the National Child Labor Committee revealed that in 181 families visited, 251 children under 16 were found at work. Wherever the investigators for the State Factory Commission explored, they found children of elementary school age working alongside of their mothers, even four- and five-year old children making flowers. Here are some of the replies received by the inspectors:

Six Year Old: "When I go home from school I help my mother to work—I help her earn the money—I do not play at all. I get up at six o'clock and I go to bed at ten o'clock."

Nine Year Old: "I have no time for play. When I go home from school, I help my mother. Half hour I make my lessons. Every morning I get up at 6 o'clock. I go to bed at 11 o'clock."

Ten Year Old: "I get up at 5 o'clock in the morning. Then I work with my mother. At 9 o'clock I go to school. I have no time for play. I must work by feathers. At 10 o'clock I go to bed."

Nine Year Old: "I earn money for my mother after school, and on Saturday, and half day Sunday. No I do not play. I must work. I get up to work at 4 o'clock in the morning. I go to bed at 9 o'clock."[44]

In return for toiling under such conditions, the typical homeworker earned the most menial wages. Working, with the aid of children, the entire family, if fortunate, might earn $5 a week. Some women earned as little as one and one-half cents an hour while five or six cents an hour was a fairly average wage. "Without doubt the vast majority of homeworkers earned less than $4 a week and many individuals were unable to reach the $2 level."[45]

Twentieth century America was also giving the world many examples of industrial feudalism—whole towns and communities were the property of giant corporations. The workers' homes, the town's police, the town's churches—quite literally everything was the physical possession of the Company. In the mining towns especially, the complete ownership of property—homes, stores, churches, saloons, hospitals, and schools—gave the companies an economic stranglehold on the miner and his family.[46]

We shall see more of what conditions were like for most American workers in the opening years of the 20th century as we examine struggles in specific industries and trades. But we have seen enough already to conclude that the average worker could find little hope in the realities of his life. An accident, a depression, or even an argument with the boss could end his earning power. The future, moreover, promised worse than the present. In middle age, he would have to suffer agonies to keep up with the younger men on the job. Old age meant no income at all.

Many skilled workers organized in stable craft unions, working for higher wages and under more pleasant surroundings than the unorganized, did not have to look forward to as bleak a future. However, the organized during these years were a small minority of all workers and their conditions and manner of living in no way reflected the norm. Moreover, all workers—organized and unorganized—had to face such questions as what would happen to them and their families in case of injury or in old age. All workers were pressed down with this sense of anxiety, an anxiety that for the majority was not helped by the fact that their wages were not enough to sustain their families.

To all this the vast majority of the capitalists and their spokesmen had only two answers. One was that the problems facing the workers were being slowly solved through natural laws of economics. "Under great economic laws," proclaimed the New York *Herald* in 1907, "more powerful than any that a legislature can enact, the share of the worker in the world's wealth is steadily increasing." The other answer was that existing conditions were not only necessary but irremediable. The capitalists and their spokesmen put forth the grim doctrines of Social Darwinism which assured success to the strong and the ruthless, and condemned the weak and the helpless to defeat. The rich were rich because they were better than the poor and the poor were poor because they were innately inferior. "We accept and welcome, as conditions to which we must accommodate ourselves," declared Andrew Carnegie, "great inequality of wealth and environment, the concentration of business, industrial and commercial, in the hands of the few, as being not only beneficial, but essential for the future of the race." Labor was admonished to "submit cheerfully to authority and learn self-control." To tinker with the laws of nature by seeking to change "faulty social conditions" would gravely imperil social order and social well-being.[47]

UPSURGE IN LABOR'S RANKS

American labor, however, disagreed and showed its disagreement in bitter struggles to remove many of these "faulty social conditions." Since capitalism was only interested in profits, declared a group of New Orleans Negro and white trade unionists in the summer of 1901, the workers must protect themselves from the ravages of the economic system through effective organization. On the one side stood the capitalists who, through their ownership and control of the means of production, were able to dictate to the workers, unless they were effectively organized, how and under what conditions they could live:

"On the other side stand the workers in their millions, without ownership in the means of life, without rights, defenseless, deprived by the State, press and pulpit. It is against them that the weapons of the police and militia are directed. . . . Individual unions must unite in one large league, which shall proclaim the unity of all and give mutual support. Soon thereafter will come the recognition of the fact that our whole society rests exclusively upon the shoulders of the working class, and that this latter can, by simply choosing to do so, introduce another and more just society. The class-conscious power of capital, with all its camp followers, is confronted with the class-conscious power of labor, the majority of the population. There is no power on earth strong enough to thwart the will of such a majority conscious of itself."[48]

This militant statement offers a fitting explanation of the resurgence of trade unionism around the turn of the century. Between 1897 and 1901, the total membership of American trade unions more than doubled, rising from 447,000 to 1,124,000. But this was only the beginning. From 1900 to 1904, union membership more than doubled, rising from 868,500 to 2,072,700, with the A. F. of L. tripling its membership from 548,300 to 1,676,200.*

The number of strikes called annually was surging upward from 1,000 to 1,300 common during most of the early and middle 'nineties to 1,779 in 1900, 2,924 in 1901, and to a high of 3,944 in 1903. And labor was winning a larger percentage of its strikes.[49]

Of the two million members in the trade union movement in 1904, about 200,000 were in the Railroad Brotherhoods, a small number were still in the once-powerful Knights of Labor, and a handful were in the Socialist Trades and Labor Alliance under the leadership of Daniel De Leon. The bulk of the organized workers were in the A. F. of L. In 1897 total membership of the Federation was 264,825 or about 60 per cent

---

* The following statistics indicate some typical examples of trade union growth:

	1899	1904
United Mine Workers	40,000	260,300
Int'l Brotherhood of Boiler Makers, Iron Ship Builders and Helpers	2,700	19,000
United Brotherhood of Carpenters and Joiners	20,000	155,400
Brotherhood of Painters, Decorators and Paperhangers	4,500	16,500
Hotel and Restaurant Employees	2,000	49,400

(Louis Lorwin, *The American Federation of Labor,* Washington, 1933, pp. 476–82.)

of the 447,000 trade unionists in the country; in 1904 the Federation included 1,676,200 out of a total of 2,072,000, or about 80 per cent. "The great growth of the A. F. of L. can be realized," wrote Frank Morrison, national secretary, in 1903, "when I say that in 1897, when I first took the office of Secretary there were only 58 international organizations affiliated with the A. F. of L., and then consider that to-day we have 113. In 1897 we received a per capita tax on 265,000 members. To-day we are receiving per capita tax on very nearly 1,700,000, a phenomenal gain, and the high water mark has not yet been reached."[50]

"THE ERA OF GOOD FEELING"

During the 1890's, and particularly within the last five years of the decade, employers in several important lines of business had begun the practice of settling all questions of hours and wages on an industry-wide basis by means of negotiated agreements with labor unions. In 1891, the Stove Founders' National Defense Association and the National Molders' Union negotiated a complete trade agreement covering the stove industry. The depression years saw a decline in the application of the trade-agreement system, but after 1897, an increasing number of trade agreements were negotiated in industries. During the late 1890's and early 1900's, the system of collective trade agreements was established in the bituminous and anthracite industries, the building trades, the printing trades,* the railroads, iron molding, newspaper publishing, stove mounting, brass polishing, machine shop, pottery, overalls manufacturing, and shipping on the Great Lakes.[51] Of these, perhaps, the most important was the agreement system erected in 1898 between the United Mine Workers and the operators in the central competitive field—the first national agreement in any important industry.

In part, this period of fairly peaceful relations between employers' associations and the unions was due to the desire of manufacturers to avoid strikes during the Spanish-American War (1898–1899) when government contracts offered huge profits. In the era of business prosperity during and immediately following the war, expectation of continued profits made employers reluctant to do anything that might interrupt the lush flow, and working agreements with benefits to organized labor became more prevalent. What is especially significant is that this period coincided with the greatest development of monopoly capitalism. In 1897 there were

---

* The printers' agreement, known as the "Syracuse Agreement," was signed with the United Typothetae, the employers' association, in 1898. It covered three unions in the industry (the International Typographical Union, the International Pressmen and Assistants' Union, and the International Brotherhood of Bookbinders), and provided for gradual reduction of hours from ten to nine. The Unions promised to do all they could to equalize wage schedules in the various competitive districts.

only 82 industrial combinations with an aggregate capitalization slightly in excess of $1,000,000,000. In the one year alone, 1898, combinations were formed with an aggregate capitalization of $916,000,000—almost equal to that of all previously organized combinations.[52]

Spurred on by the desire to limit production and raise prices, monopolies in the making resorted to any and every means to crush their competitors. In many industries efforts were made to utilize the unions for this end; through the control of labor power the monopolists sought to force the independents into the associations or conform to the prices set by the combination if their businesses were not to be ruined.

The most widely publicized illustration of this trend occurred in the building construction industry. The big associations of contractors in various cities sought to crush their competitors through control of materials as well as labor power. During the late 1890's, these contractors, with this objective in mind, recognized the closed shop, making a contract with the building trades' unions in which it was agreed that the contractors would hire none but members of the unions, and that the unions, in turn, would guarantee that none of their members would work for any contractor not in the association. In 1897 the Chicago Carpenters' Union entered into an agreement with the employers' association in which the union, in return for the closed shop, agreed not to allow its members to work for non-members of the association. With this exclusive contract in hand, the employers were able to drive out of business all competitors who would not join the organization, and thus gained complete control of the Chicago market. The union did its part by calling strikes against any employer who refused to join the combination of employers. By 1899, similar agreements existed in the Chicago bricklaying, steamfitting, plumbing, and printing trades, through which the employers' associations, with the aid of the unions, established strong monopoly control of the market.[53]

Agreements of this nature between employers' associations and unions affiliated with the A. F. of L., in which the unions were used as a club against employers who would not enter the combination, flourished in many trades throughout the country. Huge profits resulted from such alliances; $600,000 in excess profits came annually to members of the Employing Stonecutters' Association in Brooklyn which had an exclusive agreement with the Stonecutters' Union, and 10 per cent of this sum was the union's share. In return for recognition and financial reward, the union punished, through strikes, recalcitrant firms and compelled independents to join the association.[54]

By restricting supply and raising the prices of the products, the employers' associations also reaped huge profits. In return for assistance in gaining this objective, they were ready, temporarily, to concede to the craft unions a small share of the swollen profits.

The craft union leaders welcomed the formation of these employers' associations and cooperated in the efforts to establish domination of the trade. Without such an association of employers, they argued, it was almost impossible to introduce anything approaching standardization in a given industry relating to wages, hours, and working rules. An association of employers which entered into a trade agreement with a union assumed a large part of the responsibility of keeping individual firms in line with respect to the terms of the agreement. On the other hand, the maintenance of an effective trade agreement frequently was made impossible because of the existence of small firms in a highly competitive industry. For the cut-throat competition among such firms continually threatened to undermine standards which had been embodied in a trade agreement.

"The rank and file of American employers are just," an A. F. of L. spokesman declared, "and it is in this spirit trade unionists encourage their organizing. In many instances collective bargaining between well organized employers and employees regarding trade agreements, wage scales and other questions have been adjusted in an eminently satisfactory manner to both parties, for strongly organized employers and employees usually have great respect for one another.

"Good luck to employers' associations. We welcome them as necessary under present economic conditions."[55]

That workers and other members of the community would face rising living costs were not mentioned in the statements of the A. F. of L. leaders. Nor did they refer to the fact that agreements between trusts and unions were not characteristic of labor relations in the monopolized mass production industries. Agreements between combinations of employers and unions in the building construction industry and other trades existed side by side with opposition to unionism in the highly monopolized, mass production industries which were characterized by the elimination of unionism from every independent firm swallowed up by the trusts, wholesale firings, and blacklisting of trade unionists.

The A. F. of L. leaders painted a roseate picture of what the trade agreement could do. They spoke of "The Era of Good Feeling" between capital and labor. But they ignored the other side of the labor picture, conclusively established in the steady stream of reports from unions in the trustified industries. They lived in sweet dreams of complacency, stimulated by the concessions to the craft unions by the employers' associations. "Combinations against labor are fast disappearing," declared a leading West Coast labor paper at the turn of the century, "and those who still persist in ignoring the workman's demands for fair hours and fair pay will soon learn the hopelessness of the position they have taken."[56]

They were in for a rude awakening. The concessions to the unions were only temporary. A monopoly, once established, no longer needs to deal with the union to help it crush competition. On the contrary, it quickly becomes as ruthless in crushing the unions as it had its competitors. The so-called peaceful relations existing between the employers' associations and the craft unions during the period of transition to monopoly came to an end when the monopoly was established. They were replaced by the Open-Shop drive.

CHAPTER 2

The Open-Shop Drive

In his presidential address of 1899, Samuel Gompers characterized as "noteworthy" the fact that "while in every previous industrial crisis the trade unions were literally mowed down and swept out of existence, the unions now in existence, have manifested not only the power of resistance, but of stability and permanence." Five years later, at the 1904 A. F. of L. convention, Gompers assured the delegates that the growth of the labor movement, based upon the leadership of the Federation, would continue unchecked.[1] The words—"the high water mark has not yet been reached"—were echoed in speech after speech by A. F. of L. leaders.

DECLINE AFTER 1904

Those who knew what was taking place in the industrial world did not share this optimism. They knew that at the very moment these officials were voicing such rosy predictions, the labor movement had already been caught in a "tide of reaction."

A general slump in the American labor movement occurred after 1904. The growth of union membership as a whole was stopped in its tracks for the remainder of the decade, while the A. F. of L. lost 220,000 members between 1904 and 1906 and did not surpass its 1904 figure until 1911*

* The trade union and A.F. of L. membership for these years was as follows:

	Average union membership	Average annual A.F. of L. membership
1904	2,072,700	1,676,200
1905	2,022,300	1,494,300
1906	1,907,300	1,454,200
1907	2,080,000	1,538,970
1908	2,130,600	1,586,885
1909	2,005,600	1,482,872
1910	2,140,500	1,562,112
1911	2,343,400	1,761,835

(Leo Wolman, *Ebb and Flow in Trade Unionism*, New York, 1936, p. 16.)

32

The Federation's financial receipts were equally discouraging. Total receipts in 1904 were $220,995.97, compared with $247,902.96 for the previous year. In August 1904, Gompers informed the members of the A. F. of L. Executive Council that "due to the reduced revenue coming from per capita tax of our affiliated organizations, both international and directly affiliated locals," the Federation had found it necessary "to largely reduce the number of salaried organizers." In 1905 this decline continued, with the receipts at only $207,417.62. As in the case of membership, not until 1911 did the Federation's financial receipts equal the 1904 figure.[2]

The initial cause of the slump in trade union membership was the sharp industrial depression which set in during the fall of 1903. Though it was of a partial and temporary nature, it gave the employers the opportunity to intensify "a crusade against unionism in general."[3] Employers' associations assumed the offensive against the labor movement on a nation-wide scale.

In June 1901, the San Francisco *Star* observed: "The few men who are in the places of real power in our industrial life have determined that trade unionism shall be suppressed . . . The few owners of the great industries are forcing the fight."[4] The observation was correct, even though the "few men" referred to were not actually the owners of the great industries. By means of stock control, interlocking directorates, holding companies, mergers, etc., the House of Morgan, the Rockefellers, Harriman, and Kuhn, Loeb & Co. had acquired a dominant position in American industrial life, and exercised economic dictatorship over the industries in which the vast majority of American workers were employed. By 1904 it was recognized publicly that "two-thirds of the country's manufacturing capital was controlled by monopolistic combines" at the head of which stood "the House of Morgan and the Standard Oil 'crowd.'"[5] Great aggregations of capital concentrated in the hands of a few powerful individuals was now available to crush trade unionism.

THE ATTACK BEGINS

Immediately after it was organized, U.S. Steel launched a series of planned wars for the purpose of rooting out and destroying every labor organization encroaching upon the steel empire or its peripheries. "I have always had one rule," said a member of the billion-dollar corporation's Executive Committee. "If a workman sticks up his head, hit it." Another member declared that there was only one thing to do with "the union . . . wipe it out. . . ." J. P. Morgan agreed. "There can be no compromise," he announced. Unionism had to be crushed. Referring to a union shop agreement in one of his affiliated enterprises, Morgan declared: "If I have any authority to cause that agreement to be broken, it will be broken." To the applause of the *Wall Street Journal* and other spokesmen for big business, the agreement was broken and the union destroyed.[6]

"In 1902," writes Robert H. Wiebe, "U.S. Steel destroyed the feeble remains of the Amalgamated Iron Workers, and with so much general attention focused upon the new giant, its example heartened innumerable employers to try for similar freedom from labor organizations." Noting this trend, the *Coast Seamen's Journal* cautioned trade unions throughout the country "to take every precaution against being placed at a disadvantage . . . and in general to remove those elements of weakness that offer a tempting invitation to attack." The growth of union membership since the end of the depression had "inspired the employing class . . . with the spirit of organization . . . for the purpose of wresting from the employees the advantages already gained. . . . Indications point to the resuscitation in the near future of the Employers' Association with the sole objective of destroying unionism. The prospect must be seriously reckoned with."[7]

It was a timely warning. Employers' Associations, organized solely to destroy the trade unions, were already in the process of formation in various cities and plans were already laid to convert these communities into open-shop citadels. The Employers' Association of Dayton, Ohio was organized in June 1900 under the leadership of John Kirby, Jr. Thirty-eight firms became charter members of the Association, and organized into an anti-union united front.

On July 25, 1901, the Davis Machine Co. and Computing Scale Co. closed down ostensibly for repairs, but the following notice was distributed to its employees:

"This factory will resume operations on or about August 19 as an *open* shop. All employees desiring to return to their present position must make written application on enclosed card and return same to superintendent in person not later than August 10.

"Those not willing to comply with the requirements will surrender their key at once."[8]

Other Dayton firms leaped into action and pressure was applied on still others to cooperate. Lockouts were instituted on a city-wide scale. Collective agreements, where such existed, were either broken or discontinued when their terms expired. Within a year after the offensive was launched, the Employers' Association membership had grown to 155 firms, and Dayton had become the first "completely open-shop city" of any appreciable size in the United States. "A general reactionary movement is manifest on every hand," President Kirby of the Association boasted in his report for the year ending May 1902.[9]

Similar movements were organized in other cities. In San Francisco large numbers of workers were notified in July 1901 "that they must either quit their unions or their jobs." The beer bottle workers received notice that "all union employees will be paid off in full, as we have decided to dispense with their services. *From this day forward we intend to operate our own business.*" The box makers were asked to sign a statement that on and after January 1, 1902, they would not strike nor require their fellow workmen "to join any labor union. . . . We agree upon our honor, not to interfere with the business of our employers, and agree that the signature hereon constitutes a resignation from the union to which we belong."[10]

Union after union in San Francisco succumbed before the relentless onslaught of the open-shop drive. The iron molders, boot and shoe makers, brewery workers and other trades were in turn bludgeoned into submission. When the San Francisco Labor Council invited the Employers' Association to a conference to discuss the local labor situation, it was bluntly told: "There is nothing to confer upon." One month after the employers' campaign of extirpation against San Francisco labor was launched, the Employers' Association boasted publicly:

"The general success of this Association can best be understood by the light of the fact that among the industries of San Francisco there remains but a single union which imposes its rule upon its trade. That union is the Typographical Union. The reason why this union still continues to dictate terms is because the employing printers have never combined to resist demands. . . . The Typographical Union would be no stronger than any other union against a combination of employers. . . . It is of most vital importance that this good work shall go on."[11]

And on the work did go, not only in Dayton and San Francisco, but in cities throughout the country. In June 1902 there were employers' associations in 24 large cities, each modeled after the Dayton and San Francisco pattern. Shortly afterwards, there was hardly a large or medium-sized city in the United States which did not possess an employers' association engaged in the battle for the open shop.[12]

THE CITIZENS' ALLIANCE

Side by side with the employers' associations and working closely with them as subsidiary bodies, were anti-labor organizations disguised under the lofty-sounding name, The Citizens' Alliance. Membership was open to firms, corporations, individual employers, and all citizens who did not belong to labor unions. The Alliances, careful to demonstrate outwardly, at least, that they opposed union methods rather than organized labor as such, usually required applicants for membership to "affirm that I am not a member of any labor organization which resorts to boycotting, or any form of coercion or unlawful force and fully agree to discountenance all strikes and schemes of persecution." In practice, however, they dropped the mask and required members to affirm that they did not belong "to any labor organization"—period. Elaborate rules were set up for the support of members subject to strike or boycott, with compensation of a specific sum to struck firms—usually $1 a day for each worker who had walked out.[13]

Originating in Dayton, Ohio, where it took on the name of the "Modern Order of Bees" (and was more familiarly known as the "Hooly-Goolies"), the Citizens' Alliance movement spread to hundreds of cities and towns throughout the country. Its membership varied from about 6,000 in Los Angeles to a few hundred in small localities. By November 1905, 18 Citizens' Alliances, composed of employers and business and professional men, had been formed in the state of Colorado, and there was hardly an important mining town that did not have its "Citizens' Alliance along with its mine-owners' association." James C. Craig, president of the State Citizens' Alliance, estimated membership in Colorado to be about 30,000.[14]

Everywhere the Alliance functioned as an auxiliary of the employers' association; indeed, membership in the two organizations was often overlapping. "We, the Union workmen of the little town in [Freeport] Illinois are being hemmed in and confronted by the Citizens' Alliance and the Employers' Association," wrote a trade unionist to Gompers in April 1904.[15]

The American labor movement was confronted with an entirely new problem. Employers' offensives, of course, were not new, but heretofore the opposition had been conducted by special groups of employers against a particular labor organization, such as the Knights of Labor, or against a specific demand, such as the eight-hour day. The new offensive was a general employer and community movement on a national scale, directed against all unionism and all labor demands.

NATIONAL ASSOCIATION OF MANUFACTURERS

Although the open-shop drive was widespread, it still lacked the cohesion of national leadership. In 1902, John Kirby, Jr., called for a national federation of employers' associations and Citizens' Alliances to better pursue their united attack against unionism. "In the matter of organization we have much to learn. We are mere novices as compared with the professional leaders of organized labor. . . ."[16] Kirby's appeal was hailed by David M. Parry, president of the National Association of Manufacturers, and he set about at once to supply the deficiency in the open-shop movement.

Organized in 1895, the N.A.M. had originally concerned itself with the promotion of trade and commerce. "To Extend American Trade—Object of a Patriotic Organization," a newspaper summed up the N.A.M. shortly after it was organized. As the organization was later to say of its original declaration of principles: "There was not a hint or threat in it of an organized front against organized labor." There was more than a "hint" in 1902 when the N.A.M. effectively lobbied in Congress against the anti-injunction and eight-hour bills which the A. F. of L. had sought to have passed. The following year, it took "formal cognizance of the increasing activity of organized labor." Early in 1903, Parry issued a call for the organization to take on the leadership of the "crusade against unionism."[17] In response to the call, the N.A.M. met in conference in April 1903 at New Orleans to formulate plans and provide cohesion and unity on a national scale for the open-shop drive.

Parry accused organized labor of having "exactly the same end and aim as Socialism"—with the difference that organized labor proposed "to gain its ends by force and arbitrary power and the Socialists gain the same end by the ballot." He warned the delegates that "unless Gomperism, 8-hour laws, boycotts, anti-conspiracy bills, and making of Socialists by the A. F. of L., etc." were checked, the United States would face "a reign of terror" which would make the French Revolution appear like a tea party. As a remedy, Parry urged the complete and perfect combination of employers throughout the country into an organization "which shall embrace the last employer in the United States, the various organizations to be combined in one grand national federation."[18]

John M. Kirby, Jr. of the Dayton Employers' Association and subsequently N.A.M. president from 1909 to 1913, endorsed Parry's proposal in these words: "Shall Americanism or Unionism rule? . . . Shall we then, as Americans, sacrifice all that is American by sitting idly by and permitting agitators to hold their jobs through such dastardly methods, or shall we organize into a solid, coherent mass, which cannot be penetrated by these destroyers of peace and prosperity and thus discharge a solemn duty which we owe to our country."[19]

The business men who attended the New Orleans conference were themselves actively combining corporate enterprises. They were organized in chambers of commerce, trade associations, corporations, and trustified combinations of corporations—to say nothing of employers' associations and Citizens' Alliances. But the right of labor to combine had to be denied. Labor must be disorganized, unprotected by the might of combination.

The liberal Toledo business and political leader, Samuel "Golden Rule" Jones, urged the delegates at New Orleans to repudiate "the monstrous doctrine that labor was a commodity like brick and sand and coal, etc., to be bought and sold." But the delegates enthusiastically endorsed Parry's belligerency toward organized labor and his vicious language, which became known as "Parryism." The convention adopted a "Declaration of Principles" of nine resolutions (a tenth was added in 1904) in which the N.A.M. stated that it did not oppose "organizations of labor as such" and then set forth a long list of provisos which would render such organizations ineffective. The "Declaration" endorsed the unrestricted supremacy of employers in the conditions of work: "Employers must be free to employ their work people at wages mutually satisfactory, without interference or dictation on the part of individuals or organizations not directly parties to such contracts." It declared "unalterable antagonism to the closed shop," and disapproved absolutely of strikes as well as "boycotts, blacklists, and other illegal acts of interference with the personal liberty of employer or employee."[20]

With its principles adopted, the N.A.M. issued a call for a convention to be held in Chicago during October 1903 for the purpose of establishing a national organization to carry on the fight against unionism. The call went out to national and state trade associations, employers' associations, Citizens' Alliances, and other anti-labor groups.

The Chicago convention, attended by 250 delegates from 124 employers' organizations, set up the Citizens' Industrial Association of America as a national federation of employers' associations, selecting Parry as head. The meeting adopted a constitution which attacked the closed shop as contrary to the principles of American government, and called for the formation of local associations in each trade and their affiliation with the National Association of Manufacturers. James A. Emery, secretary of the C.I.A.A. from 1905 to 1908 and N.A.M. counsel until 1938, described the purpose of the new organization as follows to a Senate Lobby Investigating Committee: "The chief object of those who organized it was to concentrate under one organization, for the purpose of cooperation, all the organizations that were interested in the open-shop propaganda." The C.I.A.A., in short, sought to organize the employers of the country to annihilate unions.

In public, the N.A.M. and the C.I.A.A. maintained the fiction of two separate entities. Actually, they were one and the same organization with identical leadership,* working hand in hand for the achievement of a common objective—the open shop.[21]

The newly-formed C.I.A.A. immediately launched a vigorous anti-union campaign, fostering the local organization of employers and the

---

* From 1903 to 1905 President Parry of the N.A.M. was also president of the C.I.A.A. In 1905, a member of the executive committee of the N.A.M., C. W. Post, became president of the C.I.A.A. to succeed Parry, and in 1906, the successor of Parry as president of the N.A.M. was James W. Van Cleave, the first vice-president of the C.I.A.A. In 1905 the board of directors of the N.A.M. was composed of "twenty-one well known manufacturers from different parts of the country." Every one was an active figure in the C.I.A.A. (New York *Tribune*, Aug. 13, 1905.) However, one student of the two organizations maintains that the Citizens' Industrial Association never functioned effectively because of suspicion of the N.A.M.'s board of directors that the C.I.A.A. was "trying to take possession of the [N.A.M.'s] treasury." (Robert H. Wiebe, *Businessmen and Reform: A Study of the Progressive Movement,* Cambridge, 1962, p. 29.)

public, encouraging the use of non-union goods and the employment of non-union men, boycotting union label goods, patronizing firms at odds with organized labor, dispensing information on "undesirable workmen" —i.e. union men—and publicizing the virtues of the open shop. The organization grew so quickly that by the time of its second meeting in February 1904, 247 employers' organizations were represented. In January 1906, the association claimed to have affiliated local organizations in almost 450 cities throughout the country. The membership was very large in some cities—in San Francisco, 12,000, and in St. Louis, 7,000.[22]

AMERICAN ANTI-BOYCOTT ASSOCIATION

Another type of general employers' association was the American Anti-Boycott Association, organized in December 1902. Membership, which was kept secret, was open to manufacturing concerns. By April 1903, 100 charter members had been secured; in May of the same year, a permanent board of 20, representing as many different industries, was elected. Charles H. Merritt was chosen chairman of the General Executive Board.

Almost immediately it went into action. On May 7, 1903, a strike was called against the Kellog Switchboard and Supply Co. of Illinois. The firm, employing about 800 workers, refused to sign a closed-shop agreement. The Teamsters' Union declared a boycott. On May 25, 1903, application for an injunction was made to the state court. It was granted and later affirmed on appeal. Contempt proceedings were brought against the union leaders, and all but one were found guilty. An appeal to the Supreme Court of Illinois brought affirmation of the decision.[23]

This incident illustrates the methods employed by the Association. This litigation was brought in the state court and included: (1) an injunction against the union's activities, and (2) proceedings for contempt against the union leaders. Where possible the Association proceeded on a larger scale. When the boycott was invoked against interstate products, actions were usually brought in both the state and federal courts. A victory in the federal courts defeated the boycott in all states, while the victory in the state courts stopped the boycott in that state alone. The Danbury Hatters' Case, which will be discussed in detail later, is an example of an action brought by the Association on a national scale. The Supreme Court decided in 1908 that the union had violated the Sherman Anti-Trust Act in stimulating a nation-wide boycott of a hatter's product.

Despite its name, the Association did not confine itself to the battle against the boycott. It spearheaded one of the most important phases of the entire open-shop campaign, "the prosecution in the courts of trade union officials and members by injunction proceedings and damage suits," and it initiated such prosecution against all forms of trade union activity, not merely the boycott. In 1904 the press reported that the Association had "a lobbyist in Congress working to defeat the Eight-Hour Law, on the grounds that it is a socialistic measure." George P. B. Brenta, a leading member, conceded the accuracy of the report, and asked: "Why should printers, or anyone else, only work eight hours? Is that a divine sacred limit beyond which no one should or may go?" He answered that there should be no "limit," and assured employers that there would be none as long as the Association and its sister organizations could keep the unions and their members from the factories and plants.[24]

OTHER OPEN-SHOP ASSOCIATIONS

The efforts of the local, state, and national general employers' associations were supplemented by those of several national trade associations. The National Metal Trades' Association, formed in 1899 by the manufacturers, abrogated its contract with the Machinists' Union in June 1901,* adopted the open shop as its policy, and operated on that basis from then on. The National Founders' Association refused in 1904 to deal any longer with the Molders' Union, promoted the open shop, and furnished monetary aid to members engaged in strikes and lockouts. In 1905, the National Erectors' Association, organized among firms engaged in steel erecting, broke off relations with the International Association of Bridge and Structural Ironworkers, and announced its intentions to institute and maintain "the Open Shop principle in the employment of labor in the erection of steel and iron bridges and buildings and other structural steel and iron work." The Association hired Walter Drew, one of the nation's outstanding exponents of the open shop, to carry out the details of smashing the union, and it announced publicly that it "stands ready to lend its whole power and influence to the open shop cause in any of the other building trades. . . ."[25]

In 1907 the Citizens' Industrial Association, composed of local employers' groups and Citizens' Alliances, the national employers' groups, the American Anti-Boycott Association, and other aggressively open-shop, anti-union groups, joined together under the guidance of the N.A.M. to form a powerful national federation of Employers' Associations which came to be known as the National Council of Industrial Defense (later to become the National Industrial Council). The primary purpose of the Council was political; it served as the legislative pressure group for the Employers' Associations in defeating legislation and candidates favorable

---

* The agreement, signed in May 1900, forbade discrimination against union members, provided that within six months, weekly hours of work would be reduced to 57, and within a year to 54. A nine-hour day would finally go into effect on May 20, 1901.

to labor and promoting those favorable to the objectives of the open-shop employers. Like the other associations, the N.C.I.D. was dominated by N.A.M. "From the beginnings," a contemporary noted, "this council was run by a self-perpetuating committee of three, and was composed from the beginning of the chief officers of the N.A.M. James A. Emery, counsel of the N.A.M., was retained by the new organization. A blank form of 'power of attorney' was drafted, which all Employers' Associations were invited to sign. This form entrusted Emery with full authority to represent these associations 'in all matters pertaining to labor legislation.' "[26] We shall see below the results of this concentrated political campaign against labor.

The conspiracy was now perfected. While one group of employers' associations was molding public opinion and legislation against organized labor, another was actively opposing union organization at the plant level. And behind both groups stood the finance capitalists, the monopolists who dominated American economic and political life. The network of finance capital extended into every industry. This gigantic power, wielded from a single center, Wall Street, dictated the strategy of destruction of all effective labor organization throughout American heavy industry and planned the offensive to destroy even the narrowest craft unions where they showed the slightest tendency to affect production by enrolling all in a skilled craft. The Parrys, the Merritts, the Kirbys, and the other titular heads of the employers' associations were only the agents of the powerful finance capitalists, as were the men in Congress and the state legislatures who furnished the legal apparatus for the open-shop drive. Just as American industry was controlled by finance capitalists through interlocking directorates, holding companies, and other devices, the employers' associations were controlled by their agents through a chain of varied interrelations. N.A.M. which supervised and spearheaded the open-shop drive, was intimately linked to every one of the employers' associations in the country. And the men at the helm of the N.A.M. were the finance capitalists. Indeed, Professor Selig Perlman notes that the whole "new anti-union pattern that came to be the model for the American employer . . . was developed by the United States Steel Corporation. . . ."[27]

Actually, Morgan's Steel Corporation did more than serve as a model for the employers. It organized and dominated the National Erectors' Association, and many local employers' associations were reported to have been "instigated by the Steel trust influences." In 1901, the Lake Carriers' Association came under the domination of the Pittsburgh Steamship Co., largest on the Great Lakes and a subsidiary of U.S. Steel Co. In 1908, the Lake Carriers' Association applied the open-shop U.S. Steel policy to maritime and coldly broke off relations with the International Seamen's Union. The union was defeated in a long strike, and the open-shop policy, inspired by the shipping companies under the domination of U.S. Steel, persisted up to our own day.[28]

With good reason, the N.A.M. boasted that it was U.S. Steel that best symbolized the association's policy toward organized labor. The N.A.M.'s official organ declared in August 1909:

"A hint to you Mr. Employer. The United States Steel Corporation employs 120,000 expert workmen. In 1901 three-fourths of the force consisted of union men; today every single one of its many plants is conducted upon open shop rules. The great corporation believes in the labor principles of the National Association of Manufacturers that 'employers must be free to employ their own people at wages mutually satisfactory, without interference or dictation on the part of the individuals or organizations not directly parties to such contracts.' "[29]

OPEN-SHOP TECHNIQUES

Throughout the first decade of the century, the various employers' associations perfected their anti-union techniques. They boycotted union goods and union concerns, gave financial and other assistance to employers contending for the open shop, furnished strikebreakers, boycotted unfriendly newspapers, bribed union officials, blacklisted union workers, employed labor spies, forced workers to sign iron-clad oaths and yellow dog contracts if they wanted to work,* disseminated propaganda painting union leaders as corrupt officials existing parasitically from the dues paid by duped workers and unionism as "un-American," used the police, militia, and private agencies to break strikes, used the courts to attack and cripple the unions, and organized powerful lobbies against labor legislation.

A number of employers recognized that these anti-union techniques, intimidating though they might be, were merely negative tools which failed to get at the reason why the workers had organized unions in the first place. They cast about for a different program that could supplant unions, and believed they found the answer in "Welfare Capitalism," particularly in "fair" wages, safety devices, clean washrooms, clubhouses or gymnasiums, and, especially, profit-sharing through bonus plans and stock ownership. This scheme was designed primarily to assure the loy-

---

* A typical iron-clad oath of the period read: "I, the undersigned, in consideration of the Oliver Typewriter Company [of Woodstock, Illinois] giving me employment, do hereby agree with the said company to withdraw from any and all labor organizations during the time or term of employment with said company, and I further agree not to urge, request or try any means whatever to induce others to join such labor union or organization during said time." (Included in letter of John Mulholland, President, International Association of Allied Metal Mechanics, to Gompers, Feb. 13, 1903, American Federation of Labor Correspondence. Hereinafter cited as *AFL Corr.*)

alty and cooperation—the uninterrupted labor—of the workers by making them feel that they were partners in the business, to reduce turnover, and avoid industrial disputes. But the main motive was to convince the workers that membership in the union was not necessary to secure fair treatment and a proper regard for their interests. As Charles Macfarland pointed out in 1909, "these employers try to buy off the laboring men and get them to forsake their unions by offering them lunch counters, porcelain bath tubs and ready-made houses." As for profit-sharing and the annual bonus, the employers' goal was "obvious: draw workers away from unions and strikes by withholding a portion of their earnings as conditional gifts."[30]

The profit-sharing aspect of the welfare program convinced few workers. For one thing, for the millions in the mines and mills, most of whom made less than $800 a year, a bonus of a dollar or two could scarcely increase the feeling of loyalty to the company. Few of these workers, moreover, could afford to buy the company's stock. The stock of U.S. Steel was offered in 1903 and sold to employees at $82.50 a share. About 10 per cent of the 12,000 workers who made less than $800 a year signed up for a single share. Very few of these were able to keep up the payments. "The real benefits went to executives and the skilled employees who earned enough to pay for the stock."[31]

Another aspect of the anti-union offensive was the development of company unionism. The first company union was organized in 1901 in the plant of the Nernst Lamp Co. in Pittsburgh. In 1903, the Everett Syndicate, operating street railway lines in Ohio, set up the Brotherhood of Motormen and the Brotherhood of Conductors as rivals to the A. F. of L.'s Amalgamated Association of Street and Railway Employees of America. In 1907 the Nelson Valve Co. of Philadelphia instituted a similar organization, and about the same time, C. W. Post, a prominent leader of the open-shop drive, and owner of the Post Cereal Company, organized a "Trades and Workers' Association" in his plants.[32]

While the company union movement did not get well under way until the Rockefeller-dominated Colorado Fuel and Iron Co. founded its plan of "Employe Representation" following the bitterly fought coal miners' strike of 1914, these earlier organizations set the pattern for the entire movement. They emphasized that they would never engage in any strike or other labor dispute, opposed trade unionism of the A. F. of L. and other varieties, and asserted the identity of interest between labor and capital. "That an organization of this kind can do a great deal to disrupt the labor movement, there is no question," W. D. Mahon, president of the A. F. of L.'s Street and Electric Railway Employees' Union, wrote to Gompers in September 1903.[33]

Still another aspect of the anti-union offensive was the spread of scientific management. Frederick W. Taylor's system was introduced in many plants not only because it promised higher profits by speeding up the workers, but also because it was based on the theory that the interests of the employers and workers were mutual,* that the workers should be dealt with as individuals rather than collectively, that they should have no voice in fixing standards, and that slow or recalcitrant workers should be replaced by "cooperative and loyal workers" who would act as pacemakers. Scientific management not only left no room for collective bargaining, but regarded it as a handicap if not a downright evil. "Stripping the unions of collective bargaining rights," notes Milton J. Nadworny, "meant a de facto destruction of organized labor, since collective bargaining gives it meaning and direction."† As for the labor leaders, Taylor, like Parry, regarded them all as misleaders and demagogues. "Gompers and his allies have to be destroyed," Taylor wrote to one of his associates.[34]

STRIKEBREAKING AND VIGILANTISM

On October 18, 1902, *The Public,* a liberal weekly, reported that "a new business has sprung up under the pressure of that thickening conflict between labor and monopoly, which is so often miscalled labor and capital. It is the business of supplying 'Strike breakers.' " To illustrate the character and scope of the "new business," the magazine reprinted the advertisement of a New York Detective Agency which engaged in it on a large scale:

"Special.—We are prepared to furnish strike-breakers, men to take the place of strikers, in every capacity from messenger boys to locomotive engineers on reasonable notice. This includes machinists, boilermakers, blacksmiths, carpenters, conductors and brakemen for steam roads, conductors and motormen for trolley roads, etc."

Such advertisements filled many pages of the employers' association's official journals. "We help eliminate the agitator and organizer quietly and with little or no friction," read an advertisement in December 1903, "and further, through the employment of our system, you will know at all times who among your employes are loyal and to be depended upon." The following advertisement by the Joy Detective Service of Cleveland,

---

* Under the present system of unionism, Taylor emphasized, "of necessity their [the workers'] employers are looked upon as their antagonists, if not even their enemies, while they should be the best friend of the men who are working under them." (Frederick W. Taylor to General William Crozier, April 15, 1909, Frederick Winslow Taylor Collection, Stevens Institute of Technology, Hoboken, New Jersey).

† "The Taylor system," James O'Connell, president of the International Machinists' Union and an A.F. of L. vice-president, pointed out, "wants individual agreements, instead of collective bargaining, which, if secured, would mean the destruction of labor unions." (Boston *Traveler,* undated clipping in Frederick Winslow Taylor Collection.)

Ohio, appeared in the May 1905 issue of *American Industries,* official publication of N.A.M.:

"WE BREAK STRIKES

"Also handle labor troubles in all their phases. We are prepared to place secret operatives who are skilled mechanics in any shop, mill or factory, to discover whether organizing is being done, material wasted or stolen, negligence on the part of employes, etc., etc.

"We guard property during strikes, employ non-union men to fill the places of strikers, fit up and maintain boarding houses for them, etc. Branches in all parts of the country. Write us for references and terms."[35]

These services were widely used. In a two to three year period, the National Erectors' Association alone spent $50,000 for espionage work. The National Metal Trades' Association publicly informed its members that it could provide "a secret service system by which members can place in their shops *special contract operatives* who will report on the loyalty of the workmen and even foremen. Through these, the employer can learn of any agitator in the shop almost as soon as the agitation begins."[36]

James Farley, known as the King of the Strikebreakers, had as many as 35,000 men on his lists, all of whom he could summon in the case of emergency. "It is Farley's business to 'break strikes.'" reported the St. Louis *Globe Democrat* of March 12, 1905, "and so well has he prospered at this unique occupation . . . that he is reputed to be worth several hundred thousand dollars, owns a fine house in Pittsburg and has a racing stable for a plaything that would do Edward VII's heart good to gaze upon. . . . He serves the corporations faithfully, has never failed to accomplish the task for which he was employed, and the street railway officials know him as a giant of strength in time of need. The Amalgamated Association of Street Railway and Electric Employees would have been a mighty power but for Farley, the man who is the cause of most of its failures in strike episodes." The paper quoted Farley as saying: "I do not want to be considered an enemy of labor unions, for I am not, but this thing is merely a matter of business with me."

Much of the espionage work for the various employers' associations was coordinated through the N.A.M.; its official strikebreaker, "Colonel" Martin M. Mulhall, was available, with ample funds, at the call of any employer engaged in a strike. A Senate Investigating Committee in 1913 disclosed that Mulhall had disbursed thousands of dollars for the hiring of secret service men, for bribing workers to abandon a strike, and for other strikebreaking activities. It also made public scores of telegrams Mulhall had received from grateful employers. The owners of the Selby Shoe Co. wired: "Permit us to thank you very cordially for services you have rendered us in closing up our labor troubles and ending the strike in our shoe factories."[37] The strike had ended in a smashing defeat for the union.

Not only were "operatives" placed in the shops; they were also placed inside the unions. Special reports to Gompers from A. F. of L. affiliates revealed that there were local officers of many unions, including even presidents and secretaries, who were discovered to be in the employ of detective agencies. "They furnish lists of membership of Local Unions to the Detective Agencies, who in return report to the Employers' Associations," wrote an A. F. of L. investigating committee set up to study the problem, "and many a poor fellow is discharged and deprived of a livelihood by this system, especially members of a union who take an active part in the working of the organization." The United Mine Workers was a particular target of this espionage system. "We have information," U.M.W. President John Mitchell wrote to Gompers in November 1905, "that fifty secret service men left Chicago about three weeks ago and are now members of our local unions in the anthracite field."[38]

Vigilantism against organized labor was a regular feature of the open-shop drive, and employers' associations publicly encouraged it by giving favorable publicity to such extra-legal activities. The August 15, 1903, issue of *American Industries,* N.A.M. official organ, urged employers to follow the example set by Tampa:

"A few years ago the leading citizens of Tampa made up their minds that there could be no industrial peace in their city so long as certain labor agitators, members of a cigarmakers' union, were allowed to remain there. They were constantly ordering strikes which interfered greatly with business. The labor men in question were seized, put on board a ship and landed on the coast of Honduras, where they slowly made their way back to the United States. The action of the leading citizens was illegal, but it pacified Tampa. The kidnapped agitators have not deemed it advisable to make any more trouble in that city."[39]

Enough examples of this type accumulated during the open-shop drive to warrant the conclusion that the employers' associations and the Citizens' Alliances might better be named Vigilante Associations and Alliances.

PRESSURE TO JOIN OPEN-SHOP DRIVE

It must not be assumed that the employers were undivided in their opposition to unionism. Some more responsible employers preferred to deal with the unions rather than to fight them. They were guided by the practical consideration, based on experience, that there was more profit in dealing with the unions, particularly with organizations led by conservative trade unionists, than in joining a war against them.

"There are many business men who are not in sympathy with them [the employers' associations]," wrote a reporter in 1904, "but there is some mysterious force used to force all to join." This force was actually not so "mysterious." For business men who recognized unions, the open-shoppers had only one name: "Traitors to America." Said the *Square Deal,* official organ of the Citizens' Industrial Association: "Don't boycott him, just let the public know it ... and his cowardice and traitorous attitude ... will bring its own reward." This, of course, was an open invitation to a boycott against the offending firm, and the very groups who protested loudly against a trade union boycott had not the slightest hesitation in boycotting employers who recognized the unions. One machine-manufacturing firm wrote to Gompers in April 1903 that its business had suffered severely because members of the National Metal Trades' Association "condemn and oppose our action in the recognition of the union and will not purchase our goods with union label."[40] A report in the Denver press about the same time tells its own story:

"A committee of representatives of the Citizens' Alliance and the employers' association visited various firms and requested them to abrogate their agreements with unions. They were given until tomorrow 3 in the afternoon to do so. If this was not done the offenders would find no buyers for their products and would be charged considerably more for any supplies needed, and would not, therefore, be able to compete with other firms in their trade."[41]

Such brazen intimidation was too much even for some conservative papers to swallow. Commenting on this particular report, the Denver *Post* editorialized: "The Citizens' Alliance and the employers' association have adopted one of the very methods of unionism that they condemn so vehemently—the submit or be destroyed method—to bring offending employers in line. They certainly can no longer wonder where laboring men get their ideas for pushing strikes and boycotts. If these steps had been taken by unions, all the better class, so-called, in the city would be loud in denouncing them." The Citizens' Alliance responded by passing a resolution calling upon the Denver Advertisers' Association to place advertising in such a manner that newspapers would see the advantage of a "conservative policy" friendly to "business interests."[42]

In September 1904, the Clothiers' Association of Boston announced that they had voted "not to recognize the Garment Workers' Union," and warned the contractors that if they "made any agreement with the union whatsoever," they might as well forget about doing business for the members of the Association. A month later, the Association gleefully announced that several contractors who had refused to heed the warning were no longer in business.[43]

Even when a majority of the employers in a particular trade recognized the union, the local Alliance would take firm steps to force these employers to break their agreements and institute the open shop. "The worst features with which we really have to contend," John B. Lennon, general secretary of the Journeymen Tailors' Union of America, wrote to Gompers in October 1903, "is with what is known as the Businessmen's Alliance. This is a local organization in the various cities, but in our trade can wield a very great influence, for as you can readily understand members of our union work on material that is only purchased by well to do people. They are not in sympathy with the Trade Union movement in mass, and these Business Men's Alliances hold all Merchant Tailors in the cities where we have agreements in fear by the threat that if they continue to recognize our union they will refuse to buy any goods of them and as they are their principal customers this threat is quite effective."[44]

Coupled with the boycott of goods manufactured by firms which continued to recognize the union was the refusal to furnish supplies to such employers. Thus the Frick Co., the main source of coke for the manufacture of steel, refused to furnish the product to the independent iron and steel manufacturers of the country—"the only firms employing union men, nearly all of which are compelled to purchase their coke from the Frick Co."[45]

In communities where a major corporation exercised dominant influence over the area's business, its threat to move unless all employers joined the open-shop drive was usually enough to produce the desired results. A report from Illinois in 1903 related: "Whitworth's threat to move the plant from Woodstock caused a panic among the business men and merchants of Woodstock, and they, well knowing that if the threat was carried out it would practically mean the ruin of the town, immediately yielded to Whitworth's ultimatum, severed their relations with the unions, and joined the Citizens' Alliance, headed by James A. Whitworth himself."[46]

It was widely reported throughout the country that the banks put the screws on employers who refused to join the open-shop campaign "under the threat of cutting off accommodations in a financial way." "The banks in this city are all controlled by members of the Parry Association," wrote John Golden, president of the United Textile Workers from Fall River, Massachusetts, in December 1904, "and as they are very much opposed to organized labor, they make it difficult, if not impossible, for firms with whom we have agreements to get a loan when needed."[47] On the other hand, the banks were quite ready to assist employers engaged in a struggle to establish the open shop, and the employers' associations often underwrote such loans. Joint support was given in cases involving legal action.

Funds were raised by the employers' associations for the erection of armories and the purchase of rifles and other equipment for the National Guard. Such expenditures were to be regarded as "merely an insurance," since employers "would lose more in one successful strike" than they had contributed to the militia. The *Financial Record,* published in Wall Street, flatly stated in June 1903 that the most efficient and least expensive way to handle a labor dispute was "with a whisp of grape," and assured employers that had there been "a more liberal expenditure of ammunition" at the beginning of the upsurge in trade union membership following the depression, "it is quite likely that there would be at the present no labor problem worth speaking of in the United States."[48]

THE ANTI-UNION PROPAGANDA FRONT

To make up for lost time, the anti-union associations launched a vast campaign to mold public opinion in favor of the open shop. Initiated early in the open-shop drive, the campaign was immensely intensified in 1907 when N.A.M. voted to implement its expanding anti-union crusade with a $1,500,000 fund for "educational purposes." In 1909 the Association launched its "Educational Literature series," publishing pamphlets which reflected the ideas of the open-shoppers. Millions of copies were distributed to schools, colleges, churches, and libraries by the N.A.M. and other employers' associations. The character of this literature can be discerned from the titles alone: "Eight Hours by Act of Congress—Arbitrary, Needless, Destructive, Dangerous," "The Disadvantages of Labor Unionism," "The Mob Spirit in Organized Labor," "Cruel Unionism," "Open Shop Encyclopedia for Debaters," "The Labor Trust," "Monopoly of Labor," "The Practical Value of Employers' Associations in Resisting Unjust Union Demands," "The Road to Industrial Peace."[49]

The road to industrial peace was, of course, through the open shop. It was necessary for "the workingmen of this country to understand that their employers are their best friends." As for the class struggle, it did not exist. "Let not the word class or classes pass our lips," said one of the publications of N.A.M. "We have no classes in our country."[50] This from an organization that was constantly appealing to the class interests of the employers to urge them on to greater organization and activity against the trade unions!

Unionism was depicted as an un-American importation and trade unionists as foreign-born anarchists of the same breed as Leon F. Czolgosz* who had assassinated President McKinley in September 1901. The leaders of the A. F. of L. were pictured as the most dangerous radicals, and Gompers was described as a "dangerous fomenter of socialism."†

---

* Not only was Czolgosz native-born, but he had only very limited contacts with the anarchist movement.

† In a survey of the "Educational Literature" series for the period 1909-1913, George Douglas Blackwood found that about 75 adjectives, nouns or phrases "with hyperbolic effect" were used at least three or more times in relation to organized labor. Among the most commonly used expressions were: unprincipled, radical, unconstitutional, illegal, autocratic, anti-American, corrupt, socialistic, monopolistic, irresponsible, promoters of class ideas, a menace to society, thieves, anarchistic, an enemy to America, anti-Christian, criminal, terroristic, murderous, unholy,

The Federation itself was "saturated with socialistic tendencies and anarchistic impulses," and its demand for shorter hours was bringing the United States close to the "horizon of communism."[51]

"10,000 Preachers to Attack Unions," a newspaper report noted in 1906, explaining that N.A.M. had completed plans to have "Ministers go after Federated Labor." Many of these sermons were reprinted in pamphlet form and widely distributed. The American Anti-Boycott Association reprinted in pamphlet form, with his permission, the text of one of Cardinal James Gibbons' sermons in which this powerful dignitary of the Catholic Church expounded views which fitted squarely into the open-shop drive.[52] Judicial decisions denouncing trade unionism as "treason" were likewise reprinted in pamphlet form and distributed. Thousands of copies were distributed of Judge John J. Jackson's opinion in the Circuit Court of West Virginia on July 24, 1902, justifying the issuance of an injunction against organizers for the United Mine Workers. The Judge declared: "No publicist or statesman loyal to his country ever claimed that free speech gave the right to any one to advocate and defend treason to his country, or destruction to its institutions. . . . Are communism and anarchy, and all the dire evils which follow in the train of such people . . . who are preaching the most destructive heresies and doctrines, to be protected by the Constitution of the United States? Never, never, never, never. . . ."[53]

Widely distributed also was the speech of Chancellor Day of Syracuse University in which the educator praised the open shop, and declared that "the workmen receive too much for their labor and are poverty-stricken because they spend too much money in saloons." But the most effective use was made of the speech of President Charles W. Eliot of Harvard University before the Boston Economic Club in 1902 in which he attacked the closed shop, praised the open shop, and expressed the opinion that "A strikebreaker is a good type of the American hero." At a convention of the American Anti-Boycott Association it was proposed that Eliot's speech should be circulated in every school throughout the country as part of the campaign to educate the young to think "open shop."[54] Other employers' associations picked up the cry, turned Eliot's declaration into a slogan of their movement, and an intensive drive was undertaken to use it in converting the schoolroom into an ally of the open-shop crusade.*

---

foreigners, network of organized crime, alien ideas, perverts, animals (or beasts), communists, a menace to Western civilization, network of organized crime. (George Douglas Blackwood, "Techniques and Stereotypes in the Literature of the National Association of Manufacturers Concerning Industry and Labor," unpublished M.A. thesis, University of Chicago, Department of History, Aug., 1947, pp. 58–59.)

* Day and Eliot were not the only college presidents whose speeches were used by the open-shoppers. The National Founders' Association printed and distributed an anti-labor speech by Nicholas Murray Butler, president of Columbia University.

The employers' associations gave wide publicity to President Theodore Roosevelt's decision of 1903 reinstating William A. Miller, an employee in the bindery of the Government Printing Office who had been discharged after he had been dropped from the Bookbinders' Union for anti-union activities. Roosevelt's charge that trade unions were attempting to usurp "governmental functions," coincided with the oft-repeated charge of the open-shoppers that the unions were seeking to usurp "management functions." And the President's declaration that the government would defend the right of an individual not to join a union fit right into the union-smashing drive of the period. The Kansas City Employers' Association, a member body of the Citizens' Industrial Association, praised Roosevelt enthusiastically for his action in the Miller case. A staunch newspaper supporter of the open-shop drive editorialized: "It makes the American heart beat high with pride in the present and with a hope for the future of this nation to read the Roosevelt 'obiter dictum' in the Miller case." The Washington *Post* even credited Roosevelt with coining the phrase "open shop," and while it was clearly in error, the statement revealed that Roosevelt's action in the Miller case "lent prestige to the employers' associations and their supporters."[55]

The press was an active agent in the open-shop drive. In no city throughout the country was this campaign so vigorously conducted as in Los Angeles, and here the entire open-shop campaign was sparked by the Los Angeles *Times,* owned by Harrison Gray Otis. In 1890, the *Times* locked out its union printers. After an aggressive fight by Typographical Union No. 174, Otis was forced to sign an agreement under which he was to unionize his newspaper within a specified time. But Otis repudiated the agreement, and not only launched an attack against the printers' union, but dedicated his paper to establishing the open shop in Los Angeles. "It was the *Times,*" writes Grace Heilman Stimson, "that rallied employers and the public behind the slogan of industrial freedom. . . . Otis used his newspaper with telling effect to justify employers in labor disputes, to upbraid and ridicule businessmen too friendly to unions, to harass organized labor at every turn, to elevate nonunion workingmen to a pinnacle of nobility, and to commend various nonunion workers' organizations, such as the Printers' Protective Fraternity. Anti-union devices, like lockout, the blacklist, and the discharge of union members, received the *Times* approval and encouragement. . . ." "It is coming to pass," declared the *Times* on October 3, 1903, "that the sympathetic lockout must be resorted to by employers as a means of combating the sympathetic strike and the boycott." Typical headlines in the *Times* read: "Union Labor Against Army," "Labor Unions Destroy Meaning of Stars and Stripes." Journalists throughout the country called the city, not Los Angeles, but Otistown.[56]

While the Los Angeles *Times* was, as Gompers correctly put it, "one of the most malicious antagonists of organized labor in the United States," it had plenty of companions in the field of journalism. Throughout the United States, with few exceptions, trade unions were treated in the press as enemies of American society. If accepted it was only grudgingly as a necessary evil and unavoidable concomitant of industrial development. Beyond this, the press viewed labor's aims as inimical to the general welfare. On almost every major issue—the use of strikes and boycotts, the union shop, labor legislation—the press was almost unanimously hostile. Throughout the period 1900–1914, the newspapers castigated organized labor as an un-American element— "how many of the most active leaders of labor unionism are of American blood?" asked the New York *Journal of Commerce* rhetorically—pictured it as an unchained beast ready, if given the opportunity, to pounce upon a helpless public, and portrayed labor unions as one with thuggery, dynamiting, and the employment of all forms of and variety of terror. Labor's favorite weapons were referred to in the *New York Times* as "the bludgeon, the bullet, the dynamite cartridge, and the terrible boycott." Its record was one of "outrages and oppression, of riot and bloodshed, of cruel boycotts, of defiance of the law." The characteristics of unions made "organized labor the enemy of society and put it in the attitude of rebellion against the law."[57]

"Labor Tyranny" was made synonymous with organized labor in the press. "It is indisputable," declared the New York *Herald* in 1908, "that as at present constituted the labor unions, dominated as they are by a few dictatorial spirits and self-seeking demagogues, are simply organized tyrannies." Organized labor's sole accomplishment throughout history, according to the New York *Evening Post* was the substitution of the "tyranny of the organization for liberty, the liberty of rigid averages for the hope of individual progress." As the New York *Sun* viewed history: "If . . . labor union rule had been imposed from the beginning [of civilization] mankind would still be in a state of savagery."[58]

The closed shop was a special target of the press. It was described as "un-American and unconstitutional." The United States Constitution, argued the New York *Sun,* held "as the most sacred and vital and indispensable element Liberty of Contract, the right of every man to work for whom he will for such prices as he is willing to accept." The *New York Times* agreed: "The right of every man to work at such wages and on such terms as he chooses to accept from any employer with whom he may choose to engage is a fundamental right, for the perfect protection of which all the powers of the State must be used wherever necessary. . . . Freedom of contract is, and should be the basis of everything in the industrial relation."[59]

The press, of course, was fulsome in praise of the open shop. Typical was the editorial comment of the *New York Times* in 1904: "The movement for the open shop comes at a time when something is needed in the way of effective opposition . . . to save organized labor from destroying itself . . . It is about all we have in sight which gives even the suggestion of a promise of industrial peace." "This government is based upon the open-shop principle," the *Times* added two years later, and in 1909, it hailed the open shop as embodying "the spirit of true Americanism."[60]

All of these newspapers and their counterparts in the magazine field were highly recommended by the open-shop associations to businessmen as warranting their "patronage in preference to those whose columns and pages are filled with cheap sensational trash tending to breed discontent, chaos and anarchy. . . ."[61] Newspapers and magazines which dared to carry even occasional articles friendly to organized labor were threatened with withdrawal of advertising, and those that refused to heed the warning faced extinction. In 1904, the Citizens' Alliance and the Mine Owners' Association in Colorado began a vigorous boycott against the *Rocky Mountain News* and the Denver *Times,* owned by Thomas McDonald Patterson, which were friendly to organized labor. The Advertisers' Association, all of whose members belonged to the Citizens' Alliance, announced a one-month advertising boycott of the papers. Since nearly all the important business interests of Denver were in the Advertisers' Association, such a boycott or threat of it, was a devastating weapon. Moreover, businessmen who advertised in these papers were made to understand that they would not obtain loans from the banks, goods from their suppliers, and orders from their customers.[62]

Although the motion picture industry was still in its infancy, the employers' associations were quick to realize the important role this new medium could play in the open-shop drive. Scores of anti-labor films began to appear during and after 1907 whose plots fitted precisely into the propaganda campaign of the open-shoppers. "Labor unrest" was attributed in these films either to jealousy, laziness or drunkenness on the part of the workers or to mob violence incited by foreign agitators. The films bore such titles as "Lulu's Anarchists," "Gus, the Anarchist," "The Dynamiters," "Murderous Anarchist," "Dough and Dynamite," "Lazy Bill and the Strikers," "The Long Strike," "When Women Strike," "The Riot," and "Good Boss." "It is suspected," noted a contemporary journalist, "that behind this class of pictures, if the veil is removed, would be the National Association of Manufacturers."[63]

The plots of the movies clearly showed the influence of the open-shop drive. Most of the films blasted unions and pictured strikes as futile. Strike leaders were dynamiters, killers, aliens who not only gained nothing for the workers but left them worse off than before. Workingmen who followed the advice of their union leaders were described as "dupes of rascals." One film showed a labor leader ruining the entire town by persuading the men to strike for better conditions. The movie ended with the factory owners moving their plant elsewhere to "teach the workers a lesson never to listen to agitators."

The scab in these early movies was, of course, a social hero, while the boss was a good man. In the widely distributed film, "Right to Labor," an "alien agitator with tremendous personal magnetism" persuaded the union to strike for more pay. Everyone went out but John—"the loyal one"—who defied the strikers, saying: "This is a free country. You have the right to strike. I have the right to labor." In reply, the strikers "plot to blow up John's house." The plot fails; the scabs take over the leadership of the strike, and the film ends with the workers driving the "alien agitator" out of town, and voting to return to work at the same wage scale. The "loyal one" is promoted to superintendent. A few weeks later the men get their ten per cent wage increase after all. "The boss said it was due to John's good work during the strike."

Vitagraph's film, "Capital and Labor," released in 1910, argued that the church could do more to improve the conditions of the workers than their unions. This film was advertised as having "a soothing charm of a most delicate love story" in which "the man of heart and moral courage (the minister) proves superior to the man of power and violence (the union organizer)." The film's message that capital would bow to labor's demands if "approached properly by the right people," prompted the *Motion Picture World,* chief spokesman of the rising industry, to call "Capital and Labor" "one of the most extraordinary motion picture dramas of the year ... powerful in its purpose."[64]

These anti-labor films were so numerous that in 1910 the A. F. of L. convention devoted special attention to the problem. The convention endorsed resolutions advising workers to protest, and protest strongly, to the local theater management whenever these movies were shown, and if the protest did not produce results to resort to other methods. Special instructions were issued to central labor bodies and local unions to protest "against the unwarranted misrepresentations in motion pictures of occurrences in strikes."[65]

While major attention was paid to newspapers, magazines, and motion pictures, the open shoppers did not neglect books. The spate of anti-labor novels that appeared after 1901 was directly connected with the open-shop campaign, and many were subsidized by the employers' associations. (N.A.M. pushed the distribution of *The Plunderer,* a novel by George Crockett, a Maine doctor, which attacked unions in general and the A. F. of L. in particular.) *The Industrial Crisis,* a novel by F. C. Lange, published in August 1903, is typical. Not only are "profanity, drunkenness, and godless living ... the shameful causes of our laboring people's outrageous conduct," but the novelist has his leading character exclaim: "As a member of organized labor, a person is actually walking in the council of the ungodly. God's name is used in vain. His supremacy is fiercely denied, and the Lord's prayer sneered at or forgotten." The employers, on the other hand, are described as "The Lord's Stewards," and but for the fact that the ownership and control of industry was under their "wise guardianship," the "masses, having wasted their substance, extravagantly, would be crying 'Bread! Give us Bread!'" Trade unionists are described in the novel as "organized anarchists," and their leaders as conspiring to create a revolution so that the United States may "in a few years, be in the hands of . . . the beasts from out of the bottom-less pit."[66]

THE TRADE UNION REPLY

For the first few years after the launching of the open-shop drive, the majority of trade union leaders were not unduly alarmed by the employers' associations' propaganda campaign. The general reaction was that the "false notions" spread by the N.A.M., the Citizens' Alliances and other open-shop associations were so exaggerated that they would be derided by intelligent people. One trade union journal summed up the early reaction: "The arguments advanced by the Parryites are so superficial and the alleged statements of facts so palpably unfair, that many unionists do not think them worthy of reply."[67]

By the end of 1903 it was already clear that the open shop propaganda campaign was having serious effect and materially assisting employers in checking the progress of unionism. Gompers sounded the warning when he told the delegates to the A. F. of L. Convention in November 1903 that the time had already passed when the employers' associations' propaganda could be dismissed with the observation that nobody would be taken in. The fact was that many had "been persuaded that the [open shop] proposition on the surface appears to be ethical." Organized labor had to answer the falsehoods of the open-shoppers with the truth of unionism, and had to do so immediately.[68] In the next few years, the trade union reply was set forth in speeches, articles, leaflets, and pamphlets.

To the charge that the trade unions were "conspiracies hatched up by certain wild-eyed foreigners with criminal tendencies and imported to America for the purpose of injuring the welfare of the people," organized labor answered with historical evidence proving that unions had existed in ancient times, in the Middle Ages, and in the United States from colonial days. True, the names of these organizations of workers varied "with time and locality," but unionism was "a universal fact," the "natural product of the present industrial system," and "no agitator or body of labor leaders" had created it. "Forced into existence by oppression," the unions continued to exist to root out oppression.

They could not be destroyed. "If they were done away with to-day, they would spring up again tomorrow."[69]

To a chief argument of the employers' associations that organized labor, by insisting on the exclusive employment of union men, was depriving nonunion men of their liberty and their right to earn a livelihood, organized labor replied that this argument overlooked the fact that unionists were justified by reasons of fair play in demanding a union shop. "When the members of a trade union have by the expenditure of their own time and means created certain conditions necessary to their safety and well-being in a certain industry or institution, it is morally their right and logically their duty to insist that the nonunionist who seeks to share these conditions shall first agree to share the labor and expenditure necessary to their maintenance—in other words to insist that he shall join the union." Then again, this argument overlooked the fact that the nonunionist by aiding the employer in defeating a union that protected the workers from deprivation and misery, was destructive to the welfare of his class, and therefore committed an injustice that eventually reached himself. "This he has no moral right to do. Nor, under the principle of group justice has he the right to take the place of the union man who is striving to maintain the objects of trade-unionism—the welfare of the group."[70]

To the charge that the closed or union shop meant tyranny and the open shop freedom, organized labor replied that this was a complete reversal of the actual facts. The trade unionists ridiculed Parry's assertion that the aim of the open-shop drive was "to reaffirm and to enforce those fundamental principles of American government guaranteeing free competitive conditions," pointing out that the trusts who controlled the N.A.M. and most of the other employers' associations were the very forces who were strangling competition. The only freedom the open-shoppers wanted was the freedom to monopolize and exploit. What freedom did an employer have when he was forced by threat of business ruin to hire only nonunion men? "He is running a free shop, but his freedom does not extend to the hiring of the men he employs." What freedom did a worker in an open shop have when he knew from bitter experience that if he dared to "exercise the rights of free men," he would instantly be discharged and blacklisted? "The glorious open shop is not so free after all. Not only differences in politics, but in religious, national, and even fraternal relations may result in the banishment and blacklisting of workmen in such institutions!"[71]

Replying directly to the question raised in a public debate, "What are the reasons for the demand for the Union Shop?" Gompers declared: "The division and subdivision of labor and its specialization, brought about by inventions of machines and new tools of labor, have robbed workingmen of their power of individual freedom of contract with their employers. Their only opportunity for anything like fair or advantageous terms under which to sell their labor, is in associating themselves with their fellow workmen, in making a collective bargain, a working agreement; in other words, a union and a contract by the union with employers for their labor, and the conditions under which it shall be sold."[72]

Organized labor distributed copies of "Mr. Dooley on the Open Shop" in which Finley Peter Dunne summed up the purposes of the open-shop drive in the dialogue between Mr. Hennessy and Mr. Dooley which concluded:

" 'But,' said Mr. Hennessy, 'these open-shop min ye menshun say they are f'r unions if properly conducted.' "

" 'Shure,' said Mr. Dooley, 'if properly conducted. An' there we are; an' how would they have thim conducted? No strikes, no rules, no contracts, no scales, hardly any wages an' dam few members.' "[73]

Writing to Gompers from Detroit in September 1904, President W. D. Mahon of the Amalgamated Association of Street and Electric Railway Employees, gave a good illustration of the trade union reply to a favorite charge of the open shoppers:

"We have just had a big Parry meeting in this town. It was addressed by Kirby of Dayton and Job, the second, of Chicago. The papers have given them columns. Kirby started out by saying the Trade Unions were directed by foreigners and socialists, so on and etc. I replied through interviews in the press here by calling attention to the first statement of his speech which was founded on a falsehood and asked what the people could expect from the rest of it. I said in my interview that out of the 65 International Organizations affiliated with the American Federation of Labor I personally knew that fifty of the heads of these organizations were American born, and many of them coming from old revolutionary stock. I called attention to John Mitchell, Dan Keefe, Jno. B. Lennon, the grandson of John Brown, and to many others. I might have called attention to my own ancestors, who were revolutionary soldiers, but my modesty would not permit, but I said enough along that line to show in plain English that Mr. Kirby was a liar. I also showed that Messrs. Kirby and Job were neither of them employers of labor but the paid agitators of the corporations. The papers gave me a pretty fair deal in the matter, and I think that my interviews had some effect for many persons outside of the ranks of organized labor have congratulated me upon it."[74]

Mahon's experience in Detroit was by no means typical. Much more customary was the situation described by one trade unionist who wrote in the same year: "Mr. Parry will get two columns of space for his vindictive actions against organized labor, but we cannot get an inch of space for reply." In the main, the press eagerly opened its front pages to the open shoppers, and kept these and other pages closed to the trade unionists or relegated their replies to obscure columns far inside or to the "letters to the editor" columns.[75]

This statement of affairs did not surprise most trade unionists. ("The millionaire stockholders of the newspaper associations," an Ohio labor paper pointed out, "must be protected, the powerful corporations which support the newspapers must be shielded from the 'encroachments' and 'exorbitant' demands of organized labor. From the unorganized hordes of labor there is nothing to fear."[76]) But it did seriously limit the effectiveness of labor's reply to the open-shop propagandists. To be sure, articles in the labor press sometimes reached an audience much greater than the readers of these periodicals.* To be sure, too, the unions occasionally sponsored special campaigns to reach the general public. But the fact that so much of labor's answer appeared in the labor press meant that it failed to reach the mass of the population which was being deluged with open-shop propaganda and whose attitudes were being shaped by it. In 1907, *The World To-Day* estimated that there were 185 monthly and 179 weekly journals in the United States and Canada "devoted exclusively to the advocacy of trades-unionism," and that these 364 publications, which number did not include Socialist periodicals, reached about five million readers.[77] Even if this readership figure is accurate—and it is probably an exaggeration—the main audience for the reply of organized labor was less than one-tenth of that reached by the open-shoppers. And this audience was precisely the one that needed the least convincing.

RESULTS OF THE OPEN-SHOP DRIVE

David Parry was only slightly exaggerating when, in his presidential address of May 1906 at the annual convention of N.A.M., he declared: "Only a few years ago trades unionism unrestrained and militant was rapidly forcing the industries to a closed shop basis. . . . But a change has come and this Association is largely responsible for it." C. W. Post, head of the Citizens' Industrial Alliance, boasted in the same year: "Two years ago the press and pulpit were delivering platitudes about the oppression of workingmen. Now all this has been changed." Newspapers which dared to champion the "tyranny" of organized labor now faced ruinous loss of advertising revenue, and ministers who followed suit, the loss of their pulpits. Local and Congressional candidates who showed sympathy for the same "tyranny" were defeated at the polls if they were lucky enough to be nominated. The eight-hour and anti-injunction bills before Congress had been defeated and stood no chance of being

---

* In a brochure circulated at the A. F. of L. booths in the St. Louis Exposition of 1904, articles from the *American Federationist*, defending the union shop, were reprinted. (*See St. Louis Exposition, 1904: Exhibit of American Federation of Labor*, n.p., 1904.)

enacted, and in case after case the courts had virtually outlawed the "despotism" of sympathy strikes, boycotts, and the union label. Much credit, Post said proudly, redounded to the Citizens' Industrial Alliance, for its "work of moulding public opinion" had helped considerably in bringing about the change.[78]

While unionism did not disappear, the attack led by N.A.M. and its associate employers' associations checked the progress of unionism in general, and wiped out the foothold the unions had acquired in some of the most important industries and trades. The extent of this trend will be seen more fully in discussions of struggles in specific industries in subsequent chapters. It will suffice now to cite just a few of the victories of the open-shoppers during the period 1901–1909 which Selig Perlman and Philip Taft have correctly characterized as the "Employers' Mass Offensive."[79] In 1901, U.S. Steel crushed a strike of 62,000, and practically annihilated unionism in the iron and steel industry. During the same year, the National Metal Trades' Association smashed a national strike of 58,000 machinists, driving the union out of most of the big plants. In 1904, the Packers' Association broke a strike of packing-house workers in Chicago, Kansas City, Omaha, and other places, and knocked the union out of the meat-packing industry. In 1905, the employers' association dealt a crushing blow to the teamsters' union of Chicago. After a long and bitter strike, the union was practically wrecked, and less than 20 per cent of the 5,000 workers reinstated, and these only when they had signed contracts agreeing not to become members of or affiliated with any labor unions. In 1908, Lake seamen constituted a formidable part of the labor movement. By 1909, their union had been smashed.

From 1899 to 1904, an annual average of 45.3 per cent of the strikes undertaken had been won conclusively by labor. But in 1905, labor won only 39.5 per cent of its strikes; in 1906, 35.0 per cent; in 1907, 25.3 per cent; in 1908, 29.6 per cent; in 1909, 33.1 per cent, and in 1910, 34.4 per cent.* But the effects of the open-shop drives was reflected even more in the number of strikes in which labor failed completely. Between 1899 and 1904, the annual average of strikes lost, in percentage of those undertaken, was 36.1 per cent. In 1905, labor lost 46.1 per cent of its strikes;†

---

* Although the number of strikes called annually during these years did not change appreciably, a sharp decrease occurred in the number of workers involved. During the period 1899–1904, 603,000 workers on the average had been involved yearly in labor strikes. For the years thereafter the number of men involved fell far below the previous average: 302,000 in 1905; 383,000 in 1906; 502,000 in 1907; 209,000 in 1908 (the lowest figure since 1888); 452,000 in 1909; and 824,000 in 1910. It is clear that due to the open-shop drive, labor was less inclined to resort to strike action. (John I. Griffin, *Strikes: A Study in Quantitative Economics,* New York, 1939, pp. 13, 38, 43.)

† In 1904 labor lost 50.6 per cent of its strikes. (*Ibid.,* p. 91.)

in 1906, 48.8 per cent; in 1907, 57.6 per cent; in 1908, 55.2 per cent; in 1909, 51.0 per cent; and in 1910, 47.2 per cent.[80]

At the same time, as we have seen, a leveling-off of growth of union membership took place during these years. The period 1899–1904 had been one of rapid expansion from 611,000 in 1899 to 2,072,700 in 1904, but after 1904, further growth ceased almost completely. In 1905, union membership dropped to 2,002,300, and in 1906, to 1,907,300. Thereafter, the unions just continued to hold their own, with 2,080,400 members in 1907; 2,130,600 in 1908; 2,005,600 in 1909; and 2,140,500 in 1910.[81]

As the open-shop drive progressed, the unions were driven out of all the trustified industries, except the railroads, and in the few cases where they were granted a meager recognition, they agreed not to endeavor to organize nonunion mills, factories, and workers. In an article entitled, "The Decline in Trade Union Membership," published in 1910, Professor C. H. Parker noted that as a consequence of the open-shop drive:

"It now appears as if assured success in trade unionism would be, for the time at least, limited to the building trades, to those occupations entailing great personal responsibility as well as skill, notably the railroad unions, and to the small highly skilled trades. . . .

"Many great companies have discontinued formal relations with their associated employees. . . . Even where trade agreements have been renewed, they have been made under less advantageous terms so far as labor is concerned. . . . In short, collective bargaining on a large scale in the United States seems to be for the moment upon the decline."[82]

Yet it would be incorrect to conclude that this situation was solely the result of the open-shop drive. There were, as we shall now see, other forces at work within and outside the labor movement that effectively deprived the trade unions of the power and militancy effectively to resist the powerful employers' offensive.

CHAPTER 3

The National Civic Federation, I: Organization and Ideology

While the open-shoppers attacked labor frontally, other forces worked obliquely for the same end. "Our experience has convinced us," declared a spokesman for this group of employers in 1903, "that the best way to control labor organizations is to lead and not to force them. We are also convinced that the conservative element in all unions will control when properly led and officered." Such unions would not only keep the workers within bounds as regards their demands and action, but would be a barrier to all forms of radicalism.[1] The objective was clear. Rather than smash unionism, this section of the employing class sought to emasculate it, to ensnare the labor leaders into a conscious program of collaborating with the employers, robbing the workers of their vigor, militancy, and the spirit of their class.

The embodiment of this concept of allying the labor movement with the employers is found in the National Civic Federation, founded in 1900 after months of preliminary preparations.*

COMPOSITION OF THE N.C.F.

At the N.C.F.'s first national conference in December 1900, the chairman emphasized that "nothing is more pressing than a method of adjusting the differences of capital and labor." Towards this end, the conference established an Industrial Department whose purpose was to promote peace and harmony in the industrial world, and "when requested

* For details on the origin of the National Civic Federation, *see* Philip S. Foner, *History of the Labor Movement in the United States,* vol. II, New York, 1955, pp. 384–87.

Local branches of the N.C.F. were set up in New York City, St. Louis, and Chicago in 1903, and in Cleveland and Boston a year later. (*National Civic Federation Review,* April, 1903, p. 20; June, 1903, p. 20; June, 1904, pp. 4, 11, 16. Hereinafter cited as *NCF Review.*)

to by both parties to a dispute, would act as a forum to adjust or decide upon questions at issue between workers and their employers." The Department, headed by Marcus Alonzo (or Mark) Hanna, the Ohio industrialist who became a commanding figure in the Republican party,* was composed of representatives of capital, labor, and the general public. Heading the labor representatives were Samuel Gompers, president of the·A. F. of L., John Mitchell, president of the United Mine Workers and vice-president of the A. F. of L., and President Daniel J. Keefe of the International Longshoremen, Marine and Transport Workers' Union and a member of the A. F. of L. Executive Council.[2]

Gompers and Mitchell were charter members of the N.C.F. Among the other labor leaders who became active in the organization were the heads of the Railroad Brotherhoods, the presidents of the iron, steel and tin workers, granite cutters, longshoremen, machinists, iron moulders, printers, garment workers, carpenters and joiners, bricklayers and masons, street railway employees, boot and shoe workers, bottle blowers, stationary firemen, and textile workers' unions.[3] This small group of men controlled the A. F. of L. and the Railroad Brotherhoods and determined their policies. They joined hands in the N.C.F. with the leaders of the trustified, finance capital-dominated industries and their representatives.

In an interview with the press, Mark Hanna, N.C.F. president, hailed the Civic Federation as providing the means "for the total abolition of strikes in the United States." John Mitchell agreed, and in a letter to Hanna predicted that as the objectives of the N.C.F. became more widely understood, "strikes and lockouts may become unnecessary."[4] As Mitchell expressed it, the N.C.F. was based on this fundamental conception: "There is no necessary hostility between capital and labor. Neither can do without the other; each has evolved from the other. . . . There is not even a necessary fundamental antagonism between the laborers and the capitalists . . . broadly considered, the interest of one is the interest of the other, and the prosperity of the one is the prosperity of the other." With good reason, one student of the N.C.F. has written of Mitchell: "Here was a labor leader upon which the Federation could count."†[5]

---

* Hanna directed the successful Presidential campaigns of William McKinley in 1896 and 1900, and he served as U.S. Senator from Ohio. Cartoonists at the turn of the century would often portray "big business" simply by showing Hanna in garments bedecked with dollar signs.

† The public statements of no American labor leader of this period were as widely reprinted in the commercial press and as widely distributed through employers' publications as those of John Mitchell. Mitchell's book, *Organized Labor,* published in 1903, was endorsed by employers' publications because it had a "conservative" approach to the "labor problem." The *Wall Street Journal* in its review of the book hailed the fact that "conservatism is very much the keynote throughout. . . . Mr. Mitchell may be counted among the ablest, most responsible and most far-sighted of the labor leaders in power today." (Oct. 28, 1903.)

Mitchell's thesis was officially advanced by the N.C.F. at its second annual industrial conference in 1901. "The laborer of today is the capitalist of tomorrow," the conference announced. "That the wage earners form the primary schools for the millionaires is evidenced every day." The evidence did not include the vast majority of American workers who, as we have seen, earned about $10.50 a week or even the 16.2 per cent who received $15 or more per week!

"Tribunal of Peace," was the headline in the Chicago *Tribune* over the report of the proceedings of the N.C.F.'s second annual conference.[6] Yet for all its inspirational talk about labor-capital harmony, the N.C.F. conceded that there were conflicts between workers and employers. These conflicts, however, were neither inevitable nor difficult to eliminate, for there were no classes in America, and thus there could be no real class conflict as in Europe. In the United States there were only "misunderstandings" between employers and workers. The object of the N.C.F. was to avoid these "misunderstandings," first, by bringing business and labor leaders together in mutual conference at meetings, dinners, and banquets, and, when a "misunderstanding" such as an industrial dispute arose, to act quickly to achieve peace.[7] There were three parties to every industrial dispute—capitalists, workers, and the general public—and by living up to the principle of the "Golden Rule," these three parties could achieve peaceful settlements of all disputes which would be satisfactory to all of the parties concerned. Corresponding to this idea, the N.C.F. was made up of representatives of the three bodies—labor, capital, and the general public.

Leaving aside for the time being, the question of how truly the representatives of labor represented the real interests of the workers, let us consider the spokesmen for capital and the general public. Mark Hanna, president of the N.C.F. until his death in 1904, was publicly considered to be J. P. Morgan's representative in the organization. To be sure, he was praised by Gompers and Mitchell as the epitome of a "fair" employer, but those who knew his activities as an employer did not share this feeling. Protesting to Gompers over the publicizing of Hanna in A. F. of L. publications as "fair, if not fairer, than any other mine owner," a U.M.W. organizer wrote: "I have only this to say in reference to this matter that if this is the case it is no wonder that the miners of America are the most downtrodden case of workmen on the face of the earth to-day. I have never visited his mines, but I understand from my colleagues, who have been there, that the employees of the Hanna interests are in a deplorable condition." The U.S. Industrial Commission's investigation of labor conditions in 1900 bore out the truth of this statement.[8]

After Hanna's death, in February 1904, it was suggested that Andrew Carnegie replace him as N.C.F. president. But Carnegie was so hated in labor circles because of his part in breaking the Homestead Steel

Strike in 1892 that it was decided to give the post to August Belmont.[9] This prominent finance capitalist, as we shall see, was soon to prove himself as adept in breaking strikes as Carnegie had been.

Among the spokesmen for the employers in the N.C.F. was J. Ogden Armour of Armour & Co., whose workers in the trustified meat-packing plants were described by an A. F. of L. investigating committee as "white slaves," and whose products were being boycotted by many trade unions because of the trust's anti-union policies. Another was Louis F. Swift, head of Swift & Co. who had agreed with other packing-house firms never to sign a written contract with a union. Another was Charles M. Schwab of the U.S. Steel Corp. and still another was Elbert H. Gary, president of the Federal Steel Co., a U.S. Steel affiliate. Both of these men played leading roles in wiping out unionism in the steel industry, and worked closely with J. P. Morgan in eradicating unionism from every company in the newly organized steel trust. Still another was Cyrus H. McCormick, president of the McCormick Harvesting Machine Co., who had broken with the union in this giant industry as far back as 1886 and thereafter had blacklisted all workers who had anything to do with labor organizations.* Other representatives of the employers in the N.C.F. had also gained notoriety for their anti-union policies. The heads of the railroad corporations in the organizaton bitterly fought every attempt to organize the mass of the railroad workers. The only unions they tolerated were the conservative brotherhood crafts which represented a small minority of the workers in the industry.[10]

The apologists for the new form of brotherhood of labor and capital embodied in the N.C.F.—among whom Gompers was a leading spokesman[11]—argued that the whole question of the fairness of the organization and its possible influence in industrial relations turned not so much on the composition of the representatives of capital and labor as it did upon the character of the men who were selected as the "representatives of the public." For these were the men whose votes, in case of a tie between capital and labor, would decide the outcome of a dispute submitted to the N.C.F.

If one examines the list of the men who functioned as representatives of the public, from the time of the formation of the N.C.F. to December 1908, and studies their associations as revealed in such contemporary works as *Who's Who, Directory of Directors, Financial Red Book, Moody's Manual of Corporations,* and John Moody's *Truth About*

* "Time and again in the next fifty years [after 1886] Cyrus McCormick was to make concessions to workers while withholding that essential to union survival —recognition of the union and the workers' right to participate in union activity without discrimination." (Robert Ozanne, "Union-Management Relations: McCormick Harvesting Machine Company, 1862–1886," *Labor History,* vol. IV, Spring, 1963, pp. 153–54.)

Trusts, one quickly discovers that the representatives of the third party in industrial disputes were none other than the finance capitalists and their agents:

1. *Grover Cleveland.* Trustee, New York Life Insurance Company. (As President, he had sent federal troops to break the Pullman strike.)

2. *Cornelius W. Bliss.* Ex-Secretary of the U.S. Treasury; director, American Cotton Co., Equitable Life Insurance Co., Fourth National Bank Insurance Co.; trustee, American Surety Co. and Central Trust Co.

3. *Oscar S. Straus.* Millionaire merchant and diplomat. President, New York Board of Trade and Transportation; trustee, New York Life Insurance Co.

4. *Charles Francis Adams.* Former president, Union Pacific Railroad; director, Kansas City Stock Yards Co. and Westinghouse Electric and Manufacturing Co.

5. *Isaac N. Seligman.* Banker; member, Advisory Committee of Stockholders' Audit Co. of New York; treasurer and director, City and Suburban Homes Co.

6. *David R. Francis.* President, Louisiana Exposition; vice-president, Laclede National Bank; director, Mississippi Valley Trust Co. of St. Louis and Waters-Pierce Coal Co., a branch of Standard Oil Co.

7. *James Speyer.* Director, Baltimore & Ohio Railroad; trustee, General Trust Co.; director and trustee of a dozen or more companies which were mainly Standard Oil concerns.

8. *Franklin McVeagh.* Merchant and reformer; trustee, Chicago Penny Savings Bank and several other Chicago institutions.

9. *James H. Eckels.* Former Comptroller of the Treasury; director in a long list of companies, mainly controlled by the House of Morgan.

10. *John J. Cook.* Corporation lawyer; trustee, American Surety Co.; director, Equitable Life Insurance Co., International Banking Corp., Mercantile Trust Co., Wells-Fargo & Co.; trustee, Sun Insurance Co.

11. *John M. Milburn.* Corporation lawyer; partner of Lewis C. Ledyard, Milburn, Ledyard & Carter of New York; director in a long list of corporations mainly controlled by the Standard Oil-Rockefeller interests.

12. *Everett Macy.* Listed as "Capitalist"; director of a long list of corporations including Standard Oil and Grand Mining Co.

13. *Charles J. Bonaparte.* Leading Baltimore capitalist; director of many corporations controlled by the Standard Oil-Rockefeller interests.

Besides these supposed representatives of "the public" there were Archbishop John Ireland, several of whose sermons were reprinted and distributed by the open-shop associations; Bishop Henry C. Potter, commonly known as J. P. Morgan's preacher; Nicholas Murray Butler, president of Columbia University, a darling of the open shoppers, and Charles W. Eliot, president of Harvard University, whose statement that the scab was the American hero, was one of the most widely distributed pieces of literature in the whole catalogue of open-shop propaganda.[12]

According to the above classification, practically 100 per cent of "the public" was composed of men intimately linked to finance capitalism, the majority actually being House of Morgan and Standard Oil-Rockefeller officials and lawyers. Yet these were the men to whom the labor movement was supposed to look for an "impartial" decision in the settlement of industrial disputes! Certainly the composition of the N.C.F.'s spokesmen for "the public" shows how ridiculous was the idea, enthusiastically endorsed by Gompers and other labor leaders in the organization, that there was a third force apart from the capitalists and organized labor that would be the salvation of the working class.[13]

The essential and all-important fact is that the N.C.F. was dominated from top to bottom by businessmen. As Gordon Maurice Jensen points out in his study of the N.C.F.: "From the very beginning, one element of the National Civic Federation's membership occupied a position of clear preponderance . . . that element was business." It was not merely businessmen but big business that dominated the N.C.F. Nearly 70 per cent of the most influential groups within the N.C.F. "represented enterprises distinctly larger than average and . . . 56 per cent represented very large enterprises." Of the 190 business leaders "who held the *topmost* positions in the largest business companies in the United States during the decade, 1901–1910, 43 were members of the National Civic Federation." "In all," Jensen concludes, "a very considerable segment of the nation's big business was represented in the National Civil Federation."[14]*

ROLE OF RALPH M. EASLEY

The composition of the "public" members of the N.C.F. was no accident. It was Ralph M. Easley, N.C.F. secretary, who decided which men should be invited to membership in the organization. From the outset, he made sure that the representatives of labor should be "conservative, practical men," and that the spokesmen for "the public" be mainly big

---

* Jensen points out that of the 241 men who constituted the inner group in the councils of the N.C.F., 177, or 73 per cent, held positions of importance: 111 were corporation presidents, three were corporation board chairmen, three were corporation committee chairmen, 26 were corporation vice-presidents, 12 were business partners, 17 were banking partners, and five ran their own business. Furthermore, almost one-third of the 367 corporations in the country with a capitalization of $10,000,000 or over had one or more members active in the N.C.F., and of the 67 railroads with a capitalization of $10,000,000 or over, 16 had members in the N.C.F. (Gordon Maurice Jensen, "The National Civic Federation: American Business in an Age of Social Change and Social Reform, 1900–1910," unpublished Ph.D. thesis, Princeton University, May, 1956, pp. 59–60.)

corporation executives. There was no room for "cranks, hobbyists or revolutionists" or radical preachers and charity workers," and there was certainly none for advocates of militant trade unionism. Although he had once been the owner and publisher of a newspaper, Easley was not a business man himself. But through long contact with businessmen, he had become a leading spokesman for the capitalist point of view. "Easley . . . was completely in accord with them [the businessmen] on most fundamentals and had so thoroughly absorbed their ideas, their habits of thought, and even their prejudices that he could and did think entirely in their terms."[15]

Easley edited the *National Civic Federation Review,* the first number of which appeared in April 1903, and, all in all, ran the N.C.F. as his "own little business." (The Chicago *Tribune* referred to the N.C.F. as "absolute management from one center—namely the secretary of the National Civic Federation.") He was accountable only to the financial contributors whose support kept the organization operating. A study of the unpublished records of the N.C.F. reveals that these contributors were the leading monopoly corporations and capitalists. Among them were: J. P. Morgan & Co., Andrew Carnegie, Kuhn, Loeb, & Co., International Harvester Co., National Cash Register Co., American Telephone & Telegraph Co., American Car & Foundry Co., American Locomotive Works, American Smelting & Refining Co., American Woolen Co., Electric Bond & Share Co., Otis Elevator Co., E. I. DuPont de Nemours Powder Co., U.S. Steel Corp., Metropolitan Life Insurance Co., Westinghouse Electric & Manufacturing Co., and Commonwealth Edison Co.[16]

Most of the corporations listed above operated as open shops—a fact that is hardly surprising since nearly all of them were controlled by the House of Morgan which, as we have already seen, was a prime force behind the open-shop drive.*

The labor unions contributed nothing to the support of the N.C.F. Indeed, big business even paid the salary and expenses of John Mitchell when he came to work for the N.C.F. full-time as salaried head of the

---

* The presence of so many Morgan firms in the list of contributors is due to the fact that Easley concentrated from the beginning on these firms. In April 1901, he stressed to Gompers the "tremendous importance to the industrial welfare of the country that every influence be brought to induce Mr. (J.P.) Morgan and his friends to start right." (Easley to Gompers, April 1, 1901, *AFL Corr.*) The absence of Rockefeller-dominated corporations from the list of contributors is clarified in a letter from Mitchell to Gompers, March 9, 1911: "As you know, the Standard Oil folks, with the exception of Mr. Vanderlip of the National City Bank, have not had much to do with the N.C.F. They seem to hold aloof from us." (*Ibid.*) However, as we have seen above, several directors of Standard Oil-dominated corporations were among the representatives of "the Public" on the N.C.F.'s Industrial Department.

Trade Agreement Department.* Andrew Carnegie contributed $2,500; George Perkins of the House of Morgan gave the same amount, while others pledged the $10,000 more needed to cover salary and expenses.

"Considering that the organization could not have remained in operation had it not been for the employers' contributions," writes one student of the National Civic Federation, "it was extremely unlikely that Easley would have done anything to lose the favor of his patrons. For example, even if he had wanted to advocate the closed shop, it would have been extremely unprofitable for him to have done so. But no one ever had reason to fear such a move from Easley. . . .

"To some extent, [Clarence E.] Bonnett was not too far off when he included the N.C.F. in his study of employers' associations [*Employers' Associations in the United States*], for the employer third of the Federation could wield a silent influence through the power of the purse."[17]

Actually, this should read "two-thirds," since, as we have seen, "the public" representatives were themselves members of the employers' class or closely linked to it.

What did the employers get for their money? They obtained the services of a widely-publicized organization which nominally had for its purpose the civic-minded task of solving labor difficulties peacefully in the interest of labor, capital, and the public, but actually functioned to further the interests of the employers, an organization that worked steadfastly to permeate the labor movement with conservatism, and to utilize the trade union leadership as a barrier against militant unionism.

THE N.C.F. AND THE OPEN-SHOP DRIVE

The champions of the N.C.F., past and present, have insisted that the concept of the Federation as an employers' association is ridiculous in light of the fact that it was attacked by the leading spokesmen for the

---

* In 1908 Mitchell suffered a breakdown and did not run for reelection as President of the United Mine Workers. He was then only 38 years old, and he asked Easley for a position in the N.C.F. He was offered the post in the organization, but it was not announced since he was still acting as President of the U.M.W. He started to work full-time for the N.C.F. after the U.M.W. convention in April 1908. He still continued to hold his position as 2nd vice-president of he A.F. of L. (John Mitchell to Ralph M. Easley, Oct. 21, 1907, John P. Mitchell Papers, Catholic University of America. Hereinafter cited as *JMP*.)

While Mitchell himself had no objection to receiving his salary from the leading capitalists, he was anxious that this information be kept private. In a letter to Easley, marked "Personal," he wrote: "I drop you this line to say I deem it of the highest possible importance not only to myself but also the Industrial Department of the Federation, that nothing be said concerning the conditions of my contract with the Civic Federation." (Mitchell to Easley, June 21, 1908, *JMP*.)

N.A.M. and the Citizens' Alliances.* It is true that such attacks did occur, especially after Parry became president of the N.A.M. (In 1902 President Theodore Search of N.A.M. was a member of the Civic Federation's Executive Council.) Parry, Kirby, and others active in the open-shop drive labeled the members of the N.C.F. "industrial doughfaces," and the organization itself "an adjunct of the A. F. of L.," "the facile instrument of the closed shop combine," and an exponent of "the most virulent form of socialism, *closed shop* unionism." But while Easley was quick to make use of such attacks in helping Gompers and Mitchell answer the growing criticism of the Civic Federation in labor circles, he also sought to persuade the big industrialists that there was really no basic difference between the Parryite and the N.C.F. approach to organized labor. Both, he wrote in the *NCF Review* were not really out to smash the unions; many of Parry's statements had been "misinterpreted" by radicals and thus the "erroneous impression" was conveyed that the open shoppers were bent upon smashing unionism.[18]

As we have already seen, many of the industrial and financial magnates who were the real power behind the open-shop drive were active in the N.C.F. (Easley boasted in December 1904 that the Civic Federation included more leaders of the N.A.M. "than the whole Parry outfit.") Many of the important employers' associations which were leaders of the drive to destroy the unions were represented in the N.C.F. in the person of their officers: the National Founders' Association, the Stove Founders' National Defense Association, the National Metal Trades Association, the National Street Railway Association, the National Association of Clothing Manufacturers, the American Newspaper Publishers' Association, the Lithographers' Association of the United States, and the Glass Bottle and Vial Manufacturers' Association.[19] The National Metal Trades' Association broke its agreement with the Machinists' Union in June 1901 at precisely the same time that the leaders of the Association were serving with the Machinists' representatives on the Civic Federation's conciliation committee.† In November 1904, the National Founders' Association, several of whose officers were among the first members of the Civic Federation, abrogated its agreement with the Iron Moulders' Union, whose president was also a member of the N.C.F.

* In his study *Businessmen and Reform* (*op. cit.,* pp. 30–31), Robert H. Wiebe makes much of these attacks upon the Civic Federation, but he later concedes that fundamentally there was no basic difference among the businessmen on the issue of unionism and that "antiunionism best unified businessmen." (p. 81.)

† Even Marguerite Green in her laudatory study of the National Civic Federation concedes that the presence of the leaders of the National Metal Trades' Association in the N.C.F. made "the Federation appear ridiculous before the public." (*The National Civic Federation and the American Labor Movement, 1900–1925,* Washington, D.C., 1956, p. 21.)

The same dual role was played by the representatives of the House of Morgan in the Civic Federation. Charles Schwab of U.S. Steel was a member of the N.C.F.'s Executive Committee and an active promoter of the open-shop movement. So were members of the N.C.F.'s "public" group. Thus President Charles W. Eliot of Harvard was head of the Industrial Economic Department of the N.C.F., formed in December 1904, and a number of his utterances in this capacity—including opposition to the closed shop, to the boycott, to sympathetic strikes, and to compulsory use of the union label, as well as his statement that there should be "no sacrifice of the independent workman to the labor union"— were featured in every issue of *Square Deal,* organ of the C.I.A. and the leading journal published by the open-shoppers.[20]

The Civic Federation did not affirm labor's right to organize until April 1908, when in response to an editorial statement in the *Union Labor Advocate* that "the Civic Federation had never specifically recognized the right of labor to organize," August Belmont, then president of the Federation, acknowledged that "labor has every right to organization." He went on, however, to denounce many of the "methods employed by organized labor to secure its industrial right." Seth Low, who succeeded Belmont as president of the N.C.F. in 1912, coupled his belief in labor's right to organize with a statement characterized by many trade unionists as a defense of the open shop. He said: "The pathway to industrial peace and industrial efficiency is to be found in the hearty cooperation of employers with labor unions, in the confident expectation that when the right of workingmen to collective bargaining passes unchallenged in practice, *the right of other workingmen to forego collective bargaining, if they wish to do so, will be equally unchallenged.*" Articles in the *NCF Review* asserted that the basic error in the Parryite movement was that it sought to make the open shop universal. This was going too far; the open shop was necessary and even "beneficial" in parts of American industry, but in others, it was unnecessary and even "dangerous" to try to institute it.[21]

THE N.C.F. STRATEGY

The idea behind this differentiation between the open shop as "beneficial" in certain parts of American industry and "dangerous" in others had been spelled out by Easley as early as October 1900, when he pointed out to Gompers the reasons why the A. F. of L. leaders should support the newly-organized N.C.F. The craft unions would win recognition from the leaders of the trustified industries for a small minority of the workers on condition that they would "not make trouble" for the corporations by organizing the mass of the workers in their plants and factories; that they would not challenge the control exercised by the finance capitalists over the American economy; that they would also agree "to 'keep politics out!' " of the unions, and thus avoid challenging the control exercised by the finance capitalists over American government. The industrialists, in return, would grant the skilled workers recognition and certain concessions.[22] Thus through the Civic Federation, the big employers and the trade unions would come to an implicit agreement. If the unions would make no real effort to organize the unskilled workers (especially the foreign-born and Negro workers), the corporations would make certain concessions to the craft unions. Business could afford to pay higher wages to a small number of skilled workers so long as the great body of unskilled workers were unorganized.

Capital was thus able and willing to share some of its profits with skilled labor, but to warrant these concessions, the craft unions would have to rid themselves of any taint of radicalism, the labor leaders of these unions would have to cooperate to combat radicalism and keep the masses of workers unorganized. Easley submitted the following Declaration of Principles to Gompers as ideally suited for the purposes of the Civic Federation:

"A Labor Union, guided by proper rules and governed by judicious and conservative leaders, is of advantage to employers and employees. Such unions should be fully recognized. Employers should encourage their most intelligent and conservative men to attend the meetings of such unions and keep them within proper limits. In return for such recognition, the union agrees that there shall be no interference with the employment of non-union unskilled labor in any department."[23]

Gompers, Mitchell, and the other labor leaders affiliated with the N.C.F. consciously adopted the trade union strategy outlined by Easley. Gompers was convinced that unionism could exist in the trustified industries only on the sufferance of the employers, and that they would tolerate it only if it confined itself to certain prescribed limits: it must confine itself to the skilled trades, maintain a sacred compliance with contracts, repress militancy and radicalism in the labor movement, and generally manifest a "reasonable" attitude. Unionism, if it accepted moderation and sanctity of contract as the twin keys to success, could gain the endorsement of the business world. On these terms, business could not only tolerate unionism but accept it as "the ally of capital for its own advantage."

Naturally, in following a "reasonable" approach, any reference to the existence of a class conflict was out of the question. How could capital be expected to negotiate with trade union officials and recognize unions if labor maintained a posture of implacable hostility to capitalism? Workers, therefore, had to be convinced that their material success and future progress were inextricably bound with that of their employers, that wages and profits proceeded from the joint efforts of both parties. To be sure, a measure of friction would always exist, but this could be ironed out once both parties recognized their mutual interests. As Henry White, secretary-treasurer of the United Garment Workers and one of the most ardent champions of the N.C.F. in the A. F. of L., put it: "Like the captain and crew of a ship, whatever differences there may be between them as to treatment, both are equally interested in bringing the vessel safely into port. That is the truth we have been trying to impress upon employers and workmen alike." The class war had to be replaced by argument and diplomacy; lockouts by arbitration between contending parties. Labor unions should not aim at the overthrow of capitalism, but rather should attempt to convince employers, through the N.C.F. "that they can just as well carry on their business under union control as without it, and that, in fact it pays them better to agree with us, to be at peace with our Organization than fight us."[24]

With this policy in mind and with the assistance of Easley, the labor members of the N.C.F. set out to ingratiate themselves with the industrialists and politicians who seemed inclined toward a live-and-let-live policy with the craft unions, and to convince the open-shop employers that they had more to gain than lose by recognizing the craft unions. These organizations were the real bulwarks against socialism, and to try to institute the open shop where they held sway would be "dangerous" to the interests of the capitalists, since it would remove "an obstacle in the path of socialism." Gompers even advised Easley how to get more information about the Socialists so as to make more effective his work with employers, and recommended that he attend Socialist meetings that he might better understand those who were "hostile to the effort to maintain industrial peace."[25]

Easley constantly sought to keep the Civic Federation's business members informed as to the facts of socialism's growth in the United States, and to impress upon them that the A. F. of L. was one of their major protections against its further advance. "It is imperative," he wrote to Gompers in 1907, "and logical at this time for employers of the United States to stand with the American Federation of Labor in the fight against socialism. . . . Within the last ten days I have spoken to six large employers on the subject . . . and all agree with the proposition and that the thing to do is to join hands with the A. F. of L."[26]

The N.C.F. campaign, under Easley's direction, championed the unionism of the A. F. of L. leadership "as an antidote for socialistic propaganda." The *NCF Review,* edited by Easley, sought steadily to convince employers that organized labor as represented by the A. F. of L. and the Railroad Brotherhoods was "conservative," perfectly respectable and reasonable, and quite willing to aid capital fight radicalism if given a chance. Endorsing this campaign, the *Wall Street Journal* declared:

"Unionism is the strongest bulwark in the body politic today against the encroachments of socialism."[27]

To prove his thesis that "trade unions were becoming more conservative," Easley arranged for the labor leaders affiliated with the N.C.F. to address meetings of industrialists and bankers. But the main method he used to promote his thesis was the annual dinner of the Civic Federation. Here "around the same dinner table of large captains of industry, leading representatives of organized labor, college presidents, and publicists . . . [and] their wives and daughters," 600 to 1,000 strong, the capitalists could see for themselves that the leaders of the craft unions were "conservative" men who should not be confused with those with "socialistic" ideas "who claim to be representing the interests of Labor." Here, too, the labor leaders could see for themselves that the captains of industry and finance were "human beings just like themselves," and "meeting on the same democratic footing," could clearly grasp that in the United States there were no "distinctions between rich and poor."[28]

The N.C.F. could point to positive effects of its policies. After a meeting with Gompers, arranged by Easley, James E. Craig, president of the open-shop Denver Citizens' Alliance, wrote: "Samuel Gompers, president of the American Federation of Labor, I regard as a comparative conservative, and the employers of the West would be glad to see him succeed in extending control of the American Federation of Labor throughout the West."[29] Darwin P. Kingsley, president of the New York Life Insurance Co., told a meeting of businessmen held in Florida in 1913: "When I tell you that the trade union movement in this country stands for private property and law and order I know what I am talking about. I met Mr. Gompers recently at a luncheon in New York given by Mr. Seth Low [president of the N.C.F. at that time] and at this luncheon I heard Mr. Gompers say just that thing. I want to say to you gentlemen that I never had my mind so quickly and so completely changed on any matter as in regard to my opinion of Mr. Gompers. I entertained the same feeling towards him that you have until I saw him. I think now that he is a great man."[30]

One cannot overlook the fact that the limited support the craft unions received from the N.C.F. was predicated on their functioning as a conservative bulwark against radicalism. No clearer illustration of this is needed than the evidence contained in an unpublished letter to Easley from Herman Ridder, German-American publisher, head of the Newspaper Publishers' Association, and an active member of the Civic Federation's executive committee. Ridder sent Easley an article in the *Machinists' Journal* of August 1908 which pointed out that the skilled workers in the craft unions could not really improve their conditions as long as the unskilled workers in the basic, trustified industries were unorganized. In an attached note, Ridder wrote: "It seems to me that the labor magazines have a pretty liberal sprinkling of this sort of stuff—straight socialist doctrine very thinly veiled at that. Are we as sure of our ground as we think in counting the union movement as a solid bulwark against socialism?"[31]

By the "union movement," Ridder meant, as did all the leaders of the N.C.F., the unions affiliated with the A. F. of L. and the Railroad Brotherhoods. The *Machinists' Journal* was the official organ of the International Association of Machinists, an A. F. of L. affiliate, whose president, James O'Connell, had been a labor member of the N.C.F.'s executive committee for years. When this union's journal spoke up for militant unionism, it filled a top leader of the Civic Federation with alarm. The whole purpose of the N.C.F. was exposed in the process. Its objective was to permeate the labor movement with conservatism, to prevent it from organizing the mass of the unskilled workers, to control it, and to deprive it of militancy.

WELFARE WORK AND LABOR LEGISLATION

"At our meeting in Washington . . . we are going to exploit our welfare work as an antidote to Socialism," Easley wrote to a member of the N.C.F.'s executive committee in April 1908.[32] We have already seen enough to realize that to Easley and others in the N.C.F., "socialism" often meant militant unionism, and this is further revealed by the nature of the Federation's "welfare work." On the surface, the purpose of installing libraries, gymnasiums, proper ventilation and lighting, sanitary workrooms, adequate toilet facilities, lunch rooms, and shower rooms in shops and factories was to present "a picture of a wise, benevolent, and paternal social capitalism doing its utmost in recognition of its important position in society, to care for the happiness and well-being of its people." Basically, however, the system was carefully calculated to assist employers in keeping unions out of their plants. "Welfare work," Dr. Jensen points out, "offered . . . the employer . . . the possibility of meeting some of the difficulties of the labor problem by means of which, to a great extent, [he] would circumvent the unions. Officially, the [N.C.F.'s] Welfare Department disclaimed any such intentions, but certainly for many employers, especially those who joined the National Civic Federation after 1905, welfare work seemed to offer an attractive alternative to the fetters and uncertainties of trying to work with the unions."[33]

This was clearly the case in the mutual benefit associations established among employers all over the country, with the assistance of the N.C.F.'s Welfare Department, to cover the cost of accident insurance and the institution of "profit sharing" plans among the corporations. For one thing, if the worker lost his job, he would lose the money paid into the mutual aid association, and contemporary evidence makes it clear that the one sure way the worker would lose his job in many of the corporations operating under the N.C.F. welfare program was if he joined a union. For another, the whole system of "profit sharing" was designed to assist the employers weaken the unions, and even labor members of the N.C.F., apart from John Mitchell, were not enthusiastic, to say the least, about its efforts to institute "profit sharing" plans. Referring to the plan established by U.S. Steel, in cooperation with the Civic Federation,* the A. F. of L. Executive Council declared indignantly: "Its [U.S. Steel's] crowning criminality, however, is its bold and heartless enserfing of labor. To disarm public indignation against its industrial and social crimes in this respect the Trust has instituted the so-called 'profit sharing' system which even the slightest examination proves to be a transparent deceit, through which a small minority of its employes are sought to be bribed to help in daily sweating the vast majority in preventing the others from joining labor organizations and in breaking down the spirit of manliness that has been cherished characteristic of American Labor."[34]

It is significant that the Welfare Department of the N.C.F. was the one committee to which no labor leaders were invited. It would be a bit too embarrassing even for those conservative trade unionists to participate in the operations of a Department whose main purpose could not be camouflaged by idyllic-sounding phrases like "hands across the table," and which, by a whole system of paternalism, erected strong barriers against the spread of unionism.[35]

The N.C.F.'s "welfare work" did not include support for social legislation outlawing child labor and improving working conditions of women workers. In 1907 the Civic Federation's Child Labor Commission was established to investigate the problem, but the outcry of protest from businessmen members of the organization, particularly Southern cotton manufacturers and coal operators who claimed that "light work" was not harmful to children, caused the Commission to be still-born. The proposed investigation was never carried out, and the Commission disbanded in the same year it was formed.[36]

In general, the N.C.F., with Gompers' support, opposed most social legislation as government interference with the rights of employers.†

---

* U.S. Steel Corp. had a president and three directors—Charles M. Schwab, Henry Phipps, Marvin S. Hughitt, and George W. Perkins—active in the Civic Federation. Perkins, who was especially active in and an "enthusiastic supporter" of the Civic Federation, was largely responsible for U.S. Steel's "profit sharing" plan. "The plan is to keep the men quiet, and it does too," one steel worker declared. (John A. Garraty, "U.S. Steel Versus Labor: The Early Years," *Labor History,* vol. I, Winter, 1960, pp. 18-21.)

† The letterhead of the N.C.F.'s appeal for funds with which to fight old age pensions included the name of Samuel Gompers. (National Civic Federation Archives, New York Public Library, hereinafter cited as *NCFA;* Louis S. Reed, *The Labor Philosophy of Samuel Gompers,* New York, 1930, p. 117.)

John Mitchell expressed the Civic Federation's attitude clearly when he declared that voluntary action by employers would "prove more effective in the maintenance of industrial peace than any program instituted by the Government."[37]

In the entire area of labor legislation, the N.C.F.'s record was a shoddy one. At the request of the labor members, a Commission on Government by Injunction was established to investigate this problem, so important to the trade unions, but the Federation's business members were so decidedly opposed to any move to upset one of their most powerful weapons against the labor movement, that no action was ever taken by the Commission. The business members of the Federation were unalterably opposed to labor's demand for the exemption of unions from the operation of the Sherman Anti-Trust Act, and while the N.C.F. did give lip-service support to labor's campaign for revision of the law, even so enthusiastic an admirer of the organization as Marguerite Green concedes that its support was "neither inspired nor productive of important results." Yet N.C.F. support for labor's legislative program, had it been sincere, could have brought "important results." George W. Smith of the Lackawanna Steel Co. wrote: "I have talked with many state and national legislators and there is no question but the lawmakers pay considerable attention to what the Civic Federation advocates or opposes. . . . Also there are many big men on the inside of the Federation's affairs who are able to inform and influence the action of legislators. . . ."[38] But these "big men" were not disposed to deprive the capitalist class of its ability to make use of the Sherman Anti-Trust Act to weaken the labor movement.

In truth, a study of the N.C.F. archives reveals that more energy was devoted by Easley and Low to persuade the A. F. of L. leaders not to follow the path of the British labor movement and sponsor an independent labor party than to the campaign for labor legislation. Indeed, when, as we shall see, Gompers was forced by events and pressure of the membership to take the A. F. of L. into political action, the businessmen members of the Civic Federation were furious. "I am surprised," wrote Charles A. Moore, president of Manning, Maxwell, Moore, and Co. of New York City, and chairman of the N.C.F.'s Welfare Department, to Easley in 1908, during the height of labor's participation in the presidential campaign, "to know the injury that has been done to our getting desirable members by the presence of Mr. Gompers in such a prominent position in our organization, and this recent exhibition of his endeavor to carry labor organizations into politics has developed expressions from friends of mine that I never heard before. And they are most pronounced. His attitude, as you know, in this campaign, has injured our organization very seriously, as they say we have made him prominent and possible through the prominence we have given him. I have felt this myself. I mention it to you just now, as no doubt you are aware of it and have heard of it from other sources, but this campaign has developed it so that men are coming out in the open and expressing themselves where they did not do that before." Easley, who knew that Gompers was being pushed by the A. F. of L. towards greater political action than he wanted, tried to persuade the businessmen in the N.C.F. that "Gompers had to yield to pressure from the rank and file or open the door to more radical groups." But the businessmen were not satisfied. They expected the Civic Federation to lead the labor members in "conservative" directions, and they insisted that the organization fulfill its objectives.[39]

What, then, was the difference between the N.C.F. and the open-shop employers' associations? Lewis Lorwin sums up the answer in one sentence: "The Civic Federation proceeded with more sophisticated and enlightened methods; but [like the open-shop employers' associations] it was bent on pulling the teeth of aggressive unionism." Lorwin goes on to point out that the N.C.F. "did not assist labor in organizing a single non-union industry, although large non-union interests were represented in it." As for its key work in settling strikes, he notes that "often settlements it applauded were disastrous to unionism."[40]

This is in sharp contrast to Gompers' conclusion. In the *NCF Review* of May 5, 1905, defending the Civic Federation, Gompers stated baldly that "in no instance have either strikes or conflicts been avoided or adjusted when they have been other than helpful to labor."[41] What, then, are the facts?

CHAPTER 4

The National Civic Federation, II. Role in Strikes

THE STEEL STRIKE OF 1901

In 1901, the membership of the Amalgamated Association of Iron, Steel and Tin Workers was less than 10,000 out of a total of some 160,000 workers employed in the industry at the time.* Its members and leaders knew that some drastic action must be taken if the organization was not to disappear and organized labor barred from the most important industry in the country. They understood, too, that no progress could be made in the industry unless the union dropped its exclusive trade unionism under which for the past 20 years it had organized mainly the highly skilled craftsmen—the puddlers and rollers—and declined to organize all the workers in a plant.

The formation of the U.S. Steel Corp. in February 1901 pointed up the inadequacies of the rigid craft unionism practiced by the Amalgamated Association. The vast majority of the billion-dollar corporation's 148,000 employees were unskilled workers. Only by organizing all the steel workers, skilled and unskilled, in one union—integrating unionism to parallel integrated industry—could this giant trust be organized. Particularly was this true in the face of the policy of the large multiplant corporations in the industry to shut down organized plants while allowing non-union properties to operate. Once this policy was put into effect by U.S. Steel, the union would find itself eliminated from the plants over which it still exercised power and eventually extinguished. It is true that U.S. Steel was willing to avoid a battle with the union for the time being by retaining the status quo in the individual companies that had merged into the trust. But it would not permit the unionization of mills then unorganized. And for the union to accept the fact that some mills should remain non-union would make it only a matter of time before it would be completely driven out of the industry.

* Ten years before, the union's membership was over 24,000. Its defeat in the Homestead Strike of 1892 began the rapid decline in membership.

To meet this danger, the union at its 1901 convention, on the eve of the formation of the Steel Trust, unanimously resolved: "Should one mill in a combine or trust have a difficulty, all mills in such combine or trust shall cease work until such grievance is settled." The discussion at the convention demonstrated that the steel workers were convinced that if the union "were unable to establish itself before U.S. Steel had solidified its financial position . . . it would be virtually banished from the industry."[1]

Negotiations of a new contract between the Amalgamated Association and U.S. Steel's operating subsidiaries began in the spring of 1901, and started with the American Sheet Steel and the American Steel Hoop companies. The union, speaking through President T. J. Shaffer, demanded that the union wage scale be signed for all the mills of the companies, and that the union be recognized. American Sheet Steel and American Steel Hoop refused to sign for the mills which had not been under contract in the preceding year.

The strike to win recognition of the union began on June 22, when 28,000 workers at American Steel Hoop, the vast majority of whom were not members of the Amalgamated, walked out. By July 10 the mills of American Sheet Steel were also tied up when 8,000 more workers, again most of them hitherto unorganized, answered a strike call. A general strike call was issued by President Shaffer on July 19, and a second strike call on August 10, bringing the total of strikers to 62,000.

Shaffer predicted that the Amalgamated would shut down the whole U.S. Steel Corp., a prediction based on his confidence that all of organized labor, and the miners and railroad brotherhoods in particular, would come to the support of the strikers, realizing that if the House of Morgan smashed the union in steel, it would not be long before it started out to destroy unionism in the other industries over which it was the absolute dictator. To be sure, Shaffer knew even before the strike started that Gompers' support of the steel strike could not be counted upon.*

* Two months before the union's demands were made on the Sheet Steel Co., Shaffer wrote to Gompers that the company's McKeesport mill was discharging men for joining the union and that a strike was likely, which might involve the entire steel corporation. He urged that Gompers instruct his organizers to keep men from going to McKeesport. Receiving no reply, Shaffer wrote two weeks later, repeating his request and this time suggesting that if the expected strike came in July, the A.F. of L. should call out all other trades employed in the steel industry to support the Amalgamated. Ten days later Shaffer again wrote, asking Gompers for his views regarding concerted action by all trades. Finally, Gompers answered. He coldly informed Shaffer that the workers would not support a call for a general sympathetic strike in the steel industry, and stated his belief that they would be right in refusing to support it. It was clear that Gompers would not approve or support the Amalgamated's strike, to say nothing of a sympathetic strike. (T. J. Shaffer to Gompers, April 16, 30, May 10, 1901; Gompers to Shaffer, May 15, 1901. *AFL Corr.*)

What he did not know was that forces were at work to frustrate any attempt to achieve the solidarity necessary to win the battle against the Steel Trust. These forces were represented by the leaders of the National Civic Federation and their allies in the leadership of the A. F. of L.

Shaffer was a member of the N.C.F.'s labor committee, but he had been selected reluctantly. Easley had been unhappy about his presence in the Civic Federation even before the strike started; he informed Gompers on January 2, 1901, that some of Shaffer's militant speeches convinced him that he would prove to be "unreliable," and he wondered if someone else "would be a better representative of his organization on the committee." Gompers shared Easley's opinion, and was especially annoyed by Shaffer's statements that the craft union policies pursued by the A. F. of L. leadership were not suited to the needs of organized labor in 20th century America. The fact that Shaffer had participated in a conference early in 1901 where craft unionism was declared outmoded certainly did not endear him to Gompers.[2]*

The news that Shaffer was counting upon wide support of the steel strikers by organized labor, including, if necessary, a sympathetic strike, frightened the N.C.F. leaders. Mark Hanna, N.C.F. president, wrote to Mitchell in alarm asking him to "do something" to stop such a movement. He felt that the union should never have attempted to defy the Steel Trust, and that "a few conservative labor leaders" must move into the picture and try to settle the strike before Shaffer began to take "desperate measures." "It seems to me," Hanna wrote to Mitchell on July 22, 1901, "that Shaffer has made a great mistake as he has taken a position never before taken by the Amalgamated Association." Mitchell, in turn, failed to point out that the "position" previously taken by the union had only resulted in gradually eliminating it from the industry.

At two conferences between J. P. Morgan, Charles M. Schwab, and the officers of the Amalgamated, held on July 27 and 29—arranged by George Harvey, editor of *Harper's Weekly*—the steel executives granted the union the wage scale demanded, but specified that the union was not to organize the non-union mills. Morgan assured the strike leaders that he was not hostile to organized labor, and predicted that "within two years the corporation would be ready to sign a contract with the union for all its plants." At the present time, however, the situation was so complicated that it was impracticable to unionize all the mills. The trouble was not so much with the directors of U.S. Steel Corp., Morgan insisted, as with the men in charge of the subsidiary companies.[3]

* Gompers suspected that Shaffer favored the formation of an industrial union movement, to include an industrial union of steel workers, outside of the A.F. of L. But while it is true that Shaffer was thinking about an industrial union of steel workers, he made it clear in all his correspondence to Gompers that he wished to work inside the A.F. of L., and opposed the formation of a separate organization.

Morgan did not disclose that the board of directors of U.S. Steel had already taken a diametrically opposite position. In 1911 the Stanley Committee of the House of Representatives, investigating U.S. Steel, revealed the fact that at a meeting of the Executive Committee, at which Morgan was present, a resolution was unanimously adopted which read: "That we are unalterably opposed to any extension of union labor, and advise subsidiary companies to take a firm position when these questions come up and say they are not going to recognize it; that is, any extension of unions in mills where they do not now exist. . . ." Here, baldly stated, was the Steel Trust's fundamental opposition to the principle of labor organization, but at the conferences Morgan masked this opposition behind protestations of friendship for organized labor. The N.C.F., through Easley who attended the conferences, assured the labor leaders that they could take Morgan's assurances at face value.

Prodded by Easley, Gompers, and Mitchell to have faith in Morgan's intentions towards organized labor, Shaffer accepted the Steel Corporation's proposition. But the Amalgamated Association's Executive Committee refused to ratify it. The proposal was condemned as a betrayal, since it excluded the union from practically the entire industry, and secured better conditions for a small section of the steel workers—the skilled workers. "Morgan's offer will in time kill the Amalgamated," the strikers insisted.[4]

Once its proposal was rejected, the Steel corporation began to import strikebreakers to start up the mills. The Amalagamated replied by appealing to Gompers, who was in Pittsburgh with Frank Morrison, A. F. of L. secretary, to call all the unions of the A. F. of L. into an emergency conference or at least a meeting of its Executive Council. Shaffer pointed out to Gompers the necessity of making the steel strike "the central fight for unionism," and called for a sympathetic strike of miners and railroad workers. Gompers quickly rejected the request for a conference, insisting that it would be a sign of weakness! Although it had been arranged for Gompers to meet J. P. Morgan in New York to propose arbitration of all matters in dispute, Gompers, without giving any explanation, called off the meeting and returned to Washington. "Mr. Gompers and Mr. Morrison left the city," Shaffer reported, "and we felt convinced that the A.A. need not look for help from the A. F. of L."[5]

From the beginning of the strike, the Civic Federation's Conciliation Committee, composed at this time of Hanna, Easley, Gompers, Mitchell, Frank S. Sargent, Grand Chief of the Brotherhood of Locomotive Engineers, and Professor J. W. Jenks, had been exerting pressure on Shaffer to act moderately. (Easley felt that Shaffer was entirely too militant, and appealed to Mitchell and Gompers "to tone him down.") With the appeal for a sympathetic strike, the N.C.F. Conciliation Committee decided not to rely on persuading Shaffer to act moderately, and instead went directly ot the heads of the trade unions who might be expected to respond to the appeal. Members of the Conciliation Committee held conferences with trade union leaders in the large cities of the east, and succeeded in convincing them that it would be folly for them to heed Shaffer's appeals for a sympathy strike.[6]

But in a number of unions, particularly among the miners, pressure for sympathetic action was still considerable. On August 10, despite efforts on Mitchell's part to prevent it, the National Executive Board of the United Mine Workers adopted a resolution requesting Gompers "to call a meeting of the Executive Heads of the various organizations affiliated with the A. F. of L. to outline a policy to assist the Amalgamated Association of Iron and Steel Workers in their strike."[7] Mitchell was instructed to do all he could to assist the steel workers win their strike.

Gompers ignored the request for the conference, not even bothering to inform the union that he had received the appeal.* But Mitchell, under pressure from his own union to help the steel workers, assured the strikers that if they accepted a reasonable proposal for settlement and this was rejected by the corporation, sympathetic action of some sort would be forthcoming. In a letter to Shaffer (a copy of which he sent to Easley), he proposed that the Amalgamated give up the idea of unionizing the nonunion mills, and accept a settlement which would grant the union scale at the mills which had gone on strike—with the understanding that the strikers would be reinstated without discrimination. This proposition was to be offered by the Amalgamated to the Steel executives, and, Mitchell concluded: "If the terms outlined in this proposition are not accepted the steel strike will have the unqualified support of the American labor movement; and President Gompers will unquestionably call the Executive Council of the A. F. of L. together for the purpose of devising methods to help them . . ."

Having received a copy of this letter, Easley concluded in great alarm that a sympathetic strike was again a possibility. He knew, too, from private conversation with the Steel executives that Mitchell's proposal for a settlement would not be accepted. He worked more actively than ever to persuade Mitchell to abandon the whole idea of sympathetic action, and he succeeded in this objective. The officials of the steel corporation rejected the proposition which Mitchell had advanced and which was

---

* On September 8, 1901, T. L. Lewis, vice president of the U.M.W., informed Gompers that many members of the union were asking him why the A.F. of L. president had done nothing about the miners' appeal for a conference, 'and in order to intelligently answer them, I would be pleased to learn from you why such a conference was not called." (*AFL Corr.*) Actually, Lewis was not in favor of a sympathetic strike, claiming contractual obligations prevented it. (New York *Tribune*, Aug. 1, 1901.)

presented by a committee representing the Civic Federation.* They offered to sign the agreement for all the mills which were union the previous year except nine, which were to become nonunion; no worker would be discriminated against for participation in the strike or union membership. The N.C.F.'s committee transmitted this counter-offer to Shaffer, with the advice that it be accepted as the best and final offer of the corporation. The union's Executive Board refused to accept the counterproposal, and the union waited for Mitchell to call out the miners as he had promised.[8]†

But the miners were not called out, and the Amalgamated Association had to go it alone. The Steel executives, fully aware of this, stood by their guns, and continued to import strikebreakers. "It will be better for the business interests now the fight is on, to let it go to a finish, which means the defeat of the workers," declared a company spokesman.[9]

The strike lingered on in diminishing force, but the "finish" was not far off. The strike was doomed to fail. A rigid craft union could not overcome at one stroke the years of resentment built up among the mass of the steel workers previously scorned, and many refused to help the Amalgamated when called upon to strike. More important, the failure of the A. F. of L. leadership, influenced by the Civic Federation, to support the strikers made defeat inevitable. Neither the A. F. of L. nor the U.M.W. contributed a cent to the strike fund, yet, as the *Journal of the Knights of Labor* correctly pointed out, soon after the strike began, money would be a key factor in the outcome. It urged the A. F. of L. to heed the strikers' appeal for financial aid: "When the trust magnates learn that Organized Labor is a unit behind the strikers and that moral and financial support are assured for an indefinite period, they will speedily come to terms."

Gompers turned a deaf ear to such appeals. He later claimed that the Federation had not helped to raise funds for the strikers because Shaffer had publicly appealed for money without first asking for A. F. of L. endorsement.[10]

On September 14, a settlement, worked out through the interposition of the N.C.F., was signed by the Steel Corporation and the union in

---

* The committee consisted of Mitchell, Easley, Henry White, Professor Jenks of Cornell University, Gompers, and Frank Sargent of the railroad trainmen. White, president of the United Garment Workers, and a member of the N.C.F. arbitration committee, had suggested early in the srike that the way to settle the strike was for the union to waive recognition of the union. This, of course, was the real point at issue. (Henry White to Gompers, July 19, 1901, *AFL Corr.*)

† Not only had Mitchell promised this action in his letter to Shaffer, cited above, but Shaffer asserted that in a visit to the office of the Amalgamated Association on August 23, the U.M.W. president had given him the assurance that if the corporation rejected the offer, the miners would go on strike in sympathy with the steel workers, (T. J. Shaffer to members of the Amalgamated Association, Sept. 21, 1901, in *American Federationist,* Oct., 1901, pp. 415–17.)

J. P. Morgan's office. Under its terms the nonunion mills were to remain nonunion, and "no attempts to organize" were "to be made" and "no charters" were "to be granted." Thus the union agreed not to endeavor to organize nonunion mills in return for recognition in the few union mills where it had been previously recognized—*except in the 14 mills which had become nonunion during the strike.* "The outcome of the strike," Philip Taft correctly concludes, "was disastrous to the Amalgamated Association of Iron, Steel and Tin Workers, and to the labor movement generally."[11] *

For several weeks following this disastrous settlement, the labor press was filled with charges and countercharges regarding the responsibility for the great defeat. Shaffer, in press releases and in a special circular to the members of the union, denounced Gompers and Mitchell for their conduct during the strike. He criticized Gompers for refusing to call a meeting of the labor leaders or of the Executive Council to aid the strike, for failing to give any financial assistance, and for accepting the counter-offer of the steel executives. He attacked Mitchell for the failure to carry out his promise to call a sympathetic strike. He claimed that the coal miners and the railroad workers had been ready to join in a sympathy strike, and the failure to call them out had doomed the strike to defeat.

Gompers and Mitchell immediately wrote to Shaffer demanding an investigation of the charges. They proposed that a committee of three be selected by Shaffer from a list of union officials nominated by Gompers and Mitchell. If the committee found them guilty of the charges, they promised that Gompers would resign as president of the A. F. of L. and vice-president of the Cigarmakers' International Union, and Mitchell would resign from the presidency of the United Mine Workers and the vice-presidency of the A. F. of L. Shaffer rejected the proposal, arguing that all the persons nominated were friendly to Gompers. He proposed, in turn, a committee to be composed of one person named by himself, one by Gompers and Mitchell, and one by the other two. Gompers and Mitchell turned down this offer.[12]

In a 15-page article in the *American Federationist,* Gompers replied to Shaffer's circular. He scornfully and indignantly denied Shaffer's charges. He stated, for example, that his refusal to call a general labor conference was due to his conviction that it could accomplish no good

* It did not take long for organized labor to feel the effects of the defeat in the steel strike, and ironically it was the miners who felt it first. In July 1902, in the midst of the great coal strike, Pat Dolan, president of District 5 of the United Mine Workers, centered in Pittsburgh, wrote to Gompers: "We not only have the Coal Operators . . . to fight, but we have the United States Steel Company, as they have several Mills in that locality, which are all non-union and they are assisting the coal operators to win out, knowing that if we win it will stimulate their men with Trades Union principles." (Pat Dolan to Gompers, July 1st, 1902, *AFL Corr.*)

results. He denied that there was any foundation for the statement that Mitchell had promised to call out the miners. "Mr. Shaffer," he commented caustically, "may not appreciate to the same extent as Mr. Mitchell the justice and value of maintaining agreements entered into between a trade union and employers, and therefore may have assumed or imagined that Mr. Mitchell . . . would lightly and ruthlessly break agreements. . . ." Gompers concluded by accusing Shaffer of rebuffing the good will and kindly assurances of J. P. Morgan that the steel corporation might recognize the union in a few years if the union would not now "attempt to drive him further than it was possible for him to go."

Mitchell, on his part, categorically denied that he had ever promised to call a sympathetic strike. He blamed the defeat of the steel workers on Shaffer's "radicalness and incompetence." Mitchell appealed to Easley, among others, to refute the charge that he had promised a sympathetic strike. This put Easley in somewhat of a spot, since he had received the copy of Mitchell's letter to Shaffer which he interpreted as meaning that a sympathetic strike would be called if the proposal were rejected by the company. However, he assured Mitchell that he had probably "put too serious an interpretation upon that letter," a conclusion with which Mitchell completely agreed.[13]

Although Gompers and Mitchell were exonerated by the A. F. of L. convention in November 1902, many workers at the time, and not a few labor historians since,* were convinced that the real force responsible for the defeat was the National Civic Federation; that the influence of the N.C.F. was decisive in convincing the A. F. of L. leaders to abandon any thought of a sympathetic strike, or, indeed, of any substantial support for the strikers in any form. It was felt at the time that although the union was not equipped to challenge the mighty Steel Trust because of its narrow craft union policies of the past, if organized labor as a whole had supported the strike, there could have been a victory for union recognition. But with the Civic Federation dominating the scene, the possibility of such support disappeared early in the strike. With good

---

* Norman J. Ware, for example, regards the failure of the strike as an example of how the A.F. of L. became a "Morgan partner" under the influence of the Civic Federation. Such cooperation, the strike proved, only served to "cut the claws of aggressive labor leadership." Ware also asserts that Gompers accepted the corporation's terms and agreed to pass them on to the Amalgamated in exchange for support by the Steel executives of an eight-hour bill then pending before Congress. (*Labor in Modern Industrial Society*, New York, 1935, p. 323.)

In his study of the strike, which is primarily a denunciation of the Amalgamated Association's leadership, John A. Garraty makes no mention of the role played by the Civic Federation. ("U.S. Steel Versus Labor: The Early Years," *Labor History*, vol. I, Winter, 1960, pp. 11–14.) Neither does David Brody in his discussion of the strike which is also critical of the union's leadership. (*Steelworkers in America: The Non Union Era*, Cambridge, Mass., 1960, pp. 61–67.)

reason, the N.C.F. publicly claimed credit "for having prevented sympathetic strikes by the miners and railroad men."[14]

After the defeat of 1901, the Amalgamated Association's policies and activities met with the approval of the Civic Federation. The union, now under the conservative leadership of President Michael Tighe, abandoned any attempt to organize the industry. Instead an effort was made to cultivate what Tighe called a "business relationship" with the Steel Corporation. This meant, he explained, "giving way to every request that was made by the subsidiary companies when they insisted upon it," and agreeing not to extend the organization of the industry. This policy was based on a fear of the strength of the trust and a decision to try to buy a limited security for the skilled workers at the expense of the unskilled and unorganized workers.[15]

The official journal of the Civic Federation praised this policy, and declared that now the union could rely upon its full support. "The Convention of the Amalgamated Iron, Steel and Tin Workers now in session is not expected to develop any unreasonable demands," the *NCF Review* declared approvingly in April 1903. A year later, the *Review* hailed as a victory for the union the fact that due to the intercession of the N.C.F. in its behalf, "the manufacturers [of Steel Sheet and Tin Plate] acquiesced in a reduction of 18 percent [in wages] instead of their original demand for 20."[16]

What were the fruits of this policy? A study of the U.S. Commissioner of Labor showed in 1910 that of the 153,000 employees in the blast furnaces, steel works, and rolling mills, 50,000 customarily worked seven days a week, and 20 per cent of them worked 84 hours or more a week, which meant a 12-hour day, including Sunday. Labor conditions in the company's plants were far below "the American standard of living among laborers in our country. Some of the details are revolting, both as to sanitary and moral conditions." The wages paid, assuming constant employment and the ordinary family as the basis, "are barely enough to provide subsistence."[17]

THE ANTHRACITE COAL STRIKE OF 1902

Despite the United Mine Workers' spectacular growth since April 1897, when it had only 10,000 nominal members, there were 300,000 miners still outside the union at the turn of the century, about half of them in the anthracite (hard coal) regions of Pennsylvania.* Since 1880 the

---

* The anthracite coal deposits of Pennsylvania were monopolistically controlled by the coal railroads. These deposits are found in an area of less than 500 square miles in eastern Pennsylvania. They are in the counties of Lackawanna, Luzerne, Carbon, Northumberland, and Schuylkill.

anthracite fields had been virtually unorganized; the hard coal miners had received no wage increases for 20 years, and working days had been decreased to 190 yearly. Annual earnings varied from $210 to $616, with the mean about $375. This was not sufficient for the maintenance of a family and most miners were forced to send their children to work.

In addition, proper weighing of coal was nonexistent. Miners were forced to produce between 2,600 and 3,190 pounds of coal before being credited with one "ton." However, when selling the coal, the operators included only 2,240 pounds to the "ton." Docking bosses made arbitrary deductions from the weight of coal mined for alleged impurities. Charges at the company stores were so excessive that most of the miners were in debt to the companies.[18]

In August 1900, the United Mine Workers presented a series of demands to the operators,* and invited them to attend a joint conference for further discussion. The operators ignored the invitation. On September 17, the strike call went out to the hard coal miners. Within two weeks, 90 per cent of the workers had joined the walkout.

Coming in the midst of the presidential campaign of 1900, the strike alarmed the leaders of the N.C.F., especially President Mark Hanna, who feared that a prolonged struggle would have unfavorable repercussions on the Republican ticket by exposing its campaign slogan of "The Full-Dinner Pail" for American workers. Hanna and a group of Republican financiers intervened in the walkout, and convinced the railroad presidents who controlled the coal companies that it was to their interest to settle before election day. The settlement included an increase in wages of 10 per cent, some improvement in working conditions—there was to be a decrease of almost 100 per cent in the price of powder charged by the companies—and recognition of workers' committees in adjusting grievances. This inconclusive agreement was to last until March 31, 1901. Although the companies refused to negotiate with union representatives and the agreement was a verbal one, they posted notices in the mines embodying the compromise terms, and the union ordered the men back to work on October 29, 1900.[19]†

* The demands included: (1) union recognition; (2) the right of the miners to employ their own men to check on the weighing and docking for impurities; (3) payment by weight and use of the legal ton of 2,240 pounds instead of the "long" ton (2,600 to 3,190 pounds); (4) reduction of hours from ten to eight hours per day; (5) elimination of company stores, company houses, company doctors, and other similar company monopolies; elimination of the compulsory purchase of powder at the company store. The price paid there was $1.75 per keg; in the outside market it was $1.10. (Robert J. Cornell, *The Anthracite Coal Strike of 1902*, Washington, 1957, pp. 42–43.)

† The United Mine Workers entered the strike with scarcely 9,000 enrolled members and emerged with over 100,000. (*Minutes of the Twelfth Annual Convention of the United Mine Workers of America*, 1901, pp. 35–36.) In a call he issued

Friction between the miners and the companies continued, for the mine owners regarded their decision to yield to the union as a strategic retreat rather than a surrender. Despite the agreement, the operators refused to negotiate with union committees, insisting that they did not represent the workers. The settlement remained a dead letter, the companies simply ignoring the improvements they had agreed to grant. "The men," Mitchell wrote to Hanna in March 1901, "are chafing under alleged violations of the agreement on the part of the companies, and particularly do they feel discontented and restless at what appears to me to be an unwarranted opposition to the organization."[20]

The U.M.W. convention, meeting early in March, voted to strike unless the union was recognized and some method provided for settlement of grievances. But Mitchell, fearing the consequences of "radical action," mobilized the "conservatives," and obtained the convention's consent for the U.M.W. president and the Executive Committee of the three anthracite districts "to exercise full power in arranging terms of settlement." "This places the matter practically in my own hands," he informed Hanna and Easley, urging them to assist him in arranging "a conference with the proper people in New York." He assured the N.C.F. leaders that he would do everything in his power to prevent the "radical element" in the union from putting the strike vote into practice. "Personally," he wrote to Hanna, "I believe you know that I am in favor of peace and the establishment of harmonious business relations with the employers of labor, to the end that strikes and lockouts may become unnecessary." But if the companies maintained their uncompromising attitude, refusing to negotiate with the union, he would not be able to hold off strike action. He was sure that if only an interview could be arranged with the presidents of the railroads, they could reach an understanding "without loss of dignity" on the part of the businessmen. About this same time, Mitchell addressed a letter to the presidents of the railroads urging them to recognize the union on the ground that "the miners' organization is a responsible institution, conducted on conservative business lines."[21]

Easley and Hanna went directly to J. P. Morgan who had a controlling interest in the railroads. Although Morgan at first refused to do anything on the ground that he could not interfere with the operation of the railroads, he finally agreed to arrange an interview between Mitchell and the Reading Railroad interests. At this meeting an agreement was concluded that the wage scale, adopted at the end of the strike of 1900, would be continued; that each company would discuss grievances with

---

to the members, Mitchell stressed that while the workers had not received full justice, a powerful union had been built, which, "if maintained and conducted on business principles," would enable the men to redress many of the local grievances. (Copy of call, dated Oct. 25, 1900, in *JMP*.)

committees of its own men, whether union or nonunion, and that if Mitchell could show that the U.M.W. could discipline and control its members, the operators would consider signing a written contract with the organization, beginning April 1, 1902.[22]

It is clear that the negotiations had really accomplished nothing but a postponement of the conflict. However, Hanna assured Mitchell that his ability to forestall "radical action" and his conservative management of the situation had greatly enhanced the prestige of the U.M.W. Mitchell was pleased, of course, but he did not entirely fool himself. He pointed out to Hanna that the miners were not pleased with the settlement, and were convinced from past experience that only union recognition would prevent "violations of the agreement on the part of the company."

It was clear in the fall of 1901 that unless the operators granted union recognition by April 1902, a strike was inevitable. In an effort to prevent the inevitable, Mitchell and a union committee tried to meet with President Thomas of the Erie Railroad, representative of the coal operators, to persuade him to convince his colleagues that it was impossible to hold off strike action unless the union was recognized. Thomas refused even to grant Mitchell and his associates the courtesy of a hearing.[23]

Once again Easley and Hanna took action. Easley held a long conference with Thomas, and spent most of his time describing the "conservative and valuable service" rendered by the A. F. of L. leaders, including Mitchell, in the recent U.S. Steel strike. He was sure that such union men could be relied upon to prevent the U.M.W. from taking any radical action against the operators' interests. He informed Mitchell that he had left Thomas "in a very friendly state of mind," although he was still opposed to the miners' demand for recognition. Mitchell, for once, was not so easily won over by Easley's honeyed words; he informed the N.C.F. president that he was getting fed up with demeaning himself before the company presidents in order to prevent a strike, and that if the operators were so sensitive that they could not receive a union committee with their mines in operation, then they would have the opportunity of receiving one "with their mines idle."

Such unprecedented militant language from Mitchell alarmed the N.C.F. leaders, and they exerted new pressure on the operators to meet with the union representatives. This came to nothing so they applied pressure on Mitchell to hold back the miners. Mitchell tried desperately to avoid an open break, but the attitude of the operators and the determination of the miners to win union recognition made this exceedingly difficult.

On February 14, 1902, Mitchell and the representatives of the three anthracite districts, in a joint request, asked the leading operators to meet them in a conference. The proposal was promptly rejected by the heads of the coal companies, and they also turned down an appeal from the leaders of the Civic Federation for a conference between the union officers and the operators. Following these failures to obtain a favorable response from the companies, the three anthracite districts of the union met in convention and drew up demands for wage increases, changes in working conditions, and recognition of the union. The U.M.W. officers were authorized to call a strike if these demands were not granted by April 1.[24]

Meanwhile, Mitchell, Hanna, and Easley were exerting every effort to avoid a strike, and a meeting was finally arranged for Mitchell with J. P. Morgan. Mitchell asked Morgan for only one thing: to arrange a conference with the operators, and he assured the finance capitalist that if this could be accomplished, an agreement could be reached. Morgan replied that he could not order the operators to confer with the union —Mitchell would have to arrange this himself—but he assured the U.M.W. president that he would "do what was right when the opportunity for action came," that "if the railroad presidents were wrong he would not sustain them; if the miners were wrong he would not help them." This left matters standing exactly where they were before the meeting, but Easley tried to buoy Mitchell's spirits by excusing Morgan's refusal to act; and assured him that, in the long run, all would work out well: "I find that Mr. Morgan is a good deal in the same fix with these coal roads, as he was last summer with the Steel Corporation. He has a lot of unruly presidents on his hands who are willing to resign any minute if he undertakes to coerce them. He has not got a lot of men standing around to put in their place. . . . That in time will all work itself out though, and we will have friendly men instead of hostile old cranks at the head of these things."[25]

This attempt to disassociate Morgan from the railroad presidents and to picture the leading finance capitalist as being at the mercy of his underlings was, of course, later proved to be ridiculous. But Mitchell had to cling to something in his effort to stave off radical action by the miners.

Several further attempts were made to obtain the conference of union representatives and operators, but no progress was achieved by the time of the miners' convention on March 18, 1902. To stave off a strike call, Mitchell had Easley accompany him to the convention, and together the two men worked to line up the conservative forces against strike action. They succeeded in having the convention direct Mitchell to appeal to the Industrial Department of the N.C.F. to act in an official capacity to do all that was possible to bring about a peaceful settlement.[26]

The long-desired conference was finally held in the New York offices of the N.C.F., but it resulted only in heated denunciations of the U.M.W. by the coal presidents, several of whom declared that they would rather go into bankruptcy than recognize the union. The conference was adjourned for 30 days, at the end of which representatives of the union and the operators met again. Nothing was achieved at this conference either, though Easley saw a triumph for the Civic Federation in the very fact that the coal presidents had been willing to sit down with Mitchell and his associates since it indicated that the business leaders were beginning to understand that they could achieve more by dealing with national officers who were "more conservative" than local officials.

In a feverish effort to hold off the strike, Hanna urged Mitchell to name the lowest possible figure the union would accept as an increase in wages in place of the 20 per cent the miners were asking. Mitchell suggested that the union might settle for five per cent. Hanna relayed the compromise offer to the companies, but the coal presidents were convinced that the union's gesture was a sign of weakness and spurned the offer. As Mitchell himself later conceded, his compromise offer was "mistaken for weakness and each attempt at conciliation increased the obduracy of the railway presidents."

Meanwhile, in the coal fields the miners were growing disgusted with the policy of hesitation and vacillation conducted by their leaders under N.C.F. influence. Mitchell was still pressing Easley for help in preventing a strike, but he knew that he could no longer hold off the men. With great reluctance, he joined with other leaders of the anthracite miners in ordering a temporary work suspension pending the determination of the steps to be taken by a convention. On May 12, 1902, 140,000 miners joined in the "temporary suspension" of work.[27]

Mitchell was now hard-pressed. On the one hand, the Civic Federation leaders were urging him to hold off further strike action, assuring him that if the strike could be postponed for another month, the coal presidents could be persuaded to see the need for a peaceful settlement. On the other hand, he knew that the miners would no longer tolerate postponement. He decided to throw his lot in with the Civic Federation and make a last effort to prevent further action. At the convention at Hazleton on May 15, Mitchell spoke against the strike, endorsed the policy of the Civic Federation, and read a telegram from its Conciliation Committee requesting that a strike be postponed until an impartial committee could make a full investigation of working conditions in the mines. Mitchell pleaded vigorously for this proposal. But the miners had had enough of stalling,* and the convention voted overwhelmingly to continue the strike.

* The miners were greatly influenced by an appeal from Eugene V. Debs, leader of the Socialist Party, advising them "to keep away from the capitalistic partnership of priest and politician, to cut loose from the Civic Federation, and to stand together to a man and fight it out yourselves." (Milwaukee *Social-Democratic Herald,* reprinted in *Literary Digest,* vol. XXIV, June 7, 1902, p. 758.) Debs' reference to "priest" was undoubtedly to the efforts of the Bishop of Scranton to stave off a strike call. (Cornell, *op. cit.,* p. 91.)

"I was hopeful," Mitchell wrote mournfully to Mark Hanna, "that the anthracite strike would be averted, or at least delayed; and I used all the power at my command to bring this about; but it developed in the Hazleton convention that our delegates were almost unanimous in their determination to enforce some concessions. The strike sentiment was crystallized when the coal operators refused to arbitrate or agree to any method of adjustment which would be fair to all alike. I should have succeeded in securing a postponement had our delegates not been under iron clad instructions from their constituents."[28]

These "constituents"—the miners—now staged one of the greatest strikes in American labor history. In Pennsylvania alone the number of strikers involved was 147,000, as virtually all the anthracite mine workers, as well as many engineers, firemen, and pumpmen employed in and around the mines, were out on strike. Strikes were also in progress in other states, and altogether 184,000 miners were involved in the great battle. Miners of many nationalities joined to sing this parody of the popular tune of the day, "Just Break the News to Mother":

> *Just break the news to Morgan that great official organ,*
> *And tell him we want ten per cent of increase in our pay,**
> *Just say we are united and that our wrongs must be righted,*
> *And with those unjust company stores of course we'll do away.*[29]

In the closing moments of the Hazleton convention, a resolution had been passed directing Mitchell to call a national convention, the purpose of which was to involve the mine workers of the whole country in the strike. The anthracite miners hoped for all-out support from the well-organized bituminous fields, convinced that with this aid victory would come quickly. Although many of the soft coal miners worked under a trade agreement which was not due to expire until the following year, there was a strong feeling among them that their future too was at stake, and talk of sympathetic action mounted rapidly.

Reports that the bituminous workers were discussing laying down their tools and blowing out their candles filled the Civic Federation leaders with consternation. On May 20, Hanna hurriedly sent Mitchell a letter on U.S. Senate stationery marked "Personal," which opened: "I view with *alarm* the talk about a sympathetic strike." He warned that if the bituminous workers ignored their contractual relations, "it would be the worst blow that could come to organized labor"; reminded Mitchell that "one of the fundamental principles of the Civic Federation is opposed to sympathetic strikes," and predicted that if the bituminous workers should actually go out, it would immeasurably damage Mitchell's reputation as a

---

* On the eve of the strike, the miners' original demand for a 20 per cent wage increase had been replaced with the demand for a 10 per cent increase and a nine-hour day.

responsible labor leader. "Even if the Bituminous and Anthracite interests separate," he concluded, "you cannot permit this strike to extend to the soft coal interests where you control." In other words, the union could go to pieces but sympathetic strike action must be prevented!

The following day Easley added his voice to that of Hanna. He warned Mitchell that a sympathetic strike would be "suicidal," reminded him of Morgan's promise—"When it gets to me I will do what is right" —and assured him that the Civic Federation was taking preparatory steps "to bear down on Morgan" at the right time to make him fulfill his promise. Any sympathetic strike action would doom these efforts to failure.[30] In short, the interests of the striking miners should be left in the hands of Morgan!

Actually, Mitchell needed no persuasion. He assured the N.C.F. leaders that, like them, he had opposed the strike, and that it had been called over his opposition. Like them, he was unalterably opposed to sympathetic strike action by the bituminous miners. But it was not a simple problem for himself alone to prevent it. The resolution calling upon him to convene a national convention had been "railroaded through" at Hazleton over his objections, and under the U.M.W. Constitution, he was compelled to call a national convention upon the application of five districts: "Five Districts have already petitioned me to call a convention, although I have kept these requests from the public and even from my own colleagues, with the hope that something might occur which would bring about a peaceful settlement."

If the efforts of the Civic Federation to get Morgan to act right proved fruitless, he would "be forced even against my own judgment and desire, to call a National Convention at an early date."

"Of course, I believe that a large majority of the bituminous miners who are working under contract will oppose, strenuously, any attempt to abrogate their agreements; but we have so many bituminous miners outside the central competitive field who are not working under joint agreements, and there are so many others on strike in Michigan, Kentucky, West Virginia, Colorado and other outlying districts that I fear that the anthracite delegation, which will attend our Convention in full force, may be able to round up a majority of the votes.*

* It is significant that Mitchell pointed out that sympathetic strike action could be taken by many bituminous miners without violating their contractual agreement since they were not working under a contract. But in all of the public statements by the Civic Federation leaders and by Mitchell and other labor men associated with the N.C.F., as well as by most historians who have written of the strike, the impression has been definitely left that the basic issue involved here was the violation of existing contracts, and that the opposition to a sympathetic strike stemmed from the conviction that "the future of the labor movement depended upon obedience to contractual commitments." (Cf. Philip Taft, *The A.F. of L. in the Time of Gompers,* New York, 1957, p. 247; Green, *op cit.,* pp. 48–49; Cornell,

"Then again, you know that there are elements in our organization not in accord with the policy of conservatism that I have tried—in my own humble way—to establish. What the attitude of these elements may be I cannot say, but it is more likely that they will oppose any course which I may recommend, so that, after viewing the situation as it really exists, I am anything but satisfied with the prospect.

". . . If a majority of the delegates in a National Convention decides that there shall be a National suspension of work there is not the slightest doubt in my mind that all the miners will obey. They may—those working under contract—disagree, they may condemn the National Convention, but right or wrong, the will of the majority will be complied with by all of them. It is this feature that is causing me so much worry, and is rendering me helpless to avert the calamity."

Hanna assured Mitchell that he realized his predicament, but vigorously urged him to delay calling the National Convention as long as possible so that "time should be given to do missionary work among the bituminous coal men to prevent a sympathetic strike. . . . That *must* be prevented at all hazards."[31]

Mitchell did his part, postponing calling the convention despite repeated appeals for immediate action from the striking anthracite miners and their brethren in the soft coal fields. Meanwhile, the Civic Federation went into action to help Mitchell build a solid bloc of conservative delegates to rally behind his policy at the National Convention. Hanna, it was reported in the press, sent agents into every soft coal district to work against a strike. With Mitchell's blessing and assistance, the labor men on the N.C.F.'s Conciliation Committee did "six weeks of hard, educational, missionary work" throughout the coal fields. Secret meetings were held in eight or ten different places at which it was made clear that if the National Convention called out the bituminous workers, the A. F. of L. would disown the U.M.W.[32]

The Special National Convention met at Indianapolis on July 17. Easley, Hanna, Mitchell, and Gompers worked energetically behind the scenes to muster opposition to a sympathy strike. In opening the convention, Mitchell stressed the importance of upholding contractual agreements, and said nothing about sympathetic action by the bituminous miners who were not working under any contract. Indeed, he read the delegates a lecture on the past history of the labor movement, asserting

---

op. cit., pp. 100–02.) The truth of the matter is that Hanna, Easley, Mitchell, and other labor leaders affiliated with the N.C.F. made clear in their correspondence (as well as in their conduct during the steel strike of 1901) that they were opposed to the strike in the first place, and were opposed to any kind of sympathetic strike action, regardless of whether or not contracts would be violated. Basically, the Civic Federation leaders believed that it was right for the miners to demand redress of grievances but not "to have the miners' union recognized." (Oscar S. Straus to Gompers, Oct. 6, 1902, Oscar S. Straus Papers, Library of Congress.)

that he did not know of "one solitary sympathetic strike" which had been successful. (He overlooked the successful general strike in New Orleans in 1892 and the spectacular victory of the American Railway Union against the Great Northern Railroad in the spring of 1894.*)

When the vote was recorded, the fruit of the Civic Federation's work was revealed. The convention rejected both a general strike in the mines or any other type of sympathetic strike action by bituminous workers, including those who were not working under contracts. Instead, it voted to donate $50,000 from the national treasury to the anthracite districts, and request the districts to contribute whatever sums they could. Every working miner was to contribute $1.00 weekly to the anthracite strike fund.[33]

The action of the convention was loudly applauded by the commercial press. "The cause of organized labor will thrive," editorialized the Minneapolis *Journal*, "when it commits the guidance of its affairs more generally to men of the Mitchell stamp." Easley agreed. He called the convention's action "a high water mark for organized labor." Hanna was overjoyed, and hastened to congratulate Mitchell "on the successful outcome of your convention." Mitchell thanked him, and assured him that "I am well pleased with the result."[34]

Later, Easley wrote that the result at Indianapolis was due primarily to the missionary work of the labor members of the N.C.F.'s Conciliation Committee in the six weeks prior to the special convention. He observed that "if the inside story" of this work "could be written, it would be one of the proudest pages that organized labor could contribute to the industrial history of the United States."[35] It might more properly be one of the most remarkable illustrations of how to sabotage a strike!

The strike continued throughout the summer and early fall. All anthracite mines were closed, guarded by 3,000 Coal and Iron Police, employed by the mine owners, and 1,000 secret detectives. On July 31, 1,200 guardsmen, under the command of "Shoot to Kill" Brigadier-General H. P. Gobin,† arrived on the strike scene. (Later, the Governor of Pennsylvania sent the entire state National Guard of 9,000 men into the coal fields.) Still no coal was obtainable. About this time, a full strikebreaking campaign was launched. Arrests, court action, and rumors that the strikers were being abandoned by other trade unions were used. But all were unsuccessful. Strikebreakers could not be found in sufficient numbers to reopen the mines.[36]

Winter was approaching and the nation was faced with a serious coal shortage. Plants began to shut down for lack of fuel. Popular opinion

* See Philip S. Foner, *History of the Labor Movement in the United States,* vol. II, New York, 1955, pp. 200–03, 257–59.
† Gobin ordered his men to fire upon persons who might attack their columns with stones or, in any other way, interfered with their operations.

all over the country swung more and more to the side of the strikers as the operators remained adamant in their refusal to come to terms. A letter written on July 17 by the chief spokesman for the operators, George F. Baer, president of the Philadelphia and Reading Railway Co., a Morgan subsidiary, intensified popular discontent over the attitude of the operators. In responding to a private appeal by a clergyman, W. F. Clark, urging a fair settlement to prevent the severe suffering that would descend upon householders dependent upon anthracite fuel, once the cold weather set in, Baer said in part that "the rights and interests of the laboring man will be protected and cared for—not by the labor agitators, but by the Christian men to whom God has given control of the property rights of the country." The minister turned the letter over to Henry Demarest Lloyd, the Chicago pro-labor reformer, who sent it to the press. Its publication throughout the country aroused widespread indignation. Clarence Darrow dubbed Baer "George the Last," and the majority of the press denounced his "Divine Right" theory. Referring to Baer's assertion in his letter that the operators were doing God's work by upholding "law and order" against the strikers' "lawlessness," the Chicago *Tribune* commented angrily: "It is impudent, it is insulting, it is audacious, of the coal presidents to speak of 'lawlessness' in the coal regions when they themselves are the greatest offenders of the law. They are the real anarchists, the real revolutionists, the real subverters of law and order."[37]

As the strike dragged on, a strong movement arose demanding the nationalization of the mines. In New York the Democratic State Convention came out for government ownership of the anthracite mines, and at a mass meeting held at New York City's Madison Square, on September 20, attended by 10,000 people, a resolution was adopted supporting the strikers, denouncing the arrogance of the operators, declaring that "the time has come when no individual or corporation may longer be allowed to remain in sole ownership, or control of a prime necessity for the whole people," and demanding the "collective ownership and operation by the people of the coal mines and the railways dependent on them as the only way out of the present state of social war between a few capitalists who own all the means of production and the masses of the toiling people."[38]

In the strike region, the Pennsylvania Socialists were gaining recruits at a phenomenal rate. Four Socialist locals were established every day after mid-July, and within a few weeks, the membership of these locals increased from 25 to 340 each. "The Coal Strike has done more for the cause of Socialism," wrote a Socialist organizer, "than all the events that ever happened in the United States before. There is nothing like an object lesson for instructing the people."

The "object lesson" was also being taken to heart by the business interests and their spokesmen. Seriously alarmed by the growing demand for government ownership, the Civic Federation leaders intensified their efforts to bring about a quick settlement, regardless of the terms. "The men *must* be put back to work before the thing breaks down," Easley wrote to Gompers in mid-August. Morgan must be made to see that it was necessary to act to stave off radicalism stimulated by the obstinacy of the coal presidents. In a letter to George W. Perkins urging him to use his influence with J. P. Morgan to help bring about a settlement, Easley stressed the fact that if the strike continued, it "would open the flood gates to all kinds of hostile legislation, political moves, etc.," and increase the influence of "the radical element, composed of the socialists, populists, and blatherskites generally [who] are fighting capital at every turn and trying hard to create class prejudice."[39]

Gompers and Mitchell shared Easley's concern over the stimulus the strike was giving to the "radical element." Mitchell wrote worriedly to Hanna that the Socialists were holding "immense meetings in every mining town," and that "there is a great and growing independent political sentiment in the coalfields." He had taken the attitude up to the beginning of September that "it must be victory, defeat or arbitration,"[40] but right after Labor Day, after consulting with the Civic Federation leaders, he proposed that the entire issue be placed in Morgan's hands, and that the financier be trusted to use his influence with the operators to achieve a fair settlement. The miners, Mitchell assured George W. Perkins, would abide by any agreement Morgan could work out.

Morgan was approached, but refused to take any action. At a Civic Federation Conference in New York on September 20, attended by Perkins, Hanna, Gompers, and Easley, Morgan's decision was discussed, and it was decided to abandon all further work along this line. In a letter to Gompers, Easley excused Morgan's refusal to act on the ground that "He does not control all the roads. The anti-Morgan faction of Wall Street control two of the most important ones and they are not in any compromise mood."[41] A few weeks later, Morgan himself proved how ridiculous Easley's rationalization was: realizing that the position of his lieutenants "was untenable and must be given up," the financier applied the necessary pressure on the operators, and they agreed to arbitration.

Morgan acted after President Theodore Roosevelt had sent Secretary of State Elihu Root to confer with the financier on his yacht in New York. Pressure on President Roosevelt to intervene had mounted during the late summer, and even conservative Senators were urging him to seize the mines by applying the law of eminent domain. Jacob A. Riis, the immigrant journalist, wrote Roosevelt "that a remedy must be found or the arrogance of the money power will bring a revolution." Later, Roosevelt told a Boston editor that he had been "fairly haunted with the thought of the misery that would come to the poor people in our great cities and of the terrible convulsion that might be produced." He was convinced that we had been "within thirty days and perhaps less of the most awful riots which this country has ever seen, and of a winter which would have left a hideous stain upon our annals as a nation."[42] Thus, as one student notes, "it was with the knowledge that his every action could have decisive effects on our entire system that Roosevelt stepped into the picture."[43]

Actually, Roosevelt vacillated until it became clear that prolongation of the strike was threatening a decline in Republican and an increase in Socialist votes in the forthcoming gubernatorial and congressional elections. As Henry Cabot Lodge, a leading Republican Senator and Roosevelt's close adviser, pointed out: "It is difficult to consider with calmness the attitude of the operators. Anything more worse or more foolish than the manner in which they are behaving is difficult to conceive. They are not only going to cause great suffering and probably defeat the Republican Party but their attitude is a menace to all property in the country and is breeding Socialism at a rate which it is hard to contemplate."[44]

Roosevelt decided to act. A conference of U.M.W. officials and the heads of the coal-carrying anthracite railroads was held at the White House on October 3. After long drawn-out discussions, Roosevelt suggested to Mitchell that the miners return immediately to work, after which he would appoint a commission to investigate the issues in dispute. The President promised to use his influence to obtain the operators' acceptance of the commission's recommendations.

The Civic Federation leaders, advised by Roosevelt of his proposal to Mitchell, began immediately to put pressure on the labor leaders to accept the offer. "I earnestly urge you to cooperate with a view to its acceptance," Hanna wired Gompers on October 7, "as the best solution possible under present circumstances."[45] It was, of course, no "solution" at all, since there was no guarantee that the union would be recognized in the final settlement or be unmolested in carrying out its activities. Furthermore, the operators had not only not committed themselves to accept any recommendations proposed by a Presidential commission, but had been unwilling even to consider arbitration.

On October 8, the miners met in mass meetings and overwhelmingly adopted resolutions asserting that they would not return to work until their demands had been granted. A vote was taken in every lodge throughout the anthracite region, and every local union reported that the vote was unanimously against terminating the strike.[46]

On October 11, Elihu Root and J. P. Morgan met on the *Corsair*. Two days later, Morgan informed Roosevelt that the operators would agree to an arbitration commission of seven men to be appointed by the President, and that they had promised to accept the recommendations. The operators specified the kind of individuals to be appointed to the tribunal and their qualifications in order to insure that no man friendly to organized labor would be appointed. Roosevelt, however, assured Hanna that he could inform Mitchell that one union man would be appointed to the commission. But the operators balked; they were "prepared to sacrifice everything," Roosevelt said later, "and see civil war in the country rather than . . . acquiesce." Roosevelt solved the dilemma by naming the labor representative, E. E. Clark, Grand Chief of the Order of Railway Conductors, as an "eminent sociologist." The operators had specified that one member of the commission could be "a man of prominence, eminent as a sociologist."[47]

On October 21, more than five months after the beginning of the strike, an anthracite convention accepted the President's terms, and the miners went back to work.

The operators' acceptance of Roosevelt's plan of arbitration was hailed as a great "moral victory" for the United Mine Workers. But there was considerable disappointment among many trade unionists that the union had ended the strike without victory in its hands. The fact that the arbitration commission was made up primarily of the type of men specified by the operators was viewed with great suspicion. "The mine owners," a trade union leader complained, "have practically dictated whom they wanted to serve and made the carrying out of the arbitration idea dependent upon those suggestions." Again, the failure to make union recognition a *sine qua non* of any settlement was a betrayal of the whole purpose of the strike. "To give in without insisting on the recognition of the union," a New York labor leader wrote to Gompers, "means that there is a danger that all that has been fought for will be lost, and this will be bad for all unions as well as for the miners." Finally, everything pointed to the fact that the miners, with the other trade unions and citizens throughout the country, could force the operators to grant the conditions demanded at the outset of the strike. The miners still had plenty of money to continue the struggle—in January 1903, there was still more than a million dollars in the union treasury—and the public, though suffering serious discomfort from the coal shortage, "strongly supported the miners' cause," and were ready to continue giving the strike this support.

"They [the operators]," declared G. Y. Harry, president of the Oregon State Federation of Labor, "are getting alarmed at the turn of public opinion in favor of the miners. They see that the country has become electrified with the spirit of giving great amounts of money for the benefit of the strikers. They must, if possible, stop this wave of financial assistance which has set in from the furthermost parts of the United

States, and the best way in which to accomplish this purpose is to agree to the appointment of the commission."[48]

The President's commission handed down its decision on March 22, 1903.* The award provided a ten per cent increase in wages, a nine-hour day, and instead of recognition of the union, the creation of a six-man conciliation board on which workers' organizations were to be represented. This board was to adjudicate all disputes arising between the miners and their employers. In the section of the award relating to non-union workmen, the commission stated: "No person shall be refused employment, or in any way discriminated against on account of membership or non-membership in any labor organization; and there shall be no discrimination against or interference with any employee who is not a member of any labor organization by members of such organization." But the report of the Commission did not stop here. It went on to emphasize that "the rights and privileges of non-union men are as sacred to them as the rights and privileges of unionists. The contention that a majority in an industry, by voluntarily associating themselves in a union, acquire authority over those who do not so associate themselves is untenable. . . . The right to remain at work where others have ceased to work, or to engage anew in work which others have abandoned, is part of the personal liberty of a citizen, that can never be surrendered, and every infringement thereof merits, and should receive the stern denouncement of the law. . . . No one can interfere with their [non-strikers'] conduct in choosing the work upon what terms and what time and for whom it may please them so to do."[49]

No wonder Clarence Darrow denounced the report as "a most cowardly document." No wonder the open-shoppers hailed it as a defeat for

* A total of 558 witnesses were examined before the commission. Louis D. Brandeis, Henry Demarest Lloyd, Clarence Darrow, and Isaac Hourwich, presented the case for the miners as well as Mitchell and other U.M.W. officials. More than 200 miners appeared before the commission, and so terrible were the descriptions of their working and living conditions that the tribunal found it impossible to listen to further testimony from this "moving spectacle of horrors." Many priests in the coal areas, most of whom had supported the strikers, corroborated the testimony of these miners.

Baer presented the case for the operators, claiming that the miners were well off compared to other groups of workers. Darrow tore his testimony to shreds, showing that as of 1903, 49 per cent of the miners were getting less than $200 yearly; nine per cent between $200 and $300, and only five per cent, an annual wage of more than $800.

Mitchell's role at the hearings was in keeping with the part he had played throughout the strike. He was most anxious to prevent any hostile attitude towards the operators on the part of the spokesmen for the miners, and forced Darrow to tone down his speeches to the commission. When Baer finished presenting the operators' case, Mitchell shook his hand and congratulated him. (Elsie Glück, *John Mitchell, Miner,* New York, 1929, pp. 114-17, 130.)

unionism or that they moved swiftly to circulate select passages from the report, especially those quoted above. "The Commission's findings," a student of the subject points out, "were tailored to specifications for the employers' drive against unions."[50]

Mitchell, Gompers, Easley, and other Civic Federation leaders hailed the Commission's award as constituting a greater victory for the miners than could have been hoped for.[51] But many trade unionists felt that it was hardly a proper reward for the militantly conducted strike, and it proved how unwise it had been for the union to have ended the struggle before complete victory was achieved.

"After reading the award of the Coal Commission," Andrew Furuseth, leader of the Sailors' Union of the Pacific, wrote to Frank Morrison, "I am sorry there ever was one. They have laid down some principles which if not checked will bring the whole labor movement to a standstill for years. Yet Mitchell is lauded to the skies for such things. Such are the victories won on the field of Diplomacy, where our own strong men are purposely kept out. The labor man who would sign it, could be Clark only or of that type. No member of the Ex[ecutive] Board would have signed such a document."

One of the principles laid down in the Commission's report to which Furuseth objected vigorously was the recommendation that businessmen establish relations with "responsible" trade unionists and thereby make certain that "conservative" union members "come to the front and gain general control and direction of its [the union's] affairs." Opposition to this type of trade unionist would cause "the more radically inclined members" to gain control. In a letter to Gompers, Furuseth asserted that the purpose of this recommendation was to tie the labor movement to the business interests, and "to get us all off the real trades union work."[52]

Since the Commission pointed to Mitchell as the type of labor leader with whom businessmen should establish closer relations, the U.M.W. president was elated. During the four months of hearings, he had repeatedly stated that there was no conflict of interest between the miners and the operators, and when the hearings finally closed, he repeated this doctrine in a speech to more than 6,000 workers in Chicago, adding that it was no fault of the capitalists that the American workers lived in poverty. "We are all poor simply because we cannot get rich honorably," he declared to his astonished listeners.[53]

In speech after speech, Mitchell asserted that the credit for the Commission's award should go to the National Civic Federation, and declared that it was a "vindication" of the organization's activities in the strike. He particularly praised the Civic Federation leaders for the help they had given him in preventing a sympathetic strike by the bituminous miners.[54]

In 1904 it was the turn of the bituminous workers to feel the results of the Civic Federation's intervention in industrial disputes. The coal agreement of 1904, negotiated with the assistance of the N.C.F., was hailed by Easley as marking a "red-letter day" in industrial history. Easley claimed that the agreement "meant the prevention of a strike whose possible consequences no men could foretell. It is plain enough . . . that the business interests have escaped a disturbance potentially even more gravely disastrous than that which was caused by the anthracite coal strike in 1902."[55]

In this lauded agreement the bituminous workers, like the Steel Sheet and Tin Plate Workers, had agreed to take a disastrous cut in wages!

Even as conservative a trade union leader as John B. Lennon, head of the Journeymen Tailors' Union and a member of the A. F. of L. Executive Council, was disturbed by the agreements for the miners and steel workers negotiated with the assistance of the Civic Federation. "The acceptance of the reduction by the Miners and the Steel Workers," he wrote to Gompers, "is also a decided handicap to all the Unions that I know of. I do not desire to criticise their efforts—possibly they used their very best judgment they could under the circumstances, but it is hurtful to everybody else, even if that is conceded."[56]

THE INTERBOROUGH RAPID TRANSIT STRIKE

In February 1904 Mark Hanna died of typhoid fever and was replaced as president of the National Civic Federation and chairman of its Industrial Department by August Belmont, the New York financier and traction magnate. His election was hailed by the labor members of the N.C.F. who had assisted in making it possible. No one had been more active in Belmont's behalf than W. D. Mahon, president of the Amalgamated Association of Street and Electric Railway Employees.[57]

In September 1904, Belmont's Interborough Rapid Transit Co. took over the Manhattan Elevator Co. and announced that it would train men to operate the new subway, and that they would work at longer hours and lower wages than those that prevailed for the elevated workers. The three unions represented on the elevated—the Brotherhood of Locomotive Firemen, Brotherhood of Locomotive Engineers, and the Amalgamated Association of Street Railway Employees, objected and demanded that preferential employment be given to their members, that seniority of service on the elevated be counted in making the promotions on the subway, that the medical examination of applicants be less severe, and that the subway workers be granted the same wages and hours as the elevated employees, which was $3.50 for a nine-hour day. The company was ready to make concessions on seniority and preferential employment, but rejected the wage and hour demands. The three unions voted overwhelmingly for a strike, and the company began recruiting strikebreakers. The Civic Federation proposed arbitration, and Belmont agreed to meet the union representatives. He offered $3 for a ten-hour day, to be increased to $3.50 after one year. The unions accepted the offer, and the Brotherhood of Locomotive Engineers signed a three-year contract.[58]

Belmont, a leading figure in the Democratic Party, was anxious to avoid a strike at the time because of the difficulty it would create for his party in the Presidential election. But when the election was over, Belmont made preparations to rid the Interborough of unionism, and took steps which indicated that he was ready to provoke a strike. Dissatisfaction soon arose among the workers on the Interborough over violations of the agreement by the company, including discharge of employees, reduction of the rest period, and unreasonable daily runs of 160 miles. Meanwhile, the Amalgamated Association had begun an organizing campaign, which had to be done secretly because of the company's policy of firing men it discovered to be joining the union. The company tried to head off the organizing drive by announcing that non-membership in the union would have no effect in the matter of preferment or promotion. But the campaign continued, and the union organized 80 per cent of the workers eligible for membership.[59]

At this time Belmont's reelection as President of the Civic Federation was due. He consulted the labor members, and told them, "It will be a mistake for me to be re-elected because we may have a strike and it would embarrass you, the National Civic Federation, and the Interborough." Gompers and the other labor members, including Mahon and Warren Stone, Grand Chief of the Brotherhood of Locomotive Engineers, assured him that they wanted him for another year, and Stone promised him that there would be no strike. Belmont was unanimously reelected. Planning to depart for Florida, Belmont again consulted the labor members of the Civic Federation as to whether he should leave the scene. He was assured that he need not delay his departure. Stone put it to Belmont succinctly: "There will be no strike. You need not hesitate to go away on your vacation." If any disagreement arose, he stated, it would be referred to him and Belmont, and if they could not agree, they would select a committee to arbitrate it. Mahon endorsed Stone's guarantee to Belmont.[60]

Neither of the two union leaders had bothered to consult their members employed by the Interborough. Had they done so, they might have learned, among other things, that the Interborough was rounding up strikebreakers. Belmont left for his vacation. Meanwhile, the grievances of the subway workers remained unsettled. On March 4, 1905, Secretary Madden of the Amalgamated local wrote to Mahon urging him to come to New York, as the situation was critical. Mahon arrived two days later and was shown a copy of the union's demands: a nine-hour day with a maximum run of 100 miles, a 10 per cent wage raise for all except the motormen, and substitution of a road test for the physical examination. Mahon urged the union not to strike for these demands, first, because they included those of the motormen, for whom the B. of L. E. had signed a three-year agreement, and, second, because the constitution of the Amalgamated required that controversies should be submitted to the international before a local went on strike. Nevertheless, the joint union committee decided to present the demands to the company.

The company rejected the demands as a violation of the agreement. On March 7, tired of the company's refusal to act, the Interborough workers struck. At the same time, they indicated they were ready to submit the dispute to arbitration. The New York *American* endorsed this stand. "Arbitrate this strike," it appealed on March 8. "The leaders of the striking men are willing to submit the case to a court of arbitrators. We understand, however, that Mr. Hedley, who prepared for the strike and who is acting for Mr. Belmont, has refused to arbitrate. Belmont himself, who got the Subway franchise for nothing, is in Florida enjoying a life of leisurely ease. . . . The immediate thing to do is to arbitrate the strike. The men who work for the company say they are willing. What do you say, Messrs. Hedley and Bryan, who manage for Mr. Belmont?"

But the company refused to budge. Mahon, moreover, refused to support the demand for arbitration. He had only one suggestion to the strikers: return to work. "Nothing now remains for me to do," he told the press on March 9, "but to declare that the present strike is neither authorized nor approved by the Amalgamated Association of Street and Electric Railway Employees of America, and I therefore advise all our loyal members to report for duty at once."[61]

Gompers, Mitchell, Stone, and Mahon issued a public statement repudiating the strike as being in direct violation of the existing agreement, and ordering the men back to work. To make their position even clearer, the international officers of the Amalgamated Association and the Locomotive Engineers revoked the charters of the locals. The combination of repudiation of the strikers by the A. F. of L. and International officials and the invasion of 1,000 strikebreakers that the company had been recruiting for some time by arrangement with James Farley, the King of the Strikebreakers, broke the strike. Although the strike had been solid on the first day, in four days the workers were forced to return, or, at least, those whom the company would take back. Two-thirds of the workers lost their jobs, and the union was destroyed.* The com-

---

* The company was not only able to smash the union but it gained financially. By dating seniority from the day before the strike, hundreds of veteran employees were either driven from the service or forced to start anew at reduced wages, netting a million dollars a year for the company. (New York *Tribune,* March 14, 1905.)

pany insisted on establishing an open shop both on the subway and elevated trains. After 1905 the Interborough remained an open-shop organization, presided over by August Belmont, president of the National Civic Federation.[62]

Embarrassed by this clear contradiction, the leaders of the Civic Federation did make a half-hearted attempt to convince Belmont that he should permit the organization of the Interborough's employees. But he rejected the proposal flatly. Nevertheless, he continued to enjoy the support of the A. F. of L. leaders during his three-year term as president of the N.C.F. On October 13, 1905, Easley wrote to Gompers concerning Belmont who was then in the hospital: "I know you will be pleased to hear that the flowers we sent to Mr. Belmont Monday, with a card containing the names of yourself, John Mitchell, D. J. Keefe and R. M. Easley, were so much appreciated by him that he sent out of the room some forty floral offerings from his business and social friends and kept only the one we sent. . . . He was quite touched by this little act of ours."[63]

Flowers for the man who had broken the strike and smashed the union. But for the strikers Gompers had only words of denunciation, "I think that their strike was unjustifiable," he declared a few weeks after the strike was broken, "for the simple reason that the employees violated their agreement and verbal contract. The most important object in the labor organizations today is the honor of agreements between employee and employer. The violation of agreements was the main cause of the strike. . . . It was a simple case of the members of the union flying off half-cocked and not taking the advice of the men who have made the labor organizations in the United States what they are today."[64]

Twenty years after the Interborough strike was crushed, at a memorial meeting sponsored by the Civic Federation in memory of Belmont and Gompers, Alton B. Parker, then president of the N.C.F., recalled how the labor members of the Civic Federation had helped Belmont break the strike. After relating the promise to Belmont that there would be no strike, he concluded: "Mr. Belmont . . . left at once for Florida. He had no more than reached his destination than the whole Interborough System was tied up by a strike. Messrs. Gompers, Mitchell, Stone and Mahon, who were on the ground, immediately issued a public statement declaring that the strike was in direct violation of orders—aye, that there was no occasion for it and ordering the men back to work, *thus virtually breaking the strike and making good their promise to Mr. Belmont.*"[65]

Rowland Hill Harvey, Gompers' laudatory biographer, characterizes Parker's story as "illustrative of the value of such contacts as were possible in the National Civic Federation." These contacts, the story indicates, were extremely valuable to the big capitalists; they were tragic for the American workers. "The relations between Gompers and August

Belmont," Harvey adds, "were particularly happy." (The same could be said for John Mitchell who wrote to Easley of Belmont: "You know I am very fond of him."[66]) The Interborough workers who saw their union smashed, who lost their jobs as a result of the betrayal of the strike by the labor leaders associated with the Civic Federation, did not have happy relations with August Belmont.

The repercussions of the sell-out of the Interborough strikers were widespread both within the Amalgamated Association and the entire labor movement. The effect on the members of the Amalgamated is clearly revealed in a letter to Gompers from Daniel J. Keefe, A. F. of L. vice-president, who wrote on September 30, 1905, on the eve of the union's convention: "I have learned from various sources that there is considerable discussion within the ranks of the Amalgamated Street Railway Employees on account of the position taken by Brother Mahon in connection with the New York Subway strike." He urged Gompers to come to the convention and "give Brother Mahon a helping hand."[67] Although Mahon's machine, with Gompers' assistance, prevented the passage of a resolution condemning the International officers' role in the strike, the issue long remained a thorn in Mahon's side.

In the labor movement, as a whole, the sell-out of the Interborough strikers confirmed the steadily growing feeling that the N.C.F. was an important agency of the employers to weaken the trade unions, and that the labor members should immediately disassociate themselves from the organization.

BATTLE OVER THE NATIONAL CIVIC FEDERATION

There were workers who were impressed by the press buildup of the labor members of the Civic Federation, picturing them as "respectable" trade unionists. That Gompers, Mitchell, and others could sit down to dinner and drinks with millionaires filled such workers with pride. There were others who felt that the role played by the A. F. of L. leaders in the Civic Federation was a logical one, in keeping with the basic policy of the A. F. of L.

"The policy of the A. F. of L.," declared the British Columbia *Federationist,* organ of the Vancouver Trades and Labor Council, "has always been to recognize the 'identity of interest' idea—that the interests of the workers and the interests of the employers were essentially the same, that the workers must organize up to the 'pure and simple' point of trade unionism—but not beyond that—in order that they might collectively bargain with the employer for a 'fair share' (whatever that may mean) of the results of industry. The 'get-closer-together-in-order to avoid trouble' idea has been the policy of the A. F. of L., and it seems to us that Gompers and the others who hold that view have been entirely logical in seeking the society of the employers via the medium of the Civic Federation."[68]

But there were many workers who opposed the whole idea of the Civic Federation from its inception, and continued to do so with increasing vehemence with the passing years. Opposition to affiliation of labor with the N.C.F., expressed in editorials and letters to editors of the labor and Socialist press, speeches at union and Socialist conventions and resolutions introduced at these gatherings, were based on the following reasons:

1. The basic N.C.F. principle of identity of interest between labor and capital was rejected as fallacious. "It is claimed that the interest of capital and labor are identical," wrote a trade unionist when the Civic Federation was first organized. "If such is the case, why do they antagonize one another?"[69] The question was asked again and again during the ensuing years.

2. Under the N.C.F. influence of alliance of labor with the employers and "the public," it was argued, main stress was placed on appealing to the civic responsibility of big business to recognize unionism. Instead of relying primarily upon organization of the workers in the factories and shops, the A.F. of L., under Civic Federation ideology, concentrated on winning favor from employers through the intercession of the N.C.F.* This took the minds of these union leaders away from the major problems with which they should have concerned themselves.

3. By associating with men who had bitterly fought unionism and continued to do so, the union leaders in the N.C.F. clothed these enemies of labor with an air of decency which made it easier for them to carry out their warfare against organized labor. As a result of these associations, the labor leaders began to regard these men as honest and sincere philanthropists who been painted blacker than they actually were in real life. Instead of fighting the enemies of unionism, they found reasons to excuse or defend their anti-labor activities, often blaming the workers for having allowed radical elements to blind them to the real truth about the capitalists. The workers in the factories and shops knew that these men were discharging and blacklisting them if they dared to unionize, but the labor members of the N.C.F., who met these capitalists at dinners, assured the workers that when they came to know them, they

---

* A striking illustration of this point is revealed in the case of the Tobacco Workers' International Union. "We would like to have your opinion as to the possibility of securing the good offices of the Civic Federation, in bringing about a recognition of our Union by the Trust," Secretary-Treasurer E. Lewis Evans wrote to Gompers in March 1902. Encouraged in this direction by Gompers and Easley, the union leadership did nothing to organize the tobacco trust. In the end, it discovered it was pursuing a myth as the trust continued to operate as an open shop. (E. Lewis Evans to Gompers, Mar. 28, April 8, 1902; Gompers to Easley, April 4, 1902; Gompers to E. Lewis Evans, April 4, 1902, *AFL Corr.*)

would discover that they were really trying to establish friendly relations with labor. No wonder the foes of the Civic Federation charged that by attending N.C.F. functions and fraternizing with corporation executives, the A. F. of L. leaders lost the point of view of the workers whom they were elected to represent.[70]

4. The Civic Federation claimed that it sought to educate public opinion to develop a more enlightened attitude towards the demands of organized labor, yet it refused over and over again to publicize the refusal of employers to sit down with union leaders or consider negotiation on any level. Had it done so it might have made a contribution to mobilizing support for labor's demands during strikes, but its opposition to such publicity against the interests of the employers clearly revealed that it would do nothing to interfere with their unlimited domination over industry.*

5. The Civic Federation's policy of ending strikes posthaste, regardless of the consequences to the unions involved, had resulted in disastrous settlements for these unions. By championing these settlements as "victories," the trade union leaders had made it difficult for other unions to gain better conditions than those embodied in the settlements produced under N.C.F. auspices.

6. Basically, the Civic Federation was a cunning device of the big corporations to check the rising discontent of the workers by winning over the trade union leaders to serve as "lieutenants" of the captains of industry. In this way, the N.C.F., as Eugene V. Debs put it, aimed to "take it [labor] by the hand and guide it into harmless channels." Morris Hillquit, the Socialist lawyer, summed up in a brilliant paragraph:

"The game played by the Civic Federation is the shrewdest yet devised by the employers of any country. It takes nothing from capital, it gives nothing to labor and does it all with such an appearance of generosity, that some of the guileless diplomats of the labor movement are actually overwhelmed by it. To the organized labor movement the policy of the Civic Federation is the most subtle and insidious poison. It robs it of its independence, virility, and militant enthusiasm, it hypnotizes and corrupts its leaders, weakens its ranks and demoralizes its fight."[71]

On May 26, 1902, the Denver *Post* featured the following comment on the N.C.F. by Thomas I. Kidd, president of the Amalgamated Wood Workers International Union and a member of the A. F. of L.'s Executive Council:

---

* An illustration of this argument occurred during the Anthracite Coal Strike of 1902. Pressed by the strikers, Mitchell asked Easley late in August "that the Civic Federation should be convened and should declare specifically and emphatically that the side which refused to arbitrate was pursuing a policy inimical to public welfare and against the best interests of the country." (Mitchell to Easley, Aug. 25, 1902, *JMP.*) Easley absolutely refused to consider the idea and it was quickly dropped.

"Personally I have absolutely no use for it and think that nothing can be gained by it. I have several times been invited to take part in its proceedings, but have refused and in the official Wood Workers journal have even 'knocked' the Civic Federation. It is hard to make the workingman believe that any good can come to them from an organization in which [Grover] Cleveland and [Mark] Hanna have a prominent place, both of whom at one time went out of their way to destroy labor unions."*

At every convention of the A. F. of L. from 1901 on, a resolution was introduced calling for a declaration of non-confidence in the Civic Federation. At first this resolution "was laughed down and sneered at."[72] But the outrageous conduct of Belmont in the subway strike of 1904 aroused tremendous outbursts against the Civic Federation. The Central Federated Union of New York sent a committee to Belmont to ask for the reinstatement of the strikers. When they were rebuffed, the body ordered any of its members or members of affiliated unions who belonged to the Civic Federation to resign from it.† Encouraged by the action of the New York labor body, Victor Berger, the Milwaukee Socialist leader, introduced a resolution at the 1905 convention of the A. F. of L. It denounced the "hypocritical attempt of the Civic Federation plutocrats to convince organized laboring men that the interests of capital and labor are identical," and the "close intimacy and harmonious relations established between Samuel Gompers and other labor leaders with the great capitalists and plutocratic politicians." Although the resolution was overwhelmingly rejected, the discussion revealed that elements in the A. F. of L. leadership were beginning to have serious doubts about the value of ties with the N.C.F.‡ This was apparent also at the 1907

* A year later, American workers had further evidence of Hanna's real attitude towards labor unions when his company, the Buffalo Union Co., with his backing, refused to arbitrate a dispute with the Brotherhood of Blast Furnace Workers after the union members employed by the company had been provoked into a strike. "If Hanna is as friendly to labor as he says, it is time for him to interfere," wrote James McMahon, president of the National Association of Blast Furnace Workers. But Hanna refused to interfere, and the union was forced to surrender. (Hanna to Gompers, July 23, 29, Aug. 3, 1903; Gompers to Hanna, July 28, Aug. 4, 1903; James McMahan to Gompers, Aug. 5, 1903, *AFL Corr.* and *GLB.*)

† The Central Federated Union, however, refused to censure Gompers for his role in the strike. Gompers came to New York to defend his actions. (*New York Times,* June 5, 1905.)

‡ This feeling was given impetus early in 1906 by a widely-discussed editorial in Hearst's New York *Journal* which advised the following procedure as the first step in a labor offensive "to defeat this big [open-shop] movement for the destruction of the unions": "Today we suggest that . . . Mr. Gompers . . . and all other union men to give up their association with August Belmont and the Civic Federation. . . . What have half a dozen big labor men to do with the Civic Federation —a body that is the direct agent of the would-be scab employers?" (Feb. 2, 1906.)

convention, even though the Resolutions Committee voted non-concurrence to a resolution urging disassociation from the Civic Federation. Soon after the convention, the *Union Labor Advocate,* usually most friendly to Gompers' policies, spoke out for disassociation from the N.C.F., reminding Gompers and Mitchell that the Civic Federation had "never specifically recognized the right of labor to organize." When Gompers pointed to the response of the Civic Federation's president in which he asserted that labor had every right to be organized—he said nothing about the fact that the statement included an attack on trade union methods—the *Union Labor Advocate* commented wryly: "The most optimistic among trades unionists can hardly expect the millennium this year, but that we are making substantial progress the above [statement] surely indicates."[73]

We will examine, in a subsequent volume, the continuing battle against the N.C.F. inside the A. F. of L. But in a sense this battle was academic, for by 1908 the Civic Federation had already accomplished most of what it had set out to achieve. As Professor Norman J. Ware notes: "It united A. F. of L. officialdom and powerful financial interests against all aggressive labor leadership in the United States. The A. F. of L. became a 'Morgan partner' in attacking radicalism wherever it appeared."[74]

CHAPTER 5

The Church and Labor

Among the editorial comments following the second annual convention of the National Civic Federation in December 1901, one that Easley found especially gratifying appeared in the *Catholic World*. "For the first time in the history of the country's industrial life," the leading journal of the Catholic hierarchy in America editorialized, "did the accredited leaders of hundreds of thousands of toiling masses look into the sympathetic eyes and grasp the friendly hands of men who control much of the invested wealth of the country." The editorial was entitled, "Marriage of Capital and Labor."[1]

ROLE OF THE CATHOLIC CHURCH

The blessing bestowed on the policy of class-collaboration embodied in the Civic Federation was not an isolated incident. It reflected the program of the Catholic Church in its activities to exert influence on the thought and practice of the American labor movement. In 1933, David J. Saposs called attention to this aspect of labor history, emphasizing that the "significant and predominant role of the Catholic Church in shaping the thought and aspirations of labor is a neglected chapter in the history of the American labor movement. Its influence explains, in part at least, why the labor movement in the United States differs from others, and why it has become more and more reactionary."[2] Since Dr. Saposs advanced this thesis, a number of studies, published and unpublished, have provided important evidence to substantiate his conclusion.[3] The unpublished correspondence in the Archives of the A. F. of L., the Papers of John P. Mitchell and Archbishop John A. Ryan at the Catholic University of America, and the Archives of the National Civic Federation add still further substantiation. It is clear today that the Catholic Church made intensive and successful efforts to permeate the American labor movement, particularly the A. F. of L., with social principles based fundamentally on the ideology of class collaboration, the ideology of conservative "pure and simple" trade unionism.

Although no statistics are available on the religious affiliation of union members, there is abundant evidence to prove that the Irish Catholics were the largest single group among the membership of the A. F. of L., America's largest labor organization of the period. Another sizeable nationality group in the A. F. of L. was the German-American, a large segment of which was also Catholic. A study of the A. F. of L. leadership reveals also that in this period the Irish Catholics were dominant in it. Of the eight vice-presidential officers on the A. F. of L. Executive Council, at least four during any one year were Catholic. More that 50 Irish Catholics were presidents of A. F. of L. unions in the same period— and these included the key unions in the Federation with the greatest influence in determining its policies. Among the unions headed by Irish Catholics were: Leather Workers, Meat Cutters and Butcher Workmen, Sheet Metal Workers, Metal Polishers, Brass and Silver Workers, Pressmen, Typographers, Hatters, Lathers, Moulders, Electrical Workers, Photo-Engravers, Hotel and Restaurant Employees and Bartenders, Retail Clerks, Paper Makers, Switchmen, Longshoremen, Glass Bottle Blowers, Plumbers and Steam Fitters, Textile Workers, Iron, Steel and Tin Workers, and Miners.[4]

In short, Catholics, especially the Irish Catholics in the skilled trades, were the dominant religious group among the rank and file of the A. F. of L. unions, among the officers of the International Unions that comprised the Federation, and on the Executive Council of the A. F. of L.

PAPAL ENCYCLICALS

Keenly aware of the composition of the trade union membership and leadership after 1900, the Catholic Church made a concerted and well-organized effort to impose its views of the labor-capital conflict upon the labor movement. Catholics might be trade unionists, the church dignitaries made it clear, but they could only be good Catholics and trade unionists if they accepted the doctrines of the church on social issues and applied them in their activities in the labor movement.

These doctrines were set forth in a series of Papal Encyclicals, the most important of which was issued in May 1891 by Leo XIII, entitled *On the Condition of Labor,* otherwise known as *Rerum Novarum.* Acknowledging that the position adopted heretofore by the church on the labor question had caused most workers "to look upon Christianity as a mockery and religion as an enemy,"* the Pope determined to rectify the

* The view that the church—Protestant and Catholic—was a capitalist tool was voiced frequently by unions and the labor press during the 1890's and 1900's. During a strike of street car workers in Terre Haute, Indiana, 1902, *The Toiler* observed: "Let the workers also remember that from no single Christian pulpit has there come in this sore hour a note of cheer. No, not one. The Church is true to its historical mission. It has ever been on the side of the oppressor. There it stands to-

situation, so far as the Catholic Church was concerned, by proving that it was not indifferent to the fact that too many workingmen were "broken down in spirit and worn down in body by the inhumanity of the employers." During the past century, the Pope declared, "working men have been given over, isolated and defenceless, to the callousness of employers, and the greed of unrestrained competition." And he asked, "Is it right that the fruit of a man's sweat and labor should be enjoyed by another?" He answered: "As effects follow their cause, so it is just and right that the results of labor should belong to him who has labored." The encyclical proceeded to advocate labor unions, asserting that "a worker's right to join a union is his by his very nature as man, and even the State cannot take it from him."

Up to this point, Leo XIII's encyclical was a great advance over the position taken by the Catholic Church until that time, for it indicated that the church recognized that the employers were responsible for the unbelievably long hours of labor, starvation wages, filthy and inhuman working conditions in industry; denied that these conditions were a natural order of things with which the workers had no right to interfere, and accepted the right and necessity of workers to organize into trade unions. No militant worker, regardless of his religious persuasion, could disagree with these sections of the encyclical, and the Socialists could and did point out that the Pope's statement—"it is just and right that the results of labour should belong to him who has laboured"—was in keeping with their own objectives.

But the Pope went on in the rest of the encyclical to outline the conditions under which the organized workers must operate if they were to win the Catholic Church's approval. The workers were bound "never to injure capital"; to reject the doctrine of the class struggle; to refrain from joining unions which sought "to get within their grasp the whole field of labour, and force workingmen either to join them or to starve," and, especially, to condemn socialism which, the Pope declared, "would injure those whom it is intended to benefit . . . would be contrary to the natural rights of mankind, and . . . would introduce confusion and disorder into the Commonwealth." In essence, *Rerum Novarum* made it clear that the church would accept the existence of trade unions and not oppose them as long as they operate along conservative lines in harmony with Catholic principles. It also made it quite clear that should the trade unions develop a socialist orientation, the church would condemn them and expect Catholic workers to leave them.[5]

---

day. When a rich and soulless corporation assaults its weary, worn, half-homed, half-fed workingmen, the pulpit is as dumb as death and no echo of the voice of Christ is heard in the temple that profanes its name." (*The Toiler*, Feb. 7, 1902, in Eugene V. Debs Scrapbook, Tamiment Institute Library, New York City, No. 5, pp. 278–79. Hereinafter cited as *TIL*.)

After 1891, it was no longer proper for the Catholic hierarchy to oppose trade unions in general. But it was both proper and necessary for the hierarchy and all devout Catholics to work for the ideal of Catholic ethics in the trade unions and to seek vigorously to keep the trade unions from succumbing to socialist principles.

Pope Pius X reiterated the church's opposition to socialism in his Encyclical Letter of 1903, asserting that "apostasy from God was the great evil dragging society to destruction." In 1912, Pius X again warned Catholic trade unionists that ". . . unions, in order to be such that Catholics may join them, should abstain from all principles and acts which are not in accord with the teachings and regulations of the Church or the legitimate ecclesiastical authority. There should be nothing reprehensible regarding these principles in their writings, their words, or their acts."[6]

One Catholic historian has declared that the result of these three papal announcements was that "opposition to socialism was acknowledged by devout Catholics to be the fundamental issue [within the trade unions]." It is important to note that when the Pope releases an Encyclical, he calls upon the entire apparatus of the church—from cardinals, archbishops, bishops down to parish priests—to devote their "full energy of mind and power of endurance" to carrying his message to members of the church and to applying its principles in their daily activities. In addition to the clergy, it also becomes the duty of the vast Catholic lay apparatus—newspapers and magazines, universities and schools, war veteran associations, pious associations, fraternal organizations, and nationality groups—to propagate the Pope's message and carry it into effect.[7]

The Papal Encyclical letters summoned Catholics to a dual crusade—a crusade to assist the workers in their organized efforts to remedy the intolerable conditions afflicting them and a crusade to eliminate radical and militant objectives and methods from the organizations of labor. While a few Catholic clergymen, particularly those on the lower branches of the hierarchy who were in closer touch with the working class, tended to place stress on the first objective, the vast majority laid complete emphasis on the second. And even those who emphasized the first always made sure to couple it with the second.* Acknowledging the danger that some Catholic clergymen might overemphasize the first part of *Rerum*

---

* This is illustrated in the work of Rev. Peter C. Yorke in San Francisco during the period, 1900-10. Father Yorke actively assisted the unions in their strikes and in their campaign against the open shop which he vigorously condemned. But after he had established a reputation among workers as a champion of organized labor, he devoted much of his energy to warning the workers "of the dangers offered to Trade Unionism by Socialism." He founded a publication, the *Leader,* which he used primarily to warn trade unionists against independent political action which he labeled a socialist plot to weaken and destroy the labor movement. (See Bernard C. Cronin, *Father Yorke and the Labor Movement in San Francisco,* Washington, 1943, pp. 55-74, 75, 79, 87, 90, 92, 97-98, 105, 113, 119-20, 127, 139.)

Novarum to the neglect of the second, which it considered to be more important, the *Catholic World* warned:

"We are to be careful to distinguish between the lawful sympathy we may and should have for injustice done to the laboring classes and the unlawful sympathy we feel disposed to indulge for their lawless methods of seeking redress. Nor can we afford to adopt the error that capitalists need all the corrections that is to be given in the solution of this problem; working men also need to have their erroneous views corrected, the more so that for the most part they have become too willing disciples of the perverse propaganda conducted by the materialistic and atheistic Socialists of our day."[8]

ATTITUDES OF CARDINALS AND BISHOPS

It was not until after 1900 that the Catholic Church in the United States began to play an active role in correcting the "erroneous views" current in the labor movement. In 1896, Archbishop Ireland observed that there was nothing to be feared from socialist influence in the trade unions since full reliance could be placed upon "the good sense" of the American workers. After 1900, this attitude of complacency disappeared. The formation and growth of a unified Socialist Party in 1901 and the break from Daniel De Leon's sectarian approach to the existing and established trade unions,* filled the church with consternation. Within a few months after the Socialist Party was organized in July 1901, Archbishop Michael Corrigan, in a series of sermons delivered at New York's St. Patrick's Cathedral, condemned the new movement. Socialists, said the Archbishop, were bent on dominating the trade unions and turning them into engines of "social discontent," and Catholic workers must be on their guard to prevent this development. In Buffalo, in 1902, Archbishop James E. Quigley issued a pastoral letter to the churches in his diocese in which he exorted the priests "to warn the people against the theories advocated by the socialists through the trade unions." Quigley warned that "no Catholic can become a member of a Social Democratic organization, or subscribe for or in any way contribute to the support of a Social Democratic newspaper organ." The *Catholic Union and Times,* a weekly published in Buffalo, featured articles by Quigley and others warning Catholic trade unionists of "the danger of Socialism."[9]

In Peoria, Illinois, Bishop Spalding called the preaching of socialist doctrines to American workers "criminal and ought to be punished by law." William Strang, Bishop of Fall River, urged trade unionists to turn to the church and not to the Socialists for the answer to social evils: "In the confessional men will find more peace of mind and rest of heart

* For the story of the formation of the Socialist Party, the doctrines of Daniel De Leon and the break from them, *see* Foner, *op. cit.,* vol. II, pp. 388–403.

than all the fanatic schemes of socialism can furnish." In Milwaukee, Archbishop Sebastian Mesmer echoed Quigley's sentiments by warning the Catholic workers: "A man cannot be a Catholic and a Socialist. . . . Consequently, the fight is on and will be continued as long as the Church is a power in the history of the future."[10]

The three American Cardinals also undertook the task of warning Catholic workingmen that they could not join the Socialist Party and remain in good graces of the church, and they emulated Bishop Quigley in applying *Rerum Novarum* in the United States. Cardinal James Gibbons declared in one of his addresses, reprinted by the American Anti-Boycott Association, that trade unions "have need of leaders possessed of great firmness, tact and superior executive ability" who would strive to improve the conditions of the membership "without infringing on the rights of their employers." They should work incessantly to prevent the labor movement from falling under the control of "designing demagogues . . . who would . . . convert it into a political engine. They should, therefore, be careful to exclude from their ranks that turbulent element composed mostly of men who boldly preach the gospel of anarchy, socialism and nihilism." Cardinal William O'Connell issued a pastoral letter to be read in all churches of the Archdiocese of Boston on Sunday, December 1, 1912, in which he urged Catholic workers to combat socialist influence in the trade unions. "There is not and cannot be a Catholic Socialist," he warned.* Cardinal Farley of New York outlined a whole series of methods for Catholic trade unionists to "combat the common enemy" of church, employers and workers—socialism.[11]

CATHOLIC MESSAGE TO THE A. F. OF L.

Sermons and writings of other Catholic clergymen followed the same pattern. These emphasized that labor and capital had common interests; that the "most sacred right of man is his right to private property"; that Catholics must support conservative trade unionism, and, above all, must not let socialism attract them or let it become affixed to their trade unions. These principles were directed at the A. F. of L. leadership as well as the Catholic unionists' rank and file. But the Catholic hierarchy went even further. The A. F. of L. leaders were specifically reminded that the Catholic workers were the backbone of the Federation's mem-

---

* Actually, there were a few Catholic Socialist labor leaders such as Frank J. Hayes who was elected president of the United Mine Workers after John P. Mitchell resigned in 1907. There was at least one Socialist Catholic priest, Father Thomas J. Haggerty. Even after he was suspended from parish duties for his socialist activities, Haggerty maintained that he was still a Roman Catholic priest in good standing. "I am a Catholic priest, as much a Catholic as the Pope himself," he told an audience in 1902. (Robert E. Doherty, "Thomas J. Haggerty, the Church, and Socialism," *Labor History*, vol. III, Winter, 1962, p. 44.)

bership. The church made it clear that it was not unwilling for Catholic trade unionists to participate in the A. F. of L. In fact, the church offered to assist the A. F. of L. in its struggle for recognition. On the other hand, it would only be a friend as long as the A. F. of L. conformed to the church's idea of how a trade union should function. Should the A. F. of L. ever depart from Catholic principles of labor organizations, should it veer toward a socialist ideology, then the Federation would find in the Catholic Church an implacable enemy. The church would not only withdraw its support of the A. F. of L., but would instruct the body of Catholic workers in the Federation to leave.[12]

To prove its conservatism to the Catholic Church it was not enough for the A. F. of L. to condemn socialism. It had also to concentrate on limited economic demands, avoiding strikes in the process, and not become involved deeply in politics. Independent political action for the working class was the same as socialism in the eyes of the church, and any endorsement of it by the A. F. of L. would bring down upon it the church's condemnation. On the other hand, the limited type of political action espoused by the A. F. of L., the details of which we will discuss below, won the endorsement of the Catholic hierarchy and lay organs of opinion. Reverend Marshall Boarman (S.J.) wrote that the "A. F. of L. . . . is respected [because] it has been conducted on sane and conservative principles [and] because of its independence of political parties." The German Roman Catholic Central Society hailed the A. F. of L. because "it intends to be a purely economic organization."[13]

Catholic spokesmen were very specific in charting the course workers should follow in the field of politics. Father William S. Kress of Cleveland used the question-answer method:

"*Question:* Can the working class secure protection without going into politics?

"*Answer:* . . . Labor Unions have gained many notable concessions from employers and have secured a considerable amount of legislation without going directly into politics, or what is the same thing, forming a distinct political party.

"*Question:* What political principles would you advise the working class to adhere to?

"*Answer:* To vote for capable and honest men, whom no amount of money can corrupt."

Here was outlined "the precise political philosophy being followed by the A. F. of L."[14]

The *Central Blatt and Social Justice,* official organ of the German Roman Catholic Central Society, advised Catholic trade unionists, among whom it was widely distributed, "to prize what their unions have gained for them through their economic methods and to avoid any political policies that would be a departure from the slogan, 'reward your friends, punish your enemies.'" It continued:

"'No politics in trade unions' may be trite, but it is a true guide to safe conduct. The attempt to commit our unions to a specific political party should not be tolerated in our midst, neither by resolution, by financial aid, by giving politicians special privileges to carry on a campaign in our unions or in our official journals. . . . Our business is not politics, but economics. The friends of labor are the men for unionists to support and the policy of unionists is well expressed in the shibboleth that 'we should reward our friends and punish our enemies.'"[15]

The phrase, "Reward your friends and punish your enemies" was, of course, the political slogan of the A. F. of L.!

CATHOLIC LABOR SOCIETIES

As early as 1902, Catholic Workingmen's Associations were established in several cities. (The St. Anne's Workingmen's Society of Buffalo, New York, founded by the Reverend H. J. Maeckel, S.J., was the first such society formed in the United States.) In a number, priests who were members of unions affiliated with the A. F. of L. played leading roles. These men were also "quite influential" in bringing the Catholic position to the unions of which they were members.

The *Arbeiterwohl* or Catholic Workingmen's Welfare Association, came into existence in St. Louis in 1909. It was founded by F. P. Kenkel, then editor of the German Catholic daily, *Amerika,* and the Reverend Albert Mayer of one of St. Louis' industrial parishes, St. Andrews. These men feared the influence of the Socialists in the local trade unions, especially among the brewery workers, and, with the assistance of a number of employers, they organized the Association. It issued a paper which "was read by every German speaking priest in St. Louis and could be found in most of the taverns frequented by German speaking workingmen."

It its annual convention in 1909, the German Roman Catholic Central Verein's President asserted that the duty of the members was to contact Catholic unionists in the A. F. of L. to arouse them against Socialist penetration, and to teach them Catholic social principles. For this purpose, he declared:

"The Central Society is urging its more influential members in the various cities of the U.S. to gather around themselves in groups and circles, Catholic laboring men, members of the American Federation of Labor to instruct them on their duties and the Christian principles in the Labor Question, to enable these to counteract the baneful activity displayed by Socialistic agitators among the laboring men of the United States and thus while leaving intact American organized labor yet safeguarding Catholic religious and civic rights. . . . As a permanent solution of the problem of safeguarding Catholic laboring men, the Central Society advocates the formation of Catholic laboringmen's organizations, of course, without detriment to the American Federation of Labor."[16]

These organizations, it is clear, were not to function as trade unions and were in no sense to be competitors to the A. F. of L. As articles in *Central Blatt and Social Justice* pointed out: "Catholic Workingmen's Societies will prove indispensable to the trade-union movement for they ought to form the natural focus from which to project the rays of Catholicity into its heart." They. were to operate as an education apparatus to instruct Catholic trade union leaders and rank and filers "as to their special duties to church and society according to precepts laid down by Leo XIII . . . only when so instructed and fortified will Catholic laboring men be able to do their full share in preventing this insidious enemy from capturing the Trade Union movement and turning it into a recruiting ground for Socialism, into an appendix of the Socialist Party of the United States." With this objective in mind, the Central Society formed Catholic Workingmen's Societies in several cities.[17]

THE MILITIA OF CHRIST

The Central Society was only one of several Catholic organizations that devoted themselves to combating socialist influence in the labor movement and to directing the trade unions along the lines of "pure and simple" unionism. Most of them, however, were not organized specifically for this purpose, and were not primarily composed of trade unionists. The most important organization of this type was the Militia of Christ for Social Service, the brain-child of Reverend Peter E. Dietz.

Father Dietz's activity in the labor movement began at the convention of the Ohio State Federation of Labor at Toledo in 1909 which split over the issue of independent political action. When the Socialist delegates carried the convention on this question, Father Dietz led the defeated minority out of the hall, and assisted in establishing a new anti-socialist Federation of Labor. For years, the two Federations fought for supremacy in Ohio.

Having contributed towards splitting the labor movement in Ohio, Father Dietz turned to the national labor scene, and in the same year, he attended the annual convention of the A. F. of L. at Toronto. Before the convention closed, Dietz organized a rally for Catholic delegates after which a committee was set up to establish a national organization of Catholic trade unionists to combat radicalism in the labor movement. In February 1910 the committee, headed by Father Dietz, met in St. Louis with Most Reverend John J. Glennon, Archbishop of St. Louis who endorsed the plan.

At the 1910 A. F. of L. convention, Father Dietz appeared as a fraternal delegate from the American Federation of Catholic Societies. Addressing the convention, following an enthusiastic introduction by Gompers, Father Dietz assured the delegates "of the Church's support of conservative trade unions." On November 21, 1910, during the progress of the A. F. of L. convention, the Militia of Christ for Social Service, the first national organization of Catholic trade unionists in the United States, was organized. Its Constitution and Charter Laws stated that it was "founded by a band of ardent Catholic Trade-Union Leaders" as "a religious, patriotic and unionist fraternity" and that it "champions, coordinates and unifies the legitimate interests of all classes of society as against the teachings of class-hatred."* Its chief objective was set forth in Section 3:

"This shall be henceforth the proper dominant note of the Militia of Christ: to cultivate the aspirations of the workers to better their conditions through organization in conservative trade-unions, through collective bargaining and trade agreements, conciliation and arbitration of industrial disputes. . . ."[18]

Father Dietz was the executive secretary, and the other officers and the directorate "included an imposing array of Catholic trade union leaders in America at that time." P. J. McArdle, head of the Amalgamated Association of Iron, Steel and Tin Workers was chosen president; Thomas J. Duffy, leader of the Brotherhood of Operative Potters, secretary. The other officers were: John S. Whalen, ex-secretary of State of New York, Peter Collins, secretary of the Electrical Workers, and John Mangan, editor of *The Steamfitter's Journal,* vice-presidents. The directorate was made up of four members of the A. F. of L. Executive Council: Denis A. Hayes, head of the Glass Bottle Blowers; James O'Connell, president of the Machinists; John R. Alpine, head of the Plumbers and Steam-Fitters, and John P. Mitchell, former president of the United Mine Workers.† T. V. Connor, president of the Longshoremen, and John Golden, head of the Textile Workers, made up the rest of the directorate. Noting its composition, the Socialist journal, *The*

---

* As Father Dietz wrote: "In the Catholic bosom there is no necessary conflict between the rich and the poor; the employer and the employe; the trade-unionist, the laborer and the farmer. What is to the interest of one is to the interest of all." (Peter E. Dietz, "The Metamorphosis," *Central Blatt and Social Justice Review,* vol. II, July, 1909, pp. 7–10.)

† John Mitchell was not born a Catholic but became converted to the Catholic religion in 1907. His wife was a Catholic, and in October 1907, she had written to Father Curran of Wilkes-Barre to pray that her husband would embrace the Catholic faith and save his soul. Two months later, Mitchell became ill and thinking he was dying, asked for a priest so that he could join the Catholic Church. He lived on as a Catholic; indeed, he usually dressed like a priest, wearing a long ministerial black coat and a white collar.

Masses observed: "The American Federation of Labor is getting more and more into the hands of the Militia of Christ."[19]

In the first year of its existence, the Militia of Christ depended almost entirely on Dietz; the directorate, he complained to John Mitchell, was doing "little beyond lending their names." But in 1912, the organization began to obtain active support both from the Catholic trade union leaders and the church. With the assistance of the A. F. of L., the Militia furnished weekly newsletters to nearly 300 labor papers; and sent lecturers to hundreds of trade union meetings and conferences which it sponsored. By the end of the year, Dietz was able to report that "the idea of the work is now spreading very rapidly." The American Federation of Catholic Societies praised his work: "Through correspondence, conferences, the weekly news service, he was able to exert a strong influence in the interests of legitimate trade unionism."[20] Saposs is more specific, describing the Militia of Christ as "a secret organization of Catholic labor leaders designed to combat radicalism. It counted among its members the leading Catholic labor leaders, and had the approval of Gompers and the conservative labor leaders. The Militia of Christ was an auxiliary of the Church. It had large funds at its disposal. It was manned by an able staff. It immediately became a formidable factor in the fight against radicalism. It issued literature and retained a corps of propagandists and lecturers. In addition it routed outstanding labor leaders and priests who had distinguished themselves in labor affairs on tours where they spoke to working class audiences against radicalism and for the conservative brand of laborism."[21]

Two of the Militia's corps of propagandists and lecturers were Peter W. Collins and David Goldstein. In the Preface to Collins' *Triplets of Destruction,* there is the comment: "Perhaps more than any other man in America, he has for nearly twenty years made a nation-wide campaign from the lecture platform, through the magazines, the press and by special pamphlets, running into the millions of copies, against the menace of Socialism. . . . He was International Secretary of the International Brotherhood of Electrical Workers for eight years, resigning that position to devote all his time to fighting Socialism and Radicalism. He was Editor of the Electrical Worker for eight years. . . . Over fifteen years ago (1904) he served as President of the Boston Central Labor Union, and was instrumental as President of that body in organizing the first national movement for bringing Labor and Capital together to settle their differences by conference and agreement, rather than by lockouts, strife and strikes."[22] One item is conspicuously absent from these biographical details—that Collins was part of a machine that ran the Brotherhood of Electrical Workers in the most corrupt and undemocratic fashion, making deals with the employers at the expense of the workers, and that he was forced to resign as Secretary of the Union by the opposition of the rank and file.*

David Goldstein was a Jewish Socialist who was secretary of The Boston School of Political Economy, founded by Mrs. Martha Moore Avery. Originally established in 1899 as a study center for the Boston Socialists under the name of "The Karl Marx Class," Mrs. Avery changed its title in 1901 with the aim of teaching Marxist economics minus Marxist philosophy, whatever that meant. In 1903 both Mrs. Avery and David Goldstein repudiated socialism, and in September of that year, the two collaborated in the publication of an attack on socialist philosophy and practices entitled, *Socialism: The Nation of Fatherless Children*. Endorsed by Gompers in 1904, more than 50,000 copies of the book were sold. In 1904 Mrs. Avery became a convert to the Catholic faith, and Goldstein did likewise in 1905. The Boston School of Political Economy became a source from which emanated publications and lectures hostile to the "threat of Socialist encroachment" on the American labor movement and for the propagation of Catholic principles in the trade unions.[23]

Father Dietz erroneously claimed credit for being "instrumental in bringing Peter Collins and David Goldstein to the Catholic platform,"† but an examination of their speeches and writings reveals why he took such pride. They emphasized only one theme—the necessity of uprooting socialist influence in the labor movement, preventing its future growth, and imbuing the trade unions throughout with Catholic principles of unionism.

Touring the industrial areas under the Militia of Christ's auspices, Collins and Goldstein preached that "workmen have a common interest with their employers," that the capitalists were friends of labor, and that the labor movement had only one enemy—"That enemy is Socialism." The chief target of this enemy was the A. F. of L.: "Socialists are battering from without and boring from within—for many are still intent on the capture of the American Federation of Labor by the peaceful means of shelving the time tried and true officials, and elevating to their places, 'class conscious' socialists." The chief bulwark against this enemy were the Catholic workers:

* *See below,* pp. 166–67.

† In 1910 Archbishop William O'Connell invited Goldstein to participate in a series of public educational meetings "to give workingmen an understanding of the basic principles that underlie the problems that affect their interests, to show them the value of the remedies which the Church proposes." Sixteen meetings were held. In 1911, under the auspices of the Central Bureau of the Central Society, Goldstein began a speaking tour during which he made 90 addresses to trade unions all over the country. (David Goldstein, *Autobiography of a Campaigner for Christ,* Boston, 1936, pp. 117, 120–55.) Collins also addressed trade union meetings under Catholic auspices, before he began this type of work for the Militia of Christ.

"The work which the Catholic men of labor have to do is an important one and to a large extent it rests with them, whether or not the pernicious and insidious propaganda of socialism will succeed within the trade-union movement. . . . Almost one half of the men of organized labor are Catholic workingmen . . . almost half of the delegates to the conventions of the American Federation of Labor are loyal members of the church. . . . These men and their fellows are a factor in the labor movement. . . . It rests with them whether or not the pernicious and insidious campaign of socialism will succeed with the organizations of workers."[24]

As a result of the educational activities of the church and of such organizations as the Militia of Christ, Goldstein emphasized, the Catholic workers could be relied upon to assist the A. F. of L. leaders defeat the "Socialist conspiracy" to unseat them. But to merit such support the A. F. of L. leaders must continually prove that their policies were based on Catholic social principles. Devout Catholics would be obliged to leave the A. F. of L. if that organization departed from the principles, and the Federation's leadership would lose "its best support, those great masses of men who stand for the moral principles which are the bulwark of the family, the Church and the State." Once this element had departed, the A. F. of L. "would sink to its death." Nevertheless, Goldstein continued, the Catholic Church was confident that it had good friends among the leaders of the A. F. of L., and that these conservative officials were in agreement with the church on the principles that should govern trade unions:

"Fear not!" he assured Catholic workers. "Such men as Samuel Gompers and John Mitchell stand as good security against so dreadful a fate [as the capture of the A. F. of L. by the Socialists]. They are too well versed in the principles of socialism not to heed the danger—they are too well acquainted with socialist tactics not to understand their modes of attack—the A. F. of L. is too strong in honor and in purpose of integrity to sink to a lower place. Its prospects are bright and its face is squarely set toward the night."[25]

RESPONSE OF A. F. OF L. LEADERS

Goldstein cleverly coupled praise for the A. F. of L. leadership with a threat to their power and, indeed, to the entire existence of the Federation if these men departed from Catholic social principles in operating the organization. This practice, as we have seen, was common among Catholic spokesmen. Usually this was left as a threat hanging over the A. F. of L., but in one case at least it went further. On the morning of October 13, 1909, the Spanish monarchy executed Professor Francisco Ferrer, founder of the Modern School of Barcelona, the pioneer of secular education in Spain, a champion of trade unionism in that country, and known as "the Tolstoy of the Latins." (Ferrer was found "guilty" of inciting the riots which occurred during the Barcelona general strike in the spring of 1909, but his real "crime" was his opposition to church domination over education in Spain.*) Joining the world-wide protest movement, the A. F. of L. denounced the execution, the Executive Council declaring: "The cause of free speech, free press and free education have found in Ferrer another martyr, the more regrettable in an age when civilization boasts of having replaced the tortures and brutality of mediaevalism by toleration and enlightenment." The resolution was published in the *American Federationist,* and aroused the anger of many Catholic clergymen who charged that Ferrer was a "radical atheist" who deserved to be executed. Reverend J. B. Cenler of Moline, Illinois, protested to John Mitchell that "the resolution seems ill-advised in as far as it is not calculated to gain for the Federation the support of the large body of Catholics in this country." He continued in a mournful tone: "There was a time when the Catholic press of this and other countries openly applauded the Federation for its clean-cut opposition to the introduction of socialist tenets in its program. But at present voices are being raised here and there to point out that the Federation is deviating—not officially, but none the less certainly—from its former position, and drifting toward Socialism, and all it implies."[26]

The *Catholic Colombian,* published in Columbus, Ohio, was so enraged by the resolution that it ran an editorial under the caption "Get out of the Labor Federation," telling "union workmen who are Catholics that they should withdraw from the American Federation of Labor." Concerned by this action, the A. F. of L. assigned John Mitchell to write to James T. Carroll, manager of the journal. Mitchell urged Carroll to reconsider the advice to Catholic unionists. "It seems to me," he wrote, "that this editorial advice is not warranted, because it is based upon the incorrect assumption that the Executive Council of the American Federation of Labor had in some way criticized the Catholic Church." He pointed out that this could not possibly be the case since "five of the eleven members of the Executive Council . . . are members of the Catholic Church" and the others would not think of criticizing the Church.[27]

The incident revealed how sensitive the A. F. of L. leadership was to threats from the Catholic Church. Gompers may not have been in complete accord with all the principles laid down for the trade unions by

---

* "Ferrer Day," commemorating the anniversary of the Professor's death, was celebrated for many years after 1909 throughout the world. The meetings always featured Ferrer's last words before he was executed by a firing squad: "Shoot, and shoot straight. Long live the Modern School." (*Industrial Worker,* Oct. 9, 1911.)

the church,* but as a practical man, he knew what Reverend Marshall I. Boarman, S.J., meant when he warned in 1908 that "were it [the A. F. of L.] to fall down before Socialism, it would immediately burst asunder. The great majority of the A. F. of L. are Christians and Catholics, and President Gompers, the English Hebrew, knows it."[28] In other words, the Jewish president of a labor federation, the bulk of whose members and officials were Catholic, was acceptable to the Catholic Church only so long as he proved himself a proponent of its concept of trade unionism. Gompers surely knew that an exodus of Catholic membership from the A. F. of L. would end his tenure of office, for it would have placed the balance of power in the hands of the large bloc of remaining Socialists. In a sermon delivered on September 2, 1951, at St. Patrick's Cathedral in New York City, entitled "The Catholic Tradition in the Labor Movement," Father Henry J. Browne declared: "Generally Samuel Gompers is given credit, and rightly so, for keeping down socialist control in the Federation, but who can gainsay the influence of those Catholic members and leaders of organized labor in whose ears there echoed such words of the Vicar of Christ as these: 'It is clear that the main tenet of Socialism, the community of goods must be utterly rejected; our first and fundamental principle, when we undertake to alleviate the condition of the masses, must be the inviolability of private property.' "[29] Another Catholic historian, Professor Aaron Abell, uses more concrete language to make the same point. Speaking of the Militia of Christ, he observes: "Members of that Society, mostly Catholics in key positions in labor unions, helped conservative trade unionists, 'the pure and simplers,' to thwart the continuous endeavors of the Socialists to capture the A. F. of L."[30]

Gompers took pains to convince the church's emissaries to the labor movement—particularly Father Dietz, Father John A. Ryan, and Father

* While Gompers was quite willing to accept church support in combating radical influences in the A.F. of L., he rejected attempts to build such close relations with Catholic organizations that might lead to the Federation being taken over by them in an organizational sense. Thus when Father Dietz called for closer affiliation and a "virile relationship" between the A.F. of L. and the American Federation of Catholic Societies on the ground that their objectives were basically the same and recommended cooperation by committees from the two organizations on issues such as industrial education, legislation and social service, at the same time warning that there "could be no compromise on policies that would adopt fundamental tenets of Marxism," Gompers wrote the Executive Council's rejection of this proposal. He acknowledged that there were many issues on which the two organizations saw eye-to-eye, but pointed out that it was impossible for the A.F. of L. "to enter such agreement with a religious body as you propose." The Federation was anxious to continue existing relations with the Catholic Societies, but to take the step recommended by Father Dietz would create a real danger of splitting the A.F. of L. (Peter E. Dietz to the Executive Council of the A.F. of L., Jan. 12, 1915; the Executive Council of the A.F. of L. to Father Dietz, Sept. 24, 1915, *AFL Corr.*)

William J. Kerby with whom he was on close personal terms—that he gave careful consideration to the church's social program in his role as A. F. of L. president. He praised the Militia of Christ, and even conceded that Father Dietz held "the unique distinction of having secured a reversal of decisions by the Executive Board of the A. F. of L." On December 14, 1911, on the occasion of the publication of *The Common Cause,* an anti-socialist Catholic journal which was to concentrate on educational work among trade unionists, Gompers wrote: "In 1891, Pope Leo XIII laid down in *Rerum Novarum,* a Gospel for the social problem. We in the American Federation of Labor are proud to admit that this Gospel has served as an important guide for our own activities in the whole area of capital-labor relations."[31]

It was in December 1911, too, that Gompers received his reward. F. P. Kenkel, director of the German Roman Catholic Society's Central Bureau, assured him that the Society was pleased with the A. F. of L. because it was in consonance with the social principles expounded by the Catholic Church, and that, under his leadership, the Federation had advanced a major objective of the church—"prudent cooperation between Capital and Labor." "In principle," Kenkel declared, "the Central Verein and its Central Bureau are in sympathy with your movement, and with the principles of the National Civic Federation."[32]

THE N.C.F. AND CATHOLIC ORGANIZATIONS

The leaders of the National Civic Federation were fully aware of the valuable role the Catholic Church could play in influencing the American labor movement, particularly the A. F. of L., in the direction of class collaboration, and they cooperated with the church's campaign. "I expect to have a conference tomorrow," Easley wrote to Gompers in April 1906, "with David Goldstein and Martha Moore Avery, and will try and help them get some writing and speaking in a number of organizations." In 1908, Easley invited Father Francis W. Howard, later bishop of Covington, Kentucky, and one of the leading Catholic speakers and writers for the trade unions,* to become a member of the N.C.F. with whose cooperation he increased his activity in the labor movement. In January 1912, Easley hailed "our Catholic friends" for their contributions to the conservative program of the A. F. of L.† During the spring and summer

* On May 14, 1908, Father Howard gave the leading address to the Brotherhood of Locomotive Engineers at their national convention in Columbus, Ohio. In 1911 John P. Frey, offered Father Howard the columns of *The Molders' Journal,* and he wrote regularly for the labor paper.

† Easley specifically cited "three very strong anti-Socialist movements" of "our Catholic friends": *Common Cause,* the American Federation of Catholic Societies, and the German Catholic Central Society. (Ralph M. Easley to Nicholas Murray Butler, Jan. 8, 1912, *NCFA.*)

of 1912, the Civic Federation held a series of conferences in New York City on the problem of defeating the efforts of the Socialists to unseat the conservative leaders of the trade unions and to influence the A. F. of L. along more radical lines. After prolonged discussion it was finally decided that two types of campaigns should be waged against the Socialists. They were to be conducted separately. One part of the work was to be taken over by the Catholic organizations such as the Militia of Christ, the "Common Cause" group, and the German Catholic Central Society. The other was to be conducted by the National Civic Federation.[33]

James Wilkinson, delegate of the Amalgamated Carpenters' Union of Canada to the 1911 A. F. of L. convention, returned to Vancouver alarmed by the enormous influence of the Catholic Church at the meeting. The Vancouver *News-Advertiser* on January 5, 1912, featured Wilkinson's report to that city's Trades and Labor Council: "Under normal conditions the Jesuits control 65 per cent of the vote of the Congress of the American Federation of Labor, and under extraordinary circumstances they can control 75 or 85 per cent of the vote. I made the discovery at the Congress that nine-tenths of the responsible officials of the American Federation are men who are owing allegiance to a religious body that usually demands first rights to a man's intelligence. Such a state of affairs is not a thing that should be present in a gathering of the kind and I think that if some of the unions knew more about their delegates the latter would be forced to relinquish their connections with these societies, such as the Militia of Christ." Although Wilkinson's picture was exaggerated, it was widely reprinted in the radical press and caused concern among many A. F. of L. members. At the 1912 convention of the International Molders' Union of North America, delegate Thomas J. Mooney, representing Local 164 of San Francisco, introduced the following resolution: "No member of the International Molders' Union of North America shall be a member of the National Civic Federation and the Militia of Christ for Social Service." The resolution was defeated by a vote of 221 to 148,[34] but the large vote cast for it showed that there was a growing realization in the American labor movement that the N.C.F. and the Catholic Church were seeking the same objective in their relations with the trade unions—to foster the principles of class collaboration and rob the labor organizations of militancy.*

* In his work, *The A.F. of L. in the Time of Gompers* (New York, 1957, p. 336), Professor Philip Taft asserts: "The theory that Catholic influence prevented American Labor from endorsing socialism and independent political action never gained a following outside of radical and anti-Catholic circles." This is not entirely accurate, for the radical circles charged that "Catholic influence" was only one of the forces responsible. More important, Professor Taft completely ignores the evidence presented by numerous scholars that "Catholic influence" did exert a power-

PRESBYTERIAN DEPARTMENT OF CHURCH AND LABOR

"Why should the Roman Catholic Church insist on meddling with the internal affairs of our American labor organization?" a group of A. F. of L. trade unionists protested. "Other churches don't do it."* This, of course, was not true. The Catholic Church was not the only religious body in America to show interest in guiding the labor movement along conservative lines. The Protestant churches similarly expressed fear that workers would entrust "class agitators" with leadership of the trade unions, and determined to assist the conservative leaders in forestalling it. "There is going to be trouble," Reverend R. L. Paddock, a leading Protestant minister declared in 1902, "unless the good men take the situation in hand. If they do not, when the storm breaks, others will lead."[35] At precisely the same time, it will be recalled, Bishop Quigley of Buffalo, New York, was issuing the same warning.

The Presbyterian Church was the first Protestant denomination to take such action. In 1903 the Presbyterian Department of Church and Labor, the first of its kind in any denomination, was organized, and Reverend Charles Stelzle appointed its superintendent with instructions to function as a special missionary to the workingmen. "The hold of the Church on this large and important element of the population is not what it should be," the Board of Home Missions declared in announcing Stelzle's appointment. "The past year has signally illustrated the power of the workingmen at any moment serious to affect economic conditions.† It is believed that only the gospel of Christ can solve the great problem which is thus presented to the Church. It is of the utmost consequence that the Church should be aroused to the necessity of doing more than she has done to strengthen her hold upon the working class."[36]

---

ful effect on the thinking of the A.F. of L. leaders along conservative lines. Dr. Thomas J. McDonagh sums up the conclusion of these scholars when he writes: "Basically conservative as an institutional force, American Catholicism had a significant . . . role as one environmental factor which influenced American unionism's 'economism.'" ("Some Aspects of the Roman Catholic Attitude toward the American Labor Movement, 1900–1914," unpublished Ph.D. thesis, University of Wisconsin, 1951, p. 188.) In his book, *Workers and Utopia: A Study of the Ideological Conflict in the American Labor Movement, 1865–1900* (Northwestern University Press, 1961, pp. 165–66), Gerald N. Grob dismisses the issue with the statement that "the antisocialism of the Catholic Church served to reinforce that which already existed within the framework of trade-union ideology." He totally ignores the wealth of evidence revealing that it was not so much "Socialism" but militant, class-conscious trade unionism in the economic and political arenas that the Catholic Church opposed and equated with "Socialism."

* The protest was directed at Bishop Carroll for having threatened "that if Socialism entered our A.F. of L., they would withdraw the Catholic membership." (Leaflet, Rochester, N.Y., Nov. 21, 1912, *JMP*.)

† The reference is to the anthracite coal strike in 1902.

Reared on New York's Bowery, Stelzle had been a machinist and labor leader—he was still a member of the International Association of Machinists—before ordination as a minister. He was the moving spirit behind the Presbyterian Church's approach to the labor movement. During 1903 and 1904, he spent most of his time studying conditions throughout the country, and preaching to workers in shops, halls, and churches. By 1905, the headquarters of the Department of Church and Labor were bustling. An extensive number of pamphlets were printed and widely distributed, some gaining a circulation of nearly a quarter of a million copies. During 1906, Stelzle's Department directed shop campaigns at the noon hour in six cities for 60 days. Four hundred shops were visited by 500 ministers who addressed 200,000 workingmen and distributed 150,000 pieces of literature. All this was apart from Stelzle's own extensive work in addressing labor meetings throughout the country. He toured the country to address "noon-hour shop meetings . . . attended by one to ten thousand men."[37]

Starting in 1905, the Department of Church and Labor's Press Bureau furnished every week an article for the labor press of the United States and Canada (usually written by Reverend Stelzle), syndicating it to 250 weekly papers and 100 monthlies. "The author speaks every week to millions of working people through articles syndicated to two hundred and fifty Labor papers," the Department reported proudly. In 1906 Stelzle announced that "nearly three hundred labor papers print regularly a syndicated article" which he furnished with "plenty of religion."[38]

The Department also sponsored conferences between employers and workers for the purpose of discussing upon "a Christian basis" the industrial problem. In language similar to that employed by the N.C.F., the Presbyterian Church announced that as a result of these conferences: "Men who cursed one another for years, came to know each other better. The ethical basis upon which both sides must rest their case was discussed, and misunderstanding which had been a chronic source of friction were explained away." Explained away—but not removed!

Another important activity undertaken by the Department of Church and Labor was the exchange of fraternal delegates between Central Labor Unions and ministerial associations. In 1905, following a plea by Stelzle for support of his Department and its activities, the A. F. of L. annual convention gave its endorsement, and recommended to all affiliated city and state branches that whenever practicable, they exchange fraternal delegates with the various city and state ministerial associations. In 1906, the A. F. of L. Executive Council voted to seat a fraternal delegate from the Department of Church and Labor. Stelzle attended as a delegate from 1906 to 1915.[39]

By 1906, ministers appointed as fraternal delegates to labor unions had been slated in more than 75 cities; the next year, the number of these cities had increased to about 100. A large number of A. F. of L. unions established the office of chaplain for these fraternal delegates. The minister, supplied by Stelzle's Department, opened and closed union meetings with a prayer, and addressed the gatherings. "Their influence in social, economic and moral questions," the Presbyterian Church announced, "has been such as to revolutionize completely the discussions and tendencies of the labor element in the labor unions."[40]

The nature of this "influence" is revealed in the literature issued by the Department as well as in the speeches of its emissaries, especially Stelzle, to the labor movement.* Stress was placed on the point that "the Church and Labor have much in common," this mutuality being partly a matter of historical relationship, since there was much evidence to prove that "Christianity was simply a great labor movement, that the early Church was a great labor union." Like the church, the labor movement was a permanent feature of society. It was here to stay, and all efforts to destroy it was as doomed to fail as were those to destroy the church. The labor movement could not be annihilated by outside forces, but it could be destroyed from within by the adoption of incorrect policies and the election of "professional agitators" (i.e. Socialists) to leadership. The church was prepared to stand with organized labor in its struggles for conditions which were basically "just and fair," but it could do so only if the unions abided by correct policies and tactics in securing their goals. "The approval of the church of the methods whereby these conditions are to be obtained should be given only when they are lawful and moral." This approval could never be given to "unreasonable strikes" and other policies concocted by "unscrupulous agitators" who sought to arouse in the workers feelings of discontent with their lot in order to increase "class division and class warfare."[41] In his articles syndicated in the labor press, Stelzle regularly offered the following credo:

"*An Every-Day Creed for the Man Who Works.* I believe *in my job*. It may not be a very important job, but it is mine. Furthermore, it is God's job for *me*. He has a purpose in my life with reference to His plan for the world's progress!!"

And again:

"*The Man on the Job.* Those who succeed get there principally because they hang on—hang on when others let go. It isn't because they possess more originality or because they give greater knowledge. It's because they stay on the job.

"It's the man who can stay on the job in spite of all supposed wrongs,

---

* Apart from his weekly releases to the labor press, Stelzle was also the author of several books on religion and labor, and of one pamphlet, *An Open Letter to Ministers of the Gospel*, Washington, 1905, published under the A.F. of L. imprint, but without the author's name.

the one who has learned how to laugh them in the face—who will win out in the end."[42]

Small wonder that Stelzle and the other Department's emissaries were welcomed by employers in hundreds of shops to address workers on their Christian duties. Small wonder that the Department could boast that "a large number of business men, who are leaders in the industry, have been secured as sustaining members." Small wonder that Easley hailed Stelzle's work and placed him on important committees of the N.C.F. The real wonder is that labor leaders should have turned over the facilities of the trade unions to such propaganda.* But, then, it was better for such leaders to have Stelzle's articles in the labor press than those by radicals; indeed, the Department pointed with pride to the fact that since syndication of Stelzle's weekly articles, "radical articles are now rarely printed in the labor press." Moreover, Stelzle's articles continually reminded the rank and file that the conservative leadership of the A. F. of L. was the type approved of by the church: "Follow the leader who is quiet, thoughtful, conservative. This is the type of man who is coming to the front in labor circles, and it prophesies better things for the workingman."[43]

"Statesmanship" was needed for labor leadership; the day had passed when the counsel of radical "blatherskites" should be heeded. Statesman-like labor leaders, learning through personal contact that the captains of industry were sincere, religious-minded people, could be relied upon to show the workers that the labor-capital relationship could be solved without bitterness. The A. F. of L. was fortunate in having such leaders, and as long as they remained at the helm, the members of the Federation need have no concern about receiving the church's support.[44]

As in the case of the Catholic Church, the theme of social justice became secondary in the Presbyterian Church's approach to the struggle against radical influences in the labor movement and support for existing conservative leadership. Indeed, the theme of social justice was little more than a vehicle to push the main objective. The major objective, one student points out, was "the desire of circumventing the development of labor extremism. . . . Protestantism in America assumed a cast of social liberalism in the attempt to guide the direction of the labor movement. This *rapprochement* was aided by the fact that the destiny of

* At a meeting of the Chicago Federation of Labor, however, a bitter attack was launched upon the A.F. of L. leadership for endorsing Stelzle's "doctrine of brotherly love." (Terre Haute, Indiana, *Gazette,* April 12, 1904, in Eugene V. Debs Scrapbooks, No. 6, p. 195, *TIL.*) In 1910, the Spokane *Labor World* criticized Stelzle for knowing nothing about actual conditions facing the working class and advised him to "quit trying to 'teach' the working class. . . . He is another example of the worker graduating into a parasitical position and keeping his place at the expense of those whom he boasts of trying to help. Out on such hypocrites!" (Reprinted in *The Workingman's Paper* (Seattle), June 18, 1910.)

the labor movement was now in the hands of the conservative leadership of the American Federation of Labor. Dignity and rectitude in the Church found mates for themselves in the ranks of labor." Frank Morrison, secretary of the A. F. of L., provided substance for this statement when he publicly declared that the A. F. of L. leadership found in the Department of Church and Labor a most useful ally in the battle against radical forces who threatened their position.[45]

FEDERAL COUNCIL OF THE CHURCHES OF CHRIST

In 1908 the Federal Council of the Churches of Christ in America, which included Baptists, Episcopalians, Methodists, and Presbyterians, adopted a platform of 16 articles called "The Social Creed of the Churches." The platform, supplemented and readopted in 1912, opened with the sentence: "We deem it the duty of all Christian people to concern themselves directly with certain practical industrial problems." It then called for the protection of the worker against dangerous machinery, occupational disease, and injury; the abolition of child labor; the regulation of conditions of toil for women; the suppression of the "sweating system"; the establishment of the six-day week, and suitable provision for the old age of workers.

Largely the work of Rev. Harry F. Ward, pastor in the stockyard district of Chicago and secretary of the Methodist Federation for Social Service, the "Creed" was the most advanced position adopted by the Protestants on the labor question during this period.* The Federal Council openly acknowledged that "the masses of those who toil have drifted from the Church and lost faith in the Church," and that to win them back, it was necessary for the church openly to ally itself with organized labor. The Federal Council asserted that its interest lay with the labor movement, and that "the fundamental purposes of the labor movement were ethical."

"Despite the errors of individuals and groups, the fault of spirit, the imperfection of methods, and, in some instances, most deplorable results, organized labor is to be regarded as an influence not hostile to our institutions, but potent in beneficence . . . trade unionism should be accepted not as the Church's enemy, but as the Church's ally."

But the Federal Council also made it clear that its chief objective was to eliminate the class struggle, the existence of which it did not deny, and that its support for organized labor was for those unions which

---

* The National Council of the Congregational Churches adopted the "Creed" in 1910; the General Assembly of the Presbyterian Church in the U.S.A. in 1910; the Northern Baptist Convention in 1911; the Seventh Day Baptist General Conference in 1913; the General Conference of the Methodist Episcopal Church, South in 1914. ("The Churches and Industrial Questions," *Federal Council Bulletin*, vol. IV, April–May, 1921, p. 53.)

proclaimed class collaboration as their goal. "With Christ's example before us," declared the Council in 1908, "it is impossible to accept a class Gospel." The Federal Council threw its support to employers' "welfare" programs as a means of eliminating class conflict. It regarded them "with the greatest satisfaction" as an evidence that some employers had "a paternal spirit and a disposition to deal justly and humanely with their employees."[46]

The Federal Council concentrated its entire aid to the labor movement behind the leaders of the A. F. of L. and the Railroad Brotherhoods whose conservative policies, it declared, were helping to eliminate class conflicts in the United States and keeping the trade unions free of "Socialist control."* As William John Villaume points out in his study of the Federal Council and labor problems, the Council was primarily interested in "supporting the American Federation of Labor and the railroad brotherhoods which were the only socially acceptable organizations working to organize American labor." It showed no interest in labor organizations which advocated industrial unionism and independent political action, and none in the problems of the great mass of the unskilled workers, Negro and white, who were excluded from the A. F. of L. and the Railroad Brotherhoods by "the exclusiveness of craft unionism." Frank Morrison and John B. Lennon, secretary and treasurer of the A. F. of L., worked closely with the Federal Council.[47]

Even Stelzle recognized that the indifference of the Federal Council to the plight of the unskilled, the majority of the workers in the United States, limited its appeal to the working class.† In 1910, Stelzle declared that "the immigrant workingman is alienated from the Church." To gain the respect of these workers, the Federal Council had to concern itself with their problems, and the church had to "take sides." To be neutral in the class struggle only earned it "the contempt of all classes." It was "neither respected by the powerful, whose interests are conserved because of its silence, nor honored by the lowly whose struggles it ignores."‡[48]

* Some Council leaders, notably Harry F. Ward and Charles Macfarland, endorsed socialism, but they were decidedly a minority. (Charles Macfarland, *The Christian Ministry and the Social Order*, New Haven, 1909, p. 20.)

† This was also brought out in the Federal Council's investigation of the steel strike of 1910 in South Bethlehem. (*Report of the Federal Council of the Churches of Christ in America Concerning the Industrial Situation at South Bethlehem, Pa.*, pamphlet, New York, 1910, p. 14.)

‡ Stelzle's remarks shocked the leaders of the Presbyterian Church, and charges were raised that he was a Socialist. Although he denied the charges, he was forced out of his position in the Presbyterian Church by the conservative elements. (C. H. Hopkins, *The Rise of the Social Gospel in American Protestantism, 1865–1915*, New Haven, 1940, p. 283.) One labor paper commented: "Poor Rev. Chas. Stelzle! 'Machinist preacher,' he struggled to bring the workers from whose ranks he sprung, 'to understand capital.' The results were, first, labor distrusted him;

In general, the influence exerted by the Protestant Church on the direction of the American labor movement could not equal that of the Catholic Church. As one student correctly notes: "Probably none of the larger Protestant denominations are representative of the working man as are the Catholic and Jewish groups in foreign industrial centers."[49]

ROLE OF THE JEWISH RABBIS

Of the three denominations mentioned above, the Jewish was the only one whose religious leaders did not make an effort to influence the ideology of the American labor movement along conservative lines. For one thing, socialist thinking was the main force in organizing the Jewish trade union movement, and any efforts on the part of the rabbis to influence the policies of these unions or the ideology of their leaders would have brought down severe condemnation on their heads. For another, any leader of the Jewish trade unions who would have tried to establish close relations with the rabbis or help them in bringing their message to the rank and file would have been denounced.

In a few cases, rabbis were called upon to intervene with Jewish employers in strikes, and they were even asked to act as judges in labor disputes and in issues involving arbitration, but any effort on their part to influence the policies of the unions would have been keenly resented. Knowing the strong anti-religious sentiment among large sections of the Jewish workers who were Socialists and Anarchists, the rabbis refrained from interfering. The theme of social justice was the major one struck in Jewish religious circles. "Between 1900 and 1915," concludes one student of the subject, "social justice became almost an obsession with the rabbis. The pulpit spoke of it incessantly."[50] While the rabbis were against socialism and all radical plans for the remaking of industrial society, they emphasized that poverty was "man-made and not the inevitable consequence of the operation of economic law. Labor was held to have the right to organize and to share in the determination of its destiny." Rabbi Stephen S. Wise of the Free Synagogue in New York advanced this theme vigorously, carrying the fight for the right of labor to organize "into the very halls of the economic barons, excoriating the profit system in their presence." The largest contributors to his Free Synagogue deserted him when he participated in a series of union meetings, but Wise continued to insist that "no genuine betterment in working conditions could come about without collective bargaining."[51]

---

second, he is now facing charges of being a socialist, before the Presbyterian Church General Assembly. Moral: no man can serve both God and Mammon." (*Solidarity*, May 22, 1915.) Although he was a leader in the Christian Socialist Fellowship, Stelzle rejected the class struggle. In 1912 he declared that socialism could not mold "a highly moral being" and was "non-effective." (Charles Stelzle, *The Gospel of Labor*, New York, 1912, p. 91.)

CONCLUSION

Had the theme of "social justice" been the only one stressed by the Catholic and Protestant churches, the course of American labor's development would have been different. Unfortunately, this theme was subordinated to the task of preventing organized labor from adopting a militant program of action and of fastening upon it a conservative leadership which would uphold the church's doctrine of class-collaboration. And all in the name of combating socialism! It is indeed ironic that the very labor leaders who were most vehement in their opposition to the Socialists on the ground that they represented an "outside force" seeking to control and shape the policy of the trade unions, not only did not oppose the church for doing precisely this, but actually joined hands with its emissaries to maintain a labor program that would win approval of this outside force.

In Belgium, Germany, and other European countries, trade unionists separated themselves from unions that reflected socialist policies and leadership and established Christian (Catholic) unions.[52] Although the organizations which sought to imbue the American labor movement with Catholic social principles, established relations with the Christian union movement in Europe, and though they and the church hierarchy threatened to establish such unions in the United States, no unions of this type were actually organized in this country during the period under discussion. Their absence was due in part to the fact that Catholics occupied a minority position in the American scene—though they did occupy a majority position in the unions affiliated with the A. F. of L.—and Catholic unions would probably have brought down the condemnation of anti-Catholic organizations in this country. But, in a real sense, the Catholic unions were not needed, for as one writer in the first issue of *The Common Cause* pointed out: "In Europe workers have had the need to establish special Catholic unions to carry out the labor philosophy set forth in Pope Leo XIII's Encyclical. But this has not been necessary in the United States. Thanks to conservative leadership this is the attitude generally taken by organized labor in this country."[53]

What had happened, in effect, is that the church had agreed to support the A. F. of L. leadership as long as it adhered to a conservative labor program. In exchange, this leadership proved to the church that its policies and activities merited this support.*

---

* Since the above was written, two new articles on Charles Stelzle have been published, both by George H. Nash, III: "Charles Stelzle: Apostle to Labor," *Labor History*, XI, Spring, 1970, 151–74, and "Charles Stelzle; Social Gospel Pioneer," *Journal of Presbyterian History*, L, Fall, 1972, 206–28. *See*, however, my letter in answer to the article in *Labor History*, published in *ibid.*, XI, Summer, 1970, 396–97.

CHAPTER 6

Business Unionism

In February 1901 the Atlantic City (N.J.) *Union Herald,* under the heading, "Managed by Business Methods," boasted editorially: "Trade Unions are more and more being based on business principles, and are more and more being managed by business-minded leaders who operate according to business methods. The more completely the mastery of these principles the greater the success attained." In November 1909, the official organ of the Bricklayers' and Masons' International Union quoted with approval the following comment by a leading commercial paper: "In practically every trade we now have one strong organization of labor, with large funds, and more than that, able business men and more and more conservative field generals at the helm, with the unions conducted in a business-like and conservative manner."[1]

As we have seen in previous volumes,* the original objective of business unionism was to enable the unions to function efficiently and effectively as tightly-knit, well-organized, soundly-financed instruments of the working class in their day-to-day struggles. Indeed, efficient internal organization was crucial, especially in the years after 1873, to trade union survival and growth. Major innovations associated with business unionism were: centralized control, especially of strikes; benefit payments for sickness, unemployment, and death; high dues and high initiation fees. To be sure, even in the early development of business unionism, there were union leaders who became so obsessed by the accumulation of funds *per se* that this was for them the sole objective of trade unionism; such leaders were reluctant to engage in struggles lest they cut into the union treasuries. But so long as business unionism in the main sought

---

* *See* Foner, *op. cit.,* vol. I, pp. 346–47, 515–16; vol. II, pp. 93–96. Philip Taft traces the origin of business unionism to the very beginnings of trade unionism in the United States in the 1790's, but his definition of what constitutes business unionism is so loose as to make his analysis fairly meaningless. (*See* Philip Taft, "On the Origins of Business Unionism," *Industrial and Labor Relations Review,* vol. XVII, Oct. 1963, pp. 20–38.)

as its basic objective the creation of labor organizations able to fight effectively for the improvement of the wages, hours, and working conditions of the membership, its adoption by the labor movement was inevitable and necessary.[2]

EMERGENCE OF BUSINESS-MINDED UNION LEADERSHIP

Unfortunately, by the turn of the century, the business unionism concept that was beginning to rule many unions meant application of the ethic of the market place, the ethic of the businessman to the labor movement—the ethic which justified the use of position and influence for the self-enrichment of the union leadership and the increased profit of the employers. The majority of union organizers were men and women who willingly faced loss of job, blacklists, and other hardships in order to organize and unite the working class in struggle. Their only reward was the greater militancy and class solidarity resulting from their labor. As Debs wrote of one such organizer in a letter to Morrison: "He has the spirit of self-denial and energy . . . his very heart is in the work. He has suffered much and done much and is capable and willing to do more."[3] The Secretary of the International Association of Blast Furnace Workers and Smelters of America wrote to Gompers in 1903: "My salary is but $15.00 a month, but I do the best I can at that knowing that the Association is not able to do any better at this time, and all the money that comes in can be used to build up the organization instead of paying salaries."[4] Of such men, Debs wrote: "The labor movement is his monument, and though his name is not inscribed upon it, his soul is in it, and with it marches on forever."[5]

This spirit never entirely died in the American labor movement. Unfortunately, a different spirit also emerged, represented by the type of union leader who saw the developing labor movement as a lush business through which he could enrich himself.

In the late 'eighties and early 'nineties, the trade unions faced savage attacks by employers. Spies infiltrated and wrecked local after local; militant unionists were blacklisted. If a committee of workingmen approached an employer with demands for improved conditions, they were likely to be fired. In the face of this employers' offensive, the youthful A. F. of L. unions found it necessary to delegate authority to organize workers and represent them in negotiations to full-time organizers who would not be dependent upon employers for their livelihood. The man who filled this job was the "walking delegate," also called the business agent. He was employed by the union on a salary and was usually an appointed official on the payroll of a local union or a city-wide federation. He had the power to grant or withhold work; he examined the work of the members of the union; organized nonunion men; penalized the boss for infraction of rules; called strikes; controlled payment of benefits and the collection of dues, and represented the local union in the Central Labor Union.[6] Since his was a full-time job, his power might easily overshadow the authority of the elected officer of the union who stayed at his trade and devoted himself only part-time to the union.

When employers lost the power to intimidate union leaders by discharging them or threatening to do so, they tried the next best thing— to buy them out. They quickly learned that it was cheaper and more expedient to pay off union officials than to meet the demands of the rank and file. The mere savings to employers if they could shave even one dollar per week off the wage demands of the workers was considerable. Assuming a union of ten thousand men, it would mean more than half a million per year. And $50,000 to a "leader" who "negotiated" such an attractive agreement would be a small price to pay.

The new type of labor leaders fitted in neatly with the employers' designs. Most of the business agents were, to be sure, honest and sincere men at the outset. They had actually worked in their trade, and had engaged in voluntary organizing long before they became paid union officials. They were still workers at heart, and many remained this way during their entire career. But others found the opportunity to supplement their union salary with employers' contributions too much to resist; they gradually lost their initial zeal and became interested primarily in augmenting their income.

Then there was from the beginning the type of business agent who was well described by a rank and file unionist in 1904 as "nothing more nor less than a saloon bum." He was hardly an example of a man who had risen in his own trade. Although he had spent years working at various jobs, he had done little work in the trade in which he now operated as a union leader. It is doubtful that he would even know how to hold, much less use, a working tool of the men he ruled. Much of the earlier life of this type of business agent had been spent in activities which had enabled him to acquire a formidable reputation as a tough guy, and some of it in prison. Some had been arrested from 12 to 20 times on charges ranging from gambling and disorderly conduct to robbery, larceny, and assault and battery. But accusers had a way of clamming up when trials came around, and they usually went free.

These kinds of union leaders shared none of the zeal of the earlier organizers who thought in terms of serving the workers' interests; indeed, they viewed their predecessors with scorn, labeling them as "fools," "starry-eyed idealists," and "asses guising under the name of organized labor."[7] To these labor leaders, the trade union was not an institution to improve the lot of its members. "To them," as one student notes, "trade unionism was primarily business and, in business, one's principal object is to acquire more and more money."[8] As one of these men wrote in 1900: "The union should be run on just the same business principles as a business firm is. The union needs a man to manage it just as much as a business house needs a manager. Then why not reward him as the business firm rewards its manager?"[9] In short, these labor leaders regarded themselves as businessmen whose business was trade unionism. They had a vested personal financial interest in the union business.

THE CORRUPTION SYSTEM

Once they took over as union leaders, these men extended their outlook. Gompers could still define trade unions as "the business organizations of the wage-earners to attend to the business of the wage-earners."[10] But the new labor leaders regarded the unions as *"their business organizations"* to be run primarily for *their profit,* and only incidentally for the welfare of the wage earners.

From his union position—or positions—this type of union leader drew more or less legitimate salary of $5,000 to $8,000 a year plus expenses.[11] However, his illegitimate earnings were often far greater and might even be more than ten times the above figures. In the latter category would fall the following:

1. *Income derived from robbing union treasuries.* The new-type union leader collected the hundreds of thousands of dollars in dues, as the case might be, paid into the union local which he controlled, but he seldom kept a bank account or even bothered to record the payments in a book. A common complaint found in letters from A. F. of L. members to Gompers or Morrison was that their union leader "receives every dollar that goes into the local and gives no receipt for the same." Union funds dwindled away on "swindle sheets" which recorded their payments merely for "the good of the local." Although the union constitutions provided for the issuance of financial reports, none were issued by these leaders, or, if issued, proved meaningless.* An example which aroused widespread attention involved Peter J. McGuire, secretary-treasurer of the United Brotherhood of Carpenters and Joiners, a pioneer founder of the A. F. of L., and a powerful force in its Executive Council. An audit of McGuire's books by the Carpenters' Union revealed shortages and discrepancies. Even McGuire's associates in the A. F. of L. leadership conceded that no one could make sense of his books. McGuire was replaced as union secretary-treasurer and later arrested, but the matter

* A financial report by the national office of the International Hod Carriers, Building and Common Laborers' Union, A.F. of L., although it covered a period of ten years, *consisted of three lines!* (Michael A. Saracino, "International Hod Carriers and Common Laborers' Union of America: A Case Study of Corruption," unpublished M.A. thesis, Sociology, New York University, 1955, pp. 48–49.)

was settled when he agreed to return to the Brotherhood the funds which were missing.[12]

2. *The payment of large sums of money by employers for preventing or calling off strikes, negotiating "reasonable" contracts and neglecting contract clauses.* On June 22, 1903, the Terre Haute (Indiana) *Gazette* carried the following report under the headline, "Walking Delegate Blackmail": "District Attorney Jerome, of New York, has caused the arrest of two walking delegates on charges of extorting money from employers to end strikes. Two thousand and $300 were the amounts paid by contractors in these cases to have strikes 'called off.' In another case the district attorney says that $17,500 was paid by contractors for the Union club to five walking delegates as a bribe to call off a strike. . . . One of the walking delegates arrested appears to have made a regular business of calling and settling strikes for his own profit." By the turn of the century, such payoffs by employers to union grafters became standard practice in a number of industries, particularly in the building trades. ("Graft was not the exception but was the rule in building construction," one investigation concluded. "Union labor was exploited in the interests of dishonest leaders who amassed fortunes for themselves.") Usually employers paid a certain percentage of the total amount of their profits—from one to three per cent—to union leaders to assure themselves of peaceful labor relations. In most cases, the original demand for strike insurance came from the employers' side; in others, the employers went along, many willingly, some reluctantly, even fearfully.[13]

"The feeling of the membership is intense against the agreement but they have been forced to accept." This sentence appeared in scores of letters from union members to the A. F. of L. leadership. When it was revealed that the union leaders who negotiated these agreements were paid off by the employers in sums varying from $1,000 to $21,000 and $50,000, it was clear why the demands of the workers were nowhere to be found in such agreements.[14]

Even the most praiseworthy agreements from the workers' standpoint became worthless scraps of paper in the hands of the business-minded union leaders. The employers simply ignored the agreements, and the business agents kept their eyes closed and pocketed the bosses' bribes, presented to them ostensibly for being "a good guy."[15] Naturally, employers who refused to pay off were forced to live up to the terms of the union contracts. Finding their competitors enjoying quiet advantages through the intercession of the union leadership, these employers usually joined the company of those who paid off. In no time, the wage scales and working conditions throughout the entire trade were completely undermined.

3. *Income derived from cooperating with employers to form monopolies in their particular trade.* The power to call strikes made the new-

type union leader especially valuable to emerging monopolists. For a payment, the union official would call strikes against competitors who refused to join the monopoly or do its bidding. Agreements were drawn up under which the union leaders were to share some of the increased profits resulting from the monopoly control of the industry. In a secret agreement drawn up between the A. F. of L. Building Trades' Council and the Millowners' Association of San Francisco, the union leaders guaranteed that no material would be used in building construction that was not made in the mills controlled by the Association. Out of the enormous profits resulting to Association members from higher prices, a percentage specified in the secret agreement went to the union leaders. Under an agreement between the Window Glass Co., the Trust which controlled 1,800 pots of the 2,800 in the United States, and the leaders of the Window-Glass Workers' Association, a bloc of stock with par value of $500,000 was placed in trust to be paid out to these leaders in accruing dividends. The union was required, under the agreement, to furnish the company an adequate number of skilled workers to run its plants even if it had to take them out of the plants of the company's competitors. Simon Burns, president of the union, was made a director of the company.[16]

Here, as in numerous other cases, the union leaders became part owners of the companies which belonged to monopolistic associations. (Sometimes the ownership was placed in the name of their wives.) Thus they had a double interest in using their union power to kill off competitors and increase the profits of the companies in which they were owners. In collective bargaining, these leaders had an interest on both sides. Indeed, there were instances in which these union leaders actually supplied scabs to the companies in which they owned interests to help break strikes that threatened their personal profit.[17]

4. *Income derived from the sale of union labels.* To many A. F. of L. leaders, the union label was "A Magic Talisman" for the organization of labor and the improvement of its conditions. As they saw it, the major attention of the labor movement should be devoted to promoting the use of the label by employers and its recognition and demand among consumers, both union and non-union. As Thomas H. West, composer of the official A. F. of L. psalm, "Stick to your Union," wrote in the song, "Don't Forget the Union Label":

> *There's nothing can your rights so well defend*
> *So help it on with deed and word*
> *In every way you can.*
> *Don't forget the Union Label, it's your friend.*[18]

As we shall see, this emphasis on the union label as a chief organizing weapon was short-sighted and naive. But more shocking is the fact that the label became an integral part of union corruption. Once employers learned that the producers of a label product had a ready market among union men and their families, many were ready to pay for its use. An A. F. of L. organizer wrote to Frank Morrison from Los Angeles in 1900: "There is a manufacturer of Overalls and Shirts here and he is simply crazy to pay me to organize his help; he wants the label." In 1904, in return for the use of the union label on its paints, the Liberty Paint Co. of Liberty, Indiana, offered the Brotherhood of Painters, Decorators, and Paperhangers of America $25,000 preferred stock calling for the payment of dividends out of the annual profits of the company, and, in addition, it promised "that when the sales of the paints shall have increased by three million gallons per annum, the company was to pay the Brotherhood the sum of $100,000 in cash."[19]

Here, then, was a lucrative field for profit, and the profit-seeking union leaders were quick to take advantage of it by entering into agreements with employers for the sale of the union label. "That sort of unionism," a union official (himself guilty of the practice) conc- led in 1903, "is only a burlesque." The companies would ostensibly recognize the union, but continue to operate, in practice, either as an open shop or completely ignore the rules governing the union label and the union conditions the label was supposed to guarantee.* After an investigation, the District Council of Cincinnati, Ohio, complained to the Brotherhood of Painters, Decorators and Paperhangers: "The Liberty Paint Company of Liberty, Indiana has the label of the A. F. of L. stating that it is union made. . . . Our investigation proves that the Liberty Paint Company had only unionized their business so they could get use of the label and after having obtained same, did not insist on the men being union." Neither did the union leadership which had obtained a sizeable income from the agreement granting the company use of the label.[20]

In many instances, the union label was nothing but a selling point from which the union leadership derived an income.[21] And of none was this more true than of the leadership of the United Garment Workers. Henry White, general secretary of the U.G.W. and an active labor representative in the National Civic Federation,† devoted most

---

* The A.F. of L. set up a series of nine rules governing the union label issued by the Federation itself or one of its affiliates. These included provisions for union wages and hours (eight per day usually), for employment only of A.F. of L. members, for enforcement by the employer of all union rules, and for the guarantee by the employer that should he violate the rules he should return the labels to the union or union officers from whom he received them. (Leaflet, 1900, AFL Corr.)

† White constantly lauded Ralph M. Easley and praised his "tact and enterprise." In the steel strike of 1901, White worked actively to get President Shaffer to waive his demand for union recognition. (Henry White to Gompers, July 19, 1901, *AFL Corr.*) For White's role as a defender of the trusts, *see* Foner, *op. cit.,* vol. II, p. 377.)

of his time to the sale of union labels. No labels were issued unless arrangements were made through White and unless he received proper compensation. When a group of A. F. of L. organizers unionized the garment workers in Columbus, Ohio, the local received a charter from White, but the request for labels was rejected. After investigating the matter thoroughly, the Columbus Central Trades and Labor Assembly protested to Frank Morrison:

"In our opinion, based on our experience and knowledge of organized labor in general, and information received from some prominent international officers of other organizations, we have arrived at the conclusion there is something very rotten in the management of this organization. . . . We have been reliably informed that the garment workers national organization, or at least the secretary thereof [Henry White] does not put out the label, except under certain conditions, and those conditions are *arranged privately with the party who is asking for the label and for a certain consideration.*"[22]

A student of the United Garment Workers notes that: "During his nearly ten-year tenure of office of general secretary . . . Mr. Henry White succeeded in making the label business the paramount issue of the organization. . . . As a result of this policy the bulk of the workers were left unorganized and oppressed, and their only means of seeking relief from the horrors of the sweating system were the sporadic strikes than convulsed one market after another. These strikes interfered with the orderly sale of labels, and, at times, involved some expense to the national treasury, and the business-like officers of the United Garment Workers terminated many strikes by expelling the locals that initiated them and ordering the strikers to return to their job."[23]

White resigned as general secretary of the Union in 1904 after he was unable to prevent a major strike which interfered with his sale of labels. "I hold," he wrote in explanation to Gompers, "that if the chief officials of a National Union allow themselves to be overridden by the members on a question which they are not in a position to determine, to surrender the right to decide whether a strike should take place or not, the union cannot endure." This remarkable piece of arrogance fooled nobody; the members of the union made it quite clear to Gompers that what really concerned White and led to his resignation was his realization that once he lost the power to prevent strikes, his label "racket" could not "endure" much longer.[24] *

* The label "racket" was not the only one White was guilty of. It was disclosed after his resignation that he was a member of a company from which he regularly purchased union supplies, including the labels. In 1907 White was ordered by the Supreme Court of New York to pay back to the union "the profits he derived from the transaction." (*Industrial Union Bulletin,* March 23, 1907.) In 1913 White appeared on the public platform under the auspices of N.A.M., denouncing trade unionism. (New York *Call,* July 2, 1913.)

5. *Income derived from sale or rental of union working permits.* The work permit system refers to the arrangement whereby unions, for a fee, give permission to nonunion members to work temporarily in an enterprise, in which hiring or continuation in employment is controlled by the union. Union leaders, finding it necessary to supply workers on a job, but having no desire to jeopardize their control by opening the union to thousands of newcomers, solved the problem by issuing "work permits" that enabled outsiders to work on the job by paying the union a fee. That brought thousands of dollars into the union treasuries supervised by the business-minded union leaders. In other cases, the union leaders rented "working permits" to an employer who was hiring nonunion labor, and received an income directly from these businessmen. They, in turn, deducted it from the wages of the temporary workers. Once the job was finished, the "permits" were returned. In either case, the union leaders derived large incomes from the wages of the unorganized workers. In most unions which used this system, no record of the "permit" cards issued was kept, nor of the fees paid for them.[25]

There were other sources of illegitimate earnings for business-minded labor leaders which helped them pyramid their incomes. In this category fell (1) collection of "gifts" from members of the union and from employers (the latter often in the form of loans which were never repaid); (2) pocketing of high fees for granting membership in the union; (3) payments from employers for permitting union workers to work on non-union goods; (4) kickbacks from the members' wages (workers, under this arrangement, are required to return part of their day's pay to the union boss in order to assure themselves a job, and, with hundreds of men kicking back, this quickly became big business); (5) payments from big business organizations for mobilizing trade union support behind programs and policies favored by the corporations, thereby helping these corporations defeat legislation demanded by organized labor.

The last-named source of income merits further comment. In 1913 occurred what has been described as "one of the most disgraceful incidents in American history."[26] On June 29, 1913, the editions of the New York *World* and the Chicago *Tribune* carried huge front page headlines: "Lobbyist Bares His Ten Years' Work as Tool of Officials of Manufacturers' Association." Under this heading came the first of a series of exposures made by the so-called "Colonel" Martin M. Mulhall, for many years lobbyist for N.A.M. and its subordinate organizations. Among other things, these articles disclosed that hundreds of union officers throughout the country had accepted bribes from the N.A.M. agent to support the political program of the open-shop movement, a program which included opposition to any attempt to remove the use of injunctions in labor disputes. In addition, these leaders had been paid off to throw support of their unions behind N.A.M.-sponsored political candidates and oppose A. F. of L.-sponsored candidates. Later, in testimony before the Senate Lobby Probe Committee, Mulhall confessed that he "hired labor leaders from Philadelphia and New York to turn over to the chairman of the Republican committee in the congressional district of New Jersey where William Hughes [a labor-supported candidate] was a candidate, 75,000 circulars prepared by the A. F. of L. to aid Hughes. These circulars were destroyed and thus kept out of the hands of the voters. Then these men, all holding cards as members of organized labor, worked day and night and finally accomplished Hughes' defeat. And they were paid from the funds of the N.A.M." Mulhall told various other stories of similar exploits in different states, including aid given by labor leaders, hired by him, towards the election of the arch-reactionary Senator Nelson P. Aldrich and his N.A.M. followers in Rhode Island. Mulhall revealed that for years Frank Feeney, president of the Philadelphia Central Labor Union, had accepted $40 a week from N.A.M. In return, Feeney had betrayed the printers' union during the strikes of 1905 and 1906, and helped Mulhall secure the defeat of William Hughes.[27]

In January 1910, the *Saturday Evening Post* featured an article entitled, "A New Kind of Organized Labor," which perfectly illustrated business unionism in operation. The article described the formation of the American Railroad Employees and Investors Association at a meeting attended by the presidents of the leading railroad corporations and the presidents of the four Railroad Brotherhoods. The Association was headed by P. H. Morrisey, formerly president of the Brotherhood of Railroad Trainmen, who, the article proudly pointed out, had distinguished himself as "a good business man" during his 14 years as head of the Brotherhood, and upon whose retirement in 1908 was presented by the general managers of the railroads "with their portraits inscribed with their names." The executive board of the Association was composed of the presidents of the Chicago, Milwaukee and St. Paul, the Chicago, Burlington and Quincy, the Atchison, Topeka and Santa Fé, the Chicago, Rock Island and Pacific Railroad companies, and the four Brotherhoods of railroad employees.

The purpose of the Association was to lobby for legislation—not to protect the railroad workers from one of the most hazardous occupations in the country nor to improve other working conditions on the lines. Rather it was to mobilize public opinion against laws regulating railroad rates, requiring the elimination of dangerous grade crossings, and the end of discriminatory practices by the railroads in favor of monopolistic corporations. Already, the article reported 25,000 railroad workers had been organized by the Brotherhoods in local branches of the Association, most of whose expenses were paid by the companies. "That the American Railroad Employees and Investors Association is certain to exert a considerable influence on future legislation can hardly be doubted. It has large financial backing and, in Morrisey, a leader who unites, more than does any other man, the confidence of railroad managers and labor unions."

But when a branch of the Association was set up in Toledo, Ohio, early in 1910, the Toledo *Union Leader* labeled it "one of the most artistic pieces of labor skinning yet devised."

"A careful reading of its objectives," the *Union Leader* commented, "will show that the railroads receive all the benefit, and care is taken that Brother Capital will not be used to give Brother Labor a share of the profits, for it is specifically provided that the new organization shall take no part in controversies between railroad employers and employes, but the latter is privileged to maintain lobbies at Columbus [the state capital] to work against any legislation that impairs dividends.*

"At the present time railroad workers are demanding wage increases, but the American Railroad Employees and Investors Association has guarded against taking part in these differences despite its claims that it intends to work 'for the benefit alike of their employes, investors and the public.' "[28]†

"LIVING STANDARDS" OF BUSINESS UNION LEADERS

From the varied sources we have just examined (as well as others), the business-minded union leaders extended their bankrolls until their annual incomes bore no relationship whatsoever to their union salaries. Between 1901 and 1903, to cite but one instance, Sam Parks, corrupt leader of the Housesmiths' Union in New York, deposited thousands of dollars into his own bank account on a weekly salary of $48!

These men felt a terrific compulsion to act big, to look big, and to live big in order to prove that they were operating a successful business. Newspapers and magazines disclosed their plush living; showed them parading their wealth with great ostentation—strutting about at high-priced dining places, at exclusive hotels, and at fashionable resorts frequented by the wealthy. They told of union officials who spent money on lavish parties while most of their members were having difficulty keeping their families fed; officials who lost thousands of dollars in one night

---

* One of the by-laws of the Association stated: "The Association shall at no time be used for partisan political purposes, nor shall it take any part in controversies, if any, which may arise between railroad employees and railroad officials."

† It did not take long for the rank and file members of the Brotherhoods to see through the Association. Opposition to the Association grew rapidly among the railroad workers, especially after it lobbied against the ten-hour law for women workers in Illinois. In 1913 the Association had to disband and Morrisey lost his job as president at $15,000 a year. Upon its dissolution, Morrisey became assistant to the vice-president of the Chicago, Burlington and Quincy Railroad. (*The Syndicalist,* June 1, 1913; New York *Call,* June 8, 1913.)

at gambling resorts; officials who lived in opulent houses in exclusive residential sections and conducted their union business in big, expensively furnished offices with gleaming desks and numerous secretaries.[29]

From Atlantic City, New Jersey, the famous seaside resort, came an interesting dispatch which was featured in the press during the summer of 1910:

"Engaged in a game of bathing suit baseball with President Sam Gompers, Secretary Frank Morrison and other leaders of the A. F. of L., on the beach this morning, John Mitchell, former head of the mine workers' union, lost a $1,000 diamond ring presented to him by his admirers after the settlement of the big Pennsylvania coal strike. Capt. George Berke, a veteran life guard found the ring, whereupon Mitchell peeled a hundred dollar bill from a roll he carried in his pocket and handed it to the captain as a reward for his find."[30]

In deadly seriousness the New Orleans *Daily Picayune* drew the following lesson from the incident: "It must be a matter of much pride and self-congratulation by the millions of organized workers who acknowledge allegiance to Mitchell and those other distinguished chiefs that are able to sport such magnificent gems and pay such royal rewards ($100.00) for their recovery after they have been lost. This mere incident shows that labor organizations are great blessings to their millions of members and that, at a small cost to each, the members are able to maintain their chiefs in opulence and splendor!"[31] But the Socialist *Appeal to Reason* was quick to note that the "admirers" who had presented expensive gifts to Mitchell were none other than the mine operators. It commented further: "Labor leaders who sport thousand dollar diamond pins presented to them by capitalist 'admirers' and peel off hundred dollar bills a la Harry Thaw, belong bodily to the capitalist class."[32]

In August, 1909, the Chicago *Examiner* carried in its society columns a report of a dinner given by Mrs. J. Borden Harriman at her home in New York State:

"The entertainment consisted of a dinner, 'al fresco,' with the stars as a canopy and the trees and flowers of her beautiful home as accessories. Dinner was served on the lawn at three long tables. From tree to tree long strings of Japanese lanterns lent their charm of fairyland to the scene. Waiters in gorgeous livery served, pretty misses in costumes led by Miss Edith Harriman, posed in quaint tableaux and sang patriotic songs, and Mrs. Harriman, John Mitchell and Tim Healy delivered addresses.

"Mrs. Harriman later posed specially with John Mitchell and Tim Healy in a souvenir photograph of the occasion, after a flashlight had been taken of the dinner party on the lawn.

"The tables were laid upon the lawn in the shape of the letter E. Mrs. Harriman presided at the center table. To the right and left of her sat Mitchell and Healy. Others present were Frank J. McNulty of Springfield, Ill., grand president of the International Brotherhood of Electrical Workers; Thomas B. Levy of Isaac G. Johnson & Co., of Spuyten Duyvil, N.Y.; Edward A. Moffett (former editor of the Bricklayers' and Masons' Journal, Camden, N.J.; C. L. Shamp of Omaha, Neb., secretary of the International Stationary Firemen's Union."[33]

One labor paper commented caustically: "Every coal miner's shack should be ornamented with a copy of the photograph which was taken of the revellers."[34]

Whether or not such type of living, as the *Appeal to Reason* argued, placed these labor leaders in the capitalist class may be debated, but it certainly caused them to grow apart from the union membership and to lose real touch with the current needs of the rank and file. Furthermore, it contributed to their thinking like capitalists. These men were not opposed to capitalism. They talked the same language as businessmen, and felt more at home with them than they did with the members of their unions. They loudly proclaimed that cooperation was much more reasonable than resistance, and, in the midst of struggles waged by their members, they could be found enjoying themselves in the company of the very employers against whom the workers were striking.[35]

Labor leaders were invited to meet important figures in the social, economic, and political world, and they quickly learned to fit into this environment. In December 1907, at the height of the depression of that year, the foreign editor of *La Petit Journal* of Paris attended the dinner of the National Civic Federation at the Hotel Astor in New York. He reported his amazement at the spectacle of leaders of organized labor enjoying the best of food and wine in luxurious surroundings at the same time that hundreds of thousands of workers were unemployed.* He added:

"I was amazed to see well known labor leaders like Samuel Gompers, John Mitchell, Timothy Healy and Samuel Prince on good terms with great capitalists like August Belmont, John D. Rockefeller, Jr., Andrew Carnegie, and James Speyer. I could hardly credit the spectacle of John Mitchell sitting between Mr. Charles A. Moore, the manufacturer, and Mr. Percy A. Rockefeller, the capitalist, and later between Miss Morgan

---

* When Gompers and his family visited Paris in the summer of 1909, several American labor papers carried reports of the amazement of Parisian journalists at the contrast between Gompers' style of living and that of the French labor leaders. "Gompers, his wife and daughter occupied an expensive suite of rooms in a fine hotel. The newspapers remarked that French labor leaders cannot afford such luxury; when they visit another city they are glad to share a bedroom with one of their associates. . . . Gompers calmly pointed out that while the Confédération Générale du Travail (Confederation of Labor) here has only about 300,000 members with perhaps $75,000 in its treasury, the American Federation of Labor has 2,000,000 members. 'It counts its deposits in banks by millions of dollars.'" (*Industrial Worker*, Aug. 19, 1909.)

and Mrs. Harriman. In France, the workers would regard what happened at the Hotel Astor as proof that labor's leaders were playing into the hands of the capitalists."[36]

In the United States, too, there were labor papers that voiced the same opinion. "While Gompers and his aristocratic friends were enjoying a sumptuous banquet in a fashionable hostelry," commented the *Miners' Magazine,* "hundreds of the *common working people* gathered on the outside of the banquet room to watch the festivities and to wonder if a time would ever come in our civilization when the man with the horny fist and the shoddy clothes, who furnished the per capita tax that paid the salaries of 'labor leaders,' would be permitted to sit down at a table and enjoy a 'square meal' washed down by high-priced beverages." "Mother" Mary Jones was more terse. "Poor John," she said of John Mitchell's presence at such banquets, "he couldn't stand feasting with the rich. He is no good to his own people any longer."[37]

Apart from enjoying the luxuries of good food, good liquor, and the best Havana cigars, these meetings brought the labor leaders important contacts which enabled them to increase their incomes. Mitchell found these associations useful in playing the stock market, and he was occasionally good enough to pass on to other labor leaders the advice he received from leading financiers as to what stocks and bonds to buy and when to buy and sell them.* When he died in September 1919, at the age of 49, Mitchell's estate was valued at almost a quarter of a million dollars, largely in coal, railroad, and steel securities. (Later, the estate was valued at $347,151.) George L. Berry started out as president of the A. F. of L. Printing Pressmen in 1907 with a pair of patched pants. He left a $750,000-fortune when he died in 1948.[38]†

John P. Frey candidly summed up the effect of the living standards enjoyed by the business-minded labor leaders: "Their environment tends to make the labor leaders conservative. When the leaders get away from the bench, their environment becomes more of the character of the employers than the workers. Moreover, the leader who rises from the rank and file at once encounters temptations hard to withstand. Many go

---

* Ralph M. Easley, the Civic Federation secretary, often acted as Mitchell's contact man in obtaining such advice from Wall Street finance capitalists. On November 16, 1907, Mitchell wrote to Easley: "After you wrote telling me that you had assurance [from August Belmont] that the [Interborough-Metropolitan] bonds were o.k., along with some relatives I purchased some of them." The bond's having fallen in value, Mitchell was anxious to know whether he should sell or continue to hold them. He asked Easley "if Mr. Belmont would tell you as to what the possibilities are," and convey the information to him. (Mitchell to Easley, Nov. 16, 1907, marked "Personal," *JMP.*)

† Part of Berry's wealth came from kickbacks he received from building contractors during the construction of the tuberculosis home of the Pressmen's Union at Rogerville, Tennessee. Berry had the union spend $200,000 on the home which left the union bankrupt. (*Solidarity,* May 25, 1912.)

wrong because they cannot stand prosperity. The sudden release from the bench, from machine power, unsteadies them; they become dissipated and dishonest. They may fall victim to the 'mahogany table,' and to what is on it."[39]

"JUSTIFICATION" OF BUSINESS UNIONISM

These union leaders were not embarrassed by reports of their wealth. They "justified" their conduct on various grounds. They argued that "union leaders should be in a position to make a good showing when they meet with the employers"; that businessmen had more respect for a union when they saw it could afford to provide its leadership with a "living standard" comparable with that of heads of corporations, and that the social acceptance of union leaders by the capitalists at meetings and dinners helped to break down the widespread opinion in the United States that representatives of organized labor were "undesirable citizens." They conceded that there were elements who objected to a labor union being run as a business from which labor leaders profit, but these men were, by nature, "misfits" and "trouble-makers," "radicals of all sorts," and they certainly did not represent the viewpoint of the mass of the union membership. The members were not concerned about ethics; what concerned them "is what they find in their pay envelopes," and as long as their leaders "delivered" the goods in wages, hours, and working conditions, it did not matter what their leaders put into their own pockets. "What they [the rank and file] demand of the leaders," declared John P. Frey, "is that they deliver the goods,' that is, in terms of high wages, short hours, and good conditions. So long as they do this they do not care how they do it. They are not surprised if the leader is crooked, or gets his 'rake-off.' "[40]

There is, of course, some truth to this. It is true that the corrupt union leaders, in order to obtain some base of support within their unions, did win certain concessions for the membership. The employers, moreover, were prepared to pay a better than average wage to the skilled minority of the workers in these unions in the hope that they would remain content with a leadership that practiced class collaboration and did nothing to organize the unskilled. And as long as these improvements were handed down, there were workers who were prepared to condone their leaders' unethical practices. A member of the Housesmiths' and Bridgemen's Union, which Sam Parks ran as a labor racketeer and despot, exclaimed: "Once a workman in the iron trade got $1.50 a day. Parks arose, became our Moses, and led us in the promised land of $5.00 a day. Suppose Parks grafted more or less, and made a bunch of money, he did not get it out of us."

Such workers were indeed short-sighted, for Parks, like other labor racketeers, did get it out of the union members as well as the employers. They got it by playing fast and loose with union treasuries filled with the dollars of membership dues, and they got it from the members' wages. Workers in corruptly-led unions never obtained what they were entitled to; they received just enough to keep them from revolting. Employers who said they would rather put the money they were using to pay off the corrupt leaders into wage increases or other benefits for the union rank and file soon discovered that this was not an adequate substitute. They were usually told, as the business agent of the Painters' Union told one such employer: "Don't be a fool. Who tells you to pay the donkeys $5 a day. Who pays union wages these days. Give them $2 and $3 and they'll be glad of it." To be sure, $2 and $3 were more than the unorganized workers were getting, and, in this sense, the members even of racket-ridden unions could feel they were not too badly off. But the whole point is that any chance they had of making much more was hampered by a leadership which was paid off precisely to keep the workers' demands in check. The hundreds of letters to the A. F. of L. leadership from union members accusing their officials of betraying the workers' interests proved that most rank and filers were not content with corrupt control of their organizations.

"Had wages and working conditions of Philadelphia reflected a bright picture," notes one student, "self-interest might explain the anomaly of labor unions allowing their leaders to be allied with industrialists and political bosses. But it was not so. On the contrary, Philadelphia wages in organized trades lagged behind most of the other larger cities of the country. A machinist was paid 62½ cents per hour in 1907 while his professional colleagues in New York received 70 cents; for a linotype operator the comparison in 1907 was 41.67 to 70; and for bricklayers in 1912 it was 62.50 to 70. As for the working conditions, Pennsylvania failed to keep pace with its Northeastern neighbors in passing statutes designed to correct abuses. . . . To complete the picture it is necessary to add that Philadelphia workers were bedeviled by insecure tenure . . . that the labor turnover each year equalled the total number employed regularly. Thus, Philadelphia offered relatively lower wages and insecure employment, while the state legislature lagged in providing the kind of laws wanted by union men."[41]

A major justification advanced by the business-minded union leaders was that they were no more guilty of crimes against their members than were scores of respectable businessmen of crimes against the public. "Show me an honest man and I will prove to you he is a fool," one labor leader declared. Another quoted the following comment by the *American Banker:* "No man succeeds unless by hook or crook or threat he forces or bribes other men to assist him." "This habit of thought is to be admired," the labor leader commented.[42] Was this not, after all, part of the American tradition? In every field where there was the possibility of profit, a racket existed. The land-grabbers had defrauded the government wholesale; the nation's natural resources had been pillaged by the businessmen who had constructed the railroads; there were the peddling of worthless stocks, market manipulations, and cheating of small investors; there were the insurance rackets, the adulteration of meats and other foods, the steals by traction and other utility companies. Indeed, was it not recognized in our "American way of life" that the "mighty dollar" is king and that the highest success one can achieve is in some form of extraction of profits—legally or illegally? Why should labor leaders who pursued the same goal be treated otherwise?

They were not! In the main, the commercial newspapers hailed these union leaders as "constructive forces in American life." Their major contribution was the creation of a "Potent and Restraining Influence Against Radicals." Under their leadership, trade unionism was "sensible and conservative." Business needed such leaders to keep the rank and file in check. "The rank and file are ignorant and impulsive, they do not know anything about business and market conditions and trade. They think all businesses are making enormous profits, and that there is no limit to the amount they can squeeze out for themselves if strong enough." Business-minded union leaders knew differently, and they could be relied upon to be sensible in their dealings with employers. What if they were corrupt? As a New England paper said in 1907 when leaders of a United Textile Workers' local were exposed as racketeers: "This may or may not be true. But what is definitely true is that they are thoroughly opposed to any radical action of any kind, and have proved that they are for the most part conservative in their conduct. It is this conservatism that commends them to the confidence of the business men with whom they are from time to time called upon to deal."[43]

"Business," a student of labor-racketeering correctly writes, "prefers to deal neither with honest nor dishonest unions; but given a choice it chooses the latter, encourages them and frequently makes them an integral part of its labor policy."[44] The corrupt union leaders were worth their weight in gold to business, for they did their utmost to prevent any expression of the militant mood of the workers. More than one industry spokesman boasted that such union leaders were good for business because "they keep the worker in his place and maintain order." After Sam Parks was sent to Sing Sing for extortion,* employers worked for his

---

* For various sums, ranging from $100 to $500, Sam Parks called strikes and called them off, made contractors rich or ruined them." (William Haber, *Industrial Relations in the Building Industry,* Cambridge, Mass., 1930, pp. 318–20.) Parks was sentenced to prison for two and one-half years, but served less than a year. He died in the prison hospital on May 4, 1904. Needless to add, the employers who bribed Parks to declare strikes against their competitors to drive them out of business, did not go to prison.

pardon so that he could, upon his release, make his contribution "to soften, or even wipe out, any ill feeling that may at present exist in the ranks of organized labor toward the employers."[45]

The businessmen and the business-minded union leaders had the same foe to combat: the militant workers who believed that a union existed for the interest of the rank and file and not to increase the profits of the employers and the incomes of the union leaders. "We both have the same enemies—your opposition is our opposition," the President of the Texas & Pacific Coal Co. wrote to John Mitchell. Mitchell agreed; he even instructed the company president on how to deal with the leader of the opposition:

"I wish to assure you that I have no sympathy with men like him and I would promptly have him expelled from the organization if we could get a clear case against him. . . . I would suggest that you permit him to remain in your employ, having your manager watch him carefully, and if it is demonstrated that he creates trouble, have him discharged and we will sustain you in your action. Of course, it would be advisable to get a clear case against him, so that he could not have any grounds upon which to appeal from my decision."[46]

DESPOTIC CONTROL OF UNIONS

"For selfish reasons they do not want to turn over a good graft," an A. F. of L. member noted in a letter to Frank Morrison, describing his union's officials.[47] To protect their lucrative union business, the business-minded union leaders organized an entire system to entrench themselves in office. While an analysis of union constitutions reveal that many of the major labor unions were structurally authoritarian, or almost so, there still did exist in these documents provisions for the basic elements of trade union democracy. But when one looks beneath the outer trappings of the union constitutions, it is easy to discover that in many unions some of these democratic procedures were not practiced, and in some of the major ones, none were.

There is not space enough here to describe the hundreds of tricks bureaucratic union officials developed for securing and maintaining power in their organizations. Let us, however, examine the most basic of these:

1. *Building up of a paid clique that maintained the union leadership in power.* This was achieved, first, by the leadership's control of the union's finances, either personally or through subservient committees,*

---

* Many union constitutions empowered the president and the majority of the Executive Board to disburse the funds of the International in whatever manner they decided upon. This placed the finances of the union completely in the hands of the machine.

and second, by control of the appointing or nominating power of officials. Thus the president of the United Mine Workers had the power to fill by appointment all vacancies occurring in any international office, except executive board members who were to be elected by the district; he could appoint such organizers, field or office workers as might be necessary to conduct the affairs of the union; he could suspend or remove any international officer or appointed employee for insubordination, for just or sufficient cause, and he was the sole judge of the justice or sufficiency of the cause. In most unions, the president had similar powers, though few gave him as much authority as did the mine workers. In every union, however, "loyalty" to the president was the price for appointment to and for remaining in office, and on this "loyalty," along with the power to disburse union funds, the bureaucratic machines in the American labor movement were based.[48]

2. *Fraudulent elections.* In nearly all American unions, the top officials were elected, on the record at least, by conventions or referendum. But in unions dominated by the bureaucratic machines, the elections were meaningless. Ballot boxes were stuffed; those who took part in opposition slates were intimidated, and in other ways elections were manipulated to guarantee victory for the incumbent leadership. So cut and dried was the procedure at union elections that opposition came to be the great exception. A study of union elections reveals that between 1910 and 1941, of 764 officers who won the election in seven A. F. of L. unions, 634, or 83 per cent, ran for office unopposed. These were all national officers. In the 86 presidencies, 63 were unopposed elections. Faced with the threat of expulsion if they dared to challenge the union leadership, opposition candidates simply refused to accept nominations for office.[49]

3. *Control of union conventions by the local and national machines in the organization.* The bulk of the delegates were paid officials, the majority International organizers, chosen in elections which were very questionable, to put it mildly. In most unions, as we have seen, the president had the authority to replace these officials by other appointees. So the delegates to the convention were on a "good behavior" test.

Delegates often came from "paper" locals which were created simply to provide votes for the union bureaucracy. Other locals, known as "trustee" locals, were denied self-rule altogether; their delegates were appointed by the national officers who kept them under trusteeship—in some instances for as long as 30 years. Delegates who were not regarded as trustworthy were limited as to the number of votes they cast, whereas those who were part of the machine were given a greater number of votes.[50]

Since the Credentials Committee was appointed by the union leadership, the seating of delegates pledged to the bureaucracy was a foregone conclusion, regardless of whether they came from "phoney" locals or were chosen in invalid elections or through no elections. Naturally, opposition delegates failed to obtain certification. A local of the Tobacco Workers' Union protested to Gompers in 1902: "We elected delegates to the Convention, and just as soon as the international officers found out that these delegates were not going to sustain them, they objected to them on technical points. They finally did seat a few of the delegates whom they were able to buy out to sustain them in their re-election."[51]

Evidently there were men who specialized in crooked work at union conventions, for a group of New York unionists published the following indictment in the labor press: "Trade Unionists! What think you of one who boastfully tells how successfully he managed to stuff the ballot box at the recent convention of the [New York] State Branch of the [American] Federation of Labor to secure the election of the candidate from Syracuse! It may also be interesting to read of the same individual being denounced in the *American Craftsman* for performing the same sort of work at the convention of the International Typographical Union, held at Colorado Springs. As a person is judged by the company he keeps, we would like to ask his two chief lieutenants, who served as delegates to the Albany Convention from [United Garment Workers' Local Union] No. 18, whether they could give an accounting of the time which they spent at the capitol—the city of interesting resorts—during the week of the convention?"[52]

Operating on the principle that "money makes the mare go," the union leadership spent the organization's money lavishly to insure that the delegates would enjoy themselves at the convention. A group of rank and filers published the following description of events at the 1905 Convention of the International Brotherhood of Teamsters:

"Steering committees were sent to meet each train on its arrival [in Philadelphia], and all delegates were urged to locate at the Columbia Hotel. On arriving at the Hotel, delegates received a most royal and cordial welcome, and there was plenty of money in sight to make every poor delegate who was in danger of becoming short of cash, feel that he had certainly fallen in with the right bunch. The delegates were told that there was plenty of money available and that everything had been arranged to look out for their interest and welfare during the entire convention. For the whole period of the convention, the delegates were wined and dined to their entire satisfaction."

These workers also charged that the most important business at the convention was delayed to the last day and transacted "with less than fifty men in the hall," the majority of the delegates having already left the city. This procedure was a violation of the union constitution which "provided that it should take a majority of all delegates to constitute a quorum; that fake names appeared on all the roll calls and that objections to this procedure were put in a basket." The minutes of the convention were not accurately kept in order that it would be impossible for local unions who had sent delegates under instructions to know "how they voted."[53]

This picture of an international union convention is fairly typical of proceedings in unions dominated by the "business-minded" union leaders. From a union suite of rooms whose luxuriousness rivaled the sanctums of great corporations, these leaders ruled the convention with an iron hand. Discussions were usually limited to finding better ways of operating the union as a private business and to long speeches praising the "great talent" of the national officers. Most of the proceedings were deliberately filled with unimportant details—"for the purpose," one group of trade unionists pointed out in 1905, "of consuming so much valuable time as possible thus robbing the membership of the opportunity to investigate the transactions of certain questionable characters more closely." The problems of organization of the unorganized, working conditions and many other matters vitally affecting the lives of the membership were subjects that were tabooed. If such issues arose, the top officials juggled parliamentary rules to table them. "We attempted repeatedly to secure the floor, to explain what we sought to accomplish for the union," a group of delegates to the Shirt, Waist and Laundry Workers' Convention complained to Gompers. "But to no avail. To make it brief. Our President assumed the role of a *Czar* and practiced *Czarism* throughout the entire proceedings."[54]

But even these emasculated gatherings put too much of a strain on the time and patience of some "business-minded" union leaders, and, in a number of unions conventions were done away with altogether or their frequency drastically reduced. The Hod Carriers convention in September 1941 was the first in 30 years. The Granite Cutters did not convene for 30 years between 1880 and 1912. Nineteen years went by before the United Leather Workers met. For eight years the Journeymen Tailors went without a convention, and from 1896 to 1912, the Cigar Makers held no convention, nor thereafter until 1920. The Tobacco Workers met in 1939 for the first time in 39 years.[55]

The abolition of conventions, the leaders of these unions argued, would save the union a great deal of money. Another argument was that issues of importance facing the union could be settled by a referendum vote of the membership. But as a group of local unions of the International Union of Brewery Workers pointed out in exposing this argument: "We know from past experience that when matters are left to a Popular Vote, the opponents of the schemers in the International Board are always at a disadvantage, because they flatly refuse to print our arguments and proofs in the 'Brauer-Zeitung' [the union's official organ], though they publish their side of the story very plainly."[56] (This last, incidentally, was a common complaint registered with the A. F. of L. Executive Council: the leaders of quite a few International unions were accused of using the union's funds, full-time apparatus and the official journal exclusively for the election of pro-administration candidates, with opposition slates not even able to get their names into the union paper.)

The fact is that when the union leadership was convinced that it could not prevent a thorough investigation of its misdeeds at the convention, it solved the problem by doing away with the convention. But with this type of leadership, the presence or absence of conventions was largely academic—in either event, the membership was deprived of the opportunity to express its sentiments.

4. *Perpetuation of the union leadership in office.* In 1899, John B. Lennon, general secretary of the Journeymen Tailors' Union and A. F. of L. vice-president, commenting on the discontent of the rank and file in his union over the absence of regular international conventions, wrote to Gompers: "You are well aware from long experience that a man who is for years at the head of any organization finally comes to be considered, by some people at any rate, a dictator." As this comment reveals, the question of longevity in office was already creating resentment in union circles in 1899, but the problem at this time bore little relation to what developed in ensuing years. Daniel Tobin became president of the Teamsters' Union in 1907 and continued to head the Brotherhood for 45 years, no one even opposing him after 1910.* William D. Mahon became president of the Street Railway Workers in 1908, held the office for over 40 years, and was unopposed after 1918. Andrew Furuseth headed the International Seamen's Union for 52 years. By 1940, George L. Berry had been president of the Printing Pressmen for 33 years, William Hutchinson president of the Carpenters' and Joiners' Union for 22 years. The average length of term of office of presidents of international unions affiliated to the A. F. of L. proved to be about 26 years. Samuel Gompers was President of the Federation for 38 years. The membership of the A. F. of L.'s Executive Council did not change at all for 11 years.[57]

Few union leaders were able to arrange to have themselves elected for life, as did Martin B. ("Skinny") Madden who forced the Steamfitters' Helpers' Union of Chicago to elect him president, treasurer, and business agent for life,[58] a feat later accomplished by Joseph P. Ryan, the notorious president of the A. F. of L.'s International Longshoremen's Association. But, for all practical purposes, all of the "permanents," as the leaders of the international unions came to be called, did hold lifetime jobs. No limitations being placed on the number of times a union leader could serve, he remained in office as long as his machine was dominant. Some

---

* When Tobin retired and became president emeritus of the Teamsters' Union, he continued to draw an annual salary of $50,000. Upon his death it was reported that he had left "a trust fund of undisclosed size." (*New York Times,* Nov. 20, 1955.)

unions held no meetings for over 10 years,* and elected no new officers for over fifteen. As long as no new officers were elected, the old clique remained in power. It required a "little revolution" to displace the autocrats who dominated such unions.

5. *Prohibition of all criticism of the union leadership.* "We are never allowed to say anything at meetings," a group of workers complained to a labor paper in 1901. "If one of us gets up to say anything, they tell us to sit down. If we persist, they call us 'troublemakers,' and threaten to throw us out of the union." The *Union Herald* of Atlantic City, New Jersey, in printing the complaint, added the editorial comment that in too many unions such conditions prevailed: "The union leader in such organizations wins his position in a questionable election, and as soon as he is installed, he assumes authority not within the province of the union constitution and by-laws, surrounds himself with a gang who know nothing about honest work, and persecutes any of the more manly members of the union who challenges his rule in every conceivable way. *Such a union leader is the hyena of the labor movement.*"[59]

Unfortunately, there were not a few such "hyenas." Year after year, reports told of suspensions and expulsions of members and even whole locals when they dared to challenge the corrupt union leadership. Many unions provided for expulsion without a trial under such vague provisions as "undermining the union, and creating dissension" or even "when the evidence is plain and the circumstances require immediate action."[60] For daring to oppose the policies of the international leadership of the Amalgamated Meat Cutters and Butcher Workmen, Local No. 1 of Syracuse, New York, was expelled from the union at the turn of the century. A trade union committee of Syracuse, after an impartial investigation, concluded that the charges against the local union—"undermining the union and creating dissension"—were "fake," and merely raised to hide the real reason for the expulsion, opposition to the leadership's policies. Likewise, a committee which investigated the expulsion of the Brockton local of the Boot and Shoe Workers' International Union about the same time and on the same charges—a local which, incidentally, was composed of 3,100 of the 8,000 members of the national organization—concluded that the real reason for the expulsion was the local's opposition to the undemocratic methods of the national leadership.[61]

In 1900, four southern lodges of the Boiler Makers' and Ship Builders' Union were expelled on the grounds of undermining the union. The real reason was opposition to the international leadership's action in abolishing union conventions. These lodges had dared to condemn the leadership publicly, and to assert as a basic trade union principle: "We believe

* On December 9, 1951, the *New York Times* reported that Local 118 of the International Longshoremen's Association had not met in 28 years!

that the only way to have a progressive order is to meet annually or bi-annually in convention to discuss the greatest good for all concerned." Shortly thereafter, they were suspended and then expelled.[62]

In 1904, the North Adams, Massachusetts, local of the Shirt, Waist and Laundry Workers' International Union was expelled as "agitators." "We were expelled," the local protested to Gompers, "without even a hearing which is prescribed by our constitution. This is an act which merits the severest condemnation of all workingmen and workingwomen." In the same year, the officers of Local No. 18 (Milwaukee) of the Tobacco Workers' International Union were suspended by President Henry Fischer because they had dared to expose his sale of the union's label to a non-union firm.[63]

Another way of disciplining members who were opposed to the officials who ran the union as a private business was to fine them heavily, and when, as was inevitable, they were unable to meet the payment, to suspend them from the union. While they were suspended, they could not work at the trade in shops controlled by the union. Employers were only too willing to cooperate with the union leadership in refusing employment to these "trouble-makers."[64]

6. *The Use of Terror.* To combat the strikebreaking tactics of employers and protect picket lines from attacks by employer-hired strong-arm squads, by sheriffs and their deputies, and by the police, the unions gradually organized committees of robust members. These members were usually assigned to what was euphemistically called, "The Entertainment Committee." Many strikebreakers and their strong-arm protectors were "entertained" by the committees, and, in the process, lost their appetite for scabbing.

By the late 1890's, the membership of the "Entertainment Committees" was supplemented, in a number of unions, by thugs furnished by gangster leaders. The "wrecking crew," as the hired thugs were called, was paid out of the union treasury—usually about $6.50 per day during the duration of the strike.

It did not take long for the trade union bureaucracy to use the strong-arm methods not primarily for the defense of the union against employer-sponsored strikebreakers, but for the protection of the leaders' "vested interests" in the union. Sam Parks ran the union meetings with his "Entertainment Committee," made up of six-foot, hired sluggers, paid out of the union treasury. These goons and hoodlums were particularly adept at stemming opposition to Parks with the toe of a brass boot or by tearing the cheek flesh of rebellious rank and filers. "We're afraid of the goons!" This refrain, in various words, was repeated often in letters to Gompers and Morrison from rank and file A. F. of L. members—some of them sent anonymously for fear of reprisal. The letters told how hired thugs, gangsters, and professional criminals of all sorts were employed by union leaders, and paid out of union treasuries, to slug, maim, shoot, break up meetings, tear up ballots—do whatever they were commanded, no matter how rough the job. "We're afraid to lose our jobs," was another common refrain in this correspondence; the writers told how faithful followers of the union leadership got the best jobs at the highest wages, while men and women who opposed the leaders either received no employment or the lowest paying jobs at the most dangerous work.[65]

Terror and starvation thus became powerful weapons in the hands of the corrupt union officials in maintaining control. Together with the other methods described above, they enabled the "business-minded" union leaders to become a law unto themselves. One correspondent correctly sized up the situation in a letter to Morrison in 1903: "As the situation prevails now in quite a few of the unions, there are no restrictions whatever on the officers."[66]

THE A. F. OF L. AND CORRUPTION ISSUE

"People should not judge the whole labor movement by gangs of this kind," the *Labor Record* of Newburgh, New York, pleaded in 1898 as it conceded that labor corruption was becoming more widespread. "In our Revolutionary army we had our Benedict Arnold and unfortunately in the labor movement, as in all others, we have our Arnolds."[67] The *Labor Record* was correct in calling attention to the fact that the entire labor movement should not be judged by dictator-run bureaucracies. While it is impossible to estimate even in the roughest terms the exact extent of corruption that existed in the labor movement in the period we are discussing, it is certainly true that it did not bulk large in the total orbit of union operations. Of the thousands of union officers in this period, only a small percentage were exposed or convicted as racketeers.

The problem, however, is not so much the percentage as it is the fact that corruption was already entrenched in the most influential sections of the labor movement, such as the building trades' and teamsters' unions, and that, like any cancer, it tended to mushroom when left unchallenged. Nothing could be gained by ignoring, ostrich-like, the rise of corrupt practices or minimizing them by arguing that they tended to be concentrated in a relatively small number of unions. Unfortunately, the A. F. of L. leadership did precisely this.

During the early years of the A. F. of L., Gompers frequently emphasized that the principles of decency, honesty, and democracy were the key to the growth of a "progressive labor movement," and that the evil power of corruption would, if not checked, destroy the vitality of the trade unions. In 1887, he wrote: "You will of course understand that our organization must be the very essence of honesty of purpose and methods, so that it may stand out in bold relief and contrast to those who are following the tactics of the capitalistic class." In 1892, Gompers urged the dismissal of a union organizer because "his whole being is controlled by money considerations." Two years later, he spoke out sharply against a high-salaried labor leadership: "It is a mistake to pay a man so high a salary in the labor movement that he shall be in his method of life so far removed from the wage-workers as probably to wean him from their conditions and interests and possibly from sympathy with his fellow-workers."

Yet, as we have seen, precisely what Gompers feared soon came to pass. Nevertheless, Gompers and his associates in the A. F. of L. leadership either ignored this development or dismissed it as not worthy of attention, because only an infinitesimal part of labor was actually implicated. A resolution was introduced at the 1902 A. F. of L. convention calling upon the organization to investigate the giving of bribes by employers and their acceptance by union officials. Gompers opposed the resolution, and it was defeated. "An isolated case of bribe-giving," went the report of the committee urging the resolution's defeat, "does not warrant the conclusion that dishonesty on the part of organized labor prevails. [A conclusion nowhere to be found in the resolution.] On the contrary, we are convinced that the representatives of organized labor are by far the most reliable, honest, and trustworthy in any walk of life."[68] That became the traditional view of the A. F. of L. for many years. Its leadership remained deaf and blind to some of the most shocking exposures of racketeering in the top circles of some of its affiliates.

But the rank and file refused to remain deaf and blind, and the demand for action against corrupt forces in the labor movement mounted after 1902 as the open-shop drive increased in intensity. The open-shoppers spent money lavishly, as was revealed by "Colonel" Mulhall, lobbyist for N.A.M., to buy up labor leaders to support their program, and, at the same time, made effective use of racketeering in the trade unions in their drive to eliminate unionism from American industry. The failure of the A. F. of L. to act on the issue enabled the open shoppers to build up a Sam Parks, a "Skinny" Madden, an "Umbrella" Mike Boyle,* a "Rough House" Frank Feeney as the very personification of American labor leadership, and by creating an atmosphere of distrust of unions, to create an atmosphere for repressive legislation and judicial decisions.

Some of the top A. F. of L. leaders privately conceded that corruption in unions was "a stumbling block to the labor movement," but contented

---

* Boyle, a leader of the building trades' unions in New York City, obtained his sobriquet from his practice of receiving payoffs from employers and kickbacks from workers in his open umbrella as he sat in his favorite bar with the umbrella hanging from the rail. (*See* William Z. Foster, *Misleaders of Labor,* New York, 1924, pp. 129-30.)

themselves with the consoling thought that "when you compare unionism and its leaders with capitalism and its leaders, unionism will take the
prize from any fair-minded jury." In any event, in the end, justice would
win out, as it always had in the past. "The influence of those who are
sincerely working for the collective benefit of the working class," wrote
an A. F. of L. Executive Council member, "will, for a time, perhaps be
nullified by those who have only personal ends to serve, but in the end
those who best serve their fellow-workers will triumph." Or as Gompers
put it: "In every great movement the world has ever witnessed, it has always been attended by some characterless monstrosity. Need I call your
attention to Judas Iscariot or Benedict Arnold? . . . But such traitors never
prevented the onward movement of humanity and progress, and neither
will despicable figures who for a few dollars lend themselves to the injury
of the cause of the working people of the country."[69]

But others in the labor movement were not content to leave the future
of organized labor to pious wishfulness. In 1904, Joseph R. Buchanan,
the militant, pioneer labor leader,* declared emphatically that efforts
by the unions to stem the open-shop drive were being frustrated "by the
intrusion [into the labor movement] of that cub of corrupt municipal politics known as the 'grafter.' " It was pointless to deny, he argued, that "men
holding responsible positions in trades unions in some of our large cities
have used their positions to extort from workers and employers money
which they appropriated to their own private uses." These developments
produced disillusionment and cynicism among union members, the kind
of apathy which resulted in poorly attended meetings, in a breakdown
of union discipline and solidarity and the paralysis of organizational activity. Buchanan publicly demanded that the A. F. of L. leadership
immediately take steps to eliminate these corrupt elements:

"The trades union must sit down upon the 'grafter,' and sit down hard.
He has no proper place within the labor movement. It may be true that
he is a natural product of the conditions which have grown up in the
country's industrial centers. So is quack grass a natural product of the
soil, when the seed is sown or the roots creep in. The capable and far-
seeing gardener roots out and destroys the quack grass. The trades unions
must uproot and cast out forever the 'grafters.'

"It is not enough to say—though it is undoubtedly the truth—that the
employers are responsible for the 'grafter,' that their crooked dealings
created him and gave him the opportunity to grow. While the 'grafter'
carries a union card the union must answer to the public for his vicious
career. Union labor cannot confidently face a crisis with a 'grafter' on its
back."[70]

---

* For Buchanan's role in the labor movement prior to 1900, see Foner, op. cit.,
vol. II, pp. 51, 90, 92, 141, 150, 162, 245–46, 249–50, 413. See also his autobiography
The Story of a Labor Agitator, New York, 1903.

Buchanan's appeal for immediate action was endorsed by A. F. of L. unions and members. The secretary of the Hod Carriers' and Building Laborer's Union supported his call, citing the dishonesty of local officers as "the principal cause delaying the advancement of the organization," for corrupt officers "not only disrupt a local union, but make future organization doubtful." The official organ of the Hotel and Restaurant Employees' Union agreed:

"First and foremost, the greatest evil we have to contend with [in the labor movement] is dishonesty. Officers to the number of over two hundred have been accused, and in the major portion, found guilty of embezzlement of the funds of as many locals. Some of the unions have been scorched several times, and all without exception suffer, while a large number have quietly laid [sic] down and ceased to exist. Reasonable allowance is made for other causes of numerical decrease, but the flagrant dishonesty of financial and other officers is actually responsible for better than two-thirds of the falling off in membership, and the setting forth of scandalous stories that have been used to the disadvantage of organizers who sought to perfect locals in territory contiguous to where such things happen."[71]

Occasionally, in special cases of malfeasance by officers of central labor bodies and federal (local) unions, the A. F. of L. Executive Council did step into the situation and assist in cleaning out a crooked leadership. In 1908, the A. F. of L. Executive Council unseated Frank Feeney and his clique from leadership of the Philadelphia Central Labor Union after it was proved that the election was stolen.* Secretary-treasurer Morrison presented the Federation's decision in person at a meeting in Philadelphia on August 10, 1908—a meeting marked by hand-to-hand clashes among the delegates.[72]

But this occasional gesture against corruption was not convincing. For one thing, it was not sustained. (When Feeney and his clique regained control of the Philadelphia Central Labor Union by "rough-house" tactics and stealing elections, the A. F. of L. Executive Council ignored appeals from protesting delegates to the Council.[73])† For another, on the major aspect of the problem, that involving the international affiliates, the A. F. of L. refused to budge from its do-nothing policy. Confronted with glaring exposures of racketeering in the international affiliates, Gompers conceded that these conditions were "deplorable," and that there

---

* Feeney, it was also disclosed, was on the payroll of the Philadelphia building contractors, and was on the city payroll as well, receiving $3,500 annually as chief of elevation inspection. (Philadelphia *North American,* Aug. 10, Sept. 15, 1908; Frank Morrison to A.F. of L. Executive Council, Aug. 14, 1908, *AFL Corr.*) It was later revealed, as we have seen, that Feeney was also on the payroll of N.A.M.

† "We, of the minority, have been bulldozed and browbeaten in every quarter," the delegates protested. (Philadelphia *North American,* Aug. 25, 1913. *See also ibid.,* July 28, 1911.)

was "some justification" for the demands of A. F. of L. action to clean up these unions. But he insisted that under the A. F. of L.'s constitution, this was impossible—each international union had full autonomy to carry on its internal affairs.[74] This was the explanation and the threadbare excuse put forth again and again by the Federation's governing hierarchy for failure of the A. F. of L. to bring to account racketeering elements in its affiliates. It added up to a policy of passive acquiescence and complacency in the face of corruption.

The excuse of autonomy did not hold water. As we have already seen in a previous volume, the A. F. of L. did not hesitate, in its early career, to invade the jurisdiction of unions which discriminated against workers because of race, creed or color,* and, as we shall see, it did exactly the same thing in the case of unions where radical elements gained control. In both instances, it acted to purge its affiliates. Then again, the A. F. of L. Executive Council threw its support behind corrupt elements in the international affiliates; it never lifted a finger to help the anti-racketeering elements in these unions, but, instead, put obstacles in their path, and even refused to recognize them after they had succeeded in cleaning up their racketeer-infested organizations. In short, the argument that the A. F. of L. was forced to remain aloof from the corruption issue, as it applied to its international affiliates, because of the principle of autonomy, was proved to be a hollow fraud by its support of the leadership of the unions infested with corruption.

The most glaring illustration occurred in the widely publicized battle in the International Brotherhood of Electrical Workers. For years the membership of the Brotherhood had sought to rid the organization of the corrupt leadership headed by President F. J. McNulty (a labor representative on the National Civic Federation) and Secretary Peter W. Collins (later an organizer for the Militia of Christ and the German Catholic Society, and, as we have seen, one of the most active propagandists for the Catholic Church's concept of the correct type of trade unionism).† Finally, in 1907, the members of the Brotherhood decided to call a special convention as provided for in the union constitution.‡ Resolutions

* See Foner, *op. cit.,* vol. II, pp. 195–200.

† It is significant that during this period, neither the National Civic Federation nor the Catholic Church ever condemned the corrupt leaders of the trade unions nor threw their support behind the clean-up efforts of rank and file members. The attitude of both groups could well be summed up in the expression: rather conservative corrupt leaders than radical honest leaders of unions.

‡ Section 3 of Article XVII of the Brotherhood's constitution read: "On motion of five local unions in good standing, no two to be in the same Executive Board district, a convention can be called by a two-thirds vote of the locals voting, each local having only one vote, the votes to be decided by a two-thirds vote of its members." (Michael A. Mulcaire, *The International Brotherhood of Electrical Workers,* Washington, D.C., 1923, p. 16.)

from scores of local unions demanding that a special convention be called were ignored by the union leadership. On September 1, 1908, after Secretary Collins had refused again and again to issue the call for the special convention, Local No. 39 of Cleveland sent out a call for a convention to be held in St. Louis, September 15, 1908. In its call, the local accused the McNulty-Collins leadership of repeated violations of the union constitution, stealing union funds, making deals with employers at the expense of the membership and for their own profit, and rigging regular union conventions so that the proceedings were fraudulent and farcical.

One hundred and ninety-three delegates, representing as many locals— which constituted 95 per cent of the total number of locals in the Brotherhood—responded and presented their credentials at St. Louis.* After endorsing a lengthy document outlining the dishonest and tyrannical practices of the international officers, the delegates deposed the leadership and elected a new slate of officers, headed by President J. J. Reid, a former vice-president.

The action at St. Louis aroused nationwide interest; for the first time, a rank and file membership had succeeded in ridding their union of a corrupt leadership, despite the whole evil system developed to maintain such leaders in power. The electrical workers had set a precedent under which the leaders of a union became accountable to the rank and file membership, and, in so doing, encouraged workers in various unions to begin preparations to clean their own houses.

But not for long!

Although the A. F. of L. Executive Council conceded that the action taken at St. Louis represented the sentiments of over 80 per cent of the Brotherhood's membership, although it acknowledged receiving hundreds of letters and telegrams from city central labor councils, local unions, and rank and file unionists hailing the steps taken by the special convention and urging the Federation to endorse them, the Council lined up solidly behind the discredited officials, and declared the action ousting the McNulty-Collins clique illegal and as constituting secession from the Brotherhood. Furthermore, all State Federations of Labor and City Central Labor Councils were ordered to recognize only representatives of the ousted officials and to expel any from the new leadership. Those who refused to abide by this order were threatened with expulsion from the A. F. of L.

The Executive Council's edict stirred a storm of protest in labor circles. Two State Federations of Labor and 18 city central labor bodies re-

* In his study of the Brotherhood, Charles Franklin Marsh points out that the St. Louis gathering was "considered [by the representatives of the 193 local unions] to be an official convention of the Brotherhood." (*Trade Unionism in the Electric Light and Power Industry,* Urbana, Ill., 1928, p. 55.)

jected the ultimatum. The Iowa State Federation of Labor protested vehemently to Frank Morrison:

"It is true, the Executive Council of the American Federation of Labor can revoke our charter. No doubt such revocation would satisfy the ousted officers of the International Brotherhood of Electrical Workers. Of that craft there are nearly 600 organized in Iowa, 75% of whom conscientiously believe those officers scoundrels, the other 25% willing to let it go at that. Will the revocation of our charter bring these men back into the confidence of the membership, and if not, who is to be benefitted? The Electrical Workers of Iowa, under their new leadership, have been as active in securing for their membership improved conditions as any other craft organization. They have rendered as many services in procuring better conditions for other unions as any other organized craft. Who has been injured by these actions?"

Another forthright protest came from the United Trades and Labor Council of Cleveland which had also rejected the ultimatum. The Council insisted, in a letter to Morrison, that what was at stake in the battle in the International Brotherhood of Electrical Workers was "the inalienable right of the members to revolt against International officers who are wrongfully carrying out the purposes of the organization, and who refuse to recognize the members' appeals for a Convention to right these wrongs, also the inalienable right of the majority rule, and that of the International Unions to the autonomy or self-government guaranteed by the A. F. of L. constitution, and which at the present time you are denying to a three-fourths majority of the Electrical workers and with all your might using the *Big Stick* to *Club* the three-fourths majority to bow to the will of the one-fourth minority."

The Cleveland Council made it clear that it could not be true to the basic principles of trade union democracy and endorse the A. F. of L.'s Executive Council's autocratic action.

These appeals to reason made absolutely no impression on the A. F. of L. leaders. Nor did appeals from the membership of the Brotherhood. When they tried to communicate with Gompers or Morrison, they were never available. When they wrote to the A. F of L. leaders, they were never answered.

The two State Federations and the 18 city central labor bodies who had refused to comply with the autocratic ultimatum had their charters revoked. And in their fury against workers who had dared to rise up against a corrupt leadership, the A. F. of L. leaders cooperated with key employers to break strikes waged by the electrical workers under their new leadership—even aiding the companies to import strikebreakers.

In the end, the corrupt "McNulty faction," materially assisted by the A. F. of L. Executive Council, regained control of the International Brotherhood. The outcome of the struggle was a tremendous setback to the whole battle against corruption in the labor movement. A. F. of L. members who had been rallying their forces to rid their unions of despotic leaders had received a clear object lesson. They knew now what to expect from the A. F. of L. Executive Council—bitter opposition.[75]

After an analysis of the history of labor racketeering, a student concluded in 1948: "The question might be reasonably raised as to what, if anything, the American Federation of Labor has done concerning the various evils that have been discussed. The answer is practically nothing."[76]

WHY THE A. F. OF L. REFUSED TO ACT

Samuel Gompers did not share in the loot derived by the union racketeers. But he did not dare to oppose them nor even to publicly criticize conduct which he had once predicted would be disastrous to the growth of a "progressive labor movement."* Not only did he keep silent, but he actually came to their defense when their crimes were exposed, and they were unmasked as betrayers of organized labor. It was Gompers who joined with the top command of several A. F. of L. affiliates in urging that "Umbrella" Mike Boyle be released from jail after this notorious labor racketeer was imprisoned for extortion.[77]

The corruption of Gompers was of a more subtle kind. "One of Gompers' passions was to keep the presidency of the Federation till he died," writes Louis S. Reed in his book, *The Labor Philosophy of Samuel Gompers*.[78] He relished the prestige that went with the office, the opportunities it offered for meeting important figures in the social, economic, and political world, the world of corporation executives, bank presidents, Congressmen, Senators, and even the President of the United States. He liked nothing better than to wine and dine with these leading figures in the nation, and to have his picture in the newspapers and magazines with these tycoons and politicos. "You know," Warren S. Stone, Grand Chief of the Brotherhood of Locomotive Engineers wrote to Ralph M. Easley, "Sam likes to be in the public press, and in fact if he were going to walk around the block, he would want to be preceded by a brass band."[79]

Gompers had great power on his own in the A. F. of L. As editor of the *American Federationist,* he could and did build up his prestige

---

* John P. Frey conceded that "publicly I don't recall his [Gompers] ever having said anything about it [racketeering in A.F. of L. affiliates]." (Harvard University Seminar, May 11, 1948, John P. Frey Papers, Library of Congress, Manuscripts Division. Hereinafter cited as *JFP*.) Actually Gompers advised A.F. of L. leaders to write and talk about only those things "which are commendable . . . and try to cover up those things which will have a tendency to discourage or mislead." (Gompers to John F. O'Sullivan, Oct. 12, 1898, Samuel Gompers Letter-Books, American Federation of Labor Archives. Hereinafter cited as *GLB*.)

and converted it into an organ for the promulgation of his principles of unionism.* He wrote all of the editorials himself and very often the leading articles as well, and generally published excerpts from his addresses besides. The other articles were usually written upon his invitation, often with suggestions as to how they should be written.

Gompers used his position as president of the Federation to weld together a group of loyal supporters whom he could always count on to stand with him against his opponents. They were his organizers, labor men whom he selected and commissioned as official representatives of the A. F. of L. in various localities throughout the country. In 1888 he issued about 80 commissions, but before long, he had several thousand organizers, a few of whom were employed on a full-time basis with regional offices. They were responsible to no one but Gompers, and their jobs depended on being loyal to his policies.

At A. F. of L. conventions, Gompers exercised great control by his power to appoint committees, to which he always selected a majority of his cronies, with members of the Executive Council generally receiving appointment as chairmen of the most important committees. "He," John P. Frey pointed out, "determined who the chairman of the committees would be. He was the only one. He didn't consult at all."[80] Often when his cronies were thrown out of the leadership of their international unions by a revolt of the rank and file, Gompers would appoint them to an important position in the Federation, and they would continue to work for him at A. F. of L. conventions.† Often, too, Gompers increased the representation of his supporters by paying the delinquent dues of their unions from A. F. of L. funds, thus entitling them to send delegates to the convention. Gompers also influenced the outcome of deliberations by his rulings as chairman of the convention, and he even ignored decisions of the convention, refusing to enforce them when they were not to his liking.[81]

On August 18, 1906, the Lewiston (Maine) *News* noted that com-

---

* Gompers was severely criticized for opening the advertising columns of the *American Federationist* to leading open-shop corporations. "Why should Standard Oil, that greatest and most powerful of all trusts in the United States," wrote one critic, "advertise not once, but eight times, in one issue (September 1908) of the official organ of the American Federation of Labor? ask workingmen? . . . Standard Oil is not in the habit of throwing away its money. It is usually put where it will do Standard Oil some good." (Clipping headed "Gompers Prints Advertisements of Standard Oil," Eugene V. Debs Scrapbooks, No. 8, pp. 192–93, *TIL*.)

† When James O'Connell was removed as president of the International Machinists' Union, Gompers immediately appointed him president of the Metal Trades Department of the A.F. of L. and retained him as third vice-president of the Federation. "This," one commentator observed, "in spite of the nation-wide agitation at the time against 'lame ducks'." (M. Rhea, "Organized Labor or Business?" *New Review*, Sept. 1, 1915, p. 206.) Rhea observed of O'Connell: "He has the business mind."

pared with Gompers' well-organized powerful machine in the A. F. of L., the ones forged by Powderly in the Knights of Labor and even by P. M. Arthur in the Railroad Brotherhoods were exceedingly primitive. "Gompers alone has endured and has accumulated strength as the years have passed." Yet fundamentally Gompers was dependent upon the business-minded labor leaders for the fulfillment of his passion to remain president of the A. F. of L. The building trades' unions were the most powerful group of labor organizations in the country, and represented the largest constituent element within the A. F. of L. The leaders of these unions were the most notorious racketeers in the labor movement. Yet if Gompers were to oppose these corrupt leaders and expose their misdeeds, he would be seriously endangering his tenure of office. "Fearing that the corrupt element in his constituency had sufficient strength to turn him out of office," Harold Seidman points out, "Gompers did not dare to antagonize them by proposing even the mildest reforms."[82] Matthew Woll, one of the "permanents" on the A. F. of L. Executive Council, summed it all up when he told William F. Morgan, Commissioner of Markets of New York City who had urged the A. F. of L. leaders to do something to eliminate the corrupt, gangster leadership of the Federation's affiliates: "We can't do anything about it, Commissioner. You see, we got to look to the vote of the boys down the line to hold our own jobs."[83]

Yet there was still another reason for the A. F. of L.'s reluctance to wage a struggle against corrupt labor leadership. The key to the struggle, of course, is the issue of democratic unionism. When unions become dictator-run bureaucracies and the membership, in effect, lose their democratic right to decide union policies, then the door is open to all forms of racketeering. For the A. F. of L. leaders to raise the banner of democratic unionism would be to focus attention on their own bureaucratic control of the Federation.

"We are a democracy," declared the call to the A. F. of L. convention held at Scranton in 1901. At this convention, eight unions with 32 delegates had 3,686 votes, and 233 unions with 278 delegates had 3,583 votes.[84]

Three elements were present at the annual conventions of the A. F. of L. under Gompers' leadership:

1. *An element made up of the self-perpetuating officers of the national and international unions.* They had one vote for every hundred members of their respective unions so that they had a large voting power. About 150 delegates of the 350 who made up the 1906 convention were controlled by this element. Thus about one dozen of the top union leaders controlled almost the majority of the votes cast at the convention.

Most of these union leaders were also represented on the A. F. of L. Executive Council, thereby constituting an important section of the machine that controlled the Federation. The Executive Council, meeting four times a year, was the body which really formulated the policies of the A. F. of L.

2. *An element made up of the general organizers of the A. F. of L. who were appointed by Gompers and controlled by him.*

3. *An element made up of the representatives of the State Federations, of the Central Labor bodies of the cities, the federal labor unions, and unaffililated labor unions.* These delegates were usually closer to the rank and file membership of the Federation than any of the others at the convention, but their influence was limited, since they had only one vote each, no matter how large the body they represented. Thus the delegates from the State Federation of New York and the delegate from the Central Labor body of Kenosha, Wisconsin, had one vote each.[85]*

There were frequent complaints that the whole voting procedure at A. F. of L. conventions was undemocratic. A delegate to a convention from Kansas City wrote to Gompers:

"It is my humble opinion that the A. F. of L. will make a mistake by continuing to curtail the privileges of state federations, central labor unions, and federal labor unions by restricting their representation at the conventions. It seems to me to be a mistake to show such great partiality in favor of national organizations as against these other organizations. I think if any favors are shown it should be in favor of the organizations which come directly from the common laborers, as do those, for example, from the federal labor unions. It looked unfair to me that I should have only one vote while representing 700 men in a federal labor union and Delegate Keneshaw have *twenty* votes, while representing 2100 men in a national organization—in other words he represented three men to my one, and cast *twenty* votes to my one. This don't look right and I can't see any good reason why it should be so. I would advise you and others who have influence in these matters to take heed of the past history of the labor movement. No labor organization ever reached the acme of success if once despotism took firm root therein. The leaders of organized labor must learn the lesson of democracy and *honesty* if success shall crown our efforts."[86]

Such appeals were filed and forgotten.

In March 1909, Austin Davis, secretary-treasurer of the Utah State Federation and a delegate to the 1908 A. F. of L. convention at Denver blasted the proceedings in his report to the State Federation:

"I proceeded to Denver to the 28th A. F. of L. convention for 15 days as your representative and on this trip I learned more to make me pin my

---

* The fact that the A.F. of L. Executive Council did occasionally move against corrupt leadership of some Central Labor bodies should be weighed against the limited power these organizations had at the annual Federation conventions. The delegates from these bodies did not threaten the continuation of the A.F. of L. leadership in office.

faith to the State Federation than by any other union lesson I have ever experienced. I found there that the 24 men representing state federations and the 36 who were there from city central bodies almost to a man observed the [union] label, and were fearfully careful as to union precepts. They were from the rank and file of every-day life. Quite to the contrary most of the delegates and officers from the higher realms of international unions and officers of the A. F. of L., ate, slept and even drank at places notoriously non-union. The greatest were no exception and I call attention to this common laxity to show that although all men are merely human, how much superior is the real, actual producer, whether farmer or mechanic to those 'who toil not, neither do they spin'—to those surfeited in the power given them for real good. As we ask for the election of senators by a direct and popular vote of the people, so let us have a general federation composed directly of men from factory, forge, lathe, or mine, to strike at the living, real evils that beset us from day to day. As it now stands at the A. F. of L. Convention, there is too much attention paid to securing votes and too little time devoted to the welfare of the rank and file."[87]

But the A. F. of L. leaders had long before decided against rank and file control of the organization. In 1897 Gompers had recommended that the officers of the A. F. of L. should be elected by referendum as a means of placing more responsibility upon all the workers and of furthering the achievement of a labor movement of the workers, for the workers, and by the workers. Within three years, however, he changed his mind on the question, for when Max Hayes, the delegate of the Cleveland Federation of Labor, introduced a resolution to that effect, Gompers opposed it in debate and helped to secure its defeat. He and most of the other leaders of the A. F. of L. had lost confidence in the wisdom of the rank and file to control their affairs in a labor movement "of the workers, for the workers, and by the workers." In 1888, Gompers warned the A. F. of L. against entrusting great power to the executive officers of the labor movement, particularly in the matter of strikes, and urged that the power should be vested in the masses who must learn to govern themselves in labor organizations as well as in the state. But ten years later he was urging that the question of strikes and boycotts should be determined by the "calm judgment of experienced officers" rather than by the membership, which was "prone to do many things, under the influence of enthusiasm." And he thought it very "peculiar" when, in 1903, the machinists' union conducted a referendum vote on the issues of socialism and industrial unionism. Gompers thought that after nine or ten hours of labor, the workers had neither the time nor the inclination to make a study of these questions which would qualify them to pass an intelligent judgment. Such questions should not be decided by the rank and file.[88]

The increasing loss of confidence in and fear of the rank and file was reflected in the organization of the A. F. of L. conventions. The will of the membership could not be adequately expressed. The conventions were dominated by the top officials of the various internationals; these delegates were elected at machine-controlled conventions or appointed by the national executive boards of the unions. In this manner, the A. F. of L. conventions were controlled, year after year, by an entrenched bureaucracy who were without mandate from the membership.*

The process of corruption thus became part of the warp and woof of the A. F. of L. even though most of its affiliates were not racketeer-infested unions. It seeped up through the Federation from key unions to the top leadership of the organization. Many of the local unions of these key affiliates were controlled despotically by known racketeers. Members of the Federation's Executive Council were heads of the national unions in which these piratical local bosses operated. But they refused to take action to clean out the labor racketeers because this would threaten their sinecures. The top leadership, headed by Gompers anxious to perpetuate themselves in office, depended, in turn, upon those heads of national unions and local bosses for their own self-advancement. The result was an organization that was beginning to be dominated from top to bottom by men who made a private business and career out of trade unionism. As Isidor Feinstein pointed out in a study entitled, "Racketeering and the American Federation of Labor":

"Racketeering represents big business control of the unions; it represents the infiltration into the labor movement of criminal elements, the perversion of trade unionism into a device for maintaining business monopolies and prices, the terrorization of the workers, and the infection of the American Federation of Labor hierarchy, which draws Peter's pence from the racketeers—being dependent for votes or revenue upon racketeer control."[89]

In 1904, Joseph R. Buchanan offered a solution for the corruption problem beginning to plague the American labor movement. It bears repeating today: "Organized labor must come again under the influence of the spirit of the olden days when 'grafters' were unknown. The spirit and ideals of a dozen years ago, supported by the ten times greater numerical strength of today, would make the trades union movement the greatest agency for the uplifting of the poor and lowly that the world has ever known. Those ideals are not dead, though they lie stunned at

---

* Between 1896 and 1906 Gompers was a perennial delegate to the A.F. of L. convention from the Cigarmakers' International Union without having been elected as one. Since there had been no convention of the International since 1896 and since delegates were elected by the convention, his election in that year remained in effect until another convention was held.

the feet of a rampant commercialism. Let us drive out the spirit of commercialism from the trades unions and put in its place the belief in the glorious mission of united labor."[90]

Fifty-three years later, at their convention in Atlantic City, the United Automobile Workers reaffirmed Buchanan's doctrine in the declaration: "The labor movement is not a business. It is and it must remain a crusade."

CHAPTER 7

Reaction to Technological Change

At the opening of the century, the American Federation of Labor "was composed primarily of unions of skilled workers who were employed in the building trades and in small establishments, such as cigar, printing, tailor, and barber shops. The unions in several mass production industries—steel, textiles, glass, and shoes—consisted almost entirely of the skilled crafts in those industries." The affiliated organizations of the A. F. of L. in 1900 included less than 20 per cent of the entire working class; the vast majority of the unskilled workers, Negro and white, women and men, native and foreign-born, and the so-called, "common and general laborers," such as the men "who built the roads and railroads, lumberjacks, foundry laborers and stevedores, were largely unorganized, as were the migratory and agricultural workers."

Despite the fact that the A. F. of L. was comprised of a small minority of American workers, the leaders of the Federation spoke of their organizations as representing "the industrial force" of the nation.[1] The fact that such an overwhelming percentage of the working class was still unorganized was, in the eyes of these leaders, the fault of these workers alone. As Gompers put it in a report to an A. F. of L. convention: "That it [the trade union movement] has not made faster progress, is not due to us who have done our duty to our fellow-workers, but to those who have failed to ally themselves to our noble cause."[2] In oft-repeated writings and speeches, Gompers spelled out precisely what he meant by the expression, "done our duty." He pointed out that one of the primary purposes of the A. F. of L. was the organization of new unions, the objective being the complete unionization of all wage earners. He stressed that the A. F. of L., "guided by the experience of the labor organizations of the past," had, by 1900, evolved a labor program that was designed to meet the needs of all workers, regardless of skill or lack of skill, race, creed, sex, or national origin. Moreover, it went to great pains to acquaint "all unorganized workers" with its program, in an effort to convince them that "the principles for which we stand will bring greater relief to oppressed, over-worked and low-paid wage earners, male and female, than any other form of relief heretofore advocated in their behalf."[3] "The coming of the twentieth century found the Federation with well-developed policies and methods," was the way Gompers summed it up in his autobiography. The Federation was aware that "the first step in securing permanent betterment for the wage-earners of America was to organize them into bona fide unions of trades or callings, skilled or unskilled," and it had "by the beginning of the Twentieth Century . . . developed concrete and comprehensive methods of work." Recognizing that the working class was confronted by "the rapid development of large-scale organization and trusts," its "work of organization was extended along lines paralleling industrial developments," and it paid its greatest attention to "the extension of the principle of organization to workers in what were then called the 'unskilled' occupations."[4]

In short, according to Gompers, the A. F. of L. had, by the turn of the century, developed the correct "machinery" to organize the unorganized, and the will to do so. The rest was up to the unorganized workers themselves, and, in the long run, they would recognize that the A. F. of L.'s "well-developed policies and methods" held out the only hope for them, and would of their own will join the ranks of their trade union brothers.[5]

These bald efforts of the A. F. of L. leadership to place the onus of blame for the unorganized status of the bulk of the American workers upon the unorganized themselves, have rarely been equaled for arrogance and cynicism. For the truth is that the Federation never had a plan suited to meet the needs of the unorganized workers, nor the will to organize them.

THE WILL TO ORGANIZE

From 1899 to 1914, the A. F. of L.'s average annual expenses reached $180,000, of which 30 per cent, or about $54,000 a year, was spent for organizing activities. Not many organizers could be kept in the field with these amounts, and their time was not entirely devoted to the work of organization. In 1912 the Federation had only 23 salaried organizers on its payroll. Actually, Gompers and the other A. F. of L. officials were not anxious to see a widespread organizing drive undertaken to recruit the unskilled workers in the basic industries. Gompers felt that a rapid growth in the membership of the trade unions was unhealthy and would usually end with a serious collapse, which would be more dangerous than a slow and steady growth and development. Then again, the A. F. of L. leaders realized that the backbone of the Federation was the international unions of skilled workers, and that it was from these unions that they derived their support. The masses of unskilled workers in the basic industries were generally more radical, and their entrance into the A. F. of L. would shift the balance and alter the entire character of the Federation and thus jeopardize the position of those who had a vested interest in maintaining the traditional composition.[6]

A basic reason for the failure of the A. F. of L. to achieve greater success in organizing the unskilled workers was the selfish and narrow outlook of the affiliated organizations. Ready and eager to buy a limited security for the skilled workers at the expense of the unskilled and unorganized workers, many of the craft unions in the Federation entered into agreements with the corporations, including the commitment to refrain from organizing the unskilled workers, thus sacrificing their interests in return for a minimum of union security for themselves and a relatively high wage differential for the skilled craftsmen. In 1908, in a letter to Mary E. McDowell, Chicago social worker and friend of the working class, Homer D. Call, president of the Amalgamated Meat Cutters and Butcher Workmen of North America, spelled out how these agreements worked:

"I am going to write you frankly in this matter, feeling assured that you will treat it as confidential. You, of course, have observed in Chicago that the sheep and cattle butchers claim to be the aristocracy of the butchering industry and what you have observed in Chicago in a small way, is duplicated several times over in the other packing centers, notably New York City. The sheep and cattle butchers in New York City have by virtue of their affiliations been able to maintain splendid conditions. Fifty, sixty, yes even seventy dollars a week, is often made by the cattle butcher of New York, for from 35 to 40 hours work. . . . But to receive that consideration they have been compelled to enter into an agreement with the packers to prevent the large percent, of what they term, the unskilled laborer, from receiving living wages. . . . While I am glad to see the sheep and cattle butchers, who constitute only about from 5 to 8 percent of the people in the industry, receiving these conditions, my heart goes out to the other 90 or 95 percent of the workers who are not receiving wages enough to barely exist. . . . Of course, I have been freely criticized by the sheep and cattle butchers for my position in asking to organize all who are working in the industry under one head, but I yet believe that is the only practical plan by which we can secure results and benefit all of those who are working in the meat industry.

"The packers are working hand in hand with the sheep and cattle butchers to prevent the organization of the unskilled laborers and the growth of the International organization. The moment a man in any of the large packing centers become active in the organization of the unskilled, he is at once let out. . . ."[7]

The correspondence in the A. F. of L. Archives is filled with similar examples of the aristocratic exclusiveness of the craft unions at the expense of the unorganized workers. Many of the craft unions frankly told Gompers that they did not want the unskilled workers in the industry brought into their organizations. They should be allowed to organize as local unions directly affiliated with the A. F. of L. or remain unorganized.[8]

Another reason for the Federation's failure to secure impressive results in the organization of the unorganized was that frequently instead of relying primarily upon organization of the workers in the shops and factories, the A. F. of L. concentrated on appealing to the public to buy only union-labeled goods. Today the union label is understood to be a minor instrument in the labor movement, one which basically records the gains made by trade union *organization*. But in the period after 1900, the label was put forward as the main weapon, as labor's "battle flag on the industrial field." Armed with the union label, the A. F. of L. could force all employers to recognize the right of their workers to organize. In achieving the organization of the unorganized, it was "more powerful than strikes and picketing."[9]*

The A. F. of L. often spent more money in promoting the activity of its Union Label Trades Department than it did in sponsoring organizing campaigns to organize the unorganized. In 1911 the Union Label Trades Department reported that a motion picture dealing with the label had been exhibited during the preceding year to 44,223 people in nine states and Canada. And this at a time when, as Gompers himself admitted, the A. F. of L.'s financial resources were strained to meet the demands upon them for strike aid and organizing expenses. This, too, in the face of mounting evidence that the union-label agitation had proved generally ineffective in organizing the unorganized and that many A. F. of L. organizers had consistently complained that "the label method of organization is barren of results." A. F. of L. publications in this period failed to reveal any concrete illustrations of where the use of the label had helped to achieve the organization of the unorganized or even strengthened an A. F. of L. union in a particular trade. If anything, it had had a misleading influence on those workers, especially in the garment trade and the textile industry, who had been led to believe that the label would be the salvation of the working class.[10]

* The union label, A.F. of L. leaders also emphasized, "brings about a more friendly feeling between the employer and the worker." Henry White, who, it will be recalled, made a lucrative racket for himself out of selling labels to employers, was fond of pointing out that the union label "puts the unions upon a business footing with the employers, identifies to a larger extent their joint interests and reduces the friction between them to a minimum. It reconciles and broadens the minds of both." (*American Federationist*, Aug. 1901, pp. 293-94, July, 1902, pp. 365-66.)

INDUSTRIAL CHANGES

At the time Gompers was proclaiming that the A. F. of L.'s organizing program was suited to meet the needs of all workers—the unskilled and semi-skilled, as well as the skilled—the character of American industry was undergoing changes that made a mockery of his words. New industries were rising which almost from the beginning were mass production in character. Old industries were being revolutionized through the introduction of new machines and processes and the spread of new forms of business organization.

By the end of the 19th century the large-scale corporation had acquired a dominant position in American economic life. In 1900 two-thirds of all manufacturing was done by corporations. By 1909 only 25.9 per cent of the nation's manufacturing establishments were owned by corporations, but this 25.9 per cent employed 75.6 per cent of all wage earners attached to manufacturing enterprises. In 1914 the value of the products of individually-owned enterprises, numbering 148,436, amounted to $1,925,518,298, while the value of the products of corporation enterprises, numbering only 78,151 in the same year, reached $20,181,279,071, or 83 per cent of all industrial products. At the same time, the individually-owned enterprises employed only 707,658 workers, while the corporation-controlled factories had 5,649,646 workers.[11]

Changes in basic production processes and techniques accompanied the development of large-scale industry. After 1900, mechanization and minute sub-division of labor, already developing after the Civil War and increasing rapidly in the 1880's, became widespread in almost every phase of American industry, with the exception of the building industry.* By the 1880's, the fundamental technological changes had already taken place in shoemaking, but inventors perfected and speeded up the machinery, designed new machines to take advantage of the division of labor, and agreed upon measurements for all parts of the last. By the turn of the century, the skilled shoemaker was a thing of the past. A writer of the 1900 Census noted: "At the present time, the genius of the American inventor has provided for every detail of shoemaking, even the smallest processes being performed by mechanical devices of some kind. This has naturally made the shoemaker of today a specialist who very seldom knows anything of shoemaking apart from the particular process in the performance of which he is an adept." The same trend was taking place in the textile industry. Although the major textile machines

---

* There were some innovations even in the building industry in the period 1898–1905 such as the pneumatic riveter, the power shovel, the electric and gas hoist, and cement gun, but there was little effect of large-scale operations. Few machines were used in house building; masonry, roofing, carpentry, plastering, painting, and tile-setting were all hand operations.

had been invented by 1870, in the next half century, engineers speeded them up, made them more simple to operate, and harnessed them to electric power. The skilled worker, who had often employed children as helpers, was replaced by a mass of adult immigrants fresh from the docks of the port cities. They took the less skilled and the heavier jobs attending the new automatic machinery. As these changes accelerated in the early years of the 20th century, the skilled workers—mulespinners, loomfixers, and weavers—became an ever-decreasing minority in the industry.[12]

The spread of mechanical typesetting and typecasting after 1899 revolutionized composing room technique. In place of laborious, handicraft typesetting in which words were built letter by letter by the hand compositor, the pressure of a finger on the keys of the linotype machine did the setting swiftly and automatically. Soon the old hand compositor found himself superseded by the machine operator and his auxiliary workers. Soon, too, the old hand press feeders were supplanted by mechanical feeding attachments and automatically fed presses.[13]

The machinists' craft, one of the traditional homes of the skilled craftsman, was also being undermined by important technical developments. Certain of the standard machine shop tools were becoming more automatic, accurate, and costly. A good deal of work that was formerly done on the lathe, planer, and drill press, or at the bench, was being done by more complex planing machines, slotters, turret lathes, and milling machines. Towards the end of the 19th century, grinding machines, formerly used only for sharpening tools, were being used for finishing work. Previously this work had been done with lathes and hand files.

Improvements in the standard machines, the increased utilization of special or single purpose machines, and the greater size of many industrial units made it possible for a marked change to take place in the methods of making machinery. Some machine shops and factories, instead of building machines as in the past, started to manufacture them. Formerly, only a small number of machines were built in a single lot. They were seldom worked upon in any consecutive order and generally stood around the shop in all stages of construction. Under this method, during the same day, a machinist might, for example, perform lathe work, milling, drilling, bench, and floor work. But in machine manufacturing, machines were made in large lots and each operation on each machine was consecutively performed. Under this system it was easy to subdivide and specialize jobs so that a man might be required to do a single type of work. The manufacturer found it easier to train a man to do nothing but lathe work than to train him to do every kind of job performed in a machine shop. It look less skill as a rule to run a specialized machine than a general machine.[14] George W. Crouse, president of a company manufacturing harvesting machines, explained to Gompers in 1900 why his firm no longer needed skilled machinists:

"Now to illustrate; the men required to do work on a moulding machine must possess good, healthy bodies and be industrious. Skilled labor is not required. We have taken unskilled labor right out of the ranks of men who have been in the habit of working for what is commonly known as 'day laborers.' I hardly think a position can be called one that demands the services of skilled labor when you can take the men who were day laborers and never saw a moulding machine, and in two weeks time can produce more than a skilled mechanic could in two months."[15]

The requirement that the machine workers "possess good, healthy bodies" was frequently waived, for all too often child labor replaced skilled mechanics. In a letter to the American Cereal Co. of Cedar Rapids, Iowa, January 25, 1900, the secretary-treasurer of the Coopers' International Union protested: "We entertained a hope that your company [in introducing labor-saving machinery] would be merciful enough to employ as many journeymen coopers as would be necessary to operate the machine cooper shop. We had hopes that you would at least be willing to divide the enormous saving that will result from the use of machinery with the class who are now thrown mercilessly upon the charity of the charitably inclined. We now learn with a deep sense of regret of the policy that you propose to pursue, that you have discharged the men [coopers] and supplanted them with children, whose natural right it is to be in school learning the things that are essential to existence in this enlightened age." In a letter to Gompers, written on the same day, the Union's secretary-treasurer wrote: "Before they placed the machinery they employed from 30 to 40 coopers and with their present policy they will require one or two as foremen."[16]

At the Bethlehem Steel Co. in the 1890's, Frederick W. Taylor carried through his methods of speed-up and break-down of operations in the plant so that each worker had as few functions as possible to perform. In 1903, in his paper "Shop Management," delivered at a meeting of the American Society of Mechanical Engineers, Taylor described how he had succeeded in eliminating the skilled workers through his system and undermining their craft unions. Immediately businessmen requested Taylor to advise them on the methods they should use in their shops to achieve the same result, or for him to recommend someone who was capable of introducing his methods. The Taylor system, glorified under the title of "Scientific Management," spread to industry after industry, breaking down craft skills and weakening the skilled workers' control of their jobs. The whole purpose of "Scientific Management," wrote Gompers, was to "reduce the number of skilled workers to the barest minimum and impose low wages upon those of the skilled workers who would be thrown into the army of the unskilled."[17]

On January 13, 1900, in an editorial entitled, "The Passing Mechanic," the Columbus (Georgia) *Herald* commented: "The revolution in industry is doing its work so quietly and so quickly that most people fail to note the great changes that are taking place. Machinery is not only displacing human labor, and re-arranging it under a new relationship, but it is rapidly destroying the skilled trades. The tendency is towards a common level in labor, and that level has hitherto been known as unskilled labor. This revolution is not simply destroying the skilled crafts by diminishing the per cent of skilled mechanics as compared to the unskilled, but it is lowering the grade of skill of those who remain." Fifteen years later, the *International Molders' Journal* observed that the "revolution in industry" had almost been completed: "There is no body of skilled workmen today safe from one or other of these forces—the introduction of machinery and the standardization of tools, materials, product, and process, which make production possible on a large scale, and the specialization of workmen—tending to deprive them of their unique craft knowledge and skill. Only what may be termed frontier trades are dependent now on the all-around craftsman. These trades are likely at any time to be standardized and systematized and to fall under the influence of this double process of specialization."[18]

CRAFT UNIONS FAIL TO ADJUST

Although it did occasionally make concessions to the unskilled and semi-skilled workers when it was first organized and during its early, formative years, the A. F. of L. was based on the needs of the "all-around craftsman." The foundation of a craft union is that each member of the organization performs or is capable of performing all the tasks included in the occupation. A secure basis for craft unionism is thus found in those industries in which the individual skill and craft knowledge of the workers is of predominant importance. If, through the introduction of machinery and new processes, minute subdivision of labor occurs, the basis for craft organization tends to disappear. With the further development of mechanization, the blurring and obliteration of craft lines, the entrance of unskilled workers in large numbers into industry and the concentration of industry in gigantic corporations and trusts, the craft union in its turn became obsolete.

It was impossible for any intelligent union leader to be unaware of the undermining of craft unionism by the industrial changes. Unfortunately, the majority of the craft unionists in the A. F. of L. ignored this development. Industry was rendering more and more operations automatic, but the craft unionists still maintained the fiction that the possession by the worker of a personal skill enabled him to bargain effectively for better conditions, and also the confidence that the organization along trade lines, based on the skill of the members, could enable each craft union to present a strong front to management.[19]

For many years trade unions had tried various methods to prevent the introduction of machinery. English handloom weavers wrecked the new power looms; the Knights of St. Crispin refused to run shoe machines; the Stone Cutters limited the output of stone planers. But none of these methods prevented the displacement of skilled hand craftsmen by new machines, and the craft unions which sought to meet the problem of changing technique by the above methods passed out of existence. As Gompers pointed out: "Many workmen in trades have fought and borne awful sacrifices in the fight against the introduction of a new machine or a new tool, and some have gone so far as to violently destroy the machine, but it did not destroy the idea." The only result of such efforts was that the new machines and tools were introduced against the wishes of the workers, without consideration of the men who performed the labor by hand, the trade unions went down, and the skilled union workers were replaced by unskilled, unorganized workers at lower wages. The intelligent course for labor to follow was to accept industrial progress, insist that the machine work be given to union members at union standards, and that the machine workers be brought into the union so as to protect those standards against unfair competition.[20]

Occasionally, technological changes were recognized in time by the craft unions affected, and they made the necessary adjustment. Instead of ignoring technological innovations in the printing process, the Typographical Union accepted the inevitable and asserted its claim to operation of the linotype machines. It announced in 1889 that "in all offices in its jurisdiction where typesetting machines are used, practical printers only shall be employed to operate them." Within the next few years, agreements were concluded with employers and with the Mergenthaler linotype interests which provided that the union would not fight the introduction of the machine and would encourage union printers to acquire the necessary skill for machine operation. In turn, the employers and the linotype company agreed that only union members would be permitted to operate the machines.[21]

By these means the printers evaded, or at least cushioned, the disastrous effects upon craftsmen of the transition from hand to machine processes. But the case of the printers was exceptional. To be sure, there was a difference between the Typographical Union which had, prior to the introduction of the linotype, most of the craftsmen in its ranks, and unions which had organized only a small part of the industry. But the same problem confronted all of the unions: would the union recognize the machine and organize the machine workers or would it cling to old, conservative craft pride?

Several craft unions slowly and reluctantly made some minor adjustments to technological changes without ever really dealing with the basic problem. A good case in point is that of the International Association of Machinists. At convention after convention in the closing years of the 19th century and the opening years of the 20th, the question of admitting specialists and helpers (workers on automatic machinery) into the union was debated. From 1897 to 1901, the efforts of those who wished to broaden the union's membership failed.* A month before the 1903 convention, P. J. Conlon, a militant union officer, printed an article in the *Machinists' Journal* which advocated that the I. A. of M. should control the machine shop, and for this purpose "admit any workman engaged in any manner with the making or repairing of machinery." He pointed out that new machinery was so rapidly transforming the status of the all-around craftsman that "very soon it will be a difficult matter to tell a general machinist, unless you tag him, and if he gets a job in a specialist shop his general skill does not amount to so very much. These men's conditions is [*sic*] bad and gradually getting worse."

Conlon's proposal provoked a long and heated discussion at the 1903 convention. The discussion revealed that most of the delegates were conscious of important technical changes which had taken place in their trade, or, at least, that the changing relations between the machinists and the specialists and helpers ("handy-men" as they were repeatedly referred to by the craftsmen) were not satisfactory. Some refused to do anything to meet the problem. They insisted that their aristocratic ranks would be polluted if others than all-around machinists became their brothers, and they shuddered at the possibility of being controlled by their "inferiors" in skill and social prestige. "We do not want to lose sight of the fact that we belong to the International Association of Machinists, and not to the handy-men," one delegate observed. "If we take these men in we will have to change our name to International Association of Machinists and Handy-Men. I want to belong to an association of machinists and none other." Another delegate, agreeing, declared: "I am not in favor of taking the handy-man into the organization because I believe they are not intelligent to vote on a subject to our interest and to help us." "We ought to preserve our dignity," still another delegate declared.

Other delegates declared emphatically that the position of the skilled craftsman could only be protected by taking handy-men into the union on an equal basis with machinists. "I believe that all men are born

* The majority opinion was summed up by one of the union leaders who declared at the 1897 convention that admitting specialists and helpers "would ruin" the machinists' trade (*Machinists' Journal*, vol. IX, 1897, p. 258.)

equal," a delegate declared earnestly, "and if they are not born equal, the employers are making them equal by reducing the machinists to the equal of the handy-men. I say, take them in and we will make them better unionists or machinists than they ever were. If we build up their standard, our standard will go up in proportion to what they get." Another delegate agreed: "I say take him [the handy-man] in on equal rights. Fitchburg [Grand Lodge] wants to go on record as not in favor of aristocratic movements, and that we are in favor of taking them in one and all, on an equal basis. We are here for the extension of this organization, and we want an organization of 250,000." Still another delegate declared: "I hope you will lay aside this discrimination against the men who are working alongside of us and who will assist us to boost ourselves as well as themselves."

Between these two groups were the compromisers who realized that the encroachments of the handy-men could no longer be ignored, but who shared the fears of the aristocrats. They proposed to meet the problem by establishing auxiliary locals for handy-men which would be under the control of the machinists—in other words, to place the unskilled in the status of second-class union citizens without any of the rights, privileges, and protections of the machinists. "We must have these men in our organization, not with equal rights and privileges, but in order to have them under our control," one of the compromisers said flatly. He was answered by another delegate who warned: "I do not believe that this thing of establishing an auxiliary will go. Do you think these men will bind themselves to join you and be controlled by you and not have anything to say about their welfare? If they did they would be fools."[22]

When the delegates finally voted on the issue, a majority (280–241) favored admitting to membership "any person working in a machine shop and engaged in making or repairing machinery." Apparently this opened the way for the admission of specialists and helpers. But the General Executive Board construed the amendment to the union's constitution to mean that only specialists in addition to all-around machinists could be admitted. Operators of machinery where skill was required might join the union, but operators of automatic machinery where no skill was required were excluded.[23] Since the majority of the handy-men fell in the excluded category, the G.E.B. ruling effectively undermined the purpose of the vote at the 1903 convention.

After 1903 the conservative aristocratic elements were in complete control. The trend in the union leadership was to restrict the organization to all-around machinists even though, as we have seen, the trend in the industry was to reduce them to a minority status. President James O'Connell publicly espoused a progressive position. Writing in the Boston *Herald* in 1905, he pointed out that the machinists, by the nature of their trade, were highly skilled workmen and supporters of the "purely trade [craft] organizations," but since they were constantly confronted by changing methods of production, the machinist was becoming rarer and the specialist and helper more common, and the union must cover all. But O'Connell's theoretical discussion was not followed by concrete action. Although a number of specialists were admitted to membership, the union continued to be dominated by the all-around men and to function as an association of highly skilled craftsmen. Helpers were not admitted into the I. A. of M. until 1911, and then only into separate lodges in which they shared few of the rights and privileges of the machinists. Although a special organizer was sent into the field to organize helpers, the results justified the warning of the delegate to the 1903 convention who had said: "Do you think these people [the handy-men] will bind themselves to join you and be controlled by you and not have anything to say about their welfare? If they did they would be fools." The machine workers, the majority in the industry, proved not to be fools. They remained aloof from a union which made a slight gesture of welcome but also made it quite clear that they really did not want them.[24]

The old conservative, aristocratic craft unionists had won out, but the victory left the union with a small fraction of the workers in the industry. The vast majority remained unorganized. The membership of the I. A. of M. declined from 75,000 in 1907 to less than 50,000 at the close of 1908, and while it recovered its 1907 figure by 1914, it still represented only a small fraction of the organizable workers in the industry.[25]

As in the case of the machinists, progressive-minded forces in the coopers', blacksmiths', and boiler makers' unions forced the conservative, craft aristocrats to accept the machine and make a gesture towards adjusting to technological changes. Typical of the stand taken by the progressive-minded forces is the position outlined by James A. Cable, National Secretary-Treasurer of the Coopers' International Union:

"I realize," he wrote to Gompers, "that the position taken by our Nat'l President and others on this question of machinery [opposing the introduction of machinery and refusing membership to machine workers] does not meet with the approval of the advanced thinkers in the cause of organized labor. I have drawn up a plan which I intend to submit to the next convention, which, if adopted will enable us to organize these people [the machine workers] throughout the entire country. My idea is, that instead of following the foolish policy of refusing to organize them and refusing our stamp on machine made cooperage, we should organize these machine workers, and thereby assist them in maintaining good wages, and doing away with child labor which is invariably employed in the machine factories, and by so doing we can bring the cost of producing the machine made cooperage up to such an extent that it will be possible for a man running a hand shop to compete with them, and at the same time protect the machine workers and bring to them better wages and conditions. . . . I will say that my reasons for writing this as a personal letter is that I am duty bound officially to carry out the plan which refuses the machine workers the right to be organized, but conscientiously I know that it is a wrong policy."[26]

Part of Cable's policy was adopted by the Coopers' Union and by the boilermakers' and blacksmiths' organizations, but the same self-defeating principle of setting up separate locals for unskilled workers, depriving them of equal rights and privileges, was followed.[27] Still even this was more than most of the craft unions in the A. F. of L. were willing to do. The majority refused to do anything at all to cope with the adverse effects of the introduction of machinery on skilled craftsmen.

A typical example is illustrated in the history of the National Window Glass Workers' Union. This union was organized in 1880 as a local assembly of the Knights of Labor with the brave motto of "Never Surrender." Later, it affiliated with the A. F. of L. At the turn of the century, the union was in a powerful position and was recognized by the employers' associations in the industry. In 1910, it controlled almost every shop in the trade. Its membership at that time was 7,000. Thereafter its membership declined steadily, except for a slight upturn during the first World War. In 1928, the union that would "never surrender" passed out of existence.

The Window Glass Workers' Union went down to defeat for one simple reason: its refusal to recognize technological changes that were transforming the industry. Prior to 1905, the work in the craft, notes Professor Norman J. Ware, "was highly skilled, requiring some knowledge of the chemistry of glass, the lung capacity of a prima donna, and the heat-resisting qualities of a stoker." The introduction of the cylinder blowing machine in 1902 and other devices undermined the basis of skill upon which the industry had formerly rested. After visiting a plant which had just installed an automatic machine, the union president wrote to Gompers in December 1904: "The machine works out eleven tons of glass in twenty-three and a half hours. Thirty minutes is the only time lost in twenty-four hours. In about two years this machine will displace over one-third of our members."

But the union refused to recognize the machine or to admit workers in machine plants to membership. It decreed that any member going to work in a machine plant automatically suspended himself from membership in the union. As for the machine workers, they were told quite bluntly that "they should not expect this Association to lift them bodily, as it were, from the non-union to the union factory." No wonder it was reported that the union's policy had made "every man who operates one of those machines a mortal enemy of the organization."[28]

Rather than organize the unskilled and semi-skilled machine operatives, the union persuaded the skilled hand glass-blowers to take drastic cuts in wages to compete with the machine. In 1924, the union leadership even set up a hand manufacturing glass plant in Huntington, West Virginia, as a means of proving that glass could be manufactured profitably without machinery by skilled workers. The venture, as was to be expected, proved to be a fiasco. The union lost $84,000, and the plant was closed in 1927.

Throughout the steady decline of the hand industry and the rise of the machine process, the progressive element in the union continued to point out that "the future belongs to the automatic machine," and to agitate for adjustment to modern conditions by the organization of the unskilled and semi-skilled machine workers. But since no conventions were held, their agitation could not force any change in the union policy. Finally, in 1927, the leadership admitted defeat, and called a convention to meet the problem that was driving the union out of existence. The convention ruled that members could accept work in machine plants and still retain union membership, and it called for an intensive campaign to organize the machine plants. But it was too late to save the organization. As the last president of the union sadly observed: "No human agency could have saved the hand craft. It was in the way of progress and it had to go. Human agency could have saved the organization, but they chose not to, and the organization, too, passed into history. The mistake we made was clinging to the old guild idea. That has no place in modern industry."[29]

A similar mistake was made by the cigar makers. In 1909, the International Cigar Makers' Union had 51,500 members; by 1929 its membership had declined to 12,900 even though the number of workers employed in the industry had increased four-fold. The reason for the union's decline is the same as that which caused the disappearance of the glass workers' union: failure to appreciate the significance of the machine and an unwillingness to organize anyone but skilled, hand cigar makers. Indeed, for some time, the union scoffed at the idea that the machine could be a threat. "No one will acknowledge," wrote a reporter in 1900 after a discussion with the union officers, "that there is a possibility of a machine being invented that will do away with cigarmakers." International President Perkins told the reporter: "There is nothing to fear from machinery in our trade. A machine that can make cigars is an impossibility—even in this advanced age."[30]

But machines did make cigars! For a while, the union sought to use its blue label as a weapon to prevent the introduction of the machine, and it broadcast the news that "no union shall be allowed to furnish the label for cigars made in whole or in part by machinery." It was a futile gesture. The machine spread rapidly, and with it went a transformation in the industry from the small shops of the craftsman era to large corporations. Mass production by machinery changed the cigar industry from one of small hand labor plants to one of large-scale factories. In 1930, 0.46 per cent of the factories produced 49.8 per cent of all cigars manufactured. It is estimated that 21,356 employees had been displaced by machinery between 1917 and 1932.[31]

In the factories, the bulk of the cigar output was manufactured by girls employed on power machines. But few of the girls were brought into the union. In 1901, the union claimed 3,240 of the 22,250 women in the industry, and even this was an exaggerated figure. Yet in subsequent years, the number of women members in the union declined while their number in the industry grew apace. In 1912, the union enrolled about two-fifths of the total number of cigar workers, but none of the 19,000 machine workers and few of the 25,000 team workers.[32]

As in the case of the glass workers, the progressive elements in the cigar union called upon the organization to abandon its restrictive membership policy and organize the unskilled and semi-skilled workers at the machine. "The only thing that can save the cigar makers of the country," a group of Socialist members of the union appealed, "from the crushing power of the Tobacco Trust is the complete and systematic organization of all the workers of the industry. Wipe out aristocracy, remove apprenticeship restrictions, break down craft barriers! Go after the unskilled workers and the thousands of women and girls at the machines!" Although he did not associate himself with this appeal, Gompers did urge that all persons engaged in the cigar industry should be eligible for membership in the Cigar Makers' International Union, his own organization. He wrote to President Perkins in 1908: "I am firmly of the opinion that . . . if it hopes not only to maintain its present standing but to make progress for the protection of the cigar makers, it will be necessary for the international union to permit everyone, whether cigar maker, cigar packer, roller, filler, breaker, stripper, or those engaged in the stripping department [to] become eligible to membership in the organization, and this too, whether they work by hand, mold, suction table or machines."[33]

But these voices of reason went unheeded for many years. No union conventions were held from 1896 to 1912. At the 1912 convention, the Socialist delegates called for organization of the women workers in the industry. They argued that "the women are becoming more and more important factors in the industry, and the Tobacco Trust is trying to make it a woman's trade in order to reduce wages." To facilitate the organization of the women and other unskilled workers, they urged the adoption of an amendment to the union's constitution reducing the dues for these categories so as to enable them to join the organization. True to his pattern of behavior, Gompers, who was a delegate to the convention, conveniently forgot about his earlier demand that the union organize the unskilled, and opposed the proposed amendment. He insisted that it "would bring the international trade union back to the position it was before 1880, when no benefits were paid and when it could not hold its members in line." President Perkins supported Gompers. "The minute you break this chain of benefits by reducing the dues," he cried, "the organization is in danger." That the union was already in danger of passing out of existence because of its unwillingness to organize the unorganized did not seem to bother Perkins.*

The progressive delegates refused to be moved by Gompers and Perkins, and the amendment was adopted. But, taking a leaf from Gompers' conduct as president of the A. F. of L., Perkins simply refused to enforce the new constitutional amendment; dues remained the same for the unskilled as well as the skilled and the union did nothing to organize the former. Between 1912 and 1920 no union conventions were held so the progressive forces were unable to compel the union leadership to see the handwriting on the wall. "Perhaps," writes John P. Troxell in his study, "Machinery and the Cigar Makers," "if conventions had been held during that crucial period, when machinery was steadily encroaching upon the Cigar Makers' domain, the union might have been stirred out of its complacency."[34] He might have added that perhaps if the union leadership had carried into effect the desires of the majority of the delegates at the 1912 convention, the union might have been saved. In 1927, the union leadership was finally "stirred," and the union abandoned its restrictive membership policy. But, as in the case of the glass workers, it proved to be too late. The union that gave Samuel Gompers to the labor movement was doomed.

The glass workers and the cigar makers are only two of many examples that could be cited of old, well-established craft unions that failed to adapt their union policies to the changed technical environment in which they had to function with the result that they either disappeared or lost their importance. A. F. of L. unions like the Bakery and Confectionery Workers, United Powder and High Explosive Workers, Tobacco Workers, Quarry Workers, Laundry Workers, Boot and Shoe Workers, Leather Workers, Textile Workers, and those in the chemical, clay, and stone industries are some of the other illustrations of "decaying unions" whose decline is largely attributable to the inability to readjust to the technical progress of industry.[35] Early acceptance of the machine

---

* The conservative delegates for whom Perkins spoke conceded that it might be necessary to do something about organizing the unorganized cigar makers, but proposed only that "a general campaign for the union label be started immediately" as the method to achieve this goal. (New York *Call*, Sept. 18, 1912.)

and the workers at the machine, democratic trade unionism, a militant organizing policy, and a trade union structure suited to meet the needs of modern industry would have saved these craft unions from the tragedy that overtook them.

We get to the heart of the problem in the mass production industries, for example, the iron and steel industry. By the turn of the century, little skilled help was required at the blast furnace in the industry. The Bessemer or open hearth converter and automatic hoisting machinery had gradually replaced skilled men with semi-skilled and common labor—mostly recent immigrants from Southern and Southeastern Europe.[36] A concomitant effect of the mechanization was the growth of the large corporation. In 1890, there were a relatively few large concerns, but production on the whole was carried on by small plants. By 1910, there had been a tremendous transformation. One corporation, U.S. Steel, controlled almost half the industry; and six others dominated the other half.

A vast, heavily capitalized industry, employing a minority of skilled workers and great numbers of unskilled and semi-skilled operators and laborers, in which managerial control was highly centralized, was confronted by the Amalgamated Association of Iron, Steel and Tin Workers, an exclusive union, composed primarily of skilled workers. Oblivious of the fact that mechanization had reduced the number and importance of the skilled worker, the Amalgamated Association showed little interest in organizing the industry and clung to the craft form of union structure long after it was clear that this was utterly inappropriate in this mass-production industry. After the defeat of the union in the 1901 strike, its leadership persistently fought efforts of progressive elements in the Association to organize all the steel workers, skilled and unskilled, in one union. They took the position that the masses of unskilled workers were unorganizable, blaming this on their lack of intelligence and the impossibility of communicating with them because so few of them spoke English. Since the skilled workers were a small section of the total working force, it was a waste of time and money to conduct an organizing drive. This backward point of view was endorsed by a team of A. F. of L. organizers in the fall of 1904, after a survey of organizing possibilities in the iron and steel industry. "We find on investigation," they reported to the A. F. of L. Executive Council, "that the number of skilled steel workers has been greatly reduced on account of improved machinery, making the possible number of men whom we sought to interest in the movement, very much smaller than we anticipated. On the other hand, a large number of the unskilled workers are foreigners, hardly able to speak or understand the English language, thereby complicating and retarding our efforts. All told, the field is not a promising one."[37]

The inability to organize this vitally important industrial field, given the Amalgamated Association's reluctance to do much and the craft union structure of the A. F. of L., was demonstrated in the steel organizing campaign of 1909 and 1910. In July 1909, the U.S. Steel Corp. provoked a strike for the purpose of completely crushing the steel workers' and tin plate workers' unions. At the A. F. of L. convention in November, it was decided to call a conference of the officers of all affiliated national and international unions to meet in Pittsburgh and decide on a plan of action. Nearly 50 of the 87 internationals were represented at the conference on December 13. They decided to call upon all the national unions to furnish at least one organizer to the steel workers' union, that the A. F. of L. place as many as possible of its organizers in the field, and that in every city where steel mills were located the central labor unions appoint special organizing committees. They also planned to call for financial assistance to the strikers, a series of educational circulars, and a statement of grievances against the steel trust to the President of the United States and the governors of the states in which the corporation operated. They further urged the steel and tin plate workers to amalgamate into one union.

But after one month only five international unions besides the steel and tin plate workers had complied with the promise to send organizers, and Gompers sent an appeal to them to fulfill their obligations. But this appeal brought little more response, and about three weeks later, President P. J. McCardle of the steel workers wrote Gompers that he was going to discontinue the campaign to organize the steel trust. When Gompers called him on the phone, he learned that McCardle had already dispersed the 10 or so organizers that had been placed at his disposal by the Federation and some of the internationals. In February 1910, the A. F. of L.'s most ambitious effort to break into the trusts was abandoned.[38]

The fact that the steel union was not really interested in organizing the industry was, of course, a key factor in the failure of the organizing campaign. But the organizers were hampered from the beginning by the craft union structure imposed upon the program by the A. F. of L. The steel and tin plate workers had to be organized into 20 craft unions, each operating independently of the other. As one of the A. F. of L organizers pointed out to Frank Morrison after the campaign was abandoned: "To establish twenty different craft unions in the dominion of the Steel King —machinists, patternmakers, moulders, laborers, electrical workers, puddlers, blacksmiths, boilermakers, structural iron workers, painters, die sinkers, etc. etc.—instead of bringing all of these workers directly into one union is to enter a combat with a mighty giant, its detectives and paid hirelings, with one arm tied around ones back. To organize on this basis, I confess is no bed of roses."[39]

In an article, "Failure of a Strike," Llewellyn Lewis, vice-president of the Amalgamated Association, criticized the whole attempt to organize the steel trust on the basis of craft unionism. He blamed both his own union—from which he resigned—and the A. F. of L. He conceded that the Federation had sent organizers into the field to help the drive, but pointed out that it had hampered them by the craft union structure they were required to follow. "Its [the A. F. of L's] policies are antiquated and unfit for application to present day conditions. The policies of 25 years ago won't do for today. The world is moving and we must move onward with it or be left far behind."[40]

Having failed to move with the times, the Amalgamated Association was doomed to remain a nonentity in America's major industry. It just managed barely to maintain its existence by holding on to a small body of skilled workers (less than 10,000 in 1910), employed largely in the small, independent plants in the industry. After investigating conditions of employment in the iron and steel industry in 1910, a U.S. Senate Committee pointed out the basic cause for the lack of unionism:

"The general policy of the Amalgamated Association . . . had from the beginning been very exclusive, so that the union embraced only the more highly skilled men in a comparatively limited part of the rapidly developing steel industry and the organizations of lodges in the steel mills was in large part merely incidental to the development and strengthening of the organization in what may be called the iron branch of the industry. At no time in the history of the Amalgamated Association was any attempt made to work out a logical scheme for dealing with the highly complex situation in the steel mills."[41]

Another example of the attempt to apply an outmoded union structure to a mass-production industry is illustrated in the meat-packing industry. In no other industry had division of labor been so ingeniously and microscopically worked out. Already by the early 20th century most packing-house operations were mechanized, particularly in the "chain" line of production. Where formerly a butcher workman had to be a skilled and proficient mechanic and know every detail of his trade, he was now reduced to a mere link in a long chain of laborers. Forty-six operations, again subdivided into over 120 hand operations, were required in the beef-killing department. Each of the operations was performed by a separate worker, whose "skill" was, in most cases, comparatively slight and easily learned in a brief time. Women and children began to work in the meat-packing-plants as new machines and minute subdivision of labor pushed out the skilled men.[42]

Instead of utilizing an integrated form of unionism to parallel the integrated character of the industry, the A. F. of L's Amalgamated Meat and Butcher Workmen organized the workers in the packinghouse jungle along the lines of craft unionism. Fifty-six craft unions were set up on a department basis, each with its own council, executive board, and set of business agents, and each negotiating separately with the result that some crafts continued to work while others were on strike.

The weakness of this form of organization in a trustified, mass-production industry was pointed out by a far-sighted member of the union who wrote to Morrison in March 1900 from Chicago, the heart of the packing industry:

"Our experience proves a separation in this craft is not only detrimental to the interests of the workers but also creates the discord and dissatisfaction which injures rather than advances their cause and the cause of all workers employed in this industry. When a union or rather a divided organization attempts to secure better conditions, in most instances [it has] failed and the workers have lost hope in the union and their reorganization is a most difficult obstacle to overcome. By the separation of the workers under as many heads as there are departments, the solidarity which is fostered is destroyed."[43]

The truth of this observation was borne out in the great packinghouse strike of 1904 which, despite the militancy of the workers, was completely smashed because of the disunity among the craft unions organized in separate and jangling councils. Some 18,000 divided workers were pitted against one of the most powerful employers' associations in the country and they went down to utter defeat.* Although the membership declined from 34,400 in 1904 to 6,200 in 1905, the union leadership refused to learn any lessons from the defeat. Progressive elements demanded the reorganization of the union along the lines of an industrial federation locking the various craft unions firmly together under one council, one executive board, and one set of business agents, creating a solid front in the whole industry. But the union leadership paid no heed to this demand. "I am informed," wrote Homer D. Call, international secretary-treasurer, to

* The strike, which began on July 12, 1904, was caused directly by the refusal of the packers to accept the demand for 18½ cents an hour minimum for all unskilled workers. (There were other grievances, of course, such as the inhuman speed-up and horrible working conditions both of which affected the skilled as well as the unskilled workers.) Although the union and the packers reached an agreement on July 6 to submit the wage dispute to arbitration and for the packers to retain all workers "without discrimination," the employers broke the agreement by refusing to abide by the employment agreement. Gompers and Mitchell urged the union not to go on strike despite this violation of the agreement, but the workers insisted on striking. The strike continued for nine weeks until September 6, 1904, when the union, conceding defeat, called it off. Having opposed the strike, the A.F. of L. leaders gave the strikers no real support. (Harry Rosenberg, "Packing House and the Stockyards," unpublished paper, Chicago Historical Society, pp. 6–7, 11, 21.) The fact that two A.F. of L. unions (the Stationary Engineers and the Stationary Firemen) remained at work during the strike helped the packers defeat it. The great ice machines were in operation, keeping the meat refrigerated and in a condition that would not spoil. The meat cutters believed that the strike would have been won if the firemen and engineers had joined the walkout. (Theodore W. Glocker, "Amalgamation of Related Trades in American Unions," in John R. Commons, editor, *Trade Unionism and Labor Problems,* New York, 1921, pp. 365–66, 377–78.)

Morrison, "that there is a demand in the union that some action should be taken as to changing the form of our organization and also its policies. Why any such action should be taken, I cannot understand. It would seem to me to be more sensible to continue on the old policies." Amazingly enough, this was written by the same man who informed Morrison that "there is but very little prospect of saving anything from the wreck," and that "we have not a single local union that is today in good standing or has been since the late strike."[44]

There was an alternative to the suicidal policies which were weakening if not destroying many of the unions affiliated with the A. F. of L.: organization of the unskilled and semi-skilled machine workers, especially those in the mass production industries, on the basis of industrial unionism. But that was just what the leaders of these unions and of the A. F. of L., as we shall now see, refused to do.

CHAPTER 8

Craft versus Industrial Unionism

BASIS OF THE CONFLICT

The adverse effects of the introduction of machinery upon unions of skilled craftsmen brought sharply to the fore the whole question of the proper form of organization. It was clear to many in the labor movement that the changes in the techniques of production could only be met effectively by a change in union structure. There was scarcely a convention of the A. F. of L., even in the 1890's, where some discussion of the need for this change was not part of the proceedings. Opponents of craft unionism, even in these early conventions, drew up indictments of the flaws in this form of union structure. While its inability to cope with the rapidly changing industrial conditions was advanced as the most important objection to craft unionism, it was also criticized for giving employers a great advantage in collective bargaining by enabling them, in the process of negotiating with several crafts separately, to play one union against another, and for causing bitter quarrels among the craft unions in the form of jurisdictional disputes. Changes in techniques of industry and the introduction of new machinery and new materials, it was pointed out, had made inevitable the jurisdictional quarrels among the craft unions. It was impossible under modern industrial conditions to draw an exact line where the work of one craft left off and that of another began.[1]

The emergence of the great trusts gave special meaning to these arguments against craft unionism. "How can the trade union meet the Standard Oil Company, the Sugar Trust, or the other swindling syndicates by which prices and wages are fixed?" John Swinton asked the delegates to the 1895 A. F. of L. convention. Pointing out that profound changes were occurring in the structure of American industry, the pro-labor newspaper editor and publisher* inquired whether the trade unions were making

---

*During the 1880's Swinton had published *John Swinton's Paper,* one of the outstanding papers in American labor history. (*See* Foner, *op. cit.,* vol. II, pp. 30, 42, 48, 54, 63, 70, 81, 115, 118, 122, 153.)

the necessary adjustments to meet these changes. He was convinced that the new situation arising from the emergence of trusts could never be met "under the old methods of the trade unions," and predicted that unless new policies, new forms of organization and new tactics were quickly adopted, the 20th century might witness "the doom of labor." Swinton's warning was echoed a few months later by George E. McNeill in an article entitled "The Trade Unions and the Monopolies," in which, among other things, the veteran labor leader called for a reevaluation of the problem of trade union structure in order to arrive at the one best suited to organize the mass production, monopolized industries in which the unskilled and semi-skilled workers were becoming the majority of the labor force.[2]

In the following decade it became abundantly clear that the type of union structure best suited for this purpose was an industrial union which admits all the workers in a particular industry, regardless of skill or craft. The concentration of industry, wealth, and power on the side of capital called for a corresponding concentration of power on the side of labor.

Gompers and the craft union majority in the A. F. of L. vigorously defended craft unionism from the assault of the industrial unionists. They argued that only this type of unionism could succeed because it was based upon the principle of the self-interest of the individual worker. They contended that the growth of the Federation could be attributed to the use of the craft form of organization; that craft or trade autonomy was the keystone upon which the success of the A. F. of L. rested; and that any policy that would jeopardize the principle of craft unionism threatened the entire Federation itself. Industrial unionism had been tried before and had failed, and craft unionism had emerged from this bitter experience. "Surely," wrote Gompers, "the lessons with previous efforts in the general organization of labor have been sufficiently costly to our movement and the workers generally to bid us have a care lest we flounder upon the same shoals of industrial concentration." Specifically, industrial unionism was simply "the old K. of L. idea," and had been mainly responsible for having "finally disrupted the whole concern." The decline of the Knights of Labor was proof that it was unsuited to meet the needs of the American workers. In a letter to Gompers, P. J. McGuire sneered:

"The Brewery Workers are possessed of the obsolete K. of L. notion of bringing all branches of Labor employed in a brewery under one centralized head, regardless of their affinity.* Of course, you can readily see

* All workmen in breweries were members of the United Brewery Workers, but separate local unions were formed for various divisions of the industry—teamsters, brewers, bottlers, engineers, firemen, etc.—each meeting separately and transacting all business pertaining to its respective craft. United action by the various local

the nonsense of it, for the logical sequence would be to have every brewery, every factory, and every shop organized in toto, regardless of the distinctive industries employed therein."[3]

The United Brewery Workers had a simple but effective answer: "The chief factor is the uniting of all trades employed in the brewing industry. Experience has taught us what solidarity means. Solidarity, man for man from roof to cellar, all for each and each for all, this alone can secure our future."[4]

The champions of craft unionism made it crystal clear that what primarily concerned them was the protection of the interests of the skilled minority, even though this was an ever-decreasing minority. "There is another current of thought in the trade-union movement," declared Andrew Furuseth, A. F. of L. vice-president, "which has received the name of 'Industrialism,' the primary meaning of which seems to be the coming together in one union, or one federation, that men working for the same employer should cease work together when in their opinion such employer is unfair. . . . Carried to its logical conclusion it would be a revival of the mixed assemblies of the Knights of Labor, and the danger always will exist of a ruthless disregard of the interests of the minority, hence dissatisfaction and disintegration as a result thereof." The advocates of industrial unionism countered with the argument that this type of unionism was based on the interest of the skilled minority as well as that of the unskilled majority. Through the introduction of machinery and new processes, with its attendant breaking down of craft lines, the unskilled rapidly became the competitors of the skilled. Hence the skilled workers could no longer say that the interests of the unskilled were unrelated to their own. Either the skilled worker could prevent the introduction of machinery or they had to find some other way to eliminate the competition of the unskilled. Since the workers were learning first-hand how futile the struggle against machinery could be, the only logical thing to do, on the basis of the principle of self-interest, was for the skilled workers to bring the unskilled into the unions. This meant adjusting the union structure to meet the changing conditions of modern industry by organizing them along industrial lines. The craft union leaders who raised the scare of the "old K. of L. idea" in opposing the new form of unionism were really not interested in protecting the skilled workers by organizing the unskilled. "They are only anxious to have sufficient organization of labor to guarantee themselves positions."[5]

The advocates of craft unionism were forced to agree that industrial

---

unions was secured through a joint local executive board containing representatives of different crafts. Each craft had its own separate contract with the employers, but all contracts had to be submitted to the firm through the joint local executive board. All contracts in a plant had to expire at the same time, and rejection of one by an employer meant rejection by all. (Herman Schlüter, *The Brewing Industry and the Brewery Workers' Movement*, Cincinnati, Ohio, 1910, p. 219.)

conditions were changing rapidly, that the introduction of the machine could not be prevented, and that machinery was replacing and would continue to replace skilled hand labor. "The artisan of yesterday," Gompers pointed out at the 1897 A. F. of L. convention, "is the unskilled laborer of to-morrow, having been displaced by the invention of new machines and the division and sub-division of labor." But when asked how the Federation proposed to meet these changes, Gompers made it clear that the A. F. of L. would frown upon any policy that would jeopardize the "principle" of craft unionism. Gompers was fully aware that craft unionism was outmoded, and that industrial organization was the need of the day. As early as 1888, he had recommended to the Federation that in the near future the basis of the A. F. of L. should be modified by having the various industries classified by the divisions of those industries. Thus the metal industry might have a convention of representatives of all the trade unions in that industry, the building trades in their industry, and the railroad workers in theirs, each legislating on the subjects that affected the general interests of their particular trades and industries. These industrial divisions in turn would be represented by their proportionate number of delegates in the conventions of the A. F. of L., and each would have a representative elected as a member of the Executive Council. The Federation would in due time become a federation of industrial federations rather than a federation of craft unions.[6]

In advocating this form of organization, Gompers was more far-sighted than others in the Federation. His proposal met with such disfavor among the affiliated unions that he had to admit he was "premature" and shelved the plan. He never revived it, for he learned that his career as A. F. of L. president would come to a swift end if he did not support the position of the craft unions whose servant he was. So Gompers became the bulwark of defense for craft unionism. As Charles Madison has pointed out, Gompers was less conservative and more intelligent than most of the trade union leaders, but "he was enough like them and wanted his office badly enough to connive with them in practices that hindered the growth of the unions movement. Instead of opposing them for the greater good of millions of workers, he became their spokesman, their jolly and aggressive 'chief.' Instead of broadening and strengthening organized labor to its fullest capacity, he built up a political machine."[7]

FEDERAL LABOR UNIONS

To cover his capitulation to the craft unionists, Gompers pointed to the existence of the Federal Labor Union as the medium for the organization of the unskilled and semi-skilled. (The Federal Labor Union included workers irrespective of trade or calling and was affiliated directly to the A. F. of L.) "The A. F. L.," Gompers boasted, "has supplied a splendid haven of protection to the unskilled in the federal labor unions. They extend the hand of fellowship to the unskilled of every creed and color. They give the lie to those who talk of A. F. of L. exclusiveness."[8]

This argument was hardly convincing. It ignored the fact that the Federal Labor Unions were not permitted to organize extensively and, at best, were regarded as only temporary and, basically, as recruiting centers for the crafts in unorganized districts. As soon as their membership increased substantially, the Federal Labor Unions would find their members parceled out among the appropriate national unions. As early as 1892, when several leaders of these nascent industrial forms attempted to retain their permanency, Gompers wrote sharply: "The Federal Labor Unions are intended to be an organization of wage-workers of which there are not a sufficient number of one trade to form a union: to be in fact a recruiting ground for the trade unions and as soon as a sufficient number of one trade or calling is in the Federal Labor Union to place them upon their feet as a trade union."[9]

The Federal Labor Unions protested that the craft unions only drew off the skilled workers, leaving the unskilled and semi-skilled to fend for themselves; that the craft unions did not attempt to organize the unskilled and semi-skilled even of their own narrowly defined jurisdictions, but condemned the Federal Labor Unions when they organized these workers, and they urged the A. F. of L. leadership to permit the Federal Labor Unions to function as permanent organizations in which skilled, unskilled, and semi-skilled could unite within a single body. But the A. F. of L. leadership refused to tolerate this concept of unionism. In his report to the 1901 convention, Gompers conceded that "serious opposition is sometimes encountered from Federal Labor Unions who fear that their organizations may become disintegrated by reason of the formation of the trade unions." He went on to say: "They do not seem to understand that . . . after all the Federal Labor Unions are a recruiting ground for the trade union movement and a convenience for the workers in such localities or diverse callings where there is an insufficient number of any particular trade or calling to form a trade union."[10]

This was the role which was consistently assigned to the Federal Labor Unions. At no time within the period 1897–1910 did they constitute more than seven per cent of the A. F. of L. membership and by 1910 they represented only 1.3 per cent.* In short, to the A. F. of L. leadership,

---

* In 1902 the highest percentage was reached: 6.4 or 67,800 Federal Labor Union membership out of a total of 1,064,600 in the A.F. of L. In 1910, the percentage was 1.3 or 21,000 Federal Labor Union membership out of a total of 1,586,000 in the A.F. of L. (Leo Wolman, *Ebb and Flow of Trade Unionism,* pp. 138, 192–93.)

the Federal Labor Unions were simply a source of revenue and a convenient substitute for organizing the unorganized. They were "the
neglected stepchildren of the American labor movement."[11]

From 1901 to 1905 several attempts were made to remedy the weakness of the Federal Labor Unions by replacing them with a national
union of unskilled laborers. Gompers consistently fought and defeated
these efforts, stating that such a union would include all workers except
those organized in the unions of skilled workers and would "practically
encompass the whole labor movement." But it was obvious that he did
not want such a union under any circumstances, for he rejected adamantly
a proposal to grant it a charter with jurisdiction only over those common
and general laborers who were not eligible for any union affiliated with
the A. F. of L., and with an express stipulation that it would release
any members claimed by other affiliated unions at any time.[12]

SCRANTON DECLARATION

Although the spokesmen for the unskilled could make no headway in
the face of the stone wall erected by adherents of craft autonomy, the
pressure within the A. F. of L. for adjustment in union structure to meet
the problems of mechanization and division of labor forced the craft
union leaders of the Federation to make a few concessions. The most
important declaration on the matter of union structure was made at the
1901 convention at Scranton, Pennsylvania. In the famous Scranton
Autonomy Declaration, the principle of craft autonomy was clearly
affirmed: "As the magnificent growth of the A. F. of L. is conceded by
all students of economic thought to be the result of organization on trade
lines, and believing it neither necessary nor expedient to make any
radical departure from this fundamental principle, we declare that as a
general proposition the interests of the workers will be best conserved by
adhering as closely to that doctrine as the recent changes in methods of
production and employment make practicable." Recognition was given,
however, to exceptional cases in which all workers should be enrolled in
the "paramount organization" in the industry. The resolution also suggested that the alliance of kindred crafts might be desirable; and urged
consideration of the possibility of amalgamations.[13]

The section of the Scranton Declaration dealing with the granting of
jurisdiction to the "paramount organization" in the industry was the
major advance in the direction of reality. The idea had been proposed in
1899 by John B. Lennon, A. F. of L. treasurer, who advocated that "the
principal craft in the manufacture of any product should control the
establishment even if it does to some extent infringe upon what many
trade unionists insist upon as being trade autonomy."[14] The Scranton
Declaration did not go as far as that, confining itself largely to the in-

dustries in isolated sections of the country and to those in which "comparatively few workers are engaged over whom separate organizations claim jurisdiction." The craft unions were assured that it would operate "at least until the development of organization of each branch has reached a stage wherein these may be placed, without material injury to all parties in interest, in affiliation with their national unions." In other words, as in the case of the Federal Labor Union, the craftsmen organized in the "paramount organization" would eventually be distributed among the different craft unions.

It is true that on the basis of the "paramount organization" section of the Scranton Declaration, the United Mine Workers was granted jurisdiction over all the workers in the industry, and was permitted to retain the craftsmen employed in and about the mines who properly came under other jurisdictions. But this concession was wrung from the A. F. of L. Executive Council only because the U.M.W. was strong enough to convince the Federation that it would keep these craftsmen regardless of what it or the craft unions involved did about it. When other unions who did not possess the strength of the U.M.W. attempted to apply the "paramount organization" principle, they were quickly told off by the Executive Council, informed that their action violated the "Trade Autonomy Laws" of the Federation, and threatened with expulsion if they did not rescind this action. "I charge," the head of one of the unions so threatened wrote to Morrison, "that the United Mine Workers of America continues to hold such workmen as members in violation of said laws. Yet the United Mine Workers have not been threatened with expulsion. Shall it then be said that other affiliates cannot operate on the same basis as the mine workers?" The Brewery Workers were equally indignant in their protest to the Executive Council:

"We direct the attention of the honorable members of the executive council to their partisan attitude in this matter, and to the absence of justice which is the inevitable result of their position. On the one hand, our organization is to be disrupted by giving its different trades to various organizations as per the firemen and engineers, while other organizations, similarly situated, are assisted and strengthened by exactly the contrary attitude to the one assumed by your executive council in this matter. We refer, gentlemen, to the assignment to the coal miners of the control of the hoisting engineers, separately and individually chartered, said assignment being made for the good of the organization. Can a reason more urgent be advanced in behalf of the coal miners than could be urged for us? And if not, are we not justified in believing that we are the butt of partisan legislation?"[15]

The Brewery Workers had good reason to complain. In the very year the Scranton Declaration was adopted, the Executive Council helped to break a strike of the brewery workers in New Orleans because the union attempted to organize the beer drivers. The New Orleans Central Trades and Labor Council, under instructions from the A. F. of L. Executive Council, gave Local 701, International Brotherhood of Teamsters, jurisdiction over the drivers, notwithstanding the fact that the contract of the Brewery workers provided more pay and better conditions than did Local 701's. When the brewery workers struck, the scabs who took their places and aided the employers to break the strike were organized into a Federal Labor Union by an A. F. of L. organizer, acting on instructions from the Executive Council. In protest against the action of the Central Trades and Labor Council, many A. F. of L. unions in New Orleans broke away from the C.T.L.C. and formed the United Labor Council as an opposition organization.[16]

UNION SCABS

The type of "union scabbing" that broke the New Orleans strike was an all too frequent occurrence in the A. F. of L. One of the most shameful episodes occurred in 1900 when the International Cigar Makers' Union and the A. F. of L. Executive Council joined with the cigar manufacturers of Tampa, Florida, to wreck *La Resistencia,* the trade union formed by the cigar workers, mainly Cubans, of that city. Unlike the I.C.M.U., *La Resistencia* was an industrial union which organized all cigar workers, skilled and unskilled, men and women. Even though it did not organize members of the I.C.M.U., the international union refused to recognize the right of any other organization to speak for the cigar workers, despite the fact that it itself, as we have seen, refused to organize the majority of the workers in the trade. Joining forces with the I.C.M.U., the Tampa cigar manufacturers locked out the members of *La Resistencia.* Members of the I.C.M.U., with the approval of the A. F. of L. Executive Council, scabbed on the strikers; other members acted as deputy sheriffs, shot and clubbed the strikers on the streets, and in other ways aided to break the strike. The combined efforts of the employers, the I.C.M.U. and the A. F. of L. Executive Council were successful. The strike was lost and *La Resistencia* smashed.[17]

Such "union scabbing" was only one variety of this evil. With employers enabled by craft unionism to use time contracts, expiring at different dates, to play one craft union against another, "scabbing on the job" became a common occurrence in the A. F. of L. Craft scabbed on craft; union workers broke strikes of brother workers, and there was even the amazing phenomenon wherein A. F. of L. building trades unions built the barracks for scabs to live in who were hired to break the strikes of other A. F. of L. unions. As the Commercial Telegraphers Union, affiliated with the A. F. of L., pointed out in a resolution adopted at its 1904 convention and forwarded to Gompers:

"Whereas, owing to the fact that contracts entered into between various labor organizations and employers do, as at present conducted, begin and expire on widely different dates, and,

"Whereas, by reason of such variance, as above stated, allied bodies are frequently forced to combat the best interests of each other, thereby defeating the main objects of unionism, therefore, be it,

"Resolved, that it is the sense of this convention that as speedily as possible, consistent with existing agreements, all organizations connected with the American Federation of Labor cause such agreements or contracts to begin and expire upon a certain date, such date to be hereafter agreed upon."[18]

The solution offered by the Commercial Telegraphers was, of course, no solution at all since the possibility of obtaining such concerted time of contracts within the entire Federation was non-existent. A much more practical solution was offered by the secretary-treasurer of the National Union of Textile Workers of America who explained to Gompers why his union had decided that the only way to end the evil of "union scabbing" was by organizing all workers in the industry in a single union:

"Perhaps you have often wondered why the N. U. of T. W. of A. aims to control the industry and embraces all branches of the craft in a single organization. I will tell you. To make a strike either successful or effective, or to enforce a demand, in the textile trade, it is necessary to close the mills down from top to bottom. You will readily realize why this is so, if any other department struck for an advance in wages, or for any other reason, the manufacturer would continue to run his mill or mills as usual, and with the forces which would continue at work the aims of the strikers would be defeated. To more effectively illustrate the point I desire to convey, I would state that a few years ago the Mule Spinners of Fall River struck for an advance in wages, but the manufacturers kept the mills running and it is a lamentable fact, to be compelled to chronicle this fact which is nevertheless true, that the members of the Weavers, Cardroom, and Slashers Tenders Unions remained at work and helped defeat their fellow unionists. This has been repeated time and time again Bro. Gompers with the same disastrous results, why; because there was no bond of sympathy existing between them—how could there be with each union operating under its own contract! Hence we decided in creating the N[ational] U[nion] to make the grievance of one the concern of all by bringing all into one organization with one contract for all . . . I think you will agree with me when I say that the only way to avoid these difficulties is to remove the cause—separate contracts—and the only way to do this is to control the industry from top to bottom."[19]

The textile trade unionist was taking too much for granted when he expressed the belief that Gompers would agree with him that industrial unionism was the basic solution to the evil of "union scabbing."

Gompers like most of the other A. F. of L. leaders was fond of be-wailing this evil, but when the obvious solution was suggested, they re-treated immediately to the refuge of "trade autonomy." Yet, in a "per-sonal and confidential" letter to Gompers in 1903, John P. Frey, soon to become the ultra-conservative champion of craft unionism and the most vocal enemy of industrial unionism, explained why the policy of "trade autonomy" and "union scabbing" were interrelated:

"The policy of strict trade autonomy leads inevitably to unions strik-ing against each other to the advantage of the manufacturer. Let me illustrate why this is so. Take the Carriage and Wagon Makers' Union, an organization representing one of the oldest crafts. No carriage worker today makes the complete vehicle; each member performs but a part of the work required; some make the bodies, axles, hubs, and wheels, while others trim, paint, assemble and letter, while still another group devote their attention to bending the wood that forms the shafts and other por-tions of the carriage. All of these different groups of workmen are re-quired to make complete the finished product of the factory. By applying strict trade autonomy to this craft, as the A. F. of L. has decided should be done, the painters are forced to join the Painters' and Decorators' Union, the body makers to affiliate with the Amalgamated Association of Woodworkers, and those who work on the springs and metal fasten-ings are divided between the Blacksmiths and Metal Mechanics' Union. Thus several groups whose joint labor is required to manufacture the finished product are members of different national unions, and this re-sults not only in dividing their forces, but in making it possible for the manufacturer to play one organization against the other in the same plant, using one union or a group of unions to break the strike of an-other union."

Frey went on to point out that the same industrial development and the failure of the unions to adjust their structure to it was the basic cause of the jurisdictional disputes that were plaguing the labor movement.* "In the division of labor, with its manifold sub-divisions, it is simply

* Briefly summarized, jurisdictional disputes may result from one or more of the following causes: (1) Similarity of craft techniques which render actual de-marcation between crafts difficult; (2) Changes in the technique of industry which transform the skill requirements of a particular kind of work and thus brings a new group of workers into competition for it; (3) Introduction of new com-modities which either partially or entirely superseded the older commodity; (4) Political, social and geographical divisions among workers in the same craft, re-sulting in the formation of dual unionism; (5) Personal ambition and jealousy of leaders of different factions; (6) Structural differences of unions, which may be the result of any one, or any combination of the foregoing causes of dispute. (For a more detailed analysis of the causes of jurisdictional disputes, with special emphasis on those arising from structural differences, see Solomon Blum, *Juris-diction Disputes Arising from Structural Differences in American Trade Unions,* University of California Publications in Economics, vol. III, no. 3, 1913.)

impossible to find a term that will fit the character of work done by any set of men and not apply to some other trade. As long as the policy of strict trade autonomy is pursued so long will contentions arise among different unions as to where one type of work stops and the other begins. Conflicts are unavoidable so long as more than one union claims the right to organize a particular group of workers. The principle of one union in a trade is the answer to this problem as it is to the problem I have described to you above." Frey might have added, in his keen analysis, that many unions who made the claim to "the right to organize a particular group of workers" did nothing to organize the workers in the trade until another union took some active steps in this direction; then suddenly they would exert their jurisdictional claim.[20]

JURISDICTIONAL DISPUTES

The first jurisdictional dispute to come before the A. F. of L. was that between the carpenters and furniture workers in 1888 over the work to be done on the Exposition building in Pittsburgh. The number of appeals presented to the Federation increased steadily thereafter, and by 1900 there were 25 cases pending. In September 1899, John B. Lennon predicted that jurisdictional disputes would become so numerous "in the near future that the major attention of the men in the front rank of the Federation will be devoted to properly adjusting them and preventing conflicts that will, if unchecked, go a long way towards disrupting the trade union movement."[21] It was an accurate prediction. Hardly a day passed after 1900 that did not find the A. F. of L. Executive Council involved in trying to settle some inter-union quarrel over jurisdiction. Page after page of the *American Federationist* is filled with reports of such disputes.[22] Indeed, the casual reader easily gets the impression that the total concentration of the A. F. of L. Executive Council lay in the direction of settling jurisdictional disputes. Even Gompers conceded that such a conclusion would not be too wide of the mark. In a private letter to an A. F. of L. official, he wrote in disgust and despair:

"You may not have the experience of what jurisdictional divisions and separations mean. I have had much experience, and it is the most heart rending, most destructive, most time-consuming of anything else in our work, bringing forth less results for extraordinary efforts than any thing that has yet come to my observation in the labor movement. I have always been a great stickler for the rights of the separate organization, but I would forego much and surrender much to prevent these jurisdictional divisions and disruptions. If I had some time to relate to you in conversation some of the incidents connected with this problem I believe it would be enough to make your hair stand on end. I assure you that while I am dictating this a cold shiver runs through my frame."[23]

So much time was consumed by the individual unions involved in these disputes that it often left little for anything else. In March 1903, Thomas I. Kidd, General Secretary of the Amalgamated Wood Workers' International Union, complained to Gompers: "We have just concluded the case between the Carpenters and Woodworkers. We were in session in Indianapolis about two weeks and a half selecting an umpire. We spent about nine days submitting testimony and making arguments. We will have about nine hundred pages of type-written testimony and arguments, the other side insisting upon a stenographer being present at the conference. They also insisted upon introducing a lot of irrelevant matters and thus forced us to combat their testimony by a volume of matter which otherwise would have remained in the file of our office in Chicago. Do you wonder that we have no time for any other union work."[24]

The dispute between the Carpenters and the Wood Workers had a long history. In 1894 the Machine Wood Workers' Union and the Carpenters' Union came to an agreement under which the latter granted the former "entire jurisdiction over all millhands, except carpenters who may at times be engaged in mill work, or mill wrights, or stair builders." In 1895 the International Furniture Workers' Union amalgamated with the Machine Wood Workers to form the Amalgamated Wood Workers' International Union, which acquired the rights conceded by the Carpenters in 1894. In 1898 and again in 1900, the Carpenters abrogated its agreement and claimed jurisdiction over all wood workers. At the 1902 A. F. of L. convention, it was decided that each union name five members to a committee and if the committee was unable to reach agreement, an outside arbitrator (or umpire) be chosen by the committee. The committee, unable to agree, chose an arbitrator who ruled that "all wood workers in planing mills, furniture and interior finish factories came rightfully under the jurisdiction of the Amalgamated Wood Workers' International Union." Although both unions had agreed to abide by the umpire's decision, the Carpenters refused to accept it. At the 1903 A. F. of L. convention, the Carpenters' Union demanded that the charter of the Wood Workers be revoked. The issue was referred to the Executive Council which ruled "that the application to revoke the charter of the Amalgamated Workers be not granted," reminded the Carpenters that it had "entered into the agreement in good faith to abide by the decision" of the umpire, and ruled that this decision would have to be accepted. But the Executive Council did nothing to enforce its ruling, and the Carpenters ignored it. "The leaders of the Carpenters do not seem to have very much regard for the decisions of the A. F. of L.," Thomas I. Kidd of the Wood Workers wrote heatedly to Gompers in June 1904. The battle continued until 1911 when the Executive Council forced the

Wood Workers to amalgamate with the Carpenters or face expulsion from the A. F. of L.[25]

The classic illustrations of inter-union jurisdictional battles are in the building construction industry. It has been estimated that 95 per cent of the strikes in this industry during the years 1897 to 1914 were caused by dispute between unions as to the jurisdiction over a particular job. The jurisdictional strike became a feature of the industry.[26]

The reason for such strikes is clear enough. With advance in technology and the substitution of one material for another, a union finds its old work cut down and the new work claimed by a competing union. Since the leadership of both unions is interested in maintaining its membership and power, the dispute becomes insoluble by peaceful means, and the unions battle it out in a strike.

So, for example, the powerful United Brotherhood of Carpenters and Joiners, faced with the introduction of iron and steel frames in place of wooden frames, iron and stone staircases in place of wooden staircases, and tile and metal wainscotting in place of wooden wainscotting, found itself struggling for its life against the masons, the plasterers, the steel and iron workers, and the marble setters. The policy of the Brotherhood was to claim a vested interest in work formerly done by carpenters even though the material used was no longer wood. "It is a wonder that they do not claim the earth," the head of one of the unions involved in jurisdictional disputes with the Carpenters wrote disgustedly of the Brotherhood. The series of disputes arising out of the Carpenters' jurisdictional claims lasted for years, and during all these years, instead of uniting against the employers, the various unions exhausted their energies by calling strikes on each other's jobs. The Brotherhood's dispute with the Sheet Metal Workers, one of the bitterest jurisdictional struggles in the history of the American trade union movement, lasted 20 years. During this time, some of the largest locals of the Sheet Metal Workers were destroyed because of the dispute. A dispute in Denver involving the building trades workers led President Kirby of the A. F. of L. Building Trades Department to say: "The result of the fight has been the almost complete disorganization of one of the best organized cities in the United States, and a condition created that has held us up to ridicule throughout the country."[27]

"What has been the effect of this long struggle on organization in the industries involved?" asks a contemporary student of the jurisdictional battle between the Carpenters and the Wood Workers. He answers: "One organization, which had a membership in 1903 of approximately 30,000 has been reduced to just above 4,000 on January 1st, 1909. Has the other organization absorbed this loss of membership? The indications point in the opposite direction. The furniture factories have become practically non-union shops. . . . There has been a loss of organized labor also in those factories manufacturing office and saloon fixtures and billiard tables, etc. . . . Out of some 700 to 800 employees in Chicago, who were all members of the Wood Workers' Union prior to 1906, not more than 250 are now [May 1909] organized. It is asserted that not more than 90 were organized in New York, and only those in the departments which employ the most highly skilled workmen. . . .

"Had the same amount of time, energy and money been spent in maintaining harmony and a strong organization, both in and out of the factory. the cause of organized labor would have been better off. There has been an enormous waste of energy that should have been devoted to the improvement of the working conditions of the men who have had to support the financial burden of the fight."[28]

While most internecine wars between craft unions were not as furious as those in the building trades, they always weakened the unions involved, created chaos in the organizations, and retarded the development of organized labor. Pointing out that of over 780,000 teamsters in the United States in 1910 only something over 68,000 or 8.8. per cent were organized, a contemporary study concluded that jurisdictional disputes "have had an important influence in hindering the growth and stability of the union" and help "to account for the low percentage of organization among the teamsters as a whole."[29]

At the 1902 A. F. of L. convention, Gompers devoted a special section of his Presidential Report to the subject, "Jurisdictional Disputes Threaten Progress of the Labor Movement." He warned that "unless our national and international unions radically and soon change their course we shall at no distant day be in the midst of an internecine contest unparalleled in any era in the industrial world. . . . They mutually regard each other with hatred and treat each other as mortal enemies." In speeches delivered from convention platforms and in letters, Gompers continued to inveigh against the ever-increasing jurisdictional battles, stressing that they "retard the whole movement for the establishment of justice to labor"; that "there is nothing which so weakens the force of organized labor as internecine strife," and "if we must fight, fight our common enemy rather than fight among ourselves." "This constant friction . . . is doing more injury to the interests of the workers, and is a greater hindrance to the progress and success of our movement than all the antagonism of the enemies of our movement."[30]

Such statements were fine, but Gompers was a past master of making fine statements and then revealing no desire to develop the necessary action to give them meaning. He not only refused to couple his statements with the demand for the necessary change in union structure to help eliminate the evil of jurisdictional disputes, but he frowned on any suggestion that he do so. Thus, when it was pointed out to Gompers, on the eve of the 1903 A. F. of L. convention, that a group of machinists had proposed that he give real substance to his speeches against jurisdictional disputes by recommending to the delegates that the Federation go on record in favor of "industrial organization," Gompers replied coldly: "The proposal is worthless. Machinists working 9 and 10 hours a day, many of them so fatigued by their day's work, that in their readings and studies, they have little time to study the differentiation between the trade union form of organization and the so-called industrial organization." Likewise, when Charles O. Sherman, general secretary of the United Metal Workers' International Union, argued in June 1903 that angry-toned speeches against the jurisdictional dispute evil were not very helpful so long as the official leadership of the Federation did nothing to remedy the basic causes of this evil, he was reminded that the A. F. of L. and its affiliated unions had made great progress since the late 1890's and that all union leaders should be satisfied with these results. Sherman, however, was not satisfied. He replied:

"I am more than gratified to read the report submitted by you as to the growth and progress of our trades union movement in the past six years. While the figures show magnificent results, they are not what might be wished for but I am confident that they show all that can be expected when taken into consideration the eternal strife that has existed more or less in the past three years on the question of jurisdictional lines.

"I am not unmindful of the fact that there should be some demarcation lines, but under the system by which our product is produced and with the marked improvement of machinery and facilities, there never will come a time when there can be exact lines drawn but what there will be a lapping over occasionally, and if those at the head of the A. F. of L. and of the various organizations affiliated to it would realize this fact, abandon insistence on craft autonomy and adjust union structure along the lines of industrial production, and not spend so much time and money quarreling and fighting over jurisdictional lines, much greater progress can be achieved. We are still in a condition of very incomplete organization, and if we would only use the same energy and expense in organizing and educating the unorganized that we expend in jurisdictional fights, I am confident the results would be magnificent.

"My theory is, let us adjust our unions so that they can organize the unorganized and then let us get labor all organized. Then I am confident the jurisdictional question will be worked out to the satisfaction of the whole."[31]

Although he received no reply to his proposal, Sherman did not abandon his theory. A few months later, at the 1903 A. F. of L. convention, he helped to sponsor the first resolution on industrial unionism introduced at such a gathering. After reciting the weaknesses of the craft form of organization, the resolution proposed that "the convention appoint a committee whose duty it shall be to study the situation and report to the next convention a plan by which the trade unions can be grouped together on industrial lines, thus forcing contending factions into agreement with each other and promoting the solidarity of labor." The committee on resolutions not only reported the resolution unfavorably, but warned that it was time to "solemnly call a halt" to the attempt by some of the unions in the Federation to force industrial unionism upon the American labor movement. Gompers strongly endorsed the report and its warning. "The attempt to force the trade unions," he cried, "into what has been termed industrial organization is perversive to the history of the labor movement, runs counter to the best conception of the toilers' interests now, and is sure to lead to the confusion which precedes dissolution and disruption. It is time for our fellow-unionists . . . to help stem the tide of expansion madness lest either by their indifference or encouragement their organizations will be drawn into the vortex that will engulf them to their possible dismemberment and destruction." The resolution for industrial unionism was defeated.[32]

The warning sounded against some unions for even daring to raise the issue of industrial unionism was not specifically spelled out. But everyone at the convention knew that it referred to the fact that the forces of industrial unionism were captained by the Socialists. After the 1903 convention, the A. F. of L. leaders became more specific, repeatedly identified industrial unionism with socialism, and charged that the industrial unionists were involved in a sinister conspiracy of the Socialists to destroy the A. F. of L. This they planned to accomplish in two ways. One was by undermining the principle of craft autonomy—the bedrock on which the entire Federation rested. The other was by introducing, through industrial unionism, a host of social and political issues which would disrupt the Federation. "On the whole," a champion of craft unionism wrote to Gompers, "the skilled craftsmen, being better paid, are apt to be ultra-conservative. The unskilled, on the other hand, being poorly paid are the hardest fighters. But they are also the most troublesome, and I fear that this is the element that we will have to cope with if the Socialists behind the industrial union scheme have their way." The members of the industrial unions would not be content, as were those in the craft unions, simply to increase their control over their jobs. They would concern themselves with broader issues—independent political action and a comprehensive program for the basic alteration of the present economic system. Conflict over these issues would as surely tear the Federation apart as would abandonment of the principle of craft autonomy. In the end, organized labor would be the loser. Another champion of craft unionism, the secretary of the Brotherhood of Painters, warned that if industrial unionism were adopted, the leaders of the A.

F. of L. would be the losers, and what they would lose would be their official positions. "Some fine morning you will wake up with a revolution on your hands," he concluded his letter to Gompers.[33]

The effect of the use of an ideological weapon against industrial unionism had already been felt by one of the most militant unions in the A. F. of L.—the Brewery Workers. It was as an industrial union that the National Union of United Brewery Workmen in 1887 applied to the A. F. of L. for a charter as an affiliated organization. The charter was granted and the jurisdiction set forth in it gave the Brewery Workers the right to include in its membership "any person or persons, in accordance with its [the Brewery Workers' Union] own laws." Under this broad grant of jurisdiction, the Brewery Workers proceeded to organize the brewing industry, including within its framework the members of the various crafts who were employed by breweries.[34] The motto of the union—"Solidarity, man for man from roof to cellar, all for each and each for all"—was carried out in practice and the union organized the industry in accordance with this principle.

In 1896 the engineers, and two years later the firemen, received charters from the A. F. of L., and the teamsters also formed a national union. Although most of these unions had done nothing to organize the workers of their craft in the breweries, they soon called on the U.B.W. to turn over its members employed at those branches of work. The brewers' union refused. As Julius Zorn, national secretary of the U.B.W. pointed out to Gompers in 1899: "It seems the engineers are jealous because the brewery engineers are members of our Organization. It is a fact that some time ago when the engineers of the breweries were not yet organized, the Engineers' Union did not give the snap of their fingers for their brothers in the Breweries, but as soon as we organized them into a Local Union of our National Union, they began to raise a racket."[35]

In 1899 the Executive Council ordered the brewers to issue no more charters to unions of brewery engineers or firemen and to recognize the cards of those who belonged to their craft organizations. Individual engineers and firemen already belonging to the U.B.W. might retain their membership and their cards were to be recognized by the unions of the engineers and firemen. It was clear that this was only the first step in a drive to weaken if not destroy the union. As one of the pioneers in the movement for industrial unionism, the socialist-oriented United Brewery Workmen was a thorn in the side of the craft union leaders. In January 1900, P. J. McGuire warned Gompers that the entire Executive Council must take a firm stand to prevent other unions in the A. F. of L. from "travelling along the same impracticable Debsian road as the Brewery Workers." (By the "Debsian road," McGuire meant the principles of industrial unionism which Eugene V. Debs had advanced in the American

Railway Union during the 1890's and which he was still advocating for the entire labor movement as a leading Socialist spokesman.) The U.B.W. national secretary complained to Gompers that he had been informed by several members of the Executive Council "that since our organization is one of the most radical in the A. F. of L., we are disliked by the officers of the Federation and would not receive the assistance due to us in maintaining our industrial claims. These gentlemen even went so far as to call us anarchists and all sorts of 'ists.' "[36]

With Gompers in the lead, the anti-U.B.W. forces in the A. F. of L. intensified the offensive against the industrial union. Early in 1902, the Engineers' Union called a strike in the Cincinnati breweries to force the U.B.W. to relinquish its engineers. Both sides finally urged Gompers to go there and endeavor to adjust the matter. He accepted, after all parties undertook to abide by the decision he rendered. Gompers ruled that the engineers should end their strike against the brewers, but the U.B.W. was to revoke all charters granted to engineers and firemen during the past three months; engineers and firemen could belong to the U.B.W. only as individuals and by their voluntary action, except in cities where there was organization of their trade in which cases they must belong to their respective craft unions.[37]

This decision meant virtually the transformation of the U.B.W. from an industrial union to a craft union, and the brewers protested that the ruling was in violation of the recommendations of the 1900 A. F. of L. convention which granted jurisdiction over all brewery workers to the U.B.W. and recognized its right to keep its "composite character." At the convention of 1902, the Committee on the Executive Council's report sustained the protest of the brewers and recommended that Gompers' decision be overruled. A bitter battle ensued, during which Gompers relinquished the chair and entered the fight to oppose the committee's report. The report was defeated, and in its place a substitute was adopted upholding Gompers' decision and further directing that future disputes between the three organizations be settled within 60 days by a joint committee representing those unions and the Executive Council. Only the three large industrial unions in the Federation voted against.

The convention's decision was of little avail in the settlement of the brewery dispute. Recriminations between the brewers, engineers, and firemen continued, with mutual raiding of membership and imposition of boycotts. The U.B.W. refused to abandon its industrial form of organization while the craft union leaders insisted that it do so. At the 1903 A. F. of L. convention, the Brewery Workers was one of the unions which sponsored the resolution for industrial unionism. This further infuriated the craft unionists and at the following convention, the union was given a brusque ultimatum: it must not in the future accept any more engineers, firemen, or teamsters. A deadline of six months was fixed, upon the conclusion of which failure to comply with this ulti-matum would result in expulsion.[38]

The Brewery Workers refused to yield. It charged that it was being discriminated against because of its political policies and its champion-ship of industrial unionism. It protested that to accept the ultimatum would reduce the union to the same helpless condition as most craft or-ganizations in the mass production industries. The A. F. of L. was deaf to this appeal, and at the 1906 convention the Executive Council was ordered to expel the brewers.* On May 30, 1907, the charter of the United Brewery Workers was revoked by the A. F. of L. Immediately, the union issued the following statement:

"The Brewery Workers have not demanded anything more than was conceded to the organizations of coal miners, of longshoremen and sea-men, and other organizations; the unions named demand for their mem-bership the engineers and firemen employed in mines, on the docks, and on the ships on rivers, lakes and ocean.

"As jurisdiction is granted to the organizations named over all the workingmen employed in their respective industries, and this right of jurisdiction is denied to us, we maintain that the proceedings against our National Union of United Brewery Workmen are acts of class legis-lation and that they deprive our National Union of its guaranteed rights, privileges and autonomy."[39]

A storm of protest against the expulsion descended upon the A. F. of L. Executive Council in the form of letters and resolutions from local unions and central labor bodies all over the country. In 1909 the Executive Council restored the brewery workers' charter on the basis of the juris-dictional limitations imposed by previous conventions of the Federation. The brewery workers were permitted to keep the engineers and firemen they had already organized, if these workers wished to belong to the union, but must not recruit any new members of these crafts into their union. Even these concessions to the brewery workers were made be-cause of the mounting protests from local unions and central labor bodies throughout the country. As one student of the controversy points out: "the Federation . . . made concessions [to the U.B.W.] . . . only because it was forced to do so by the recognition of circumstances which could not be overlooked."[40]†

* The delay in carrying through the expulsion order was due to some extent to Gompers' reluctance to carry it into effect. He felt that it was a mistake to expel the union, that it would only arouse widespread resentment among members of the A.F. of L., and that a policy of patience and flexibility would gradually win the brewery workers around to a position acceptable to the craft unionists. (Gom-pers to Lennon, April 29, May 8, 1907; Gompers to James Duncan, May 1, 1907, *GLB*.)

† The jurisdictional controversy between the brewers and the craft unions con-tinued down to the mid-1930's, making it the longest jurisdictional battle in the history of the A.F. of L. For the details of this continuing conflict, *see* Benjamin C.

As the United Brewery Workers pointed out in their protests against their expulsion from the Federation, the A. F. of L. had already granted a number of unions the jurisdictional rights which it denied the brewers. But these unions were, in the main, craft unions and the ideology of the United Mine Workers, under Mitchell's leadership, was akin to that of the craft unions even though it was an industrial union.* But the U.B.W. was a militant industrial union. As Perlman and Taft pointed out:

"If the Federation repeatedly showed itself complacent to practical departures from the principle of the inviolability of chartered craft unions, when under pressure from strong craft unions or . . . in its eagerness for new acquisitions, matters were different when the attack on craft autonomy came from avowed advocates of industrial unionism. Then it became a matter of principle rather than expediency and adjustment, and the Federation, if it yielded at all, did so only in the last extremity. This was shown in the case of the brewers."[41]

AMALGAMATIONS AND DEPARTMENTS

Year after year resolutions for industrial unionism were introduced at the A. F. of L. conventions, generally by the Socialists. Just as regularly Gompers and the trade union officialdom beat them down. But even a number of them sensed that the evils flowing from craft autonomy would not solve themselves. "Since leaving Boston," John P. Frey wrote to Gompers a few days after the 1903 convention where the industrial unionism resolution was defeated, "I have become convinced that a form of industrial autonomy should prevail in certain trades, in fact I believe that in the future nothing would be of better interest to the Trades Union movement in general than to have a common sense application of this form of organization. The policy of trade autonomy adhered to by the American Federation of Labor since its inception is being carried too far, and unless some cognizance is taken of present industrial conditions there is danger ahead. The rapid introduction of machinery and the specialization that is taking place in some industries have created conditions that cannot be fully covered if rigid trade autonomy is to be adhered to, and I am convinced that the time has come when a form

Roberts, "Jurisdiction Disputes Between the Brewery Workers and Other A.F. of L. Affiliates," unpublished M.A. thesis, University of Chicago, 1936, pp. 92–163.)

* Although Mitchell was convinced that "as a consequence of the evolution of industry, there is a marked tendency toward industrial unionism," he refused to take an active part in the battle for industrial unionism inside the A.F. of L. When delegates to the U.M.W. 1906 convention urged him to support the Brewery Workers in the struggle against the craft unions, Mitchell rejected the appeal. (Mitchell to A. V. Brisson, March 6, 1911, *JMP; Proceedings,* U.M.W. Convention, 1906, pp. 55–56.)

of industrial autonomy should be adopted in certain lines of production. By this I mean that where it becomes necessary for a number of men to each contribute a share in producing a finished article, manufactured in large quantities in the same establishment, that these workmen should have an organization that would give them control of all those who were directly occupied in contributing their share to the finished article."[42]

As a principle Frey's suggestion was rejected; indeed, it was not adopted in practice until the organization on a large scale of the manufacturing industries during the great organizing drives of the 1930's and 1940's, sparked to a great extent by the rise of the Congress of Industrial Organizations, which, ironically, Frey did so much to sabotage as the bitterest enemy and red-baiter of the C.I.O. from its inception. Yet, partly as a concession to the rising tide of industrial unionism,* and partly because it was the only way the unions could function, the A. F. of L. did move somewhat in the direction outlined above. At the 1907 convention Gompers announced his "counterreformation," the "natural, orderly and well-defined course" of promoting cooperation while respecting trade autonomy. He boasted that the A. F. of L. was flexible enough to permit necessary adjustments in organizational structure without repeating "the fatal error of the past" by adopting industrial unionism. He pointed specifically to the voluntary amalgamations† and trades councils‡ as proof that "the trade unions were not rigid organizations which cannot meet new conditions."[43]

In 1907, the A. F. of L. finally decided to inaugurate the formation of industrial departments. That same year it was decided to charter a Building Trades Department, to be composed of the building trades organizations affiliated with the A. F. of L., with authority over the local building trades sections and power to issue charters to such sections. One

---

* The formation and activities of the Industrial Workers of the World (I.W.W.) were influential in forcing these concessions. We will deal with this organization in the next volume.

† Amalgamations took place after 1900: the metal mechanics with the machinists, the coremakers with the molders, the lasters with the shoemakers, and the car workers with the railway carmen. But not all were "voluntarily." The lasters were forced to join the shoemakers and the car workers the railway carmen by the A.F. of L., with the full approval of Gompers, in opposition to their wishes. This was certainly in violation of the Scranton Declaration as well as of the A.F. of L. constitution, and showed again that trade autonomy was not so sacred that it might not be sacrificed to satisfy the demands of a powerful union in the Federation or to gain the adherence of a large organization. (*See* Louis Lorwin, *The American Federation of Labor*, pp. 489-91, for a list of amalgamations after 1900.)

‡ In the 1890's the construction workers set up an International Building Trades Council. The United Brotherhood of Carpenters and Joiners subsequently took the lead in creating a Structural Building Trades Alliance which united most of the important unions in the industry.

of its main functions would be the settlement of jurisdictional disputes. In 1908, the Building Trades Department received a charter as did the Metal Trades Department, and in the next two years departments were also formed among the railroad employees and mine workers. (A Union Label Department was formed in 1909.) This action, said Gompers, "will prove conclusively that the carping critics of our movement who charge, or insinuate, that the trade union movement does not progress, advance or develop, is baseless and a mischievous untruth."[44]

In short, under pressure from within and outside the Federation for industrial unionism, the A. F. of L. had been forced to make some concessions to minimize jurisdictional difficulties, increase union strength, and achieve coordinated demands and action. But the essential character of the A. F. of L. had not changed. It still clung to the idea that union organization could be based upon craft skill. It still reflected one of the principal weakness of craft unionism—craft separatism. It still geared its structure for the improvement of the conditions of the minority of the American working class—the skilled craftsman. The vast majority of the unions affiliated to the A. F. of L. still refused to admit all workers in a particular industry, regardless of skill or craft, even though the industrial area that lent itself to organization of skilled workers had considerably narrowed. Despite the shift of power to the mass production industries, the A. F. of L. still carried out the craft idea, not the industrial idea, still refused to carry on collective bargaining on an industrial basis.

What had occurred in the various amalgamations so proudly cited by Gompers as the answer to the industrial unionists was mainly the absorption of small crafts by larger ones. Real amalgamation of powerful unions in the same industry was scorned by a trade union bureaucracy determined to maintain vested interests in their jobs. Even uniformity of action in most of the amalgamations which developed was impossible. When one group struck, the others remained on the job, for a sympathetic strike involving the breaking of a contract was vigorously frowned upon in the Federation.[45]

The Departments, the rise of which was also proudly cited by Gompers as the answer to industrial unionism and as embodying the principle of "an injury to one is the concern of all," were a far cry from meeting the demands of the industrial unionists. Structurally, they were not industrial in form; rather, they were loose, voluntary coalitions between autonomous groups which did little to obliterate craft lines. Factional divisions within the Departments prevented them from functioning effectively. When the jurisdiction of a powerful international was threatened, it vetoed the affiliation of the threatening union or seceded from the Department. Departments lacked the power to enforce any decisions formulated by them; the stronger unions simply ignored the decisions when it did not serve their interests. The Building Trades Department was rendered ineffective because of the refusal of the Carpenters, the largest and most powerful of the building trade unions, to support the Department.[46]

John R. Commons aptly characterized the Departments as "industrial unionism of the upper stratum" of the labor movement. An official of the automobile workers' union commented that "they were nothing less than a confession that greater unity is needed, but those in control of the old machinery of the Labor Movement are reluctant to give way to the new order of things. They would patch up the old vehicle; they would put a motor in the old wagon and thus make an up to date automobile of it, but would decline to accept the modern vehicle, because it means a new deal in the Labor Movement, and they are afraid they would be lost in the shuffle."[47]

Thus the attempts in the A. F. of L. to modify the single craft principle, while quite numerous, were trivial in their effects. Despite various amalgamations and the formation of Departments, disputes kept recurring. The Executive Council generally ruled in favor of the craft union claiming jurisdiction even though the development of the industry along mass production lines had rendered craft union organization obsolete. This is clearly illustrated in the Executive Council's handling of the jurisdictional disputes in the rapidly developing automobile industry. In 1912 the Executive Council granted to the Carriage, Wagon and Automobile Workers' International Union,* organized on an industrial basis, complete jurisdiction over the automobile industry. The blacksmiths, however, claimed the right to workers of their craft in the automobile plants. After some conferences between the two unions proved futile, the Executive Council upheld the blacksmiths. In subsequent decisions, it upheld the claims of the Carpenters and Joiners, the Painters and Decorators, and the Upholsterers to workers of their craft in the automobile industry. The tragic story of the complete failure of the A. F. of L. to organize the automotive industry after these decisions reveals clearly the decisive weakness of the craft approach to a mass production industry.[48]

The miscellaneous attempts at federation were shattered on the rock of "craft autonomy." Basically, the A. F. of L., dominated by craft unionists, consistently opposed any policy that would jeopardize the "principle" of craft unionism. In practice, the A. F. of L. leadership departed frequently from this principle when it came to dealing with the acquisition of weaker unions by strong craft unions. But they adhered to it steadfastly when it involved the all-important issue of organizing the un-

---

* The union, founded in 1891, was originally called the Carriage and Wagon Workers' International Union. In 1909 its name was changed to the Carriage, Wagon and Automobile Workers' International Union.

organized in the mass production industries through the only union structure conducive to the achievement of solidarity and power in these industries—industrial unionism.[49]

The success of unionism is not, of course, entirely bound up with the choice of an appropriate union structure. There were many other factors involved in the policies of the A. F. of L. which weakened its effectiveness in organizing the unorganized. As we shall now see, the struggle to revise the structure of the A. F. of L., so as to make it a more flexible instrument of labor advance, was linked to the struggle to remove other barriers set up by the Federation against the organization of the workers—the Negro workers, the women workers, the foreign-born workers, and the young workers.

CHAPTER 9

Women and Negro Workers

In an address before a trade union congress at Toronto in 1901, Gompers urged organized labor in Canada to follow the example set by the A. F. of L. in placing the abolition of various social prejudices at the head of its demands. "The American Federation of Labor," he continued, "affirms as one of the cardinal principles of the trade union movement that the working people must organize, unite and federate irrespective of creed, color, sex, nationality or politics."[1]

It is difficult, if not impossible, to reconcile Gompers' lofty assertions with the actual practice of the A. F. of L. Speeches boasting that the keystone of the Federation's policy was the organization of the working people regardless of differences of sex, color or nationality sound hollow in the face of policies and practices designed to prevent the achievement of this goal. The categories of workers listed by Gompers—women, Negro and foreign-born workers—were employed almost entirely in the semi-skilled and unskilled occupations, and, as we have already seen, the craft union structure of most of the A. F. of L. unions made it difficult, if not impossible, to "organize, unite and federate" these workers—even if these unions wished to accomplish this. On top of this, the majority of these workers were excluded from membership in the A. F. of L by a complex system of rules, regulations, and practices deliberately designed to achieve their exclusion.

HIGH DUES AND INITIATION FEES

One aspect of this policy was the heavy tax on A. F. of L. members through high dues and initiation fees. The 1900 A. F. of L. convention proclaimed that high dues and initiation fees were "an absolute [sic] necessary foundation for successful trade unionism." No one was more vocal on this theme than Gompers. In his reports to the A. F. of L., in editorials in the *American Federationist,* in his correspondence, and in his addresses to international unions, he drove home the necessity of high dues and high initiation fees. Only in this way could the A. F. of L. and its affiliated unions achieve stability. Only in this way could workers wring concessions from employers without resorting to strikes, for only in this way could they prove that their unions would not be forced to succumb because of their small treasuries. Once the unions were placed on an effective financial foundation, they would secure "the highest and best conditions of labor."[2]

There can be little doubt that a firm financial foundation was a vital necessity for the unions, particularly when they were small and weak. But the continued emphasis on this policy was incompatible with the A. F. of L's professed aims of organizing all workers. Of necessity, it limited trade union membership almost exclusively to the "labor aristocracy," the skilled mechanics and craftsmen who alone could afford these high initiation fees and high dues payments. To those who pointed out that the wages of the unskilled workers were too low to enable them to meet these financial requirements for union membership, Gompers would reply that their wages would be cut even further if they did not make the necessary financial contributions. How these workers would find the means to pay was evidently no concern of his. All he could say was that they would find a way. Once they saw that the union provided a stone wall of protection for their interests, they would soon come within its wall for protection.[3]

But many workers found that the stone wall erected by the unions was more a barrier to their entrance into the labor movement than a protection against exploitation. Dues ranging from $1 to $5 a month and initiation fees fixed at sums varying from $25 to $100, $200, $250, $300 and even $500 made a mockery of resolutions and speeches calling for the broadest organization of the working class. "The initiation fee is a barrier to poor men and women," a correspondent protested to Gompers after the A. F. of L. had approved the fixing of the initiation fee of several of its affiliates at $99. "How is it possible to obtain perfect organization of meagerly paid vocations with such high initiation fees and dues?" another correspondent asked.[4] Gompers did not bother to answer such questions. As even a champion of the A. F. of L. president concedes: "Gompers simply did not believe that the trade union movement could afford to worry about those who were either unwilling or unable to pay high dues."[5]

A student of the labor organization in this period points out that the median weekly wage in New England cotton mills for men was between $7 and $7.99 and for women $6 and $6.99, and that it was not surprising that these workers were "little inclined to contribute any large portion of it as trade union dues." But the United Textile Workers, an A. F. of L. affiliate, refused to lower its dues to enable the vast majority of the workers in the industry to become members of the union. John Golden, the U.T.W.'s class-collaborationist president, explained at the 1905 convention that the high dues did not prevent the skilled workers in the industry from joining the union, and that, fundamentally, that was all that mattered. "I find them the most intelligent and the easiest to organize. . . . They are also of more value to us than the unskilled workers."[6]

This was, unfortunately, the attitude of many of the A. F. of L. unions. The heavy financial burdens were imposed upon prospective members in order to restrict not expand membership. One union put it bluntly in 1908 when it stated that it was raising the initiation fee "as the officers are continually annoyed by prospective candidates." The corollary of this doctrine was that it was a waste of time to spend money organizing low-paid, unskilled trades whose workers could not contribute to the union's sound financial foundation. The 1900 A. F. of L. convention had endorsed high dues and initiation fees for the purpose of "building up of large treasuries to be held by the organizations themselves, available for the protection of members in all casualties which may befall them." This immediately raised the question: why should the skilled workers tax themselves for the benefit of unskilled workers who, when organized, could not assist in the "building up of large treasuries." Thus the policy of the A. F. of L., by placing the accumulation of large union treasuries above the solidarity of the working class and emphasizing the immediate needs of the highly skilled craftsmen rather than the long-range interests of all workers, made the organization of the unskilled difficult, and confined the Federation to "principally the upper-strata of semi-skilled labor."[7]

On June 12, 1900, a group of women shoe workers in Pontiac, Illinois, wrote to Morrison: "We are anxious to go into the Boot and Shoe Workers union and wrote to Mr. [H. M.] Eaton [the general secretary-treasurer] to that effect. He sent us a copy of the by-laws and when we found out what the high dues were we voted by a large majority not to go in as the dues were to [o] high, and we simply do not earn enough to pay them." They appealed to the A. F. of L. national office to urge the Boot and Shoe Workers' Union to reduce the dues. The request was forwarded, and Horace M. Eaton bluntly informed Morrison to forget the whole thing! "We have been in touch with these women right along, as their letter indicates, and there is nothing to be gained from pursuing the matter further. They evidently want to organize on the bargain-counter plan, and we can well do without such members." Learning this, the women organized a local union and asked Morrison: "Could we not get a charter in the American Federation of Labor under the head of a mixed union?" The Boot and Shoe Workers' Union vigorously protested against granting a charter to the newly formed women's local, and the A. F. of L. national office turned down the request.[8]

This story of the small group of women shoe workers buried in the archives of the A. F. of L. may not seem to loom large in the broad history of the American labor movement. Actually, it is highly significant, for it symbolizes the tragic relationship between women workers and the A. F. of L.

A. F. OF L. AND WOMEN WORKERS

From 1890 to 1910, the number of females gainfully employed doubled —4,005,532 to 8,075,772. In the same period, women workers were an inconspicuous part of the labor movement. Leo Wolman estimates that 73,800 women belonged to unions in 1910, of which the largest numbers were in the garment trades, textile and cloth weaving, book binding, shoe making, tobacco, retail, and in the musical and theatre arts.[9] This figure represented only 0.9 per cent of all women wage earners at that time!

Year after year, the A. F. of L. passed resolutions calling for the organization of women workers, and even urged "those international and national organizations that do not admit women workers to membership . . . to give early consideration to such admission." But nothing was done to give these resolutions meaning. Women, being predominantly semi-skilled and unskilled workers, did not work in appreciable numbers in the trades mainly represented in the A. F. of L. and were neglected by the craft unions. Moreover, they were denied by most of these unions the opportunity for on-the-job training, or for promotion, which would either enable them to acquire additional skills, or put such skills to use.

Women workers earned incredibly low wages compared with men whose wages were low enough. Paul Brissenden estimates annual per capita earnings of women workers in 1899 at $267, compared with $498 for men, $289 to $540 in 1904, and $339 to $631 in 1909.* During the same period, according to F. W. Taussig, the wages of young women, who constituted the bulk of those employed in factories, ranged about $6 a week.[10] Naturally, women could contribute very little in union dues; nor could they pay the prohibitive initiation fees. Consequently, the A. F. of L., for all its professed interest in organizing women workers, neglected their problems.

To be sure, the A. F. of L. advanced a theory to justify its neglect. "So far as organizing women workers is concerned," wrote an A. F. of L.

---

* Brissenden asserts that the difference in earnings between men and women workers "are often attributable less to the sex factor than to the degree of skill." But it was precisely because of their sex that women were prevented by many unions, in collusion with employers, from achieving any "degree of skill."

leader, "the over-shadowing difficulty lies in the temporary character of their employment." Women did not stay in industry permanently. They obtained jobs just for "spending money." They wanted to get married and have families, and once married, they dropped out of the industry. Why should the trade unions tax themselves and expend undue energy attempting to organize women? Once organized, they left, and the job remained to be done over again.[11]

That there was some truth to this argument goes without saying. But the fact was that women were entering industry in larger and larger numbers, and surveys disclosed that the majority depended on their wages for a livelihood, that most of them had dependents, and that the trend for women, married as well as unmarried, was towards entering factories. In its investigation, the Industrial Commission found widespread evidence in 1900 that "the wives—mothers of the family go into the factory and work for a living." In 1908, the president of Bryn Mawr College, after an exhaustive study of the subject, reported that "everything seems to indicate that women will not only make their way into all except a few trades and professions, but that they will be compelled by economic causes to stay in them *after marriage*." It was not difficult to discover the "economic causes." A married couple could hardly get along on less than $10 a week, but many men earned only $6 or $8 a week. The wives had to work too. Between 1890 and 1912, married women in industry multiplied six times over, increasing from 515,000 to over 3,000,000.[12]

Commenting on these developments, the British Columbia *Federationist* declared on December 23, 1911:

"Women are today in industry; about one wage worker in five is a woman. . . . Through the streets of all large cities, at morning and night, troop the brigades of women workers, and their number is increasing yearly. Their numbers increase for the reason that fathers and brothers are no longer able to keep the family on the wages they get and the 'self supporting' woman is forced out of her home by the necessity of having to help increase the family income. . . .

"There are some workingmen who discourage the idea of women joining their organizations. This is a short-sighted policy. The very women whom they scorn today may tomorrow be taking their places— taking them for the reason that they know no better and because the men workers did not organize and instruct them."

But such mature observations, like the evidence presented in government and private surveys, did not dispel the false cliché that women workers considered their jobs temporary, and A. F. of L. officials and many craft unions continued to justify their refusal to spend money to organize women on the ground that "most of them will be entering into the matrimonial state and consequently will drop out." Those who took cognizance of the contrary evidence advanced the argument that women should not be wage earners, that their place was in the home. "Just in proportion as woman is transferred from the home to the work-shop," George Gunton wrote in an A. F. of L. pamphlet, "is her refin-ing and elevating influence in the domestic circle destroyed, and hence the social environment, and therefore, the character of the children, the family, and ultimately that of the whole industrial community is thereby lowered." In 1905 Gompers was asked by the *Woman's Home Com-panion* to answer the question, "Should the wife contribute to the sup-port of her family by working for wages?" His answer was "positively and absolutely, 'No!' . . . In our time, and at least in our country, generally speaking, there is no necessity for the wife contributing to the support of the family by working . . . the wife as a wage-earner is a disadvantage economically considered, and socially is unnecessary." (How the family was to survive on the meager earnings of most of the male workers "in our country," Gompers did not bother to discuss.) Not only was industrial work bad for women, but even trade union mem-bership was not suited to bring out their best qualities. "Do they not tend to unsex them and make them masculine?" observed an A. F. of L. leader in a letter to Agnes Nestor, secretary-treasurer of the International Glove Workers' Union and one of the handful of women who have ever held posts as national union officers in this country.[13]

A. F. of L. unions made their contribution to maintaining the feminine qualities of women workers untouched by demanding that all women employees should be eliminated from their trades and by refusing to permit them to become union members. The Building Trades Material Council of Chicago asked the state factory inspectors to bar women on the ground that the work was unhealthy. A union in Massachusetts made a smilar attempt to force women out of the coremaking trade. Gompers gave these efforts his unqualified approval and support, main-taining that their employment was a degradation of womanhood.[14]

Nor did the militant struggles conducted by women affect A. F. of L. policy. During the 11 years 1895 to 1905, there were 15,726 strikes, and women were directly involved in 1,262 of these struggles. In 83 strikes of this 11-year period, women workers alone were involved,* representing practically all trades where women worked: bookbinders, boot and

---

* Although there is little information in the statistics, it is known that women's unions often struck in sympathy with men's unions. One such strike occurred in a Chicago nail factory where 120 women made $10 to $12 a week on piecework, while the 80 men received only $1.75 per day. The women went on strike, de-manding a 10 per cent raise for the men and nothing for themselves except that 10 of the women getting $1.25 per day should have a 25-cent increase. After a strike of only half a day, the employer agreed to the demands. (Ray Ginger, *Altgeld's America: The Lincoln Ideal versus Changing Realities.* New York, 1958 p. 246.)

shoe workers, garment workers in both men's and women's clothing industries, glove workers, hat trimmers, musicians, retail clerks, shirt, waist and laundry workers, textile, tobacco and typographical workers, waitresses and "miscellaneous."[15] The spirit and determination of these workers proved that it was possible to organize women of the most varied backgrounds and traditions. Indeed, even the *American Federationist,* viewing these statistics, conceded in 1905 that "we can safely predict that organization for women is possible and practicable in a majority of city and town employments. Of the occupations that employ women in the largest numbers, in agriculture alone and among house servants does organization seem to be impossible under present conditions."[16]

In a study of women in trade unions made in 1905, 14 national or international organizations connected with the A. F. of L. were cited to which women belonged. In 1909 there were practically no women to be found in five of these unions—Potters, Commercial Telegraphers, Bakery and Confectionery Employees, Building Employees, and Meat Cutters and Butchers. The reports of the New York Bureau of Statistics reveal that from 1895 to 1908 the proportion of women to all trade unionists in that state fell off from 4.8 to 2.9. This decline in union membership was not confined to any particular trade or locality; it occurred to the same or even greater degree in every industry and in every part of the country. In 1903 in Chicago it was estimated that there were 31,400 women trade unionists in the city in unions composed solely of women. Yet in 1908 the number had dwindled to 10,000 in unions of every kind. In 1903 women's unions included those of paper box makers, laundry workers, and more than 20 other trade organizations. The report submitted to the Senate Committee on conditions of women in industry stated that "in 1909 such organizations of women had disappeared from Chicago except for perhaps a nominal existence in one or two cases. That organizations composed entirely of women have vanished from 16 out of 25 industries in Chicago within a period of six years is a rather striking evidence of decline of unionism among women."[17]

While there are a number of factors that checked the growth of unionism among women and led to the loss of membership, general disgust among women at the hostility displayed towards them by many A. F. of L. craft unions was a major cause. In February 1904, the president of the Shirt, Waist and Laundry Workers' Union, whose membership was predominantly women, protested to Gompers:

"A major handicap to our already exceedingly difficult task of organizing our craft throughout the country arises from the fact that in many localities the Central Labor bodies dominated by unions composed almost exclusively of men refuse to recognize our locals and the women delegates duly elected by them. We feel that no results can be accomplished unless this is satisfactorily adjusted, as the female members of our craft are naturally timid about joining the labor movement, and with the evidence now apparent that the unions of men in the Central Bodies are hostile to them and unwilling to support them, they are even more timid. This condition does not have a tendency to increase their desire to become active in the labor movement. On the contrary, it is causing many of our members to think of leaving organized labor. Hence our appeal to you that you take this up at your earliest convenience."[18]

A few months later, the president of District 5, United Mine Workers, wrote to Gompers: "Several groups of the working women of the Pittsburgh area requested me to give them information on how they could get organized. I contacted the various unions of the trades involved after which the women themselves approached them. I have learned that these women were told that there was no room for them in the unions they approached. Most of the women are so discouraged that they are ready to abandon the plan to organize, and I wonder if there is not some way that they could be attached to the American Federation of Labor directly."[19]

There are many similar letters in the archives of the American Federation of Labor describing hostility or indifference of the craft unions to the organization of women workers, and urging the Federation's leadership to do something quickly to halt this trend before those women already in the unions abandoned their membership. But the A. F. of L. leaders failed to meet the problem, and Gompers' contradictory statements urging, on the one hand, the organization of women workers and the principle of equal wages for equal work, and, on the other, that women should not be wage earners and that their place was in the home, only confused matters.

Only a small number of national trade unions in this period entirely forbade the admission of women by prescribing that only men were to be eligible for membership. Among them were the Barbers, the Watchcase Engravers, the Switchmen, and the Molders. The last-named union resolved in 1907 to seek "the restriction of the further employment of women labor in union core rooms and foundries, and eventually the elimination of such labor in all foundries." A penalty of $50 fine or expulsion was levied on any member who dared to give instruction to female laborers in any branch of the trade.

But constitutional clauses barring women were only the most direct method used to achieve this end. Some unions admitted women employed in certain branches, but not those employed in others, and usually the women were excluded from the main branches of the trade. (The Upholsterers, for example, admitted women when they were employed as seamstresses.) Nearly all A. F. of L. unions refused to open new employment opportunities to women, and by restricting their apprenticeship programs to men only, confined women to unskilled jobs. "It is an evil combination," one woman protested to Gompers. "Lack of skill keeps many of us from entering the unions of skilled craftsmen, and rigid apprenticeship regulations prevents us from becoming apprentices to the trade and thereby rising to the rank of skilled workers."[20]

It is true that the A. F. of L. pointed to the fact that many of the international unions did not openly discriminate against women; that some even passed regulations reducing fees and dues for women, and adopted resolutions in favor of apprenticeship training for women and equal pay for equal work. But they failed to mention that there was a huge gap between the policy of the national unions and the practice of the locals. Actually, the local unions had final control in carrying out policy, and many simply disregarded the declarations of the national union, denied admission to women applicants, refused to permit the granting of a special charter for a woman's local, and rejected female applicants holding transfer cards. In 1902, the national secretary of the Amalgamated Meat Cutters and Butcher Workmen called upon the local unions to organize the women in the industry, pointing out correctly: "It is useless . . . to attempt to stem the tide of female workers. It now rests with us to bring them into our organization . . . to see that they are affiliated with us . . . and that we extend to them the protection which thorough organization affords . . . is a duty which we cannot shirk without grave danger to ourselves." But when the women in the Chicago packinghouses—five thousand were employed in the stockyards in 1903—formed a union, the local refused to grant them a charter, and the national union said nothing.[21] The A. F. of L. refused to act against national unions which had constitutional clauses barring women or else discriminated against women in their locals on the doctrine that each international union is autonomous and undisciplinable!

What little effort was made to help and organize women workers was sparked largely by the small group of leaders from their own ranks and from leisure-class reformers, especially women social workers. In Chicago, Hull House, under the leadership of Jane Addams, recruited a small army of young women of independent means—Florence Kelley, Julia Lathrop, Grace Abbott, Alice Hamilton, etc.—to help improve the conditions of working women. Mary E. McDowell, head resident of the University of Chicago Settlement, helped the women workers in the stockyards organize a union and, after considerable persuasion, convinced the local men's unions to grant them a charter of incorporation and equality of representation with men in local affairs. In New York's Henry Street Settlement, Lillian D. Wald played a similar role.[22]

The National Consumers League, organized in 1899, with branches in cities all over the country organized boycotts of companies that exploited women and children. Later it worked for legislation which would force

employers to conform to standards set by the state, and when such legislation was challenged in the Courts as unconstitutional, the National
Consumers League, under the leadership of Florence Kelley, led the
battle to establish governmental responsibility for the working conditions
and welfare of women workers.[23]

WOMEN'S TRADE UNION LEAGUE

In 1903 the Women's Trade Union League was founded at Boston's
historic Faneuil Hall by a group of trade unionists and liberal professional social workers interested in the organization of women.* Impressed by the accomplishments of the Women's Trade Union League of
Great Britain in aiding the organization of working women,† its founders in America sought to solve three basic problems facing working
women in this country: the unionization of women, the education of the
unions to the need of organizing them, and the enactment of protective
legislation for women and children. Membership in the League was
open to "any person . . . who will declare himself or herself willing to
assist those trades already existing, which have women members, and to
aid in the formation of new unions of women wage earners." Membership on the Executive Board was to be divided as follows: "The majority . . . shall be women who are, or have been, trade unionists in good
standing, the minority of those well known to be earnest sympathizers
and workers for the cause of trade unionism."[24] But it was not until
1907 that a majority of the Board were trade unionists; up to that time
women of independent means made up most of the Board members.‡
After 1907 working women leaders became more important—women like

* Among them were John R. O'Brien, president of the Clerks' International
Protective Union, Mrs. Mary Kenney O'Sullivan, formerly a general organizer
for the A.F. of L. and leader of the Chicago Bindery Workers' Union, and William
English Walling, noted Socialist journalist and economist.

† The British Women's Trade Union League was formed in 1874, although it
was not until 1890 that it took on its official name. Its founder, Mrs. Emma Pater-
son, had been impressed by the militancy and organizational ability of American
women workers during her honeymoon trip to the United States, and when she
returned to England, she was determined to help her countrywomen form trade
unions. Thus the British League was influenced by experiences in America, and
the American League by the experiences of the League in England. (Gladys
Boone, *The Women's Trade Union Leagues in Great Britain and the United
States of America,* New York, 1942, pp. 20–42.)

‡ The League's first officers were Mrs. Mary Morton Kehew, president, Miss
Jane Addams of Hull House, vice-president, Mrs. Mary Kenney O'Sullivan, secretary, and Miss Mary Donovan (secretary of the Lynn Central Labor Union),
treasurer. Miss Mary E. McDowell, Miss Leonora O'Reilly, and Miss Lillian D.
Wald of the Henry Street Settlement were among the members of the Executive
Board. Margaret Dreier (who later became the wife of Colonel Raymond Robins)
was elected president in 1907 and held that office until 1922.

Mary Anderson and Emma Steghagen of the shoe workers, Rose Schneiderman of the cap makers, Agnes Nestor and Elisabeth Christman of the glove workers, Melinda Scott of the hat trimmers, Josephine Casey of the railway ticket takers, Stella Franklin of the department store clerks, Elizabeth Maloney of the waitresses, and Maud Swartz of the typographers. Until 1921, the presidency of the League was held by three women of independent means: Mrs. Mary Morton Kehew, Mrs. Charles Henrotin, and Margaret Dreier Robins. In 1921 Maud Swartz became the first working woman president of the League.

In 1904 state branches were formed in Illinois, Massachusetts, and New York and by 1911 the League had grown to 11 branches, expanding to Springfield, Illinois; St. Louis, Cleveland, Kansas City, Baltimore, and Denver. The national office for years was in the office of the Chicago *Union Labor Advocate,* which also printed the League's Woman's Department. In 1911 the League launched its own monthly publication, *Life and Labor,* edited by Alice Henry.

The League was not officially affiliated with the A. F. of L., but its constitution read: "To assist in organizing women into trade unions . . . such unions to be affiliated, where practicable, with the American Federation of Labor." The A. F. of L. greeted the new venture politely, and its leaders gave it lip-service support. But the Federation did very little to encourage the League in its work, and the Executive Council as well as many of the international affiliates often threw obstacles in its path. Although the League, particularly its state branches, did set up some unions,* and took an active part in strikes of women workers, organizing the strikers, picketing, raising bail or strike funds, mobilizing public opinion, and running relief kitchens and welfare committees, its main work consisted of bringing to the attention of the public the need for improving the working conditions of women,† providing social activities

* The New York League helped to organize more unions than any other League. From 1904 to 1912, it organized or helped to organize unions among hat trimmers, embroidery workers, textile workers, bakery and confectionery workers, white goods workers, straw hat makers, laundry workers, shirt waist workers, fur workers, paper box makers. (*See Annual Reports of the Women's Trade Union League of New York,* 1907-1912.)

† In March, 1907 the Women's Trade Union League of Chicago joined with Jane Addams of Hull House and others to sponsor the Chicago Industrial Exhibit. The purpose of the display was to "reveal that hard and material side of life which goes on in factories and workshops, to epitomize the labor which clothes and feeds the modern world." Statistics produced at the exihibit showed that girls were earning an average of $7.25 per week, with many earning as little as $3.00. (*Hand Book of the Chicago Industrial Exhibit, Brooke's Casino, Wabash and Peck Court, March 11th to 17th,* Chicago, n.d., pp. 21, 28-30.) The Chicago *Tribune* dismissed the evidence presented at the exihibit with the comment that a bright girl earning such a small sum had only herself to blame, for she could easily earn more if only she applied herself (March 17, 1907).

for working women to bring some pleasure into their drab lives,* and carrying the message of unionism to women workers especially to those in the trades which came to be known as "women's industries"—the clothing, textile, laundry, glove, and hat industries. *Life and Labor* carried letters from women describing the impact of unionism on their lives. One young woman wrote:

"I . . . believe in the Union. It makes us stronger and makes us happier and it makes us more interested in life and to be more interested is oh, a thousand times better than to be so dead that one never sees anything but work all day and not enough money to live on. That is terrible, that is like death."[25]

By furnishing speakers to meetings of unorganized women and to unions who could be interested in the organization of women, the League prepared the ground for unionization of women workers. But it was primarily the job of the women themselves to organize and of the international unions in the A. F. of L., under whose jurisdiction the trade fell, to charter the group.† Too often, unfortunately, the A. F. of L. affiliate refused to follow up the League's preparatory work and complete the organizing activity "on the plea that the International Union is not ready to organize the women." Too often, as a result, the League had to report sadly that the women were forced to abandon the idea of organizing, "and as a group are lost to organized labor." Efforts were made to set up indepedent organizations for the women, but all eventually fell to pieces.[26]

The League's leaders became so disgusted with the hostile attitude of many of the A. F. of L. affiliates that they appealed to the Executive Council to take action either to compel the international unions to accept the women or charter them directly to the Federation in separate federal labor unions. But they always came up against the autonomy doctrine, and were coldly informed that "the American Federation of Labor had no authority to touch the question, either through its Executive Council or in convention—that so long as the Internationals claimed jurisdiction, the A. F. of L. could never compel them to accept women as members

* In Chicago, for example, the League offered hockey, folk dancing, outings, a library room, and a chorus to girls seeking recreation. The League organized its social activities on a ward and precinct basis. One of the Organizers reported that "the ward parties of the League continue to grow in popularity. . . . The programmes have been varied to meet the tastes of residents in each ward." An evening's entertainment might consist of a dramatic skit, music, and a speech. (*Life and Labor*, May, 1911, p. 158; *Some of the Happy Features of the Women's Trade Union League of Chicago*, n.p., n.d.)

† In its annual report for 1907–08, the New York League pointed out: "While the Women's Trade Union League has been working for the organization of women into trade unions it has recognized that the direct work of organization will be done by the women themselves and that its own work is largely educational."

nor issue federal charters to women whom the International refused to organize." In one instance, the League asked whether the A. F. of L. could not say to the International Typographical Union: "If you will not organize the [women] copyholders or accept them into your organization, you must relinquish the jurisdiction." The answer was no![27]

At the 1907 A. F. of L. convention, the League was represented by several fraternal delegates. They were treated politely as usual, and Agnes Nestor, a regular delegate from the International Glove Workers' Union of which she was secretary-treasurer, as well as a fraternal delegate from the League, was called to the platform by Gompers and asked to preside.* "Woman Presides at A. F. of L. Convention," were the headlines in newspapers all over the country the next day.[28]

The A. F. of L. leadership was not so polite when it came to dealing with the League's delegates' request that a woman organizer be appointed on the Federation's staff. The Executive Council, to whom the convention had turned over the request, kept the League's committee cooling their heels for a fortnight waiting for an interview—in vain.[29]

In 1908, Annie Fitzgerald was appointed as a general organizer by the Executive Council "for the purpose of organizing wherever possible all women who work in gainful occupations." She took her work seriously, appealing to the male members of the A. F. of L. for assistance. Conceding that employers had taken advantage of the unorganized status of women workers to beat down wages of the men, she criticized the attitude that the way to end this evil was to deny the women the right to work:

"I doubt whether any movement in that direction would be successful at this, or any other time in the near future. Hence it seems the only logical and sensible thing to do is to organize the women workers in trade unions. Personally I believe that men should first realize that we are confronted by a stern fact, that the women workers are already here, and secondly apply the only remedy at hand, organization. Organize them. Apply the rule of equal pay for equal work for both sexes, and organize, keep on organizing. Do this and I hold that much of the evil complained of in the matter of women workers will be minimized to the lowest possible point. . . . The women can be organized. Will you men do your share in the necessary work? Speaking for the women, I can say, we will do our share, if given proper encouragement."[30]

But "proper encouragement" was the one thing the women could

---

* Agnes Nestor was the first woman president of an international union—the International Glove Workers' Union—and for 35 years, from 1913 till her death in 1948, she headed the Chicago Women's Trade Union League. She spearheaded the drive for the shorter workday for working women as well as for other industrial legislation. Her papers are in the Chicago Historical Society. Her autobiography, *Woman's Labor Leader,* was published in 1954.

hardly expect from the A. F. of L. Before Miss Fitzgerald could fairly get started, her commission was revoked. The A. F. of L. remained without a woman organizer until the period of World War I.[31]

As we shall see in a subsequent volume, it was the great garment strikes of 1909–1913, in which the Women's Trade Union League played an important role, that sparked an upsurge of organization among women workers all over the country. But this took place in spite of the A. F. of L. policy, and as long as the policy remained in effect of passing resolutions urging the organization of women while the individual unions kept them out either by constitutional bars and other discriminatory practices, or by simply refusing to organize them, the over-all picture could not and did not change markedly. Among the 8,075,000 women gainfully employed in 1910, 73,800 or 0.9 per cent, as we have seen, were members of trade unions. This membership broke down as follows: (1) of the 2,407 women employed in liquor and beverage industries, from 20 to 30 per cent were organized; (2) of the 333,000 employed in the clothing and printing and bookbinding industries, from 10 to 15 per cent were organized; (3) of the 145,870 employed in leather industries and cigar and tobacco factories, from five to 10 per cent were organized; (4) of the 415,000 employed in the lumber, furniture, and textile industries, from one to five per cent were organized; (5) of the remaining 7,180,000, less than one per cent were organized.[32]

In 1900, the situation in most trades so far as union membership of women workers was concerned was epitomized in the following exchange between a member of the U.S. Industrial Commission and G. W. Perkins, president of the Cigar Makers' International Union:

"*Q:* 'Have you many female members?'

"*A:* 'Very few, comparatively speaking, to the large number of females employed in the trade.' "[33]

Twelve years later, the situation had not basically changed. In 1912, only eight unions were officially estimated to have each more than 1,000 women members: the Bakery and Confectionery Workers (1,000), the Brewery Workers (1,200–1,500), the Bookbinders (2,500), the Cigar Makers (4,000), the Typographical Union (5,500), and the United Garment Workers (26,000).[34] * The mass production industries which employed women in large numbers were unorganized.

In 1912 F. E. Wolfe summed up the general attitude of the A. F. of L. toward women workers in a single sentence: "A large portion of the na-

---

* Since these figures are based upon statements issued by the presidents or secretaries of each of these unions, it is quite likely that they are exaggerated. No estimate of the total number of women workers in the A.F. of L. at this time can be made since most international unions did not supply information on the break-down of membership according to sex.

tional trade unions are not concerned with the problems of female labor."[35]

A. F. OF L. AND NEGRO WORKERS

The A. F. of L. leaders never tired of "reiterating, re-endorsing and re-affirming" the fact that the Federation had no color bar, and of proclaiming in speeches that the "workers must organize and unite under the banner of the American Federation of Labor, without regard to race, color, creed, or nationality." But speeches and resolutions "were not actions. In fact, they were often a substitute for action."[36] In terms of declared union policy, it might seem that discrimination had all but vanished in the A. F. of L. In terms of practice, however, discrimination existed openly or with only the flimsiest concealment.

By the opening of the 20th century the A. F. of L. was in full retreat from the progressive position it had earlier taken with regard to Negro labor. The practice followed, as we have seen in a previous volume, during the first few years after the A. F. of L.'s formation, of insisting that unions desiring to enter or remain in affiliation must eliminate the color clause from their constitutions, had been completely abandoned.* About a dozen A. F. of L. unions at this time did actually bar Negroes by specific provisions.† Some accomplished this by constitutional clauses specifying that only "white-born" applicants were eligible; others, like the Machinists, had removed the constitutional ban but not its practice by transferring it to the rituals. Each member was bound by the ritual to propose only white workmen for membership.[37]

Thus the early A. F. of L. policy of equality of workers regardless of color had come to an end. To be sure, the Federation had for several years insisted that no unions could affiliate if their constitutions banned Negroes, but they were accepted if this practice was accomplished through the rituals. After a while, the A. F. of L. officials did not even bother to insist on the elimination of constitutional barriers to Negro membership, but admitted as affiliates organizations which excluded Negroes by constitutional provision. When the Order of Railroad Telegraphers and the Brotherhood of Railway Trackmen, both of which restricted membership to whites in their constitutions, affiliated with the A. F. of L. in 1899 and 1900, Gompers reported their action "with much pleasure," and ex-

---

* See Foner, op. cit., vol. II, pp. 195–204.
† In 1910 the following unions affiliated with the A.F. of L. explicitly excluded Negroes by provisions to that effect in either their constitutions or their rituals: Wire Weavers, Switchmen, Maintenance-of-Way Employees, Railroad Telegraphers, Railway Clerks, Commercial Telegraphers, Machinists, Boiler Makers and Iron Ship Builders. (F. E. Wolfe, Admission to American Trade Unions, Baltimore, 1912, p. 117.)

pressed the hope that the other Railroad Brotherhoods, who were among the worst offenders against Negro workers, would follow suit. It was clear that they could join the Federation, like the Telegraphers and the Trackmen, without altering their constitutional ban against Negroes. In 1902, the Stationary Engineers, a national union affiliated with the A. F. of L., amended its constitution so as to exclude Negroes. Not a word of protest came from Gompers and the Federation. In 1909 and 1910 the Federation admitted the Brotherhood of Railway and Steamship Clerks and the Brotherhood of Railway Carmen even though both organizations openly discriminated against Negro workers.[38]

The admission of the Railway Carmen was particularly resented by Negro workers because it was also accompanied by the departure from the A. F. of L. of the International Association of Car Workers, which refused to amalgamate with the Brotherhood, at the A. F. of L.'s insistence, because of the latter's discrimination against Negroes. The Brotherhood of Railway Carmen was organized in 1888 on the model of the other Railroad Brotherhoods and it followed the others in not affiliating with the A. F. of L. In 1901 the A. F. of L. chartered the International Association of Car Workers. Trouble ensued immediately and amalgamation was suggested. The Brotherhood insisted that if it affiliated, the clause in its constitution denying membership to Negroes must be retained. The International Association of Car Workers refused to accept this condition, and continued to maintain this position even though the leaders of the A. F. of L. urged it to be "reasonable" and proceed along the lines demanded by the Brotherhood. In August 1910, the A. F. of L. Executive Council stopped trying to persuade the International Association of Car Workers to amalgamate with the Brotherhood on the latter's terms, canceled the International's charter, and made the Brotherhood, with its anti-Negro clause still intact, as the "regular" union of the car workers. The International Association protested the decision at the 1910 A. F. of L. convention, accusing the Executive Council of violating its "sacred principle of trade autonomy" and of conspiring with the enemies of labor solidarity, but to no avail. At the 1911 convention, the International Association of Car Workers dramatically surrendered its charter.[39] *

The absence of specific clauses barring Negro members did not mean that Negroes were admitted to other A. F. of L. unions. Many unions whose constitutions or rituals did not specify membership in the "white race" as a prerequisite for admittance, and even some whose constitutions proclaimed the principle of equality of all workers, kept Negroes

---

* The International Association continued under the old name until 1915 when it renamed itself the American Federation of Railroad Workers, and announced that it would function as an industrial union which all railroad workers, Negro and white, might join. (*Proceedings*, A.F. of L. Convention, 1915, p. 177.)

out by tacit agreement. Others achieved this objective by such practices as high initiation fees which Negro workers could not pay; requiring special licenses which Negroes could not obtain; requiring applicants for membership to pass a technical examination which Negroes invariably "flunked," and prohibiting Negroes from becoming apprentices. The last device was especially important, for by refusing to open their apprenticeship programs to young Negroes, many A. F. of L. affiliates kept Negro workers from acquiring the necessary training to qualify as skilled workers.[40]

At the 1900 convention of the A. F. of L. official sanction was given to a Jim-Crow policy of organization. Article 12, Section 6, of the A. F. of L. constitution was revised to read: "Separate charters may be issued to central labor unions, local unions or federated labor unions, composed exclusively of colored workers where in the judgment of the Executive Council it appears advisable." In this way, the A. F. of L. let it be known that affiliated national and local unions could continue to refuse admission to workers because of their color. It was a signal that the A. F. of L. had abandoned even the formality of equal status for Negro workers, and had settled into a fixed policy of Jim-Crowism. Segregation, Gompers declared, was the best settlement of the problem; the separation of Negro and white workers was best for both groups and for the entire labor movement, for it would avoid "arousing bitterness."[41]

Jim-Crow unionism was not regarded by the A. F. of L. as a necessary alternative to the preferred form of organization, to be established only where local prejudice made any other form impossible, but as the only way to solve the whole problem. The A. F. of L. did not make it a condition that the Negro as well as the white workers should desire separate organizations; it did not urge the white unions to accept Negro workers before yielding to the establishment of separate unions; indeed, it specifically refused to make such requests of central labor unions. Moreover, the Federation decided as early as December 1901 that even where there were not enough Negro locals to form separate trades councils, the Central Labor Unions did not have to admit their delegates.[42]

In 1903 Gompers reversed his decision to appoint a Negro organizer for the South when it was protested by the Alabama Federation of Labor. This decision was in keeping with the general trend in the A. F. of L. of allowing the most backward sections in the Federation to call the tune on the Negro question. Even separate Negro unions were not chartered by the Federation unless the international union, affiliated with the A. F. of L. or not, agreed. On November 6, 1903, Morrison wrote to John T. Wilson, president of the International Brotherhood of Maintenance-of-Way Employes: "Your favor of November 2nd received, in which you state that there is no objection on the part of your organization to the A. F. of L. organizing the colored section. In accordance with this communication, we have today issued a charter to the union in New Orleans."[43] But the Executive Council refused to grant charters as federal locals to Negro unions when any international union would neither accept them itself nor surrender jurisdiction over them. On July 9, 1904, J. C. Skemp, secretary-treasurer of the Brotherhood of Painters, Decorators and Paperhangers, wrote to Morrison:

"I have your favor of July 7th informing me that you have received an application for a charter from Moberly, Mo. from a union of colored men with just enough members to secure a charter, that is seven, and one of the applicants is a painter. I also note you state that Organizer Willott of Moberly, who forwarded the application states that there is no objection upon the part of the Local Unions in the trades at which these men are employed, to their organizing in direct affiliation with the A. F. of L., and that there are no objections upon the part of our Local Union in that city of Moberly to the admitting of the colored painter in the Federal Labor Union.

"The International Union, however, does have a serious objection. We are of the opinion that by admitting this colored painter to a Federal Labor Union, it will cause some trouble for our members there, as he would put up the claim that he was a union man affiliated with the A. F. of L. and entitled to all the privileges, with the right to work upon any job regardless of where it may be, or who were employed thereon. If he becomes a member of the Federal Labor Union, he will certainly be required to demand the same scale of wages which is paid to our Local Union in the city of Moberly, Mo. The complications that will arise cause us to urge that the charter not be granted."

Morrison could have replied that the International should take steps to convince the Local Union to accept the Negro painter as a member. Or he might have written that there was nothing tragic in the fact that a Negro member of the A. F. of L. would seek the same wage scale as white members in the trade. But he did neither. The charter was not granted. Thus the A. F. of L. accepted the policy of its affiliates who refused to allow the organization of Negro workers under any condition.[44] In April 1903, the *Electrical World,* organ of the International Brotherhood of Electrical Workers, declared: "We do not want the Negro in the International Brotherhood of Electrical Workers, but we think they should be organized in locals of their own, affiliated with the American Federation of Labor as that organization knows no creed or color."[45] But when Negro workers, forced by discriminatory practices of unions like the Brotherhood of Electrical Workers, organized their own unions and sought affiliation with the A. F. of L., the organization that knew "no creed or color" rejected their applications if the Internationals or their locals, which kept the Negroes out, objected.

Philip Taft, a leading apologist for the A. F. of L.'s retreat from its

earlier progressive position on the question of organizing Negro workers, bases his defense on three main arguments: (1) "Whatever its own
view, the Federation could not determine the admittance policies of the
autonomous unions; as long as they met the other formal requirements
of the A. F. of L., the latter could not inquire into the conduct of its
affiliates." (2) "Prejudice against the Negro was widespread, and the
question was whether organizations of labor could be set up in the
South if the leaders insisted upon retaining white and Negro workers
in the same union. . . . Despite the efforts of the A. F. of L., unions in
Southern communities would not accept Negroes as members. The
Federation was then faced with the question of whether it would devise
some method to meet the situation, destroy its organizations in the
South, or encourage the creation of a 'purely' Southern labor movement."
(3) "The solution devised by the Federation was to permit the organization of separate locals of Negro workers and separate city central labor
bodies. . . . Neither Gompers nor the other leaders considered this solution, forced upon them by circumstances, as felicitous, but unless they
had been ready to surrender the organizations of the South, they had
to accept the compromise. . . . Gompers believed that the Negro was a
good and loyal union man, and he regarded the article of the A. F. of L.
constitution which provided for separate locals and central bodies of
Negro workers as a necessity because integrated locals and central bodies
were not possible."[46]*

Apart from the fact that the doctrine that each international union
was autonomous and undisciplinable was the same doctrine used to defend inaction against hoodlums, common thieves, and other assorted
scoundrels in the labor movement, the truth is that the A. F. of L.
did not hesitate to discard this doctrine whenever it wished to eliminate
affiliates who pursued a radical, militant economic and political program. The existence of prejudice against Negroes in the trade unions,
particularly in the South, is certainly not to be denied. But it was used
by the A. F. of L. leaders as an excuse to do nothing to overcome this
prejudice. Here was an opportunity to launch a broad program of education to convince the more backward elements in the labor movement
that discriminatory practices injured all workers, white as well as Negro.
But the fact is that during the first decade of the century, neither Gompers nor the Federation came forward with any plan for education on

* For similar defenses of the A.F. of L. policy toward Negro workers, see Gerald
N. Grob, "Organized Labor and the Negro Worker, 1865–1900," Labor History,
vol. I, Spring, 1960, pp. 173–76, Gerald N. Grob, Workers and Utopia, pp. 153–57,
and Daniel Levine, "Gompers and Racism: A Strategy of Limited Objectives,"
Mid-America, vol. XLIII, April, 1961, pp. 106–13. Levine adds a new twist to the
ideological defense of Jim-Crow unionism by asserting that Gompers' retreat from
his earlier progressive views on organizing Negro workers only proved how "class-
conscious" he was.

this vital subject. The result was that the more backward elements set the policy of the Federation, and continued to do so without resistance by the A. F. of L. leadership.

Actually, as we shall see, the leaders of the Federation shared many of the prejudices of the backward elements in the trade unions. The view that Gompers regarded the Negro as a good and loyal union man was, as we shall see, refuted by his own statements. Finally, as the A. F. of L. leaders themselves admitted, the pattern of Jim Crow unionism was not regarded as a temporary solution to remain in existence until the more backward workers learned the need for integrated unionism, but as the only, the permanent way to deal with the problem.

NEGROES DRIVEN OUT OF TRADES

Taft and other apologists for A. F. of L. policies ignore the fact that the craft union basis of the Federation was a major obstacle in any attempt to organize great numbers of Negroes. Not only were the mass of the Negro workers unskilled, but in the very years that the A. F. of L. was abandoning even the formality of equal status for the Negro, they were systematically being driven out of the skilled trades in the South. During the 1880's and early 1890's, Negro labor in Southern cities was important in railroading, shipping and building. Beginning in the late 1890's, the Negro workers in Southern cities were steadily eliminated from skilled jobs. White workers displaced Negro firemen, switchmen, and shop workers from the railroads. In the building trades the Negroes felt the sting of economic discrimination most harshly. Negro electricians, plumbers, pipe fitters, and carpenters constituted a high percentage of those crafts towards the close of the 19th century. By 1950, Negroes constituted only one per cent of the electricians and 3.24 per cent of the carpenters. The figures on Negro participation in apprenticeship programs were even bleaker. They showed one per cent for plumbers and pipe fitters, and six-tenths of one per cent for carpenters.[47]

Booker T. Washington, head of Tuskegee Institute and the outstanding Negro leader favoring accommodation to segregation, advanced the theory that the Negro was losing out in trades and occupations only because of improper training. Explaining the decline of work skills among Negro laborers, he wrote in 1903: "For nearly twenty years after the war, except in a few instances, the value of the industrial training given by the plantations was overlooked. Negro men and women were educated in literature, in mathematics and in the sciences. . . . As a generation began to pass, those who had been trained as mechanics in slavery began to disappear by death, and gradually it began to be realized that there were young men educated in foreign tongues, but few in capacity."[48] This interpretation was quickly seized upon by apologists for white supremacy, even in the ranks of organized labor, and the blame was thus placed on the radical white allies of the Negro during Reconstruction.

As early as 1903, this argument was demolished by W. E. B. Du Bois, the militant leader of the Negro rights movement, who pointed out that there were less than 3,000 living Negro college graduates in the United States, and that less than 1,000 Negroes were attending institutions of higher learning. Actually, what had happened was that the Negro was being driven out of the skilled trades by the conspiracy of employers and the craft unions. The records of various Negro conferences in the early years of the 20th century are filled with accounts of Negroes being pushed out of industries because white workers, members of A. F. of L. unions or of the Railroad Brotherhoods, refused to work beside them.* In 1909, the white locomotive engineers of Georgia removed Negro locomotive firemen from the industry by the simple expedient of striking until the Negroes were replaced by whites. With the cooperation of the carriers, the Brotherhoods also succeeded in excluding Negro firemen from service in Pittsburgh and Cleveland. At Pittsburgh, the Baltimore & Ohio officials agreed that they would make no effort to hire other Negroes, and that those already employed would be removed. As late as 1917 there was no record of a Negro engineer in road service. Warren S. Stone, Grand Chief of the Engineers, argued that Negroes would not make good engineers because they "could not keep awake and always lost their heads in an emergency."[49]†

By refusing to admit Negro members and by preventing union members from working with men who were not in the union, the craft organizations pushed Negro workers out of skilled positions. Where Negro craftsmen were organized in separate Jim-Crow locals, they received little or no assistance from the city central labor bodies, composed of white men drawn from white locals. The skilled places held by the members of the Negro local were eyed jealously by the white craft unions which waited only for an opportunity to displace the Negro workers. Smaller and therefore less powerful, the Negro local was severely handicapped. The national unions to which the Jim-Crow locals were affiliated refused to protect their jobs or wage scales.[50]

* Before the formation of the Brotherhood of Engineers and Firemen, Negroes held many of the higher paying railroad jobs. Many were firemen and brakemen. After the formation of the Brotherhood, Negroes were pushed out of these positions, and were replaced by men who were eligible for membership in the all white Brotherhood.

† In an effort to gain new members, the Brotherhood considered extending its jurisdiction to Cuba. After investigation, the union concluded that it would be impossible to draw a color line in Cuba and dropped the plan. (George James Stevenson, "The Brotherhood of Locomotive Engineers and Its Leaders, 1863–1920," unpublished Ph.D. thesis, Vanderbilt University, 1954, p. 246n.)

The institution of formal apprenticeship training, controlled by the craft unions, for "picking up" the trade was an important factor in limiting opportunities for Negroes in the skilled trades. Employers and unions conspired to confine apprenticeships to whites, and with vocational training closed to most Negroes in the South, the Negro was not only excluded from certain occupations he formerly had held, but given little or no opportunity to mount higher on the economic ladder.[51]

From the first, the practice in most Southern factories had been to employ white workers in production jobs and Negroes as janitors and in other unskilled or inferior jobs. The unions, with few exceptions, accepted the racial patterns prevailing in Southern industry. The few Negroes in the cotton mills had lowly jobs, lived apart from the white workers, and were excluded from the A. F. of L.'s United Textile Workers as well as from whatever limited plans this organization made to advance the status of the workers in the industry. In the tobacco factories of Virginia and North Carolina, the machine jobs were reserved for white workers, and the Negroes were confined to the least desirable and most unhealthy jobs. Here, too, the Tobacco Workers' International Union, affiliated to the A. F. of L., scarcely reached the Negroes in its feeble efforts to organize the industry. In November 1903, the Rucker & Witten Tobacco Co. of Martinsville, Virginia, anxious to obtain the union label, approached the Tobacco Workers' International Union with the request that it organize its plant. The offer was rejected on the ground that "nine-tenths of the labor employed is negroes, and this class cannot be successfully organized into a union."[52]

Thus the Negro was steadily driven from the ranks of skilled labor and diverted to menial occupations. Through the conspiracy between employers and many A. F. of L. unions and the Railroad Brotherhoods, "white only" signs were placed upon such trades as electricians, plumbers, gas and steamfitters, railroad engineers and firemen, stationary engineers, cranemen, hoistmen, machinists, and hundreds of other skilled and semi-skilled occupations. As a result, the Negro's place in industry was at the bottom of the scale. No matter where he was employed, he received lower wages than whites for the same job, and usually was limited to the hardest and dirtiest tasks. Negroes who managed to join craft unions found that they had gained little protection. White members received preference for jobs, and several A. F. of L. unions allowed Negro members to work longer hours than white workers and at a lower wage scale.

That the more backward white workers in the South supported this policy is true. But essentially it was part of monopoly's program of complete segregation of workers by which it was able to prevent unity of action and through which it could prevent the wages of white workers from rising much above those for Negroes. Witness after witness told the Industrial Commission of 1900 that the unorganized status of the Negro working class was "a drag on the white laboring class in the South, and tends to cut down their wages." "The white journeymen bricklayer in our section," a Southern employer testified, "gets $2.50 a day, and we are able to employ a colored bricklayer for $1.75." Asked how this affected the wages of the white bricklayer, he replied that "when the white bricklayer . . . asks for employment and makes known his rate of wages, which is $2.50 a day . . . the employer may say to him in return, I can employ a Negro bricklayer who has as much skill as you, and will do a good service for $1.75. Now, I will put you on at $2.25." To the question why not raise the wages of the Negro workers, the employers invariably had one answer: "Notoriously the negro workman of the South is spoiled by prosperity. Advancing his wages has generally tended to make him more of an idler, since at higher wages his wants are supplied by fewer days of labor." But the real key to the Southern employers' attitude was offered by John Graham Brooks in 1903:

"I asked one of the largest employers of labor in the South if he feared the coming of the trade union. 'No,' he said, 'it is one good result of race prejudice that the negro will enable us in the long run to weaken the trade union so that it cannot harm us. We can keep wages down with the negro, and we can prevent too much organization."[53]

THE ISSUE OF NEGRO STRIKEBREAKING

There were frequent statements by A. F. of L. leaders, including those by heads of unions which barred Negroes from membership, revealing that they understood that white workers could not raise their living standards while Negro workers remained on the lowest rungs of the economic ladder. At the turn of the century, Gompers wrote to an A. F. of L. organizer in Houston, Texas:

"So long as one class of workers, black, brown, or green, is left unorganized, and consequently work for long hours and for low wages, it is absolutely impossible for white workmen to make the progess which they otherwise would and should. This is not a matter of sentiment or prejudice or love for or against the colored man; it is a proposition of the most eminent practicability. It is a bald business proposition, and I hope that the opportunity to organize these colored men will not be allowed to slip by."[54]

But in public Gompers had an entirely opposite approach. Thus at the very time that he sent this stirring letter, he told the U. S. Industrial Commission that the Negroes were themselves to blame for the lack of organization among them. If organized labor discriminated against Negroes, it was not because of prejudice against their color, but because they have "so conducted themselves as to be a continuous convenient whip placed in the hands of the employers to cow the white men and to compel them to accept abject conditions of labor." In an article in the *American Federationist,* April 1901, entitled "Trade Union Attitude Toward Colored Workers," Gompers assigned two reasons for the low percentage of Negro membership in the A. F. of L. First, he said Negro workers did not possess the required skill to become members of the craft unions. (He did not mention the fact that most of these unions prevented them from acquiring that skill by refusing to accept them as apprentices.) The second reason was that in many cases, when white workers were on strike, Negroes took their places and thus helped the employers to tear down labor standards and destroy the unions. In short, the Negroes were "cheap workers," and, as such, it was hardly surprising that the unions should regard them as enemies rather than as allies.[55]

The racist approach of the A. F. of L. leadership was expressed most sharply in their efforts to place the blame on the Negroes themselves for their lack of organization and in the Jim-Crow setup in the Federation. In September 1905, Gompers wrote in the *American Federationist* that organized labor desired no controversy with Negroes, "but if the colored man continues to lend himself to the work of tearing down what the white man has built up, a race hatred far worse than any ever known will result. Caucasian civilization will serve notice that its uplifting process is not to be interfered with in any way." About the same time, he told a trade union gathering in St. Paul: "The Caucasians are not going to let their standard of living be destroyed by negroes, Chinamen, Japs, or any others." Negroes, according to the A. F. of L. leaders, like Chinese and Japanese, were not like white workers (the "Caucasians"), and lacked the necessary characteristics that would fit them for union membership. In the *American Federationist,* August 1906, Gompers published an article which referred to Negroes who had been brought to Chicago in 1904 to replace the striking stockyard workers as "hordes of ignorant blacks . . . possessing but few of those attributes we have learned to revere and love . . . huge, strapping fellows, ignorant and vicious, whose predominant trait was animalism." When criticized for this and similar racist statements, Gompers could only reply: "It cannot be expected that with all their traditions, mental, moral and social, and the fact that they are only 50 years removed from slavery, the negro can understand the fundamental philosophy of human right."[56]

In the entire discussion of this issue, the A. F. of L. leaders made not the slightest effort to understand the real reasons for "Negro strikebreaking." This is not surprising since it was the policies of the Federation and many of its affiliates that were largely responsible for this development. A report of an interview with Negro strikebreakers read: "Their defense was the anomalous position assumed by the white unions who refused to unionize colored men and at the same time expected colored men to starve and show a vicarious loyalty by not scabbing."[57] The exclusion of Negro workers from white trade unions forced Negroes to use strikebreaking as a means of getting into an industry from which they had previously been excluded.* Negroes, working in an industry largely as unskilled workers doing the dirtiest and most dangerous jobs and barred from rising to a higher level by the conspiracy between the employers and the craft unions, were forced to use strikebreaking as a means of advancing to better-paying jobs as semi-skilled and skilled workers.

The A. F. of L. leaders also failed to point out that Negroes imported by employers to break strikes did not know the purpose for which they were to be used. Rounded up largely from agricultural areas where they had no industrial contacts, they were unaware of what a strike or a union was. Frequently, when unions informed the Negroes that they were being used to break strikes and made an effort to assist them in their predicament, the Negro workers refused to take the jobs. It was not uncommon to see Negroes carrying passes with the inscription: "This is to certify that the bearer of this card was brought to—on the promise of a legitimate job. Discovering on his arrival that he was to act as strikebreaker, he refused. We kindly ask all good union brothers to assist him in returning to his home in——."[58]

Actually, the whole issue of Negro strikebreaking was exaggerated by the A. F. of L. leaders as an excuse for their own failure to organize the Negro workers. Had these men spent half as much time informing the membership of the A. F. of L. of the heroic role Negroes played in strike struggles, of the fact that in such viciously anti-union centers as West Virginia, the membership of the United Mine Workers was predominantly Negro and that many of the Negro miners made desperate sacrifices to insure the success of their union,† as they did in repeatedly

---

* As a result of the 1895 strike on the Ward Line in New York City, when the company employed Negroes to break a strike, Negroes secured a foothold in the longshore industry from which they had heretofore been excluded by the union. (E. Franklin Frazier, "A Negro Industrial Group," *The Howard Review,* vol. I, June, 1924, p. 148.)

† The *United Mine Workers' Journal* of March 5, 1903 carried a letter from Chris Evans, an official of the union, written from Charleston, West Virginia. Evans had gone to West Virginia to investigate the slaying of three militant Negro miners, leaders of the struggle in that state. These men, William Dodson, William Clark and Richard Clayton, were shot to death by Deputy Marshal Dan W. Cunningham and his deputies while they were sleeping. "This shooting," Evans wrote, "took place without anything being said to those on the inside [of the house] and the three colored men . . . were found dead on the floor. Two were in their night clothes and the other one was partly dressed, with one shoe on partly laced and the other foot bare. . . . In no instance could we find where these people had asked to surrender until after the deputies had commenced shooting at the occupants of

declaiming against Negro strikebreaking, the American labor movement would have greatly benefited. In many cases where white as well as Negro strikebreakers were used, the presence of Negroes was emphasized and exaggerated. This was the case in Chicago in 1905 during the great teamsters' strike. Of 5,800 strikebreakers used, it was estimated that 5,000 were white. And yet, although the white strikebreakers outnumbered the Negroes by more than 6 to 1, the A. F. of L. leaders singled out the Negroes for special abuse. Writing in *Charities* of October 7, 1905, R. R. White, Negro pastor of Chicago's Trinity Mission, observed correctly:

"The bulk of Negro workmen never consisted of strikebreakers. Nor are Negroes opposed to unions. Many struck with the unions and remained loyal to them at the stockyards. In the teamsters' strike, while there were 800 Negro strikebreakers, the unions held a membership of nearly two thousand Negro teamsters, and one of their number represented the coal drivers at the Philadelphia convention of the Brotherhood of Teamsters in August. . . . Yet it still remains that in times of industrial peace the more desirable places are closed against Negroes, either because the employers will not hire them or the men will not work with them."[59]

DIVISION IN NEGRO'S RANKS

Among the Negro people, the issue of strikebreaking caused considerable discussion; actually, it was part of the split in Negro thinking regarding the advisability of joining unions. Some Negroes opposed unionism and advocated a policy of planned strikebreaking to enable Negro workers to win entry into industries that usually barred them. This attitude had existed throughout the post-Civil War period, but its popularity had declined in the 1880's as a result of the direct appeal of the Knights of Labor for Negro members and the widespread organization of Negro workers by the Order.* This did much to win sentiment among Negro leaders for cooperation with the labor movement. Unfortunately, with the decline of the K. of L., and the abandonment by the A. F. of L. of its early progressive policies towards the organization of Negro workers, the old attitude reasserted itself.

Negro antagonism to unionism stemmed from three sources: (1) resentment against white displacement of Negro workers caused to no

---

the houses named." Evans called "this slaughtering of miners, simply because they are forced to struggle for a just cause . . . a sad commentary on our boasted Republic." For the role of the Negro miners in West Virginia, *see* Charles W. Simmons, John R. Rankin and U. G. Carter, "Negro Coal Miners in West Virginia, 1875-1925," *Midwest Journal,* Spring 1954, pp. 61–86.

   * *See* Foner, *op. cit.,* vol. II, pp. 66–84, 71–74, 161–62.

small degree by the racist policies of many of the craft unions; (2) the barriers to Negro membership in the craft unions, and (3) the influence of Booker T. Washington's accommodation school of thought which stressed the virtues of wealth and the duty of Negroes to win recognition through hard work and unprotesting service. This school also stressed that the Negro must avoid the stigma of association with the radical labor elements, and thus not antagonize the wealthier classes which had the power to give jobs to the Negroes. Washington boasted that the Negro was not inclined to trade unionism,* and he appealed to employers to use Negro labor on the ground that the Negro worker "is almost a stranger to strife, lock-outs and labor wars; labor that is law-abiding, peaceable, teachable . . . labor that has never been tempted to follow the red flag of anarchy."[60]

While the influence of Washington was considerable, opposition to him was developing under the leadership of William E. B. Du Bois, and this, in turn, led to the development of a new attitude towards the trade unions. Du Bois pointed out that Washington abhorred unionism at a time when Negroes were turning from the field to the factory and had to aid in the development of a powerful labor movement; that he preached the values of trusting the "best" whites at a time when these elements were barring the Negroes from the polls and conspiring with reactionary craft unions in developing patterns of segregation which were effectively barring Negroes from most fields of skilled labor. Du Bois advocated a dual position: the Negroes should work unceasingly to build Negro-white unity in the labor movement, but, at the same time, they should challenge and attack bitterly and unrelentingly the pattern of segregation and discrimination in the trade unions.[61]

This dual point of view was set forth at various conferences in the developing Negro freedom movement. The Atlanta Conference on Negro Americans recommended in 1902 that Negroes should support the labor movement where it pursued a fair policy, but denounced the unjust proscription of Negroes practiced by many unions. In 1905, the Niagara movement, one purpose of which was to bring Negroes and trade unions into mutual understanding, held up for "public execration" the practice of unions "in proscribing and boycotting and oppressing thousands of their fellow-toilers, simply because they are black." The National Association for the Advancement of Colored People, formed in 1909 under Du Bois' leadership, urged that Negroes make common cause with the working class, but pointed out that discrimination by the

---

* Actually, Washington refuted his own statement. He reported in 1913 that he had sent a query to a number of trade unions asking whether Negroes on the whole made good union men, and that he had received out of a total of 50 only two replies in the negative. (*Atlantic Monthly*, June, 1913, p. 756.)

trade unions was keeping most Negro workers in a state resembling that of peonage. In 1913, the N.A.A.C.P. put forward a "Minimum Program of Negro Advancement." Among the eleven points were: "The right to work; The end to peonage; Equal service and equal pay for the Negro." Du Bois spelled out the significance of these demands in an editorial in *The Crisis*: "Whatever the tactics, the result is the same for the mass of white workingmen in America; beat or starve the Negro out of his job if you can by keeping him out of the union; or, if you must admit him, do the same thing inside union lines." "So long as union labor fights for humanity, its mission is divine," Du Bois emphasized, but when they fought only for a clique of white skilled workers, practiced segregation and discrimination, and thereby forced competent Negro workers into starvation, "they deserve themselves the starvation which they plan for their darker and poorer fellows."[62]

Despite sharp criticism of union discrimination, every one of the Negro conferences sponsored by the Du Bois forces emphasized that the interests of white and Negro labor were identical, and proposed that the A. F. of L. (and the Railroad Brotherhoods) cooperate with the Negro freedom movement in achieving admission of black labor into the unions. These appeals fell on deaf ears. When Du Bois proposed this to Gompers in 1902, in urging the A. F. of L. president to comment on a memorandum he was preparing for publication dealing with the lack of Negro membership in the trade unions due to the discriminatory policies of these organizations and the failure of the unions to train Negro apprentices,* Gompers replied coldly: "I should say that your statement is neither fair nor accurate. . . . You are inclined, not only to be pessimistic upon the subject, but you are even unwilling to give credit where credit is due. Let me say further, that I have more important work to attend to than correct 'copy' for your paper."[63]

Actually, the A. F. of L. leadership had little sympathy with the militant policies of the Du Bois school. Although Gompers had once criticized Booker T. Washington for recommending that Negroes rely on the good will of their employers to improve their status, he was later reconciled to his conservative policy of achieving freedom "by the slow process of education and development," and by "rendering service to society that would assure their value and independence."[64]

---

* Du Bois disclosed that 43 national organizations, including the Railroad Brotherhoods, had no Negro members and that in 16 of these this was due to the discriminatory policies of the unions. His report estimated that there were only 40,000 Negroes in the A.F. of L., and that half of this number were in the United Mine Workers. It revealed further that in some of the A.F. of L. affiliates a decrease had occurred in Negro membership during the decade, 1890–1900, during which decade, it pointed out, the A.F. of L.'s policy had retrogressed from its earlier limited progressive policy.

A. F. OF L. AND NEGRO RIGHTS

The A. F. of L. rarely registered any protest against disfranchisement of Southern Negroes, lynchings, exclusion of Negroes from jury service, inferior and segregated accommodations in the public schools and colleges, railroads, and other public places, chain gangs, involuntary servitude through debt peonage, and other injustices heaped upon the Negro people. To be sure, at the 1895 convention, the A. F. of L. had denounced restrictions on the suffrage and directed the Executive Council to aid, and if necessary take the initiative, in thwarting the disfranchisement movement. But neither Gompers nor any of the other members of the Executive Council did anything to carry out the instructions. Thereafter the A. F. of L. was silent even though the movement to disfranchise and otherwise oppress the Negro people in the South was at its height. In 1900, at least 104 Negroes were lynched, and by 1914 the number of victims of murderous mobs had reached 1,079. Appeals directed to Gompers calling upon the A. F. of L. to speak out in protest against "those horrible 'lynchings' that are now disgracing the nation" were filed and forgotten. Gompers gave the reason for this indifference in an address at Jacksonville, Florida, in which he stated that neither he nor the A. F. of L. had any desire to interfere with the "internal affairs" of the South. "I regard the race problem as one with which you people of the Southland will have to deal; without the interference, too, of meddlers from the outside." To the Negro people who were calling for full equality, he had only one piece of advice: "You must hold on and hope for a time."[65]

In 1910, in the course of an address to the trades council of St. Louis, Gompers was quoted by the local press as having "read the negro out of the labor movement." This was reported throughout the country, and resulted in a flood of protests from Negro spokesmen, including even Booker T. Washington. Taken aback, Gompers stated that he had been misquoted and that the alleged remark in no way represented his attitude toward the Negroes. What he did say, he explained, was that it was difficult to organize Negro workers because they did not have the same conception of their rights and duties as did the white workers, and were unprepared for fully exercising and enjoying the possibilities existing in trade unionism.[66] Once again Gompers placed the blame for their lack of organization on the Negroes themselves. In short, he had not read the Negroes out of the labor movement; the Negro workers had read themselves out of the labor movement.

But it is quite likely that the original report of what Gompers had said was accurate. He said much the same thing on other occasions. The New York *Evening Post* struck the right note in the controversy when it commented that regardless of whether Gompers had been quoted correctly, there was "nothing in his utterances at St. Louis or elsewhere which we have seen that indicates an earnest desire to enroll many negroes among his supporters or to give them a real welcome....

"So far as the American Federation of Labor is concerned, it originally took the position that it would admit no union which discriminated in its charter against the colored man. But that high ground has been abandoned. In 1902 it recognized the legality of excluding negroes from local unions, central labor bodies, or federal labor unions. National unions which expressly exclude negroes are now affiliated with the federation, and, in 1902, the Stationary Engineers altered their by laws so as to exclude negroes. At the Atlanta University conference on the negro artisan in 1902 a list was given of 44 of the most important unions, several with a membership of over 80,000, which have not a single negro member.*

"Obviously, in view of this drift in his organization, it is highly significant that while Gompers denies having advocated putting out the negroes from the unions, he does not deny having advocated their not being admitted. Yet it must be conceded that denying them fellowship on equal basis within unions is a denial of the democracy which the trades unions have heretofore declared to be the cornerstone of their entire edifice....

"For Gompers and his workmen, in the long run, the proper policy is to admit negroes and to do their share in elevating them, in asking for them the education which, in many sections, is practically denied them, and in giving them higher standards of living and the greater responsibility which comes with a more important social and economic position."[67]

A labor leader with foresight would have distributed this editorial to the members of the A. F. of L. and called for action to carry out its wise advice. But Gompers ignored it entirely. Gompers, as Bernard Mandel points out "sacrificed both his principles and the Negro workingman as well as the broader interests of the labor movement, to the short-sighted and selfish demands of the aristocratic officialdom of the craft unions whose spokesman he had agreed to be." In an editorial in the *American Federationist* for July 1915, Gompers stated that "there are now two great groups of exploited workers in the United States—immigrants and women." He not only did not include Negroes, but even in his reference to women, he made it clear that he meant white women. He said nothing

* The Atlanta University conference, organized by Dr. W. E. B. Du Bois, also revealed that 19 national unions, with a total membership of nearly 400,000, had about 33,000 Negroes. Eleven more with almost 100,000 workers had a negligible proportion of Negro members. Twenty-three other unions reported having none, while one was undecided and another had no record. Fully 13 national organizations excluded Negroes outright. (W. E. B. Du Bois, *The Negro Artisan,* Atlanta, Ga., 1902, pp. 158, 164, 167.)

about the fact that Negro women had a double burden to bear: discrimination as a woman and as a Negro, and that they were excluded from employment and from the unions by both sex and color.* In his 1,100-page autobiography, Gompers devoted only two sentences to the subject of Negro labor: the statement that he believed Negroes should have the right to organize.[68] Indeed, the topic "Negro" does not even appear in the 70-page index to the autobiography, covering seventy years of the American labor movement.

Gompers' lack of concern and awareness of the problems of Negro workers reflected the basic policy of the A. F. of L. on this vital issue. It is hardly surprising that many Negroes became embittered and were receptive to the idea of strikebreaking as a means of gaining entry and re-entry into some of the trades.

NEGRO-WHITE UNITY

While the employers have always found it to their advantage to play off one group of workers against another, particularly by stirring up strife between Negro and white workers, there were many examples in the early 1900's of unity between Negro and white workers both North and South. In place of platitudes, so often spoken by Gompers and other A. F. of L. leaders, the Chicago Federation of Labor, representing all the organized bodies of the city, issued an appeal to Negroes in 1900 urging: "Come into our trades unions, give us your assistance and in return, receive our support, so that race hatred may be forever buried, and the workers of the country united in a solid phalanx to demand what we are justly entitled to—a fair chance of the fruits of our industry." Responding to this appeal, Negroes did join a number of unions in Chicago and became noted for their zealousness "for the cause of unionism." By 1905 there were a half dozen Negro delegates from unions to the Chicago Federation of Labor, and several Negro local union officers.[69]

Mary E. McDowell described the entrance of a Negro candidate for admission to the woman's union organized by the girls in the Chicago stockyards: "It was a dramatic occasion on that evening, when an Irish girl at the door called out—'A Colored sister asks admission. What shall I do with her?' And the answer came from the Irish young woman in

* The proportion of employed Negro women during this period was almost three times as large as that of white women, but they were confined to a narrow range of occupations. By far the greatest number of Negro women wage earners in 1910 (1,904,494 out of 2,013,981) were engaged in agriculture and domestic and personal service. They were bound to the lowest paid jobs, and, more than any other group of women, excluded from any other occupation. Manufacturing and mechanical industries which employed 1,366,959 women in 1910 employed only 16,835 Negro women. Of these 16,835 women in industrial occupations, 10,672, or 65 per cent, were laborers or semi-skilled operatives in cigar and tobacco factories. ("Negro Women in Industry," *Bulletin of the Women's Bureau*, No. 20, p. 5.)

the chair—'Admit her, of course, and let all of you give her a hearty welcome!' And as a tall, dignified, but frightened colored girl walked up the aisle between a crowd of girls, Irish, German, American, Polish, Bohemian, some well dressed, others with a shawl or handkerchief over the head, one felt that there was here a law stronger than that of Roberts Rules of Order."[70]

Stronger, too, than lofty pronouncements by the A. F. of L. leadership! The understanding that unity benefitted all workers was revealed in the fact that the Irish longshoremen of New York discovering that the Negro outside of the union was "a perpetual menace as a scab . . . decided it was better to admit him as an ally," and organized them as members of their union with equal status with the white workers.[71] It was also revealed in a remarkable agreement reached in New Orleans in 1902 between the white and Negro screwmen by which all jobs would be worked on a half-and-half basis, an equal number of whites and Negroes. The two unions, Negro and white, both affiliated with the A. F. of L., joined forces to demand regulation of the day's work. Within a month the two unions, in spite of the fact that the Negro organization had still two years to go on a three-year contract, united to regulate the number of bales the workers were supposed to load each day.[72] "In a gang of four men," the New Orleans *Daily Picayune* reported on October 22, 1902, "working in a hold, two of them must be black. If the man at a forward hatch is white, the one aft must be black. . . . If the whites and blacks stand together . . . then all will be serene again on the levee." There was to be equal wages and working conditions as well as equal division of jobs. But the white and Negro unions still met in separate places, and it was felt that to avoid misunderstanding and friction deliberately fostered by the employers,* a unifying central body should be organized. This led to the formation of the Dock and Cotton Council, a representative body composed of an equal number of white and Negro delegates. The 72 delegates, half white, half Negro, represented 36 unions of dock workers, and the offices of the Dock and Cotton Council were divided equally between white and Negro: president—white, vice president—Negro; financial secretary—white; corresponding secretary—

---

* Six years later, during a State investigation of the Port of New Orleans, E. S. Swan, president of the Colored Longshoremen, explained how the employers operated: "I knew the time when the whites wouldn't work with the negroes, and when they found that they were up against it, the two sides agreed to take separate parts of the ship and work. The negroes had the forward hatches and the whites the aft hatches, and the bosses used to go to the niggers and say, 'Niggers, them white men is beating you two to one; if you don't do better, we'll give all the work to the whites.' Then they'd tell the same thing to the whites, and they kept war to the knife, and knife to the hilt, between the two races, and a riot was likely to break out at any time. Then the two races amalgamated." (New Orleans *Daily Picayune,* March 14, 1908.)

Negro, etc. At each annual election, the rotation of officers was reversed. And delegates addressed each member and officer as "brother."[73]

In 1907, white and Negro unionists in New Orleans joined in a general levee strike which involved 10,000 workers in the following unions: White and Negro screwmen, white and Negro longshoremen, white and Negro yardmen, coal wheelers (all Negroes), teamsters and loaders (all Negroes), freight handlers (mixed white and Negro), cotton inspectors and markers (all white), scale hands (all Negroes). The strike started when the employers refused to renew the 1906 contract. It lasted 20 days, without a single break in the ranks of the men. The outstanding feature of the strike was the unity of the white and Negro workers. President E. S. Swan of the Negro longshoremen declared:

"The whites and Negroes were never before so strongly cemented in a common bond and in my 39 years of experience of the levee, I never saw such solidarity. In all the previous strikes the Negro was used against the white man,* but that condition is now past and both races are standing together for their common interests. . . . If the two would combine everywhere as they have combined here, they would have better conditions."[74]

They continued to "stand together" until the end of the strike. The New Orleans *Times-Picayune* tried to break the unity of Negro and white with a red-baiting article charging that it was a "simple fact that a number of negroes have been anarchists and fanatical denouncers of authority." But the strikers answered by solidifying their ranks even more solidly. On October 24, the employers gave in. The arbitration committee was to consist of two or four from each side with an impartial umpire to be selected by Mayor Behrman and the president of the Cotton Exchange. The screwmen named two whites and two Negroes as their representatives, "dividing the appointments," the New Orleans *Daily Picayune* noted, "just as they do their work on the levees." The employers' representatives refused to meet with the Negroes. The Mayor attempted to intimidate the Negro secretary of the strike committee with the remark: "Take these names back to your association and let the members know that interests demand that there will be no colored men on the committee." When this demand was rejected, the Mayor appeared before the Dock and Cotton Council, the labor body to which all the levee unions were affiliated, and urged that the screwmen appoint only white men. "The Mayor sagely pointed out," reported the *Daily Picayune,* "the feelings and conditions in this section, but despite the logical contentions, the

* This was not entirely accurate, for in the great national strike of 1892 in New Orleans there was tremendous unity between white and Negro workers. Indeed, one labor leader in 1907 remarked that "the city still remembers the big tieup of 1892, when all the labor unions, white and negro, walked out in sympathy with the carmen, and not even the electric lights in the city were burning." (New Orleans *Daily Picayune,* Oct. 11, 1907. For a discussion of the 1892 general strike, *see* Foner, *op. cit.,* vol. II, pp. 200–04.)

negro stood firm and the Council backed him up. . . . A well known white longshoreman and a mulatto, whose reputation as an agitator and a leader of the disturbing element among the screwmen is wide, were the committee who came downstairs to inform the Mayor that his mission had born no fruit."[75]

The Mayor then wrote sadly to the shipowners: "For your information I would state that the screwmen have selected as their representatives: Edward Nestor, James Jemison, Edward Gay and John D. Grandeson. I regret to say that the last two named are colored men appointed against my earnest appeal to the organization." The shipowners' representatives still refused to meet. "Mr. George," the *Daily Picayune* reported, "who is a Kentuckian, with all the instincts and traditions of the true Southern gentleman, stated last evening without reservations that he would not serve on the committee with negroes." Another employers' representative, the Manager of the Texas Transport & Terminal Co., was described as a "Virginia gentleman, a former major in the Confederate army," and he stated publicly "that he would not serve with darkeys."[76]

The issue was then brought to the New Orleans Central Labor Union with the plea that it use its influence to eliminate the Negroes from the committee. But this, too, was rejected. President T. R. LeBlanc of the C.L.U. declared in a public statement: "There being a controversy relative to the acceptance of negro representatives on the Port Investigating Committee, and as debarring them would only be an injustice to the thousands of negroes who constitute a majority of the laboring organizations of New Orleans, and would tend to make a settlement of the present trouble more difficult, it is to be hoped that the objections will be withdrawn. The negro has always been a strong bulwark in the labor union movement, and as he forms the greater number of the laborers in general it would be unjust and untimely to debar him."[77]

The New Orleans press desperately tried to scare the white trade unionists into retreating from their firm position by charging that the Negroes wanted representation on the committee not so much for economic reasons but to achieve social equality. They were using the strike settlement as a means of "trying to further pull down the barriers which bar them from equity in all things with the superior race." But the scare fell flat. The white trade unionists of New Orleans stood firm. In the end, the employers had to yield. They chose representatives who, reluctantly, were willing to meet with the Negroes in order to settle the strike.[78]

During the meetings of the Committee of Sixteen, the employers again tried to split the ranks of the strikers by warning the white trade unionists that they were undermining the sacred honor of the state of Louisiana. But this failed utterly. As the Negro trade union representative declared: "We are not here to save the honor and prosperity of the great

WOMEN AND NEGRO WORKERS

State of Louisiana. We are here to settle the strike." The strike settlement brought the white and Negro workers all of their original demands.[79]

The unity of Negro and white workers so manifest during the strike continued after the struggle was over. The New Orleans *Daily Picayune* of March 28, 1908, carried the following dialogue that took place before the Port Investigating Commission:

"Do I understand you to say that twelve white men, and twelve negroes dominate the commerce of this port?" Senator Cordill asked.

William J. Kearney, stevedore for the Harrison Line answered, "Yes, sir."

"Well, sir, we are practically under negro government," was Senator Cordill's comment.

The New Orleans strike was one of the most stirring manifestations of labor solidarity in American history. The leaders of the A. F. of L. would have done more for the progress of the labor movement if they had spent one day in New Orleans during this strike than all of the evenings they spent at National Civic Federation dinners and banquets.

In July 1906, the New York *Age,* a Negro weekly, reported that "New York was treated to the extraordinary spectacle of white union men striking to compel a company of contractors to recognize the Afro-American members of the union." When the Cecilia Asphalt Paving Co. began to replace Negro pavers and rammersmen with Irish and Germans, James S. Wallace, the Negro agent of the International Union of Pavers and Rammersmen, informed the officers of the union "that his men were not getting a square deal." The report in the *Age* continues:

" 'Then we'll call out all of our union members,' replied the officers; and in a short while nearly all the white workmen laid down their tools.

"The superintendent of the company hustled to the spot posthaste and tried to persuade the white men to go back to work.

" 'Beat it,' replied they, 'unless you give us a written guarantee to recognize all the members of our union, black as well as white.'

" 'I'll give you the letter tomorrow at 10 o'clock,' conceded the contractor.

" 'Then we'll be back tomorrow at 10 o'clock,' said the union men.

"The next morning the letter was forthcoming, and all the men triumphantly went back to their tools."[80]

Speaking shortly after this display of Negro and white unity, James S. Wallace said: "Years of experience have impressed upon my mind that a mutual understanding between the white and Negro men whom you may call the laborers and mechanics, or the common people, would have a good and wholesome effect upon both races. . . .

"Labor and capital will never be reconciled, and he who advances the capitalist ideas cannot be looked upon as a friend of labor. . . . When the millions of poor working people recognize that the interest of one poor man is the concern of all, and that a blow struck at the Negro's progress affects the entire working class; when they agree to stand for one object, and let the object be better conditions, racial troubles will be reduced to the minimum."[81]

Not a few white trade unionists learned from bitter experience the truth of Wallace's remarks. "We are commencing to see a few things," declared the Davenport, Iowa, local of the United Brotherhood of Leather Workers after the employers had taken advantage of the union's discrimination policy to use Negro workers as strikebreakers. "The prejudice we have held against color is beginning to vanish. A man may be white, black, brown, red or yellow, if he is a toiler he is one of us and part of us, for if his scale of living is lower than ours, our own is not secure, for 'no chain is securer than the weakest link in it.'"[82] In short, instead of using and exaggerating his role as a strikebreaker to justify the failure to organize Negro workers, this union drew the logical conclusion that the solution lay in unity and solidarity of all workers.

RESULTS OF A. F. OF L. POLICY

Unfortunately, the weak and vacillating attitude of the A. F. of L. with regard to organization of Negroes persisted. The A. F. of L. leaders continued to make declarations of the necessity of organizing Negroes, but did very little about their affiliated unions which kept out Negroes other than blaming the Negro workers themselves. The result was the effective exclusion of the vast majority of Negro workers from the Federation. In 1910–12, most A. F. of L. affiliates had either no Negro members or "a few." The largest membership was in the United Mine Workers which had 40,000. The Teamsters had 6,000 Negro members; the Cigar Makers, 5,000; the Hotel and Restaurant Employees, 2,500; and the Carpenters, 2,500. But the Printers had only 250, the Pressmen less than six, the Lithographers one, the Photo-Engravers less than six, the Iron, Steel and Tin Workers two or three, the Potters none, the Glass Bottle Blowers none, the Hatters none, the Molders 12, Pattern Makers 1, Glass Workers "a few," Boot and Shoe Workers five, and the Wood Workers "a few." These statistics clearly reveal why the annual earnings of Negro workers in 1910 approximated just about one-third of the earnings of white workers, and why a report of the status of the Negro in Philadelphia could read:

"The negroes in this section are practically shut out from all the skilled industries. The department stores may draw attention to the underpaid shopgirl, but the few colored women who find employment in them receive less pay than the sales people. The colored waitress receives a child's wage. The other opportunities open to negroes in big stores are limited to portering and operating elevators. The great railway systems, too, discriminate against the negro, and here he is limited, no matter how high a degree of efficiency he may attain, to the menial and poorly paid tasks. Our street railways, with their thousands of workmen in the semi-skilled trades, completely bar the colored man. He is excluded from practically all of the great industrial plants. This exclusion is especially striking in one great shop that at this minute employs more than 19,000 men daily, but carefully avoids the negro. In brief, the negro is denied the opportunity to earn an honest living in most of the big industries and commercial enterprises of this city."[83]

What was true of Philadelphia was true for much of the state of Pennsylvania. In the entire state, a study revealed in 1911, fewer than 200 Negroes boasted skilled union status.[84] And what was true of Pennsylvania was true for the United States as a whole! "The net result of all this," wrote W. E. B. Du Bois sadly, "has been to convince the American Negro that his greatest enemy is not the employer who robs him, but his fellow white workingman."[85]

CHAPTER 10

The Immigrant Workers

Next only to the Negro people, the immigrant masses were most seriously affected by the restrictive policies of the A. F. of L. and of most of its affiliated craft unions. Indeed, the Jim-Crow basis on which the A. F. of L. functioned paved the way for a racial approach to foreign-born workers, and the "white supremacy" theories that had been directed against Negroes were now turned against Italians, Poles, Jews, Hungarians—and especially against Asians.[*]

A. F. OF L. AND EUROPEAN IMMIGRANTS

Wave on wave, the immigrant tide rolled onto American shores. The first wave of immigrants, prior to 1880, was constituted of English, Irish, Scottish, German, and Scandinavian. The second wave represented the migration of eastern, southeastern, and southern Europeans. From 1881 to 1910, 1,562,000 Jews and 3,005,000 Italians flocked to this country. Altogether in those 30 years there landed in our ports 17,730,000 newcomers. From 1905 to 1914 over a million newcomers entered the country every year.[1]

Of the 7,048,953 immigrants admitted during the 12 years from 1899 to 1910 and reporting an occupation, 35.9 per cent were laborers and 23.4 per cent were farm workers. In the year ending June 1903, nearly one half or 46.5 per cent of all immigrants to this country were either urban or farm laborers, and only 14.5 per cent were skilled workers.[2] The overwhelming majority were thus of peasant stock, with peasant backgrounds and skills. They did not, however, become farmers or agricultural workers here. Hundreds of thousands of American farmers were moving from the land

---

[*] A number of A.F. of L. leaders referred to themselves as "white men," lumping the Italians, Poles, and Negroes as non-white. (*See Final Report and Testimony Submitted to Congress by the Commission of Industrial Relations Created by the Act of August 23, 1912,* Washington, 1916, vol. III, pp. 2069, 2125, 2159, 2171.)

into the cities and factories, and the need was obviously not for farmers to replace them, but for the immigrant farmers to join them as unskilled and semi-skilled workers in heavy industry and in construction work.

Each immigrant group was herded into a special kind of occupational concentration. The Italians were concentrated in construction work, road-building, and ditch-digging, not because the Italian farmer had come to the United States prepared to dig ditches, but because if he did not take that kind of work he found it hard to get any other. Similarly, the Slav peasants were drawn into the coal and steel areas and the Bohemians into the slaughter and packing houses of Chicago. The Jewish immigrants, unlike most of the immigrant groups, were not of peasant but of urban origin.* They came from the cities, large and small, and they had urban occupations and skills.† Occupational restrictions in Eastern Europe had concentrated the Jews in light industry. In the United States, light industry was expanding rapidly, particularly the clothing, metal-working, wood-working, building, textile, and tobacco industries. It was in these industries, and particularly in the clothing industry, that the Jewish workers concentrated, continuing the occupations they had engaged in prior to their emigration.[3]

Although industrial expansion rapidly assimilated the mass of humanity eager to find work in their new homeland, the vast majority were neglected by the A. F. of L. Not that they were not in dire need of being organized. "Many," as one student points out, "exchanged the stagnation of a feudal society for the bondage of an industrial system. The riches of the new world were frequently a mirage, and the dream of American opportunity led often to the sweatshop, where laborers slept on unswept floors littered with work refuse while their worktables doubled as dining tables. They labored fantastically long hours; a 4 A.M. to 10 P.M. day was not uncommon. . . . Immigrant workers cried out in despair: 'We worked, worked, and our profits went into the hands of others.' If they protested, they were summarily discharged by employers who easily recruited other immigrants to fill vacant places."[4]

Even if the A. F. of L. leaders had shown an inclination to organize the immigrant workers, its predominantly craft structure would have made this almost impossible. The average of skilled workers in the total immigration from 1899 to 1910 was 20.2 per cent; the vast majority, as we have seen, were unskilled and semi-skilled. (About three-quarters of the

---

* Tsarist restrictions in Russia forced the Jews into the urban centers.

† Among the Jewish immigrants from 1899 to 1910, 67.1 per cent were skilled workers. The Jewish skilled workers had a higher percentage than those immigrants who came even from industrially advanced countries like Scotland (57.9 per cent), or England (48.7 per cent); or Bohemia and Moravia (40.8 per cent). It was the skilled worker who was the main figure in the Jewish immigration of that period. (*Universal Jewish Encyclopedia,* vol. VII, pp. 547–49.)

2,250,000 Italians who entered the United States between 1899 and 1910 reported their occupations as agriculturists.[5]) The A. F. of L. leaders were hardly interested in organizing these newly arrived immigrants; they adopted the attitude that it was best for the Federation "to permit the newcomers to sink or swim by themselves."[6] At the same time, they advanced the thesis that they could not be organized; unlike the "old" immigrants, they were "a heterogeneous stew of divergent and discordant customs, languages, institutions; and they were impossible to assimilate or unionize."[7] They cut wages because they were satisfied with conditions that neither the native American workers nor the "older" immigrants would tolerate. They came not to settle permanently, to take root in America, but to earn a few dollars, primarily through strikebreaking, and return home. Their experience and background had deprived them of the unity of purpose and tenacity necessary to successfully build a stable labor movement. They had been oppressed by poverty for so many centuries and become so degraded that they were unable to lift themselves up to the high level of American workers or of the "older" immigrants from northern Europe. Even when organized and allowed to become members of the trade unions, the "new" immigrants were no asset to the labor movement. The "older" immigrants were amenable to trade unionism; they were patriotic, and democracy was in the very marrow of their bones. Not so with the "new" immigrants. They fell prey to the propaganda of the "anarchists," "socialists," and "radicals of all sorts." They started strikes without cause, and, in general, became "trouble-makers."[8] The A. F. of L. leaders agreed fully with the fear expressed by President Kirby of the National Association of Manufacturers when he warned that the large number of immigrants from Southern Europe were "nothing but seeds of socialism and anarchy with which to thistle our fertile land." Tracing the history of the attitude of both organizations on this question, one student has pointed out: "The National Association of Manufacturers and the American Federation of Labor do not differ in their avowed purpose as it relates to the immigration problem."[9]

"Despite their compelling need for labor organization," writes Melvyn Dubofsky, "the newcomers had few supporters within the ranks of the AFL. The leaders of the AFL, apparently content with their increasing stature within American society, were unwilling to damage their hard-earned reputation by associating with alien groups bearing the taint of European radicalism." David J. Saposs makes the same point: "The inclination of the immigrant towards radical doctrines made leaders of the existing unions chary of accepting them as members." This opposition to the organization of the foreign-born was reflected in special requirements imposed upon immigrant applicants for membership in many A. F. of L. unions: (1) naturalization, or declaration of intention to become a citizen (some unions even required full-fledged citizenship);* (2) payment of high initiation fees, higher fees than were demanded of other applicants (some unions fixed fees as high as $500);† approval or consent of the officers of the national unions; (4) presentation of the card of a foreign union; (5) special evidence of competency; it was not uncommon for a skilled immigrant craftsman with several years of experience to fail the union's examination. Finally, many unions simply closed their books and refused to accept new applicants for membership.

The memoirs of immigrant workers are filled with bitter complaints against the attitude and policies of the A. F. of L. unions. "The Brotherhood [of Painters]," an immigrant painter wrote, "maintained a high admission fee which was entirely out of the reach of an immigrant worker." "It was difficult for an immigrant to get into a building-trades' union," another wrote. "The smallest initiation fee was $25.00; in some cases it was as high as $100.00. Second, even when an immigrant could pay this sum, he was not sure that he could pass the required examination." Referring to another A. F. of L. union, an immigrant worker recalled later: "The initiation fee had been placed at $100. If the person seeking membership was favorably regarded, the entrance fee could be paid in installments, and if he were (an immigrant and) not so regarded it had to be paid in a lump sum." An immigrant union leader summed it up when he recalled bitterly that "the Labor Movement could have helped us but did not understand us and did not realize that we belonged to it."[10]

The immigrant workers did not wait until they wrote their memoirs to register their protests against the failure of the A. F. of L. to make an effort to organize the foreign-born. In 1909, in a speech at the New York Central Federated Union, the local A. F. of L. central labor body, an Italian immigrant leader charged the A. F. of L. with neglecting to organize Italian laborers: "The Italians have been reviled as scabs time without number. But there is a reason for this. Your delegates of unions and central labor bodies have never taken enough interest in the Italian

* On March 31, 1904, Chas. Nane, Secretary of Local Union No. 63 (Kingston, N.Y.) of the Brewery Workmen's International Union, wrote indignantly to a fellow-officer in New York City: "The man you sent arrived today. I asked you to send me a good union man, instead you sent a man only 3 months in the country. You have collected his initiation fee and sent him up here which you had no right to do since he must have his first papers out before he can join the union." (*AFL Corr.*) This letter was written on union stationery which carried the slogan: "Workingmen of all Countries, Unite!"

† A study written in 1911 revealed that many unions affiliated with the A. F. of L. in Indiana charged a "union fee of three or four hundred dollars for foreigners, altho that for natives is only five or ten dollars." (Donald G. Adams, "Foreign Born Laborers in Indiana," unpublished M.A. thesis, University of Indiana, 1911, p. 15.)

to help him to organize. I want you to understand that these men are flesh and blood—are workingmen like the rest of you, and they are willing to fight for recognition as organized workmen, and willing and anxious to stand together for a living wage."[11]

Kept out of many unions by special restrictions, the immigrants tried to enter the A. F. of L. through separate locals. Here, too, however, they frequently found the path closed. The following report submitted to Frank Morrison in April 1904 by H. A. Stembrugh, general secretary-treasurer of the International Hod Carriers' and Building Laborers' Union, describes a situation which was all too frequently duplicated:

"I beg to advise that the situation at Newark, N.J. is the result of a turn down in a certain nationality, namely Italians, by the other labor organizations in the building industry for reasons that can be explained in a very few words.

"The Italians had made several efforts previous to this time to become members of local union #122 of Newark, N.J., which is part of our organization, but were unable to obtain admittance. Finally, they appealed to the local to grant them a charter as a union for Italian workers which would allow them to work jointly together. But through some reason or other the Italians failed to receive the charter. The refusal of the charter was brought about, I believe, by the Board of Business Agents and the Building Trades Council of Newark, N.J. They simply refused to recognize that the Italians of Newark had a place in the organized labor movement.

"The Italians have not been supported by any labor organizations affiliated with the A. F. of L. They have applied for a state charter and vowed that if the labor organizations in the building industry do not wish to recognize them because of their prejudice against Italians, they are ready to come out and fight for their rights, and will do so regardless of any labor organizations in Newark, N.J.

"In view of the situation at Newark, N.J. I went to the above named city on the 15th of March in the hope of soliciting support for the Italian workers and effecting a settlement. Arriving in Newark I found that the other crafts in the Building industry were opposed to recognizing a local composed of Italians and threatened that if it were chartered by the state they would have nothing to do with it. After several attempts to effect a settlement and being unsuccessful, I decided that it was utterly impossible to bring about a settlement unless the A. F. of L. took some action. I would suggest that the Executive Council order the crafts in Newark, N.J. to abandon their bitter hostility to the Italians and allow them to be chartered as a separate local."

Morrison refused to act. The A. F. of L., he informed Stemburgh, did not have the power to tell the locals who should or should not be admitted as members, and since the crafts in Newark had jurisdictional control over the various occupations, they could not be compelled to allow the chartering of a separate union in their field.[12]

When the United Hebrew Trades, organized in 1888 by a group of Jewish Socialists on the lower east side of Manhattan,* gradually began to establish unions among the Jewish immigrant workers, these unions found themselves barred from the A. F. of L., and the U.H.T. itself was subjected to an intensive campaign of vilification by the Federation's leaders. In July 1901, the New York Central Federated Union refused credentials to a delegate from the U.H.T. on the ground that he was hostile to "American unionism." At the 1907 A. F. of L. convention, a series of resolutions was introduced denouncing the U.H.T. for destroying the solidarity of organized labor by functioning along "race" lines. The resolutions called upon all A. F. of L affiliates to withdraw their locals from the U.H.T. Although there were thousands of Jewish workers in its own ranks, whose problems it completely neglected, the United Garment Workers of America led the attack against the U.H.T. The reason for this opposition was made clear in the official organ of the U.G.W.A. The U.H.T., it charged, was "a bogus labor body . . . made up of 'Genossen' (Comrades)" who exerted "a disruptive socialistic influence upon the American labor movement."[13]†

A. F. OF L. FAVORS RESTRICTING IMMIGRATION

The A. F. of L. spearheaded the movement for more stringent legislation restricting immigration (increased head tax, sterner physical examination, more capital on entry), but its principal demand was for a literacy test for immigrants and the Federation's lobbyists in Congress pressed insistently for action on this proposal.‡ "Because of its well functioning

* For the formation and early history of the United Hebrew Trades, see Foner, op. cit., vol. II, pp. 35-36, 185, 287, 398-99.

† Gompers waged a long and bitter battle against the United Hebrew Trades, but finally accepted it as a means of introducing Jewish immigrants to the American labor movement. He justified this policy as "theoretically bad but practically necessary," and eventually even claimed credit for having helped organize the U.H.T. (Will Herberg, "Jewish Labor Movement in the United States: Early Years to World War I," Industrial and Labor Relations Review, vol. V, July, 1952, pp. 504-08; Gompers, Seventy Years of Life and Labor, vol. II, p. 153.)
Gompers maintained that his main objection to the U.H.T. was that it introduced religious issues into the labor movement. Actually, the U.H.T. was a language-oriented organization and not a religious one, and most of its members were not even religiously inclined.

‡ Early in 1897, Congress had passed legislation requiring literacy in some language of all immigrants. But President Grover Cleveland vetoed it as being against the best traditions of American democracy. The A.F. of L. leaders had supported the bill.
A literacy test bill was passed by Congress in 1909, but was vetoed by President Taft. President Wilson vetoed the 1917 literacy bill but the measure was passed over his veto. It required a literacy test for all aliens over 16 years of age.

central organization, with a full treasury, and with its hundreds of 'locals' scattered throughout the country," notes Joseph H. Taylor, "the American Federation of Labor gradually shouldered the burdens which had hitherto been borne by the more intellectual Immigration Restriction League."* The A. F. of L. widely distributed the League's propaganda directed against the "new" immigrants, and added racist arguments of its own. In placing the A. F. of L. squarely behind the Shattuck Bill in Congress in 1902, Gompers said that its literacy-test section, "will exclude hardly any natives of Great Britain, Ireland, Germany, France, or Scandinavia. It will shut out a considerable number of South Italians, and of Slavs and other equally or more undesirable and injurious."[14]

"Racial purity" was the key to Gompers' argument. Reminiscing in his autobiography years later, he wrote of the turn of the century: "That was a day before there was a general understanding of the principle that the maintenance of the nation depended upon the maintenance of racial purity and strength."[15] To this argument—if it can be dignified by such a name—was added the exaggerated fear that the "new" immigrants threatened the standards of organized labor and the very existence of the trade unions. This argument was given forceful weight by the report of the Immigration Commission, under the chairmanship of Senator Dillingham, appointed in 1907. Presented in 1910, the report comprised 42 volumes. Since the A. F. of L. not only hailed the report, but claimed that its "recommendations confirm the facts of the case as they have been accepted by the American Federation of Labor after the serious study its members had given the question for decades,"[16] it is worth examining the findings of the Dillingham Commission.

Despite its scientific pretensions, the commission conducted most of its investigations on the theory that it was the national origin and racial characteristics of immigrants which made them good or bad immigrants, and which governed the degree to which they might be assimilated. Starting out with the premise that the "old" (North and West European) immigrants were good immigrants and "quickly assimilated," the commission, as it itself stated, "paid little attention to the foreign-born element of the old immigrant class and directed its efforts almost entirely to . . . the newer (East and South European) immigrants." Throughout the 42 volumes are repeated references to the inferiority of the "new" immigrants and the menace they represented to the American people, and especially to organized labor. Twenty volumes were devoted to the economic effects of immigration, and the conclusion was that the "new" immigration had an adverse effect upon existing labor standards, lower-

* The Immigration Restriction League, an employer-financed organization, was organized in 1894 and worked as a pressure group, issuing books, pamphlets, and articles, sponsoring lectures, and influencing Congressmen to pass an immigration restriction law.

ing them to a degree that "the Americans and older immigrants have considered unsatisfactory." Without offering any evidence, the commission concluded that "the extensive employment of southern and eastern European immigrants in manufacturing and mining has in many places resulted in the weakening of labor organizations or in their complete disruption. . . . The recent immigrant has not, as a rule, affiliated himself with labor unions unless compelled to do so as a preliminary step toward acquiring work, and after becoming a member of a labor union he has manifested but little interest in the tenets or policy of the organization." It was all summed up in a single sentence: "The more recent immigrant employees from southern and eastern Europe and Asia . . . have been a constant menace to labor organization and have been directly and indirectly instrumental in weakening the unions and threatening their influence."[17]

The conclusion of the years of investigation was that the "new" immigrants—those from southern and eastern Europe—were less literate and less skilled and therefore less easily assimilated than the older immigrants from northern Europe had been, and that so far as the labor movement was concerned, they represented a danger that had to be faced and overcome or else the trade unions would be destroyed. The commission made token statements that some of the problems which had arisen from recent immigrations were due to the absence of efforts on the part of the government to foster the assimilation of the immigrants, to the evil results of private distribution of the immigrants, and to the desire of American industry for cheap, unskilled labor. But the only solutions offered were to lessen or cut off entirely immigration from southern and eastern Europe.

The A. F. of L. not only fully endorsed the commission's findings and conclusions, but called upon every trade unionist to write for copies of the "Brief Statement of the Conclusions and Recommendations to the Immigrant Commission." "Let every active unionist and every local union," Gompers appealed, "also see to it that this information has its proper and due influence on the public through the local newspapers and on the local representative in Congress." To give substance to the report, the A. F. of L. called upon the wage earners to demand from Congress legislation increasing the head tax on immigrants from $4 to $10; that each immigrant be required to bring at least $25 with him in addition to the amount required to pay transportation to the point where he expected to find employment, and that immigrants between the ages of 14 and 50 years "should be able to read a section of the constitution of the United States, either in our language, in their own language, or in the language of the country from which they come." Finally, the A. F. of L. national headquarters distributed thousands of printed petitions to Congress to the locals all over the country. The petition emphasized that "The Immigration Commission after a four years' investigation is unanimous in its recommendation that a curb be placed on the present stimulation and injection of cheap labor, and urges the enactment of the illiteracy test 'as the most feasible single method for excluding undesirable immigration'."[18]

A. F. OF L. REFUTED

The conclusions of the Immigration Commission (and the basic arguments of the A. F. of L.) were brilliantly attacked by Isaac Hourwich in his *Immigration and Labor,* published in 1912. Dr. Hourwich demonstrated that the immigration from southern and eastern Europe had actually encouraged organization of labor. He cited ample evidence in support of this contention. Thus he showed that in the years from 1901 to 1910, the period of the largest immigration from southern and eastern Europe, membership in unions increased from about 1,300,000 to about 2,625,000, in other words, doubling. He showed that in Kansas, where the immigrant population was insignificant, the ratio of trade union membership to urban population was smaller from 1900 to 1909 than in New York, where recent immigrants formed a large part of the population. He showed that in New York City in 1900, one-half of all the wage earners in non-agricultural pursuits, were foreign-born whereas in the remainder of the State, three-fourths were of native birth; yet at the same time, New York City had more than its proportionate share of trade union membership. In considering particular industries, he pointed to the success in forming unions among coal miners and the garment workers, where the influx of immigrants had been especially large—35.3 per cent of the coal miners were organized in 1910 and 17.10 of the clothing, shirt, collar and cuff workers. He also showed that in the cotton and woolen mills and in the iron and steel industry there had never been any significant organization among the unskilled workers, even before the large influx of southern and eastern European immigrants into those industries.

Hourwich also cited statistics to show the willingness of the "new" immigrants to engage in strikes not only in the United States but in their native lands. He pointed out that from 1901 to 1904 there were 3,032 industrial strikes in Italy, involving 621,737 workers. In the one year, 1905, Hourwich estimated from statistics of the Russian government, there were 3,762,000 workers on strike in the Russian Empire. "Recent immigration," Hourwich emphasized, "has not retarded the progress of trade unionism except, of course, where it is the policy of unions to exclude the recent immigrants by prohibitive initiation dues and other restrictive regulations intended to limit the number of competitors within their trades."[19]

But the A. F. of L. leaders dismissed Hourwich's study as they did similar evidence submitted by immigrant trade unionists. They continued to insist that the "new" immigrants damaged the American workers' security, even though, when pressed to provide proof, they conceded that they could not do so. "We cannot show you," James O'Connell, A. F. of L. vice-president, confessed at a conference discussing the immigration question, "we cannot prove to you, we cannot bring you chapter and verse for these things, but we meet it, and we know it. It is in our hearts, before our eyes every minute of the day. . . . You say, 'Show me.' We simply say we know it is so because we have suffered from it." As one of the speakers at the conference remarked: "If Mr. O'Connell says: 'I do not know why, but I believe it,' that is not argument."[20]

SPECIAL PROBLEMS IN ORGANIZING IMMIGRANTS

In 1909, John R. Commons of the University of Wisconsin gave the correct answer to the charge that the influx of immigrant labor made possible the lowering of wage and living standards in America. "Organization," he wrote, "is the only means by which the immigrants can rise to the standards of those whom they displace." It is true that organization of the immigrants presented special problems. There was the language barrier to overcome, especially since many companies deliberately filled their plants with workers of various nationalities as a means of preventing solidarity, and this could present a real obstacle to organizers who could not speak any other language than English. Moreover, many immigrants came from the old countries with national and religious animosities bred by generations of hatred and war, which the monopolists deliberately exploited to keep the workers disunited and away from the unions. Then again, a high rate of re-emigration often made organization of the immigrants difficult to maintain.[21]*

But these and other obstacles hindering organization of the immigrants could be overcome given the will to do so. Interpreters could be used to bring the message of unionism to the foreign-born. When C. O. Sherman, general secretary of the Metal Workers' International Union, tried to organize the mills in East St. Louis in 1903, he found that the majority were foreigners, and, as he informed Morrison, "I cannot hold a conversation with them or understand what they say." But this did not stop the organizing drive. Sherman arranged for an interpreter to assist him. "One of the members," he wrote to Morrison, "who is quite intelligent as

---

* From 1908 to 1914 re-emigration averaged from 25 per cent to nearly 40 per cent of the total number of immigrants yearly. (*Historical Statistics of the United States,* Washington, 1949, pp. 33, 38.) "The immigrant intended to return to their villages, and many did. From 1908 to 1910 . . . forty-four South and East Europeans departed for every hundred that arrived; altogether, 590,000 left in three years. But more remained." (David Brody, *Steelworkers in America, op. cit.,* p. 106.)

well as educated acted as interpreter and took the platform after I got through speaking and told them what I had to offer and, from the applause that was received from his address, I was convinced that it met with favor. My conclusion was justified, for they have all signed up." A report in the *Leather Workers' Journal* of October 1906 from Branch 80, Rockport, Illinois, tells a moving and significant story: "At our last meeting we initiated a young Russian. He couldn't understand our language, so Brother Smentek acted as interpreter. It seemed funny to hear our ritualistic work in a foreign language, but all was changed from the ridiculous to the sublime, when in a short talk, Brother Smentek acting as interpreter, the young man explained the trials and hardships he had gone through to escape from his native land, where he belonged to the revolutionists, and was hunted by soldiers of the Czar."[22]

But too many A. F. of L. affiliates made no real effort to deal with the special problems involved in unionizing immigrant workers, and, instead used them as an excuse for their failure to conduct an effective organizing campaign. Despite the obvious ridiculousness of such a course, the A. F. of L. dispatched organizers who could speak only English in the few efforts it made to unionize the foreign-born workers in the mass production industries.* The inevitable result was a failure to communicate with and understand the unorganized workers and the early abandonment of the unionizing campaign. In listing the reasons for the abandonment of the organizing campaign in iron and steel in 1904, the A. F. of L. organizers assigned to this work cited as a leading cause the fact "that a large number of the workers we approached are foreigners, hardly able to speak or understand the English language, thereby complicating, and, in the end, nullifying our efforts at every point." Similarly, in explaining the abandonment of an organizing campaign in textile, the A. F. of L. organizers wrote to Morrison in 1911: "We found that the Americans in the textile mills of New England are gradually being displaced by Poles, Italians and Greeks, and this has created very grave difficulties in establishing unionism in these mills. The employers have two, if not more, nationalities employed, and generally manage to engender more or less national dislike between them. We found, too, that there is a determined effort by these workers to retain their national customs, religion and language, in short, to form their own colonies. We found, as a

---

* Homer D. Call, secretary-treasurer of the Amalgamated Meat Cutters and Packinghouse Workers, complained bitterly that every time the A.F. of L., after much persuasion, agreed to send an organizer to help organize the stockyards, an English-speaking man was sent who knew nothing of the background of the workers he was to organize. He had repeatedly informed the A.F. of L. leaders that "if the stockyards were ever organized again, it must be done by some men who can speak the slavic language and who has the confidence of that class of people." But the A.F. of L. had ignored his complaints and advice. (Homer D. Call to Mary E. McDowell, Feb. 5, 1908, Mary E. McDowell Papers, Chicago Historical Society.)

result, that there was no way in which we could communicate with them."[23] The only thing surprising about this report is that the A. F. of L. organizers should have been surprised to find such conditions existing in the textile industry and not have made adequate preparations to cope with them.

Rather than devoting time and energy to study and solve the problems involved in organizing the immigrant workers, the A. F. of L., as we have seen, erected barriers to their entrance into the labor movement. These barriers, in turn, were pointed to by anti-union forces to convince the immigrants that they owed nothing to organized labor and were perfectly justified in "scabbing" against striking union workers.* When *Panhellenic*, a Greek-American paper was attacked in 1909 for defending the action of "Greeks who had taken the place of strikers at the packing-houses in South Omaha, Nebraska and elsewhere," it replied: "How many Greek workmen have become members of the American Federation of Labor? Maybe not even 2% of them. And why can they not become members? Because many unions in the American Federation of Labor have special restrictions against immigrant workers which are deliberately imposed to prevent them from becoming members of these unions." Even the managing editor of *Atlantis,* a Greek-American paper which proudly announced that it sought "to get all Greek workers to join the different labor unions and fought hard whenever Greeks were induced by false promises to replace strikers and pointed out to them the meaning and the disgrace that comes to every self-respecting man to become a 'scab,' " was forced to admit to Gompers that these efforts were

---

* One of the major problems reported by A.F. of L. organizers in the steel organizing campaign of 1909 and 1910 was the fact that the Hungarian workers had been enraged by John Mitchell's attack in the summer of 1909 on Hungarian immigrants as "foreign intruders" whose "standard of living was so low that they would work for next to nothing, and thus dragged down wages wherever they were employed." It was impossible to assimilate and organize such workers, Mitchell concluded. The speech was reprinted in the Hungarian language and widely distributed by the Steel Trust. As one A.F. of L. organizer wrote to Mitchell in February 1910: "The distribution of these statements has resulted in a decided coolness towards us among all the immigrants, and particularly among the Hungarian workmen, and whenever I approached them, I was told that they had been warmly disposed towards the American Federation of Labor until they read your opinion about the foreign intruders." (Jacob Tazelaar to John Mitchell, Feb. 14, 1910; Rev. Alec Varlaky to John Mitchell, 2/1910, *JMP* and *AFL Corr.; Literary Digest,* Aug. 1909, p. 119; *American Federationist,* Jan. 1911, pp. 6–8.) Mitchell always considered the new immigrant workers in coal mining a serious deterrent to unionism. To him they were "a drove of cattle, ready to stampede" at the cries of any misleader. (Mitchell to Ryan, Sept. 24, 1900, *JMP.*) Yet the actual facts showed that the immigrants from southern and eastern Europe had entered the United Mine Workers rapidly after their entrance into the industry and were among the most loyal and militant members of the union. (*See* Frank J. Wayne, *The Slav Invasion and the Mine Workers: A Study in Immigration,* Philadelphia, 1904, pp. 119–21.)

frustrated by the policies of the A. F. of L. "All over the country," he protested to Gompers, "the Greek workers are forming societies for mutual protection and are taking an interest in the affairs of the labor movement in general; and from records it will be shown that the Greeks are good, honest workmen and would be desirable members of the trade unions once they had the opportunity to prove it. But how can they ever prove it if so little continues to be done by your organization to bring them within the fold of the trade unions?"[24]

Not until this question was answered correctly could the American labor movement make effective headway.

A. F. OF L. AND THE ASIAN IMMIGRANTS

The racist attitude of the A. F. of L. towards the Asiatic people was particularly vicious. Led by Gompers, the Federation insisted at convention after convention on the inborn inferiority of the Asians. They were "people of vice and sexual immorality" who were "of inferior social standards"; they were "cunning, debased and degraded caricatures of humanity"; they could never be assimilated into American society, and had to be excluded either by law or they "will be driven out by force of arms." The A. F. of L. boasted that it had played an influential role in forcing Congress to pass the Chinese Exclusion Act of 1882, and it also took credit for the passage of the Greary Act in 1892 which extended for another 10 years the law of 1882 excluding Chinese laborers from the United States. Under the earlier act much illegal entry into this country from Mexico and British Columbia was alleged to have taken place, and the Greary Act (which the A. F. of L. had a hand in framing) was supposed to put more teeth in the law.[25]

On May 6, 1902, the Greary Act was scheduled to expire. A year before this date, the A. F. of L. went into action to campaign for its continuance. With Herman Gutstadt, San Francisco A. F. of L. representative, Gompers wrote a pamphlet which presented a comprehensive treatment of the so-called "Yellow Menace" from the A. F. of L. standpoint. Published by the A. F. of L., it bore the title, *Some Reasons for Chinese Exclusion: Meat vs. Rice, American Manhood Against Coolieism, Which Shall Survive?* In a brief introduction, the authors disclaimed biased motives in presenting the official A. F. of L. views on the subject of Chinese immigration: "We . . . desire to assure our readers that in maintaining our position we are not inspired by a scintilla of prejudice of any kind, but with the best interests of our country and people uppermost in our mind, simply request fair consideration." What followed was filled with the most vicious prejudice against the Asian people, a prime example of racist ideology.

In their native countries, the pamphlet argued, the Asians had demonstrated that they were incapable of self-government or economic improvement, "allowing themselves to be barbarously tyrannized over." In this country, they continued their frightful habits, "entirely at variance with our economic, political, social and moral conceptions." Then followed several pages detailing the allegedly low morals of the Chinese in the United States who, the authors charged, were congenitally immoral. "Ninety-nine out of every 100 Chinese are gamblers," they wrote. This was hardly surprising, since "the Yellow Man found it natural to lie, cheat, and murder." Chinatown abounded in passion and vice; opium was corrupting Caucasians in every Chinatown from San Francisco to Boston. Gompers and his co-author raised the sexual bugaboo, a favorite argument of the racists. The Chinese loved "to prey upon American girls," preferring them to their own kind, whom they willingly leave behind in the old country. After ranting on in this fashion, the authors attacked Chinese workers for undercutting white workers. A Chinese could live on next to nothing, and because he worked for so little, he was degrading the dignity of work in general and the trade he entered in particular.[26]

It is significant that Gompers thought so well of the pamphlet that he boasted to the delegates at the 1901 A. F. of L. convention that it was a key contribution in the Federation's "most active and energetic campaign " for new legislation against Chinese immigration. "No one can read this pamphlet," Gompers cried, "without feeling surprised at the wonderful patience exhibited by our fellow-citizens of the Pacific Coast in submitting to a state of affairs so horrible and degrading." "Energetic and immediate action," he continued, "is an imperative necessity. There is no question to be considered by the present Congress fraught with so much import to the American people as is the question whether or not the Chinese shall be excluded from the United States. . . . The introduction or continuance of an element so entirely at variance with our economic, political, social and moral conceptions, and so utterly incapable of adaptation to the Caucasian ideals of civilization, is not only dangerous to us as a class, but is destructive of the very institutions we are so earnestly striving to uphold, maintain or attain. Whatever may be the opinion of others, to us this matter does not permit a compromise."

Seven resolutions were introduced at the A. F. of L. convention demanding the continued exclusion of Chinese. Near the end of the convention, a special Committee on Chinese Exclusion reported a substitute proposal embodying the substance of these resolutions and demanding the reenactment of the Chinese Exclusion Act. "Their presence in considerable numbers," the Committee appealed in its memorandum to Congress, "would engender a hostility which would make them a disturbing factor in society. Their admission would provide an unfailing supply of degraded servile laborers that would affect our efforts to improve industrial conditions."[27]

When Congress convened in 1902, the A. F. of L. demanded immediate enactment of the Mitchell Bill, an even more severe proposal than the stringent Greary Act of 1892. While the law that was passed was essentially the same as the Greary Act, the 1902 measure declared that the immigration and naturalization of Chinese should be prohibited indefinitely. At the 1903 A. F. of L. convention, Gompers reiterated the familiar argument against "the Mongolian Menace," and boasted that the 1902 Chinese Exclusion Law had been "secured through our efforts."[28]

The A. F. of L. also singled out the Japanese people for racist attacks. Prior to 1903 there had been little attention paid to the Japanese in the Federation's attack upon the Asian people, but with the increase in Japanese immigration, the situation changed. "Almost from the moment of their arrival," notes Carey McWilliams, "the Japanese were caught in the crossfire of previous anti-Oriental agitations. Racial myths and ideologies dating from earlier agitations were quickly extended to them." It was not long before the A. F. of L. began to apply the racist epithets, heretofore attached mainly to the Chinese, to the Japanese (and Korean) workers. At the 1904 A. F. of L. convention, a number of delegates, led by Gompers, heatedly attacked "the Japanese and all . . . Asiatics," and demanded that the Chinese Exclusion Act be broadened to include Japanese and Korean workers. A resolution to this effect was passed by the convention. Endorsing the resolution in the *American Federationist,* Gompers demanded that the Japanese should be barred from the United States. They were as difficult to assimilate into the American culture, he insisted, as the Chinese, citing the fact that the American God was not the God of the Japanese—but failing to indicate the significance of this for organized workers in the United States.[29] In the same issue of the *Federationist,* Gompers launched a vicious attack on Sen Katayama, a Japanese Socialist and labor leader who was visiting the United States. He referred to him as a "presumptuous Jap" with a "leprous mouth whose utterances show this mongrel's perverseness, ignorance and maliciousness. . . . Perhaps this Japanese Socialist may be perturbed by the fact that the American workmen, organized and unorganized, have discovered that the Japanese in the United States are as baneful to the interests of American labor and American civilization as are the Chinese."

Writing two years later in the official A. F. of L. monthly journal, Gompers voiced public approval of the policy of the city of San Francisco in "segregating Japanese children from white children in the public schools."[30]

The A. F. of L. took considerable credit for the "Gentlemen's Agreement" negotiated by President Theodore Roosevelt in 1907. Under its terms, skilled and unskilled Japanese laborers, except for those who had formerly been residents of the United States or were relatives of residents, were not granted passports by the Japanese government. Thus nearly all Japanese workers were excluded from the United States.

WERE THE ASIAN IMMIGRANTS A THREAT?

In defending Gompers and the A. F. of L. from the criticism that their approach to the immigration question, and particularly the immigration of Oriental workers, was dominated by "racism and anti-foreignisms," Philip Taft insists that the attitude was "not based upon racism, but economic necessity."[31] Taft makes no mention of the epithets used by Gompers and the A. F. of L. in describing both the "new" immigrants from Europe and the Oriental workers, or that frequently the two groups were linked together in such attacks.* Nor does he point out that even the most vehement opponents of Oriental immigration in the Federation conceded publicly that the A. F. of L. policy was dictated by racism and not by economic necessity. In the *American Federationist* of October 1913, Walter MacArthur, one of the chief spokesmen in the A. F. of L. on Oriental exclusion, stated frankly that the problem "has at all times been chiefly, and at most times exclusively, a problem racial rather than economic in character." He continued:

"The more recent agitation against Japanese and other Asiatic immigration rests upon grounds identical with those involved in the case of the Chinese. Throughout the half century from 1852 to 1902, and even down to the present day, the attitude of the West on the subject of immigration has been inspired by racial instinct and impulse. Economic considerations have entered into the discussion of course, but even the economic feature has been grounded upon the race question. The standards of the Asiatic are low, as compared with our own, but no change in this respect can suffice to remove or offset the racial antipathy that is planted in the bone and sinew of man." He closed triumphantly: "The West, let us assume, is safe as a 'white man's country.' "[32]

The A. F. of L. gave official endorsement to MacArthur's thesis at its 1914 convention when it requested of Congress "the extension of the Chinese Exclusion Act so as to permanently exclude from the United

* In a speech in 1906, James O'Connell, A.F. of L. vice-president, said that neither the "new" immigrants from Europe nor the Chinese immigrants could be assimilated, and, as a result, the United States was in danger of becoming "Chinaised or Hungarianised." (*Facts About Immigration,* Report of the Proceedings of Conferences on Immigration, held by the Immigration Department of the National Civic Federation, New York, 1907, pp. 86–89.)

Women workers were also linked together with the Chinese. In 1908 a top A.F. of L. official was quoted as saying: "Woman is the white Chinaman of the industrial world. She wears a coiled-up queue, and wherever she goes she cheapens the worth of human labor." (William Hard, Rheta Childe Dorr, Collaborator, "The Woman's Invasion," *Everybody's Magazine,* vol. XIX, Dec., 1908, p. 798.)

States and all its insular territories all races native of Asia." This action was not asked primarily for the protection of the economic position of the organized workers, but because "the racial incompatibility as between the peoples of the Orient and the United States presents a problem of race preservation which it is our imperative duty to solve in our favor, and which can only be effectively solved by a policy of exclusion."[33]

Taft makes no effort to examine the question of whether Oriental immigration actually constituted a major threat to the standard of living of American workers, as the A. F. of L. leaders repeatedly alleged. Other scholars who have studied the problem in great detail have concluded that the Asian immigrants were in no sense a real economic challenge to most American trade unionists. For one thing, they point out, during no single decade from 1870 to 1920 did the combined number of Chinese and Japanese immigrants (who comprise nearly the whole of Asian immigrants of the period) exceed more than 4.4 per cent of the total immigration into the United States, and except for the decade, 1871–1880, the combined number did not exceed 1.8 per cent of the total. Again, at no time from 1870 to 1920 did the combined Chinese-Japanese population in the United States total more than one-fifth of one per cent of the entire population.[34]

Furthermore, the cigar, shoe, and cotton and woolen industries were the only areas where job conflict between Oriental and American trade unionists might be considered as serious. But, as Mary R. Coolidge has demonstrated after a careful study of the subject, only in cigar-making could the so-called "coolies" be said to have been a direct economic threat to the "white" wage worker; indeed, the fact that the Oriental workers were forced to take the worst jobs made it easier for the "white" workers to move to better jobs. In the cigar industry, Mrs. Coolidge points out, the chief competition to the Pacific Coast "white" workers came not from Orientals, but from Eastern cigar manufacturers. (She could have added that a chief competition, as we have seen, came from the introduction of machinery and the consequent displacement of skilled craftsmen by unskilled workers, many of whom were "white" women.) Mrs. Coolidge concludes in her book, published in 1909:

"It has been shown that the only place where the Chinese really came into serious competition on the same plane as white laborers was in certain specific manufactures; that these industries were probably initiated because of a local advantage and artificial protection; that their margin of profit was always small and their scale of wages necessarily low. . . . Further, it has been demonstrated that in recent years since the Chinese have become an inappreciable factor among operatives, and in spite of the increase of (white) women and children, these manufactures have stood still. It has been established, therefore, that such

Chinese competition as there was, was slight in degree and affected only a very small number of white wage workers. . . ."[35]

But the A. F. of L. leaders paid no more attention to Mrs. Coolidge's findings than they did to those of Hourwich dealing with the effect of European immigration. For one thing, it was easier for the officials of the Cigar Makers' International Union (and those of other A. F. of L. affiliates) to blame the Oriental workers for "undermining the American standard of living" than to organize the unskilled workers at the machines. Indeed, to no small extent, the whole anti-Oriental agitation was deliberately fanned by employers and their agents to divert the attention of American workers from the real problems they faced in the class struggle. As Fred W. Riggs points out: "There was . . . a disproportion between the many issues over which the California worker might reasonably have become exercised, and the extent to which his efforts were channeled into anti-Chinese agitation."[36] That the A. F. of L. leaders should have been the most active agent in channeling the thinking of American workers away from more basic problems into anti-Chinese agitation is not surprising when we bear in mind that this was precisely the period when these leaders developed the whole strategy of class-collaboration. That the anti-Chinese agitation was part of this strategy is clearly revealed in the pamphlet by Gompers and Gutstadt, *Some Reasons for Chinese Exclusion.* Appended to the 1908 edition, was a "Memorial to Congress," drawn up at San Francisco on November 21, 1907, in which the exclusion of Chinese workers was demanded on the ground that it was necessary in building close capital-labor cooperation. The California memorialists, among whom were several leading A. F. of L officials, declared:

"The increasing recurrence of strikes in modern times must have convinced everyone that their recent settlement is nothing more than a truce. It is not a permanent industrial peace. The new organization of capital and labor now necessary to bring about lasting peace and harmony between those engaged in production will require greater sympathy, greater trust and confidence, and a clearer mutual understanding between the employers and the employed. Any such new organization will require a closer union to be formed between them. *These requirements can never be fulfilled between the individuals of races so alien to one another as ourselves and the Chinese. The Chinese are only capable of working under the present unsatisfactory system. All progress, then, to an improved organization of capital and labor would be arrested.*"[37]

When such arguments—as well as those based on a racist foundation—failed to convince the more militant and enlightened trade unionists, the A. F. of L. leaders pulled out their trump card. As one contributor to the *American Federationist* put it: "[The Asian] must always remain the stranger. . . . Herein lies the greatest danger. . . . He cannot be *unionized!*"[38]

ASIAN WORKERS AND UNIONISM

The A. F. of L. knew very well that the Chinese and Japanese workers were familiar with union organization in their native lands. During 1903, the A. F. of L Executive Council sent Edward Rosenberg, a member of the Seamen's Union, to China to study labor conditions there. His report, published in the *American Federationist,* was filled with chauvinistic attacks on the Chinese who were described as "so brutalized and exploited by successive generations of corrupt and tyrannical governments, that it may be a sorry day for any country and its workers if the Chinese are allowed to enter such countries either as free or contract laborers." But it did demonstrate that the exploited workers of China were struggling militantly for the right to unionize, and had conducted several important strikes.[39]

For several years in the late 1890's, Gompers received regular reports from Fusataro Takano, a Japanese-American who had returned to Japan to assist in establishing trade unions in his native land.* These reports told of the upsurge of unionism in Japan, the inauguration of strikes in all industries, most of which proved to be successful,† and the general

* Describing himself, Takano wrote: "It was in the year of 1889 while I was working at a sawmill in California when fortune favored me to receive a book entitled, 'Labor Movement, the problem of to-day.' Perusal of the book aroused my interest to [*sic*] the movement and sharpened my sense to the wrongs that are endured by Japanese workers. Succeeding seven years in the U.S. was spent in diligent study and close observation of American labor movement and upon my return [to Japan] inaugurated the movement in this country by forming the Rodo Kurniae Kisi Kwai." (F. Takano to Gompers, Tokyo, Japan, Dec. 17, '97, *AFL Corr.*)

† On April 15, 1897, Takano wrote to Gompers: "I have, at last, the honor to inform you that the first public meeting ever held in this country with the sole object of advocating the cause of labor was held under the auspices of the Friends of Labor on the 6th inst. at the Kinkikay, Kanda, this city [Tokyo], when several hundred workmen attended despite a pouring rain. . . . "The friends of workers' under whose auspices the meeting was held, consists of 4 remnant members of an association formed years ago in San Francisco by some dozen Japanese living there. The remnant members are a tailor, two shoe-makers and myself, all of them, I assure you, are staunch advocators of the trade-unionism. . . .

"Within the past month, two strikes were reported in this country, one by the coopers employed in the distilling establishments of Nada, a well known distilling district in this country and located a few miles off from Kobe, demanding a raise of 10% in their wages and after 3 days of cessession [*sic*] of work, it ended victoriously to the workers; the other was by 1,500 umbrella makers of this city, who after 2 days strike succeeded to gain 15% raise of their wages. There is one conspicuous fact in connection with the strikes so far occured [*sic*] in this country, viz., all the strikes ended favorably to the strikers." (*AFL Corr.*)

determination of the Japanese workers to unite against their exploiters.[40]

In 1905 the A. F. of L. Executive Council learned with dismay that a number of local unions in Honolulu, Hawaii, including the Carpenters and Joiners Union No. 745, were urging the repeal of the Chinese Exclusion Act as special legislation for the territory. Gompers immediately wrote to Frank Duffy, International Union secretary, to warn the Hawaii union to cease agitating for entrance of Oriental workers into the territory "in order that some of the unions connected with the organized labor movement of America should not be quoted by our opponents as favoring Chinese immigration into Hawaii or any other territory or part of the United States." Duffy did as he was bid, but to his consternation Local 745 replied that it favored the admission of Asian workers into the territory, that the union's experience indicated that they would make good trade unionists, and that their presence would be "a help to organized labor here." He forwarded the letter to Gompers, at the same time assuring him: "I am as much in favor of excluding Japanese from the United States as I am the Chinese. I have no particular love for either race, and the day is coming—and is coming fast—when organized labor will be compelled to take stringent measures against allowing the Chinese and Japanese to enter the States or any territory controlled by the United States government." The fact that the Asian workers would, if allowed to enter the labor movement, make good trade unionists and would be "a help to organized labor" in Hawaii, cut no ice with the A. F. of L. leaders. Local 745 was ordered to abandon its campaign in favor of the Oriental workers or face expulsion from the International Union and the A. F. of L.[41]

In the United States proper, too, the Oriental workers demonstrated that they could be organized. Frequent strikes took place among Chinese workers in the urban areas of the Pacific Coast, and even though they were not conducted by trade unions, they were organized struggles, led by "protective associations" known as tongs. The California Bureau of Labor described these as a type of "trades-unions" which "are very rarely heard of, but nevertheless exist and are very powerful. In case of a strike or boycott they are fierce and determined in their action, making a bitter and prolonged fight."[42]

The truth is, as the United Mine Workers effectively demonstrated in Canada,* that the Oriental workers could be organized. But policy

* In the summer of 1912, the U.M.W. organized the Chinese coal diggers on Vancouver Island. Organizer George Pettigrew was sent from Seattle to Victoria, accompanied by a Chinese organizer who would assist him as interpreter. Although the Canadian authorities, fearing the organization of the Chinese coal diggers, refused to allow the Chinese organizer to enter the country, the campaign on Vancouver Island was successful. (British Columbia *Federationist*, Aug. 3, 1912.) The organizing campaign was preceded by a strike of the Chinese miners for a raise in wages of 12 cents per day. The British Columbia *Federationist* of July 20,

(apart from distinctive restrictive covenants forbidding their membership) blocked their entrance into the A. F. of L.* Gompers gave it all
away when he wrote in June 1904 to an official of the Hotel and Restaurant Employees' Union who reported that one of the locals was organizing the Chinese restaurants:

"I am inclined to believe that it would be unwise and impracticable
to unionize a Chinese restaurant. Of course I realize the desirability of
having every establishment possible unionized, and to organize our
fellow-workers, but you must take under consideration the further fact
that the American labor movement has set its face against the Chinese
coming to this country, and upon our demands the law has been passed
for the exclusion of Chinese from the United States or from any of the
territories or possessions of the United States, or going from one group
of Islands to another group of Islands which belong to the United States.
In other words, the American labor movement stands committed against
the Chinese coming to our country or any possession of our country.

"It would be the height of inconsistency of our movement to unionize
the Chinese against whom we have declared."[43]

As we have seen, the A. F. of L. took the same position towards the
organization of Japanese workers. In April, 1903, a strike of about 1,000
Japanese and Mexican workers took place in the sugar beet fields near
Oxnard (Ventura County), California, in protest against "starvation and
bad treatment." The Japanese were the first to organize and strike and
were joined by the Mexicans, and together they fought side by side until
they won a wage increase and improved working conditions. Following
the victory, the two united in forming the Sugar Beet and Farm Laborers' Union of Oxnard and applied to the A. F. of L. Executive Council
for a charter. Gompers in a letter to J. M. Larraras, the Mexican secretary
of the union, expressed willingness to grant the charter on the condition
that the organization contain no Oriental workers. "Your union must

---

1912, carried the notice: "The United Mine Workers of America have taken the
matter up and intend to stand by the Chinese in their efforts to raise wages. By the
way of showing they are in earnest, the Mine Workers have already expelled those
of their members who have taken the place of the Chinese, and are prepared to come
out in a body if the Chinese are not reinstated at the increased wages they are
asking for." The victory of the Chinese in this strike, with the aid of the U.M.W.,
was an important factor in bringing these workers into the union.

* In the constitutions of many A.F. of L. affiliates, Chinese were unequivocally
barred from membership. (*Report of the Industrial Commission on Labor Organizations, Labor Disputes and Arbitration; and Railway Labor*, Washington, 1901, vol.
XVII, pp. 270, 282.) The A.F. of L. did not exclude Oriental workers in its constitution, but Gompers stated that, for "obvious" reasons, "It is against the entire
policy of the American Federation of Labor to admit to membership in its affiliated
organizations either Chinese or Japanese." (Gompers to J. W. Wood, Aug. 5, 1903;
Gompers to T. J. Ryan, Aug. 29, 1903; Gompers to Jere L. Sullivan, June 24, 1904,
AFL Corr. and *GLB*.)

guarantee that it will under no circumstances accept membership of any Chinese or Japanese." The secretary of the union replied in a letter that should have occupied a prominent place in the *American Federationist* and distributed to all members of the A. F. of L.:

"Your letter . . . in which you say the admission with us of the Japanese Sugar Beet and Farm Laborers into the American Federation of Labor can not be considered, is received. I beg to say in reply that our Japanese brothers here were the first to recognize the importance of cooperating and uniting in demanding a fair wage scale. . . .

"They were not only just with us, but they were generous when one of our men was murdered by hired assassins of the oppressors of labor, they gave expression to their sympathy in a very substantial form. In the past we have counseled, fought and lived on very short rations with our Japanese brothers, and toiled with them in the fields, and they have been uniformly kind and considerate. We would be false to them and to ourselves and to the cause of unionism if we now accepted privileges for ourselves which are not accorded to them. We are going to stand by men who stood by us in the long, hard fight which ended in a victory over the enemy. We therefore respectfully petition the A. F. of L. to grant us a charter under which we can unite all the sugar beet and field laborers of Oxnard without regard to their color or race. We will refuse any other kind of a charter except one which will wipe out race prejudices and recognize our fellow workers as being as good as ourselves."[44]

When Gompers still refused to grant the charter, a labor paper, published in Chicago, commented angrily that he had "violated the expressed principle of the A. F. of L., which states that race, color, religion or nationality shall be no bar to fellowship in the American Federation of Labor." It went on to point out:

"It will be impossible, so long as this ruling is sustained, to organize the wage workers of California for the protection of their interests, for there are between forty and fifty thousand Japanese in this state, who hold the balance of power among the field workers, and nothing can be effectually done without their cooperation. In such a warfare to raise race prejudice is unpardonable folly, a folly for which President Gompers must soon answer to the unions of southern California who are unanimous in demanding recognition for brother wage workers, the Japanese."[45]

The comment about the unions of southern California was accurate. In April 1903, the Los Angeles Council resolved that the time had come to organize the migratory workers in agriculture on the Pacific Coast, and declared that experience had demonstrated that the only way to do so successfully was to bring the Japanese and Mexican agricultural workers into the same union with the white American field workers. "We do declare our belief," the Labor Council wrote to the A. F. of L. Executive Council, enclosing its resolution, "that the most effective method of protecting the American workingman and his standard of living is by universal organization of wage workers regardless of race or nationality." A leading official of the California Federation of Labor enthusiastically endorsed this appeal, and urged the A. F. of L. Executive Council to act favorably on the request for organization of Japanese workers into the Federation: "This is one of the most important resolutions ever brought to the attention of the executive council. . . . It virtually breaks the ice on the question of forming the Orientals into unions and so keeping them from scabbing on white people, in place of not organizing Asiatics as at present."

But the A. F. of L. Executive Council refused, again pointing out that it would be inconsistent for the Federation to campaign for the exclusion of Japanese workers from the United States, and, at the same time, to unionize them. Since the A. F. of L. was not going to upset the apple cart by countenancing the organization of the Japanese workers, the result was that the proposal to set up a union of all workers in this field came to nothing.[46]

In 1909, the A. F. of L. Executive Council learned to its horror that the Wyoming State Federation of Labor had sanctioned the organization of Chinese and Japanese workers in the mining camps at Rock Springs, that "Orientals sat in the same lodge room with whites," and that the "union demands the same wages for the yellow men as for white labor." The Executive Council immediately ordered the expulsion of the Oriental workers, and forbade any future unionization along this line.[47]

Andrew Furuseth, leader of the Sailors' Union of the Pacific and a member of the A. F. of L. Executive Council, summed up the Federation's position when he wrote: "We are in favor of Japanese being organized and Chinese being organized, but we want them organized in Japan or China, not in the United States."* The British Columbia *Federationist* summed up what the Federation's position should be in an editorial entitled "The Race Question":

"The colored races compete with the white races in the labor market, in exactly the same manner, and for the same reason that the members of the white races compete with each other. The same course of action must therefore be taken with regard to the colored races as has been pursued in connection with the white workers whom economic conditions have driven to this country.

"Organize and educate them!

---

* Ironically, Furuseth saw in this position no proof of prejudice on account of "Color or Race. The Labor movement knows no race, etc., but it knows locality," he wrote. (A. Furuseth to Morrison, June 12, 1903, *AFL Corr.*) Yet Furuseth could also write that he took pride in "being as much devoid of nationality feeling as any man." (Letter of Sept. 27, 1907, quoted in Hyman Weintraub, *Andrew Furuseth: Emancipator of the Seamen,* Berkeley and Los Angeles, 1959, p. 113.)

"It is immaterial to the master class whether the workers whom they use to beat down other workers, be black, white, or yellow. It is therefore essential that no color lines be drawn in labor organizations. It must be remembered that it is just as necessary to organize the colored races as the white. It is all labor power, and can be used to beat other workers into subjection, just so long as its possessors remain unorganized and uneducated as to their position as members of the working class.

"The colored races are members of a wage slave class, even as we, and they also must be educated to a knowledge of their position in human society, in order that the working class of the world may achieve its emancipation."[48]

Of the total number of persons employed in industry in the United States in 1910, about 16.5 per cent were below the age of twenty and of the total number of women workers, about 7.9 per cent were below the age of sixteen. The vast majority of these young workers found their entrance into the skilled trades blocked. Negro youth and young white women workers, of course, had special obstacles placed in their path.* But all young workers faced a serious dilemma which was summed up by one such worker who wrote to Gompers: "I am working in a shop organized by the above union and am denied the privilege of either joining the union or learning the trade." "Hundreds of thousands of youth have no vocational and industrial training," wrote one contemporary authority. Without vocational and industrial training during most of this period, the youth could only hope to learn a skill through apprenticeship. But many A. F. of L. unions severely limited the number of apprentices and gave preference in constitutional provisions to sons of members in selecting apprentices, and some permitted *only* sons of members to learn the trade. Those fortunate enough to overcome this barrier, often found to their dismay that they would have to spend three to five years learning to become a mechanic, and then would be unable to obtain admission to membership because they failed to satisfy the union's examining board as to their competency.[49] In commenting on the development of manual training in the school system, Gompers declared: "Manual training as a rule has simply had the tendency to improve the ability of youth to handle tools; but it has not had a great tendency to induce boys to follow certain trades." He said nothing about the fact that the difficulties these young workers encountered in becoming members of A. F. of L. unions may have been responsible for their relucance "to follow

* How little this tragic situation had changed in more than half a century is illustrated in the following item in the *New York Times* of June 9, 1963: "More often than not, Negro youths, by virtue of outright discrimination or inadequate education or guidance, are denied the right to acquire skills."

certain trades." William D. ("Big Bill") Haywood pointed to a tragic situation facing American youth when he declared in 1912: "I . . . want to assert—and I got it from knowledge gained by visiting the different prisons throughout the country—that the jails and penitentiaries of this country are filled with young men who have no trade, and a very large percentage of them have been denied the right to learn a trade by the fathers' trades unions."[50]

In sum, the practice of limiting apprentices and membership to relatives of members, the system of high initiation fees, and the rigid requirements of competence created what was called "an injurious and intolerable monopoly against the present and future generations."[51] The vast majority of young workers were forced into the ranks of unskilled labor where they composed an army of underpaid, highly exploited workers, almost completely unorganized.

CONCLUSION

When the Los Angeles Labor Council called the attention of the A. F. of L. Executive Council to the principle that the only sure way to protect "the American workingman and his standard of living is by universal organization of wage workers regardless of race or nationality," it pointed to the basic weakness in the Federation. Instead of "universal organization," the A. F. of L. had come to consist largely of skilled craftsmen, many with an open contempt for unskilled workers, a dislike for women, Negro and immigrant workers, and all others who might provide job competition. The A. F. of L.'s organizing policy was based on the unionization of a minority of the workers, a minority that was becoming smaller year by year as machinery and other modern technological innovations were transforming this organized minority of skilled workers into the majority of unskilled. "In 1910," writes James O. Morris, "most of the AFL's members came from unions (largely of the exclusive craft type) in building construction, the printing trades, and transportation and communication, and also from the United Mine Workers."[52] Manufacturing industries in 1910 contained 7,143,433 organizable workers. But unions in manufacturing industries (exclusive of printing and clothing) claimed about 430,000 members out of all organizable employees in manufacturing. Indeed, five unions alone in 1910—the Machinists, Molders, Boilermakers, Metal Polishers, Blacksmiths, and Pattern Makers—accounted for more than one third of all unionists in manufacturing![53]

The greatest impediment to the organization of American industries was the craft policy of the A. F. of L. The overwhelming majority of American workers, as we have seen, were unskilled laborers and factory workers, but the Federation's stubborn refusal to organize these classes of workers and its opposition to industrial unionism, made the organization of the workers in the mass production industries impossible.

The truth is that the A. F. of L. leaders had no real interest in organizing these groups of workers. In 1905 Gompers stated publicly that the masses of the unskilled were probably unorganizable, blaming it on their lack of intelligence. Looking back on the problem later in life, he defended the Federation's failure to exert itself in mass organizing campaigns by asserting that the unskilled were unorganized wholly because of *their* lack of courage, persistence, and vision, and that it could not be expected that the A. F. of L. should jeopardize its own organization in order to "rescue" them.[54]

The combination of craft unionism, craft autonomy, restrictive covenants in union constitutions, a male supremacist approach to women workers, a racist approach to Negro and foreign workers, and a callous indifference to the problems of the unskilled, produced the inevitable result—the unorganized status of the vast majority of the American workers.

CHAPTER 11

Political Policies and Practices, 1900-1905

Organized labor faced its enemy, organized capital, on two fronts: economic and political. As the leading spokesman for organized labor, the A. F. of L., in theory, was on record as supporting the principle that the trade unions should fight the enemy on both fronts. Gompers wrote in October 1900: "The A. F. of L. declares that every field, whether economic or political, in which the workers' class interests can be promoted, requires the attention of trade unionists. It declares, too, that while it is the duty of trade unionists to perform their duty on election day, it recognizes that on the other three hundred and sixty-four days of the year as well as on election day, it is necessary to stand in defense, and, to advance the interests of labor."[1]

A. F. OF L. ON POLITICAL ACTION

Nevertheless, year in and year out, at union meetings and conventions and in union newspapers and journals, the A. F. of L. leaders underlined the theory that economic action alone would enable labor to win in the struggle with capital. According to this line of thought, the trade union was equipped to solve all of labor's problems by its activity on the purely industrial field. "It will work out reforms and changes," Gompers wrote at the turn of the century, "and bring about the disenthrallment of the workers from every form of wrong. Economic action, through the trade union, is the only effective means for the wage earners of our time to achieve anything like progress and success."[2]

Political action was thus basically unnecessary; indeed, it would probably weaken the fundamental weapons the workers possessed in the struggle for a better life, for it would divert them from the all-important economic activity in the trade unions. Political groups were always at work trying to steal away the loyalties of the workers from their trade unions and to channelize their energy into political directions, and if they succeeded they would create conflict within the unions, make corruption inevitable, and ultimately lead to their destruction.* In 1900, Adolph Strasser, one of the men who helped shape the policies of the A. F. of L., was asked by the U.S. Industrial Commission: "Did you ever know of any trade union in the United States to live that went into politics?" He answered: "Not to my knowledge. They are all exterminated sooner or later. I mean partisan politics." In 1903, John Mitchell declared in a widely circulated statement: "Labor unions must be kept strictly apart from politics, and just as soon as they become political machines *they must die*. The mere suspicion of graft is fatal. I have tried hard to keep the mine workers as far from politics as possible. Even when our men are running for office, the local unions *do not indorse* them."[3]

In September 1902, Gompers wrote in the *American Federationist:* "I now address myself to the question of the ballot-box. What is to be remedied—the economic or the social or political life? If it is the economic life that is to be remedied, then it should be done through the economic life and through no other medium." Legislation could do little to improve the economic life. On the contrary, this type of assistance would prove more of a detriment than a benefit. Intervention of the federal or state governments in the sphere of labor relations through legislation would have disastrous consequences. Governmental assistance to workers would weaken individual incentive and enterprise and the desire of the workers to build strong unions. As John B. Lennon, A. F. of L. vice-president, wrote to Morrison in 1903: "If there is only the reason, to wit, that the more the men depend on the law, the less will they depend on their Trade Union, that would be sufficient to induce me to vote against demanding legislative reforms." But there were other reasons. Workers and their unions would eventually lose all freedom of action and would become powerless cogs in huge and all-powerful governmental machines. "The A. F. of L.," Gompers explained, "has apprehensions about the wisdom of placing in the hands of the government additional powers which may be used to the detriment of the working people." Once such power was given to the government, "you cannot avoid the danger of some form of compulsory labor."[4]

This line of argument was pursued by the A. F. of L. on the subject of

---

* John P. Frey recalls the following conversation with Gompers in the late 1890's: "Gompers asked me about my local union. 'How are they politically?' 'Well, I said, I think there are more Republicans than Democrats and we have a few Socialists.' 'Well,' he said, 'so far as your keeping them united is concerned, what would happen if you permitted a discussion of partisan politics, somebody wanting an endorsement of some political party?' The question carried its own answer." (Harvard University Seminar, May 11, 1948, *JFP*, Container 10.)

the general regulation of wages and hours in American industry by federal and state governments. Gompers and his associates never tired of repeating that, except in the case of child and women workers—who were too weak and helpless to defend their interests against the employers—and save in the case of government employees and workers under government contract, direct negotiations between the unions and the employers were infinitely more effective than any type of wage and hours legislation. For one thing, such legislation would lead workers to believe that it was not important for them to build and strengthen their unions. For another, wage rates fixed by legislation would become a ceiling rather than a floor. (The same would be true in the case of the shortening of hours by legislation.*) If government were given the right to fix minimum wages, it would assume the right not only to compel workers to work at these rates, but the right to reduce them. Wage rates increased by government, George E. McNeill declared in 1901 "may be [arbitrarily] reduced by the same forces. The gain won by unions, on the other hand, can be protected by them." Gompers told the bakers to cease seeking minimum wage and maximum hours legislation since "what the law gives or what the state gives, the state can take away; but what you get through your own exertions you can hold as long as you maintain your strength."[5]

Furthermore, progress in securing legislation to improve working conditions through governmental action was slow, cumbersome, and an unsure process at best. And even, if after much work and pressure, a union or a group of unions was able to get labor legislation through Congress or a State legislature, there was always the danger that it would be declared unconstitutional by the courts. Even when the courts allowed the laws to remain on the statute books, they were rarely enforced in the shops and factories. Thus John B. Lennon argued in justifying his stand against any concentration on legislative reforms:

"The theory often advanced is that all that is needed are good laws, labor laws. Now the fact is, that the statute books of the land are bursting with 'labor laws.' If one half of these laws were enforced, the condition of the wage-earners would be fairly good; but this, unfortunately, is not the case. We have the automatic coupler law; the factory law to protect the life and limbs of the employee; the bakery laws; the anti-truck laws; the screen laws; the anti-sweatshop laws; the anti-blacklisting laws. . . .

* For a short time, Gompers was an advocate of a universal eight-hour law for all workers. But by 1888 he had assumed the position that, except for government employees, women, and children, the workers should not invoke state interference in the matter. He maintained this principle throughout his life, in spite of repeated declarations by the A.F. of L. in favor of eight-hour laws for all workers. (*Proceedings*, A.F. of L. Convention, 1899, p. 107; 1913, p. 285.) Gompers, it is worth noting, excluded Negroes and immigrants from the group who should be aided by eight-hour legislation.

But these laws, and hundreds of others that I could mention, remain dead letters. Railroad men continue to be killed and maimed, because the railroad companies refuse to obey the automatic coupler laws; railroad employees continue to be worked over 10 hours a day, despite the 10 hour laws; employers disregard the provisions of the factory law to the sorrow of their workers; the baker shops continue to spread disease among the employees despite the baker shop laws; the mine workers continue to be plucked by the truck stores, and to be cheated of their pay, despite screen laws and anti-truck laws; women and children continue to be sweated as if no anti-sweatshop laws were there. . . .

"Why is this? Because they keep the minds of the workers off the main task of building their unions and only through their unions can the workers gain improvements in their conditions. These measures turn the workers' eyes away from the economic struggle, from which *alone* help can come."[6]

In short, the energy and funds expended by the workers to obtain legislative objectives could be much more profitably used in the industrial field. Inspired by such attitudes, the A. F. of L. set its face resolutely against a thoroughgoing program of social insurance including old age, unemployment, and sickness insurance. It held that all such legislation would render union organization less imperative, and it insisted that funds for the protection of the workers against industrial and social hazards should be provided by the union members themselves through the agency of union benefit funds, without any financial help from the federal and state governments. As Gompers editorialized in September 1900: "It [organized labor] does not depend on legislation. It asks no special privileges, no favors from the State. It wants to be let alone and to be allowed to exercise its rights and use its great economic power. . . . In fine, organized labor must depend on its own worth and superiority for continued progress."[7] What the A. F. of L. demanded from government was the guarantee of freedom to achieve its ends primarily through economic means, that is, through the unions, by protecting labor's right to organize and strike.* Labor's primary need was to be free from such legal or institutional restraints as impeded it in realizing its aspirations through economic means.

Year after year, Gompers, who largely shaped the Federation's official philosophy on this issue, reiterated this theme. Any expansion in state functions, any growth in governmental power would weaken the allegiance of workers to the trade unions, would seriously contract and eventually destroy the economic organizations of labor. How this theory

---

* The other area where government action was necessary was where legislation was the only possible method, such as immigrant restriction and the regulation of convict labor.

applied to the vast majority of Americans who were unorganized, Gompers did not bother to explain.[8]

It is clear that the A. F. of L. lacked a coherent attitude towards political action. On the one hand, Gompers insisted that the Federation upheld the doctrine that trade unionists must be simultaneously active on both the economic and political fronts. On the other, he and other A. F. of L. leaders stressed that political action was completely subordinate to economic action, while the chief purpose of political action was not to secure social legislation—which was denounced for reasons not dissimilar to those advanced by N.A.M.—but only to insure a climate favorable to the growth of the economic organizations of labor. The Federation's guiding principle in political action was set forth in the thesis that whatever part of labor's energy that could be spared from economic activity for political action—and it had to be a very small percentage—must be applied only in four directions: (1) in the nomination of candidates and in the formulation of the legislative programs of the existing major parties; (2) in elections, where endorsed candidates can be given labor's vote; (3) in the passage of specific legislation, and (4) in the process of administration. It should not and must not be exerted to nominate and elect labor candidates, to launch political programs by labor, and especially, to further the formation of a new independent party, whether labor or farmer-labor. This nonpartisan policy—bipartisan policy (support only of the major parties) would be a more correct term—was expressed in the slogan, "Stand faithfully by your friends. Oppose and defeat your enemies, whether they be candidates for President, for Congress or other offices, whether executive, legislative, or judicial."

To maintain, as the so-called nonpartisan policy did, that organized labor could bargain with both parties by offering votes in exchange for friendly candidates and favorable legislation, executive, and administrative policies was to assume, as Professor Harold J. Laski has pointed out, "that the Republican and Democratic parties are not concerned to promote class interest, but to operate for the well-being of the whole community." It was to assume further, again quoting Professor Laski, "that the American government, as the agent of the State power, is a neutral and mediating force among the different elements in society." Even Gompers knew better. "From the foundation of our Government up to the present day," he told an A. F. of L. convention towards the close of the 19th century, "the representatives of business and commerce have had absolute and exclusive representation in the Cabinet and in every Department of our Government." Labor got nothing but the run-around from both political parties, Gompers told the House Committee on Labor in 1900. "There is not anywhere that we can go for the purpose of trying to bring about some remedy, some change, some improvement, but we are met by the same position [from either party] . . . prompted by the same motive, and that is to leave the workmen helpless to the mercy of the employing class."[9]

Yet in advancing the thesis that the A. F. of L. must keep to the pure and simple path of "no politics in the unions and no unions in politics," confining its political activities to a "nonpartisan" policy, Gompers sought to convince the American workers that it could compel the government to be neutral in labor-capital relations. Actually, the basic theory of "reward your friends and punish your enemies" remained only a theory during the period under discussion. It was uttered many times before 1906, but in practice the Federation did little to translate even this limited form of political action into reality. It gave no stimulus, leadership, or direction to its affiliated unions on the manner of conducting their political action so as to elect "friendly" or defeat "unfriendly" candidates; did nothing to raise funds, print literature, send its leaders to speak in campaigns, and generally publicize the issues at stake and the legislative records of the candidates. In keeping with its general approach that the less political action the better, the A. F. of L., during this period, merely paid lip service even to the "reward your friends and punish your enemies" formula.[10]

UNION LABOR PARTY OF SAN FRANCISCO

The first large group of A. F. of L. members in the 20th century to learn, through actual experience, the fallacies of the political policy, or rather nonpolitical policy, that dominated the Federation were those in San Francisco. Here as early as 1901, the entire labor movement was in peril from the open-shop drive. By the summer, the destruction or preservation of organized labor hung in the balance. Although there were earlier skirmishes between labor and capital, the showdown came with the lockout of the union teamsters by the Draymen's Association on July 21, 1901. Labor charged that the Draymen's Association had been forced into the lockout by the Employers' Association which confronted it with the alternative of fighting the union or facing the competition of a new draying association sponsored by the organized employers.[11] The lockout spread to the entire waterfront and the teaming business of the city came virtually to a standstill.

Scabs were imported to replace the locked-out teamsters and when tension mounted, the Employers' Association called upon the police for immediate assistance. It came promptly. A special police officer was assigned to accompany each strikebreaker, and the police even acted as scabs themselves. "The police," the *Coast Seamen's Journal* charged, "are beginning to act freely in the interest of scab teamsters and their employers. . . . The police are not only helping in the work of loading scab teams under the pretense of protecting them, but they are actually driving the teams and in other ways acting with super-serviceable zeal."[12]

Labor's response was swift and unequivocal. It could not stand by while its unions were being destroyed singly. The teamsters' strike was decisive for the future of unionism on the west coast. Labor mobilized its forces. On July 29, the 14 maritime unions comprising the City Front Federation voted a general strike in support of the teamsters. Sixteen thousand sailors, longshoremen, marine firemen, ship and steamboat joiners, packers and warehousemen, ship clerks, porters, pile drivers and bridge builders, hoisting engineers, and steam and hot-water fitters walked out. The next day shipping was almost completely tied up. Vessels were deserted by their crews and remained moored to their anchors. Each day added to the number of idle vessels. Cargoes could not move. Business was at a standstill. Street traffic was effectively suspended. Farmers could not ship their produce.

The employers turned a deaf ear to proposals for a peaceful settlement of the strike. They refused steadfastly to meet labor's representatives. They were confident that if there was enough police brutality, it would only be a short time before the strike was smashed and unionism given its death blow. Mayor James D. Phelan transmitted the employers' request to the Chief of Police who ordered his men to smash the strike: "The strikers must be driven off the streets. . . . Drive the men to their homes and make them stay there. Keep the streets clear of union men."[13]

A reign of terror was unleashed. Pickets were clubbed and shot. Five deaths and 336 cases of assault were reported. Two hundred and fifty assaults required surgical attention. Police were instructed to arrest every man, known or suspected of being a member of a union, found on the water front after dark, and hundreds of union men were arrested; in fact, so many that the courts were unable to handle the cases brought them. "There are now more than six hundred mercenaries clothed with police power in this city," declared Andrew Furuseth, secretary of the Sailors' Union of the Pacific. "Among them are men lately released from San Quentin and other prisons. . . , opium fiends and other dregs of society who under ordinary conditions are kept under strict surveillance by the regular police. Men saturated with anti-social instincts, clothed with police power, furnished with clubs and guns, and feeling that behind them they have the all-powerful merchants and a friendly grand jury are not calculated to add to the peaceable condition of any city." Many of these police officers, hired for the emergency, were paid out of a fund raised by the Employers' Association.[14]

The vicious attack on labor's right to organize by the open-shop Employers' Association and the use of the police to break their strike, opened the eyes of most A. F. of L. unions in San Francisco to the weakness of their traditional approach to political action. Unions which had forbidden political issues to be discussed at meetings now began to talk of the need for making labor's strength felt at the polls as well as on the picket line. As early as June 1901, even before the lockout of the teamsters, a number of unions formed an Executive Committee to sponsor independent political action since the "appeals and supplications" which had been addressed to the muncipal authorities by organized labor "had met with scoffs and rebuffs." This movement grew enormously during the teamster-water front strike as the civic authorities repeatedly ignored labor's protest against regular police details for the protection of strikebreakers, and against the deputizing of hoodlums and other despicable characters as special officers. On July 28, Typographers' Local 15, condemning the Employers' Association, announced that "we will endeavor to make no mistake in the coming political struggle to put men in office who are broad-minded enough to recognize the fact that all American citizens have rights before the law, whether they be 'laborers' or 'employers.' "[15]

Encouraged by the growing enthusiasm in labor's ranks for independent political action, the Executive Committee decided to submit an independent ticket to the electorate. According to Section 1188 of the *Political Code of California,* three per cent of the entire vote cast at the previous election was required to petition for a new party to be placed on the ballot.

The top leaders of the A. F. of L. in San Francisco tried to halt the trend towards political action, especially toward independent political action. P. H. McCarthy, leader of the A. F. of L.'s Building and Trades' Council, warned the workingmen of the dangers to trade unionism inherent in political action, and denounced the movement for a labor party as "Socialism." Furuseth also opposed the movement, saying: "If men in the ranks of labor have any such purpose, it is a sad mistake and likely rises from resentment rather than common sense." Despite the opposition of the top A. F. of L. leadership, labor rallied to the slogan, "elect your own," and the signatures of the required number of petitioners were obtained easily.[16]

In June and early July, the *Coast Seamen's Journal,* upholding the traditional A. F. of L. policy toward political action, advised labor to avoid politics as "a movement of divisions," and warned the workers "that the idea of voting themselves into better economic conditions is a delusion and a snare." Anything of lasting value could only be won through the trade unions. By early fall, the *Journal* had changed its tune, and gave unstinting support to the movement for a labor party. It conceded that the theory that economic action alone could win what labor desired was fallacious, and the hope that government would confine itself to removing restraints from labor's economic power was not only naive but dangerous for the future of unionism. "Who can forget the shooting and clubbing of strikers, the wholesale arrests of hundreds of inoffensive men, the surrender of the entire police force to the Employers' Association?" it asked. Noting that labor had not forgotten, it observed approvingly: "A large number of men, members of trade unions of San Francisco, have organized for political purposes."[17]

In a short time, a far-flung organization for the initiation of a labor party emerged. When the convention to launch the party was called to order on September 5, approximately 300 delegates representing 68 unions were present.* Since the constitutions of some of the unions forbade direct participation in politics, the members met as political clubs after the adjournment of the regular union meetings, and elected delegates to the convention.

On the third day, the convention officially formed the Union Labor Party of the city and county of San Francisco on a platform which announced at the very outset: "We consider it of the utmost importance for the wage earners of this city, in order to better their conditions, to nominate and elect men directly from their own ranks who are eligible and place men in every office with the object of establishing the following measures." Then followed a number of progressive demands, the first of which was a call for revision of the city charter so that participation by the muncipal administration in labor disputes could be curbed. The other demands included municipal ownership of all public utilities; that all municipal supplies bear the union label; the erection of brick or stone school houses at the rate of one per year to be paid for out of current taxes; the removal of the schools from politics by making the advancement of teachers dependent on merit; the abolition of the poll tax. The platform opposed the granting of exclusive franchises to corporations unless ratified by a majority of the voters in the ensuing election after their proposal, and endorsed the popular initiative and referendum of legislative matters, the recall of officials, and proportional representation in the election of Supervisors. Unfortunately, the platform also contained a reactionary demand for the establishment of segregated schools for Asians.

Eugene E. Schmitz, president of the Musicians' Union, was nominated for Mayor,† and trade unionists were nominated for all other municipal offices with the exception of the Union Labor candidate for coroner who was chosen outside of the ranks of organized labor.[18]

The campaign was featured by red-baiting attacks on the Union Labor

* The Building Trades' Council, led by P. H. McCarthy, refused to send delegates, but two building trades' unions, the carpenters and the electrical workers, were represented. (San Francisco *Chronicle,* Sept. 6, 1901.)

† Although it was later revealed that Abraham Ruef, a San Francisco lawyer and political boss of the Republican Primary League, had a hand in the organization of the Union Labor Party and in the nomination of Schmitz, the movement sprang basically from the mass of the trade unionists in San Francisco and the lesson they had learned during the longshoremen-water front strike.

Party. The San Francisco *Bulletin* charged that the party introduced the "un-American principle of class struggle into a political campaign," that it was "dangerous because it represented a wrong political principle and because it established an un-American doctrine that a part of the people should dominate the entire people." The Building Trades' Council, acting under McCarthy's instructions, warned that the Labor Party represented a movement for class government, and declared that it desired "to impress upon every trades union man connected with the building trades industry that this muncipality is best governed when public servants are selected from the entire community without regard to any particular class." *Organized Labor,* the official journal of the Council, denounced the Labor Party as "foreign" in origin and "socialistic" in purpose.[19]

The *Coast Seamen's Journal* remarked dryly that if the Union Labor Party did represent a class it at least represented a class of the many, rather than the few. The City Front Federation, representing the teamster and water front unions, replied forthrightly that "while we are opposed to class government as such, we can see no means of resisting class government by the rich except by inaugurating, for the time being, a class government administration by those who have suffered oppression by such class government to the end that due respect and allegiance may in the future be given to the law, regardless of whose interest may be served thereby."[20]

Michael Casey, leader of the teamster-water front strike, came out strongly for the Labor Party ticket, stating publicly that independent political action was the only means of curbing disrespect for law by public officials during labor disputes. Even Andrew Furuseth had to yield before the overwhelming support for the new party in labor's ranks. When, towards the end of October, the grand jury failed to indict policemen and special guards accused of illegal activities in connection with their treatment of the strikers, he came out openly for the election of Schmitz, declaring: "I then fully realized that the employing class in this city had full control of the city's government and that the laborer and hired man had no chance. I found that we had a class government already and a dangerous one too."[21]

By the time of the election, the Union Labor Party was supported by every union in San Francisco except the Building Trades' Council, and a poll of the building trades' unions made just prior to the election, showed them to be 75 per cent in favor of the labor nominee.[22] Every commercial newspaper in San Francisco, except William Randolph Hearst's *Examiner,* bitterly opposed the Union Labor Party.

On election day labor won a smashing victory; Schmitz was elected mayor with a plurality vote of 21,806. The Union Labor Party elected three of the supervisors and lacked but 50 votes of electing at least three more. The election was a people's referendum against the employers' open-shop offensive and its active support by the city administration. The political victory insured that unionism would emerge triumphant in San Francisco. Directly after the election, the strike was settled in favor of the trade unions. The employers agreed not to discriminate against union men. Two days later, the scabs were discharged, and the strikers reinstated in their jobs, granted full union recognition and the union scale of wages and hours, including a 48-hour week. Although the unions failed to gain the closed shop, they had succeeded in checking the open-shop campaign. The battle which had begun with unionism in danger of complete and utter annihilation ended with unionism triumphant, and union labor controlling the government of the city.[23] The two developments, declared the *Coast Seamen's Journal* a week after the election, were interrelated: "San Francisco may be regarded with pride and hopefulness by every trade-unionist and lover of progress in the country. A year ago the trade unions existed, if not exactly upon sufferance, at least with very little substantial recognition from the government or the public. . . . Today the city is . . . a union town."[24]

With the Union Labor Party in power, the trade union movement in San Francisco experienced a tremendous upsurge. Assured that no policeman would assist scabs to break their strikes, the unions were strengthened in morale, increased membership, and forced the employers to recognize them. The employers knew that they had been deprived of their most powerful ally in the class struggle—the municipal government —and they were forced to capitulate. In April 1902, the Shipowners' Association came to terms with the Sailors' Union of the Pacific, signed a closed-shop agreement with the union, and made concessions in wages and hours. Thus ended a 17-year struggle by the Sailor's Union for recognition. This, in turn, increased union activity among all other water front unions, and they also gained union recognition and reduction of hours and increases in wages.[25]

In April 1902, the overworked and underpaid street car employees attempted to improve their status. The men asked the United Railroads Co., the principal employer of the carmen, for union recognition, restoration of men discharged for union activity since September 1901, a reduction in hours from 11½ to 10 hours a day, and a flat rate of 25 cents an hour instead of the current wage of $2.50 a day. The company refused to consider the demands or even to meet the representatives of the union. Thereupon, the union voted to strike.[26] On April 19, the strike was called and street car traffic in San Francisco came to an almost complete standstill. Determined to break the strike, the company imported strikebreakers and asked Mayor Schmitz for a police detail to protect the scabs. It also arranged with the Curtis Detective Agency for the employment of special police.

Up to this point, the strike was following the usual pattern, and might easily have been crushed by the power of the regular and special police. But the pattern was altered in San Francisco in the spring of 1902. Mayor Schmitz refused to grant the request for a police guard and ordered the Police Commissioners to issue no permits for any special policemen to carry firearms. Within a week, the company agreed to enter negotiations with the union representatives. Eight days after the strike had started, the company signed a contract with the union in which it agreed to all of its demands. "The Great Fight Won," the *Labor Clarion* exulted. It stressed that the refusal of labor's mayor to permit the United Railways to arm their own guards or furnish them with police guards was a crucial factor in the victory of the street car workers.[27]

The ability of unions involved in strikes during the Labor Party administration to survive employer attacks and to compel recognition is reflected in the growth of the entire labor movement. In the year 1900, there had been some 20,000 unionists in San Francisco. In 1902, a year after the election of a Labor Party mayor, the number had increased to 45,000, many of whom were unskilled workers. Nor were the unions successful only in their drives for increased membership. Union demands made upon the employers for reduction of hours of labor and wage increases also met with success. It is significant that the unskilled workers gained improvements in working conditions ordinarily enjoyed only by skilled craftsmen.[28]

With "Labor in the saddle," the Employers' Association disbanded. By the end of the Union Labor Party's first administration, San Francisco was the only closed-shop city in the United States.[29] In short, political action of organized labor not only had not weakened the trade unions of San Francisco, as the A. F. of L. leaders usually predicted, but had been extremely helpful in strengthening the entire labor movement of the city.

This significant blow to their theory did not, of course, please the A. F. of L. leadership. Gompers even considered appealing directly to the trade unions of San Francisco, warning them against continuing to support the United Labor Party. But he was dissuaded from such a step by Andrew Furuseth. Furuseth wrote from San Francisco in February 1903, that he, too, was unhappy that "the labor movement here has moved away from pure & simple trade unionism," and he agreed with Gompers that this was "a definite set-back for the policies of the American Federation of Labor. Unfortunately, the rank and file unionists see nothing wrong in this, and there is little hope in the immediate future that they will change their minds. It is pointless to try to convince them of their error. There seems to be nothing that you can do just now."[30]

The election results in the fall of 1903 bore out Furuseth's prediction. At the mass meeting on October 3, ratifying the renomination of Mayor Schmitz, George B. Benham, president of the Labor Council, warned the workers of San Francisco: "The working men hold the political

power in this city. If any other man than Eugene E. Schmitz is elected
to the office of Mayor and armed guards ride on the heads of the workers, let the workers place the blame where it belongs—on themselves."
P. H. McCarthy refused to heed this warning, and again denounced the
Union Labor Party for preaching "class hatred which scares away investors from this great and glorious city (and since it) drives capital away
from San Francisco, steals our chance of employment. But the workers,
including members of the Building Trades' unions,* thought otherwise.
Schmitz was re-elected, winning a total of 26,016 votes, and was especially
strong in working class districts.[31][†]

In the election of 1905, not a single union or union leader opposed
the Union Labor Party ticket—not even McCarthy of the Building
Trades' Council. There were two reasons for this. In the first place,
union labor was well satisfied with the two administrations of Mayor
Schmitz. The four years had been characterized by increasing strength
of the unions and well-being for the working class. While the period was
also marked by several sharp clashes between labor and capital, all of the
disputes had been settled to the advantage of the workers, and several
were prevented when Mayor Schmitz made the employers understand
that they would not get police protection.[32] The menace of the use of
the police and other law-enforcement officials, including private detectives and guards, to the detriment of organized labor, had been effectively eliminated.

The second reason was the entrance on the San Francisco scene early
in 1904 of the Citizens' Alliance, organized by Herbert George, one of
the most active of the anti-unionists in the nation-wide open-shop drive.
George introduced the Alliance into San Francisco after he had launched
a successful anti-union campaign in Denver, Colorado. Soon the San
Francisco Alliance numbered thousands of members—16,000 were said to
belong in December 1904—who pledged themselves to re-establish "the
Americanism of the Open-Shop in San Francisco" by locking out union
men and refusing to do business with union firms. To those firms which
honored their pledge, the Alliance supplied strikebreakers and financial
assistance. But San Francisco was not Denver; the employers discovered
that their inability to obtain police protection for the strikebreakers
crippled the Alliance campaign and produced meager results for its open-
shop drive. The Citizens' Alliance decided that there was only one
solution to the problem: Unseat the Labor Party mayor![33]

* McCarthy tried to "deliver" the Building Trades' Council's votes to the Republican candidate, but the resentment this created among the members of the Council
caused this maneuver to backfire and actually increased support for Schmitz.
(*Labor Clarion,* San Francisco, vol. II, no. 37, Nov. 6, 1903.)

† The Party elected only one supervisor, but the emphasis in the campaign was
on the mayoralty office.

In the 1905 election, the Alliance first tried to split the labor vote in the primaries by forming the United Labor League. It was expected that P. H. McCarthy would swing the Building Trades' Council behind the League, but the Council warned McCarthy not to do the Citizens' Alliance's "dirty work," and he was forced to support the Union Labor Party. Said McCarthy in a public statement: "The Democrats and Republicans want us to have a row so that they may fuse on a Citizens' Alliance ticket and bring Colorado to California. I shall stand by the man who has fought the Alliance, who has been true to Labor, Eugene E. Schmitz. I am opposed to those men who are advocating two labor tickets at the primaries."[34] The failure of the primary maneuver made it absolutely essential for the Republican and Democratic parties to fuse on a single ticket if there was to be any chance left of defeating the Union Labor Party. Pressured by the Citizens' Alliance, whose members controlled both parties, the Republicans and Democrats nominated a fusion ticket. The Alliance immediately endorsed the fusion ticket, and issued thousands of circulars calling for defeat of the Union Labor Party:

"All that now remains to insure San Francisco a long season of industrial peace and commercial prosperity is the election of a Mayor who will be a Mayor for all of the people and not a class of the people. With the proper maintenance of the Citizens' Alliance and a progressive Mayor in the chair and a Police Commission favoring law and order, we may depend upon a police department to be ready and willing at all times to arrest lawbreakers regardless of their religious, political, fraternal, union or non-union affiliations and this is all that is needed in any community to make it a comfortable place to live in."[35]

The brutal frankness of these circulars, the *Coast Seamen's Journal* pointed out, made the election issue crystal clear: "That issue is: Which class shall control, the working classes or the business classes represented by the Citizens' Alliance?"* Herbert George conceded that this was an accurate evaluation of the situation: the lines in the campaign were "drawn between the unions and the Citizens' Alliance."[36]

To San Francisco unionists the demands of the Alliance for "a Mayor for all the people" and "a Police Commission favoring law and order" were simply dodges to effect the election of public officials who would assist the employers to restore the open shop. "Schmitz will be beaten and organized labor with him," the San Francisco *Bulletin* predicted as it colorfully pictured the city operating as an open shop, freed from

---

* On January 13, 1904, the *Coast Seamen's Journal* announced that it would uphold the principle, "Labor Unions *Must Not* enter politics" in the 1905 campaign. But the open participation of the Citizens' Alliance in the campaign caused it to change its position and support the Union Labor Party. "Citizens' Alliance Politics" had to be answered by "Union Labor Politics." (April 26, 1905.)

control by "stupid and ignorant workers." But when the returns were in, they marked the complete triumph of the Union Labor Party. It swept its ticket into office from top to bottom. Not only was Schmitz reelected, but, for the first time, he carried into office the Labor Party's full slate of supervisors.[37]

REPERCUSSIONS ELSEWHERE

News of the three successive victories at the polls by the Union Labor Party of San Francisco was received with jubilation by unionists throughout the country. In California, labor parties were organized in a number of communities as union members decided to adopt independent political action as a means of strengthening their campaigns to win economic demands. "The unions are becoming very active in the political game," the Los Angeles *Times* reported in the summer of 1902, after a survey of trends throughout the state.[38] Beyond the confines of California, the impact of the San Francisco experience was reflected in the nomination and election of union candidates to local office from mayor down. The mayor elected to office in Marietta, Ohio, in the spring of 1903 was the president of the Federal Labor Union, the president of the City council was the head of the A. F. of L. Trades Council, and all of the other local officeholders were described as "either members of unions or else friendly to organized labor." At a meeting of the Industrial Council (central labor body) of Kansas City in the winter of 1904, the experience of San Francisco labor was cited in calling upon the unionists to take a united stand at the spring election. Each local union was requested to send delegates to a special meeting to discuss the question. Over 100 unions responded, and an organization was formed, which became known as the Voters' League. In the spring election, the League nominated labor candidates for municipal offices, and elected a majority of the city council.[39]

"The example of San Francisco has shown us our strength," the Connecticut State Federation of Labor declared in urging the A. F. of L. leadership to mobilize the labor movement throughout the nation for independent political action. From San Francisco Ray Stannard Baker, the prominent journalist, wrote worriedly to President Theodore Roosevelt in the fall of 1903, ". . . conservative [labor] leaders here and elsewhere, as you doubtless know, are having trouble to keep the lid down on the union political pot. It wouldn't take much to stampede the whole labor movement into a big national party."[40]

In 1904 the 24th annual A. F. of L. convention met in San Francisco. Representative of the San Francisco trade unions appealed to the delegates to learn the lesson of the Union Labor Party's achievement in smashing the open-shop drive and to help it establish the movement for independent political action on a national scale. "It is our boast, and a justifiable one, I hope you will admit," J. O. Walsh, president of the San Francisco Labor Council informed the delegates, "that San Francisco is one of the most thoroughly organized cities in the United States." Although fundamentally the strength of the unions, he pointed out, was the result of their own economic efforts, the fact that both workers and employers knew that the labor administration would not help break strikes was of tremendous importance. Certainly the trade unions in many communities who were facing the mounting employers' offensive could help their economic struggles by emulating their fellow-unionists of San Francisco. Even P. H. McCarthy conceded, in his speech to the delegates, that the Union Labor Party had been a decisive force in the great power wielded by San Francisco unionism. "You are in the best organized city in the world today," he concluded. "I stand ready to give you $100.00 for each and every scab mechanic that you can find."[41]

The Socialist delegates to the convention backed up these appeals with resolutions urging the A. F. of L. to go on record in favor of independent political action. But the A. F. of L. leaders turned a deaf ear to the appeals, and the bureaucracy defeated the resolutions without difficulty. The truth is that the A. F. of L. leaders had, from the inception of the Union Labor Party, viewed the movement with alarm, and had tried to prevent its spread outside of the West Coast metropolis. When the Los Angeles Council of Labor voted to nominate a Union Labor Party ticket in the summer of 1902, Gompers dispatched a warning that the Council would lose its charter if it entered partisan politics, an action that split trade union support for independent political action. In an effort to placate Gompers, the Council of Labor proposed that the Union Labor Party would only advocate "the political demands of the American Federation of Labor, present and future, and such state or municipal demands as will benefit the working class, primarily, and finally all classes."* But Gompers was not impressed. He even came to Los Angeles in person, together with several members of the A. F. of L. Executive Council, and spent a week urging the trade unions to "take the 'no politics' route." Yielding to Gompers' warnings and threats, the Los Angeles Council of Labor withdrew from the Union Labor Party, and, deprived of its main trade union base, the party was unable to roll up an impressive vote at the polls.[42]

---

* Among the demands of the Union Labor Party of Los Angeles were direct legislation, abolition of the contract system on public work, the eight-hour day on public work, the union label on public printing, civil service reform, equal pay for men and women, weekly payment of wages for municipal employees, city ownership of municipal franchises, better public school facilities, free school books, establishment of night schools and public playgrounds, ample compensation for teachers, and an adequate sewage system.

"GOVERNMENT BY INJUNCTION"

Although the A. F. of L. leaders were successful in blocking and disrupting the movement for independent political action, they could not hide the fact that events since 1900 demonstrated that their political policy was in need of drastic revision. "The paramount issue in American politics in the future must necessarily be the abolishment of Government by injunction," wrote a top A. F. of L. leader.[43] By this test alone, the A. F. of L. policy towards political action proved itself a failure.

From 1894 on, when the American Railway Union strike led by Eugene V. Debs against the Pullman Co. was broken by a government injunction, the issuance of injunctions "came in rapid succession from both state and federal courts."* The injunction became the open-shoppers' most powerful weapon, and its use became increasingly frequent for all kinds of anti-labor purposes—especially to break strikes and boycotts, and even to prevent union organization, for most injunctions could forbid the intimidation of non-union workers, and most judges held that picketing was necessarily intimidating and unlawful. If a strike was declared unlawful in itself, all actions promoting the strike were unlawful and could be forbidden by injunction, and the result of violating it was usually trial for contempt. As Louis Brandeis pointed out, such contempt charges "were tried by a single judge, sitting without a jury. Charges of violating an injunction were often heard on affidavit merely, without the opportunity of confronting or cross-examining witnesses. Men found guilty of contempt were committed in the judge's discretion, without either a statutory limit upon the length of the imprisonment, or the opportunity of effective review on appeal, or the right of release on bail pending possible revisory proceedings. The effect of the proceeding on the individual was substantially the same as if he had been successfully prosecuted for a crime, but he was denied, in the course of the equity proceedings, those rights which by the Constitution are commonly secured to persons charged with crime."[44]

"Strikes are usually won or lost in the first few days," Edwin E. Witte, the noted American jurist observes, "and it is at this crucial time that labor injunctions are most devastating." Even if the injunction was appealed and overruled by a higher court, the unions would still be involved in time-consuming and costly legal proceedings that might

* Frankfurter and Greene list in the Federal courts alone 12 injunctions from 1894 to 1901, and 18 cases from 1901 to 1905. (Felix Frankfurter and Nathan Greene, *The Labor Injunction,* New York, 1932, p. 49.) Gompers said in 1911: "As in the State of Massachusetts from 1898 to 1908, employers petitioned for injunctions in sixty-six cases, and injunctions were actually issued in forty-six, it may be estimated that the entire number granted throughout the country in that time reached not less than a thousand." (*Proceedings,* A.F. of L. Convention, 1911, p. 53.)

seriously deplete the union treasury and thereby possibly destroy the union. Furthermore, during the period in which the appeal would be pending before the courts, the union could be prevented by virtue of the injunction from continuing its organizing activities.[45]

The interpretation of the Sherman Anti-Trust Act by the courts as applying to labor unions as bodies aiming at a restraint of trade which could be acted against on these grounds, gave a basic legal justification for the use of the injunction. It became apparent that some sort of federal legislation would have to be put into effect which would outlaw the injunction and exempt labor unions from the application of the Sherman Act. This was imperative if the A. F. of L. was to retain the slow and painful gains which it had made since its formation in 1881, and if further advances by its affiliated unions in the industrial field were not to be brought to a complete standstill. "What labor demanded was relief from the injustice by which workers were singled out and judicial authority applied to them for the exercise of their personal rights and activities within the law. It demanded government by law and of law, not the manufacturing and torturing of the law by reactionary judges for the purpose of paralyzing organized labor."[46]

A. F. OF L. SEEKS TO END "GOVERNMENT BY INJUNCTION"

In 1896, soon after its headquarters had been established at Washington, the A. F. of L. began an active campaign in Congress for the repeal of the labor clauses of the Sherman Act, and for an anti-injunction law. (It also pushed for a bill establishing an eight-hour day for workers in Federal government projects, but this was considered secondary in importance to the anti-injunction bill.) In 1897, Gompers assured the American workers that "a wise and persistent course on the part of organized labor" would eliminate the threat of "government by injunction." By "a wise and persistent course," Gompers meant applying pressure on Congressmen through the A. F. of L.'s lobbying tactics, but, at the same time, avoiding any involvement in "partisan politics."[47]

It proved to be wishful thinking. Year after year the A. F. of L. Legislative Committee patiently lobbied at each session for passage of an anti-injunction bill. It would get friendly members of the Republican and Democratic parties to introduce an anti-injunction bill into the two Houses, where it was almost invariably shelved or sidetracked at some stage of the legislative process through the powerful influence of the employers' associations' lobbies: N.A.M., the Anti-Boycott Association, and the National Council of Industrial Defense. The open-shoppers had a staunch ally and friend in "Uncle Joe" (Joseph G.) Cannon, the Republican Speaker of the House of Representatives, who used his semi-dictatorial powers to appoint anti-labor members to the Committee of the House and thereby stall the bills favored by the A. F. of L. With good reason the Speaker of the House under McKinley, Roosevelt, and Taft was called in labor circles "Czar" Cannon.

The high mark of A. F. of L. success against Cannon's obstructive tactics came in 1903, when following an appeal to all unionists to apply pressure on Congress, an anti-injunction bill was passed in the House of Representatives. But it was defeated in the Senate. Alarmed by the action of the House in passing a bill which "would remove" trade unions from prosecution "under the operation of the Sherman Anti-Trust Law," the employers' lobby was determined to bar repetition of this action by any succeeding House, and brought pressure on the members of the House Judiciary Committee where the bill had originated. On April 16, 1904, the New York *Tribune* reported that "the result of extended hearings has been to convince the Committee that they erred last year in ordering a favorable report . . . This action on the part of the Committee will effectually block the attempt to nullify a just law because of alleged reckless administration." It was an accurate prediction. During subsequent Congressional sessions for the next few years, the A. F. of L.'s agitation to revive the bill came to nothing.[48]

The A. F. of L. received little help in its battle against the injunction from President Theodore Roosevelt. The Federation leaders who naively boasted that Roosevelt's role during the anthracite strike of 1902 made him a friend of organized labor were swiftly disillusioned. In the summer of 1903, in the Miller case, Roosevelt, it will be recalled, came out in favor of the open-shop principle in the federal employment of engravers. On August 20, a Presidential order extending the open shop to all branches of the executive was made public. Besides the Bookbinders' local, the members of the Typographical Union and other unions employed in the government printing office, and of the machinists' union employed in the navy yard were affected. As Euguene V. Debs noted: "A very severe blow has been struck at organized labor and its effect will be far-reaching, as it will virtually non-unionize the government printing office and other departments of the public service, and will also serve as a precedent for employers of labor generally." Members of the A. F. of L. Executive Council, led by Gompers, called on the President to protest. They accomplished nothing; moreover, when the Bookbinders' Union threatened to strike, Roosevelt wrote to Senator Henry Cabot Lodge, his anti-union friend who influenced the President considerably, that "if they did, not a man jack of the strikers would get back into the Government service while I [am] President."[49]

Before Roosevelt's administration, government workers had enjoyed the right to make direct appeals to Congress for wage increases. But

Roosevelt issued a "gag-order" prohibiting government employees from soliciting increases in pay by attempting to influence legislation, either before Congress or its committees. In the future all government employees were to be limited to working through departments or suffer the penalty of dismissal.[50]

During his first administration, Roosevelt refused to further any distinctive labor reforms. Although he admitted, for instance, that the courts abused the use of injunctions in labor cases, he refused to support the anti-injunction bill sponsored by the A. F. of L. His cabinet appointment of "Injunction Bill" (William Howard) Taft and of Paul Morton who had broken the Chicago, Burlington and Quincy and the Santa Fe strikes had been bitterly protested to no avail by organized labor. By his insistence on the right of the Federal government to intervene in strikes through the use of troops and by his attacks on the closed shop as an unjustifiable monopoly, Roosevelt merited being welcomed by the open-shoppers as an ally in their nation-wide drive.[51]

CONGRESSIONAL CAMPAIGN OF 1904

By the summer of 1904, the prospect of securing anti-injunction legislation by the lobbying efforts of the Federation's legislative committees appeared doomed. J. Mahlon Barnes, national secretary of the Socialist Party and an influential figure in the Cigarmakers' International Union, even proposed an amendment to the A. F. of L. constitution prohibiting the maintenance of a lobbying committee. "All methods of lobbying," he asserted, "are bowing the head and presenting ourselves in an undignified attitude, and the results obtained so far have not been commensurate with the efforts put forth or the funds expended in that direction." Both major parties, he insisted, were tools of the capitalist class and vied with each other in beating down the legislation requested by labor. They would respect labor only when the latter ceased to beg for its rights and organized politically to fight for them and to take them. Gompers, in reply, admitted that the Federation had not yet secured all that it demanded, that it had suffered setbacks. But he insisted that there were notable achievements secured by nonpartisan methods, and that many more would still be obtained in the future.[52] Nevertheless, it was clear that Barnes was voicing an opinion that was being expressed more and more inside the A. F. of L., and the Executive Council had to take some heed of this feeling. For the fall election campaigns, the A. F. of L. adopted a new strategy—the plan of systematic nonpartisan questioning of candidates for Congress and the state legislatures. By announcing that it would publicize the replies, the Federation hoped to force the candidates of both major parties to pledge themselves in favor of pro-labor legislation.* Candidates for election to the House of Representatives were questioned directly. Since U.S. Senators were elected by state legislatures at the time, the only method of reaching prospective Senators was to question candidates for election to the state legislatures. In areas where nomination was usually equivalent to an election—as in the South —the candidates for nomination by the party conventions would be questioned and their written answers published.

Three national measures were selected to which the system of questioning was to be applied in the campaign of 1904. These were (1) an anti-injunction bill, (2) a bill proposing to limit the hours of work in government contracts to eight hours, and (3) a proposal that steps be taken toward the adoption of an amendment to the Federal Constitution providing for the initiative and referendum on questions involving interstate railways and other corporations doing an interstate business. The text of the three proposed measures, their history before former sessions of Congress, and arguments in favor of their enactment, were published in a special number of the *American Federationist,* July 15, 1904, running to 28 pages of double columns in small print. This special publication was distributed to the secretary of every union affiliated with the Federation and the chairmen of local union legislative committees, who were asked to pass them along to candidates to be questioned, and to read the contents at regular union meetings. The circular accompanying the pamphlet emphasized: "Don't let any candidate 'bluff you off' or evade the issue by telling you the law prohibits him from making a pledge. The law does no such thing. If it did, no political party would dare make promises in its platform, and no candidate would dare pledge himself to carry out these promises. But you know they do every election." The circular stated that the issue at stake was "the establishment of the people's sovereignty. It is not only a labor question or simply a question of capitalism, but a question of monopoly. Shall the monopoly of the political power of the country be in all the people or continued in the ruling few? It is the people against the monopolies."[53]

"If the questioning of candidates is heartily pushed by all the unions," Gompers wrote to the A. F. of L.'s central labor bodies on July 15, 1904, "there is an excellent prospect of success." And success in this endeavor would prove the value of the A. F. of L.'s nonpartisan approach to political activity "without engaging in party politics." Gompers pointed

---

* This system of nonpartisan questioning of candidates was not really new. It was used in 1902 by the Missouri State Federation of Labor and a year later in several municipalities, including Detroit, Michigan, Winnetka, Illinois, Waco, Texas, and Toronto, Canada. This system was used in state elections by the Missouri State Federation of Labor as early as 1901, and, in 1903, it applied it in the Congressional campaign. (*Proceedings,* A.F. of L. Convention, 1901, p. 28; *American Federationist,* Jan. 15, 1904, p. 13.)

with pride to the fact that the literature of the A. F. of L., including the 28-page special issue of the *Federationist,* was thoroughly nonpartisan, neither political party being mentioned.[54] But Gompers pointedly ignored a question asked him by the Hartford *Times:* "If it happens that none of the candidates of either party, or only a few of them, shall obey his command as to a prompt answer, what will Mr. Gompers do about it? Will he establish a party of his own?"[55]

The A. F. of L. Executive Council did not publish a report on the number of candidates labor had been able to pledge. It did cite the fact that Missouri had pledged 12 of its 16 Congressmen, but conceded that this was not typical: "Equally good results would doubtless have been attained in most of the other states had there been an equally zealous questioning of candidates."[56] But nothing was said of the fact that there were complaints from the rank and file members that the Federation refused to outline a plan to follow up the pledge system with concrete action to elect candidates who supported the three demands in the questionnaire and oppose those who refused to commit themselves in this direction. Even the principle of "reward our friends and punish our enemies," it was pointed out, would have been better than merely to distribute questionnaires and publicize the responses. Some went further and protested to the Executive Council that the whole idea of expecting to obtain pro-labor legislation from candidates of the major parties was fallacious. Local No. 49 of the United Brotherhood of Leather Workers on Horse Goods complained to the A. F. of L. Executive Council: "Can we as progressive Trade Unionists expect the representatives of the capitalist class to legislate for the interests of the Laboring class? If we really wish to have laws passed for the interest of Labor, must we not elect men from our class to represent our own class in the same way that the capitalist does?"[57]

New Time of Spokane, Washington, made the same point: "Mr. Gompers betrays his ignorance of the class character of our government when he hopes that candidates of parties whose campaign expenses are paid by corporations, who owe their whole power to the fact that they are backed by corporate wealth, are going to vote for any bills which will interfere with their benefactors, the corporations."[58]

The N.A.M.'s role in the Congressional campaign of 1904 pointed up even more sharply the total ineffectiveness of the A. F. of L.'s concept of political action. The open-shop association singled out William Hughes, who was running for re-election to Congress from the Sixth New Jersey District, for defeat. (Hughes had incurred N.A.M.'s displeasure because he held a union card, was affiliated with the A. F. of L., and was a leading labor member of the House.) The N.A.M. sent "Colonel" Martin M. Mulhall, its lobbyist, to bribe A. F. of L. officials into campaigning for Henry C. Allen, the Republican candidate for Congress. With the assistance of labor leaders, among them George Curtin, secretary of the Allied Building Trades of Philadelphia; Frank Feeney, head of Philadelphia's Central Labor Council; Jacob Casselier, a general organizer of the A. F. of L., and William Ryan, an official of the Electrical Workers' Union, N.A.M. defeated the pro-labor candidate. The A. F. of L. leaders were too busy extolling the questionnaire method to pay much attention to Hughes' campaign.[59]

PRESIDENTIAL CAMPAIGN OF 1904

In the Presidential campaign of 1904, the two major parties displayed their contempt for the A. F. of L.'s political influence. Neither the Republican nor the Democratic platforms incorporated any of the A. F. of L.'s demands. The Republican platform praised Roosevelt's intervention in the coal strike, but it said nothing of substance on the subject of labor, contenting itself with the vague statement: "Combinations of capital and labor are the results of the economic movement of the age, but neither must be permitted to infringe upon the rights and interests of the people. Such combinations when lawfully formed for lawful purposes are alike entitled to the protection of the laws, but both are subject to the laws, and neither can be permitted to break them."[60] Theodore Roosevelt was quickly nominated the Republican Presidential candidate.

In 1904, the Democratic party was completely dominated by the Eastern industrialists and bankers who had regained control after the defeat of William Jennings Bryan in 1900. They insisted that the party "required safety and conservatism as the strongest issues," and for this it was necessary to ditch the progressive elements, including organized labor. In keeping with this approach, the party platform vaguely came out for legislation which would give labor and capital "impartially their just rights." It conceded that the rights of labor were no less vested than the rights of capital, and should be so recognized. But when it came to specific proposals, the platform contented itself with declaring for arbitration of differences between corporate employers and their employees.[61]

The labor question did arise at the Democratic convention in the battle over the Presidential candidate. William Randolph Hearst, a contender for the candidacy, had been trying for several years to line up labor support behind him by championing labor demands and opposing "corporate tyranny." While he was motivated by opportunistic reasons, Hearst did support labor's struggles in his newspapers—the New York *American,* the New York *Evening Journal,* the Chicago *American,* and the San Francisco *Examiner*—and in most of the crucial strikes of this period, these were the only commercial newspapers in these communities to stand by the labor movement. The Hearst press exposed the open-shop propagandists, defended trade unionism and the closed shop,* opposed "government by injunction," endorsed higher wages and shorter hours, and attacked the trusts and corporate control of government. They also repeatedly called upon the trade unions to fight capital on both the economic and political fronts.[62]

Hearst and his henchmen organized political clubs (called Hearst Clubs and W. R. Hearst Leagues) throughout the country for the sole purpose of promoting his candidacy for the Presidency. His papers published tributes by these clubs to him as "the workers' champion . . . and a labor leader under whose standard democracy can achieve overwhelming triumph at the polls next November." (Many of these tributes were repudiated by the men named as having been falsely attributed to them.) Democrats in Congress were inundated by a flow of petitions from workers (or said to be from workers) asking that they use their influence to secure the nomination of Hearst "as the chosen advocate of the working class in the United States." According to Ferdinand Lundberg, Hearst spent at least $1,400,000 of his own money to try for the Democratic nomination.[63]

Although Hearst failed to obtain A. F. of L. endorsement for his candidacy,† he entered the Democratic convention with considerable labor support for his nomination. The Printers and the Letter Carriers were especially active in his behalf because his newspapers had attacked President Roosevelt's "gag order" against government employees, had supported the letter carriers' plea for higher wages and circulated petitions in their behalf. In seconding Hearst's nomination, Clarence Darrow, the great pro-labor lawyer, emphasized his following in labor circles: "Nominate William Randolph Hearst, and that great army of toilers, that great industrial army, the real army of the civilized world today will look forward with gladness and hope to a victory which will mean something when it comes."[64]

Regardless of the question of Hearst's sincerity, there is no doubt but that his candidacy alarmed the conservative leaders in control of the Democratic party. August Belmont, Wall Street banker, National Civic Federation president, and president of the Interborough Rapid Transit Co., where he was to establish the open shop, led the movement to nominate Judge Alton B. Parker. Although Parker had taken a liberal stand

---

* In a signed editorial, Hearst announced that there was "no more useful, promising, and enlarging feature . . . in the nation than trades unionism." (New York American, May 21, 1903.)

† Ferdinand Lundberg asserts that just before the Democratic convention, Hearst went to Gompers in an attempt to get his support, but that the A.F. of L. President refused it. (Imperial Hearst, New York, 1936, p. 101.) Gompers made no statement on this subject in his autobiography, and there is no evidence in the A.F. of L. Archives that such a meeting took place.

on labor issues in several cases,* he had endeared himself to the million-aires in control of the Democratic Party by having ruled the New York eight-hour law unconstitutional. He was essentially a conservative, and, as such, was opposed by Bryan and the liberal forces in the party.[65] But the Eastern bankers and businessmen dominated the convention, and Parker was nominated the Democratic standard-bearer.

Labor demands fared better in the platforms of the minority parties. The Populist convention declared that labor had the right to organize and the party pledged itself to preserve that right without compromise. The Populists agreed with Lincoln that labor was prior to capital, and called for legislation that would establish an eight-hour day in govern-ment service in the belief that this would stimulate its adoption in the factories, workshops, and mines; for legislation to abolish child labor, suppress sweatshops, eliminate the competition of convict labor with free labor, and exclude foreign labor from American shores. The last demand was in keeping with the chauvinistic orientation of the Populist movement as was the nomination of Tom Watson, now a demagogic anti-Negro leader, for President.

The Socialist Party was the only one to specifically condemn the use of injunctions and military forces to break strikes. In addition, among other demands, the party called for shorter hours of labor, increase in wages, insurance of workers against accident, sickness, and unemploy-ment, and pensions for aged and exhausted workers.[66] Eugene V. Debs, respected in trade union circles throughout the country, especially among the rank and file, was nominated as the Socialist Presidential candidate.

The A. F. of L. and its affiliated unions took little part in the Presiden-tial contest. The election resulted in a two-million majority for Roosevelt who had enormous financial support from big business. Of the 13,523,519 votes cast, Roosevelt received 7,628,834 and Parker 5,084,491. However, the Socialists, with 408,000 votes, polled more than four times their 1900 vote. Some of this increase undoubtedly came from disgruntled Demo-crats, for the Democratic vote decreased by more than one quarter of a million. The total vote cast in the election was 460,000 less than in the 1900 election, and nearly 430,000 less than in 1896—and this despite the increase in population. Evidently this drop reflected the fact that many were convinced both of the major parties had avoided the main issues. Some voted Socialist, but others stayed away from the polls.[67]

One fact emerged clearly from the election—the obvious one that the

* In one case Parker had voted in favor of the right of labor unions to obtain a closed shop by threatening to strike. (170 N.Y. Reports 315.); in *People vs. Loch-ner*, he voted to uphold the constitutionality of an Act of 1897 limiting the hours of work in New York bakeries to sixty a week (177 N.Y. Reports 144); in an-other case, he insisted that a decent wage scale be given to workmen in public works and that the wage should be equal to the prevailing rate of wages in private industry. (166 N.Y. Reports 1.)

A. F. of L.'s political policies had contributed little toward solving labor's most pressing problems. In April 1905, the Pennsylvania State Federation of Labor dispatched an urgent message to trade unionists throughout the country which opened: "Arouse Yourselves! The Organized Wage Earners Must Get Busy!" It continued:

"The organized wage earners of the United States and of the several states have for years been demanding legislation to protect workingmen from injustice and oppression. Nationally nothing has been accomplished for ten years. Government by injuction is still in force, by which attorneys of corporations, through the accommodating Federal judges, restrain the right of the people to assemble, and in some instances, even to speak to their fellow workmen during a strike or lockout. The bill before Congress for some years to complete the legislation for the eight-hour workday has also been ignored by those who we have elected to represent us, and other legislation asked for has met a similar fate. In our own State inspection in factories and mines is only partially accomplished, and child labor still dwarfs the bodies and minds of our children, and it was only with great effort that the bill to tax coal production was defeated. We can not continue with this do-nothing policy and retain even the small rights that the politicians have grudgingly granted."[68]

The labor press in the opening months of 1905 was filled with similar complaints reflecting widespread dissatisfaction with the A. F. of L.'s political policy and practice. The *Leather Workers' Journal* of March 1905 carried a typical comment in a letter from Branch 49, Cincinnati, Ohio:

"Organized labor is trying to do Twentieth Century business on an 18th century plan. The A. F. of L. says politics must not come into organized labor, then turns around and sends representatives into the halls of Congress to beg and plead and pray with men to whom we have given our ballot to pass and make laws that are fair and just to all mankind. Every member of organized labor knows that all our efforts in this direction have been in vain. We say it is high time organized labor was getting up from her knees and stop begging and pleading and praying to representatives of capital to enact laws that will benefit her. It is time that we elect representatives of labor and send them to Congress, there to enact laws that will be just and fair to all mankind."[69]

In the same month that this communication was published, Morrison announced that there was no reason for the A. F. of L. to change the form of its political activity. "It is an unwritten law that the A. F. of L. should maintain a non-partisan approach to politics, should not engage in political campaigns directly, should avoid partisan politics lest the trade unions be ruined, and should constantly remind the trade unions that they must depend primarily on the use of their economic strength to advance labor's interests."[70] The A. F. of L. leadership had evidently learned nothing from events since the turn of the century!

CHAPTER 12

Labor's "Bill of Grievances" and the 1906 Campaign

A series of events occurred during the remaining months of 1905 which forced even the A. F. of L. leaders to concede that the "unwritten law" of "no politics in the unions" was obsolete. The open-shop drive of the employers' associations reached a high point, and one of its manifestations was the intensification of the antagonism which the courts displayed towards organized labor.

INCREASING ATTACK ON LABOR

1. The Supreme Court of Massachusetts decided in 1905 that a union shop agreement which existed between employer and union did not entitle the union to demand the discharge of nonunion men. The plaintiff, who was not a member of the union, claimed that he had been deprived of his right to work because of the union shop agreement in existence. The court rendered the decision in his favor, and awarded him damages against the agent of the union. It was clear to the A. F. of L. that if other courts followed the judicial ruling of the Massachusetts Supreme Court, the union shop would be doomed.[1]

2. The court in Cincinnati, Ohio, struck at organized labor in 1905 by ruling against the Molders' Union. An employer against whom the union was on strike alleged that he had lost his access to non-union labor because the union had paid the initiation fee of workers and inducted them into the union. Judge Hosea of Cincinnati sided with the employer and fined the union for the "tort" it had committed. In denouncing the decision, Gompers accused the Court of assuming that an employer had a property right in his workers.[2]

3. In a five-to-four decision, the U.S. Supreme Court ruled in 1905 that an act of the New York State Legislature which limited the working hours in bakeries to ten per day and 60 per week was unconstitutional.

The court declared that such legislation was "illegal interference with the right of individuals, both employers and employees, to make contracts regarding labor upon such terms as they may think best or which they may agree upon with the other parties to such contracts. Statutes of the nature of that under review, limiting the hours under which grown and intelligent men may labor to earn their living are mere meddlesome interference with the rights of the individuals." The court based its ruling on the due process clause of the Fourteenth Amendment which forbade any state "to deprive any person of life, liberty, and property without due process of law." In the eyes of the Court, any legislation to fix maximum hours and minimum wages would be a denial of "due process." In effect, notes Edward Berman, the Court had "interpreted the Fourteenth Amendment as prohibiting Congress from passing legislation to protect labor."[3]

4. Judge Holden of Chicago issued a judicial order in 1905 during the strike of the Chicago Typographical Union for an eight-hour day which prohibited "peaceful picketing," "any moral suasion whatever," and forbade any "attempt by the printers to induce non-union printers to join the union." Two of the officers of the Chicago Typographical Union were sentenced to jail and the union was fined $1,500 for contempt of the injunction. The strike was broken.[4]

5. The ruling of the Courts in 1905 in the Danbury Hatters' Case threatened the entire foundation of trade unionism. The epochal labor case—which was not fully decided until the Supreme Court ruled on it in 1908—developed as a result of the determination of the United Hatters of North America to organize itself nationally in the hat industry. One of the main weapons which the union found effective in accomplishing its purpose was the boycott. In 1901, the Hatters' Union, bent on organizing the shop of Dietrich E. Loewe in Danbury, Connecticut, called a strike and declared a boycott. Loewe's fight against the union was financed by a group of hat manufacturers, and the American Anti-Boycott Association agreed to give financial assistance if he would make a test case of the boycott. In 1903, Loewe filed suit against the union for common law conspiracy, claiming $100,000 damages, and another in the United States Circuit Court for violation of the Sherman Anti-Trust Act, claiming triple damages in the amount of $240,000. Simultaneously, the homes and bank accounts of 248 members of the union were attached. The suit was not against the Hatters' Union as an entity—but against individual members of the union in Danbury.

Such legal action against individual union members was a real innovation in the United States, for although unions were already well aware that injunctions could be used against them, they had not foreseen any legal instrument by which employers could sue individual rank and file members of the union. If successful, such a suit could impoverish union members.

In response to the complaint against them in the Circuit Court for the District of Connecticut, the officers of the Hatters' Union entered a plea that the complaint was insufficient. They contended that their boycott did not involve a violation of the Sherman Act, inasmuch as there was no interference with the physical transportation of the hats between the states. To the dismay and alarm of organized labor, the Court in December 1905 held "the complaint to be sufficient." About the same time, the Federal court in California granted the Loewe Co. an injunction which ended the boycott activity against it by the California State Federation of Labor. The California Court held illegal "interference with a complaint-ant's business by means of circularization of an 'unfair list' containing his name."[5]

While the onslaught of the courts on labor's right to organize and improve its working conditions through economic and legislative measures was mounting in fury, the A. F. of L.'s campaign to secure remedial legislation in Congress had ground to a complete standstill. By December 1905, the decade-long effort to secure anti-injunction legislation looked quite hopeless even to the A. F. of L. leaders. Furthermore, the attitude of President Roosevelt on this subject was no more encouraging than that of Congress. In his message to Congress, on December 5, 1905, Roosevelt declared: "There has been a demand for depriving the Courts of the power to issue injunctions in a labor dispute. Such special limitation of the equity power of our courts would be most unwise."[6]

Roosevelt's stand should not have surprised the A. F. of L. He had again demonstrated after his election in 1904 that he was a friend of the anti-union employers. During a visit to Chicago in the spring of 1905, Roosevelt helped to break the strike of the militant teamsters who had gone out in sympathy with the garment workers employed by Montgomery Ward & Co., one of America's leading foes of trade unionism.* The Employers' Association, representing the express companies ·and merchants in Chicago, locked out all of the members of the International Brotherhood of Teamsters.

When Roosevelt arrived in Chicago, there were widespread reports that the employers were planning to convince him to use federal troops against the strikers. A delegation of strikers, headed by Cornelius P. Shea, president of the Brotherhood, presented Roosevelt with a petition stating their case. The memorial outlined the history of the strike from the inception of the employers' lockout, pointed out that the strikers had asked

---

* The Teamsters intervened at the request of the Chicago Federation of Labor, and when the Montgomery Ward management refused to negotiate with the garment workers who had been out on strike for several months, the Teamsters joined the struggle.

all along for arbitration, a demand that had been repeatedly spurned by the employers, and stated that the reason for their spurning the demand was "because they openly boast that they can spurn it, and that the troops under your command will shoot down him who dares openly protest against their action." The memorial then quoted the late Benjamin F. Butler of Massachusetts who, in a speech years before, had named the corporations as the "aggressors" and declared to an assembly of workingmen: "You are stronger than they. You have your right arms and your torches, and by them we will blot out this outrage."* The memorial added: "Can a few soldiers scare the men who make armies and who compose the flower of American manhood? Are we serfs that we cringe at the mention of the troops?" The appeal concluded with a request for the President to consider carefully all the facts if he was faced with a demand for intervention.[7]

That night Roosevelt delivered a speech in Chicago in which he dwelt on the problem of class hatred. "The greatest and most dangerous rock in the course of any republic," he warned, "[is] the rock of class hatred."† He went on to praise the efforts of the city administration to protect strikebreakers and maintain law and order, and warned that in the event these efforts failed, "back of the city stands the State and back of the State stands the nation." Roosevelt had made it clear that, if necessary, federal troops would be used to help smash the strike. As he wrote to Henry Cabot Lodge, the strikers now knew that if the state and the city could not control the situation, "the Regulars will come."[8]

Chicago's anti-labor press hailed Roosevelt's warning to the strikers. "President's Visit a Boon," was the headline in the Chicago *Evening Post*. Charles G. Dawes, a leading Chicago banker, declared that "the President's address unquestionably will have a good effect." A spokesman for the Employers' Association wrote jubilantly to Roosevelt's secretary that as a result of the President's threat to use regular troops "the backbone of the strike had been broken." "We builded wiser than we knew in bringing him here," he added.[9]

The Teamsters were forced to submit to the united employer front, and the strike ended in a defeat for the union. But Roosevelt was happy. "I had a great time in Chicago with the labor union men," he rejoiced.[10]

---

* Roosevelt distorted this quotation as proving that the strikers believed that "they need have no fear of the United States army, as they had torches and arms." (Roosevelt to Henry Cabot Lodge, May 15, 1905, Theodore Roosevelt Papers, Library of Congress. Hereinafter cited as *TRP*.) Actually, the strikers' petition quoted Butler to prove that "the power of the army even rests to a great extent upon the support of the people. What would a few soldiers do against a nation?" (Chicago *Tribune*, May 11, 1905.)

† Commenting on this remark by Roosevelt, the *Chicago Daily Socialist* noted: "Whether the President knows it or not, his warning is in itself an acknowledgment of the existence of classes." (May 20, 1905.)

Later that same year Roosevelt again struck at the rights of labor by ordering that the eight-hour law for government workers or for workers employed by contractors or sub-contractors upon any of the public works of the United States be suspended in building the Panama Canal. At his insistence, Congress effectively barred the eight-hour law from the Canal Zone for alien workers, the majority of those who would be employed in building the canal. Although as we shall see in a subsequent volume, the A. F. of L. leaders enthusiastically supported Roosevelt's imperialist coup in seizing Panama from Colombia, they were seriously alarmed by the move to abolish the provisions of the eight-hour law in the Canal Zone for alien labor, fearing that it was the first step in a broad offensive against the eight-hour law for all government workers and for those employed by contractors for the government. But Gompers' protests to Roosevelt to veto the provision went for nothing. Roosevelt signed the Urgent Deficiency Bill which provided for the scrapping of the eight-hour law for alien laborers in the Canal Zone.[11]

Between 1900 and 1904, the A. F. of L. leaders, while occasionally giving lip-service support to the concept that labor must fight its enemies on both the economic and political fronts, had repeatedly advanced the theory that the unions could solve their basic problems through economic power alone. All they asked from the state was to be neutral in the struggle between labor and capital, and not limit the economic might of the unions. In the fire of the class struggle, the neatly spun theories of the A. F. of L. leadership went up in flames. The traditional A. F. of L. belief in the efficacy of economic power as the main means to advance labor's welfare had received a serious setback in the court decisions of 1905. To be sure, a decision like the one declaring the New York law limiting the hours of bakers unconstitutional did not unduly alarm the A. F. of L. After all, it did not favor legislation establishing the shorter work day except for government employees. This objective would be obtained through agreements with employers reached by collective bargaining or the strike. But then came the campaign waged by the International Typographical Union to secure the eight-hour day through collective bargaining. This met with solid opposition from the Employers' Association, and when the union initiated strikes to enforce its demand, it came up against the periodic nemesis of the trade unions—the injunction. The subsequent defeat of the union's campaign, the imprisonment of the officials of the Chicago local and the fine imposed upon that union for contempt of court, especially alarmed the A. F. of L. leaders. For the I.T.U. was one of the oldest, strongest, and most conservative unions affiliated with the Federation. It had a stable membership and a substantial treasury. Since, in addition, the particular skill of the printers made them difficult to replace, the union was the A. F. of L.'s model of a labor organization that could protect and advance itself through economic power. But the strike for the eight-hour day showed that even this union could be defeated by judicial attack, just as the strike of the teamsters showed that another powerful union could be overpowered by interference by the government. Now even the A. F. of L. leaders had to admit that no union could achieve its objective by relying only on its economic strength.[12]

IMPACT OF BRITISH LABOR EXPERIENCE

The year 1906 opened with the sensational news from England of the success of the Labour Representation Committee (forerunner of the British Labour Party) in electing 50 Members—all trade unionists—to the House of Commons. Shortly thereafter came the news that the Liberal government, which had obtained a great majority because of trade union support, had introduced a measure in Parliament which "exempts trade unions from the ordinary operation of conspiracy or combination . . . and will restore as statutory rights combination and picketing, which, under the Taff Vale decision, have been condemned as infringements upon the employers' liberty of action and consequently valid for suits for damages levied against the trade union funds." When the New York *Tribune's* London correspondent noted that "for the last five years the reversal of the Taff Vale judgment and the restoration of the previous status of absolute immunity from legal liabilities have been the supreme objects of [British] trade union agitation," his words struck a meaningful chord among American trade unionists. The conditions that had faced the British labor movement, it was clear, were similar to those confronting the American labor movement. The injunction in the Taff Vale's railroad strike and the decision by the British Law Lords in 1901, holding the Amalgamated Society of Railway Servants financially responsible for damages and costs and awarding the railroad £23,000 in damages had led in 1900 to the formation of the Labour Representation Committee at a conference of trade unionists and Socialists, to the election of 50 labor deputies to Parliament, and to the introduction of a government-sponsored bill to revise the Taff Vale decision. The injunction in the Danbury Hatters' case and the court decision with its potential threat against the financial strength of American trade unions and each of their members individually was America's Taff-Vale case and could only be met effectively as the British unionists had met the attack on the purse of their unions.[13]

In England, too, certain union spokesmen had predicted that the unions would be doomed if they entered politics. The employers and the courts had convinced British unionists that their unions were doomed if they did *not* enter politics. Or as the Labour Representation Committee put it in 1902: "Menaced on every hand in workshop, court of law, and press, Trade Unionism has no refuge except the ballot box and Labour Representation."[14]*

Almost identical words were used in letters from A. F. of L. members to the Executive Council in the fall of 1905. Although Gompers toned down the militancy of the correspondence, he acknowledged the existence of this discontent with established policy in his report to the A. F. of L. convention of that year. "From among the rank and file of the workers of our country have come impatient inquiries as to the possibility of labor legislation at the hands of Congress, and the request to know whether the time is not opportune to conduct a campaign that will impress upon the minds of those who are juggling and disregarding the legislative interests of American workers, the necessity for a more decent regard for those rights and interests."[15] By 1906 this pressure could no longer be ignored. The trade unions were being ruined by the ruthless manner in which the employers were utilizing the State against organized labor. The need for increased political activity to preserve the unions was appallingly obvious. It was a vital, practical requisite, necessitated by the elementary principles of self-defense and self-preservation. The only question left to determine was the precise type of political action the A. F. of L. would now employ.

LABOR'S "BILL OF GRIEVANCES"

On March 3, 1906, the Legislative Committee of the A. F. of L. held a conference in the office of the Federation in Washington. Gompers enumerated the efforts of the A. F. of L. to secure the passage of legislation favorable to labor, and to prevent the enactment of bills antagonistic to labor. He acknowledged that these efforts had failed dismally. He put no blame for the failure on the political policies and practices of the A. F. of L., but emphasized that a major cause was the fact that the membership of the committees of both houses of Congress had been so

* The course of events in England were fairly well-known to American unionists. In August 1903, Clarence Darrow's article, "Labor Politics in England," was widely published in the United States. Darrow, who was then in England, described the action of the British courts against the labor movement, the rise of the Labour Representation Committee, and pointed out: "It is safe to say that there is not a leading radical or trades unionist in England to-day who does not know that he must change the laws of England before he can move another step in advance; more than this, that unless he can change these laws he will surely go back to the place from which he came. All of these leaders agree that independent, political action alone can bring them any measure of relief." (Chicago *Examiner*, Aug. 29, 1903.) Since Darrow had advised the American labor movement, facing similar dangers, to learn from the British experience, the A.F. of L. leaders found his article distasteful. "About Darrow's ideas," Andrew Furuseth wrote to Gompers on August 27, 1903, "well, he simply fails like most men to grasp the tremendous importance of this movement." (*AFL Corr.*)

selected that "it would be utterly impossible to secure favorable consideration for any labor bills." A further reason was the hostility of the Roosevelt Administration to all legislation submitted by labor organizations; indeed, of all these proposals, the only measure to receive Administration support was one providing that convict labor should not go into the material, manufacture or repairing of mail bags. Meanwhile, the Sherman Anti-Trust Act was being used by the Administration as a weapon to destroy the labor unions, rather than for the purpose for which it was adopted.

Gompers conceded, however, that the time had come for reformulating the Federation's political program. To this end, a conference should be called immediately of all leading A. F. of L. officials to meet with the Executive Council "for the purpose of entering protest of organized labor to Congress against its failure to adopt remedial legislation . . . and that if legislation was not considered, then they would hold the dominant party in Congress responsible for the failure to secure its passage."[16]

On March 5, 1906, after consultation with several members of the Executive Council, Gompers sent a letter to the officers of the affiliated international unions throughout the country, asking them to be present or represented at the conference to be held in joint session with the Executive Council "to present to the representatives of our government, a united protest in the name of labor against the negligence and hostility of those legislators which have been clearly manifest within recent years." The delegates were requested to be in Washington during the week of March 19. Appointments were made by Gompers for the delegates to visit President Roosevelt, William Frye, pro-tempore President of the Senate, and Joseph G. Cannon, Speaker of the House, so that labor's "united protest" could be officially submitted to the three leaders of the nation's executive and legislative departments.[17]

This was the origin of the famous document known as labor's Bill of Grievances, drafted by Gompers and Furuseth and adopted on March 21, 1906, at the conference attended by representatives of 118 national and international unions and members of the A. F. of L. Executive Council. The Bill of Grievances complained in general "of the indifferent position which the Congress of the United States has manifested toward the just, reasonable, and necessary measures which have been before it these past several years, and which particularly affect the interests of the working people." In particular, the measures enumerated were an anti-injunction bill, an effective eight-hour law that would be extended to all federal work, a complaint against the Panama amendment to the eight-hour law, a bill to protect workers from competition of convict labor, a bill to prevent the violation of the Chinese Exclusion Act, a bill restricting immigration, a bill to free seamen from involuntary servitude, a bill to provide additional ship-safety for seamen, and a bill to make the anti-trust law more stringent as against monopoly and to end its being perverted "so far as the laborers are concerned, so as to invade and violate their personal liberty guaranteed by the constitution." The two remaining items mentioned in the document called for the restoration to government employees of the right of petition by rescinding President Roosevelt's order prohibiting this right, and the reorganization of the membership of the House Committee on Labor with a view to making the committee more sympathetic toward labor. "We present these grievances to your attention," the labor leaders told Congress and the President, "because we have long, patiently, and in vain waited for redress. . . . Labor now appeals to you, and we trust that it may not be in vain. But, if perchance, you may not heed us, we shall appeal to the conscience and the support of our fellow citizens."[18]

On the same day, the 118 union representatives and the members of the Executive Council presented the document to President Roosevelt, Senate President Frye, and House Speaker Cannon in separate audiences at intervals of one hour. No minutes of these meetings seem to have been kept, but it is clear that the Bill of Grievances did not elicit a favorable response from Administration leaders. President Roosevelt agreed in general with the items on immigration, Chinese exclusion, and particularly the eight-hour work day, but was cool to other portions of the Bill of Grievances. Senate President Frye refused to commit himself on any of the points, and Speaker Cannon not only followed suit, but repeatedly told the delegates that they spoke for only a small minority of the working class. "You are not the whole thing," he told Gompers, denying that the House Committee on Labor was antagonistic to organized labor. "You are not the only pebble on the beach." Cannon abruptly concluded the interview by brusquely telling the delegates: "Union labor is not the whole shooting match. There are the workmen to be considered who refuse to wear the shackles of unionism."[19]*

The following day the A. F. of L. Executive Council met to discuss the cool reception labor's Bill of Grievances had received from the Republican leaders to whom it had been addressed. After noting bitterly that "the toilers' appeals and petitions are treated with indifference and contempt," the A. F. of L. leaders decided that their next step would be "to take an active part in the impending Congressional election and to defeat or elect candidates for Congress" depending on whether they opposed or supported the demands of organized labor. In short, having

---

* Cannon's position was a frequent theme in the commercial press. "The trades unions cannot forever live in a fool's paradise," declared the *New York Times* of November 28, 1904. "They are not the American people. They represent but a small fraction of the American people. In its present tendencies the labor movement is becoming more and more a danger to the body politic and a menace to the best interests of the workingman."

received no satisfaction from the presentation of labor's Bill of Grievances to the officials of the Republican Administration, the A. F. of L. now prepared to carry out, to some extent, the threat contained at the close of that document—"to appeal to the conscience and support of our fellow citizens."

The first step was to bring the entire matter to the attention of the A. F. of L. membership. On April 7, 1906, a leaflet of four pages, containing the Bill of Grievances and recounting the treatment which it had received from the three Republican Party leaders to whom it had been presented, was sent to unions in all parts of the country. The leaflet concluded with a statement by Gompers of the political methods which the A. F. of L. would now bring into practice:

"Let the inspiring watch-word go forth that—

"We will stand by our friends and administer a stinging rebuke to man or parties who are either indifferent, negligent, or hostile, and wherever opportunity affords, to secure the election of intelligent, honest, earnest trade unionists, with clear, unblemished, paid up union cards in their possession."[20]

Many trade unionists who read the leaflet must have concluded that the mountain had labored and brought forth a mouse. There was nothing new or startling in the document, no departure from past A. F. of L. political policy. The Bill of Grievances itself merely recapitulated the most significant demands long pressed by the Federation. The accompanying letter did not reveal any change in political philosophy or practice. Its basic theory of "reward your friends and punish your enemies" was traditional A. F. of L. political policy, and had been uttered many times before 1906. There was no mention of an independent political party even though there was considerable demand for it, or of support for the Socialist Party—either of which would have been recognized as a definite departure from past A. F. of L. political policy. Indeed, neither labor's Bill of Grievances nor the statement issued by the A. F. of L. after its cool reception by the Republican leaders, revealed any basic change in the Federation's position toward government. Gompers himself made this quite clear when, in an address before Cigarmakers' Union No. 144 in New York City on April 27, 1906, arguing that the unions could not keep out of politics, he defined the purpose of trade union action:

"Primarily to prevent hostile legislation; primarily to prevent hostile acts on the part of government hostile to labor and to labor's interests.

"Secondly, to secure such action at the hands of the government which can not be exercised and secured by trade-union action, and

"Thirdly, to give trade unionism full and free right in the exercise of its natural functions. . . .

"We will resort to politics . . . to do the things that we can not do for ourselves to secure for the trade union movement the free hand to work the natural salvation of labor."

Gompers printed this statement in the *American Federationist* and included it in a pamphlet distributed to trade unionists all over the country to make sure that they did not misinterpret the events since March 1906 to mean that a basic change had taken place in the A. F. of L.'s political policy.[21] To be sure, the statement represents a departure from Gompers' cherished faith in the ability of labors' economic power by itself to redress the workers' grievances. Nevertheless, political action was still regarded as a necessary but temporary activity, whose main purpose was to remove all restrictions imposed by the government upon labor's economic power. The concept that labor should use its political strength to become a dominant force in government was still completely foreign to Gompers' thinking.

In his speech to the cigarmakers, Gompers was also careful to stress that the A. F. of L.'s plans for political action to carry into effect the Bill of Grievances did not envisage the abandonment by the Federation of the nonpartisan policy which it had long since adopted. There was to be no progress in the direction of support for an independent political party of labor. Gompers conceded that the demand for a national labor party was being voiced in unions throughout the country, and that many unionists were influenced in this direction by the events in the British labor movement. But he contended that this was based on a misinterpretation of what was occurring in England. "The truth is that the trade union Congress appointed a committee and called it the Labour Representation Committee, the duty of which was to try to secure the election of labor men to Parliament, regardless of party, and wherever that could not be done to secure the defeat of those who stood hostile to labor interests of Great Britain." The implication was that this type of political action was no different from that now being promoted by the A. F. of L. But Gompers said nothing of the fact that the British trade unions had made it quite clear that its procedure was *the first step* towards the organization of a labor party of their own.[22] Indeed, just as Gompers was speaking, the Labour Representation Committee was changing its name to the British Labour Party!

Gompers was correct in acknowledging that there was considerable demand after the release of the Bill of Grievances for the formation of an independent labor party. *The Independent,* a liberal weekly, reported that this sentiment was widespread in labor circles, and agreed with those who hoped that we "should soon see our two millions of workers marching to the polls and electing to office, as representatives of their class interests, the candidates of an independent labor party." But it saw no hope of such a movement from Gompers. His only purpose was "to have the workers capture the primaries of the Democratic or

Republican parties and to nominate men favorable to the demands of labor when it was not possible to find candidates who would reply satisfactorily to the questions asked them by union officials. . . . Such methods can result only in failure. . . . Petitions and questioning have failed, and must fail. Voting for 'favorable candidates' have failed. But one thing remains. If labor is to obtain these specific demands from the legislative and judicial branches of our government, it is bound to go into politics. It will organize a separate political party, nominate men from its own ranks, and elect them upon a working class program."[23]

PREPARATIONS FOR THE 1906 CAMPAIGN

Although the A. F. of L. leaders refused even to consider the question of an independent labor party, they knew that if the rising tide in its favor was to be curbed, the "reward your friends and punish your enemies" method had to produce more satisfactory results than in the past. Consequently, they had to give sustained stimulus, leadership, and direction to the affiliated unions on the manner of conducting their political action to guarantee that the support to friendly and opposition to unfriendly candidates meant more than words.

On July 22, 1906, the Executive Council issued a document of four pages entitled, *A. F. of L. Campaign Programme*, which was addressed "To all Organized Labor and Friends in the United States," and was mailed to all local unions affiliated with the Federation, with instructions that it be read at the next local meeting.* It was also distributed to working people, both union and nonunion, in every part of the United States. The document announced that Congress had adjourned without having satisfied a single demand of the Bill of Grievances. It charged that there was evidence of graft and corruption in high places of government, and that in their "frenzied rush for the almighty dollar," public officials had become indifferent or hostile "to the interests of labor" and "to the real interests of the people." "The great insurance companies, the trusts, the corporations, the so-called captains of industry, have indeed become the owners of the legislators of our country." Therefore, the time had "arrived for labor and its friends to raise their voices in condemnation of such degeneracy, and to invite all reform forces to join with it in relegating indifference to the people's interests, corruption and graft to political oblivion; to raise the standard of legislation by the election of sincere, progressive, and honest men, who, while worshipping money less, will honor conscience, justice and humanity more." To direct this

---

* Accompanying this document was a leaflet which made an appeal for funds "in order to carry on this campaign to a successful issue. Every dollar will be utilized to accomplish the largest degree of success in labor's interest." Contributions were to be sent to Frank Morrison. (Copy of leaflet, July 22, 1906, *AFL Corr.*)

campaign, a Labor Representation Committee, composed of Gompers, Morrison, and James O'Connell, A. F. of L. third vice-president, was created.[24]

The *A. F. of L. Campaign Programme* represented an advance in the Federation's political views and position over its previous statements. For one thing, it emphasized that the aim of labor's political action was not confined to achieving a free hand from government for the trade unions to operate on the economic front, but, in addition, to end control of government by "corporate interests" and to cause it to function in the interests of all people, especially the working class. For another, largely as a concession to the rising demand for independent political action, it emphasized the importance of electing trade unionists to office. In this connection, the document even referred to the experiences of the British workers, noting that "In the last British elections 54 trade unionists were elected to Parliament. If the British workmen, with their limited franchise, accomplished so much by their united action, what may we in the United States not do with universal suffrage?"[25]

Such seemingly militant language from the A. F. of L. leaders even dazzled some of the progressive forces in the Federation, and they began to express exaggerated interpretations of what the *Campaign Programme* signified. The organ of the Texas Federation of Labor, for example, saw in it the beginning of the end of pure and simple unionism. "Pres. Gompers," it asserted, has at last realized that to be successful, the unions must have the government with them, and to have the government they must elect members of their class. . . . But the new unionism involves another idea. It involves the idea of 'class struggle'. . . . Gompers has been forced to see the class struggle." But Gompers made it clear that he would rather have the campaign doomed to failure than to see it develop into a movement for an independent labor party, to the concentration on political struggles to the neglect of the economic effort. Trade unionism pure and simple was still the basic answer to the needs of the working class.[26]

On the possibility of establishing a labor party, as the British trade unionists were doing, the *Campaign Programme* was silent. Lest this be interpreted as even opening the door to discussion of this question, the *United Mine Workers' Journal* stated flatly that advocates of a labor party should not hope to see any change in A. F. of L. policy which would continue to be based on "reward your friends, punish your enemies"—regardless of party affiliation. "We do not propose to organize any new party. Our votes represent the balance of power which, if properly used, will secure us the legislation for which we are seeking."[27]

The issues of the *American Federationist* from May to December, 1906, gave attention to political action on a scale unprecedented for the journal. The editorial section of each number during these months ended with what came to be known as labor's watchword, printed in heavy, bold type: "*We will stand by our friends and administer a stinging rebuke to men or parties who are either indifferent, negligent, or hostile, and whenever opportunity affords, secure the election of intelligent, honest, earnest trade unionists, with clear, unblemished, paid-up union cards in their possession.*" At the same time, Gompers made sure that each issue of the *American Federationist* contained some argument against an independent party of labor. In August 1906, he reprinted approvingly an editorial in a contemporary journal which warned: "It will not mend matters to turn the labor union into a political party. The thing is impractical. This is not the way to get relief. Let every laborer, independent of his union, make his own policies, choose his own party. It would do incalculable injury to the cause of organized labor to become a political class. There are too many demagogues to take advantage of such a thing. Let the workingmen remember the populist movement and hesitate."[28] In his anxiety to publish any attack on the idea of a labor party, Gompers did not even hesitate to include this statement which, with its emphasis on every worker making "his own policies" and choosing "his own party," independent of his union, flatly contradicted the A. F. of L.'s plea that each worker should support only candidates endorsed by the Federation and its affiliates.

The September 1906 issue of the *American Federationist* was the largest published up to that time. Over 50 pages were devoted to the answers of Congressmen to a letter sent by the A. F. of L. on April 26, which had included a copy of the Bill of Grievances and a request for their attitude on the various legislative measures demanded in that document. The replies could be classified as straightforward, indifferent, and hostile. Of the 122 replies received from Congressmen and published in the *Federationist*, 72 were from Republicans and 50 from Democrats. Forty-seven of the Democratic Congressmen were judged to be acceptable to the Federation, and three were commented on unfavorably. Only 23 Republicans were considered as acceptable, while 49 were to be regarded as enemies in the November election. A record in Congress that failed to show support of anti-injunction legislation and an eight-hour day for all goverment employees was enough to label the Congressman as unsatisfactory. To many of the replies, Gompers added his comments so that "a clearer understanding of their position, either expressed or implied might be obtained." In some cases, the editorial comment indicated that faithful promises could not be reconciled with records in Congress that were either indifferent or openly hostile to labor's demands. In other cases, the editorial called particular attention to the candidate's favorable record in Congress. In approximately half of the cases, there was no editorial comment following the published letter. Absence of editorial comment indicated that Labor was satisfied with the promises and record of the Congressman and would promote his re-election.[29]

The work of compiling each Congressman's record and placing it in a form to be readily available was carried on at the A. F. of L. headquarters in Washington. The vote of each Congressman on labor measures was investigated for the entire time he was in Congress and made ready for use. The A. F. of L. archives show that there was a heavy demand for these records. The inquiries usually asked for the Congressman's record on particular labor measures, though they often inquired concerning his attitude towards the Bill of Grievances. Thousands of letters were written in reply to those questions, always accompanied by the complete record of the Congressman on measures of direct interest to labor. It was not unusual in the 1906 campaign for the Federation's letter giving a Congressman's record to be kept standing in display type on the front page of a progressive newspaper of his district. This was particularly true in the case where the record was a favorable one to labor.[30]

THE CAMPAIGN IN MAINE

In the 1906 political campaign, the A. F. of L. worked harder to defeat Republican Congressman Charles E. Littlefield of the Second District of Maine than any other member of Congress. There were several reasons for this. First, in the eyes of the A. F. of L., Littlefield ranked next to Speaker Cannon "as an implacable and conspicuous foe of labor legislation." As a member of the important House Judiciary Committee, he had blocked bills outlawing injunctions in labor disputes, and advanced the progress of bills providing for even stricter application of the Sherman Act to trade unions.[31] Secondly, since the election in Maine took place on September 10, almost two months before the nation's general election, the A. F. of L. could concentrate all its strength in a limited area. In Littlefield's district there were said to be "three thousand union men," and with these workers fully mobilized, his defeat seemed highly likely, since he had won his previous election by a plurality of 5,419 votes. Finally, a triumph in Maine would have great significance in the campaign in other parts of the country, for the Maine election was generally regarded as a political barometer. It would mark an auspicious beginning for the A. F. of L.'s new political program, intensify the rising interests of trade unionists in the coming general election, and increase labor's prestige among the existing political parties.[32]

On August 15, Gompers informed the A. F. of L. Executive Council that he had been directed by the Labor Representation Committee to "proceed to Maine and endeavor to secure the defeat" of Littlefield, and remain there until the close of the campaign; that several A. F. of L. organizers had been directed also to go to Maine, and that a number of officers of International Unions had been requested to send representatives into Littlefield's district.* A. F. of L. headquarters during the Anti-Littlefield campaign would be maintained at Rockland.[33]

The first meeting of the A. F. of L.'s campaign to defeat Littlefield was held in the city hall at Lewiston, August 18, 1906. Preceded by a huge labor parade, the gathering was attended by over 2,000 people. Gompers was the chief speaker, and for two and a half hours he presented labor's case against the Republican Congressman. He reviewed Littlefield's position on Congressional committees, accusing him of opposition to the anti-injunction bill and the eight-hour bill, his failure to say a word for the bill prohibiting the employment of railroad workers for more than 16 hours a day, and his support of a ship subsidy bill opposed by labor. Discussing the use of injunctions in labor disputes, Gompers declared: "I charge that these injunctions are issued at the behest of the powerful and the strong, of the wealthy against the man of labor, and I charge the Hon. Charles E. Littlefield to be so much enmeshed in corporate influence that he must ever raise his voice and vote against a measure that promises some relief from corporate power." There was only one choice open for men of labor and its allies in Maine's second district, Gompers concluded, and that was to "bury this misrepresentative of yours under the avalanche of your votes on election day. Men of Labor, men who love our country, Organize, vote together and stand together."[34]

From the time of his August 18 speech until the balloting exactly one month later, Gompers delivered 14 major addresses of a similar nature against Littlefield in various parts of the district. Apart from Gompers' efforts, addresses were also made by more than a dozen labor leaders. In addition, a house-to-house canvass was made throughout the district; the assistance of the wives of workers was enlisted, and thousands of leaflets were distributed urging Maine citizens to "Vote against Charles E. Littlefield, the enemy of the common people—he is owned and pledged to defend the trusts."[35]

Although the A. F. of L. conducted a spirited campaign, a number of weaknesses soon became apparent. Most serious was the question of for whom the anti-Littlefield citizens should vote. When Gompers first arrived in Maine, he stated in an interview with a reporter from the Lewiston *Morning News* that American workers should learn the lessons from "the success which has attended political action [by labor] in Great Britain." Immediately, the impression was created that Gompers was advocating the formation of an independent labor party to nominate a trade unionist against Littlefield; indeed, so strong was this impression that, at first, Maine newspapers referred to Gompers and other A. F. of L. spokesmen as "the labor party leaders." Gompers moved swiftly to dispel this impression, and Collis Lovely, a leader of the Boot and Shoe Workers'

* About 15 A.F. of L. leaders from states outside of Maine assisted Gompers during the anti-Littlefield campaign, and worked under his direction.

Union, was assigned the task of speaking all over the district on the subject, "Non-Partisan Politics."[36]

For several days, Gompers avoided even mentioning the name of any candidate against Littlefield, and the press emphasized that his meetings were "non-political in character"—meaning that they were designed to defeat Littlefield rather than elect anyone in his place. But by the end of August, the A. F. of L. campaigners made it clear that they hoped to "bury Littlefield" by getting labor and its friends to vote for his Democratic opponent, Daniel J. McGillicuddy. Many workers were disappointed, for they had little enthusiasm for the Democratic candidate. Up until the eve of the election, McGillicuddy declined to state his position on the issues Gompers had raised in denouncing Littlefield, particularly the question of an anti-injunction bill. (Indeed, McGillicuddy even denied for some time that he was in any way "allied with Mr. Gompers.") One prominent magazine writer, who had come to Maine specifically to study the effect of the entrance of organized labor in the political arena, declared, after interviewing scores of workers, that many had expressed dissatisfaction with the Democratic candidate's stand. One trade unionist was quoted as saying: "Many members of organized labor will not support either Littlefield or McGillicuddy. They would support McGillicuddy if that gentleman had the courage to come out flat-footed for even a part of our demands. But when he refuses to take a stand for a single one of our demands then the honest union man may well hesitate before casting a ballot for either a coward or unsafe friend." The journalist concluded: "It looks to me as though it would be better for labor men to put up their own candidates—real labor men, and then make a concerted fight for them."[37]

Not a few of the workers interviewed felt that the only man who merited labor's support was Walter A. Pickering, a trade unionist and the Socialist candidate for Congress. "Mr. Pickering is the only one of the three who stands for the demands of organized labor," was a common statement. A Maine Socialist leader addressed an open letter to Gompers in which he asked: "Should not the union men of this district vote for a union man? . . . Is it not true that Candidate Pickering is the only one of the three who stands squarely and honestly for every demand of the Federation of Labor? If you are sincere and honest yourself, Mr. Gompers, and your demands are sincere and honest, there is only one thing for you to do and that is to advise the union men of the Second District to vote for Walter Pickering." The letter was wasted on Gompers; indeed, he charged that the Socialists were subsidized by the N.A.M., and that money was furnished them by "the trusts, the corporations, and the railroads in order to divide the opposition to Littlefield."[38]

On the eve of election day, McGillicuddy did finally announce his support of an anti-injunction bill and other labor measures. But it was difficult at that late date to undo the damage; nor, for that matter, were many workers convinced that his belated support of labor's program was anything but a political maneuver.

At first the Republicans dismissed the A. F. of L. activity in Maine as insignificant, and contented themselves with accusing the Federation of "political blackmail." But this attitude was quickly abandoned, and the Republicans began to register real alarm. The New York *Journal of Commerce* warned that if Littlefield were defeated practically any representative could be "coerced" into submitting to labor's wishes.[39] President Roosevelt and other Republican leaders became so anxious that they took steps to send the party's big guns into the district to bolster Littlefield. Secretary of War Taft, Senators Beveridge and Lodge, Speaker Cannon and several other Congressmen hastened to Maine to campaign for Littlefield. Lodge, fearful of the effectiveness of labor's campaign, wrote to Roosevelt that the question of whether a Republican or Democrat was elected was insignificant compared to the question "whether Gompers shall dictate the choice of Congressmen." Roosevelt, who agreed fully with Lodge, himself sent a letter to Maine stating that he would consider Littlefield's defeat "a positive calamity to his district and to the country at large." In a letter to Littlefield, Taft wrote: "There is no election that has taken place in a long time that I think is more important than this, for the reason that should they succeed in beating you, it would frighten all Congressmen, and would enable Gompers to wield an influence which would be dangerous and detrimental to the public weal." Taft told Roosevelt that a Republican defeat would be regarded as a labor victory, whereas should the Republicans emerge victorious, it would draw "the claws of such a bumptious demagogue [as Gompers]."[40]

Money was spent lavishly in Littlefield's behalf, much of it raised by the commercial, railroad, and shipping trusts and by the N.A.M. The N.A.M. sent the following "confidential" circular appealing for funds to every manufacturer and business man in Maine and to many outside of the state:

IMPORTANT TO YOU, AS AN EMPLOYER OF LABOR

Do you realize the great moral effect we shall all have to overcome if Gompers, as President of the American Federation of Labor is able to successfully interfere in the election of Congressmen, by throwing the immense strength of the Federation into one district after another, browbeating the candidates and obtaining sufficient support to change the natural balance of majorities. . . . Future freedom from such outrageous assaults on the ballots will depend on how successful we are in making Gompers' defeat sufficiently marked to be an object lesson. . . .

You will observe there has been no mention made of Hon. Charles E. Littlefield, the courageous lawyer, and champion of the sanctity of the Courts in injunction matters, because we feel he is only an incident in this fight, the principle of which we feel is important enough to justify our bringing this to your attention by this confidential circular.

To defeat "this first attempt at outside dictation," employers were directed to send their contributions either to Littlefield's campaign manager or to Marshall Cushing, secretary of the N.A.M.[41]

The tone of the Republican spokesmen in the campaign followed the pattern outlined in the confidential circular. They emphasized that Gompers had instituted "an un-American political blacklist," that the A. F. of L. had introduced "class issues" into American politics, and that the campaign waged by the Federation against Littlefield was stirring up "class hatred." Indicative of this last point is the Republican treatment of a strike in Rumford Falls, part of the Second District. Two hundred and fifty girls at the Continental Paper Mill struck in late August for an increase of $1.50 per week. (They were receiving $6 per week.) Immediately, the Republicans shrieked that "it was the labor propaganda spread by the imported labor leaders that caused the discontent resulting in the strike," and the loss of business to the community. Speaker Cannon used the strike to illustrate the point that if the A. F. of L. leaders had had their way in Congress, similar strikes would have raked the nation from one end to the other, and had it not been for the fact that men like Littlefield had stood firm against the Federation's demands, "the country would have gone to the devil long ago."[42]

Even some conservative journals found it difficult to swallow the Republican charges. Thus the *Wall Street Journal* admitted that Gompers and the other A. F. of L. spokemen "had fully as much right there [in Maine] as Secretary Taft and Speaker Cannon had. . . . We may deplore the entrance of labor organizations into politics, because this promotes class animosity and leads to class legislation; but, after all, the labor organizations have ample precedent for political action in the conduct of leading organizations of business men."[43]

On August 26, Gompers sent a hurried "personal" call to John Mitchell urging him to come to Maine. "According to present appearances, and the general consensus of opinion, Mr. Littlefield can and will be defeated," he assured the U.M.W. president. "But it is also true that in his desperation he has called upon Speaker Cannon and others to come to this district and make speeches in his favor. This no doubt will have considerable influence and everyone who has spoken to me upon the subject suggests that if you could and would come here and make two or three speeches, however brief, following Mr. Cannon, it would have the determining influence upon the campaign and Mr. Littlefield's defeat would be assured." But the U.M.W. president refused to come; he informed Gompers that he was "overwhelmed with work."[44]

The Republican press made much of Mitchell's failure to appear in Maine as proof of his disagreement with Gompers over the anti-Littlefield move. Much was also made of the fact that James Duncan, international secretary and treasurer of the Granite Cutters' Association, a union with a large membership in the state, failed to come to Maine, and it was reported that he "considered Gompers' action in Mr. Littlefield's district as unwise, etc." Although Duncan denied the report, these apparent rifts in the A. F. of L. high command weakened the campaign against Littlefield.[45]

Although Littlefield was re-elected, his plurality of 5,400 in 1904 was reduced to 1,362. The A. F. of L. immediately announced that the reduced plurality was a moral victory, and, in a leaflet distributed "To Organized Labor and Friends in the United States," the Executive Council declared:

"Every wage-earner, every member of organized labor, and every sympathizer with our cause must feel gratified with the result of Labor's first skirmish in Maine, where a stinging rebuke was administered to Mr. Littlefield and his allies. All the trust forces, all the resources of corporate wealth, all the prestige of administrative power were thrown into the fight to save Mr. Littlefield from utter defeat. Labor with very slender financial resources,* made a clean-cut straightforward contest, purely on the ground of securing justice for Labor and the common people. . . . Though Mr. Littlefield slipped in, the vote was a moral victory for our cause and will have great influence in the general campaign."[46]

The opponents of labor were quick to point out that the entire Republican vote in the state was reduced; that all the Republican candidates in Maine were hurt by their stand in favor of prohibition, and that this issue was a major factor in reducing Littlefield's plurality as it was in reducing the pluralities of the Republican candidates in three other Congressional districts where the A. F. of L. had not conducted a campaign. But most political commentators did not belittle the significance of the reduced plurality for Littlefield. "If the labor movement could all but defeat Littlefield," a leading New York newspaper editorialized, "in a Republican stronghold of a state where the labor element does not exercise the power it has in other districts and states, what may it be expected to do where Republican lines are less strong and where there is a greater force to the labor movements and to the parties that are akin to it—in New York, for example. In Maine, there flies a storm signal for November. What Gompers undertook to do in Maine is only the beginning of the

---

* The total expense of the Maine campaign was $918.95. ("Financial Report of the American Federation of Labor for Political Campaign of 1906," p. 16, *AFL Corr.*)

work he and his followers have cut out for themselves in other places."
"The lesson to the country at large is plain," observed the New York
Commercial. "The American Federation of Labor is in politics to stay."
Gompers agreed, and predicted that when the results were in in No-
vember, "one of its results will be to make labor's opponents less arrogant,
indifferent, or hostile."[47]

THE CAMPAIGN ELSEWHERE

The A. F. of L.'s campaign throughout the rest of the country could not
be compared with the vigor it had exhibited in Congressman Littlefield's
district. A major factor limiting political activity was the slender financial resources available to the Federation for this purpose. From the beginning, it was decided that no contributions would be accepted from
candidates, and no money was to be taken from the treasury of the
A. F. of L. to conduct the campaign. Consequently, the Federation was
forced to rely on direct appeals to unions and to individual members.
Such an appeal was made on July 22, but by September 18, the Labor
Representation Committee complained that adequate funds were not
available to bear the cost of printing and speakers, and it requested the
Executive Council to issue a second call for contributions. This appeal,
issued on September 24, asked that "each and every trade union member
. . . immediately contribute the sum of $1 to the campaign fund." The
secretary of each local union was asked to read the appeal at the first
meeting of the union.[48]

It is impossible to determine how thoroughly this request was complied
with. The United Mine Workers' National Executive Board did, however, supplement the A. F. of L.'s appeal with a circular to officers and
members of local unions recommending "to all of our members . . . to
contribute whatever they can toward the advancement of this cause, and
that they organize committees or clubs for the purpose and for the general advancement of the movement."[49]

The total sum received from the two appeals during the period July
26–December 24 was $8,147.19.[50] Lack of funds thus hampered the
entire A. F. of L. campaign. Another factor was the refusal of a number
of important leaders of the A. F. of L. to support candidates endorsed by
organized labor and their insistence on campaigning for candidates
singled out for defeat by the Federation. Mitchell's refusal to play an active part in the anti-Littlefield campaign certainly hurt the Federation's
activities in Maine. In a larger sense, the alliance of corrupt labor officials
and the political machines and the open-shop organizations, already
demonstrated, as we have seen in the Congressional campaign of 1904,
was again evidenced in 1906. In one case, where union officials even campaigned against Congressman George A. Pearre of Maryland, a leader of

the A. F. of L.'s anti-injunction drive,* Gompers wrote privately to these men, reminding them that they were betraying the entire labor movement. "If labor does not stand faithfully in support of men who prove their friendship, and who are sincere, faithful representatives of the interests of their constituents, and of the people generally, how is it possible for us to expect that such men shall remain true? How can we hope to win friends to our cause, the cause of righteousness and justice?" But union officials who made a practice throughout the year of collaborating with the enemies of labor on the economic front, refused to change their pattern of behavior in the political arena. Moreover, many of these leaders were tied to local political machines, dominated by big business, and they refused to cut their connections to advance the A. F. of L.'s political campaign.[51]

Still another factor was the discontent among A. F. of L. members over the tendency of the Federation's leadership to link political activity in 1906 to the kite of the Democratic Party. Not only were many of the Democratic candidates endorsed by the A. F. of L. anything but champions of organized labor, but the Federation refused to take up a battle against a single Southern Democratic Congressman who had contemptuously thrown Labor's "Bill of Grievances" into the wastebasket. Yet it was precisely through an alliance between the Republicans and the Southern Democrats that labor's bills had been overwhelmingly defeated time and again in Congress.[52]

The refusal of the Socialist members of the A. F. of L. and others who favored the formation of a labor party to respond enthusiastically to the Federation's appeals was another factor limiting campaign activity. On September 11, 1906, Typographia Union No. 7 of New York City wrote to the A. F. of L. Executive Council:

"After years of opposition to independent political action of the working class, after years spent in declaring that there must be 'no politics in the unions,' after years of denunciation for those of us who stood for such

---

* Pearre was the sponsor of the Anti-Injunction Bill, prepared by the A.F. of L. In the early spring of 1906, the Federation employed a group of lawyers to make a study of the jurisdiction of the courts to grant injunctions with a view to recommending what might be done by Congress to end this evil. As a result of this investigation, a bill was drafted which, in substance, prohibited U.S. courts from issuing injunctions in any case between employers and workers unless necessary to prevent irreparable injury to property or to a property right of the party making the application, for which injury there was no adequate remedy at law. The bill was introduced into the House of Representatives by George A. Pearre. On May 12, Gompers and a committee representing the A.F. of L. Executive Council called on President Roosevelt and urged him to announce his support of the Pearre Anti-Injunction Bill. Roosevelt refused to act, and the bill remained bottled up in the House Judiciary Committee. No action was taken on the bill before Congress adjourned. (Gompers and Committee of Executive Council to President Roosevelt, May 12, 1906, *TRP*.)

action—you have at last been compelled by the logic of events to admit that we were right; that the methods of trade unionism alone are not sufficient to procure economic justice for the wage-workers; that union in the shop must be supplemented by union on the political field. We congratulate you on this step. We rejoice that we have pushed you forward.

"But your forward step is too short. The methods which you propose will not serve the purpose. You talk of independent political action; but in practice the action which you advise is not independent at all. In fact, it is really hardly an advance over your old begging policy. . . . In a word, you still advise us to cast our votes for men nominated by capitalist influence and pledged to capitalist platforms, if they will only give us some empty words of friendship during the compaign. This would simply put a premium upon anti-election [*sic*] buncombe and post-election fake in order to gain your endorsement."[53]

When the ballots were tabulated in the 1906 Congressional elections, it was found that the Republican majority in the House of Representatives was decreased from 112 members to 56, and many of the Republican incumbents were returned with a smaller plurality than in 1904.[54] Gompers claimed that the decline in the Republican majority "demonstrated beyond doubt the practicability and influence of the A. F. of L. plan of campaign." He conceded that the re-election of Speaker Cannon with a plurality of over 10,000 votes which was even better than his total of 1902, despite the A. F. of L. campaign waged to achieve his defeat, was a bitter pill to swallow.* But he took special satisfaction in the fact that the Federation's first real campaign had secured the election of six Congressmen with active membership in the trade unions: Wilson and Nicholas of Pennsylvania, Sherwood of Ohio, Hughes of New Jersey, McDermott of Illinois, and Carey of Wisconsin.[55]

To the forces who favored independent political action by labor the chief significance of the 1906 campaign was the promise it held that the political action momentum which had begun could be accelerated further until it resulted in the formation of a labor party. "Brothers," Typographia Union No. 7 wrote in concluding its letter to the A. F. of L. Executive Council, "you have made one step forward by recognizing the necessity for independent political action by the wage-workers. In view

---

* President Roosevelt rallied to Cannon's support and sent leading Republicans into his district to line up votes for the Speaker. Nicholas Longworth, Roosevelt's son-in-law, spoke as a personal representative of the President and told the voters: "The President has done his greatest work in the last five years, during which time his right hand and helper has been Speaker Joseph G. Cannon, your own distinguished citizen." (Blair Bolles, *Tyrant from Illinois,* New York, 1951, p. 50.) Roosevelt maintained that "it is a simple absurdity to portray him [Cannon] as an enemy of labor." which was an absurd statement. (Roosevelt to E. E. Clark, Sept. 5, 1906, *TRP.*)

of strikes broken with police and military force by officials of both old parties, in view of injunctions and anti-labor decisions by judges of both old parties, let us hope that in the near future you will take another step, will learn *what* independent political action really means by sponsoring the formation of an independent party of labor." Max Hayes, Socialist Party national committeeman and leader in the International Typographical Union, was convinced that the 1906 campaign marked the "death knell" of "pure and simpledom" in the A. F. of L., that "the bars are down," and that if the Socialists were active in pushing for a labor party in the Federation, "it won't take long to completely down reaction and fossilized conservatism."[56]

THE 1906 A. F. OF L. CONVENTION

But the A. F. of L. leaders were equally determined to keep the bars up against any attempt to involve the Federation more deeply in political action in the future beyond what had been adopted in the campaign of 1906. In his opening address at the 1906 A. F. of L. convention, Gompers warned that the delegates should not regard the past campaign as signifying any deviation in the Federation's traditional concept of regarding economic power as the key to labor's future. He urged them to reject any attempt to alter this approach, and "that no hard and fast rule be established that will in the slightest impair the great economic power of our movement; for after all is said and done, there is no escape from the conclusion that in all the activities in the life of the wage-workers, there is no effort within measuring distance so potent as to accomplish tangible results in the material, economic, moral or social conditions as the great economic power of the trade union movement."[57] The strategy of the A. F. of L. leadership was clear. It was to identify any attempt to develop political action beyond the philosophy, practice, and methods exhibited in the campaign of 1906 with weakening and eventually destroying the economic power of organized labor. This approach was endorsed by the Committee on the President's Report which warned that there should be no change in the concept that labor's economic power was the most effective weapons in its arsenal:

"We hold with the President, that the economic function and power of trade unionism is by far its greatest instrument for good. We further hold that the solidarity of our movement must not for a moment be permitted to be endangered by the attempt to identify it with a partisan political movement. . . . The attempt to delegate any authority by this convention, to form political organizations on any specific lines, would to that extent identify the Federation of Labor with a party movement and inevitably violate one of the most fundamental principles of trade unionism. *Political movements are ephemeral. . . .*"

The Commitee recommended that the convention go on record as opposing the endorsement of any political party or any plan for the formation of a political party. Instead, they favored a continuance of the plan of having the Executive Council "carry on an aggressive educational campaign" by furnishing statistics, literature, and speakers to interested unions.[58]

The Report touched off a debate between administration supporters who did not want to see the organization extend its political activity any further than it had gone in the past campaign, and the delegates who wished to see a further increase in political action—leading soon to the establishment of a labor party.

The administration's supporters argued that the trade unions had already accomplished a great deal by the political pressure applied upon the two major parties; that an independent political party of labor would not win enough votes to elect "a corporal's guard in Congress"; that all past American labor movements that "identified themselves with a political machine" had gone "down to destruction"; that the introduction of "class spirit of hatred and bitterness" into the unions through an independent labor party would jeopardize the chance of obtaining "the fullest support for the measures that most deeply concern us"; that the whole idea of a labor party was a Socialist plot to weaken the economic power of the trade unions and thus destroy the A. F. of L.; that it would be a disaster for the American workers "to crucify the cause of trade unionism upon the cross of political activity," and that the fruits of the Federation's 1906 Congressional campaign would soon prove to the workers that its political policies were more than sufficient to meet their needs.[59]

The administration's opponents, led by the Socialists, insisted that the working class had sufficient strength by itself to win elections, but it had to be properly mobilized; that the way to do this was by organizing a party for the working class "along working class principles" which would rally "every working man—young and old, black and white, skilled and unskilled," and through which "the working people will then control the government"; that the policy of bringing pressure to bear on the Republicans and Democrats was fruitless, since they always promised to support labor before election and promptly broke their promise after election; that the candidates of the major parties could not really fulfill their pledges to labor, since they were dominated by the "political bosses and their machines," who, in turn, were controlled by big business; that the argument that introducing politics into the trade unions, made up of members of different creeds and parties, would disrupt and injure the unions, had been raised in England, too, but British labor had discovered that "there was nothing left for the trade unions to do but to enter politics, whether they liked it or not," and they had correctly decided to have a party of their own which they could control;* that the reason for organizing trade unions was that workers recognized their interests as a class, and it followed logically "that we must get our rights politically by organizing as a class"; that by securing such rights, the workers would be in a better position to advance their economic demands, hence the argument that political action would weaken the economic struggles of the workers was a spurious contention that had no basis in the actual day-to-day experiences of labor.[60]

After a speech by Gompers supporting the committee's report as covering the subject of political action "fully and safely," the vote began. The Committee's Report was upheld. The convention, dominated by the administration's machine, made it clear that the A. F. of L.'s increased political activity in the 1906 election was not to be interpreted as a prelude toward still greater political action—especially in the direction of an independent labor party. "The principle of non-partisan politics, summed up in the dictum 'to defeat labor's enemies and to reward its friends,' received official sanction," writes Lewis Lorwin.[61]

CONGRESSIONAL SETBACK

In closing the debate on political action, Gompers had predicted that the A. F. of L.'s role in the 1906 campaign would have "magical results," and "our opponents will not be so arrogant toward the representatives of labor as they have been in the past. . . . I feel confident that we have enough Congressmen elected and pledged to the rights of labor and the people so as to make it impossible for another 'hostile or indifferent' Congress to treat labor's demands in the future as they have been treated in the past." But N.A.M. President Kirby was equally confident that the results of the election would prove beneficial to the open-shop employers, and that the new Congress could be counted upon to resist any attempt to pass "the anti-injunction and eight-hour bills."[62]

Kirby proved to be a better prophet than Gompers. Cannon had been re-elected to the House, and continued as Speaker, more hostile than ever to organized labor because of its campaign to defeat him. He continued the practice of appointing anti-labor men to the committees which considered the legislation demanded by the Federation. The Republicans, in the main, continued to show "hostility or indifference," while many of those legislators who had "pledged themselves to the rights of labor" forgot their pledges when in office. During the second session of the 59th Congress, which followed the election of 1906, not a single measure to limit the use of injunctions in labor disputes even came before the House for a vote. The only measures enacted of special interest to labor

---

* This point had also been emphasized in a speech to the convention by a fraternal delegate from the British labor movement.

were a bill for the investigation of women and child labor, and one to reduce the hours of labor for railroad men. The latter measure, however, was so ineffective in shape and form that labor opposed its passage. Lewis Lorwin sums up the situation accurately in a single sentence: "The House of Representatives after the election of 1906 turned even less friendly to labor than before."[63]

CHAPTER 13

Political Policies and Practices, 1907-1909

The time seemed ripe for increased activity in behalf of an independent party of labor. One of the most effective arguments against the movement for a labor party at the A. F. of L. convention had been the assurance by the Federation's leadership that the policy of "reward your friends and punish your enemies," so vigorously pursued in the 1906 election, would pay off in the new Congressional session. Certainly, then, the barren fruits of that session so far as labor was concerned should have stimulated an increased demand for the labor party.

LULL IN 1907

But the year 1907 saw instead a setback for the labor party movement. It was the year of revelation of graft and corruption in the municipal administration of San Francisco where the Union Labor Party had been in power since 1901. The investigation showed that the Labor Party and the mayor, the union musician, Eugene E. Schmitz, were controlled by the Boss Abe Reuf who, under the guise of legal fees, was able to extort large sums of money from the public utilities, gambling houses, and houses of prostitution in return for favors and protection. In the spring of 1907, at the height of the graft scandals, the Union Labor Party was driven out of office.

Actually, in the course of the investigation and the trials that followed, it became clear that Ruef was a tool of big business which used him as a means of gaining control of the public utilities. The Graft Prosecution showed that it was big business that corrupted politics, but of all those accused, only Ruef went to jail. Indeed, as soon as it was evident that the investigation would touch the wealthy bribers as well as the bribe-takers, big business changed its attitude and demanded that the Graft Prosecution be called off. "As long as only Ruef and Schmitz had been under indictment," writes Walton Bean, "the business class in San Francisco had supported the prosecution and had praised it for trying to rid the city of corrupt union labor politicians who had been 'holding up' honest businessmen. But as soon as [prosecutor] Henney's real beliefs and objectives became apparent, opinion among the wealthier classes and those often known as the 'best people' in San Francisco underwent a violent change. It began to be pointed out that the whole thing was very bad for the city's business and was 'hurting business.' "[1]

Although, as Lincoln Steffens made abundantly clear in his book, *The Shame of the Cities,* Pittsburgh, Cleveland, Cincinnati, Philadelphia, Chicago, New York and other large cities were even more corrupt than San Francisco, the commercial press paid special attention to the exposure of the Graft Prosecution in the West Coast city. It was determined to prove that a labor party and a corrupt administration were an inevitable combination. Thus the Philadelphia *Public Ledger,* published in a city described by Steffens as "Corrupt but Content," commented: "In San Francisco . . . labor is a synonym for the ruling political power, and that political power and labor element are thoroughly corrupt and frankly inimical to decency, and are arrayed in active hostility to the courts, to the law, to plain honesty and to all the common safeguards of any social order, to all the elementary props and foundation stones of a government of whatever character and form."[2]

Although they could point to many gains won by labor in San Francisco during the regime of the Union Labor Party, the Graft Prosecution made it difficult for the advocates of independent political action by labor to win new converts. As *The Nation* noted gleefully: "A defender of organized labor as a political force must be speechless in view of its San Francisco record."[3]

One group of trade unionists, however, refused to remain speechless. Under the slogan, "The Trade Union in Politics," the unions of Rockford, Illinois, organized a Union Labor League, and on April 2, 1907, elected the mayor, three aldermen, five supervisors, and the city assessor. Mayor Mark Jardine was the former president of the United Brotherhood of Leather Workers on Horse Goods, and most of the other victorious candidates were members of Local No. 80 of this A. F. of L. union. In May 1907, in a letter to A. F. of L. unions, the Union Labor League announced its victory at the polls, and appealed: "Come, brothers from other cities, fall in line."[4]*

---

* While Rockford was a small city (40,000 inhabitants) it sprang into prominence, first, as a result of the sweeping victory by independent political forces of organized labor, and later, by Mayor Jardine's activity in ferreting out dishonest aldermen and bringing them to public view. Pointing out that this activity would do something to overcome the impression created by the Graft Prosecution in San Francisco, the Rockford *Morning Star* declared in an editorial entitled, "A Labor Mayor Who is a Credit to the Community": "Mayor Jardine should be upheld for

But the A. F. of L. was not listening. Indeed, throughout the winter, spring, and summer of 1907 there was hardly any discussion of political action in the *American Federationist* or at meetings of the Executive Council. The first reference to the subject that year occurred in connection with the impending fall elections, and it was confined to a single circular, "To All Organized Labor," in which the Executive Council called upon all workers to compel candidates for legislative and judicial offices to express their attitude towards the A. F. of L.-sponsored Pearre Anti-Injunction Bill. Upon their attitude towards the measure, "candidates for judicial or legislative office should be pledged, repudiated, or opposed."[5] But beyond this feeble attempt, the Federation did nothing in the 1907 elections.

The only other political activity during the year was an attempt by the Executive Council to mobilize labor's opposition to Cannon's re-election as House Speaker at the opening of the 60th Congress in December 1907. On October 28, 1907, it released a circular, "To All Organized Labor," recounting Cannon's past role as "the strategic center of opposition to Labor," and concluded with the request that all central bodies and local unions pass resolutions calling upon the Congressmen from their districts to vote against Cannon's re-elecion and send committees "to personally wait upon the Members of Congress from their respective districts and present the urgency and the need of these members to vote against Mr. Cannon for the speakership."[6] Here, too, the Executive Council did nothing beyond issuing the circular. Soon after the 60th Congress convened, Cannon was re-elected Speaker of the House.

The decline in the Federation's political activity took place precisely at a time when the N.A.M. was intensifying its work in this area. While the *American Federationist* was either silent about the need for increased political action or warning the affiliated unions that they should be careful not to weaken their organizations by going into politics, *American Industries,* official publication of the N.A.M., carried the following in large type on the front page of every issue:

"Go into Politics! Employers must fight labor class legislation, and must fight it now. The battle is for good government for capital and labor alike, for personal liberty for every man in the community, of every station and occupation, and for honest, stalwart, clean-handed Americanism. Go into Politics!"

The N.A.M. went into politics with a vengeance. It strengthened its lobby in Washington to obstruct labor legislation, concentrating on making sure that the appointments to the House and Senate Committees

---

his demand that dishonest men be driven out of the council. He has worked hard, and early and late, to ferret out this rascality . . . He has run down these aldermanic rascals and will help put them behind the bars." (Reprinted in *Leather Workers' Journal,* May, 1908, p. 487.)

which considered such legislation were such as approved by the N.A.M. In the first session of the 60th Congress, the N.A.M. succeeded in getting the Committee on the Judiciary to bury the bill to exempt labor organizations from the application of the Sherman Anti-Trust Act.[7]

The N.A.M. poured money lavishly into the 1907 campaign—raising a fund of $1,500,000 for its activities along this line—and used it to support candidates who were outspoken in opposition to labor's political program. It rallied support behind the re-election of Cannon as House Speaker. It employed detectives and kept them scattered over the country collecting information concerning the members and officers of the A. F. of L. which, exaggerated and distorted, could be used to discredit organized labor. There were successful efforts at bribing local union officials to support N.A.M.-sponsored candidates, and there were even outright attempts made to bribe the top officials of the A. F. of L.[8]*

ANTI-LABOR OFFENSIVE BY THE COURTS

The lull in labor's political activities was broken by two historic court decisions: the Bucks' Stove and Range Co. and the Danbury Hatters' cases.†

James W. Van Cleave, president of the Bucks' Stove and Range Co., a manufacturing company located in St. Louis, was also president of the N.A.M. and a member of the American Anti-Boycott Association, both leading open-shop organizations. The Stove Founders' National Defense Association, of which he was a member, had a detailed plan of mutual assistance to drive unionism out of the industry, and Van Cleave, with the cooperation of the three anti-union organizations, began to establish an open shop in his own company. He placed spies in his shop, refused to confer with the representatives of the union, and secretly plotted to substitute nonunion for union men. He hoped to provoke the union into

* An effort was made to bribe Gompers himself. The plan involved paid agents of the N.A.M. and was engineered by James W. Van Cleave, its president. Gompers told the complete story to the delegates at the 1907 convention, and was corroborated by two A.F. of L. vice-presidents. (*Proceedings*, A.F. of L. Convention, 1907, pp. 260–67.) At the time, Gompers' story was widely ignored in the press, but a few years later, a House Lobby investigation disclosed the facts in the story as Gompers had told them. (*See "Synopsis of Report of the House of Representatives Lobby Investigation*, 1913, pamphlet.)

† Another important decision that rocked the labor movement was handed down by the Supreme Court in the Adair case in 1908. The Court declared unconstitutional Section 10 of the Erdman Act of 1898 which made it unlawful for an employer to discriminate against or discharge any employee because of the latter's membership in a union. In the case before the court a worker had been discharged because he would not give up his union membership. (Adair v. United States, 208 U.S. 161, 1908.) The decision, in effect, gave constitutional sanction to "yellow-dog" contracts and the blacklist.

committing an overt act which would give him an excuse for cancelling existing contracts between the Founders' Association and the Iron Moulder's and Metal Polishers' Union. When a dispute arose in the nickel plating department over an increase in the hours of labor, Van Cleave refused to arbitrate. The men were dismissed, and when negotiations between the Metal Polishers Local No. 10 in St. Louis and the company failed to adjust the matter, the union went on strike to enforce the nine-hour day.

The union declared a boycott against the company, and, following an inquiry, the Executive Council of the A. F. of L. found that Van Cleave would not consider an adjustment of the dispute. The Council, therefore, endorsed the boycott and published the name of the company on the "We Don't Patronize" list of the *American Federationist*. Van Cleave served notice on the Federation on August 19, 1907, that business had been seriously affected, and the company was threatened with ruin because of the boycott against its goods. This, in turn, led the A. F. of L. to issue a circular calling upon all the affiliated unions to intensify their boycott activities. Van Cleave, assisted and financed by the American Anti-Boycott Association, requested an injuncion from Justice Ashley M. Gould of the Superior Court of the District of Columbia against the A. F. of L., its officers, and the Metal Polishers' Union to prohibit them from carrying on the "conspiracy" to boycott.

On December 18, 1907, Justice Gould granted all the company wanted and more. He issued a temporary injunction against the A. F. of L., its officers, "each of their agents, servants, attorneys, confederates, and any and all persons active in aid or conjunction with any of them," and enjoined them as officials, or as individuals from conspiring, agreeing, or combining in any manner to restrain or destroy the business of the company or its agents, from publishing the company's name in the "We Don't Patronize" or "unfair" list, or from calling attention to the existence of a boycott.[9]

"This injunction is the most sweeping ever issued," Gompers wrote in the *Federationist*. "*It is an invasion of the liberty of the Press and the Right of Free Speech.*" It was not an issue that concerned labor alone. "It is the *American Federationist* that is now enjoined. Tomorrow it may be another publication or some other class of equally law-abiding citizens, and the present injunction may then be quoted as a sacred precedent for future encroachments upon the liberties of the people." He announced that the A. F. of L. intended to fight the case until a final decision was rendered by the Supreme Court.[10]

To implement this intention, the Executive Council retained the services of several lawyers, including Alton B. Parker, former Chief Justice of the New York State Court of Appeals, and appealed the injunction to the District of Columbia Court of Appeals. On Parker's advice, and with the consent of the Executive Council, Gompers removed the name of the Bucks' Stove and Range Co. from the "We Don't Patronize" list of the *Federationist*, but continued to discuss editorially the principles involved in the controversy. It is clear that he was aware that he was risking a contempt of court citation.[11]*

To secure funds for the legal battles that lay ahead, the 1907 A. F. of L. convention authorized the levying of an assessment of one cent per member of affiliated organizations, and empowered the Executive Council to levy additional assessments, if necessary. On January 24, 1908, the Council distributed a circular "To All Organized Labor," entitled: "An Urgent Appeal for Financial Aid in Defense of Free Press and Free Speech." It appealed "to all unions and union members, and the friends of justice to contribute as promptly and as generously as they can, in order that a legal defense fund may be at the disposal of the American Federation of Labor to defend the rights of labor, and the rights of our people before the courts." Funds were forthcoming—the U.M.W. alone contributed $2,000 in addition to the assessment.[12]

On March 23, 1908, the injunction was made permanent and Gompers filed an appeal in the Court of Appeals. In July, a petition was presented by the Bucks' Stove and Range Co. in the Supreme Court of the District of Columbia that ordered each of the defendants—Gompers, Mitchell, and Morrison—to "show cause . . . why he should not be adjudged to be in contempt of the order and decree of the court." It was alleged that Mitchell, as vice-president of the Federation, violated the injunction in authorizing and permitting acts to be done by the organization's officers, and that he, as president of the U.M.W., "entertained a resolution at the Mine Workers' Convention, last January, calling upon the miners of the country to refrain from purchasing the products of the Bucks' Stove and Range Company." The charges against Secretary Morrison were that he had sent out or caused to be sent out copies of the *American Federationist* containing editorials and other utterances concerning the company after the permanent injunction became effective. The charges against Gompers were based on the allegation that he had violated the injunction "in doing or authorizing, or directing the doing of these acts, the sending out of an appeal for funds for legal defense in the suit and

---

* The idea of labor leaders risking a contempt citation in the fight against the injunction was advanced earlier by John B. Lennon, A.F. of L. Treasurer. On March 20, 1903, he wrote to Morrison: "Until there are some prominent men willing to go to jail and serve terms in defense of their rights as American citizens and trade unionists, there will be no public sentiment that will affect the issuance of injunctions, or the curtailment of the law restricting their issue. The very opposite you will find will be true. The injunctions will be increased in their scope all the time, and unless the trade unionists of this country have sufficient courage to defy them, they will soon wield a tremendously injurious effect upon our movement." (*AFL Corr.*)

injunction proceedings on the platform in public speeches, and in editorially discussing the fundamental principles involved in these proceedings."[13]

The labor movement was still considering how best to meet the problems it faced as a result of the court's action in the Bucks' Stove and Range Co. case when, on February 3, 1908, the Supreme Court issued its decision in the Danbury Hatters' case, described by Gompers as "the most drastic and far-reaching decision which it has ever handed down," and which a contemporary journal characterized as "worthy to stand with the infamous 'Dred Scott' decision of fifty years ago." In a unanimous opinion, the Court declared that the Sherman Anti-Trust Act applied to organizations of labor. "The Act," read the decision, "makes no distinction between classes and records of Congress show that in fact attempts have been made to exempt organizations of farmers and laborers by legislation. As no such legislation has been enacted, the Anti-Trust Act applies to the case at hand." It ruled further that interference with the physical transportation of an article was not necessary to cause a violation of the Sherman Act, and that the Loewe company of Danbury, Connecticut, could sue the United Hatters of North America for three times the amount of damage it had suffered by reason of the union's boycott of the company's products.* The defendants, the court declared, were members of "a vast combination engaged in a combined scheme and effort to force the plaintiffs against their will . . . to unionize their shops, with the intent thereby to control the employment of labor in the operation of said factories . . . and to carry out such schemes, effort, and purpose, by restraining and destroying the interstate trade and commerce of such manufactures, by means of . . . boycotting them."[14]

As Chief Justice Melville W. Fuller read the decision, organized labor knew that it was facing extinction. While the decision applied only to the Hatters' Union, its force and effect applied equally to all labor organizations in the country. Here, for the first time, the Supreme Court stated clearly that trade unions came within the provisions of the Sherman Anti-Trust Act. All labor organizations were held to be trusts, combinations, and conspiracies in illegal restraint of trade, and they and

* It was left up to the jury alone to decide the amount of damages which the company sustained. Judgment of $240,000 was obtained against the members of the union in 1909, and six years later, the Supreme Court put its approval on it, ordering a collection of the full amount with additional penalties and interest. (235 U.S. 522, 1915.) Finally, a compromise was arrived at under which settlement was made for $234,000, but it is estimated that the case cost the union membership over one million dollars. In April 1910, the A.F. of L. Executive Council announced that it had been informed that the union and its membership "have exhausted their financial resources and are unable to take an appeal to the higher court unless financial assistance is rendered." The Council, as authorized by the A. F. of L. convention, levied an assessment of two cents per member of the entire Federation. (Cleveland *Citizen,* April 30, 1910.)

each of their members were not only liable to three-fold damages claimed by anyone, but each member might be punished by a fine of $5,000 and imprisonment for one year. For as the Court now interpreted the law, individual members became liable for the actions of union officers and other members. There were 197 defendants named in the case, and only two were prominent as union leaders. Every union, under the decision, might find its strikes, picket lines, and boycotts classified as "conspiracies," and its very existence threatened because of the damage suits against them by employers eager to see the organization wrecked.[15]

That the open-shoppers intended to do precisely this was made clear in the comment on the decision by James M. Beck, general counsel of the American Anti-Boycott Association. He urged all employers to intensify their offensive against the A. F. of L. assuring them that they could rely even more than in the past on assistance from the federal government. And this assistance was crucial: "As in the great Pullman Strike only the U.S. Government was effectual to stop it by its injunction against Debs, similarly only the Federal Government can effectually destroy this wide-spread conspiracy of the Federation against the freedom of commerce and the liberty of the individual."

The employers had a new, powerful weapon in the Court's decision, Beck concluded, and it would be well if they began immediately to make effective use of it.[16]

LABOR'S REACTION

As the A. F. of L. viewed the scene in the opening months of 1908, it was clear that a specter hung over the labor movement. Either this would be destroyed or the labor movement would perish. The combination of the new decisions of the courts, enforced by the injunction, threatened to cripple the whole policy of economic action which the A. F. of L. had so laboriously built up and upon which it staked so much. In addition to hampering labor's freedom of economic action, the ceaseless litigation was draining union treasuries, and paralyzing labor's ability to withstand the open-shop offensive.

The decisions of the courts in the Bucks' Stove and Range Co. and the Danbury Hatters' cases, Gompers pointed out, made "it an essential duty for us to fight for the very life of our organizations." But what should be done? How should labor fight to preserve its existence? Gompers answered: "We must secure Congressional legislation, and secure it now." Should Congress "fail to heed our request for justice we shall at once appeal to all people to help us right our wrongs by electing representatives pledged to the interests of the people."[17] Not even the prospect of the total annihilation of the economic power of organized labor could budge Gompers from resorting to the already tried-and-proved defective policy of seeking relief within the framework of the two-party system, the policy of electioneering for the defeat of labor's "enemies" and for the victory of its "friends" on the basis of the candidates' pledges.

But from every side pressure was mounting for a more effective way of fighting for the existence of the trade unions. From the mid-west, John B. Lennon, A. F. of L. treasurer, wrote to Gompers late in February, informing him that "the working people here are demanding that something be done that will prove more effective in achieving legislation we seek than what we have previously depended on; they are beginning to listen more eagerly than I have ever before seen to those who criticize our policies and advocate either the formation of a new, independent labor party or support of the Socialist Party, and we are going to have the most terrible problems to face on this issue, unless we can do something quickly along the lines we approve of." Gompers knew from correspondence pouring into A. F. of L. headquarters that Lennon was not exaggerating. There are scores of letters in the A. F. of L. Archives from local unions and individual trade unionists stressing the same point that the workers told Lennon. A typical one came from a local union in Illinois:

"Do any of the old parties care for the labor class? No, with a capital N. Mr. Gompers, don't you think it is time you quit dabbling with the old political parties, and support the only means by which laboring men can elect our own representatives, as the capitalists do theirs now— a party of the laboring people. Let's stop working for those who will promise anything to get our votes and as soon as elected will drop us like hot cakes and enact laws by which we can be pushed further down than we are now. Have not the events since 1906 taught you anything?"

Quoting Lennon in a "Confidential" letter to John Mitchell, Gompers wrote: "If I tried for a whole day to describe the situation, I could not do it better, and perhaps not nearly so well as he has stated in his letter, and which I have just quoted. And if this is the situation—and no thinking man can dispute it—it is the imperative duty of everyone of us to lay everything else aside to avoid just such a chaotic condition which must prove disastrous." It is obvious that Gompers felt that it was absolutely imperative for the A. F. of L. to meet the workers' insistent demands for action without letting the movement for independent political action gain the ascendancy, to head off the rising discontent lest it crystallize into a labor party or close association with the Socialist Party. This meant that the A. F. of L. leaders would have to adopt a more militant program of political pressure methods. As Daniel J. Keefe, president of the Longshoremen's Union, put it in a letter to Ralph M. Easley in mid-February 1908: "The wage earners of America are worked up to a very high pitch, owing to recent decisions of the United States Supreme

Court, and I am of the opinion that President Gompers and his associates will be called upon to take a more radical position than they contemplate."[18]

On March 3, 1908, Gompers took the first step in this direction. He wrote a "Confidential" letter to the members of the Executive Council informing them that he was "in receipt of quite a number of communications and resolutions adopted by various organized bodies affiliated to the American Federation of Labor, in some form or other, expressing themselves that a definite course be pursued by our Federation relative to the new conditions that have arisen resulting from the decisions of the United States Supreme Court." He went on to point out that the decisions had created an "unsettled state of mind among a large number of our fellow-workers throughout the country as well as those most active in the ranks of our movement." Already, "a number of central bodies have under consideration resolutions declaratory in some form or another of a movement wholly independent and divergent, while others have taken action for the creation of an independent labor party, and in the event this is not done by a specified time, that they themselves will inaugurate such a movement." He was pleased that "others have shown their intelligence and devotion to the cause of labor by expressing themselves as willing to fall in line with the course laid down by the Executive Council." To make certain that the course advocated by the Council and endorsed by workers of "intelligence and devotion" would be the one pursued in the immediate future, Gompers called the Executive Council to a meeting on March 16, 1908, in Washington. He also proposed that the heads of each national or international union, affiliated to the Federation, be invited to meet with the Executive Council two days later after the beginning of its meeting "for the purpose of taking such action as in the full judgment of all may be productive of the best results to protect and promote the lawful interests of labor." The reason for the two-day delay in the second meeting was to prevent any but the course advocated by the Executive Council from being considered: "If the Executive Council meets two days in advance of general conference above outlined, we can in a measure outline what we propose to submit to the general conference and thereby accomplish the best results with the least possible danger of any action being taken likely to result injuriously to our fellow-workers!"[19] No chance was to be taken to allow a movement to develop for an independent labor party!

On March 7, under authority granted by the Executive Council, Gompers wrote to the presidents of all national and international affiliates, inviting them to send delegates to a joint meeting with the Council on March 18, 1908.[20] The Executive Council met, as scheduled, two days before, and drew up a program to be presented to the larger meeting which was based on the "political pressure" methods pursued in the past.

Two days later, the larger meeting took place which was styled: "Protest Conference of the Executive Council of the American Federation of Labor and Executive Officers of International Unions and Farmers' Organizations to Consider Recent Supreme Court Decisions and Labor Legislation." Representatives of 118 affiliated unions, several of farmers' organizations, and an official of the Brotherhood of Locomotive Firemen were present.

There was no discussion permitted on any proposal except that presented by the Executive Council. The Conference issued two documents, drawn up by the Council: Labor's Protest to Congress and An Address to Workers. The Protest to Congress did not cover as much ground as the Bill of Grievances of two years earlier; its main emphasis was upon a single issue—the recent application by the courts of the Sherman Anti-Trust Act against trade unions. The Protest urged Congress to amend the Sherman Act so that it could not hereafter "be enforced to apply to any arrangements, agreements, or combinations" among workers or farmers; to limit the issuance of injunctions, to pass an employers' liability law and an eight-hour law for all government employees, and for those employed upon work for the government, whether by contractors or subcontractors. It closed with a threat to hold the members of Congress and the party in power accountable for the disposition of labor's demands. The document was signed by Gompers, the members of the Executive Council, and the 118 visiting representatives of national and international unions.

The Address to Workers explained why the conference had been called, summarized the Protest to Congress, and outlined the "legitimate pressure" that could "be brought to bear upon Congress in the effort to secure passage of our amendment to the Sherman Law." It called upon the American workers to hold mass meetings in every city and town on the evening of the third Sunday or Monday in April (19th or 20th), and at the meeting "voice fully and unmistakably labor's protest against the Supreme Court decision which strips labor of the rights and liberties which we had supposed were guaranteed by the constitution." In addition, every member of organized labor was urged to write a personal letter to the congressman of his district and the two Senators of his state "insisting that they use their efforts and cast their vote for the passage of our amendment to the Sherman Law and other legislation mentioned in labor's protest and warning them that labor and its friends will hold them responsible." The Appeal closed:

"We have appealed to Congress for the necessary relief we deem essential to safeguard the interests and rights of the toilers.

"We now call upon the workers of our common country to stand faithfully by our friends, Oppose and defeat our enemies, whether they be Candidates for President, for Congress, or other offices, whether Executive, legislative, or judicial. . . ."

The only reference in either of the two documents to the existence of forces in the labor movement who so alarmed Gompers, Lennon, and other members of the Executive Council was a brief statement in the Address to the Workers: "We deem it essential for the successful accomplishment of the plan set forth in the foregoing that local unions, city, central, and state federations follow closely the line of action outlined by this conference and such further plans as may be promulgated by the Executive Council or by future conferences so that our strength and influence may not be frittered away by different lines of action."[21] Having closed any opportunity for the forces favoring independent action by labor to express themselves at the Conference, the A. F. of L. leaders next warned all affiliates against associating themselves in any way with this movement.

The Protest to Congress was presented to the presiding officer of the Senate and the Speaker of the House. Simultaneously, several million copies of both the Protest and the Address were printed and distributed; a special edition of the *American Federationist* was published, and "hundreds of thousands of circulars" were issued. Mass meetings were held throughout the country on April 19 and 20, and Gompers announced gleefully that "Congressmen have been deluged and swamped with a mass of resolutions and personal letters which have poured in from their constituents demanding that the present session of Congress heed the demands of labor and enact the measures which it specifies."[22] Nevertheless, Congress adjourned in May 1908 without passing any of the measures demanded by labor. Several bills to restrain the use of injunctions in labor disputes were introduced in the House; they were referred to the Committee on the Judiciary, packed with anti-labor Congressmen, and died there.[23] Indicative of how indifferent the Republican Party was to the A. F. of L. threat to hold the party in power responsible was the refusal of Speaker Cannon to reappoint Congressman Pearre, champion of anti-injunction legislation, to the powerful Judiciary Committee. James S. Sherman, a Republican leader in Congress, boasted that "the Republican Party is responsible for legislation or for the failure of legislation," that the party was willing to assume the responsibility, and challenged the A. F. of L. to do something about it. And the majority leader on the floor of the House, Congressman Payne of New York, declared on the eve of the Congressional adjournment: "We are doing this business; we are legislating; we are responsible for what we do, and we propose to assume the responsibility for it from beginning to end." Like Sherman, he told the A. F. of L. to make the most of it.[24]

Thoroughly disgusted, though not surprised, at the failure of the Republican-dominated Congress to heed labor's appeals and warnings, a group of A. F. of L. unionists in Oklahoma, Kansas, Nebraska, and Minnesota, under the leadership of J. Harvey Lynch, general organizer of the Federation for the state of Oklahoma, began a move to form a new party of labor. A call was sent to A. F. of L. State Federations of Labor, asking their reaction to the idea of convening a convention directly after Congress adjourned for the purpose of discussing the formation of a labor party, and drawing up "a platform of demands of labor." Despite the limited resources of the campaign,* the response had been greater than the organizers had ever expected. "I am splendidly encouraged from twenty-seven State[s]," Lynch announced, "from Rhode Island and Vermont to Montana, and from Minnesota to Alabama. Several Executive Boards have acted favorably upon the matter and I am sure that a large number of States will be represented and much good will be accomplished." He urged all working people to rally behind the movement: "If we, the Laborers and Farmers, are the 'salt of the earth,' the 'bone and sinew of the land,' then let us assume our responsibilities and rise equal to our duties."

Gompers immediately took steps to stop the movement. He wrote to Lynch reminding him that the Appeal to Workers had warned precisely against such action. He assured Lynch that he did not "doubt the sincerity or honesty of your purpose," but insisted that the step he had taken "would show to those who are hostile to the cause of labor something that would bring glee and unction to their souls, demonstrating that there is neither unity, or spirit or purpose among the organized workers of the country." He concluded that "nothing could be so prejudicial to the interests and welfare of the working people of our country as an attempt to hold a convention for the purpose outlined in your circular," and he urged him to withdraw the call. Lynch assured Gompers, in reply, that once he had had an opportunity to understand the importance of the call for the conference, and the magnitude of the favorable responses—he was prepared to go to Washington to explain the issue fully in person—"you will agree with me as to the wisdom of the move." He was backed in this proposal by J. Luther Langston, secretary-treasurer of the Oklahoma Federation of Labor, who wrote angrily to Gompers: "I cannot see wherein you have cause to feel alarmed at the proposed convention of State Federations. . . . If I were in your stead I would hesitate to criticize until I was familiar with details."[25]

But Gompers was taking no chances. He sent a "Confidential" letter to the Executive Council, apprising it of the danger that a labor party might emerge from the conference of State Federations, of his letter to

* In one of his circulars, Lynch described himself as follows: "I am a Plasterer and am working at my trade and like all active Trade Unionists who are trying to push the cause, am poor. Therefore, I am directing this work at spare moments and as my means will permit." (dated April 25, 1908. *AFL Corr.*)

Lynch urging him to call off the conference, and expressing his opinion that the gathering could be exceedingly dangerous since it would cause the labor forces to "be confused" as to what policy to follow. He urged the Council members to use their influence to prevent the proposed convention from being held.[26]

Meanwhile, Lynch tried to counter Gompers' opposition with an appeal of his own to the State Federations informing them of the A. F. of L. president's request that he call off the conference, and of his determination to ignore the request: "As this is a move among the 'grass roots,' or rank and file I can readily see why the Politicians of all parties, and the representatives of corporate wealth would object to it, but just why our national president should object to it, I can not understand. . . . Brothers, this movement represents your interests, and you should favorably consider this matter, as has already a large number of states. Let me hear from you by return mail." But the pressure from the A. F. of L. leaders completely overshadowed the appeal from a poor Plasterer who was "trying to push the cause" of organized labor. The plan to hold a convention to discuss the formation of an independent labor party was dropped.[27] Heaving a sigh of relief, the A. F. of L. leaders turned their attention to preparing for the conventions of the two major parties which were to assemble in the summer to draw up platforms and nominate candidates for the forthcoming presidential elections.

THE POLITICAL CONVENTIONS OF 1908

In the summer of 1908, the A. F. of L. Executive Council, headed by Gompers, appeared at the convention of the Republican Party in Chicago to present labor's program to the platform committee. The Republicans were asked to pledge to enact legislation exempting labor and agriculture from the operations of the provisions of the Sherman Anti-Trust Act; curbing the injunction power of the courts, and providing for trial by jury when contempt punishment was being considered; guaranteeing the eight-hour day to all persons on government work when employed by contractors or sub-contractors; creating a separate department of labor and a federal bureau of mines and mining; establishing a governmental postal bank; instituting general employers' liability, and submitting a constitutional amendment for ratification to the states "for the absolute suffrage of women, co-equal with men."

Gompers and A. F. of L. vice-presidents James Duncan and Daniel J. Keefe—both known as "adherents to the Republican Party"—were selected to present these proposals to the Republican Committee on Platform. They were refused a hearing before the whole committee, and allowed only ten minutes to present their position before a subcommittee. The labor arguments were given no consideration, and a reactionary labor plank was adopted which read: "The Republican Party will uphold at all times the authority and integrity of the courts, state and federal, and will ever insist that their powers to enforce their process and to protect life, liberty, and property shall be preserved inviolate. We believe, however, that the rules of procedure in the federal courts with respect to the issuance of the writ of injunction should be more accurately defined by statute, and that no injunction, or temporary restraining should be issued without notice, except where irreparable injury should result from delay, in which case a speedy hearing thereafter should be granted." Apart from the labor plank, the Republican platform made one other reference to labor. It boasted that the eight-hour law for government employees and the child labor laws had been enacted during Republican administrations. It also made the meaningless statement: "The Republican party recognizes the special needs of wage-workers generally, for their well-being means the well-being of all."[28]

Gompers denounced the injunction plank as "a flimsy, tricky evasion of the issue. . . . It is a pro-injunction not an anti-injunction declaration."* But the N.A.M. was happy; indeed, President Kirby of the open-shop organization boasted that had it not been for N.A.M. pressure, a plank more acceptable to the A. F. of L. would have been written into the Republican platform.[29]

The nomination of William Howard Taft as the Republican standard-bearer was a bitter pill for labor to swallow. Known as the "injunction judge,"† his record was so unsatisfactory that the *American Federationist* of October 1907 carried an editorial of six pages entitled, "Taft, the Injunction Standard-Bearer." (It was issued as a pamphlet and circulated

* In order to gain labor support for the Republican Party, Roosevelt hoped to secure an injunction plank that would satisfy some labor leaders and still not offend the more conservative elements within the party. Before the convention, Roosevelt led Gompers to believe that he would favor pledging the Republicans to "progressive declarations" for labor. But when the showdown came at the convention, Roosevelt and Taft chose party harmony and unity above the desires of labor and yielded to N.A.M. and other pressures. N.A.M. claimed that it was responsible for the fact that 30,000 to 40,000 telegrams poured into the Resolutions Committee in one day demanding a pro-injunction plank. (Gompers, *Seventy Years of Life and Labor,* vol. II, pp. 260–61; Theodore Roosevelt to Henry Cabot Lodge, June 15, 16, 1908, *TRP.*)

† Through his actions on the bench, Taft had also earned the name of "father of injunctions." As Judge of the Federal Circuit Court, he had ruled against union labor in several contempt and injunction cases, and these rulings were used as the basis of anti-labor decisions by other judges subsequently. (*Taft, the Injunction Standard Bearer,* pamphlet.)

The only influence of organized labor at the 1908 Republican convention was the defeat of Harrison Gray Otis as candidate for delegate-at-large. "The selection of General Otis," a California Republican wrote Taft, "would have been considered a direct affront and insult to union labor." (Meyer Lissner to William Howard Taft, May 19, 1908, Meyer Lissner Papers, Stanford University Library.)

by the Democrats in the campaign.) But Wall Street gave its blessings to the Republican party platform and its candidates, and, as Gompers reported, "James Van Cleave [of the N.A.M.] and the Republicans jeeringly told labor to 'Go to Denver.' "[30] And to Denver the A. F. of L. Executive Council proceeded, to present labor's demands to the Democratic Convention. Here they were warmly greeted; the Democrats, being out of power, were naturally looking for allies, and the failure of the conservatives in 1904 to prove that a less progressive stand would win votes, made them more receptive to labor's proposals.

The Executive Council members proposed the inclusion in the Democratic platform of exactly the same propositions that had been presented to the Republicans. The Democratic platform incorporated provisions which were substantially what labor demanded. It gave lengthy attention to the jurisdiction of the courts with respect to the injunction process affecting labor: "We deem that parties of all judicial proceedings should be treated with rigid impartiality . . . and that injunctions should not be treated with rigid impartiality . . . and that injunctions should not be issued in any cases in which injunctions would not be issued if no industrial dispute were involved." The platform called for the amendment of the Sherman Anti-Trust Act, stating: "The expanding organization of industry makes it essential that there should be no abridgement of the right of wage earners and producers to organize for the protection of wages and the improvement of labor conditions, to the end that such labor organizations and their members should not be regarded as illegal combinations in restraint of trade." An eight-hour day on all government work and the creation of a separate department of labor were also pledged in the platform. Of the measures requested by the A. F. of L., the Democratic platform, as finally approved, pledged the party to all but those on woman suffrage and governmental postal banks. And in seconding the nomination of William Jennings Bryan as the Democratic presidential candidate, John G. M. Gearin of Oregon declared: "Labor demands the nomination of Bryan . . . whose voice has been heard everywhere in advocacy of the rights of labor and against the wrongs perpetrated or threatened against labor."[31] Bryan was again nominated as the party's standard-bearer.

The *American Federationist* of August 1908 contained an editorial by Gompers entitled, "Both Parties Have Spoken—Choose Between Them." "Labor asked the Republican Convention for bread and it gave a stone," he wrote. For the Democratic platform, he had only the highest praise. The anti-injunction plank was "good all the way through. It had a right ring in it. It will cause a stir throughout the masses of the workers." He, therefore, called upon the workers to support the Democratic Party and its candidates: "We have no hesitation in urging the workers and our friends throughout the country to support the party in this campaign which has shown its sympathies with our wrongs and its desire to remedy them and to see that the rights of the people are restored."

While the Executive Council did not officially endorse Bryan, the A. F. of L. did, for the first time in its history, ask its membership and all workers to give their votes for a specific party during a presidential election.

A. F. OF L. CAMPAIGNS FOR BRYAN

On August 27, 1908, the A. F. of L. Executive Council conferred with Norman E. Mack, chairman of the Democratic National Committee. Mack agreed to print and distribute the campaign literature of the A. F. of L., and Gompers in turn assigned several of his organizers to Democratic headquarters to work for the party.[32] The plans for political liaison between the A. F. of L. and the Democratic Party having been clearly worked out, the Federation launched its campaign to elect Bryan and other Democratic candidates. The methods followed in 1908 followed the same general pattern established two years before in the Congressional campaign. Circulars, leaflets, pamphlets, cartoons, and news stories, many incorporating letters and resolutions from trade unions endorsing the A. F. of L.'s political campaign and pledging support of the Democratic Party, were distributed in the hundreds of thousands. The September and October issues of the *American Federationist,* containing more than 30 articles by A. F. of L. union leaders explaining why labor should vote Democratic, were reprinted and widely distributed. Literature describing the records and attitudes of candidates toward labor's legislative demands was circulated on a nation-wide scale.

In addition to distributing literature as a means of bringing its message to the workers, the A. F. of L. sent Gompers and other leaders to deliver addresses to audiences of workers at mass meetings sponsored by its affiliates. Throughout August, September, and October, Gompers toured Pennsylvania, Michigan, Ohio, Indiana, Illinois, and New York, addressing meetings of trade unionists in the leading cities of these important states. While he left no doubt in his speeches that he favored the Democratic candidates, Gompers repeatedly emphasized that the A. F. of L. was not "politically partisan"; that its position was that "the interests of the wage earners would be furthered by the success of the Democratic party not because it is the Democratic party, but because that party has adopted a platform compatible with labor's legislative needs while the Republicans have only shown disdain for labor."[33]

The care Gompers took to point out that the A. F. of L. was not endorsing the Democratic Party *in general* was a reflection of the opposition with the Federation to the political policy pursued in the 1908 campaign. This opposition stemmed from three sources: (1) the trade union leaders who were traditionally Republican; (2) the Socialist element in the Federation who believed the A. F. of L. should endorse the Socialist Party ticket, and (3) the non-Socialist elements who felt that neither of the two major parties could be trusted to assist labor in its hour of crucial need.

The Republican Party, attacking Gompers for his "promise to deliver the labor vote to Bryan," tried to organize a revolt against his leadership in the A. F. of L. The Republicans spread the report that four members of the Executive Council were either non-committal or definitely opposed to support of Democratic candidates. In his Buffalo speech on October 30, Taft repeated the charge, and mentioned the names of Daniel J. Keefe, John Mitchell, Max Morris, and James Duncan, all members of the Executive Council.[34]

Gompers immediately wired the four men requesting a reply. Morris replied that the report was "unqualifiedly false, as I have and do heartily approve of Gompers' program." Duncan replied that he had not changed his mind since the meeting of the Executive Council when labor's political policy was decided. Mitchell answered that Taft's statement conveyed the wrong impression: "I am in full sympathy and accord with the non-political partisan policy of the American Federation of Labor as it has been outlined and promulgated by the Executive Council." Keefe, however, refused to budge from his position as a leading labor supporter of the Republican Party. "I have been a Republican all my life," he wrote, "and I have already indicated to the Executive Council that regardless of what promises the Democratic Convention or Mr. Bryan might make, I intended to vote the Republican ticket as I have for thirty-two years." The fact that three of the four replies repudiated the Republican charge did not halt the campaign in the party press. It continued to headline statements by Republican leaders that there were heads of A. F. of L. unions who would not relinquish their political independence to satisfy Gompers' wishes.[35]

Mitchell did not, in his reply, corroborate Taft's statement, but he did nothing to dispel the widely publicized report that, as a close friend and admirer of President Roosevelt, he supported the Republican candidate. In a statement to the *United Mine Workers' Journal*, Mitchell declared that he did not believe that the labor movement was supporting any particular party "but that their chief aim was to elect to office members of trade unions or those in sympathy with the protection and preservation of the interests of the wage earners."[36] This must have sounded strange coming from a man who refused to lift a finger to defeat a candidate for President whose court decisions had seriously hampered the mine workers, and who refused to make a single speech against Republican Congressman James Watson, a longtime foe of labor, who was seeking election as Governor of Indiana, an important state for the union.*

A. F. of L. affiliates where Socialist influence was predominant voiced vigorous disagreement with the Federation's course in the campaign, and refused to support the Executive Council's recommendations or to contribute to the political fund drive. The Cigarmakers' Union of Brooklyn wrote to Gompers: "The Democratic party is financed and managed by capitalists and their agents, and therefore cannot represent the workers." The National Brotherhood of Potters of Trenton, New Jersey, wrote: "We deprecate your efforts to make a catspaw of labor organizations through the medium of professional capitalist politicians." The Pittsburgh local of the International Union of Steam Engineers replied to Gompers' appeal for campaign funds: "With all due respect to the office you and the committee hold, we would consider ourselves traitors to the working class to contribute to the capitalist party you are supporting." The Bakery and Confectionery Workers of Brooklyn informed Gompers: "We don't endorse any capitalistic party. They don't care about us. . . . The only political party which we endorse and which is on our side is the Socialist Party."[37]

The Socialist ticket, again headed by Eugene V. Debs, was endorsed by the Wisconsin Federation of Labor, the Toledo Central Labor Union, three international unions (the Bakery and Confectionery Workers, the United Brewery Workers, the Western Federation of Miners), and locals of the mine workers, carpenters, switchmen, cigarmakers, steam engineers, and potters. The statement of the International Union of United Brewery Workers, expressed in a letter to Morrison, summarizes the position of all of these unions:

"We don't believe in so-called tail politicians voting one time for a democrat who promises to stand for labor interests and the other time for a republican, for we know that those promises do not count anything, and therefore always believed and are stronger in our belief today than ever, that it is absolutely necessary for the wage workers of the country to be independent in politics and that the only party that represents the wage earners' interests is the Socialist Party of this country and no other. We have been fooled long enough by democrats and republicans. Even if once in a while we elect a good man on the democratic or republican ticket who would like to keep his promise toward the wage workers, such men cannot fulfill their promises, as they have to adhere to the mandates and dictates of their respective party."[38]

---

* The need for Mitchell's services in Indiana was stressed by G. H. Hendren, a Democratic leader in that state, who wrote to Gompers: "We are exceedingly anxious to have Honorable John Mitchell make a speech at Linton, the center of the great coal fields in Southern Indiana. . . . Republicans are now saying that Mr. Mitchell will not help us and it is very important that he give us a date now if possible, at such time as will meet his convenience." (July 28, 1908, AFL Corr.)

Not all the A. F. of L. locals and members who differed with the organization's support of the Democratic Party were Republicans or Socialists. A third group felt that only a new, independent party of labor was the answer to the workers' problems. They agreed that the Republicans were the worst enemies of organized labor, but they could see little hope for labor in a Democratic victory. For one thing, the Southern Democrats would have the greatest influence in Congress, and these men had already demonstrated that they were as bitter enemies of organized labor as the Republicans. In none of the party platforms of the Democratic Party in the Southern States was a single labor demand adopted, and several failed to mention labor in any way. Indeed, most of the State Democratic platforms gave little attention to labor—despite Gompers' recommendation to the Chairman of the Democratic National Committee that all State Democratic conventions incorporate in their state platforms declarations similar in character to the labor planks adopted at Denver.* How then could labor expect to achieve any real gains from a Party that showed so little interest in its problems throughout the states and which was controlled nationally from the South?[39]

Gompers did not bother to answer the arguments raised by the Socialists or those who favored an independent party of labor. He simply accused them of doing the Republicans' "dirty work" and charged that their propaganda was being financed by the N.A.M. But with the Democrats worried by the lack of harmony in the A. F. of L.'s campaign,[40] and, in an effort to solidify organized labor's ranks, Gompers issued a four-page circular on October 12 under his own signature. (The circular, however, was on official A. F. of L. stationery and carried the names of all members of the Executive Council at the top of the first page.) Addressed to "Men of Labor, Lovers of Human Liberty," the message reviewed why, he had no choice but to support the Democratic ticket. Indeed, it was not even a choice; it was a duty. "Duty to preserve with my voice, pen and ballot, that form of government, for the preservation of which, Lincoln said: '*Men died at Gettysburg.*'" Then Gompers got down to the real purpose of the circular. He denied that his position represented partisan support of a political party—"in performing a solid duty at this time in support of a political party *Labor does not become partisan to a political party, but partisan to a principle.*" He denied also, that he and other leaders of the A. F. of L. who supported the Democratic ticket were motivated by the hope of receiving a political appointment. As for himself, he wished it clearly understood "that there is no

* In a study of labor provisions of State party platforms in the Election of 1908, John R. Commons concludes that the Democrats gave less attention to labor in the state platforms than the Republicans. ("Party Platforms on Labor," *Charities and the Commons,* vol. XXXI, Dec. 20, 1908, pp. 419–20.)

political office in the gift of the American people, elective or appointive, that I would, under any circumstances, accept." He concluded with the now familiar appeal for the workers and "friends of human liberty" to respond affirmatively to labor's call "to stand faithfully by our friends and elect them, oppose and defeat our enemies, whether they be candidates for President, for Congress or other offices, whether executive, legislative or judicial."[41]

Gompers' circular aroused nation-wide attention when it provoked a bitter response from President Roosevelt. In a public letter to Senator Knox, Roosevelt defended the Republican platform and made a sweeping attack on Gompers for entering into collusion with Bryan to deceive labor. He accused Gompers (and Bryan) of proposing to limit the jurisdiction of the courts in a vicious attempt to undermine the American form of government, and hailed Taft's stand on injunctions as clear and unequivocal. Gompers issued a reply to this letter, accusing Roosevelt of having capitulated to the reactionaries in the Republican Party and abandoning the fight for a "liberal platform" at the Republican convention. He charged the letter was nothing but "an exhibition of impotent rage and disappoinment, and an awful descent from the dignity of the high office of the President of the United States."[42]

Roosevelt's attack on Gompers backfired. It aroused support for the A. F. of L. president, and rallied greater enthusiasm for the Democratic ticket. "I have been throughout the entire state," the secretary-treasurer of the Minnesota State Federation of Labor wrote to Morrison, "and I can honestly say that President Roosevelt's unjustified and vile denunciation of the Federation's president is producing a stronger support for the Democratic ticket. Very few prominent labor men in the state are now against us. I am sure that 90% of the trade unionists in Minnesota will vote for Mr. Bryan next Tuesday. I can also say with the same candor that the members of the railway brotherhoods are now also in line, and they are doing splendid work in behalf of the cause. Look out for Minnesota on election day." Morrison himself had the same type of information to report from the East. Late in October, following a speaking tour through New York and Rhode Island, he wrote to the Executive Council: "Everywhere the effect of President Roosevelt's attack on Mr. Gompers is evidenced. In every city the union men now appear to be unanimous in favor of the A. F. of L. political program; in fact, during my entire trip I did not hear a discordant note and no one in the audience questioned the action taken by the A. F. of L. Many socialists say they propose to cast a non-partisan vote for Wm. J. Bryan for President."[43]

Despite dissensions in the ranks and the refusal of many local unions to contribute towards the expenses of the campaign, there appears to have been considerable confidence at A. F. of L. headquarters in the closing weeks of the campaign. Reports from Maine in the September elections were encouraging. Rockland, Vinal, Haven, Stonington, Isle au Haut, St. George, and Saco which went Republican in 1906 voted Democratic in 1908, and several of the victorious candidates were union men. The entire State went Republican by less than 8,000 votes. "The Democrats are jubilant," an A. F. of L. campaigner wrote from Maine, "inasmuch as this is presidential year and the Republicans were confident of a large majority. I am more than pleased with the results." Early in October, the A. F. of L. evaluated the situation as being very hopeful. In a "confidential" memorandum to the Executive Council, Morrison wrote: "The outlook for Mr. Taft's election as President of the United States is very slim indeed." He listed three reasons for this conclusion: "1st, that the Roosevelt policy has brought about the general depression of business which has deprived many workers almost of a livelihood;* 2nd, that Mr. Taft has promised, if elected, to pursue the same policy; 3rd, the interpretation of Mr. Taft among most workers, covering all, is that he is the father of injunctions."[44]

Although the A. F. of L. leaders may have been indulging in wishful thinking, as the election results soon demonstrated, there is no question but that the Republican Party and its allies were alarmed and intensified their drive to win the labor vote in the last weeks of the campaign. Through personal contacts, Roosevelt was able to mobilize a number of A. F. of L. leaders, notably Daniel J. Keefe and John Pringle, editor of a Pittsburgh labor paper, and several leaders of the Railroad Brotherhoods—Warren Stone, grand chief of the Locomotive Engineers and Patrick H. Morrisey of the Trainmen—into actively aiding Taft's campaign. The Washington *Star* reported that Roosevelt was "personally directing a part of the program to turn labor to the Republican ticket." Learning that the Superior Court of the District of Columbia was about to hand down the decision in the Bucks' Stove and Range Co. case and fearing that Gompers and Mitchell would be convicted and sent to jail for contempt, an outcome which would win votes for Bryan, Roosevelt advised Taft to get to Van Cleave of N.A.M. and secure a continuation in the contempt proceedings. The result was that the decision was not handed down until after the election.[45]

The N.A.M. was especially active in the campaign. It issued pamphlets, leaflets, hired speakers, organized clubs and parades, and inserted paid advertisements in newspapers throughout the country calling for Bryan's defeat. Gompers was accused of attempting "to deliver the labor vote to the Democratic party by a campaign of misrepresentation," and the

---

* This is one of the few references by the A.F. of L. during the campaign to the economic crisis following the Panic of 1907.

A. F. of L. as a whole was charged with demanding "vicious class legislation" and of seeking the destruction of the dignity of the courts, thus undermining the foundation upon which the American government rested. Bryan was depicted as a "Socialist" who, as President, would nationalize American industry thus destroying the jobs of millions of workers. Special appeals were directed towards workers in industries protected by high tariffs adopted during Republican administrations. The iron and steel workers, the window glass workers, the flint workers, the structural iron workers and all their allied trades and helpers, were flooded with N.A.M.-financed literature portraying a Bryan victory as bringing in its wake low tariffs, unemployment, and low wages for those fortunate enough to find work, and a Taft victory as bringing a continuation of high tariffs, work for all, and high wages.[46]

After the election, the N.A.M. boasted that the employers had enthusiastically responded to its appeals: "Never before in any campaign, not even in 1896, did the business element of the country rally so promptly or work so harmoniously, enthusiastically, or effectively, as in 1908." The N.A.M. raised hundreds of thousands of dollars to finance its campaign to elect Taft. The total collections of the A. F. of L. during the entire campaign was $8,469.98![47]

RESULTS OF THE ELECTION OF 1908

The results of the A. F. of L.'s first big drive in a national election were disappointing. Taft was elected with a majority of well over a million popular votes, and with 321 electoral votes to Bryan's 162. (Debs polled 424,483 votes, a slight increase over his 1904 total.) What was a particularly bitter pill for the A. F. of L. to swallow was that a large popular vote for Taft was concentrated in the northeastern states, the very area where the Federation had its greatest membership.[48] To be sure, the Democrats made important gains in the Congressional districts where the A. F. of L. had campaigned actively; nevertheless, the control of the conservative and anti-labor Republicans over both Houses was unbroken. The new House of Representatives was made up of 213 Republicans and 172 Democrats. "Uncle Joe" Cannon, despotic boss of the House, whom the A. F. of L. had marked as enemy number two, giving Taft first place, and against whom it campaigned actively, was returned to Congress.

There were a few comforting results for the labor movement. James R. Watson, Republican candidate for Governor of Indiana, whom N.A.M. wanted especially to see elected and who had been vigorously opposed by labor, was defeated. Ten Congressmen were elected who held active membership in the trade unions—the six elected in 1906 were all re-elected and four new ones were added to the group of union card-holding Congressmen.*

These victories could not obscure the basic failure of the A. F. of L. to "reward the friends and punish the enemies of labor." Gompers tried to console the membership and justify the efforts to secure a Democratic victory by pointing out that labor's voice had been heard as never before, that the issues with which it was concerned had been fully presented to the people, and that a more respectful hearing would have to be given to labor's demands in the future. "Though temporarily defeated, labor is not conquered," Gompers announced to the press on the day after the election.[49]

There were several contemporary explanations for the stunning defeat suffered by the A. F. of L. In *Charities and the Commons* of December 1908, Graham Taylor, the noted sociologist, argued that the "union leaders had overestimated the strength of the labor vote and the efficiency of their organization to rally and wield it effectively." The A. F. of L. had succeeded in rallying most of the top union leaders and many of the subordinate ones behind its political policy, but the rank and file had not gone along. "Their rank and file have been and are still an unknown quantity politically." Taylor also argued that many skilled workers in the A. F. of L. were frightened by Republican and N.A.M. propaganda picturing Bryan as a "Socialist," whose election would place their jobs in jeopardy. As Robert F. Hoxie, the noted labor economist, pointed out in an article, "Gompers and the Labor Vote" in the *Journal of Political Economy* of December 1908, the A. F. of L. consisted mainly of skilled workers, and its appeal for political support was thus limited in the numbers it could influence; moreover, it could influence precisely the type of workers who would be most frightened by Bryan's reputed radicalism. In short, the failure of the A. F. of L. to organize the unskilled and semi-skilled workers in the mass production industries seriously weakened its political efforts. Hoxie noted further that not a few unions in the A. F. of L. had gained special concessions from Republican employers in order to keep them from organizing the unskilled, and that these unions were not seriously affected by court decisions. Having

* William B. Wilson and Thos. D. Nicholas, both Democrats from Pennsylvania, held membership in the U.M.W.; William J. Cary, Republican from Wisconsin, and T. J. McDermott, Democrat from Illinois, were members of the Commercial Telegraphers; Isaac K. Sherwood, Ohio, and Wm. D. Jamieson, Iowa, both Democrats, were members of the Printers' Union; John A. Martin, Democrat, Colorado, Brotherhood of Locomotive Firemen; Arthur P. Murphy, Republican, Mississippi, Railroad Trainmen; Carl C. Anderson, Democrat, Ohio, Musicians' Union. Wm. Hughes, Democrat, New Jersey, was not a member of organized labor, but had been made an honorary member of the Steam Shovel and Dredge Engineers and Cranemen's Union because of his stand in favor of labor legislation. (Frank Morrison to John Mitchell, April 27, 1910, *AFL Corr.*)

developed an indifference to the principles of working-class solidarity on the economic front, they carried this attitude over to the political arena, and refused to assist weaker unions who were menaced by injunctions and hoped to strengthen their economic power by a political victory.* Finally, Hoxie pointed out that the very political tradition the A. F. of L. leadership had nurtured for so many years had now returned to plague it. From the inception of the A. F. of L., Gompers "preached such a crusade against political action that in the minds of many of the workers the separation of unionism and politics has become as thoroughly canonized as the separation of church and state."[50] In other words, during the whole history of the A. F. of L. since 1881, Gompers had constantly warned, "Stay out of partisan politics." Politics, he had repeatedly insisted, must be subordinated to economic action, the only means through which labor could gain results; moreover, politics was a breeder of discord and disruption, a game of cunning in which workers could not hope to compete. Now, in 1908, partisan politics had been treated as the medium of the labor movement's deliverance. To be sure, Gompers claimed that the A. F. of L. was not engaging in "partisan politics" in actively supporting the Democratic ticket, but was only "partisan to a principle." But this fine distinction fooled nobody and only served to heighten the contradictions in the Federation's political policy. No wonder many A. F. of L. members were confused.

Neither of these two distinguished contemporary commentators emphasized another factor: the disgust of many rank and file A. F. of L. members with the "reward your friends and punish your enemies" policy, and their conviction, based on experience, that both major parties were controlled by the capitalists, and, despite pledges in party platforms, would never really help labor to secure the necessary legislation to enable it to emerge triumphant in the struggle against the very class that controlled these parties. Some of these workers showed their disgust with the A. F. of L. policy by voting for Debs, but many did so by refusing to vote for any candidate.[51]

1908 A. F. OF L. CONVENTION

The defeat of 1908 was very much in the minds of most delegates as they gathered in Denver on November 25, for the annual A. F. of L.

---

*In a letter to Gompers, accompanying resolutions condemning the action of Gompers and the Executive Council in endorsing Bryan and campaigning for the Democratic ticket, the officers of the International Longshoremen's Association wrote: "As far as our organizations are concerned, Mr. Taft has shown that he has been fair and just toward us." (Aug. 27, 1908, *AFL Corr.*) The fact that so many sister unions had been seriously affected by Taft's decisions on the injunction issue, which served as precedents for other anti-labor court decisions, did not seem to bother the Republican-dominated Longshoremen's Association.

convention. Badly shaken by the Federation's poor showing in persuading Congress to treat with labor's needs and the inability of its political policy to achieve electoral success, many delegates looked to the convention to advance a new political program. In discussions at union meetings prior to the convention, many workers had demanded independent political action through a labor party, not unlike the British Labour Party.

Gompers came to the convention well prepared to deal with the demands of the militant forces, and by the opening of the sessions, the bureaucratic machine was ready. An observer at the convention, writing in *The Outlook,* noted: "He [Gompers] had carefully prepared not only the general but the specific lines of action to be taken at the convention. Every player had his part and all parts fitted into a harmonious whole."[52]

The Gompers' "steam-roller" was first applied to the members of the Executive Council who had disagreed with the support of Bryan. In his report to the convention, Gompers proposed that executive officers of the A. F. of L. should resign when they found that they could not support the policies of the organization in its political endeavors. The Committee on the President's Report recommended that this proposal be adopted, and the machine carried it through. Daniel J. Keefe then announced that he would decline to run for re-election to the Executive Council on the ground of the policy "restricting members of the Council as to what they shall or shall not do in political contests. I have voted the Republican ticket in National affairs for thirty years and will continue to vote the Republican ticket." Keefe was probably looking for an excuse to justify his refusal to run for re-election—he was appointed by President Roosevelt to the position of Commissioner of Immigration on December 1, 1908, as a reward for his campaign work for Taft—but this did not obscure the fact that the administration was determined to crush any opposition to its political policies.

The Socialists and other forces favoring independent political action through a labor party came next under attack. Gompers accused the Socialist Party of being a part of the Parry, Post, Van Cleave, Taft-union-smashing trust, and, at his instigation, a resolution was introduced calling for a committee to be appointed to investigate the books of the Socialist Party and determine where its funds came from. This was probably too much even for the machine delegates to swallow, and the resolution never came to a vote.

Gompers bluntly told the advocates of a labor party that the Federation's nonpartisanship would continue. The thought of any identification of the A. F. of L. with a third party movement was ridiculous. The A. F. of L. would continue to support one of the major parties. Very likely, this would be the Democratic Party, but Gompers warned that this should not be taken for granted. "If the Democratic party retreats from the position which it has taken in support of labor's just demands,

I shall be the first to repudiate it."[53] Where the A. F. of L. would then go, if anywhere, was not indicated.

The pro-labor party forces could not cope with the power of the Gompers' "steam-roller." As one of the delegates wrote after the Convention: "The political policy will as usual remain the same although many of the delegates expressed the hope for an independent labor party. But they did not stand a chance against the well-prepared machine that controlled the convention."[54]

The news of the defeat of the pro-labor party forces at the Convention did not appease the open-shop enemies of organized labor. John M. Kirby, Jr., who replaced James W. Van Cleave as N.A.M. president, vowed to continue the onslaught against the trade unions in the shops and factories, the courts and legislatures as persistently as had his predecessors. He announced his intention "to go after the American Federation of Labor as a body," dismissing the defeat of the pro-labor party forces as unimportant since Gompers and his associates on the Executive Council were just as guilty as the more militant elements in the Federation of "planting the seeds of Socialism and anarchy everywhere." A leading employers' journal urged Kirby on, assuring him that he could look forward to ample support from the Republican administration: "In the work which Mr. Kirby contemplates, he will have the assistance of the President, the Courts and Congress."[55]

THE COURTS AGAIN

The 1908 A. F. of L. Convention was barely concluded when the reasons for the employers' optimism became apparent. On December 23, 1908, in a speech replete with bitter invective and abuse, Judge Daniel T. Wright found Gompers, Mitchell, and Morrison guilty of contempt in refusing to abide by the injunction issued in the Bucks' Stove and Range Co. He upheld all of the contentions of the company's attorneys, maintaining that the A. F. of L. coerced union members and dealers into supporting the boycott in order to destroy the business of the company and that the defendants had unlawfully combined to restrain trade and commerce among the states. They had continued the conspiracy even after the injunction was issued. "The position of the respondents involves questions which smite the foundations of civil government, and upon which the supremacy of law over anarchy and riot verily depend." Even if the injunction was wrong, he contended, "yet it must have been obeyed." The issue involved, he concluded, was "between the supremacy of law over the rabble or its prostration under the feet of the disordered throng . . . those who would unlaw the land are public enemies."

After reading his decision, Wright asked if the defendants had anything to say why judgment should not be passed. Gompers made a moving speech:

"Your honor, I am not conscious at any time during my life of having violated any law of the country or of the District in which I live . . . . the freedom of speech and the freedom of the press has not been granted to the people in order that they may say the things which please, and which are based upon accepted thought, *but the right to say the things which displease,* the right to say the things which may convey the new and yet unaccepted thoughts, the right to say things, even though they do a wrong, for one can not be guilty of giving utterance to any expression which may do a wrong if he is by an injunction enjoined from so saying. It then will devolve upon a judge upon the bench to determine in advance a man's right to express his opinion in speech and in print. . . ."[56]

After hearing this statement, Judge Wright proceeded to pass sentence, which was unprecedented both as to the nature of the acts which were held as contemptuous and as to the length of the sentence. Morrison was sentenced to six months in the United States jail in the District of Columbia, Mitchell to nine months, and Gompers to 12 months. They appealed to the Court of Appeals and were released on bail of $3,000, $4,000, and $5,000 respectively. In a plea for voluntary contributions to a fund to bear the expense of the appeal, the Executive Council declared: "From the expressions of our fellow-workers and friends in all walks of life we find that they are in absolute accord with us on the determined stand taken by Messrs. Gompers, Mitchell, and Morrison in the assertion of their and our inalienable rights of free speech, and the determination that these cases be pressed to a final conclusion." This was a correct evaluation. Regardless of their attitude toward the policies generally pursued by the three labor leaders, the workers rallied to their support. Eugene V. Debs appealed to all workers, Socialist and non-Socialist alike, to act immediately in defense of the A. F. of L. leaders:

"I have nothing to say about Gompers, Mitchell and Morrison as labor leaders. Their official attitude, views and policies I have no sympathy with, not the slightest;* but this is not the time nor the place for such discussion, nor for the exploitation of any other differences or disagreements.† In this fight, forgetting all else, I am with them, not half-

---

* Victor L. Berger put it more sharply. He came to Gompers' defense although "there could be no question that Sam Gompers deserves a prison sentence" for his policies and tactics. ("Now's the Time for Labor to Awaken," *Social-Democratic Herald,* Jan. 2, 1909.)

† Debs, however, was critical of Gompers' decision to halt publication of the "unfair list" in the *American Federationist.* He would have ignored the injunction, continued to publish the "unfair list," and "advised all labor papers not carrying the list to incorporate it in their columns. And they would have done it, and in so doing would have been backed up by three million union men. Then let

heartedly, but as thoroughly in earnest as if they were my Socialist comrades, and I shall gladly give them all the support in my power . . . Whether this decision of Justice Wright is allowed to stand and Gompers, Mitchell and Morrison go to jail depends entirely upon the working class. Upon this issue they can all unite—radicals and conservative, organized and unorganized—in such widespread, emphatic and determined protest—as will not only rebuke the court and prevent the sentence from being carried into execution, but absolutely secure them against any such despotic decision in the future."[57]

Gompers received hundreds of letters and telegrams pledging support in the fight for the rights of labor and the freedom of speech of the American people. Many of them came from Socialists, including some of his bitterest opponents. Deeply moved, Gompers expressed the hope that the injunction fight might help unite the labor movement in the struggle for human liberty. Morris Brown, the Socialist secretary of Local 144, Cigarmakers' Union, called upon his union to make a large contribution to the legal defense fund; Gompers thanked him and stated that "all union men, so long as they are decent union men, look alike to me, without regard to their theoretical or political preference."[58] Had Gompers practiced what he now preached, the history of the American labor movement would have been quite different and the A. F. of L. would have served the interests of the workers far better than it did.

The court action against the A. F. of L. leaders pointed up sharply the importance of securing immediate relief from Congress. But it soon became apparent that there was little disposition either on the part of President Roosevelt or Congress to enact legislation labor needed to obtain relief from court decisions. In the President's message to Congress, the section dealing with labor contained only a sharp criticism of the role played by the A. F. of L. in the past campaign, and a gleeful reference to "labor's failure in the last election."* The *American Federationist* charged the President with libeling organized labor, but the N.A.M. praised the message and viewed the forthcoming Congressional session with complete confidence. And with good reason! Charles E.

---

the Supreme Court of the trusts and the corporations put the American labor movement in jail for contempt. It is just such spineless submission that invites such judicial contempt." ("The Gompers' Jail Sentence," *Solidarity*, Feb. 15, 1909, pp. 11–12.)

* Two weeks after the 1908 election, President Roosevelt held a "labor legislation dinner" at the White House at which a number of labor leaders who attended received the impression that some of their suggestions for modification of injunctions and elimination of labor unions from the operation of the Sherman Anti-Trust Act "might bear fruit in his message." (Washington *Herald*, Nov. 18, 1908.) But nothing of the sort happened. Roosevelt had refused to invite Gompers to the dinner, and, as a consequence, Mitchell, Duncan, Keefe, and other top A.F. of L. officials declined his invitation.

Littlefield, a member of the House Judiciary Committee, informed the N.A.M. that the Committee appointed by Speaker Cannon would "be a committee that will see that nothing but wise and judicious legislation is reported therefrom."[59]

POLITICAL INERTIA

There were several attempts made by the A. F. of L. to amend the Sherman Act during this session of Congress, but the N.A.M. succeeded in having all of these bills referred to the Committee on the Judiciary, the personnel of which, as Littlefield had indicated, guaranteed that the measures would not even come before the full House for a vote. The same state of affairs prevailed in the state legislatures. At the 1908 N.A.M. convention, Parry told the assembled delegates: "What we have just done and are doing in Washington we must do in Albany, Harrisburg, Boston, Columbus, Springfield, and the capitals of all the rest of the great industrial states. The machinery for this broadening of the scope of our work is already in operation." In 1909, this "machinery" effectively blocked pro-labor legislation in most of the industrial states.[60]

At the 1909 A. F. of L. convention in November, Gompers conceded that the year had brought nothing of any importance for organized labor either from Congress or the State legislatures. "The need for adequate, remedial, definitive, and protective legislation is as great as when I had the honor to submit to you my report a year ago." Nevertheless, although he had just returned from a European tour* and had seen in person the way in which the British Labour Party was winning important legislative victories for the English trade unions, including the outlawing of injunctions,† Gompers still offered no further concrete plan or method that would enable the A. F. of L.'s legislative program to be achieved other than the traditional policy of "reward your friends and punish your enemies." He admitted that one of the past weaknesses in the Federation's political activities was its inability to arouse the support of the unorganized workers, and he called upon the A. F. of L. membership to

---

* Gompers returned from Europe in mid-October 1909. He was greeted in Washington, D.C., by a stupendous parade of nearly 15,000 union marchers, representing all sections of the country and including delegations from Hawaii and Puerto Rico. The parade was mainly called to support Gompers in his battle against the jail sentence imposed upon him by Judge Wright. (Washington *Herald*, Oct. 13, 1909.)

† Years later, John P. Frey reported Gompers' reaction to his personal observations of the British Labour Party: "He believed that the more the British trade union movement centered its efforts on political action, the greater its problems would become, and that if the trade union movement supported it and carried the Labour Party into victory so that the Labour Party became the government, that the final results could not help but react unfavorably on itself." (Harvard University Seminar, May 11, 1948, *JFP*, Container 10.)

operate as an educational force among these workers, and endeavor to familiarize them with the organization's political program. Just how these members could enlist the unorganized workers behind the A. F. of L.'s political policies while they were being neglected by the Federation on the industrial front, Gompers did not bother to discuss.

Gompers concluded his discussion of political action at the 1909 Convention with an appeal to union labor to enter all primary elections with a view to nominating men on both the Republican and Democratic tickets who were friendly to labor. He called upon the unions "to begin agitation and to organize so as to be prepared to take action in the next Congressional campaign."[61]

There was hardly any discussion of Gompers' report on political action at the 1909 convention. The gathering had taken place shortly after the District of Columbia Court of Appeals had upheld the sentences against Gompers, Morrison, and Mitchell, and Gompers, particularly, was the hero of the convention.* His leadership completely solidified by the action of the Courts, there was no challenging Gompers' policies at this time. Though convinced that they could have won the support of from 10 to 25 per cent of the delegates for a resolution in favor of an independent labor party, the Socialist delegates decided not to introduce any motion criticizing the Federation's policies while its leadership was under indictment and facing prison. The only voice raised in behalf of a labor party at the convention was by the delegation from the Women's Trade Union League which presented a resolution adopted by its convention on October 1. This declared that "the time is now ripe for the Working Classes of the United States to forward their legitimate interests by political action"; that this end could "best be served by the formation of a political party independent of all other political parties," and, therefore, urged the A. F. of L. "to take action toward the formation of a Labor Party, which party shall be pledged to forward the higher interest of the toiling millions as against the selfish interests of a privileged minority." But the A. F. of L. told the women to concern themselves with problems other than political action and tabled the resolution.[62]

With the Socialists no longer providing a militant spur to the A. F. of L. leadership, the Federation's political activity fell into a state of lethargy. The *American Federationist,* before and immediately after the convention, was silent on political issues, and once again the official organ was filled with Gompers' proclamations announcing that the

---

* When Gompers' name was put in nomination for re-election to the presidency, the convention broke loose into a five-minute demonstration, and, after the unanimous vote of the convention was cast for the "old man," a new demonstration lasting fifteen minutes broke loose, featured by a parade of the delegates around the hall.

A. F. of L. intended first and foremost to adhere to its belief that economic activity would solve labor's basic problems.[63]

On June 18, 1909, the *Spokane Labor World* wrote a fitting epitaph for the A. F. of L.'s political policies since the turn of the century:

"Last fall the organized workers of the state made a campaign for the enactment of needed labor laws and nearly every man who was elected to the legislature pledged himself to vote for such laws. The end of the legislature came and not a single labor measure was put upon the statute books. Labor, as usual, was kicked, spit upon and betrayed. In the Spokane city election this spring every candidate pledged himself to the eight-hour day and the doing of municipal work by day's labor. Almost the first act of importance of the new city council was advertising for bids to build city bridges by contract instead of by day's labor. Labor is kicked, spit upon and betrayed again. Will labor ever get sense enough to quit voting for 'friends of labor' and put into office men from labor's ranks who will put into active force labor's demands, and do it from the standpoint of conviction and principle?"

CHAPTER 14

The Socialists, 1900-1905: "Boring from Within"

In many accounts of the American labor movement during the opening years of the 20th century, the role of the Socialists constitutes but a few stray footnotes to the history of the period. Too many labor historians have made little if any distinction between the different variety of Socialists, although they followed very different trade union policies. In general, this difference revolved about the tactics to be followed for the penetration of the American labor movement by Socialist views and doctrines. Popularly they were known by the expressions "boring from within" and "boring from without."

"BORING FROM WITHIN" AND "BORING FROM WITHOUT"

The theory of "boring from within" emphasized that the Socialists should work inside the existing unions, especially the A. F. of L. and its affiliates, helping the unions in their economic struggles, and in this way win support for the Socialist Party in its political struggles and gradually convert the trade unionists of America to socialism. As Job Harriman, Socialist Party leader, told the Socialists in a public debate with Daniel De Leon, leader of the Socialist Labor Party, on November 25, 1900:

"Go into your Union; when a strike comes on, espouse the cause of the Union, take up the fight of the Union, make their interests your interests, and when you do, you will find that they will open their ears to every argument that promises a benefit and a means to further their ends. . . .

"I say to you men that the possibility of boring from within is infinite in scope. Because you work with the laborers in their struggles and in their strifes and when they are in their fight and the party backs them in their struggles, you open their ears not only to political action, but to the political philosophy that lies behind the political action that is taught;

and all over the country there are today Unions taking up the proposition of the collective ownership of the means of production . . . simply because those who have been patient and who have worked within have gained the confidence of the people, and they have gained an advantage by gaining a hearing before those men."[1]

De Leon who had established the policy of "boring from without" in December 1895, with the launching of the Socialist Trade and Labor Alliance,* answered Harriman's arguments. " 'Boring from within' amounts to nothing but a pretence," he declared. It "meant to throw up the sponge, sheathe the sword, and become a traitor to the working class" —as complete a traitor as the leaders of the "pure and simple" unions. This was the case because essentially " 'boring from within' meant that you had to keep quiet, and get the applause of the labor fakir, so that he might do what he wanted to." Citing his own experience in the "pure and simple" trade unions,† De Leon ridiculed the optimism of the "boring from within" adherents:

" 'Bore from within?' We tried it. We went into the unions and bored from within. We tried to teach the class struggle. . . . We struggled and we struggled with the labor lieutenants of the capitalists; it came to hand encounters; finally, we landed on the outside. . . .

" 'Boring from within' resolved itself accordingly, into this: either you must bore to a purpose, and then you land quickly on the outside; or you don't land on the outside, but then you knuckle under, a silent supporter of the felonies committed by the labor lieutenants of capitalism. Such was the experience, and this will be the experience every time. 'Boring from within' with the labor fakir in possession, is a waste of time."

It was a "waste of time" primarily because the old trade unions were "hopelessly gangrened," too corrupt to be reformed. There was a "correct alternative," De Leon emphasized, to "the idiotic utopianism of the 'boring from within' theory." "We call upon the Socialists of the United States to get out of the pure and simple organizations and smash them to pieces." "Up and at them militants. 'Bore from without'!"[2]

Only the Socialists in the S.L.P. responded to this appeal; indeed, at its convention that same year, the S.L.P. adopted a prohibition against members of the party holding office in any pure and simple trade union. The proposal was in the form of an amendment to the constitution on qualification for membership. It read: "If any member of the Socialist Labor Party accepts office in a pure and simple trade or labor organization, he shall be considered antagonistically inclined towards the Socialist Labor Party and shall be expelled. If any officer of a pure or simple trade or

* *See* Foner, *op. cit.,* vol. II, pp. 296–98, 389–90, 398–401, for the story of the launching of the Socialist Trade and Labor Alliance.

† De Leon was referring to his experiences in the Knights of Labor and the A.F. of L. *See ibid.,* pp. 281–87, 296–97.

labor organization applies for membership in the Socialist Labor Party he shall be rejected."[3] The regulation was not rescinded until 1908.

By 1900, when this resolution was adopted, the S.L.P. had so completely isolated itself from the American working class that its "boring from without" amounted to little more than a whisper, and it declined even further during the next few years. In 1898 the S.L.P. boasted 6,000 members, about twice the number it had in 1889. By 1905 it had only 1,400 members. Its dual union offspring, the Socialist Trade and Labor Alliance, consisted "for the most part of Socialist 'leaders'—a sectarian and impotent letter-head organization."[4]

In 1901 the Social Democratic Party merged with a faction of the Socialist Labor Party that had become fed up with the doctrinaire and autocratic leadership of De Leon and his dual unionism, to form the Socialist Party of the United States. The vast majority of its members upheld the "boring from within" doctrine from the outset. Yet, by 1905, many of the most militant elements in the Socialist Party were echoing De Leon's remarks in his debate with Harriman, and advocating complete abandonment of "boring from within." To understand the reasons for this transition, it is necessary to examine the ideology of the newly formed Socialist Party, especially its trade union policies.

IDEOLOGY OF THE SOCIALIST PARTY

At its founding convention, the Socialist Party pledged itself to give moral and financial support to the trade unions in all their economic struggles, and all party members were instructed to join the unions of their trade.[5] These members were to conduct a patient struggle within these unions, leading them in day-to-day battles to improve the conditions of the membership, uniting the workers for independent political action, and gradually converting them to Socialism. This was the theory of "boring from within." But, in practice, the precise role the Socialist members were to play in the existing unions was never made clear.

In a large measure, this was due to an opportunistic attitude with respect to the trade unions adopted at the Socialist Party's first convention in 1901. This was the policy of "non-interference" in union internal affairs. The resolution asserting this policy, adopted in 1901 and reaffirmed at the 1903 convention, stated that the trade union movement and the Socialist movement were "inseparable parts of the general labor movement," that "the interests of labor as a whole will be best conserved by allowing each of the movements to manage the affairs within its sphere of activity without active interference by the other," that the Socialist Party would "take no sides in any dissension or strifes within the trade union movement," and would support all organizations of labor "without allowing itself to be made the ally of any one division of the trade union movement as against another."[6]

Undoubtedly, this policy was an inevitable reaction to De Leon's insistence upon the total subservience of the trade union movement to the Socialist Labor Party. Over and over again, De Leon asserted that "the party must dominate the trade union movement. . . . The disagreeableness of the trade union can be held in check only by the party's taking the trade union movement in hand. It must either dominate or be dominated by the union. . . . The judgment of the party is final and controlling."[7] But the correct alternative to De Leon's totally incorrect approach was not for the Socialist Party to remain neutral on the fundamental issues facing the trade unions and especially in the struggle against the conservative policies of the A. F. of L. bureaucracy. When the Socialist Party was formed, many of the A. F. of L. unions were just beginning to be dominated by a corrupt leadership. These bureaucratic machines were not yet so deeply entrenched, and trade union democracy was still sufficiently prevalent to permit the launching of a well-organized campaign to oust the bureaucracy. But instead of mobilizing the A. F. of L. unionists against the emerging bureaucracy, the Socialist Party, through its policy of "non-interference," surrendered the control of the unions to the bureaucrats just as surely as did the dual unionist Socialist Labor Party which wanted to have nothing to do with the A. F. of L.

Basically, the incorrect trade union policy of the Socialist Party flowed from the total ideology of the Party. Ideologically, the Socialist Party from the time of its first convention in 1901 was split into several wings, all of whom used Marxist terminology but disagreed sharply as to how Marxism was to be applied to America. By 1904, there were already three loose factions in the party—Right, Center, and Left.* The Right, led by Victor Berger of Milwaukee, its ideological and political leader, emphasized that socialism could be achieved city by city, through the advocacy of muncipal ownership and good government, and as the Socialists won control of more and more city governments, they could gradually transform the capitalist system into a socialist one. Berger often quoted from the writings of Eduard Bernstein, a German Socialist who formulated the theoretical basis of evolutionary socialism,† to the effect that Socialists

---

* Reporting the 1904 Socialist national convention, Algernon Lee spoke of the "right" and "left" and a "center" made up of "the majority and the very large majority of the convention." (*The Worker*, May 15, 1904.)

† Eduard Bernstein (1850–1932) published many articles and books on his theories. Publication of his book *Die Voraussetzungen des Sozialismus und die Aufgaben der Sozialdemokratie* (The Premises of Socialism and the Tasks of Social-Democracy) aroused tremendous discussion in Socialist circles. Bernstein's theory was denounced as heresy at the Luebeck Congress of the German Social-Democratic Party in 1901 by Karl Kautsky and Rosa Luxemburg. They effectively demonstrated that his views were anti-Marxist.

must constantly work for socialistic reforms under capitalism, and that these would gradually lead to socialism. The "American Bernstein," as Berger was called,* sneered at the revolutionary element in the S.P., and boasted that the Milwaukee movement, which he headed, was "absolutely in favor of socialistic *reforms*—'one step,' two steps or six steps at a time— as many as we can make—and we are deadly opposed to the impotent and good for nothing *revolutionary phrases* that are the stock in trade of certain hypocritical or ignorant Socialist 'leaders.'" Only if the national Socialist Party and its separate locals adopted the same outlook would the movement make headway in the United States.

The Right conceded the existence of classes in America and affirmed its belief in the class struggle. But socialism, it asserted, was not a class movement. It sought to benefit all classes, not merely the working class; consequently, it was only right and proper that all classes, including the capitalist class, should join the Socialist Party. Moreover, the Right warned that if socialism were just a proletarian movement, it could have no hope of success in the United States. The working class was not "ripe for Socialism," and it would take centuries before enough workers could be converted to the cause to bring about even the "gradual transformation to Socialism," envisaged by the Right. Meanwhile, unless there were intelligent men to guide the Socialist movement, the most ignorant and desperate workers would try to obtain the goal by force and bloodshed. Hence the middle classes and even the rich owed it to themselves to join the Socialist Party and help prevent violence by working for the gradual inauguration of socialism.[8]

The Center, led by Morris Hillquit, the New York Socialist attorney, and the Left, led by Eugene V. Debs,† made the concept of the class struggle the key to their ideology.‡ In capitalist America, as in all capitalist societies, there were two classes, capitalist and proletariat. The former consisted of the owners of the great trusts and monopolies, and of the

---

* Actually, Berger denied that he was a Bernsteinian. (*See* his letter to Morris Hillquit, April 8, 1905, Morris Hillquit Papers, Wisconsin State Historical Society. Hereinafter cited as *WSHS*.) But his views entitled him to the appellation of the "American Bernstein." In October, 1901, he wrote an editorial in his paper, the *Social-Democratic Herald*, entitled "The Bernstein Doctrine for America," in which he came out strongly in favor of Bernstein's theory.

† Although Debs was the national leader of the Left, his influence in the Socialist Party leadership was never as great as it might have been because of his persistent refusal to run for party office. (H. Wayne Morgan, *Eugene V. Debs: Socialist for President,* Syracuse, 1962, pp. 34–36.)

‡ "In the party's first two or three years of activity," notes Ira Kipnis, "the Center and Left were almost indistinguishable as far as public pronouncements of doctrine were concerned. Distinction between them during this period is perhaps attributable more to historical hindsight than to differences recognized by the members themselves." (*The American Socialist Movement, 1897-1912,* New York, 1952, p. 107.)

small business men who wished to restore a competitive society by destroying or controlling the monopolies. The working class had no interests in common with either of these two groups, and its real interests would only be served when it ousted the capitalists from the control of the productive forces and of the machinery of government. In the course of their battles for higher wages and better working conditions, the workers would gradually become class conscious, and join the Socialist Party. They would learn, and the Socialists should play an active role in educating them on this point, that the U.S. government, instead of being the government of the people, was being used by the capitalist class to aid in the exploitation of the proletariat.

Socialism, said the Center-Left, would be achieved when the working class captured the existing machinery of government and used it "to make the instruments of wealth production the common property of all." And this was not difficult to achieve. "Once the workers, who far outnumbered the capitalists, learned to transfer the economic class struggle to the political field and struck at the ballot box, the battle for socialism would be won."[9]

By 1904 the difference between the Right and Center narrowed as the Hillquit Center wing accepted more and more of the Right ideology and came to resemble the Berger Wisconsin school even though it clothed its position in more Marxist terminology. The Center, for example, completely accepted Berger's "two-armed labor movement" doctrine in which "each party member devoted one arm to union work on the economic field and the other arm to political work through the Socialist Party," with neither arm "interfering" with the other. The Left refused to accept this distinction between party and trade union work. However, all three factions continued to adhere to the principle that the trade unions and the Socialist Party were separate entities, each with a specific duty to perform, and each to refrain from interfering in any way with the other. The unions fought within the framework of capitalism for higher wages and better working conditions in the economic field. The Socialist Party fought for workers' rights on the political field, through the ballot. Each should concede the other priority in its own particular area without interference from the other—the trade unions in the economic field and the Socialist Party in the political field.[10]

The three factions of the Socialist Party were not motivated by the same reasons in supporting the policy of "non-interference." The Right was confident that its program of replacing capitalism with Socialism by a gradual process of growth could be made attractive to the leadership of the A. F. of L. and its craft union affiliates, and was determined to avoid any action that would antagonize them. The Right-wing Socialists agreed that Gompers' opposition to their party had been justified in the past because of its dual union tactics, under De Leon's leadership, and its belief, under the same leadership, that the trade union struggles for economic improvements such as higher wages and shorter hours were not only a waste of time under capitalism, since "the abolition of the system of private ownership in the means of production . . . is the only thing that can bring redress and improvement,"[11]* but, even if achieved, these gains retarded the coming of socialism by making the workers contented with their lot. It was these policies and not the leadership of the A. F. of L., according to the Right-wing Socialists, that had impeded the growth of Socialist influence in the American labor movement. Thus Max Hayes wrote in July 1900:

"The writer is firmly of the opinion that the Federation and many national unions would have declared in favor of socialism some years ago if certain fanatical leaders, so-called, had not kept up a running fire against trade unions, and made loud boast and bluffs of disrupting the 'pure and simple' organization. . . . Had there been some diplomacy used, had an honest and persistent and tolerant effort been made to educate the worker, the American labor movement would now undoubtedly be abreast of the European movement."[12]

But now with the new policy of "non-interference" in internal union affairs, the Socialists could win the good will of Gompers and other labor leaders towards the Socialist Party and its program,† and by working for measures supported by these leaders, they could convince them that the political aims of the Socialist Party and the economic aims of the unions were not antagonistic. Meanwhile, all criticism of the A. F. of L. leadership was to be avoided as interfering with the objective of converting these leaders to socialism. Not all Right-wing Socialists adhered to the doctrine of holding back criticism of Gompers and other A. F. of L.

* De Leon completely disparaged trade union activity as a means for improving labor's position under capitalism. He spoke of the "futility" of the strike weapon which "a century of conflict has proved to be utterly worthless," and described the boycott as "a farce," insisting that "in the face of modern industry the boycott is even more weak than the strike alone." (*Weekly People,* Sept. 29, 1900, Feb. 3, 1901.) De Leon even proposed to those who led the great coal strike of 1902 that they call off the stoppage by frankly telling the workers: "Boys, we have been travelling along a false road. It leads to a blind alley. Turn back. There is no hope for you while this social system of capitalism lasts. . . . You are bound to go down unless the working class owns the land on, and the tools with, which to work. . . . Organize yourselves into the Socialist Labor Party." (*Weekly People,* May 24, 1902.)

† On August 8, 1900, Rudolph Benz, A.F. of L. general organizer in St. Louis, reported to Gompers that he had had a long talk with Leon Greenbaum, national secretary of the Socialist Party, who outlined to him the "non-interference" policy and then "he asked me what would Gompers say if he would hear my [Greenbaum's] remarks. I assured him that Gompers would approve of this policy." Benz reported that Greenbaum was delighted, and would immediately inform the Socialist Party that its policy would certainly meet with Gompers' approval. (*AFL Corr.*)

leaders. (Berger in the period under discussion, as we shall see, tried to unseat Gompers at A. F. of L. conventions—unsuccessfully to be sure—and denounced his policies and his iron rule of the Federation.*) However, most Right-wing leaders frowned upon too sharp criticism of A. F. of L. policies, arguing that it smacked too much of De Leonism and would isolate the Socialists from the organized workers as it had already done the followers of De Leon.[13]

The Center-Left did not interpret "non-interference" as meaning support of "the traitors to the working class who are wrecking the unions," and the Left-wing, particularly, denounced the Federation leaders for their opposition to industrial unionism, for participation in the National Civic Federation, for the conservative and cautious strike policies, their nonpartisan politics, their business unionism, and their opposition to socialism. But they bent over backwards to refrain from telling the members of the unions what to do in fighting these "traitors." As Debs, leader of the Left, put it in 1902: "The attitude of the Socialist Party toward the trades-union movement broadly endorsing it and commending it, but stopping there, and allowing it to manage its own affairs is, without doubt, the correct one, as any intermeddling must result in harm with no possible hope of good."[14]

The opposite policy to "non-interference" did not mean "intermeddling." On the contrary, it meant exerting the influence of the Socialist Party to help the trade unions in their struggles and assisting their members in making the unions function as militant, democratic organizations. If the Party was to remain aloof from these activities, to fail to give leadership to the struggle against the reactionary policies of the trade union bureaucracy, how were the members to function as intelligent, enlightened Socialists in the day-to-day battles of the workers? How were they to show the relationship of these struggles for immediate gains to the movement for socialism, if they were to avoid raising the issue?

The issue came to the fore during the great anthracite coal strike of 1902. The Pennsylvania Socialists took on the task of helping the strikers, working actively among them and organized Socialist locals to which the miners flocked. "We came with a new message to the strikers, and they heard us gladly," William Mailly reported from the coal districts. "In my

* Late in 1904, Bergert boasted that in the eyes of the A.F. of L. leadership he was a "'wicked fanatic,' a 'trouble-maker,' and the embodiment of the 'red spook.'" ("Another Light That Failed," *Social-Democratic Herald*, Dec. 31, 1904.) There was some truth in this, but mainly it reflected Berger's extreme egotism. A typical example of this egotism is Berger's remark at the 1906 A.F. of L. convention to which he was a delegate: "Our worthy chairman [vice-president Duncan] gets shivers down his back when he sees me coming. . . . But I want to tell you the capitalistic class in Milwaukee are shivering all the time. I am a live Resolution there; I have resolved to abolish the system there; I am a walking resolution." (*Proceedings*, A.F. of L. Convention, 1906, pp. 186–88.)

experience I have never seen men who listened so eagerly and with such unfeigned enthusiasm to the Socialist presentation of the situation as did these strikers. I think the members of the Socialist Party are justified in believing that the presence of their representatives in the field was beneficial to the strike and the miners' union. We preached the necessity of Solidarity and explained the industrial situation so that the miners could not help but become imbued with an increased faith in themselves."

The Socialist Party National Executive Committee frowned upon the activity of the Pennsylvania Socialists, regarding it as violating the Party's "non-interference" policy, and ordered them to desist all further work in this direction and disband the Socialist locals in the strike-bound areas. It was perfectly acceptable for the Socialists to raise funds for strike relief, but beyond this they were not to go. Participation by Socialists in the strike itself was to be avoided on the ground that this was "exclusively the area of the union."[15]

On the basic question of whether to call a general coal strike, the Socialist Party took no official position. The Right-wing element in the leadership agreed with the A. F. of L. leaders that a general strike would be a "breach of contract." The Center-Left elements held that only a general strike could produce a clear-cut victory, but refused to do anything to influence the miners in its favor on the ground that this would violate the policy of "non-interference" in union internal affairs.* It is hardly surprising that the vast majority of the miners, who, as we have seen, favored a general strike, felt that Socialist criticism of the strike settlement came in bad taste from a party all of whose factions had remained aloof from the struggle and whose leadership had rebuked the local Socialists for helping conduct a militant strike.

In the eyes of all three factions in the national Socialist Party leadership—Right, Center, and Left—the proper share of activity by Socialists in the trade unions was to work towards converting trade unionists to socialism by propaganda for the cause. Berger boasted that this had already been accomplished in Wisconsin, and that the policies pursued by the Social Democratic Party of that state in relation to the trade unions could, if followed nationally, produce similar results on a higher level.† (He was later to concede that it was a good deal harder, if not impossible,

---

* The Right-wing leaders, however, did not hesitate to interfere in the union discussion of the general strike. Leon Greenbaum, national secretary of the Socialist Party, used his influence among the Socialist delegates to the U.M.W. convention to help defeat the proposed general strike. (Chicago *Socialist,* July 19, 1902; *Social-Democratic Herald,* Oct. 11, 1902.)

† By 1903 Berger claimed that the Milwaukee trade unions were the backbone of the Social Democratic Party and that they regularly endorsed its program. ("Is A Revolutionary Body," *Social-Democratic Herald,* Oct. 31, 1903. *See also* Frederick I. Olson, "The Milwaukee Socialists, 1897–1941," unpublished Ph.D. thesis, Harvard University, 1952, pp. 89–95.)

to convert the A. F. of L. to the endorsement of socialism than it had been to get the Wisconsin State Federation of Labor to do so.*)[16]

All three factions in the national Socialist Party leadership agreed that the economic struggles of the workers were to be supported morally and financially, but the trade unionists had to be constantly reminded that the working class had little to gain from higher wages and better working conditions under an economic system which robbed them of the full fruits of their labor. There was, to be sure, a group of Socialists, called the "impossibilists," who believed that the struggle for immediate demands, including higher wages, shorter hours, and improved working conditions, was a waste of time, and that the only activity that counted was the circulation of propaganda for the immediate inauguration of socialism. But up to 1905, this theory, representing the remnants of De Leonism in the Socialist Party, was criticized by all three factions.† Economic struggles were not a waste of time,‡ but Socialist members were to leave the work in the economic field to the union leadership and to devote themselves to educating their brothers and sisters to the need of voting Socialist. This was to be done through general discussions at union meetings, introduction of resolutions favoring socialism, distribution of Socialist pamphlets, the sale of Socialist papers to union members and the use of the "letters to the editor" columns of trade union journals. A typical sample of such propaganda, published in 1904, reads:

"American workingmen: have you stopped to think that while shorter

---

* Actually, the Wisconsin Federation of Labor toned down its original stand in favor of socialism by qualifying its definition. At first, the Federation came out flatly for "The collective ownership by the people of the means of production and distribution." Later, it diluted this firm stand by adding the qualifying clause: "By this we mean that when an industry becomes so centralized as to assume the form of a trust or monopoly and hence a menace to the best interests of the people, such industry shall be assumed by the government." (*Proceedings of the Wisconsin State Federation of Labor*, 1906, p. 4.)

† After 1905 the term "impossibilists" was applied by the Right to all Socialists who opposed the achievement of socialism through "step-at-a time" tactics.

‡ The Right, however, often emphasized that strikes were useless and resulted only in suffering for the workers involved. "Strikers will get empty pockets, will get hungry, their families will suffer," G. A. Hoehn wrote, and he asked: "Will a Socialist striker's family stand the suffering and privation more patiently than the family of the conservative?" (*International Socialist Review*, vol. III, Jan. 1903, p. 410.)

By 1904 the Center had come to agree with the Right that strikes were futile. "Is the Strike Played Out?" *The Worker* headed its leading editorial in its October 2, 1904 issue. It asserted that "the day of winning great strikes is over," and concluded: "The Socialist Party now forms the only rallying ground for the hard-pressed workers—a position from which they can advance to the attack in the assured confidence of victory and make the one great strike at the ballot box, accomplish permanently and with infinitely more thoroughness what a thousand futile economic strikes have failed to gain."

hours and an increase in wages will undoubtedly be a great help in the cause of labor, as long as the pernicious capitalist system continues, there is little hope of lasting benefits.

"While trade unions may raise wages within their own craft, they cannot to any extent improve the conditions of the whole class, and what is more, can have no influence in determining the price of an article that workers must buy in the market.

"Can trade unions solve this problem? They can if their members will vote Socialist. By using their political power which is even greater than their economic power, they can take over the machinery of production, their own creation, which now enslaves them but which, owned and operated by the working class, can be made an eternal source of supreme happiness for all people...."[17]

Socialist Party propaganda did not entirely dismiss the trade union struggles for immediate economic gains, but it emphasized that these were really secondary to the role that labor should play on Election Day by voting Socialist.

THE SOCIALISTS AND LABOR POLITICAL ACTION

"One trouble with the trade unionist is he strikes one way and votes another," a Socialist wrote in a union journal. "Strikes for more of what he produces, then on election day votes for a government which supports a system that is forever and continually grinding the wage slave lower and lower." Such a trade unionist was really a scab, and, indeed, a worse scab than one who crossed a picket line. "He is not in fact a union man at all who, though a member of the union on the economic side, is a non-unionist on the political side; and while striking for, votes against the working class. . . . The fully developed labor unionist uses both his economic and political power in the interest of his class."

The Socialist Party made it clear, however, that there was only one way in which "the fully developed labor unionist" could use his "political power in the interest of his class": voting for the Socialist Party. A worker who voted for a labor party was as much a scab as one who voted for the Republican or Democratic Party. Since labor parties, even when organized and dominated by the trade unions,* failed to raise the

* The *International Socialist Review* dismissed the argument that the role of the trade unions in initiating the labor parties should be weighed in evaluating whether or not Socialists should support them. "We see an exaggeration of the importance of the organized labor movement," it commented. (Vol. III, Jan., 1903, p. 427.) It also emphasized that it was not the business of the trade unions to go into politics. The unions were to devote themselves to the economic field, while the Socialist Party would express the demands of the working class in the political field. This was the philosophy of a two-armed labor movement—the unions having jurisdiction in the economic arena and the Socialist Party in the political arena.

issue of socialism, they were little more than appendages of the capitalist class. They actually served only one real purpose: to divert the attention of workers from the Socialist Party, the only true party of the working class.[18] As an editorial in the *International Socialist Review* put it in January 1903:

"The only thing which determines whether a party is a working class party in the sense in which the Socialists used the word is whether it stands upon a platform expressing the mission of the working class as the future ruling class, and whether the attitude and spirit of the new party indicates that it is inspired by a consciousness of the functions of the working class as the collective owners of the instruments of production and distribution, and the rulers of the social organism.

"Judging by these standards, not one of the so-called 'union labor' parties has any right whatever to be called a working class party. Their principles are much more in accord with small capitalist interests than with those of the working class."[19]

The Socialist Party unalterably refused to support any attempts by the trade unions to form local or national political parties around the crucial issues facing the labor movement: injunctions, labor legislation, political corruption, etc. All locals of the party were ordered to nominate a full slate of candidates in every local and national election. If for any reason the local branch or state organization could not make such nominations, it was ordered to boycott the election. No member of the party was ever to support or vote for candidates of any other party. Socialists who violated this fundamental principle were suspended or expelled. Locals that participated in "fusion" with any reform, radical, or labor party had their charters revoked if they ignored the national committee's demand that they cease such activity immediately.[20]

But the Socialists went even further in their opposition to labor parties; wherever possible, they prevented the formation of such parties. When Chicago unions attempted to form a labor party in December 1901, 200 Socialists packed the meeting. As soon as it was called to order, the Socialist majority secured passage of a resolution declaring "that the laborers of Chicago do not need the help of a gang of grafters meeting in the wine room of a saloon to organize a Labor Party for them." They then adjourned the meeting. *The Workers' Call,* a Socialist weekly published in Chicago, praised the Socialists for their work, and reminded the trade unions that there was "already a 'Labor Party' in the field [the Socialist Party] definitely committed to the interests of the workers." The Socialist journal warned the trade unions not to try to form a new labor party in the future: " 'there will be a warm time in the old town' for any gang of fakirs that tries to start a 'Union Labor Party' in Chicago. These Socialists in the Chicago trade unions know that the man who attempts any such dirty work is ten times as bad a scab as the poor devil who takes the place of a striker, and they will treat him accordingly."[21]

In Colorado early in 1904, in the midst of the bitter strikes of the western miners, a three-day conference was held by 400 labor leaders to discuss the advisability of independent political action. The Socialist delegates defeated the motion for a union labor party, and the movement disintegrated. In St. Louis, the Socialist-controlled Central Trade and Labor Union rejected local union demands for a broad labor party.[22]

In only one city in this period, Los Angeles, did the Socialists endorse and actively campaign for a union labor ticket.* In the fall of 1902, Local Los Angeles decided to flout national policy by supporting the Union Labor Party instead of entering their own ticket in the city elections. In response to widespread criticism of its decision by the Socialist Party leadership, Local Los Angeles argued that a Socialist Party, to be powerful and effective, must have its roots in the working-class movement, must recognize its identity with the workers, and must encourage political activity by organized labor and cooperate with it in this activity. "Comrades," the Los Angeles *Socialist* asked in a valiant appeal to the National Committee, "do you still insist that we should stand aloof from the trade unions until such time as their vision is so broadened as to enable them to grasp, theoretically, the Socialist movement as a whole?" It was a futile plea. The National Committee condemned Local Los Angeles for betraying the socialist cause, and, yielding to pressure, the Local voted in January 1903 to sever all relations with the Union Labor Party. It declared that the party leadership was correct in regarding the encouragement of union labor parties as a "menace" to the Socialist Party.[23]

Thus the Socialist Party leadership frequently removed the party from the struggles of the organized workers in both the economic and political field. It acknowledged the trade unions' exclusive rights in the field of economic organization and activities without "interference" from the Socialist Party. And it would have nothing to do with the formation of labor parties by the trade unions. It argued that just as the Socialist Party respected the trade union's exclusive rights in the economic field, so the unions should recognize the Socialist Party's exclusive rights in the political field and get their members to vote Socialist. This was the "two-armed labor movement—a labor movement with a political arm and with an economic arm. Each arm has its own work to do, and one arm ought not to interfere with the other." Both arms would form "a grand army moving on *two roads* for the abolition of the capitalist system."[24]

* In San Francisco the Socialist Party did not put up a ticket against the United Labor Party in the state election in the fall of 1902. (A year before it had attacked the U.L.P. as a "scab" and "capitalist" party and urged all workers to vote Socialist.) But it did not, as in Los Angeles, endorse the Labor Party. (San Francisco *Advance,* Dec. 20, 1902; Chicago *Socialist,* Jan. 24, 1903.)

But what of the organized workers who were not yet ready to vote Socialist? Their efforts to express themselves politically through independent action must not be supported. Thus the influence of the party was removed from the day-to-day struggles of the workers in the trade unions in both the economic and political arenas.

SOCIALISTS AT A. F. OF L. CONVENTIONS

In the early years of the 20th century, the Socialist Party was less concerned with strikes and day-to-day work in the unions than it was in attempting to win support at annual conventions of the A. F. of L. for resolutions sponsored by the party. The nature of these resolutions reflect the outlook of the party leadership towards the labor movement. In the main, they dealt with the overthrow of the wage system and the establishment of a society based on the collective ownership of the means of production. They rarely dealt with the question of organizing the unorganized, particularly the foreign-born, Negro, and women workers; the kind of trade union structure required to accomplish this; the need for labor solidarity, especially native-American and foreign-born and Negrowhite unity; and the need for an independent party of labor, sponsored by the trade unions.

On the matter of craft versus industrial unionism, the Socialist Party indicated its preference for industrial unionism in party publications, but refrained at A. F. of L. conventions from outright condemnation of craft unionism or wholehearted endorsement of industrial unionism on the ground that to do so would create dissension in the labor movement. True, Socialist delegates gave lukewarm support to the battle for industrial unionism, and spoke on the advantages of industrial organization during the jurisdictional disputes at the 1902 and 1903 A. F. of L. conventions. But they never made it a real issue or declared themselves vigorously in favor of industrial unionism.[25]

On the question of independent political action of labor, Socialist delegates at A. F. of L. conventions indicated repeatedly the necessity of the labor movement breaking away from reliance on the two "capitalist parties," and just as repeatedly condemned the Federation's "reward your friends and punish your enemies" policy. But, in keeping with the Socialist Party outlook, they just as continually emphasized that the only type of independent political action that they considered worthwhile was support of the candidates of the Socialist Party. Thus while the Socialist delegates effectively exposed the weaknesses of the "reward and punish" doctrine of the A. F. of L. leadership, they reduced their influence in helping to achieve independent political action by the labor movement through their insistence that this must be achieved *only* through the Socialist Party.[26]

With respect to the issue of labor solidarity in the trade unions, the Socialist delegates to the A. F. of L. conventions played a totally passive role. This was a reflection of the Socialist Party's official position on this crucial matter. Although a good percentage of the party membership in 1901 were foreign-born, the party showed little interest in the struggle for their economic, civil, and political rights. It was not until 1907 that a statement on the rights of the foreign-born was passed by the National Committee, and nothing was ever done to implement the resolution. It is hardly surprising, then, that in the period 1900–1905, the Socialist delegates at A. F. of L. conventions hardly ever bothered to raise the question of discrimination against foreign-born workers flowing from the Federation's policies. On the question of restricting immigration, these delegates were fully as chauvinistic as were the Federation leaders themselves.[27]

Only one resolution was adopted by the pre-World War I Socialist Party dealing with Negro rights, and this, passed at the time of the party's formation in 1901, urged the Negro to join the Socialist movement and vote his way to emancipation. On the question of discrimination against Negroes, the party was officially silent; no resolution was adopted prior to World War I condemning such discrimination. Indeed, several Socialist leaders, especially among the Right wingers, were unabashed racists. In an article curiously entitled "The Misfortune of the Negroes," in the *Social Democratic Herald* of May 31, 1902, Victor L. Berger wrote: "There can be no doubt that the negroes and mulattoes constitute a lower race—that the Caucasians and indeed the Mongolians have the start on them in civilization by many thousand years—so that negroes will find it difficult to overtake them." Berger declared further "that the free contact with the whites has led to further degeneration of the negroes." About the same time, the *Social Democratic Herald* declared editorially that the whites disliked Negroes because the latter were inferior, depraved degenerates who went "around raping women [and] children."[28]*

Although Debs strongly condemned anti-Negro prejudice, refused to speak before segregated audiences even in the South, repeatedly emphasized that any racial division was harmful to the labor movement and that the white workers could not elevate themselves so long as the Negroes were held in an inferior position, he did nothing to mobilize the Socialist Party to battle for Negro rights and even refused to support a special fight in the movement for the rights of Negroes. Thus, when at the

---

* Berger was subjected to sharp criticism for his anti-Negro expressions, and as Congressman he did try to rectify his earlier stand. On April 17, 1911, he wrote to A. B. Wesley: "In voting . . . for the amendment to the election of Senator's bill, which would have given federal supervision to the primaries in the South, I, of course, had in mind the protection of the rights of the negro." (Victor L. Berger Papers, Milwaukee County Historical Commission.)

1903 party convention, proposals were introduced to develop such a special struggle, Debs opposed the action, arguing: "We have nothing special to offer the Negro, and we cannot make separate appeals to all the races. The Socialist Party is the party of the whole working class, regardless of color—the whole working class of the world." Writing that same year in the *International Socialist Review,* Debs declared that only socialism would solve the problems facing the Negro people, such discrimination, lynching,* etc. The Chicago *Socialist* agreed: "After all that has been written and said is summed up and analyzed, the negro must learn that the only emancipation is that that will come by adoption of all races of the science of Socialism. That is the negroes only hope. It is the only hope of all races."[29] Under capitalism, then, the struggle against discrimination was a waste of time!

The attitude of the Socialist Party toward the question of equal rights for women bore a striking resemblance to its approach to the question of Negro equality. As in the case of Negroes, the status of women was part of the general "labor question" and could be fundamentally improved only by the overthrow of capitalism and the establishment of socialism. But the Socialist Party did little to involve women in the work of building this new social order, for the white chauvinist attitude of many Socialist leaders was matched by their male supremacist views. In 1904 *The Worker* admitted that too many men in the Socialist Party, "good Socialists in most respects," look with a disapprobation or with more irritating contempt on any participation by women in the affairs of our movement."[30]

With such attitudes dominating the Socialist Party, it is hardly surprising that Socialist delegates to the A. F. of L. conventions failed to raise the demand to end Jim-Crow unionism in the Federation and discriminatory practices against foreign-born and women workers, or to raise the demand for a specialized program to organize these workers. It was much simpler for the Socialists to argue that the real solution for *all* problems facing *all* workers lay in achieving socialism and to concentrate all of their energies towards winning A. F. of L. support for this goal.

At the turn of the century, the Socialists in the A. F. of L. were optimistic that this goal would soon be achieved. Reviewing the 1900 convention in the *International Socialist Review,* Max Hayes predicted that it would only be a year or two before the control of the Gompers' leadership was "broken into smithereens" and the Federation went on record for socialism. "As a matter of fact," he noted, "nearly one-half of the vote in the convention was pledged in favor of a declaration for socialism but

---

* In 1903, the International Socialist Bureau, with which the American party was affiliated, inquired of the attitude of the Socialist Party toward lynching. The National Quorum, the executive board of the party, replied that there was only one solution to the problem—socialism. (Chicago *Socialist,* Nov. 28, 1903.)

when the conservatives opened fire many ran to cover for fear of arousing antagonism for their organization." As soon as the conservative power was broken, the declaration for socialism would be adopted by a huge majority.[31]

Two years later, at the 1902 convention, it seemed that this prediction might come true. Hayes introduced a resolution which read: "That the twenty-second annual convention of the A. F. of L. advise the working people to organize their economic and political power to secure for labor that full equivalent of their toil and the overthrow of the wage system and the establishment of an industrial co-operative democracy." Adoption of this resolution, Hayes explained, did not constitute an endorsement of the Socialist Party. It would, however, signify that the A. F. of L. recognized the principles of the class struggle and socialism.

When it became obvious that the resolution was too radical for most of the delegates, Hayes accepted a compromise amendment, introduced by William B. Wilson, which deleted all reference to overthrow of the wage system and the institution of co-operative democracy, and stipulated only that the A. F. of L. "advise the working people to organize their economic and political power to secure for labor the full equivalent of its toil." Berger, attending as a delegate from the Milwaukee Federal Trades Council, supported Hayes in accepting this emasculated version of the original resolution: "To those who believe that whatever is must remain so forever, I have nothing to say. But trade unionism itself is a living witness of the constant change of economical and political systems. Capitalism has succeeded feudalism and slavery, and capitalism by the force of the same evolution will have to make room for socialism, if our civilization is to survive. Socialism is not a theory, it is a phase of civilization."

A fierce fight broke out on the floor of the convention over the adoption of the "socialistic" resolution. Gompers trained his full guns on the Socialists, accusing them of wishing to disrupt the American labor movement for their own selfish ends, and linking the sponsors of the resolution with the dual union activities of the Socialist Labor Party (Gompers conveniently overlooked that the Socialist delegates to the A. F. of L. convention bitterly condemned De Leon's dual union tactics.) But the miners, carpenters, and brewers supported the resolution, and it was narrowly defeated by a vote of 4,897 to 4,171 with 387 delegates abstaining.[32]

The majority of the Socialist press hailed the vote as indicating the extent of Socialist strength in the A. F. of L. Hayes thought the balloting showed a significant near-majority for socialism even though the heart had been taken out of his original resolution. Berger, however, was more realistic. "The vote . . . is very deceiving. It was not a vote for Socialism. It [the amendment] was interpreted by Delegate Reese of the Mine

Workers as meaning a resolution for the Democratic party."* The resolution "was tame enough, the discussions had an 'academic value' only
and the votes are in no way an indication of our strength in the American Federation of Labor." Berger estimated that the actual Socialist votes
in the convention had numbered not more than 2,000; the remainder
were obtained by tactical means. Berger, in fact, was convinced by his
experience at the 1902 convention that the A. F. of L. was so conservative
that any attempt to "capture" that organization was useless in its present state of development.† He was still convinced, however, that this
would inevitably occur. "We are so thoroughly convinced of the victorious
power of Socialist ideas and the force of our unanswerable arguments,
that we know that our party will take possession of the laboring classes
even if we do not preach the 'party' day after day in the trade unions."[33]

Although there was considerable disagreement over what the vote on
the amended resolution signified, events demonstrated that this was the
high tide of Socialist influence in the A. F. of L.‡ Socialist delegates at

* Reese voted for the resolution even though he was not a Socialist. Indeed,
the fact that the United Mine Workers cast 1,855 votes for the resolution and the
Carpenters 799 votes, was pointed to as proof that the Socialist strength in the
A.F. of L. did not equal what the vote indicated. At the 1903 convention, the
mine delegates voted against a similar resolution proposed by the Socialists. Probably the experiences of the miners in the coal strike of 1902 swung the U.M.W.
delegates over to support the resolution at the 1902 convention.

† Berger was furious because the convention voted down his resolution advocating
for all wage workers who had an average income of less than $1,000 an old-age
pension of at least $12 a month beginning at the age of 60, provided the worker
was a citizen and had lived in the United States at least 21 years continuously. In
view of the fact that the Republican Party had favored old-age pensions in its 1900
platform, that Bismarck, "the great enemy of international Socialism" had originated the German old-age pension law, and that practically every civilized country
in the world was considering such a measure, Berger felt that the vote of the
A.F. of L. "speaks volumes" and was characteristic of "the spirit that holds sway
in the A.F. of L." ("The American Federation of Labor and Socialism," *Social-
Democratic Herald*, Dec. 6, 1902.) Berger felt this way about the convention even
though that body had adopted his resolution calling for the procurement "of national laws to protect disabled workmen, and to provide a system of national insurance for their assistance during enforced idleness." (*Proceedings*, A.F. of L.
Convention, 1902, pp. 101, 225.) It was not until 1932 that the A.F. of L. came
out in favor of state legislation.

‡ Noting that after 1902 Socialist strength declined in the A.F. of L., Daniel Bell
observes: "This is an incongruous fact, for 1902 was the beginning of rising socialist political influence in the United States. The answer to this paradox is that the
socialist vote never was drawn primarily from organized labor—a fact that was
one of its fundamental weaknesses." ("The Background and Development of
Marxian Socialism in the United States," in Donald Drew Egbert and Stow Persons, eds., *Socialism and American Life*, Princeton, 1952, vol. I, p. 254.) This statement does not apply with equal force to Milwaukee in the period under discussion
where the Socialist vote was primarily drawn, though by no means entirely, from
organized labor. (*Social-Democratic Herald*, March 5, 1904.) Nor does it, as we
shall see in a subsequent volume, apply with equal force to other areas after 1909.

the 1903 convention again offered their resolutions on the need for labor to use its economic and political power along class lines to secure the full product of its toil. But this time the Gompers' machine was fully prepared to deal with the situation, and Gompers launched his most vicious assault upon the Socialists.

Until this time, Gompers and other A. F. of L. top leaders had taken pains to distinguish between socialist ideas and the persons who held them, had made explicit their approval of some socialist principles, and even stressed the similarity in outlook of the trade union and Socialist movements. Gompers had always insisted during the 1890's that he was not anti-Socialist, that he shared the goals of the Socialists, and that he could work with them as long as they did not attack the trade unions. Socialist principles were worthy of respect, and the trade unionist "has all respect for the sincere socialist," but it "has no use for those" who form "dual trade societies," an action which was equivalent to "bear[ing] the dagger of the assassin which they strive to plunge into the vitals of trade unions." However, Socialists who did not form dual unions but remained within the A. F. of L. would find a welcome in that organization. Indeed, the A. F. of L. was only too ready to gain the support of the Socialist Party. "We heartily recommend the cordial acceptance of all assistance that may be given the trade union movement by all reform forces, the socialist party included," Gompers wrote in 1899. "The hope and aspiration of the trade unionist is closely akin to that expressed by the socialist."[34]

But all this was essentially a pose. For, notes Bernard Mandel, "as Gompers moved within the orbit of the National Civic Federation, he began to talk less and less about the fact that 'the hope and aspiration of the trade unionist is closely akin to that expressed by the socialist.' References to 'wage slavery' and the 'emancipation of labor,' with which he would sprinkle his speeches during the 1890's, dropped out of Gompers' vocabulary. He no longer gave even lip service to the notion that labor would some day come into its own as the controlling element in society, and there was not even any more talk about subordinating the final emancipation of labor to the attainment of immediate goals, but with the understanding that this emancipation was labor's ultimate goal. Improvement of labor's conditions under capitalism became synonymous with emancipation."[35]

As Gompers dropped the mask behind which he had given lip service to socialist objectives, he came out openly as a bitter opponent of Socialists and began to attack not only the Socialists but socialism itself. He had hinted at this at the 1900 convention when he charged that "when men become imbued with socialism, they actually lose interest in their union."[36] But it was at the 1903 convention of the A. F. of L., during the debate on a labor party, that Gompers announced his first clear-cut expression of opposition to socialism in a speech which he later reprinted in the *American Federationist* under the revealing title, "Trade Unionism versus Socialism." He spoke in the beginning in his old vein, suggesting that he was simply attacking the Socialists because they did not live up to the high principles of their movement. "It is because their professions are in entire discord with their actions in this convention that it is necessary to call their position in question." But at the close of the speeches he gave vent to the statement which made it clear that he no longer drew any distinction between socialist principles and practices:

"I want to tell you, Socialists, that I have studied your philosophy; read your works upon economics, and not the meanest of them; studied your standard works, both in English and German—have not only read, but studied them. I have heard your orators and watched the work of your movement the world over. I have kept close watch upon your doctrines for thirty years; have been closely associated with many of you, and know how you think and what you propose. I know, too, what you have up your sleeves. And I want to say that I am entirely at variance with your philosophy. I declare it to you. I am not only at variance with your doctrines, but with your philosophy. Economically, you are unsound; socially, you are wrong; industrially, you are an impossibility."

Before Gompers' forceful opposition and the control of his well-prepared machine, the Socialists went down to overwhelming defeat The Socialist-sponsored resolution was rejected by the vote of 11,282 to 2,145.[37]

As a result of Gompers' onslaught against socialism, he was hailed by the press as a hero. The National Civic Federation printed a picture of him on the front page of its journal with the caption, "Socialism's Ablest Foe." This pleased Gompers, for he wrote to a friend that his renunciation of socialism "largely disarmed our opponents and clarified the air of the prejudice of public opinion which was leveled against us last year, and it will undoubtedly take away much of the sting of antagonism directed against our movement by Mr. Parry and those who follow him." But Gompers, as we have already seen, badly misjudged Parry, for the open-shop spokesman was soon to declare: "The A. F. of L. voted down the socialism that aims for peace through the means of the ballot, but it did not vote down the socialism that President Gompers stands for—mob force socialism. It is this mob force socialism that we have to combat as much as the other."[38]

Gompers' renunciation of socialism came as a heavy blow to the Socialists who had been taken in by his earlier endorsement of socialist objectives, and the vote at the 1903 convention heightened the impact. They decided that the whole strategy of advancing the socialist cause by getting resolutions in its favor adopted at A. F. of L. conventions was a mistake. Education would bring this about, and if the unions only opened their doors to study and discussion, the workers would automatically reach conclusions favorable to socialism. At the National Convention of the Socialist Party held in Chicago, May 1 to 6, 1904, several delegates urged the party to speak out firmly in favor of industrial unionism and to denounce "the treacherous, deceitful work of the conglomeration between several labor leaders so-called, and the captains of industry such as the National Civic Federation and other like institutions, and brand these federations as instruments of the capitalist class to perpetuate the system of to-day and to use organized labor as a tool for that purpose." But Hayes and Hillquit opposed the stand, arguing that it would retard the efforts to educate the members of the A. F. of L. "in Socialistic principles." The delegates finally adopted a vague resolution on trade union policy which emphasized that trade union activity was secondary to political action, that while the trade unions were of great value in the struggle against the exploitation of labor, this could only be achieved by a political revolution which would give ownership of the instruments of production to the entire people for the equal benefit of all. "Every trade unionist who realizes this should join the Socialist Party and assist in arousing the working class to political action, so that it may secure the powers of government, and by abolishing wage slavery and establishing the co-operative commonwealth, achieve its own emancipation."[39]

At the 1904 A. F. of L. convention, the Socialist delegates presented no Socialist resolutions as had been introduced in previous years. Instead, they pushed for a resolution introduced by Berger recommending that trade unionists should discuss economic and political subjects in their local meetings. On other issues, the Socialist delegates did not even act as a united group. Although it had been agreed before the convention that if one Socialist delegate were involved in a debate, the others present, about a dozen, would join. But when Berger publicly called upon his fellow-Socialists to help him defend his resolution favoring the principle of industrial unionism, no one responded. "This created no little wonderment and glee in the ranks of the opponents," Berger wrote disgustedly later.[40]*

"There was no Socialist resolution introduced in the convention," Max

---

* Berger introduced ten resolutions at the convention, the most important of which advocated old-age pensions, industrial unionism, and the study of economics in the organizations affiliated with the A.F. of L. The first two were non-concurred in, while the third was approved after the following clause was struck out, with Berger's approval: "Whereas, The unprecedented concentration of wealth in the United States and the rapid development of the trusts in almost every branch of industry make it obvious that capitalism will soon reach its culmination point, and will have to make room for another phase of civilization." In demanding the omission of this clause, Frank K. Foster, chairman of the resolutions committee, declared: "Your committee are not yet so engulfed by the vaporous atmosphere of dreamland, so entirely under the influence of illusive metaphysical dope that they are ready to proclaim a doctrine of that nature." (*Proceedings,* A.F. of L. Convention, 1904, pp. 185–88.)

Hayes explained. "It was unnecessary. Socialism is receiving plenty of notice at present as much as is necessary to insure solid and substantial growth." But Berger accused Hayes of capitulating completely to the Gompers' machine, of having played "good politics," swapping votes so that he could be the fraternal delegate to Great Britain, of having made but one speech at the convention and that a stereotyped one, and of having done no fighting for socialism. Hayes defended his conduct, though convincing few Socialists, but it was clear that as a militant, fighting force, the Socialists counted for very little in the A. F. of L. In fact, the Socialists had been thoroughly humiliated at the 1904 convention when Berger was forced to apologize for an editorial in his *Social-Democratic Herald* entitled "Are They Traitors?" which contained the story of Gompers' and John Mitchell's private dinner with President Eliot of Harvard who had publicly approved of the "scab," a remark which the A. F. of L. convention of 1902 had condemned.* Little wonder Berger described the 1904 convention as "a wretched affair" from the standpoint of Socialism.[41]

The new policy of educating A. F. of L. members to vote for socialism led to the gradual dropping or the soft-pedaling by the Socialists within the Federation of any agitation in the A. F. of L. for union organization along industrial lines, independent political action, and a militant program of labor solidarity. The dominant Socialist approach to the A. F. of L. and its affiliates, as expressed by the Right and Center factions which were now closely linked, was that Socialists in the unions must devote themselves almost exclusively to educating workers in the benefits to be gained from an intelligent use of the ballot—since "the only salvation of the workers is to go into politics: Socialist politics." Regardless of what policies were adopted in the economic field, union members would learn through experience under capitalism that they would solve their basic problems by voting Socialist. Education would not only hasten the process, but would teach the workers how to get rid of leaders who did not serve their interests. "Educate the rank and file," wrote G. A. Hoehn. "Let them elect Socialist delegates, representing the carpenters, miners, cigarmakers, machinists, printers, etc., and you will soon get rid of leaders who you consider detrimental to the progress of the movement."[42] Other Socialists active in the A. F. of L. now stressed, however, that it was no longer important to wage a struggle against the leaders of the Federation since the workers were bound to learn that

---

* The editorial was reprinted in a leaflet and distributed among the delegates. Mitchell declared angrily: "He [Berger] will have to prove that I am a traitor or he will have to stand convicted before this Convention as a liar." Gompers explained the dinner with Eliot with the statement: "I will go anywhere to preach the gospel of trade unionism." When Berger apologized for the editorial, claiming he had not written it and disapproving of its contents, Mitchell accepted it, and his remarks were ordered stricken from the record. (*Ibid.*, pp. 198–202, 215–16.)

they could only fundamentally help themselves by supporting the movement for socialism.

It is not surprising that the Socialist delegates, with the exception of Berger, now refused any serious effort to depose Gompers from the leadership of the Federation.* In 1904, Max Hayes, having been elected an A. F. of L. fraternal delegate to Great Britain, stated that it did not "matter much to the trade unionists of the country who are chosen to transact the Federation's business." The Socialists put up no opposition candidates from 1904 to 1912.

Thus the Socialists, operating on the principle of "boring from within" the A. F. of L., became completely quiescent, and the whole tendency was to soft-pedal criticism of the A. F. of L. leaders and their policies. To do otherwise, it was argued, was to make it difficult for the Socialists to gain access to trade union councils where they could reach the members with the message to vote Socialist. Vote-getting activity for the Socialist Party, after all, was what really counted. The labor movement consisted, to be sure, of two arms—an economic arm and a political arm—but it was the political arm, that is, the growth of the Socialist vote, that, in the long run, would determine the future destiny of the American workers. What did it really matter, then, if the economic arm remained under the control of men who used their power to crush proposals aimed at ameliorating the condition of the laboring class?[43]

SOCIALIST GROWTH AND ITS NATURE

When Max Hayes wrote in explanation of the failure of the Socialists to introduce any resolution in favor of socialism at the 1904 A. F. of L.

* Berger liked to boast that beginning with the 1904 A.F. of L. convention, and at each subsequent convention that he attended, except for the 1907 and 1910 meetings, he had cast his vote against Gompers, sometimes standing alone to do so. (Berger to E. Edelmar, July 11, 1916, Victor L. Berger Papers, Milwaukee County Historical Society.) After the 1904 convention, he denounced Gompers as a "vain sycophant" who acted as if he were being paid by the capitalist class instead of the laboring class, and as though he were trying to make the A.F. of L. a "tail of the capitalist kite." (*Social-Democratic Herald,* Jan. 7, 14, 1905.) In his private correspondence, Berger referred frequently to "the reactionary, rotten and drunken Gompers clique," and when Job Harriman, the California Socialist leader, cautioned him against such criticism of Gompers, Berger characterized the A.F. of L. president as "one of the most vicious and venomous enemies of socialism and progressive trade unionism in America. The time to fight him—is all the time, because the American labor movement will remain ultra-reactionary as long as he has any influence." (Berger to Murray E. King, Mar. 4, 1914; Berger's penciled notes on Harriman to Berger, July 2, 1912, Berger Papers, *ibid.*)

Sometimes Berger expressed admiration for Gompers' organizing ability, but he coupled this with the accusation that he was a self-seeker who used his power to maintain himself in office. Since Berger was accused of precisely the same practice with respect to the Milwaukee Socialist movement, it might be said he knew what he was talking about. (Olson, *op. cit.,* pp. 153-54, 179-80.)

convention that it was "unnecessary" because "Socialism is receiving plenty of notice at present as much as is necessary to insure solid and substantial growth"—he was asserting the main line taken by the Center-Right group dominant in the Party. They pointed with pride to the spread of Socialist propaganda, Socialist electoral victories, and membership growth as justifying their policies. They noted that at its second convention, in May 1904, the party had 184 delegates, representing 1,200 locals in 35 states, and that the party's dues-paying membership had doubled since 1901, being 15,975 in 1903 and 20,768 in 1904. The party press was also growing rapidly, with several dailies in German and other non-English languages and over 100 English-language weeklies and monthlies. In 1898 the total circulation of the Socialist press was about 25,000. In 1903 the weekly *Appeal to Reason* alone had a circulation of 50,000 and the monthly *Wilshire's Magazine* sold 100,000 copies. Between 1898 and 1903, the number of Socialist pamphlets and leaflets published increased from about a dozen to 500. The party's success in the 1904 national elections was striking. Eugene V. Debs and Ben Hanford, the Socialist presidential and vice-presidential candidates, polled 408,000 votes, or about a 350 per cent increase over the vote in 1900, and almost twice their 1902 total.

The party's trade union influence, the Center-Right insisted, was also on the rise. Did not the Springfield *Republican* of January 30, 1903, state that "Socialistic sentiment is plainly growing among labor unionists throughout the country?" Did not the Los Angeles *Times* of September 18, 1904, declare that "the natural drift of labor unionism in the United States is toward Socialism"? Were not unions passing resolutions introduced by Socialist delegates? Were not Socialists Fred Heath and Victor Berger the leaders of the Central Labor Union of Milwaukee; James H. Maurer, leader of the Reading (Pennsylvania) Federated Trades Council and the Pennsylvania State Federation of Labor, and Max Hayes leader of the Cleveland Central Trades Council; was not Morris Hillquit attorney and advisor to several trade unions, and J. Mahlon Barnes a powerful figure in Gompers' own Cigarmakers' Union? Certainly the party had gained considerable following among the brewery and bakery workers, the clothing and millinery workers, the ladies' garment workers and a number of other affiliates of the A. F. of L. Several of these unions were, to be sure, small, particularly the United Cloth Hat and Cap Makers of North America, formed in 1901, and the International Ladies' Garment Workers' Union, founded in 1900. But their membership was socialist-minded and were becoming more so due to the consistent education of the members in the principles of socialism. Had not the 1904 convention of the Ladies' Garment Workers resolved "to permit the discussion of socialism at the convention of the I.L.G.W.U."? Soon other unions affiliated to the A. F. of L. would be following the example set by this socialist-minded union. In short, "boring-from-within," despite what might appear as "surface indications of slow progress," was a success. As Max Hayes summed it up in advancing this thesis:

"This is demonstrated by the steady increase of the Socialist party vote throughout the country, by the more tolerant spirit with which Socialists and their doctrine are received among the heretofore most unyielding unions and members, and by the emphatic refusal of the organized workers to allow their organizations to be used by political adventurers in the interest of capitalist politics.

"The trade union movement is naturally and logically developing into Socialism. There is no necessity to become worried or discouraged. The organized workers are learning that there is no escape from capitalism except by inaugurating a co-operative commonwealth. Let every wide-awake Socialist assist in the work of education."[44]

Certainly the array of statistics testifying to Socialist electoral victories, membership growth, and increasing influence among all sections of the population was impressive. But they did not convince those members of the Socialist Party who were growing more and more alarmed by the watering down of socialist principles to attract an ever-increasing following regardless of its class composition, the soft-pedaling of criticism of the class-collaboration policies of the A. F. of L. leadership, and the increasing tendency of the party leadership and control to fall into the hands of the middle class. These members were not overly impressed by the fact that the party's membership was rising since they saw it attracting more membership from the middle class than from the working class, and increasing the danger that a movement that had to be rooted into the working class would soon be inundated by middle class recruits. They were not impressed by the mere passage of resolutions introduced by Socialist delegates at union conventions since they were rarely backed up with concrete action, and, in most cases, the value of the resolutions ended after they had been recorded by the secretary. They were not impressed by the influence of the party in a number of unions since it was obvious that most of these socialist-minded members had been converted to socialism in earlier years in Europe. But where were the workers who had been newly converted to the ideas of the Socialist Party, and where, particularly, were the workers in the mass production industries who were sorely in need of organization? What contribution to rallying these workers to the party did the Center-Right policies make? And how could they contribute when the Socialists, influenced by the Center-Right approach to the labor movement, refrained from participating in the everyday struggles of the working class, and when Socialist delegates who made their annual pilgrimage to the A. F. of L. conventions abandoned altogether the battle against the Federation's narrow, craft, "pure and simple" trade unionism? How could the party win converts among the workers when some of its most important leaders publicly asserted that employers who joined the party were not to be criticized for joining employers' associations which had as their purpose the destruction of the trade unions?[45]

As the years passed with no organized work by the A. F. of L. among the mass of the unorganized workers, and with no effort by the Socialists in the Federation to force this issue, those Socialists who felt the urgency of such work among the unorganized became increasingly disillusioned with the "boring from within" doctrine. Instead, they turned more and more to the movement for a new, militant, class-conscious labor federation, based on industrial unionism, emerging from the West.

CHAPTER 15

The Western Federation of Miners

"There never was a labor organization that encouraged such opposition from companies as we encountered from the mining companies, opposed to organized labor." So wrote the editor of the *Miners' Magazine,* official organ of the Western Federation of Miners, in 1901.[1] What was true in 1901 was true throughout this entire decade. There is hardly a year in this period when the very life of the W. F. of M. was not endangered in some area or other. In these years the W. F. of M. was involved in ten strikes or lockouts of importance.* Two things particularly stand out about these struggles: first, they represent some of the most violent examples of class conflict in the whole of American history, and second, they reveal a developed pattern of employer resistance to unionism. Both are interrelated.

EMPLOYERS' OFFENSIVE AGAINST W. F. OF M.

The western metal miner was employed in what was probably the most dangerous of America's major industries. The miner faced the risk of accident at almost every point in his daily work, in his handling of explosives, in traveling up and down the mine shafts, from cave-ins or fires while at work in the drifts and the stopes. The preamble to the first constitution of the W. F. of M., adopted in 1893, emphasized that "the men engaged in this hazardous and unhealthy occupation of mining should receive a fair compensation for their labor, and such protection from the law as will remove needless risk to life and health." But the miners soon discovered that the system of "corporate avarice and lust for gold" gave no thought to the conditions of the men who produced the wealth. Managers representing absentee owners, the finance capitalists of the East—the Standard Oil combine, the House of Morgan, the Gould and Guggenheim interests—were interested only in increasing profits from

* For the history and struggles of the Western Federation of Miners before 1900, *see* Foner, *op. cit.,* vol. II, pp. 223–24, 244, 379–80, 422.

the mines. They fought every attempt of the miners to change the terrible conditions of work. Through their domination of the economic life of the western mining states, these interests exercised a dominant influence over the entire political and legal life of these states. They purchased legislators and other public officials to pass laws to serve the interests of the absentee capitalists and to defeat legislation in the interests of the workers.[2]

Citizens' Alliances, Pinkerton detectives, labor spies, state and federal troops, the blacklist and discharge of union members, "ironclad" oaths and "yellow-dog" contracts, force and violence, were all part of the pattern developed by the big corporations to destroy the W. F. of M. By 1904 it was reported that 20 to 25 local Citizens' Alliances, the leadership drawn from the Mine Owners' Association, and the membership from bankers and small businessmen, had been formed in Colorado alone. Detectives were employed to act as spies within the unions; sometimes they secured responsible positions and attempted to destroy the union. A Pinkerton detective was actually in charge of relief administration for the local union during the 1903 strike in Colorado, and attempted to cut down the relief as much as possible "so as to cause dissatisfaction and get the men against the union." Another Pinkerton detective attempted to cause a trainwreck during the strike in order to discredit the union. The train was warned in time and passed in safety, but had the plot succeeded, it would have resulted in a frightful loss of life, for the cars were crowded with passengers among whom were a number of union members. During the trial, H. H. McKinney, the Pinkerton detective, testified that he had been paid $500 by a representative of the Mine Owners' Association to wreck the train and place the blame on the union. His testimony reveals that the mine owners were ready to employ the worst type of criminals in their attempt to destroy the union:

"*Q.* Mr. McKinney, as I understand you, you agreed to wreck a railroad train for $500, is that correct?

"*A.* I believe so, yes.

"*Q.* And you were going to share that with your partners in crime, is that correct?

"*A.* I suppose so.

"*Q.* So that for $250 you were willing to plunge the souls of men into eternity in that way by wrecking the train; you were willing to kill men for $250, is that correct?

"*A.* Looks that way.

"*Q.* You undertook the job of killing them for $250?

"*A.* Yes, sir.

"*Q.* Now are you in that same frame of mind now that you would kill men for $250?

"*A.* I might under the same circumstances."

The jury, composed of ranchmen and timbermen and without a single miner or union man on it, brought in a verdict of "not guilty" within a half hour after the trial closed.[3]

Discharge of workers for union activity was a frequent occurrence in the western mining regions. In Coeur d'Alene after 1899 every employee was required to secure a "rustling card" from a central employment office, and to pass a "critical examination as to membership in the union." The same system was adopted in Cripple Creek in 1904, with its avowed purpose to "throw out all those who are in harmony with the unlawful methods adopted by the Western Federation of Miners on so many occasions." The 1909 lockout in the Black Hills of South Dakota was caused by the demand of the Homestead Mining Co. that every employee sign a statement asserting: "I am not a member of any labor union and in consideration of my being employed by the Homestead Mining Company, agree that I will not become such while in its service."[4]

MILITARY DESPOTISM

On February 14, 1903, 76 members of the Colorado City Mill and Smeltermen's Local No. 125 of the W. F. of M. left their jobs at the Standard and Colorado reduction mills. Within nine months strikes had spread over the entire state, beginning first with members of the allied unions in the W. F. of M., and later spreading to the coal miners organized by the United Mine Workers of America. The demands of the W. F. of M. were for the eight-hour day, recognition of the union, wage raises, and reinstatement of the workers who had been fired for joining the union. Of these issues, the major one was the struggle for an eight-hour day. Since 1894 the W. F. of M. had fought for a statute limiting the working day in all underground mines and in reduction and refining mills to eight hours. In 1899 the Colorado legislature passed such an act, but the employers refused to comply with the law, and began a campaign to have it declared unconstitutional. This the State Supreme Court obligingly decreed in 1901. The following year, however, the miners believed they had finally achieved victory. By an overwhelming vote, the Colorado voters adopted a referendum authorizing the legislature to pass an amendment to the constitution that would legalize the eight-hour measure, and elected a Republican governor, James H. Peabody, who pledged his support to the legislation. But the powerful mining interests of Colorado moved to sabotage the will of the voters, and the legislature, responding to the pressure of the mining lobby, failed to pass the eight-hour law. As Ray Stannard Baker noted: "Rarely, indeed, has there been in this country a more brazen, conscienceless defeat of the will of the people, plainly expressed, not only at the ballot box, but by the pledges of both parties." President Charles F. Moyer of the W. F. of M. expressed the feelings of the miners when he declared: "What is the use of your ballots anyway? You might as well tear them up and throw them into the gutter."[5]

The W. F. of M. knew now that the miners could not achieve their demands through legislation and resolved to strike. After conferring with the mine owners, Governor Peabody sent in troops to prevent picketing, but public opinion forced the governor to bring the contending parties into conference. The independent mills granted the union's demands, including the eight-hour day. But the Standard Mill refused to accede, and the union placed a boycott on the mill and struck the mines which refused to stop shipping ore to the mill.

Over the protest of the sheriff and city council, the governor sent in 1,000 soldiers and a number of mines resumed operations with nonunion men. As there were no State funds available for the pay, transportation and maintenance of the troops, the officials of the Mine Owners' Association informed Governor Peabody that they would advance to the state the money required. It was clear that the troops were nothing more than hired tools of the mine owners, and that they had been brought in not to prevent violence, but to break the strike. This was too much even for the *Army and Navy Journal,* a prominent organ of military opinion. It observed: "The arrangement virtually placed the troops for the time being in the relation of hired men to the mine operators and morally suspended their function of state military guardian of the public peace. It was . . . more likely to invite disorder than to prevent it."[6]

The City Council wired a protest to Governor Peabody, and well over 3,000 citizens sent a petition to the legislature requesting the removal of the soldiery. These protests were to no avail; Governor Peabody replied: "The soldiers will stay in Cripple Creek until the strike is broken."[7]

With the arrival of the troops there began one of the most flagrantly brutal instances of military rule and vigilantism in American history. The Citizens' Protective League deported 18 miners who had been seized in their homes, although no charges were placed against them. Arrest of strike leaders began on grounds of "military necessity." The union instituted *habeas corpus* proceedings, and when the case came before the court in September 1903, General Chase threw a cordon of 90 cavalrymen around the trial room, and soldiers with fixed bayonets escorted the petitioning unionists into the building.* Judge Lafferty, not to be intimidated by this shocking procedure, adjourned his court and ordered General Chase to produce the petitioners. Chase and his superior, Adjutant General Sherman Bell, however, continued to intimidate and even openly to defy the court. The courthouse was surrounded by an army

---

* Brigadier-General Chase had headed an investigating committee sent by Governor Peabody to determine the nature of the strike and the need for troops. General Chase took testimony from the mine operators but ignored the strikers.

of troopers, sharpshooters were posted on surrounding roofs, and a Gatling gun was mounted in front of the courthouse. Nonetheless, Judge Lafferty granted writs of *habeas corpus,* ordering the miners released. He pointed out that there was no serious violence in the strike zone, and that, if there had been, the military officials were still subject to the civil authority. This decision brought General Chase to his feet with the announcement that he would refuse to honor the court's order on the grounds that he was subject only to orders from the governor. The men were thrown into makeshift stockades or "bull pens," where they remained for months.

In an effort to break the resistance of the strikers, the militia arrested the men without specific charges and held them in the "bull pens" for extended periods. Even the staff of a local newspaper, the Victor *Record,* was imprisoned in the "bull pen" for an editorial criticizing the tactics of the militia commanders. In some cases town officials were arrested and warned to stop sympathizing with the miners.

An ex-rough rider under Theodore Roosevelt, General Bell summed up his conception of duty in the strike in his statement: "I came to do up this damned anarchistic federation." The counsel for the militia, Judge Advocate Major Thomas McLelland maintained that under martial law the militia was justified in ignoring or circumventing civil processes. When it was suggested to him that this was an unconstitutional interpretation of military powers, he replied: "To hell with the Constitution! We aren't going by the Constitution. We are following the orders of Governor Peabody." Speaking from the bench, Judge Stevens declared: "A grave question is presented as to whether it is the striking miners or the Governor of Colorado and the national guard that are engaged in insurrection and rebellion against the laws of the State. If there is to be a reign of military despotism in this State and civil authority is to have no jurisdiction, the latter might as well go out of business."[8]

"If there is to be a military despotism in this State. . . ." The Western Federation of Miners stated that there was no "if" involved. In one of its statements to the people of the United States, it declared:

"Is Liberty Dead!

"The People vs. Military Despotism in Colorado!

"Never in the history of the United States of America have the rights of citizens been so ruthlessly torn and trampled, as during the last few weeks in Cripple Creek District, Colorado.

"Innocent men have been arrested without charge! confined for weeks in a bull-pen! and denied the writ of Habeas Corpus! The civil process of law is ignored! Women and children terrorized, and threatened with imprisonment! The freedom of press and speech is throttled!

"These terrible outrages are but chapters in the dark and subtle conspiracy to defeat the will of the people of this State, where a majority of forty thousand electors declared for an eight-hour law for persons employed in mines, mills, smelters, reduction works and blast furnaces.

"To prove that a conspiracy exists, it is only necessary to say that the military is rented to the Mine Operators, 1500 armed men hired out like convicts, to shoot down the strikers if need be, anything to break strikes."[9]

But even worse was yet to come. In June 1904, nearly a year and a half after the beginning of the strike, the railroad depot at Cripple Creek was blown up, killing 13 and wounding 16 men. The W. F. of M. not only disclaimed any connection, but its convention was in session at this time and the union offered a reward of $5,000 for the arrest and conviction of those responsible for the crime. The officers of the W. F. of M. were indicted for murder as a result of the explosion, but the case was later dismissed for lack of evidence. But the Mine Owners' Association, having failed in a year and a half to break the spirit and solidarity of the strikers, used the incident to launch its most vicious offensive to destroy unionism. A mob organized by the Citizens' Alliance and the Mine Owners' Association forced the sheriff to resign, and the militia attacked the miners' halls, destroyed the furnishings in them, and rounded up union men. Then in one of the most brutal actions ever perpetrated against trade unionists, the militia, with the support of the operators and the Citizens' Alliance, engaged in a series of deportations of union men and sympathizers. Large numbers of strikers were herded into "bull pens" or driven out of the district. General Bell ruled over the strike zone as though he were an occupying commander in the territory of an enemy. At his command on June 10, 1904, 79 men were forced into box cars, transported to the Kansas line, and left on the prairies with orders never to return to Colorado, a volley being fired over their heads to emphasize the military nature of the operation. Another deportation sent 33 men to New Mexico. These men, including a prominent lawyer, were cruelly mistreated by their militia guards. A third major deportation occurred on June 28, with 39 men being shipped out of the district.

These men, torn away from their families and threatened with violence if they returned, were in some cases not even directly involved in the strike. Some business and professional men who sympathized with the union were treated in the same fashion. Not only were properties of the W. F. of M. destroyed by angry mobs, with the assistance of the militia, but the militia commander forbade local merchants from dealing with the union. Even private relief was denied families of deported men.[10]*

Civilian and police officials sympathetic to the miners were forced to

---

* The W.F. of M. called on President Theodore Roosevelt to investigate the deportation of union miners and give them the protection guaranteed by the law. Labor unions from coast to coast took up the cry for presidential intervention. John W. Murphy, attorney for the union, wrote to the President in August 1904, asking for federal troops to be sent to Colorado to prevent further outrages against

resign and were replaced by Alliance men. As if to throw off all pretense of impartiality, the seven-man military tribunal held court in the office of the Mine Owners Association. Small wonder the union asked: "Is Colorado in America?"* Because of one of the posters issued by the union which asked this question in the title, W. F. of M. President Charles E. Moyer was imprisoned and charged with desecrating the flag.† The poster carried the American flag on it and the following statements across each of the stripes:

"Martial law declared in Colorado!

"Habeas Corpus suspended in Colorado!

"Free Press throttled in Colorado!

"Bull-pens for union men in Colorado!

"Free speech denied in Colorado!

"Soldiers defy the courts in Colorado!

"Wholesale arrests without warrants in Colorado!

"Union men exiled from homes and families in Colorado!

"Constitutional right to bear arms questioned in Colorado!

"Corporations corrupt and control administration in Colorado!

"Right of fair, impartial and speedy trial abolished in Colorado!

"Citizens Alliance resorts to mob law and violence in Colorado!

"Militia hired by corporations to break the strike in Colorado!"

Below the flag was a picture of a union miner shackled to a telephone pole.[11]

When the militia left the strike zone on July 26, 1904, it turned the city over to the mob, headed by the Citizens' Alliance. Union stores were wrecked and robbed. The Victor *Record* was again invaded, the presses destroyed, and the staff put in the "bull pen." Strike sympathizers were

---

the miners by the militia and the Citizens' Alliance. But to all requests for intervention, Roosevelt replied that he did not have the power to intercede to protect the rights of Colorado citizens. (*Miners' Magazine,* Dec. 10, 1903, p. 8; Roosevelt to William H. Moody, Aug. 24, 1904, *TRP.*) President Roosevelt followed the advice of Commissioner of Labor Carroll D. Wright, which was to let the public know that he was conducting an investigation, while actually allowing the matter to drift. (Wright to Roosevelt, June 21, 1904, *TRP.*)

* Some newspapers headlined reports from Cripple Creek: "Happenings in Color-Russia!" (New York *American,* June 12, 13, 1904.)

† Moyer was seized at Ouray, Colorado, on March 26, 1904, and turned over to the militia on the charge of desecrating the flag. When the military authorities refused to produce Moyer in court on a writ of *habeas corpus* by District Judge Theron Stevens, the case was carried to the Colorado Supreme Court. The court avoided giving any answer to the basic issue of whether the governor, as commander-in-chief of the militia, could declare martial law and suspend the writ of *habeas corpus.* In a two-to-one decision, the court simply decided that the arrest and detention of Moyer in this specific instance was justified. ("A Report on Labor Disturbances in the State of Colorado from 1880 to 1904, Inclusive." 58th Congress, 3d Session, *Senate Document No. 122,* p. 229–46.)

terrorized, robbed, or deported by white-capped Alliance men. These included not only miners, but lawyers, among them the former attorney general of the state, the former county attorney, and a judge. Also a widespread blacklisting system against union men was developed.[12]

Although the strike in the Cripple Creek district was not officially terminated by the union until 1907, it had run its course by the end of 1904, ending in a defeat for the miners. The eight locals in the district were all destroyed and it became virtually impossible for a union miner to get work in the area. The Mine Owners' Association reigned supreme.[13]

Major strikes at Telluride and Idaho Springs, Colorado, growing in large part out of the struggle to secure the eight-hour day, were smashed by the same tactics used at Cripple Creek. Again the mine owners, Citizens' Alliance men, and the militia engaged in a reign of terror against the strikers including mass deportations, blacklisting, arrest and detention, censorship, and intimidation. By the end of 1904, through activities of the militia, businessmen, and mine operators, the strikes had been broken.* The fight in Colorado, as "Big Bill" Haywood, W. F. of M. secretary-treasurer, put it, had been for the "principles of this Republic,"[14] but the giant corporations, assisted by the state authorities and local vigilantes, had made a mockery of these principles.

GROWTH OF THE W. F. OF M.

In area after area, the finance-capital dominated corporations continued to fight the W. F. of M. with "reckless, unscrupulous and maddening insolence."[15]† The growth of the union, in the face of the tremendous opposition it faced throughout these years, is truly remarkable. From 1893 to 1910 the union grew from 15 locals scattered over five

---

* The strike of District 15, United Mine Workers, in Colorado was broken by the same methods. Governor Peabody ordered the militia into the strike zone on March 22, 1904, and the militia was no sooner in the field than it inaugurated the same tactics that were used at Cripple Creek. On March 26, 1904, "Mother" Jones and another U.M.W. organizer, as well as the editor and publisher of a Trinidad newspaper, were deported from Trinidad and ordered never to return. A week later, eight strikers, most of them local union officers were ejected from Colorado. When the militia commander, Major Hill, was asked if there were any specific charges against the men, he replied: "No, but I believe their absence is better for the people than their presence." Faced with a powerful alliance of corporations and state authorities, and deprived of further financial support from the national office of the U.M.W., the Colorado coal strikers abandoned the battle on October 12, 1904. (Edmund Philip Willis, "Colorado Industrial Disturbances, 1903–1904," unpublished M.A. thesis, University of Wisconsin, 1955, pp. 78–114.)

† An important part of the employers' offensive was one of the most colossal frameups in American labor history—the Moyer, Haywood, Pettibone case. Since Moyer and Haywood were also officers of the I.W.W. and the case is intertwined with that organization to some extent as well as with the W. F. of M., it will be discussed in the next volume which deals with the I.W.W.

states, to 177 locals, located in 13 states, Alaska, British Columbia, and Ontario. In terms of actual membership, the earliest figures we have are for October 1896, when James Mahrer, secretary-treasurer, reported "fifteen thousand members in good standing." This may have been an exaggeration;* still by 1907, the membership had reached a high point of 44,000. At times, the Butte local alone had a membership of 8,000.[16]

The chief strength of the W. F. of M. was concentrated in the Western states; British Columbia, Colorado, and Montana were the main areas of organized strength in 1900, and by 1910, Arizona, California, and Nevada were added to this list. The number of locals in those six states grew from 75 in 1900 to 120 in 1910.† and, in 1910, 62 per cent of the total membership was located in them.[17]

The metal mines and smelters of the mid-West remained, however, a vast unorganized sector, constantly threatening the standards of the organized miners. By 1910 the W. F. of M. had only organized some 14 per cent of the metal miners of the United States, with 28 per cent of the membership in Montana alone. The lead mines of Missouri, the iron mines of Minnesota, the copper region of Michigan, were low wage areas—in Missouri, for example, the average daily wage for miners in 1910 ran from $1.77 in the eastern district to $2.32 in the western district, while in Colorado and Montana, it ranged from $3.37 to $4.00 a day. These depressed areas were a source from which employers could secure strikebreakers. In 1900 there was only one local in the entire mid-West area, and in 1910 there were six in Missouri and 13 in Michigan. But combined membership of these 13 locals in 1910 was only 2,300.[18]

As an industrial union, the W. F. of M. sought to bring within its jurisdiction all those employed in the copper, silver, and gold mines, cutting across craft lines which separated the skilled from the unskilled.‡ Its constitution was amended in 1899 to state specifically that the union

---

* Leo Wolman lists 8,000 members for the W. F. of M. in 1897 (*Ebb and Flow of Trade Unionism,* pp. 172–73.)

† In 1900 these locals were distributed as follows: British Columbia, 18, Colorado, 27, Montana, 21. In 1910 they were: Arizona, 15, British Columbia, 18, California, 16, Colorado, 19, Montana, 22, Nevada, 30. (*Miners' Magazine,* Dec. 1900, pp. 60–61, Oct. 6, 1910, p. 15.) The decline in Colorado, of course, was the result of the loss of the 1903–04 strikes.

‡ The union also sought to bring wage levels of the unskilled up to that of the skilled. In 1910 Tom Mann, the British labor leader, reported having met Haywood in England and that the latter had told him "that although the W.F.M. have had many fights for wages they have never had one directly on behalf of the skilled men who received the highest money, but always in behalf of the lowest paid to raise them to the standard of the highest. He declares this has worked exceedingly well for all concerned, and as a result all those working about the mine get a minimum wage of three dollars a day, the labourer just as much as the skilled man. . . . This is splendid testimony to their good sense and to their faith in the principles of brotherhood." (*The Industrial Syndicalist,* vol. I, No. 4, Oct. 1910. Copy in library of the London School of Economics.)

included "all persons working in and around mines, mills and smelters."[19] The membership was thus open to miners, miners' helpers, timbermen, laborers, engineers, and those employed in the smelters, and it was open to them regardless of race, creed, color, or nationality. At the 1903 convention, former president Edward Boyce urged the delegates to pay special attention to organizing immigrant workers because "foreigners are leaders in labor movements." The convention voted to publish its by-laws and ritual in Austrian, Finnish, and Italian to help those nationalities understand W. F. of M. objectives. Later, replying to a criticism raised because the union had organized Italians who were said to be "by nature" scabs, the W. F. of M. retorted vigorously:

"It is true that a majority of the men employed at that time on the Revenue Tunnel [in Ouray, Colorado] were Italians, but nevertheless, they were fellow working men and we were bound not to discriminate against a fellow working man on account of creed, color or nationality. And we believe that the fact that they were out on 'strike' is ample proof that they are not 'scabs,' for scabs never strike, and immediately after coming to Ouray on the following day they joined the Western Federation of Miners. A large number of them are already members in good standing."[20]

Mexicans and Navajo Indians were members of some locals, particularly those in Durango and Telluride, and the W. F. of M. urged its members to make special efforts "to induce the Mexican miners to join the union." The 1906 convention adopted a resolution on a strike for higher wages of Mexican miners in the mines of La Cananea, Mexico, which was accompanied by a great deal of violence and terror against the strikers:

"Whereas, The Western Federation of Miners recognize the class struggle throughout the world, and know no race or creed in the battle for industrial freedom; therefore, be it

"Resolved, that while we deplore the loss of life and property, the Western Federation of Miners in convention assembled, send greetings to the Mexicans, trusting that their efforts for a higher standard of living will be crowned with success."[21]

At the 1910 convention, the constitution was amended to provide that "no charter shall be issued the effect of which is to segregate the crafts engaged in the mining industry." In general, all those working in and around the mines were organized in one local, and members of the executive board were elected by districts, rather than as representatives of specific crafts or occupations.[22]

The first charter issued to coal miners was granted in 1905. In 1906–07, as we shall see, the W. F. of M. became the mining department of the I.W.W. with jurisdiction over all miners. In 1908, however, the convention voted that it was not "to the best interest of the W. F. of M. and the working class in general to issue any more charters to workers in the coal mining industry," but it recommended that "locals of coal miners already organized be maintained."[23]

CONSTITUTION AND OBJECTIVES

The constitution of the W. F. of M., with all the amendments which were attached to it during the years of our study, was thoroughly democratic, and the changes made were directed towards an increasing participation of the members in policy making. After 1902, the initiative and referendum governed all amendments to the constitution, and, after 1903, all major policy decisions were submitted to referendum vote of the membership. The conventions allowed for the fullest discussion of significant policy questions, and usually almost every delegate spoke on important motions. In 1906 the process of amending the constitution was made simpler by changing the number of locals necessary for ratification from two-thirds to a simple majority. Organizers were at first appointed, but were later elected at the annual convention and served as members of the executive boards for the various districts.[24]

Control of strikes and finances was fairly centralized. Strikes were called by a vote of three-fourths (later two-thirds) of the resident members of the local unions, but, in order to receive the financial support of the Federation, they had to be approved by its executive committee. Strikes were generally approved where it was felt that the organization could support the strikers, where there was a chance of success, or where the strike was forced by an employer lockout. The executive board and the annual convention had the power to levy assessments above the normal charter and per capita taxes.[25]

Conscious of the existence of a class struggle in society, the W. F. of M. was convinced that the resolution of that struggle required something more than the strike and boycott. But it did not repudiate the struggle for improvement of immediate working conditions through the strike and boycott. As Boyce pointed out in 1902: "The principle objects of this organization, like all other labor organizations, is for a higher wage schedule and a shorter work day." The W. F. of M., as we have seen, engaged in many strikes for these "objects" in this period, and fully supported, except for a short period, the demand for union label products "regardless of national affiliation."[26]*

But these methods, in the end, were regarded as inadequate, for the gains secured through them could only be temporary. "We are well aware," declared the union's Executive Committee, "that the increase in

* After a report on the misuse of the A.F. of L. labels, the 1906 convention decided to recognize only the I.W.W. label (*Proceedings, W. F. of M. Convention* pp. 248–53.) Later it changed its position once again.

wages is no remedy to the industrial controversy, as such increases are often appropriated by those who control the necessities of life." Or as the *Miners' Magazine* put it: "Nothing save the getting of all that labor produces will ever solve the vexatious struggle between the producers of wealth and organized greed."[27] And this end could only be achieved, in the W. F. of M. view, through the establishment of a socialist society.

At the time of its formation and during the years of its early growth, the W. F. of M. did not reject the framework of the society in which it operated. It believed that through industrial unionism and independent working class political action the major evils of capitalism and the power of monopoly could be curbed. In September 1899, an A. F. of L. organizer in the West emphasized that the most important influence in the W. F. of M. was "not so much a socialist sentiment but really a purpose to enter the political field to obtain legislation to protect the wage earner." Through independent political action, the W. F. of M. was able to force the legislatures in several states to pass eight-hour laws covering workers in mines and smelters. But the mining and smelter trusts, having failed to prevent the passage of these laws, either refused to comply with them or succeeded in having them declared unconstitutional by the state supreme courts. Where the constitutionality of the laws was upheld, the trusts simply evaded them. The Colorado law was fought by the smelter trust, and it was not "until 1913 that an enforcible law was put on the statute books." In Montana, an eight-hour law covering workers in the mines and smelters was passed and put into effect on May 1, 1901. Evasion of this law was widespread, and it was not until 1906 that an actual eight-hour day was instituted in Butte, Anaconda, and Great Falls at which time it was reported that 6,000 men had had their time reduced one-half hour to one hour each day. By 1910, every major mining state in the West had an eight-hour law on the statute books, but the union was constantly involved in battles to enforce these laws.[28]

The discouraging experience with these laws, the vicious attacks of the trusts, assisted by city, state, and federal governments, the brutal use of the state militia and federal troops, the subservience of the courts —all contributed towards convincing the W. F. of M. of the need for a new society, a new economic system which would "in the end result in the emancipation of the laborer from the thralldom of monopoly." At its 1901 convention, the union adopted resolutions demanding "a complete revolution of present social and economic conditions," and declared that since "the working class has nothing in common with the capitalist class; either politically or industrially—we take such steps political as to completely separate us as a political body from all parties controlled by the capitalist class." The resolutions accepted socialism, but they did not endorse any party of socialism. But in July 1901, a month after the above resolutions were adopted, the Socialist Party of the United States was born at a unity convention in Indianapolis. The W. F. of M. hailed the event as marking a new era for the American working class. A year later, at its 1902 convention, the union endorsed the Socialist Party in these terms: "We, the tenth annual convention of the Western Federation of Miners, do declare for a policy of independent political action, and do advise and recommend the adoption of the platform of the Socialist Party by the locals of the Federation in conjunction with a vigorous policy of education along the lines of political economy."[29]

Even though there was always a minority group that opposed such action, this policy was reaffirmed at subsequent conventions until 1906 and the union went on record each time as favoring independent political action on behalf of the Socialist Party. At the 1906 convention, in order to put an end to wrangling over the endorsement of socialism and the Socialist Party, the union eliminated the word "Socialism" from its objectives and the endorsement of the Socialist Party was stricken from the constitution and by-laws. However, the union still insisted that "We demand the full product of our labor." The 1907 convention declared: "We assert that the working class, and it alone, can and must achieve its own emancipation. We hold finally that an industrial union and the concerted political action of all wage workers, is the only method of attaining this end." Continuing to reject capitalism, the W. F. of M. called for "the election of class-conscious representatives of the working class, who will endeavor to remedy the evils and ultimately overthrow the capitalist system which rests upon the misery and exploitation of the workers."[30]

In addition to serving as a vanguard in the struggle for improvement of conditions of workers under capitalism, the W. F. of M. sought to become an organizing center and a vast educational apparatus working for socialism. From 1900, the year in which it was established, and even after the specific endorsement of socialism and the Socialist Party was removed from the union constitution and by-laws, much of the space in the *Miners' Magazine,* the union's official organ, was devoted to articles about socialism. As early as 1902, a labor journal declared: "The *Miners' Magazine* is one of the strongest Socialist publications in the world." As part of their educational activities, local unions established libraries, which were open to the public as well as to members and in which socialist literature was featured.* The W. F. of M. sponsored Eugene V. Debs and Father T. H. Haggerty on speaking tours for the Socialist Party; union leaders ran as Socialist candidates in many places in the West, Haywood running for governor of Colorado on the Socialist ticket

---

* In 1905, Carroll D. Wright said of the W. F. of M. locals: "Many of them maintain libraries and reading rooms in connection with their meeting halls." (U.S. Senate, *Senate Documents No. 122,* 58th Congress, 3d Session, p. 43.)

while in prison in Idaho in 1906. In general, the W. F. of M. lent strength to the Socialist Party in the West, and in 1905 its members were advised "as individuals to commence immediately the organization of the Socialist movement in their respective towns and states, and to cooperate in every way for the furtherance of the principles of socialism and the Socialist Party."[31]

As was to be expected, the aggressive role played by the W. F. of M. in furthering the cause of socialism was pointed to by employers as proof of their charge that the union was an advocate of force, violence, and terrorism against capitalism and capitalists.* The union's policy on political action gives the answer to these charges: peaceful political action was regarded by the W. F. of M. as the means by which capitalism would be overthrown. It is undoubtedly true that members of the W. F. of M. participated in acts of violence during strikes, particularly against strikebreakers, but that violence was a deliberate and official policy of the union, as the employers charged, is an allegation which cannot be substantiated.

President Charles F. Moyer made the position of the union clear when he said in 1904: "There are but two ways to meet the policy outlined by the corporations and the Citizens' Alliances, one, the rifle, the other the ballot. Which will organized labor choose? Which will the leaders of the great army of organized wage workers advise to be placed in the hands of their followers? There can be but one answer—the ballot. Were I the anarchist claimed by those who would destroy our organization, if my only desire were the destruction of property and the taking of human life as has been charged, then surely I would advise the rifle." The *Miners' Magazine* repeatedly condemned acts of terrorism. When Arthur Collins, a mine manager, was shot and killed by an unknown assailant, it denounced "the degenerate who slaked his insane thirst for revenge in the annihilation of human life." In 1903, commenting upon a letter to the editor counseling the miners to arm themselves, the magazine, although recognizing the employers' provocations which prompted such advice, stated that "the advance guard in the ranks of organized labor are appealing to the reason and intelligence of the world to use the bloodless weapon." In 1904, it pointed out: "The charge of inciting to crime cannot be sustained by one private or public utterance of these men. The leaders of the Western Federation of Miners are not making the fight along these lines."[32]

The W. F. of M. constitution, adopted in 1903, asserted the right of the miners "in all lawful ways to cooperate with one another for the

---

* The minority group in the union that opposed independent political action and endorsement of socialism argued that they would give the employers a weapon to attack the union as an advocate of force and violence. (*Proceedings,* W. F. of M. Convention, 1903, pp. 209–10, 261–71.)

purpose of procuring a just share of the product of our toil," and pointed out that its objects were "proper and lawful." The 1904 convention urged all members "to use their peaceful conciliation and social persuasion to induce others to join hands with them at the ballot box in securing the overthrow of the present iniquitious system of government."[33] In short, the union's policy advised political action for the overthrow of capitalism, not force, violence, or terrorism.

At the same time, however, the W. F. of M. asserted the right of the workers to defend themselves against the use of force by employers. If the employers chose to use force to invade the rights of the miners, then force in retaliation or self-defense would be justified. Thus the 1901 convention adopted this carefully phrased declaration: "We advise the toiler to be ever on the alert in defense of his rights, educate himself to protect those rights by a peaceful use of the ballot so long as the feasibility of such means will justify the end in view; when not, let us be prepared to meet the enemy with weapons of his choice." Boyce took this position in defending the advice he gave that every miner should arm himself to protect himself and his union against the employers' hired gunmen, and Haywood developed the same theme in 1906: "The Western Federation of Miners has engendered the intense hatred of the capitalists and corporations, not because the organization at any time advocated violence, but because you have at all times demanded recognition and obedience of law by the master class, who seem to think that law and regulation are only intended for those who labor. When the inevitable conflict comes, it will be precipitated by the class that ignores and tramples under foot the mandates of civilized society."[34]

This then was the W. F. of M., a union industrial in structure and possessed of a deep sense of class solidarity, a union which called for class conscious political action, rejected the framework of capitalism and looked forward to a socialist society under which poverty and exploitation would be abolished. To be sure, there was a minority group in the union that did not go along with these advanced views, and as we shall see in a subsequent volume, their influence was to increase in the latter part of this period. But, in the main, this militant, class-conscious union and its membership were correctly described by a contemporary paper as follows: "They are men of such rugged independence and unwavering loyalty to union principles that their organization stands almost without a peer in the field of organized labor."[35]

W. F. OF M. AND THE A. F. OF L.

It is indeed unfortunate for the American labor movement that this militant union, composed of men who were so deeply imbued with "unwavering loyalty to union principles," did not exert its power together with other progressive forces in the A. F. of L. to combat and defeat the conservative, class-collaboration policies of the Federation's leadership. But throughout the period when these policies were being developed and becoming fixed into the framework of the A. F. of L., the W. F. of M. stood apart from the struggle inside the A. F. of L. against these policies.

At its 1896 convention, the W. F. of M. affiliated with the A. F. of L. This step, discussed in the union for over a year, was finally decided upon because, as President Edward Boyce wrote: "We believe that the only true system of accomplishing this [the elevation of the laboring masses of our country] is the federation of all organizations under one head working for the same cause and voting as one man."[36] Barely was affiliation achieved, however, when a bitter dispute arose between the W. F. of M. and the A. F. of L. The ostensible issue was lack of support by the A. F. of L. Executive Council for the Leadville strike being conducted by the W. F. of M. to defeat a wage reduction.* Actually, the lack of financial help from the A. F. of L. leadership was a secondary reason for the dispute between the two organizations. At the root of the conflict was a sharp difference over ideology and tactics. Edward Boyce returned from the 1896 A. F. of L. convention a disappointed and disillusioned man. In a statement to the 1897 W. F. of M. convention, he declared that during the six days of proceedings at the A. F. of L. gathering, "there was nothing accomplished in the interests of labor." He had been sickened by "the centralization of control in a few hands and the dearth of rank-and-file influence, as well as the low intellectual plane of the program." He was convinced, he later informed Gompers, that it was "time to do something different than to meet in annual conventions and fool away time in adopting resolutions indorsing labels and boycotts." He was further convinced that the increasing concentration and combination of capital, culminating in the rise of giant monopolies, had rendered the craft unionism of the A. F. of L. obsolete.[37] "I am convinced that the day of its usefulness is past," he wrote to Gompers, emphasizing that it divided the workers rather than uniting them."[38]†

* The strike was broken in the fall of 1896 when over 600 militiamen were sent into the area. Some of the strikers still held out, and the troops remained at full strength until February 1897, and were not entirely withdrawn until March 10, 1897.

† Throughout its history, the W. F. of M. repeatedly criticized craft unionism. Its point of view was perhaps most succinctly stated by the executive committee in its report to the 1907 convention: "Wealth and control of industry accumulate constantly in fewer and fewer hands, and experience proves that the old craft or trade unions are unable to cope with the growing power of the employers. The trade unions foster a condition in which one set of workers are pitted against another set to the injury of both, and misleads the workers to believe that their interests are identical with the employers. When one set of workers is in-

Although the W. F. of M. at its convention in May 1897 did not formally withdraw its affiliation with the A. F. of L., it paid no per capita tax so that the affiliation was purely on paper.* By 1900 all connections between the two organizations had ceased.

In May 1904, a committee of four officials appointed by Gompers visited the W. F. of M. convention in Denver to invite the union to re-affiliate with the A. F. of L. They reported that they had been "well received," that their remarks "urging affiliation" were "highly appreciated," and that "there was a strong feeling on the part of the delegates to affiliate with the American Federation." It appears that the committee exaggerated the extent of sentiment at the convention for affiliation, for by this time, the western miners "were overwhelmingly wedded to the principle of industrial unionism," were fairly well convinced that there was little chance of achieving a more effective organization of the working class through the A. F. of L. and its dominant form of craft unionism, and were further convinced that "Samuel Gompers, John Mitchell, and others [in the leadership of the A. F. of L.] were misleading the labor movement."[39] But even if the report of the A. F. of L. committee was accurate, the reprehensible conduct of the Federation's leadership in the Colorado struggles in which the W. F. of M. was then engaged, doomed all hope of achieving affiliation.

Despite the mounting terrorism against the W. F. of M. and the protests of many A. F. of L. affiliates over the attacks on the civil liberties of the striking miners, the Federation's leadership maintained a strict silence on the subject all through 1903 and the early months of 1904. The Erie *People,* official organ of the Central Labor Union of Erie, Pennsylvania, expressed the feeling of many A. F. of L. members when it noted bitterly that the April 1904 issue of the *American Federationist* devoted 17 pages to Gompers' report on his journey through Puerto Rico, and not a single line about Colorado. "The stirring events in Colorado, the infamies of Telluride and the unspeakable outrage committed on union labor should certainly furnish a theme worthy of the pages of the first union publication in the land. But there isn't a word about these things in it. Not a blamed word."[40]

The truth is that the A. F. of L. leaders had been in close touch with the situation in Colorado, and were receiving reports from its organizers

---

jured, all are injured, and it should be the concern of all." (*Proceedings,* W. F. of M. Convention, 1907, p. 143.)

* Vernon H. Jensen asserts that "the W. F. of M. at its convention in May, 1897, formally withdrew its affiliation with the A.F. of L." (*Heritage of Conflict: Labor Relations in the Nonferrous Metals Industry up to 1930,* Ithaca, New York, p. 62.) This is not correct. There was no formal act of disaffiliation. On March 30, 1898, the W. F. of M. was described by the A.F. of L. as "members of the A.F. of L. . . . not in good standing with the A.F. of L. (Jas. O'Connell to Gompers, Mar. 30, 1898, *AFL Corr.*)

in the area. These reports emphasized that the attack on the miners was not an attempt "to crush out organized labor. It is more a question of tramping out Socialism than anything else. The cause of the trouble is the adoption of socialistic ideas by the Western Fed. of Miners." Since the A. F. of L. leadership was not loath to see the "tramping out of Socialism," it decided to say nothing about the military despotism in Colorado. But this placed the leadership in somewhat of a dilemma. "If we say nothing about it I fear we will be severely criticized and if we say what we would like to and reveal what we have learned from these reports, it will be equally hurtful," John B. Lennon wrote to Morrison on March 8, 1904. The decision was to say nothing.[41]

But by June 1904, it became impossible for the A. F. of L. leadership to keep silent any longer. The Chicago Federation of Labor requested Gompers to call a conference of all delegates of all central labor bodies in the United States to consider the situation in Colorado. A few other central bodies and international union leaders endorsed the plan, but Gompers refused to call such a meeting.* However, under pressure to do something for the miners, he issued an appeal for financial assistance in which while denouncing the fact that all civilized law and constitutional rights in Colorado were being trampled under foot, he hinted that he thought the W. F. of M. had probably committed some of the "crimes" it had been accused of, and made it clear "that there are certain policies pursued by the Western Federation of Miners that run counter to those advocated by the American Federation of Labor." Gompers appealed to all organized labor and its friends to send financial assistance to aid the arrested miners to secure redress through the federal courts.[42]

The W. F. of M. welcomed the appeal for financial assistance, though it was annoyed by Gompers' implication that the strikers were probably guilty of the "crimes" of which they were accused. But neither it nor the Chicago Federation of Labor was satisfied that Gompers' appeal was sufficient to meet the situation. On July 2, the latter body resolved that since "President Gompers has taken no action in this direction up to this time, notwithstanding the appalling condition of our Brothers in Colorado," it would call the conference of central bodies itself, to meet

* This was not the first time the A.F. of L. leadership refused to call a convention to aid the hard-pressed miners in the West. In the Coeur d'Alene strike in 1899, W. F. of M. President Boyce had wired Gompers urging him to call a national union labor convention in Chicago "to protest against the usurpation of power by Military authorities in Idaho." Gompers rejected this appeal and he received immediate backing from the A.F. of L. Executive Council. Gompers was denounced by the W. F. of M. as being "a tool of the Trust," and charged with having refused to call the conference because he did not want to antagonize the Standard Oil combine. (Ed Boyce to Gompers, June 28, 1899; Gompers to Edward Boyce, June 30, 1899; D. C. Coates to Gompers, July 24, 1899. *AFL Corr.*)

in Victor, Colorado, on August 25 "for the purpose of considering the effect of the official lawlessness of the Officials of the State of Colorado, on the movement of America, and devising ways and means of meeting this new capitalistic method of dealing with labor organizations." The call was handed to Gompers while he was in Chicago, and he was asked to endorse it; in addition, he was informed that President Moyer of the W. F. of M. was of the opinion that such a convention "would be of great benefit to organized labor, and to the country in general, in showing up the deplorable state of affairs that exist at the present time in the State of Colorado," and that he had pleaded that "everything possible should be done to secure Pres. Gompers' endorsement to the call."[43]

Gompers refused. "I have declined to give my sanction to calling such a congress or to encourage it," he informed the A. F. of L. Executive Council. He explained that he could not sanction a meeting which might commit the labor movement to some declaration by men "who can not represent the rank and file of the bona fide labor movement of the country."[44] Of course, it was precisely for the purpose of securing the expression of the rank and file that the conference was called, for the city centrals were closer to the ranks than were the leaders of the international unions or even the conventions of the A. F. of L.

Early in August, Gompers made a speech to the Baltimore Federation of Labor. He felt impelled to take notice of the charge that he lacked sympathy for the striking miners in Colorado. He denied this and asserted that their cause was just, but went on to say that they had made many mistakes. Although no evidence had been presented connecting the union with any violence, and the arrested strikers had not yet been brought to trial,* Gompers denounced the W. F. of M. for not adhering to the principles of law and order and for not obeying the authorities. "No strike succeeds," he stated, "that disobeys the law and no union man attains the end who resists those who are sent to enforce the law."[45]

"Gompers in League with Western Mine Owners to Defeat Colorado Strike," ran a headline in a western labor paper, and, in an angry editorial, it accused the A. F. of L. leaders of being "willing to sacrifice the hopes of the working class at the beck and call of capitalism." As long as men like Gompers stood at the head of the A. F. of L., declared the *Miners' Magazine,* it was useless to talk further of affiliation with it by the W. F. of M. "We have the warmest fraternal feeling for the rank and file of the men whose names are enrolled upon the register of the American Federation of Labor, but we have no bouquets to present to the vice-president of the Civic Federation."[46]

The refusal of the W. F. of M. to reaffiliate with the A. F. of L. does not mean that it pursued a policy of going it alone. Not long after it

---

* It was not until January 1905 that the officers of the W. F. of M. were brought to trial, and the case was dismissed for lack of evidence.

severed its relations with the A. F. of L., the W. F. of M. began using whatever energy and funds it could spare from its own continuous struggles to build a federation based on industrial unionism to organize all workers, regardless of race, creed, color, sex, national origin, or skill. Starting in the West, this Federation, it was hoped, would eventually encompass the entire nation.*

* Since Chapters 15 and 16 were written the following works have appeared which are also worth consulting in addition to the sources referred to in the Reference Notes: Melvyn Dubofsky, "The Leadville Strike of 1896–1897: An Appraisal," *Mid-America,* XLVIII, April, 1966, 99–118; "The Origins of Western Working Class Radicalism, 1890–1905," *Labor History,* VII, Spring, 1966, 131–54; "James H. Hawley and the Origins of the Haywood Case, 1892–1899," *Pacific Northwest Quarterly,* LVIII, January, 1967, 23–32. Much of this material appears also in Melvyn Dubofsky, *We Shall Be All: A History of the Industrial Workers of the World,* Chicago, 1969, 19–80.

CHAPTER 16

The American Labor Union

In 1906 President Charles F. Moyer declared proudly that for nearly ten years the W. F. of M. "has been in the vanguard of a movement which is arousing the great majority of the army of labor to a realization of their power."[1] The movement referred to was one that sought to organize the American workers, and especially those in the trustified, mass production industries, by means of industrial unionism. Moyer placed the beginning of the W. F. of M.'s real activity in this movement in 1897 when it took the initiative in forming a federation of the workers in the West.

A FEDERATION OF WESTERN WORKERS

The idea of such a federation was not a new one. Even in the late 'eighties and early 'nineties, various western unions, charging that the A. F. of L. had done nothing for the workers in the West, raised the question of a separate western federation. Gompers himself acknowledged the existence of this feeling as early as 1891 when he wrote: "For years the Trade Unions of the far West and the Pacific Coast have been complaining that they are entirely neglected in the consideration of the Trade Unionists of the East and North."[2] The A. F. of L., however, did little to overcome this feeling.

In November 1897, the State Trade and Labor Council of Montana, on independent organization not affiliated with the A. F. of L. because it felt that the western workers were neglected by the latter, met in convention and adopted a resolution calling for a general "western federation" of labor. A month later, the W. F. of M. took similar action. At its executive board meeting on December 28, 1897, it was decided to circularize all locals on the question: "Do you favor extending an invitation to various labor organizations of the West to meet with us for a two or three day discussion for the purpose of bringing all labor organizations in the West into closer touch?" When the majority answered affirmatively, an invitation was sent announcing a conference at Salt Lake City on May 10, 1898.[3]*

Delegates assembled at Salt Lake City from Rossland, British Columbia; Galveston, Texas; San Francisco, and from South Dakota as well as Colorado, Montana, Wyoming, and Washington. Boyce told the gathering that in sponsoring the western federation, the W. F. of M. had no intention of disrupting the American labor movement. Its purpose was to join with other laboring men and women who "irrespective of occupation, nationality, creed or color, are determined that no corporation, trust, syndicate, or injunction shall longer deprive them of their inherent rights." One of the major objectives of the new federation would be to eliminate "inattention to the unskilled workmen" who, under existing industrial conditions, were becoming more and more the major force in the working class.[4]

THE WESTERN LABOR UNION

Following Boyce's statement, a Committee of Five proposed the establishment of the Western Labor Union. The W.L.U. was not to be a dual union, and the members could "continue their affiliation with existing national trades organizations and their respective state central bodies." In its future organizing work, the W.L.U. would concentrate on "unattached bodies of workmen," particularly the unskilled, and, wherever possible, concentrate on the industrial form of unionism. Labor had to adjust itself to the changes in the methods of production, and its form of organization had to reflect these changes. "The method of production of 50 years ago would be ridiculous today: the employer has changed from the single individual to the corporation, and from the corporation to the trust, while the plan of unionism (adopted by most unions) is still practically that of our grandfathers. . . . Through the medium of the Western Labor Union, such rights as the tradesmen now enjoyed will be extended to the common laborer." In this way, skilled and unskilled would be united in a struggle against their common foe: the trusts.

By a vote of 101 to 7, the Salt Lake City conference adopted the report and formally established the Western Labor Union. The W. F. of M. became the first chartered body and the Montana State Trades and

* The A.F. of L. Executive Council sent Gompers to attend the Salt Lake City conference "to place the A.F. of L. before [the] assembled delegates in its true light," and try to head off the formation of the western labor federation. But it was to no avail. On the contrary, the westerners were furious that the A.F. of L. thought of sending emissaries into the area only when there was a threat to its power. (H. E. Garman to Gompers, Feb. 23, 1898; Gompers to A.F. of L. Executive Council, May 16, 1898, *AFL Corr.* and *GLB;* Pueblo *Courier,* June 3, 1898.)

Labor Council the second. Daniel McDonald, leader of the Molders' Union of Butte, Montana, and vice-president of the Montana State Trades and Labor Council, was elected president of the new organization. The Pueblo *Courier* was made official organ.[5] In accepting the "honor," the *Courier* declared: "We hail with joy the formation of the Western Labor Union which has progress for its main object. This forward movement so auspiciously begun in the West, will permeate the labor movement in the East, and when that is accomplished we may look for the laboring man to come into his own."[6]

In October 1899, there were 65 trades and labor unions in Montana, Colorado, and Idaho, and one in Rossland, British Columbia, affiliated with the W.L.U. The W. F. of M. was the largest and strongest of these unions, and others consisted of cooks, waiters, butchers, clerks, musicians, lumbermen, bricklayers, and stonemasons.[7]

WAR BETWEEN A. F. OF L. AND W.L.U.

Michael Raphael, A. F. of L. organizer in the West, urged Gompers "to recognize the W.L.U.," pointing out that the movement reflected the sentiments of many western workers, including most A. F. of L. members in the region. Since most of the W.L.U. branches were also affiliated to A. F. of L. unions, it would be wise for the Federation not to take any step that would force them to decide between the A. F. of L. and the W.L.U.[8]

Raphael was correct in pointing to the dual affiliation of western unionists. The W.L.U. did not insist that its members choose between it and the A. F. of L. Moreover, even A. F. of L. organizers conceded that the W.L.U. and its members loyally supported all boycotts of A. F. of L. unions, both of eastern and western affiliates, and the boycotted products were driven from every mining camp and town where the W.L.U. had influence. But the A. F. of L. leadership refused to tolerate the existence of the W.L.U.; the only prospect they held out to the western movement was to abandon the field. When the W.L.U. refused to commit suicide, the A. F. of L. leadership decided that it must be destroyed. A. F. of L. organizers in the West were instructed to devote themselves entirely to splitting away branches from the W.L.U. On January 18, 1900, W. G. Armstrong, A. F. of L. organizer, reported to Morrison from Seattle that he was zealously carrying out the instructions from national headquarters with the following results:

"We got the Bakers out of the Western Labor Union and they are now only in the national [of the A. F. of L.]. The ice men, upholsterers and laundry workers are on the edge of sending back their charter. After I clean them up here I will try and kill them off in Spokane. . . . In this connection I might say, that one or two other organizations in

Seattle will return their charter to the Western Federation within the next week or ten days. The only other stronghold in the State is at Everett. I have been up there twice and believe we'll have them in line in a very short time."

Armstrong was anxious that his activities be kept secret, for he added: "Now Frank, what I have written is for the Ex[ecutive] Council and yourself of the A. F. of L., and don't let it get out. I am giving the Western Federation what they need in my own way, and don't want them to 'get on.'" Armstrong's "own way" consisted of organizing men who scabbed during strikes conducted by W.L.U. affiliates, and bringing them into the A. F. of L. Protests against this anti-union conduct directed to the A. F. of L. leadership from Seattle were ignored.[9]

Despite the "rule or ruin policy of the paid agents" of the A. F. of L., the W.L.U. continued to grow. Between May 1901 and February 1902, it issued 71 charters, 17 to unions in Denver, and the other 54 to unions throughout the intermountain states. So remarkable was this achievement in Denver where little organizing work of any consequence had been done in over a decade, that in March 1902 the Denver Trades and Labor Assembly voted by a substantial majority to return its charter of affiliation to the A. F. of L.[10] On March 29, 1902, an A. F. of L. leader in the West wrote confidentially to Frank Morrison in response to a request asking him to report frankly on "the strength of the Western Labor Union":

"In re strength of W.L.U.—McDonald claims membership of 40,000. If you or others at the head of the A. F. of L. would visit this country, you would be very much surprised at its strength. The slogan 'Its a Western Union for Western men' holds the ear of the enthusiastic and hardy Westerners and the quick and ready response which the W.L.U. makes to appeals for aid, gains their sympathy and co-operation. Several Spokane locals have been thus aided when they sorely needed it in a hurry. An instance—last fall the Bakers who were affiliated with their [A. F. of L.] international and also with the W.L.U. (5 or 6 other Spokane locals in same condition) had trouble and telegraphed both unions for aid. In three days, they received check for $50.00 from W.L.U. and in six weeks received check for $50 from their International. There are numerous cases of this kind in W.L.U. centers and is one of the chief reasons for supporting the W.L.U."[11]

The report convinced the A. F. of L. Executive Council that steps had to be taken immediately to halt the further growth of the Western movement.[12] The W. F. of M. and the W.L.U. were holding conventions simultaneously in Denver in June 1902. (A third convention was held at the same time in conjunction with the other two, that of the United Association of Hotel and Restaurant Employes, affiliated to the W.L.U.) Morrison and Vice-President Thomas Kidd were designated to represent the A. F. of L. Executive Council and convey the Federation's demand that the two organizations affiliate with the A. F. of L. in the interest of labor unity.

At first Morrison and Kidd were well received, and a resolution was adopted by the W. F. of M. thanking them for coming and extending "good wishes . . . for the success of the General Movement." The delegates to the W.L.U. convention were impressed by the peaceful overtures of the A. F. of L. emissaries, and were prepared "to bring about reconciliation between the A. F. of L. and the W.L.U." But the atmosphere changed when Morrison and Kidd told the W.L.U. that unless it immediately affiliated with the A. F. of L., the Federation would take steps to destroy it by setting up rival unions in all of the western states, and that within six months, the W.L.U. would be a thing of the past.[13] This threat of "annihilation" by men invited to present the need for labor unity infuriated the delegates. The finishing touch came when the delegates learned that Morrison and Kidd were busy helping J. D. Pierce, A. F. of L. organizer in Denver, already notorious for his collusion with employers against W.L.U. unions, to smash a building trades strike in the city led by the W.L.U. A. F. of L.-sponsored scabbing in the building trades strike "turned the stomach of all who before had an appetite for peace."[14]

The infuriated delegates called on Eugene V. Debs, a convention guest, to answer the A. F. of L. threats. Debs began by asserting that he, too, was in favor of labor unity, and was willing to make "any sacrifice to secure that unity save one, and that is principle and honor." With the original formation of the W.L.U., he had had nothing to do. But if the causes that led to its formation were "justifiable" at that time, "the years that have since intervened have simply served to vindicate the wisdom of such action." It was not the W.L.U. but the A. F. of L. which prevented the realization of labor unity. When the A. F. of L. refused to organize unskilled workers, particularly Negro, women and foreign-born workers, when it refused to organize the mass-production industries, when it clung to the outmoded forms of craft unionism, when its leaders spent their time consorting with the enemies of labor in the National Civic Federation instead of devoting themselves to organizing the unorganized, the A. F. of L. assumed the responsibility for promoting disunity in the ranks of labor. To achieve unity by yielding to the "reactionary outlook" of the A. F. of L. would be to sacrifice the needs of the great mass of the unorganized workers in the mass production industries. When the A. F. of L. would sever its ties with the National Civic Federation, ending an association which was undermining the very basis of the labor movement, agree to organize the unorganized into industrial unions, thereby equipping the trade unions "with a rapid-fire gun in the modern warfare instead of the old blunderbuss," and recognize the need for the trade unions to take a stand "upon a political platform"—then would be the time for unity. Meanwhile, Debs called upon the delegates to meet the threatened A. F. of L. raids by making the Western Labor Union a national movement, change its name to the American Labor Union, declare in favor of socialism, and institute a national organizing campaign, concentrating in the East, where, he assured the delegates, they would secure enthusiastic recruits.[15]

Morrison was given the opportunity to answer, and he charged that Debs was simply trying to win recruits for the Socialist Party and was not really interested in building the trade union movement. "I pointed out," he wrote to the A. F. of L. Executive Council, "that the ideas that he advocated could be accomplished under the American Federation of Labor."[16]

The delegates were not convinced by Morrison's assurance. The participation of the A. F. of L. leaders in the formation and development of the National Civic Federation where they joined hands with leaders of big business was enough to cast doubt on Morrison's statement. "The western workingmen," declared the *Miners' Magazine* scornfully, "are not yet prepared to follow Mr. Gompers into Mark Hanna's wigwam to be scalped with the knife of capitalistic arbitration and become the toy of Republican politicians. . . . The Western Federation of Miners and the Western Labor Union are ready to join forces with any labor organization that offers a remedy, but they don't propose to be led like sheep into a slaughter pen to await the butcher's knife without a struggle."[17]

FORMATION OF THE AMERICAN LABOR UNION

Every one of Debs' proposals was enthusiastically adopted. The name of the Western Labor Union was changed to the American Labor Union, thus enabling it to "unfurl its flag in every state of the union," officers were elected,* and a statement of principles adopted which asserted that the increasing exploitation of labor and the increasing might of monopoly capitalism "necessitated a class conscious movement upon the part of the toilers." Experience had demonstrated over and over again that "the older form of organization," represented by the A. F. of L., was "unable to cope with the recent aggressions of plutocracy obtained by class legislation and especially maintained through the medium of friendly courts." The A.L.U. came out for industrial unionism, independent working class political action, and adopted the platform of the Socialist

* The officers were: Daniel McDonald, Butte, Montana, president; D. F. O'Shea, Cripple Creek, Colorado, vice-president; Clarence Smith, Butte, Montana, secretary-treasurer. Members of the executive board were from Colorado, Montana, Washington, and Wyoming.

Party of America "in its entirety as the political platform and program of the American Labor Union." The statement concluded with the appeal: "Believing that complete organization is necessary for the overthrow of the present inhuman method of production and distribution, and that the above plan offers the most practical, economical and reasonable way to success, we invite the people of America to join with us in the cause of humanity."[18]

In his confidential report to the A. F. of L. Executive Council, Morrison emphasized that the formation of the A.L.U. was primarily a Socialist plot "for the purpose of agitating and creating discontent among workers in the hope of using the Western Labor Union for organizing the workers now un-organized and stampeding them into the Socialist Party." The plot, he charged, had been engineered from the national headquarters of the Socialist Party, and the leadership of the party had decided "to martial all their forces" in the West, using the new labor organization as the way "to entrench themselves in the Inter-Mountain States."[19]

Although it was quite an admission on Morrison's part to give the Socialists credit for seeking to organize "the workers now un-organized," he was way off the mark in attributing the formation of the A.L.U. to the national leadership of the Socialist Party. Actually, the majority of the party leadership viewed the formation of the A.L.U. with anything but enthusiasm. To be sure, a number of Socialist papers lukewarmly welcomed the endorsement of socialism by the A.L.U., and one or two hailed the action of the W.L.U. convention in changing its name, declaring in favor of socialism, and beginning organizing campaigns throughout the nation. According to *The Comrade*, a Socialist monthly published in New York, "no more important event, and certainly none of greater encouragement to the Socialist, has occurred in recent years . . . this action . . . is for us, full of inspiration and encouragement. Everywhere it should inspire us to further endeavor and sacrifice."[20]

The majority of the Socialist press and party leaders, however, condemned the decision of the Denver convention as fostering dual unionism, for it was obvious that "the A.L.U. cannot expand east of the Mississippi without getting into a most disastrous fight against the A. F. of L." Socialists were warned not to help build the A.L.U.; were instructed by the Local Quorum, which was empowered to make policy and issue statements for the national organization, to recognize the formation of the A.L.U. as a serious tactical error, and to help bring that union into the A. F. of L. Those Socialists who were working to build the A.L.U. were "misrepresenting the attitude of our party and compromising it in their attempts to build up a rival organization to the American Federation of Labor."[21]

This was too much for Debs, and he replied to the Local Quorum and all Socialists who endorsed its position in an article published in the *International Socialist Review*, November 1902. He began by stating that the events at Denver "so entirely compatible with the Socialist conception of class-conscious and progressive trades-unionism, should have met with the prompt and hearty approbation of every unionist and every Socialist in the land." Unfortunately, this was not the case; instead, the Socialist press, with few exceptions, and the party leadership, had displayed only an attitude of "unfairness and injustice to the Western movement." After making it clear that, in his opinion, these timid Socialists (including the members of the Quorum) were "fawning at the feet of the 'pure and simple' movement of the East," and were "in perfect accord with the capitalist press, and also the 'labor lieutenants,' the henchmen and heelers," Debs charged that they spoke only for themselves and not for the rank and file of the party who, he was convinced, hailed the events at Denver "as a happy augury for the future." He denied the charge that the W.L.U. and its successor, the A.L.U., were dual unions, arguing that an objective history of the labor movement would prove that it was the leaders of the A. F. of L. and not the western workers who had split the trade unions and prevented labor unity. While the western workers had always supported their brothers in the East, the A. F. of L. had persistently sought to destroy their organizations. He acknowledged that labor unity was important, but it could not be made an excuse to cover every crime against the true interests of the workers. The A.L.U. had publicly declared for socialism; why then should the Socialists attack it in favor of its conservative rival? There could be only one answer to this question: these Socialists had apparently decided that "it was wiser policy to curry favor with numbers than to stand by principles."

Debs declared that he was a friend, not the enemy of the A. F. of L., and he urged the Socialists who worked inside the Federation to remain there and "continue their efforts." He assured them that they would receive help from the very existence of the western movement, for the A.L.U. would serve to inspire all workers who favored industrial unionism, socialism and political action, and, in order to hold its own, the A. F. of L. would be compelled to adopt these principles and initiate new organizing efforts. In time, as a result of the work of the progressive forces, inside the A. F. of L. and the pressure from progressive forces, represented by the A.L.U., from without, the labor movement would be united. But it would never be united on the terms insisted upon by the A. F. of L. leaders which meant "to go *back* and *backward* to the American Federation of Labor" and its "pure and simple" unionism:

"There is one way and only one way to unite the American trades-union movement. The American Federation of Labor must go forward to the American Labor Union; the American Labor Union will never go back to the American Federation of Labor. Numbers count for nothing; principle and progress for everything."[22]

Debs' article aroused widespread discussion in Socialist ranks.* Hostility to the stand of the Local Quorum, headed by the national secretary, Leon Greenbaum, mounted; the question was asked over and over again by what right did the Quorum pronounce the A. F. of L. "the established trade union movement."[23]

Although Debs rarely participated in the sessions of the party's National Committee, he carried the battle against the condemnation of the A.L.U. into the Committee. As was to be expected, he met bitter opposition. Berger charged that the supporters of the A.L.U. were doing the party immeasurable harm in the trade unions, and nullifying much of the work of Socialists who were seeking to win support for the cause inside the A. F. of L. Debs countered with the argument that the only truly progressive union was the A.L.U., and that its growth would help the struggle to change the A. F. of L. from an organization tied to the National Civic Federation to one operating along the lines of the class struggle. Hillquit attempted to effect a compromise, but with Debs adamant, he ended up siding with Berger, indicating that the Right and Center were moving closer together. In the end, Debs had his way. The Local Quorum went down to defeat, and the National Committee removed it and Greenbaum from office.† In May 1903, the membership of the party, by a vote of 4,195 to 1,180, confirmed the action of the National Committee in removing the Local Quorum and the national secretary.[24]

Although there were other issues besides the dispute over trade union principles that led to the downfall of the Local Quorum,‡ the outcome gave the Socialists who were helping to build the A.L.U. a free hand to continue their work, and meant that, for the time being, the new movement would not be hampered by open opposition from the Social-

---

* It also aroused discussion among Socialists abroad. Henry Mayers Hyndman, British Socialist and founder of the Social Democratic Federation, praised Debs' article which he called "sound, sober, important & statesmanlike. It gives me a higher opinion of the man than anything I have seen of his." "It seems to me," he wrote to A. M. Simons, "you in America, though moving faster than we are, have precisely the same difficulties with the Old Trade Unions (with their 'bosses') that we have; likewise similar trouble with ambitious & mutually jealous individualists 'on the make.'" "I saw Gompers in Paris in 1889 & mistrusted him then," he added. "He made no pretence then to be a class-conscious Socialist any more than, I gather, he does now" (Letter, 1902, in A. M. Simons Papers, WSHS.)

† Greenbaum was replaced by William Mailly, a young coal miner. Greenbaum immediately left the Socialist Party, and devoted himself to assisting the A.F. of L. in its attack on the A.L.U. (*The Worker,* Jan. 24, 1904.)

‡ A major issue was the battle over whether Socialists should endorse or support, in any fashion, labor parties sponsored by the trade unions.

ist Party. This was no small victory, for the A.L.U. had its hands full meeting the opposition of the A. F. of L.

A. F. OF L. ATTACKS ON A.L.U.

In his report on the Denver Convention, Morrison urged the A. F. of L. and the national and international unions immediately to "take some preventive measures to prevent success of any kind for the Western movement." He called for "continuous agitation" in the intermountain states "to organize the crafts and callings. With such an agitation the efforts of the Socialist Agitators could be minimized and after the next election had taken place the American Federation of Labor would be in a position to absorb all unions that had any staying qualities now affiliated with the Western Labor Union." Upon receipt of Morrison's communication, the Executive Council authorized Gompers to immediately launch a campaign to combat the A.L.U. Gompers sent organizers to Colorado, Washington, and the Southwest, and asked the waiters', barbers', and butchers' unions which had the most defections to the western movement, to send organizers into the territory. He opened a branch headquarters in Denver for the A. F. of L. organizing campaign. In July 1902, Gompers embarked on a six-week organizing tour to the West. Mass meetings and parades were arranged in all the major cities from Chicago to the coast, and particularly in the strongholds of the A.L.U.[25]

Here then appeared to be concrete evidence to buttress Debs' argument that the existence of the western labor movement would compel the A. F. of L. to organize in areas which it had hitherto completely neglected. Unfortunately, events soon demonstrated that the A. F. of L. leadership was bent more on destroying the A.L.U. than on competing with it in organizing the unorganized.

Gompers' message everywhere in his six-week tour of the West was the same—the necessity for unity in the labor movement and the danger and folly of dual unionism. But the way in which the A. F. of L. organizers operated in the West contradicted this theme. In most cases, when the A.L.U. had organized a shop or mill and found it necessary to declare a strike, the A. F. of L. organizer in the vicinity stepped in, organized those who refused to obey the strike call, signed an agreement with the employers on conditions a good deal worse than those demanded by the A.L.U., and affiliated the local union with the international which had jurisdiction in the field and the A. F. of L. Naturally, the A.L.U. condemned these as "dual organizations" and "scab unions," and accused the A. F. of L. leadership of "scurrilous, treacherous, damnable methods, even more disreputable than could be conceived and executed by the direct enemies of labor in the ranks of capitalism."

Even important A. F. of L. spokesmen were disturbed by these anti-union practices. "We are getting a bad reputation through all this," Furuseth complained to Gompers from the Pacific Coast, "and such actions by our organizers are causing workers in the West to call us scabs, and, in my opinion, are responsible for increasing the drift to the American Labor Union." James O'Connell, international president of the Machinists' Union, informed Gompers that the members of his organization in the West were flooding him with complaints against the role of A. F. of L. organizers in granting charters to men who scabbed during A.L.U. strikes, and that this "has placed me in a most awkward position to our membership," since as a member of the Executive Council he was being held responsible. He urged Gompers to issue instructions to organizers to cease such activity, for it was obviously an issue that was "of great importance to the labor movement in the West and even members of our international are hammering the Federation with restraint over this issue." "I have always been a strong advocate of the A. F. of L.," he concluded, "but confess that of late my confidence is being very badly shaken." Even so conservative a labor leader as Lennon criticized J. D. Pierce, A. F. of L. organizer in Denver, for organizing "scab unions," and predicted to Morrison that unless this type of activity was cut short, the remaining unions affiliated with the A. F. of L. in Denver would join the A.L.U. "I keep constantly posted as to the situation in Denver and know that the unions that ever stood by the A. F. of L. are one at a time dropping away from the [A. F. of L.'s] Assembly; they may maintain an independent position for a while, but sooner or later they will be into the new organization."[26]

Since complaints against Pierce were widespread, Gompers went through the routine of asking him for an explanation. Pierce defended himself with the argument that the complaints came from "Socialists," and insisted that "to change our policy would place us back again where we were a year ago." He conceded that he had organized workers who had refused to leave work during strikes called by the A.L.U., but argued that any and every method was justified in fighting "Socialists and secessionists. We have got to lick them by fair means or foul; no use to pat them on the back for while you are doing that, they will stick a knife in your ribs." Finally, he demanded that Gompers endorse his work, for "I wonder how long I have got to fight not only those who would disrupt our movement, but also those who should give me their full support." Gompers assured Pierce that he had his support, and that he need not worry about criticism, whatever the source. But Lennon's prediction came true. Not only did most of the unions affiliated with the Denver Trades Council, A. F. of L., drop out, but the Council itself joined the A.L.U.[27]

Despite the attacks of the A. F. of L., the A.L.U. continued to support all strikes and boycotts of Federation affiliates. The November 27, 1902, issue of the *American Labor Union Journal,* official organ of the A.L.U., proudly reported that the Cripple Creek Trades and Labor Assembly, A.L.U., had voted to force all nonunion cigars out of the district by honoring the Cigar Makers' Union (A. F. of L.) labels. "Thus the members of the American Labor Union continue to fight for the labels of the American Federation of Labor while the paid organizers of that organization work for the disruption and destruction of the unions belonging to the American Labor Union." The *Journal* also reported that the A.L.U. in Denver was cooperating with the National Teamsters' Union, A. F. of L., in helping to organize the unorganized teamsters of that city.[28]

GROWTH OF THE A.L.U.

According to the report of Secretary-Treasurer Clarence Smith, the first year of the A.L.U.'s existence,* was significant for the addition of about 50,000 new members, bringing "the actual per capita paying membership close to the 100,000 mark."[29]† It also saw the issuance of charters for 151 local unions, five district unions and one international union. The last-mentioned was the United Brotherhood of Railway Employees which, with its reputed 35,000 members, ranked second in membership to the W. F. of M., the A.L.U.'s most powerful affiliate. The third international union in the A.L.U. was the United Association of Hotel and Restaurant Employees.

The U.B.R.E. was organized at Rosebury, Oregon, on January 27, 1901 by former members of the American Railway Union who felt that the time had arrived to put into practice the fundamental principle of that militant organization—industrial unionism in the railroad industry. Most of them were veterans of the historic Pullman Strike, and they were confident that events since that epochal, though ill-fated, struggle had demonstrated anew to the railroad workers that the craft separatism of the Railroad Brotherhoods, by dividing the workers in their battles against the powerful, finance-capital dominated railroad monopoly, guaranteed their defeat if they should ever choose to strike and constantly weakened their bargaining position. "They [the railroad workers]," declared the founders of the U.B.R.E., "have learned by bitter experience that the men who load and handle the freight, who make, build and repair the tracks, who build and repair the engines and cars, who make

---

* The A.L.U. regarded this as its fifth year of existence, dating its birth from the formation of the Western Labor Union in 1898.

† Because of the scarcity of records it is almost impossible to determine the accuracy of membership figures cited by A.L.U. officials, but it can be assumed that they were exaggerated.

the trains in every department, and who attend to the thousand and one details in connection with the running of a railroad, all depend on the other." There was no room any longer in an industry as completely trustified as was the railroad industry for the old, snobbish attitude that "the engineers are too good to associate with the brakemen, and that the firemen must have nothing to do with the section men." Engineers and brakemen, firemen and section men, and all other railroad workers had to join hands in an industrial union—"the only railway organization competent to cope with the railway trust."

The U.B.R.E. organized the various classes of workers in the railroad industry from track laborer to engineer into separate locals, but they were all united in a division covering an entire railroad system. Though each local managed its own affairs, agreements were drawn up on an industry-wide basis, covering all the workers on the system. In the event of a strike, the entire division struck. "Under this system," the U.B.R.E. explained, "a 'fair' engineer will never be found pulling a scab crew, nor a union switchman operating with a scab engineer."

The U.B.R.E. spread from Oregon into California and other points in the far West down into Texas and across the northern border into Canada. It voted to join the A.L.U. in January 1903, and George Estes, U.B.R.E. president, became a member of the A.L.U. Executive Board. In that same month, the U.B.R.E. won its first big strike on the Canadian Northern Railway, gaining union recognition for all the workers employed on the line, increased wages and an eight-hour day.[30]

The A.L.U. made important gains during its first year in the lumber industry. It was an ideal field for the industrial form of organization. It was not suited for craft organization, since there was a preponderance of unskilled, or at best semi-skilled, workers in the industry, many of whom were migratory, and even had it been possible to allot each man a particular craft, the result would have been an impossible litter of separate unions with one or possibly two or three members in each craft in the camp. The conditions were notorious; hours of work were from 11 to 12 a day and wages were miserably low. The lumberjack was hardly considered civilized by the employers and was generally called a "timber beast." Until the Western Labor Union entered the industry, these workers had been ignored by the trade union movement. The A. F. of L. showed no interest in organizing them, and its affiliate, the Shingle Weavers' Union, confined itself to organizational activity among the skilled shingle weavers, ignoring the sawmill and logging workers, most of whom were semi-skilled or unskilled.[31]

The A.L.U. carried on the work of its predecessor, and set up locals in the lumber camps in California, Oregon, Montana, Washington, and British Columbia. Two important strike victories during the first year of the A.L.U.'s existence received widespread attention in the West; the complete victory of the Crescent City, California, Lumbermen's Union in increasing wages after a fierce struggle, and that of the union in Sequoia, California, in reducing hours from 11 to 10 a day without any reduction in pay.[32]

Apart from the federal labor unions which united workers of different crafts who were not numerous enough to form a local together with semi-skilled, unskilled workers and laborers, the majority of the local unions in the A.L.U. were craft unions in the West which were under the jurisdiction of national and international unions affiliated with the A. F. of L. None of these locals had obeyed the order to withdraw from the A.L.U. In several instances the locals had openly defied the national officers, and in other cases the national unions simply decided to do nothing and allow the locals to retain their affiliation with the A.L.U. These unions of teamsters, musicians, butchers, retail clerks, brewers, meat cutters, building trades workers, etc., were mainly craft in nature, but believed in the A.L.U.'s program of labor solidarity, and, in many cases, in its vision of a socialist society. All believed, moreover, that their interests had been neglected by the A. F. of L. and could be better cared for by an organization centered in the West.

The chief strength of the A.L.U. lay, of course, in Colorado, Montana, Idaho, Washington, California, and British Columbia. (Of the 151 new local unions chartered during the year, 32 were in Montana, 23 in Colorado, 20 in British Columbia, 15 in Washington, and 10 in California.) But it began penetrating into the East during its first year of existence, and four A.L.U. locals were established in New York City, one in New Jersey, three in Ohio, and eight in Massachusetts. Of these the most important was the Lynn local of shoe workers. The A.L.U. began organizing these workers in February 1903 after receiving an appeal from former members of the A. F. of L.'s Boot and Shoe Workers' Union who had quit the organization because the national officers confined themselves to selling labels to the manufacturers while forcing contracts down the throats of workers which contained nothing of benefit to them. The A.L.U. local in Lynn, composed of former members of the Boot and Shoe Workers' Union started a drive to organize an industry which was predominantly unorganized.[33] "I have just returned from Lynn, Mass., and I tell you things are in a bad shape there and if the A. F. of L. don't do something pretty soon they are going to lose that territory and lose it for good," an A. F. of L. organizer wrote to Gompers and Morrison in March 1903. "I find that the Western Federation has already broken into Lynn, and at a street parade last night I saw workers carrying banners which ran—'A.L.U. is good enough for us and better than an outfit which sells labels to our bosses!' Something must be done and that right away. An active and aggressive campaign in Lynn and Vicinity on an entirely new basis is needed or else our movement will get a great set back." But, as we have seen, the leadership of the Boot and Shoe Workers' Union was not the only one in the A. F. of L. guilty of selling labels to the employers who could then continue to function under nonunion conditions. The A. F. of L. continued to operate in Lynn on the old basis, and the A.L.U. continued to win recruits in the shoe factories.[34]

1903 A.L.U. CONVENTION

In his opening address to the 1903 A.L.U.'s convention, President Mc-Donald spoke of the union's "rapid growth and unexpected success, which has come up to our most extravagant expectations." The same theme was struck by Secretary-Treasurer Smith, but he took pains to emphasize that the A.L.U. would have experienced an even greater growth had it not been forced to combat "the opposition not only of the capitalists themselves . . . but also of the emissaries and alleged organizers of the American Federation of Labor." Still he went on to assure the members of the A. F. of L. that "with a true regard for the principles of unionism," the A.L.U. would continue to "loyally support the strikes, boycotts and labels of that organization."[35]

A "true regard for the principles of unionism" was constantly raised at the A.L.U. convention. It arose over the question of sending a protest letter to the Secretary of State requesting the State Department to voice the indignation of the American people to the Russian government over the horrible butchery of the Jews in Kishinev, Russia, and to demand an immediate cessation of such atrocities. A minority report of the Resolutions Committee, while voicing sympathy for the Jewish victims, declared that "we do not deem it wise for the toilers of this continent to appeal to any of its governments to send strong protest and to take steps which would bring about the cessation of bloodshed of innocent people in Russia while the governments of this continent not only allow, but sanction and protect, the commercial barons of this continent in their ever-increasing slaughter of human life." Delegate after delegate condemned this stand as being a violation of "the principles of unionism," and the convention voted overwhelmingly to send the protest to the State Department.[36]

The issue arose also over the admission of Chinese and Japanese workers as members of the A.L.U. Several months before the convention, the A.L.U. *Journal* had criticized the A. F. of L. for excluding Asian workers —it used the term "Mongolians"—from the Federation and for spearheading the movement to exclude them from entering the country. The A.L.U., it declared, realized that the exclusion of "Mongolians" from the labor movement "will not help the workers but only injure them by splitting their ranks." It opposed any legislation restricting their entrance into the country on the ground that such laws never had benefitted the working class.

Evidently some A.L.U. locals objected to this stand, and at the 1903 convention these forces opposed the granting of membership to "Mongolians," claiming that the labor movement already faced difficult problems and that the entrance of these workers into the unions would only aggravate them. But the majority of the delegates united in condemning A.L.U. unions which objected to the admission of Chinese and Japanese workers, and endorsed a resolution which asserted "that we extend a hearty welcome to the Chinese and Japanese, and all other wage earners to become members of our organization; and be it further resolved that the executive board be empowered to take such steps as will see to the complete organization of these people." As one delegate put it:

"A very short time ago we refused to take the Italians, the Scandinavians and the Russians into our unions, and we protested because they took our places when we went on strike, but now that circumstances have forced us to take them into the unions, we find them among the best union men and women on the continent, and I believe that the same thing will apply to the Mongolian when we extend to him the right hand of fellowship and take him into the union as a fellow wage earner, who is being exploited the same as we are."[37]

The overwhelming vote in favor of the resolution welcoming Chinese and Japanese workers was reinforced in the constitution of the A.L.U. drawn up at the convention, Section 2 of which stated: "No working man or woman shall be excluded from membership in local unions because of creed or color."

The constitution reaffirmed the name of the organization as the American Labor Union; its jurisdiction was to extend over the United States, Canada, and Mexico, and was to consist of national and international unions, state, territorial, provincial, district, city, local (industrial and federal), and junior unions. National and international unions were to be "formed on the industrial union plan [and to] admit to membership all eligible persons engaged in the industry, irrespective of the number of crafts required in the operation of each industry." Local industrial unions were to comprise all workers of an industry irrespective of technical craft or trade line. Local federal unions were to admit to membership all eligible persons in a locality who were not united with a national or international union or a local industrial union in that locality, irrespective of the industry or industries in which they were employed. Junior unions were to be composed of boys not under eight or more than 16 years of age, and their main purpose was to "imbue the boys with the spirit of independence and educate them in the principles of unionism."

The constitution included provisions for democratic trade unionism by requiring a referendum of the membership on all important union issues* other than those relating to the calling of strikes. (Since strikes to be effective might have to be called on short notice, it was decided not to include this issue within the area over which the membership would have direct control by referendum.) It further sought to prevent the entrenchment of a trade union bureaucracy by limiting the power of the union leadership to suspend or expel locals or members, and gave those suspended or expelled the full right of appeal to an impartial body which was to exist separate and apart from the union leadership.[38]

The constitution reaffirmed the A.L.U.'s belief in socialism, endorsed the Socialist Party† and incorporated its platform as objectives of the union, and adopted as its motto, "To Labor Belongs All Wealth." (Other mottoes of the A.L.U. were: "One for All, and All for One," and "An Injury to One is the Concern of All.") But it was the provision for industrial unionism that was regarded by the A.L.U. leadership as the key to the entire document. As George Estes, president of the U.B.R.E., put it: "The entire plan of the new Constitution is founded on the principle of uniting the workers together by industries instead of by trades, that is to say, all workers in one industry are to hold membership in one union, irrespective of the number of trades involved. This combines the power of the workers whereas the trades union method, 'pure and simple,' divides that power and leaves the worker prone and helpless against the united strength of the trusts and monopolies."[39]

It is clear that the A.L.U. constitution was a product of both the experience of the western workers in the class struggle and their awareness of what they considered to be "fatal weaknesses" in the A. F. of L. It was a constitution, in the words of Debs, which established "the most advanced and pronounced type of twentieth century unionism in America."[40]

A.L.U. AND A. F. OF L. UNIONS

Although it criticized craft unionism for tending "to create an aristocracy of labor and division between the various trades and callings," the A.L.U., unlike De Leon and the S.T. and L.A., did not call for their com-

---

* The constitution itself was adopted in December 1903 by a referendum vote of the entire membership which was preceded by several months of intensive discussion of each provision in the *American Labor Union Journal*.

† During the convention a resolution was introduced by Butte Clerks' Union condemning the endorsement of the Socialist Party as being in violation of the A.L.U.'s guarantee "to every member of the right to profess any religion or political faith," and urged that the endorsement be rescinded in the new constitution. This was voted down, but later, the A.L.U. Journal took pains to point out that the endorsement of the Socialist Party and its platform "was entirely educational in character and no man forfeits his membership by a refusal to comply." (*Official Proceedings . . . American Labor Union. . . . ,* 1903, p. 47; *A.L.U. Journal,* Jan. 7, 1904.)

plete annihilation. While the A.L.U. insisted that heretofore unorganized workers, particularly those in mass production industries, should be organized directly into industrial unions, it did not advocate that unions which were already in existence should give up their careers and allow their members to join industrial unions. Rather, it recommended that the separate craft unions in a particular industry should gradually amalgamate and function through a joint board as a unified organization during strikes and other struggles, but with each union retaining its identity and control over its affairs. It conceded that this procedure was not as effective as complete industrial unionism, but it was certainly far better than the situation under which the different craft unions in an industry signed separate agreements with employers, and, in the case of strikes, scabbed on each other. Moreover, it would help to solve that "curse of the A. F. of L.—the jurisdiction dispute." This, the A.L.U. pointed out, was an evil particularly in the A. F. of L. building trades' unions, and it recommended that there be organized, through the process of amalgamation, a "United Brotherhood of Building Trades' Workers" which would admit "to general and full membership any and all tradesmen of the various building trades."[41]

It was not necessary for this amalgamation of various unions within a specific industry to take place under the auspices of the A.L.U. The A.L.U. emphasized that it would be quite happy if the craft unions carried through the amalgamation inside the Federation. The A.L.U. would do nothing to interfere with this process, and would be pleased to give it whatever assistance might be required of it.[42]

The A.L.U. stressed that it was not out to take away unions belonging to the A. F. of L., and even some A. F. of L. officials bitterly opposed to the A.L.U. conceded that it did not approve of its organizers chartering locals of A. F. of L. members unless they left the Federation. Owen Miller, secretary of the American Federation of Musicians, wrote to Morrison that an A.L.U. organizer in St. Louis was organizing a local of members of the A. F. of L. union. "I wrote to Clarence Smith about it," he continued, "and he assured me that this was against the policy of the A.L.U. and that it would be stopped. This has been done and I am going to publish the fact in the next number of our official journal."[43]

However, locals which voluntarily left the A. F. of L. because they disagreed with the policies of the international unions or felt that their interests were neglected were accepted into the A.L.U. In a frank letter to Morrison, J. C. Skemp, secretary-treasurer of the A. F. of L.'s Brotherhood of Painters, Decorators and Paperhangers of America, wrote: "If the members of our Portland union are members of the American Labor Union, it is, no doubt, due to the fact that they could not get recognition or support from the Central Body in that city and joined the American Labor Union as a last resort, thinking that perhaps it might bring about some change in condition of affairs in their city. Mr. Noffke who has, along with the others, joined the American Labor Union is undoubtedly one of the most energetic workers in the labor movement on the western coast. He is, I believe, far too intelligent to foster a dual organization which would in any way injure the interests of the organization affiliated with the A. F. of L., and although he may be a member of the American Labor Union, it is not, I believe, with the intention of destroying or tearing down the work which has already been accomplished, but rather for the purpose of redressing the grievances of the Portland local."[44] Needless to say, the A. F. of L. leadership did not publicize such confidential reports which contradicted their consistent contention that the A.L.U. existed for only one purpose—to destroy or tear down the A. F. of L.

In one case, the A.L.U. took in a whole section of an A. F. of L. international union—the Metal Polishers, Buffers, Platers, Brass Molders and Brass and Silver Workers' Union—after the majority of the union membership had voted in a referendum to withdraw from the A. F. of L. and join the A.L.U.

The referendum vote had been preceded by the most intense discussion in the union on the issue of affiliating with the A.L.U. The foes of affiliation, led by President E. J. Lynch, whose arguments were prepared for him by Gompers and Morrison, charged that the A.L.U. was nothing but a "political annex of the Socialist Party," that its policy was "one of disruption," that it had gained nothing for its members, and that nothing could be gained by affiliating with it except the "promise of an Utopian universe if we live long enough." The advocates of affiliation insisted that the A.L.U. was not a political organization, even though it emphasized the importance of political action by labor; conceded that it advocated socialism, "but does not say you must become a Socialist," and that "you may or may not be a Socialist" to enjoy the benefits of the A.L.U.'s program. They cited instances of A.L.U.'s gains for its membership: A.L.U. hotel and restaurant employees in Montana received wages higher than those paid for the same work "any where else in the world"; A.L.U. clerks had an absolutely closed shop, early closing "and a perfect industrial organization in Butte, with the highest wages paid any clerks in America"; A.L.U. laundry workers in Butte had a closed shop, reduced hours, "and higher wages than are paid any other laundry workers in the country"; A.L.U. teamsters received higher wages for an eight-hour day "than are paid any other teamsters, union or non-union"; A.L.U. lumbermen in Montana, Idaho, and California had "the only union conditions and wages for lumbermen in the United States or Canada, the minimum in Montana for the commonest labor in the lumber industry being $2.50 a day"; the A.L.U., through its affiliate, the U.B.R.E., was having success in organizing and improving the conditions of railroad workers in an industrial union "covering every employe from the section hands to the

stenographers in the superintendent's office, securing increases for all."
Finally, the advocates of affiliation contrasted the divisive craft unionism
of the A. F. of L. and the unifying industrial unionism of the A.L.U.
Within the A. F. of L. "we are going backward instead of forward, when
by concentration we could raise industrially the greatest pillar of strength
in modern times. The A.L.U. is founded upon correct principles; its plan
of organization will make the American labor movement as strong as
Gibraltar."[45]

"Many thanks for the assistance given me by Bro. Morrison and yourself," President Lynch wrote to Gompers on October 12, 1904. "From the
statement you have sent me I have gotten up a reply to the resolution
calling for affiliation to the American Labor Union that will bury it for
all time to come." On December 24, Lynch sorrowfully informed Gompers that the referendum in favor of affiliation had received a majority
vote of the membership. "A desperate condition confronts us and desperate methods have to be resorted to," he added. He was even thinking
of altering the returns. "We might throw out some of the locals' votes or
lose them, and by that method carry the proposition in favor of remaining with the Federation by a small vote. . . . This I feel we cannot do,
but I want your opinion. Would you advise this proposition?" The decision was not to tamper with the returns, but to rush through a constitutional amendment permitting five locals to retain the charter of the
A. F. of L. Although most of the members of these five locals withdrew
and joined the A.L.U., the union's leadership refused to accept the will
of the membership. "I feel that I will see the Organization go to ————
before I will let the American Labor Union bunch control it," Lynch
wrote to Gompers.[46]

A. F. of L. unions who believed in industrial unionism and sought to
practice it inside the Federation only to meet with opposition from the
Gompers' leadership and those discriminated against in decisions involving jurisdictional disputes, were invited to join the A.L.U. "The moral
of all these jurisdictional fights and one-sided decisions," the A.L.U.
Journal appealed to the United Brewery Workers and the International
Union of Carriage Workers, is: "All international unions who believe in
the industrial form of organization should get into the American Labor
Union, the organization built on the industrial plan."[47]

The A.L.U. announced that it would respect the jurisdictional claims
of A. F. of L. unions—provided they sincerely sought to organize all the
workers in the industry over which they claimed jurisdiction. But it
would not be bound by these claims if nothing was done to organize
these workers. It refused to recognize the jurisdictional claim of the A. F.
of L.'s union of telephone workers on the ground that it had done
nothing to organize the women in the industry, and it set up several
A.L.U. locals in the Bell Telephone System to which all workers in the

industry were eligible. It refused to recognize the jurisdictional claim of any A. F. of L. international union which excluded Negroes from membership, and organized A.L.U. unions in these areas which were open to all workers regardless of color. "Some men are class conscious," declared the *A.L.U. Journal* in condemning the exclusion of Negroes from a number of A. F. of L. unions, "others are 'craft conscious,' while others are color conscious. There is room in the labor movement only for the class conscious."[48]

"The machine has come and come to stay," the A.L.U. emphasized in criticizing the Cigar Makers' National Union for refusing to organize the machine workers in the industry. It pleaded with George W. Perkins, president of this A. F. of L. affiliate, to organize these workers and stated that it would be willing to lend a hand. But the leadership of the Cigar Makers turned a deaf ear to this plea; as we have seen, it was not interested in organizing the machine workers. The A.L.U. thereupon assigned an organizer to bring these workers into the A.L.U., and succeeded in setting up several locals. "These workers should have been under the control of the Cigar Makers' Union with all the tobacco workers in one organization," the A.L.U. announced in explaining its action. "But the Cigar Makers refused to organize and recognize these workers. These people have a right to organization. Since the Cigar Makers refused them, the A.L.U. was justified in organizing and helping them."[49]

A similar situation was involved in the affiliation of the Manhattan Association of Knife Cutters of New York City with the A.L.U. in December 1903. The Shirt, Waist and Laundry Workers' International Union had been given jurisdiction over these workers by the A. F. of L., but refused to allow them into the union, and repeated communications from the Knife Cutters brought no reply. When the Manhattan Association finally voted to join the A.L.U., the Shirt, Waist and Laundry Workers accused it of "treason to the labor movement for refusing to recognize our jurisdiction rights." But the I.L.G.W.U., affiliated with the A. F. of L., placed the blame squarely on the Laundry Workers' leadership. "The action of the Manhattan Association of Knife Cutters in becoming affiliated with the American Labor Union has been made possible by the refusal of the Laundry Workers to grant said Manhattans a charter."[50]

Even where the A.L.U. organized locals of unorganized workers in an industry over which the A. F. of L. union claimed jurisdiction but refusd or failed completely to organize, these unions assisted the A. F. of L. organizations in their struggles. The most widely publicized example occurred during the packinghouse strike in the summer and early fall of 1904. The A.L.U. organized the Millwrights and Machinery Erectors' Union No. 286 in the packinghouses of Chicago after these workers had been denied admission to the A. F. of L.'s Amalgamated Meat Cutters and Butcher Workmen. When the Amalgamated's strike began, the

A.L.U. union marched out of the packinghouses in a body. Although the Packing Trades' Council, which directed the strike, refused to admit delegates from Local 286, the A.L.U. members continued to stay out, and there was not a single scab among them as long as the strike lasted. During the six weeks its members were out in support of the A. F. of L. strike, the A.L.U. paid them strike benefits from its meager treasury.

This action of A.L.U. Local 286 stood in sharp contrast to that of the A. F. of L. Engineers and Firemen's Union in the packinghouses. These men, having negotiated separate agreements with the employers, remained at work, and operated the machinery which made it possible for the plants to continue operating with scabs, thereby contributing considerably to the smashing victory of the packinghouse trust over the Amalgamated Meat Cutters and Butcher Workmen.[51]

To the A.L.U. the lesson of the disastrous defeat for organized labor was obvious, and while it had refrained from criticizing the A. F. of L. union during the strike, it made its position clear once the battle was over in an appeal "To the Defeated Striker":

"Brother: Just a word with you.

"Organized Labor has been defeated in your particular strike. Why? . . .

"The membership of the American Labor Union, through bitter experience, have learned the lesson and know the answer to the question they are now asking. They know you have failed because—

"*You have never been properly organized; you are not now properly organized; your unions are divided against themselves:*

"*Each craft is independent of other crafts; each international is independent of other internationals.*

"The whole mass is loosely connected in an American Federation of Labor which is absolutely powerless to make a united successful fight against anything, and whose 'leaders' hobnob with your enemies in a Civic Federation.

"Study for yourselves the American Labor Union plan of organization and you will find:

"*Industrialism instead of Craft Division: men organized sensibly in local unions; locals united firmly in industrial organizations.*

"Industrial organizations bound together like bands of steel in the American Labor Union general organization of all industries. . . . Investigate it; unite with it; give it your help; make it supreme; it is your duty."[52]

The appeal brought a response from the disheartened packinghouse workers. One of the most active members of the Amalgamated Meat Cutters and Butcher Workmen wrote to Agnes Nestor: "I believe that the A.L.U. is the only form of organization that can stand any show of winning a fight with the masters in the future. I believe that affiliation with the A.L.U. is our only hope of salvation, that it would not only give us something to lean on, not only help us to organize, but what is more, it would put new life into us. It would revive the old fighting spirit, the old enthusiasm, the old fire, the old love of one for all and all for one."[53]

A.L.U. AND SOCIALIST PARTY

In the early period of its career, the A.L.U. supported the Socialist Party with the utmost enthusiasm. The *American Labor Union Journal* devoted considerable space each week to Socialist Party news and to articles explaining why the workers should vote Socialist. "It is a waste of energy," the *Journal* declared in March 1903, "to organize labor unions without a definite plan for the emancipation of labor from the bonds of wage slavery." This would be achieved primarily through the triumph of the Socialist Party.[54]

The Left-wing in the Socialist Party welcomed these expressions of support from the A.L.U. and called upon the Party to give the union every possible assistance.[55] But the Socialist Party leadership, under the domination of the Right and Center wings, regarded the A.L.U.'s support of the party as a source of acute embarrassment, hindering efforts to win approval of the Socialist program within the A. F. of L. They had only one piece of advice to offer the A.L.U.—disband and join the A. F. of L. This was the tenor of the resolution introduced by the Resolutions Committee at the May 1904 convention of the Socialist Party, and adopted by a vote of 107 to 52. While the resolution did not mention the A.L.U. by name, it clearly condemned it in the sentence: "Neither political nor other differences of opinion justify the division of the force of labor in the industrial movement." "I read in the resolution, as it now stands, an endorsement of the American Federation of Labor," wrote Ernest Untermann who supported the program of the A.L.U.

In opposing adoption of the resolution, a Left-wing delegate predicted that the progressive labor forces who stood for industrial unionism and independent political action would properly interpret it as "a specious endorsement of one kind of unionism," and he warned that before these forces would capitulate to those who were "playing into the hands of the capitalists," they would tell the "convention to go to hell."[56] It was an accurate warning. Not only did the A.L.U. refuse to pay any attention to the resolution, but it grew increasingly resentful of what it regarded as a conspiracy by the Socialist Party officialdom to keep the membership ignorant of what the western labor movement really stood for. The A.L.U. sent a copy of its pamphlet outlining its "principles of Industrial Unionism" to every Socialist paper in the United States and Canada in the fall of 1904, but very few of them even mentioned it. "Although the matter is one of supreme moment to the working class," the A.L.U. *Journal* complained bitterly, "the majority of the papers ignored it." The *Journal* was equally furious when it learned that *St. Louis Labor,* published by the Socialist Party, refused to take an advertisement to be paid for by the A.L.U. on the ground that the organization was a dual union bent on disrupting the labor movement. The same paper, it pointed out, had no hesitancy "in giving aid, comfort, support . . . to a person ('Slimy Sam Gompers') who has shown himself as antagonistic to working class interests as any capitalist in the land."[57]

Early in its career, the A.L.U. had repeatedly tried to convince the leadership of the Socialist Party that it had no quarrel with those Socialists who believed that the role of the militants should be to remain inside the A. F. of L. and fight the Gompers' leadership. But as it became increasingly bitter towards Socialists who criticized it and defended the A. F. of L. leaders, the A.L.U. attacked the entire concept of "Boring from Within." "The architect who remains within a crumbling structure for the purpose of pointing out its weaknesses, in the hope that the other dwellers may correct them, instead of devoting his fine talents to the new and modern steel building which is rapidly erecting across the way," declared the A.L.U. *Journal* in November 1904, "may be professionally praiseworthy, but he is not doing the positive work which the world needs." A month later, it charged that it was hopeless to attempt to convert the A. F. of L. into a militant, class-conscious industrial union. Right-wing and Center Socialists, it sneered, were transforming the Federation at a rate comparable to the growth of a coral reef: "the American Federation of Labor is to the workingman industrially what the Demo-Republican party is to him politically; the former is the union of his craft, while the latter is the party of his craft." In February 1905, the official journal of the A.L.U. declared: "We refuse to recognize the caliphate, seneschalship, suzerainty or dynastic rights of the A. F. of L. to a single toiler in any part of America—north, south, east or west. The socialist who resents the spread of the American Labor Union does so either from ignorance or from inborn craft jealousy, and not because he has at heart the industrial solidarity of the working class."[58]

DECLINE OF THE A.L.U.

To talk of the "spread of the American Labor Union" in February 1905 was to engage in fantasy. Celebrating Labor Day 1903, the A.L.U. claimed a membership in good standing of 100,000 men and women, organized in 276 unions in 24 states, territories, and provinces, "and reaching from the Dominion of Canada to Texas, and North Carolina, and from Massachusetts to Arizona and California." One A.L.U. organizer boasted in December 1903 that "the membership affiliated with the American Labor Union numbers nearly 300,000 members and the A.L.U. controls union affairs west of the Mo. [Missouri] line." Yet, in its appeal to the defeated packinghouse strikers in October 1904, the A.L.U. stated: "It has already united more than sixty thousand of the best fighters of the American labor movement."[59]

The decline in membership from September 1903 was to be explained, according to the A.L.U. *Journal,* by the fact that the dues paid by the membership were too low; locals had perished, and many more were on the point of perishing, through lack of funds.[60] Whether or not this was a valid explanation,* it was certainly true that the union was in desperate financial straits. The fact that the *Journal* was changed from a weekly to a monthly after the July 5, 1904, issue was concrete evidence of this.

In July 1904, the A.L.U. moved its headquarters from Butte to Chicago, explaining that this move was made necessary by the growth of the organization in the East. The A. F. of L. immediately charged that the move was made necessary by the fact that the A. L. U. was in serious financial trouble, and that it had been forced to leave Butte because it had exhausted its credit in that city. "The source of supply has been closed down hence the change," Morrison reported to the A. F. of L. Executive Council.[61]

In the opening months of 1905 even the A.L.U. leadership conceded that the organization had outlived its usefulness, and that it was merely marking time until a more effective organization could carry through its principles. The February 1905 issue of the *Voice of Labor,* the new name of the A.L.U.'s official journal, announced that a conference had just taken place in Chicago to lay the foundation of just such an organization. By the time the last issue of the *Voice of Labor* was published in June 1905, marking the passing of the American Labor Union, this new organization was coming into being—the Industrial Workers of the World.

SIGNIFICANCE OF THE A.L.U.

The A.L.U., at its high point, had no more than 100,000 members. But it was far more important than this figure would imply. For one thing, its activities, particularly in the West, were an influence that stimulated

---

* A.F. of L. officials in the West attributed the decline in membership to the fact that a number of Federation affiliates that had joined the A.L.U. in resentment against neglect by the top leadership and because of their hostility to the unionization of scabs, returned when these policies were changed. Max Morris, secretary-treasurer of the Retail Clerks' Protective Association, wrote to Morrison from Denver that "since this organizer [Pierce] has left this city, we have at least partly succeeded in wiping out the prejudice and antagonism existing toward the American Federation of Labor in this city, and I am of the opinion that the action of these Organizers so far prejudiced the mind of many that it extended to Montana and elsewhere, and assisted the A.L.U. in embittering the minds of the Trade Unionists against the American Federation of Labor." (Jan. 27, 1904, *AFL Corr.*)

some progress within several A. F. of L. unions. On A.L.U. initiative, in a number of unionized or unorganized fields, exemplary struggles were conducted, showing that the workers were willing to fight when given leadership. Moreover, the A.L.U. popularized the whole idea of industrial unionism during a time when this principle of labor organization was being derided by the A. F. of L. leadership. It was for this reason that the A.L.U., like the Western Federation of Miners, was regarded as a menace by the open-shop employers.*

The members of the A. F. of L.'s Metal Polishers union who advocated affiliation with the A.L.U. were correct when they pointed out that "its plan of organization will make the American labor movement as strong as Gibraltar." The A.L.U. was too weak to carry this plan into effect, but as Clarence Smith predicted, "the American Labor Union principles can only gather strength from the economic development of these times. . . . The American Federation of Labor advocates the *segregation of Labor*. The American Labor Union advocates the unification of Labor." The A. F. of L. was mainly concerned with keeping "the workers segregated into narrow craft organizations so that one will not interfere with the other whereas the great problem to be solved by the labor unions of today is how to best combine in order to combat the aggressiveness of capital. If the American Federation of Labor adheres to its declared narrow-minded policy its doom is sealed. On the other hand, the American Labor Union, with its broad and aggressive policy and its declared plan of action, will accomplish the emancipation of the workers of this country."[62]

Smith's prediction aroused widespread laughter among the leaders of the A. F. of L. But on January 28, 1905, Jere L. Sullivan, secretary-treasurer of the A. F. of L.'s Hotel and Restaurant Employees' International Alliance, wrote to Morrison: "Anybody that imagines the A.L.U. is a dead duck has another guess coming. They have the advantage over us, for the reason that most of their members are convinced that its ideas of industrial unionism and Socialism will continue to make headway even if it is not the A.L.U. itself that will carry them forward."[63]

Labor history, in the long run, was to prove Sullivan to be correct.

---

* The Kansas City *Times* of October 1, 1903, carried the text of a speech delivered by J. C. Gray, secretary of the Citizens' Alliance of Denver, at a meeting of open-shop spokesmen in Chicago. "The American Labor Union and the Western Federation of Miners must go," Gray told the delegates. "Both organizations have reached the point where they are dangerous to the community at large. . . . Samuel Gompers, president of the American Federation of Labor, I regard as a comparatively conservative man, and the employers of the West would be glad to see him succeed in extending the control of the American Federation of Labor throughout the West."

REFERENCE NOTES

CHAPTER 1

1. Milton J. Nadworny, *Scientific Management and the Unions, 1900–1932,* Cambridge, Mass., 1955, pp. 3–10.
2. George W. Edward, *The Evolution of American Finance Capital,* London and New York, 1938, p. 132.
3. John Moody, *The Truth About the Trusts,* New York, 1904, pp. 477, 488.
4. Chicago *Socialist,* Jan. 31, 1903; *Amalgamated Engineers' Journal,* March, 1901, pp. 19–20.
5. *Report of the Industrial Commission,* Washington, 1901, vol. VII, pp. 15, 739; T. S. Adams and H. L. Sumner, *Labor Problems,* New York, 1910, pp. 112–15.
6. *The Public,* Oct. 13, 1900.
7. Frederick Lewis Allen, *The Big Change: America Transforms Itself, 1900–1950,* New York, 1952, p. 55.
8. Donata Mary Yates, "Women in Chicago Industries, 1900–1915: A Study of Working Conditions in Factories, Laundries, and Restaurants," unpublished M.A. thesis, University of Chicago, 1948, p. 16.
9. *Leather Workers' Journal,* Feb. 1904, p. 365; New York *American,* Dec. 16, 1903.
10. Paul H. Douglas, *Real Wages in the United States, 1890–1926,* Boston, 1930, pp. 41, 57, 58, 582.
11. *Ibid.,* pp. 43–46; E. B. Sanford, editor, *The Federal Council of Christ in America,* New York, 1909, p. 246.
12. Testimony of Father Hussie before the Coal Commission, in "Proceedings of the Anthracite Coal Strike Commission," Washington, D.C., 1903, No. 11, pp. 1352–86.
13. *Report of Minutes, Board of Education, City of Chicago,* Oct. 2, 1908, p. 4.
14. *The Comrade,* vol. II, Aug. 1903, p. 235.
15. John Spargo, "Child Labor in 'Free' America," *ibid.,* vol. I, July, 1902, p. 222.
16. Allen, *op. cit.,* p. 57.
17. New York State Factory Investigating Commission, *Supplementary Report,* Albany, 1915, pp. 124–37.
18. Pauline Newman, "As I Remember," *25th Anniversary Booklet: New York Women's Trade Union League Clubhouse, 1922–1947,* New York, 1947, p. 4; New York State Factory Investigating Commission, *Preliminary Report,* Albany, 1912, vol. I, p. 162.
19. William J. Walsh, *The United Mine Workers of America as a Social Force in the Anthracite Territory,* Washington, 1931, pp. 83–84.
20. Spargo, *op. cit.,* p. 221.
21. *The Comrade,* vol. II, March, 1903, p. 134; "Proceedings of the Anthracite Coal Commission," *op. cit.,* No. 12, pp. 1573–74; No. 13, pp. 1618–19.
22. New York *Tribune,* Feb. 9, 1914; New York State Factory Investigating Commission, *Fourth Report,* Albany, 1915, vol. I, pp. 34–38; vol. II, pp. 193, 404; vol. III, pp. 1049, 1073; *Third Report,* Albany, 1914, pp. 40–41, 159; *Preliminary Report,* vol. I, pp. 34–36; Charles B. Barnes, *The Longshoremen,* New York, 1915, p. 92.
23. Ellen M. Henrotin, "Organization for Women," *American Federationist,* Nov. 1905, p. 825; Louise C. Odencrantz, *Italian Women in Industry: A Study of Conditions in New York City,* New York, 1919, pp. 151–52; New York State Factory Investigating Commission, *Fourth Report,* vol. V, p. 2810.
24. United States Senate, "Report on Condition of Women and Child Wage-Earners in the United States," 61st Congress, 2nd Session, *Senate Document No. 65,* Washington, 1911, vol. II, p. 158.
25. John A. Fitch, *Hours of Labor in the Steel Industry,* New York, 1912, pp. 4, 5, 6–7; Samuel Waitzman, "The New York City Transit Strike of 1916," unpublished M.A. thesis, Columbia University, 1952, pp. 29–30; St. Louis *Post-Dispatch,* March 11, July 3, 1900; *Senate Document No. 415, op. cit.,* vol. I, pp. 193–212.
26. Mary Van Kleeck, "Working Hours of Women Workers," *Charities and Commons,* vol. XVII, Oct. 6, 1906, pp. 13, 16.

27. Florence Kelley, "Industrial Democracy: Women in Trade Unions," *The Outlook*, vol. LXXXIV, Dec. 1906, p. 926.

28. New York State Factory Investigating Commission, *Supplementary Report*, vol. I, pp. 143–53, 154–57, 200–02.

29. Allen, *op. cit.*, p. 57; *Proceedings*, United Mine Workers Convention, 1905, p. 28.

30. New York State Factory Investigating Commission, *Supplementary Report*, vol. I, pp. 235–43; *Preliminary Report*, vol. I, p. 320.

31. *Ibid., Preliminary Report*, vol. II, pp. 25, 331.

32. New York *Tribune*, March 26, 1911; Leon Stein, *The Triangle Fire*, Philadelphia, 1962.

33. Report of Investigation in *Solidarity*, vol. III, June 15, 1908, p. 15.

34. Cleveland *Citizen*, Aug. 20, 1910.

35. *See especially* Reports of Colorado, New York and Pennsylvania.

36. *Industrial Relations Commission Hearings*, Washington, 1913, vol. VII, p. 6435.

37. Richard Martin Lyon, "The American Association for Labor Legislation and the Fight for Workmen's Compensation Laws, 1906–1942," M.S. thesis, Cornell University, 1952, p. 1.

38. Ives *v.* South Buffalo Railway Company, 201, N.Y. 285.

39. Herbert Hillel Rosenthal, "The Progressive Movement in New York State, 1906–1914," unpublished Ph.D. thesis, Harvard University, 1955, pp. 179–80.

40. John R. Commons and John B. Andrews, *Principles of Labor Legislation*, New York, 1936, 4th edition, p. 232.

41. William A. Marshall, "Workmen's Compensation Laws: Notes on the Beginning," *Oregon Historical Review*, vol. LIV, Dec. 1913, p. 290.

42. Melvyn Dubofsky, "New York City Labor in the Progressive Era, 1910–1918: A Study of Organized Labor in an Era of Reform," unpublished Ph.D. thesis, University of Rochester, 1960, p. 30.

43. M. E. Ravage, *An American in the Making: The Life Story of an Immigrant*, New York, 1917, pp. 66–67; *Senate Document No. 65 op. cit.*, vol. II, pp. 295–98.

44. New York State Factory Investigating Commission, *Preliminary Report*, vol. I, pp. 83–92; *Supplementary Report*, vol. I, pp. 90–123.

45. *Ibid., Second Report*, Albany, 1913, vol.

II, p. 700; vol. IV, pp. 1555, 1609–10; Dubofsky, *op. cit.*, p. 788.

46. *The Survey*, vol. XXXIII, Dec. 5, 1914, p. 246.

47. William Miller, editor, *Men in Business*, Cambridge, Mass., 1952, p. 299.

48. New Orleans *Picayune*, Aug. 16, 1901.

49. Leo Wolman, *The Growth of American Trade Unions, 1880–1923*, New York, 1924, pp. 33–34, 138; *Twenty-First Annual Report of the Commissioner of Labor, 1906*, Washington, 1907, pp. 478–79.

50. Wolman, *op. cit.*, p. 15; Frank T. Morrison to John T. Wilson, Oct. 14, 1903, American Federation of Labor Correspondence. (Hereinafter cited as *AFL Corr.*)

51. Clarence E. Bonnett, *Employers' Associations in the United States*, New York, 1922, pp. 21–23.

52. G. Warren Nutter, *Extent of Monopoly Enterprise in the United States, 1899–1939*, Chicago, 1951, pp. 25–30.

53. W. G. Haber, *Industrial Relations in the Building Industry*, Cambridge, Mass., 1930, pp. 253–54; Harold Seidman, *Labor Czars: A History of Labor Racketeering*, New York, 1938, p. 35.

54. Seidman, *op. cit.*, pp. 41–42; John R. Commons, "The New York Building Trades," *Quarterly Journal of Economics*, vol. XVIII, May, 1904, pp. 409–36.

55. *Report of the Industrial Commission, op. cit.*, vol. I, p. 30.

56. San Francisco *Voice of Labor*, April 29, 1899.

CHAPTER 2

1. *Proceedings*, A.F. of L. Convention, 1899, p. 13; 1904, p. 22.

2. Gompers to A.F. of L. Executive Council, Aug. 6, 1904, *AFL Corr.*; *Proceedings*, A.F. of L. Convention, 1905, pp. 38, 40; 1911, pp. 32, 36.

3. Selig Perlman and Philip Taft, *History of Labor in the United States, 1896–1932*, New York, 1935, p. 12.

4. Quoted in *Coast Seamen's Journal*, June 19, 1901.

5. Nutter, *op. cit.*, p. 30.

6. John A. Garraty, "U.S. Steel Versus Labor: The Early Years," *Labor History*, vol. I, Winter, 1960, pp. 6, 11; Lewis Corey, *The House of Morgan*, New York, 1930, pp. 277–78; *Wall Street Journal*, Aug. 3, 1901.

7. Robert H. Wiebe, "The Response of American Business Men to the National

Progressive Movement, 1901–1916," unpublished Ph.D. thesis, University of Rochester, 1957, p. 177; *Coast Seamen's Journal*, July 31, 1901.

8. *American Federationist*, July, 1901, pp. 529–30.

9. Perlman and Taft, *op. cit.*, pp. 129–37; *The Union Picket*, published by the Dayton Central Trades Council, May 31, 1902.

10. *Coast Seamen's Journal*, July 31, Aug. 7, 1901.

11. *Ibid.*; Clarea E. Mortenson, "Organized Labor in San Francisco from 1892 to 1902," unpublished M.S. thesis, University of California, Berkeley, 1916, pp. 32–48. Robert Knight, *Industrial Relations in the San Francisco Bay Area, 1900–1918*, Berkeley and Los Angeles, 1960, pp. 74–76.

12. Annual Report of Employers' Association of Ohio, in Chicago *Socialist*, March 7, 1903.

13. *The Union Picket*, June 7, 1902; Grace Heilman Stimson, *Rise of the Labor Movement in Los Angeles*, Berkeley, California, 1955, p. 258; "The Citizens' Alliance and Its Methods," San Francisco *Labor Clarion*, May 13, 1904.

14. *The Union Picket*, June 7, 1902; John Mulholland to Gompers, Toledo, Ohio, Dec. 15, 1902, *AFL Corr.*; Stimson, *op. cit.*, p. 258; "A Report on Labor Disturbances in the State of Colorado from 1880 to 1904, Inclusive," 58th Congress, 3d Session, *Senate Document No. 122*, pp. 47–48.

15. George W. Dipell to Gompers, April 23, 1904, *AFL Corr.*

16. *The Union Picket*, June 7, 1902.

17. New York *Tribune*, Jan. 12, 1896.

18. Albion Guilford Taylor, *Labor Policies of the National Association of Manufacturers*, Urbana, Illinois, 1927, pp. 8–25; Cincinnati *Enquirer*, April 15, 1903.

19. Report of Committee on Education and Labor, 76th Congress, 1st Session, *Senate Report No. 6*, Part 6, "Labor Policies of Employers' Associations," Part III, pp. 5–7; Chicago *Socialist*, April 18, 1903; *Proceedings*, N.A.M. Convention, 1903, pp. 7–8, 218.

20. *Proceedings*, N.A.M. Convention, 1903, pp. 163–75; Albert K. Steigewalt, "The National Association of Manufacturers: Organization and Policies, 1895–1914," unpublished Ph.D. thesis, University of Michigan, 1952, pp. 184–96.

21. 76th Congress, 1st Session, *Senate Report No. 6*, part 6, pp. 7–10.

22. *Bulletin No. 1*, Citizens' Industrial Association of America, Indianapolis, 1903, p. 18; *A Statement of the Character and Purposes of the Citizens' Industrial Association of America*, Indianapolis, n.d., p. 7; *Square Deal*, Jan. 1906, p. 15.

23. *Christian el al vs. Kellog Switchboard and Supply Company, Brief, Argument and Decision of Appellate Court of Illinois*, Issued by the American Anti-Boycott Association, Chicago, 1903.

24. Norman J. Ware, *Labor in Modern Industrial Society*, New York, 1935, p. 355; clipping attached to Frank Duffy to Frank Morrison, Feb. 26, 1904, *AFL Corr.*; *Convention Bulletin*, Feb. 1907, issued by the American Anti-Boycott Association, p. 39.

25. *Machinists' Journal*, Sept. 1901, pp. 1–4; *American Federationist*, July, 1901, p. 253; Luke Grant, *The National Erectors' Association and the International Association of Bridge and Structural Iron Workers*, Washington, 1915, p. 191.

26. Philip G. Wright, "The Contest in Congress between Organized Labor and Organized Business," *Quarterly Journal of Economics*, vol. XXIX, Feb. 1915, p. 247.

27. Bonnett, *op. cit.*, p. 239.

28. Ray Stannard Baker, "Organized Capital Challenges Organized Labor," *McClure's Magazine*, vol. XXIII, July, 1904, pp. 279–81; Stimson, *op. cit.* pp. 256–57; Charles P. Larrowe, *Maritime Labor Relations on the Great Lakes*, East Lansing, Michigan, 1959, pp. 30–40.

29. Bonnett, *op. cit.*, p. 239.

30. Charles Macfarland, *The Christian Ministry and the Social Order*, New Haven, Conn., 1909, pp. 132–33; Wiebe, *op. cit.*, pp. 185–86.

31. Garraty, *op. cit.*, p. 19.

32. *The Workers' Monthly*, Sept. 1925, p. 497.

33. W. D. Mahon to Gompers, Aug. 5, Sept. 28, 1903, *AFL Corr.*

34. Nadworny, *op. cit.*, pp. 48–49; Jean Trepp McKelvey, *AFL Attitudes toward Production, 1900–1932*, Ithaca, N.Y., 1952, p. 15; Frederick W. Taylor to Col. John T. Thompson, Jan. 17, 1910, Frederick Winslow Taylor Collection, Stevens Institute of Technology, Hoboken, New Jersey.

35. 76th Congress, 1st Session, *Senate Report No. 6*, part 6, pp. 15–16.

36. Bonnett, *op. cit.*, pp. 112, 138.

37. New York *World,* July 2, 1913.
38. Report dated 1902, entitled "Spy System Exposed"; John Mitchell to Gompers, Sept. 4, 1905; W. D. Mahon to Gompers, March 31, 1905 *AFL Corr.*
39. 76th Congress, 1st Session, *Senate Report No. 6,* part 6, p. 11.
40. *American Federationist,* June, 1904, p. 508; 76th Congress, 1st Session, *Senate Report No. 6,* part 6, pp. 10–11; Adolph Mueller, President, H. Mueller Co., Decatur, Illinois, to Gompers, April 15, 1903, *AFL Corr.*
41. Newspaper clipping attached to Max Morris' letter to Gompers, Denver, Colorado, May 18, 1903, *AFL Corr.*
42. *Ibid.;* "A Report on Labor Disturbances in the State of Colorado from 1880 to 1904, Inclusive," *op. cit.,* p. 50.
43. *The Weekly Bulletin of the Clothing Trades,* Sept. 16, 1904; *Daily Trade Record,* Sept. 16, 1904.
44. Jno. B. Lennon to Gompers, Oct. 29, 1903, *AFL Corr.*
45. Carl Wyatt to Frank Morrison, Jan. 4, 1908, *AFL Corr.*
46. *An Explanation of the Trouble Now Existing Between the Oliver Typewriter Company of Woodstock, Ill., and the International Association of Allied Metal Mechanics,* April, 1903, pamphlet, copy in *AFL Corr.*
47. *American Federationist,* June, 1904, p. 517; John Golden to Gompers, Dec. 9, 1904, *AFL Corr.*
48. *Annual Report of the New York Chamber of Commerce,* 1912, pp. 25–26; 1913, pp. 113–22; *The Army and Navy Register,* Oct. 10, 1914, p. 455; *National Guard Magazine,* vol. II, March, 1908, p. 112; vol. V, May, 1910, p. 455; vol. VI, Oct. 1910, p. 313; vol. IX, Sept. 1912, p. 368; vol. XI, Sept. 1914, p. 260; vol. XII, April, 1915, p. 73; *The Financial Record,* June 10, 1903.
49. *Proceedings,* N.A.M., 1907 Convention, p. 36; Bonnett, *op. cit.,* pp. 86–88, 125, 344–53, 465–67, 485–87, 536–38; George Douglas Blackwood, "Techniques and Stereotypes in the Literature of the National Association of Manufacturers Concerning Industry and Labor," unpublished M.A. thesis, University of Chicago, 1947, pp. 104–05.
50. Bonnett, *op. cit.,* p. 353.
51. *American Industries,* Nov. 1, 1906, pp. 10, 13; *American Federationist,* April, 1903, pp. 266–68.
52. Chicago *Daily Socialist,* Dec. 7, 1906; Cardinal James Gibbons, *Organized Labor,* reprinted by the American Anti-Boycott Association as part of a pamphlet entitled, *The Morals and Laws Involved in Labor Conflicts.*
53. *116 Fed. Rep.,* p. 511.
54. Bridgeport (Conn.) *Evening Post,* Jan. 21, 1907; *Convention Bulletin,* Feb. 1907, Issued by A.A.B.A.
55. Sterling D. Spero, *Government as Employer,* New York, 1948, pp. 378–80; New York *Press,* Aug. 22, 1903; Roosevelt to Oswald Garrison Villard, July 25, 1903, Theodore Roosevelt Papers, Library of Congress. (Hereinafter cited as *TRP.*); Stephen Steinberg, "Theodore Roosevelt and the American Labor Movement, 1901–1909," unpublished M.A. thesis, University of Wisconsin, 1959, pp. 83–84.
56. Stimson, *op. cit.,* pp. 246–47; Richard Connelly Miller, "Otis and His *Times:* The Career of Harrison Gray Otis of Los Angeles," unpublished Ph.D. thesis, University of California, Berkeley, 1961, pp. 183–94, 220–25; Los Angeles *Times,* Dec. 10, 13, 1903.
57. Gompers, "To Whom It May Concern," Oct. 5, 1903, *AFL Corr.;* New York *Times,* Nov. 16, 1902, Aug. 14, 16, Oct. 29, 1903; New York *Journal of Commerce and Commercial Bulletin,* May 6, 1904.
58. New York *Herald,* July 25, 1908; New York *Evening Post,* May 4, 1904; New York *Sun,* June 5, 7, 1901.
59. New York *Sun,* July 30, 1904; *New York Times,* July 26, 1901. See also Jan. 4, 1906, May 30, 1914.
60. *New York Times,* April 29, 1904, Feb. 28, 1906, Aug. 4, 1909.
61. Bonnett, *op. cit.,* p. 341.
62. Jno. B. Lennon to Gompers, July 11, 1904, *AFL Corr.;* "A Report on Labor Disturbances in the State of Colorado from 1880 to 1904, Inclusive," *op. cit.,* p. 50.
63. Cleveland *Citizen,* Dec. 10, 1910.
64. *Motion Picture World,* April 22, 1910, p. 46.
65. *Proceedings,* A.F. of L. Convention, 1910, p. 136; Cleveland *Citizen,* Dec. 10, 1910.
66. Herbert N. Casson, "Novelists and the Labor Question," *American Federationist,* April, 1902, pp. 172–73; Lisle A. Rose, "A Descriptive Catalogue of Economic and Politico-Economic Fiction in the United States, 1902–1909," unpublished Ph.D. thesis, University of Chicago, 1935, pp. 48–51; F. C. Lange,

The Industrial Crisis, Hartford, Conn., 1903, pp. 191.

67. *Leather Workers' Journal,* Sept. 1904, p. 7.

68. *Proceedings,* A.F. of L. Convention, 1903, p. 20.

69. *American Federationist,* Dec. 1899, pp. 239–44; May, 1900, p. 128; July, 1902, p. 376; *Trade Unions: Their Origins and Objects, Influence and Efficacy,* A.F. of L. edition, Washington, 1913, pp. 12, 16.

70. *Proceedings,* A.F. of L. Convention, 1902, p. 139; *American Federationist,* Jan. 1904, pp. 21–26; Oct. 1910, pp. 911–12.

71. Perlman and Taft, *op. cit.,* p. 134; Stuart Reid, "Freedom Through Trade Unions," *American Federationist,* June, 1904, pp. 485–86; Frank K. Foster, *Has the Non-Unionist A Right to Work,* A.F. of L. pamphlet, Washington, 1904; Samuel Gompers, *Open Shop Editorials,* pamphlet, Washington, n.d., *Proceedings,* A. F. of L. Convention, 1904, pp. 6–8.

72. Gompers to Robert A. Montgomery, Feb. 27, 1905, Samuel Gompers Letterbooks, Washington, D.C. Hereinafter cited as *GLB.*

73. Aleine Austin, *The Labor Story,* New York, 1949, p. 159.

74. W. D. Mahon to Gompers, Sept. 24, 1904, *AFL Corr.*

75. Youngstown *Advocate* reprinted in *Leather Workers' Journal,* Feb. 1904, p. 364; *New York Times,* Aug. 16, 1903; *New York World,* May 17, 1906.

76. Youngstown *Advocate* reprinted in *Leather Workers' Journal,* Feb. 1904, p. 364.

77. *The World To-Day* reprinted in *Solidarity,* Feb. 15, 1907, p. 17.

78. *Proceedings,* 11th Convention, N.A.M., New York, 1906, p. 15.

79. Perlman and Taft, *op. cit.,* p. 129.

80. John I. Griffin, *Strikes: A Study in Quantitative Economics,* New York, 1939, p. 91.

81. Wolman, *op. cit.,* p. 16.

82. *Quarterly Journal of Economics,* vol. XXIV, May, 1910, pp. 565–66.

CHAPTER 3

1. J. H. Smith, Manager, the Corporations Auxiliary Company, to "Gentlemen," Dec. 1903, *AFL Corr.*

2. National Civic Federation, *National Conference on Industrial Conciliation:* *A Report of Proceedings, December 16–17, 1901,* New York, 1902, pp. 91–92; Mimeographed Statement of National Conference on Conciliation and Arbitration, *AFL Corr.;* By-Laws of the Industrial Department.

3. N.C.F. *National Conference . . . 1901,* p. vii; *National Civic Federation Review,* November–December, 1906, p. 10, May 1914, p. 12. (Hereinafter cite as *NCF Review.*)

4. New York *Tribune,* Dec. 21, 1901; John Mitchell to Mark Hanna, March 20, 1901, John Mitchell Papers, Catholic University of America. (Hereinafter cited as *JMP.*)

5. John Mitchell, *Organized Labor,* Philadelphia, 1903, p. ix; Marguerite Green, *The National Civic Federation and the American Labor Movement, 1900–1925,* Washington, D.C., 1956, p. 38.

6. N.C.F., *National Conference . . . 1901,* p. 4; Chicago *Tribune,* Dec. 17, 1901.

7. N.C.F., *National Conference . . . 1901,* pp. 4, 5–6, 12–16, 29, 30, 38, 50, 54–57, 78, 95–96; *NCF Review,* April, 1903, pp. 8–9; June, 1903, p. 9; Jan. 1905, p. 4.

8. Ralph M. Easley, "Senator Hanna and the Labor Problem," *The Independent,* vol. LVI, March 3, 1904, p. 484; W. C. Pearce to Gompers, April 1, 1902, *AFL Corr.; Report of the Industrial Commission,* Washington, 1901, vol. VII, pp. 30–35.

9. Ralph M. Easley to Gompers, Feb. 2, 1905, *AFL Corr.;* John P. Mitchell tc R. M. Easley, Nov. 22, 1907, *JMP.*

10. Jas. O'Connell to Gompers, June 10 1897; N. D. Call to Gompers (Jul 1899); M. Donnelly to Frank Morris April 13, 1900, *AFL Corr.*

11. *American Federationist,* Jan. 1902, p. 24.

12. *New York Times,* Dec. 17, 1901.

13. *American Federationist,* March, 1902, pp. 93–113, 120–23, 175–77.

14. Gordon Maurice Jensen, "The Nationa Civic Federation: American Business in an Age of Social Change and Social Reform, 1900–1910," unpublished Ph.D. thesis, Princeton University, May, 1956, pp. 49–51, 58–60.

15. Ralph M. Easley to Gompers, April 6, 1900, *AFL Corr.;* Ralph M. Easley to William Howard Taft, Sept. 17, 1912, William Howard Taft Papers, Library of Congress; Jensen, *op. cit.,* p. 67.

16. Irving G. Cheslaw, "The National Civic Federation and Labor," unpublished M.A. thesis, Columbia University, 1948, pp. 45–46; Chicago *Tribune,* Dec.

444 REFERENCE NOTES

20, 1900; Sidney Sass, "The National Civic Federation, 1900–1914," unpublished M.A. thesis, Columbia University, 1948, pp. 150–63; Jensen, *op. cit.,* pp. 50–51.

17. Minutes of the Finance Committee Meeting, June 2, 1908, National Civic Federation Archives, New York Public Library; (hereinafter cited as *NCFA*); Cheslaw, *op. cit.,* p. 61.

18. *Proceedings,* C.I.A., 1904, pp. 128–29; *Square Deal,* Jan. 1906, p. 8; *American Industries,* Nov. 2, 1903, p. 8; A. C. Marshall to Easley, Jan. 7, 1903, in *JMP;* Ralph M. Easley, "An Interesting Disavowal," *NCF Review,* vol. I, Nov. 15, 1904, p. 9. *See also* Easley to Daniel A. Tompkins, March 21, 1907, Daniel Augustus Tompkins Papers, Library of Congress.

19. Easley to John Mitchell, Dec. 8, 1904, *JMP;* Jensen, *op. cit.,* pp. 105–06, 146; *NCF Review,* June, 1904, pp. 17–18; Easley to W. B. Wilson, Dec. 28, 1913, Department of Labor File, No. 16/18, National Archives.

20. Cheslaw, *op. cit.,* p. 35; Easley to Mitchell, Nov. 13, 1901, *JMP; Square Deal,* Dec. 1904–Dec. 1905.

21. *NCF Review,* July, 1904, p. 9; April, 1908, p. 12; *Union Labor Advocate,* May, 1908, p. 42; Philadelphia *Ledger,* March 16, 1912; Easley to Oscar S. Straus, March 25, 1907, Oscar S. Straus Papers, Library of Congress.

22. Easley to Gompers, Oct. 2, 10, 14, 16, 1900, *AFL Corr.*

23. Easley to Gompers, Dec. 8, 1906, *AFL Corr.*

24. Gompers to Easley, Feb. 3, 1902, *GLB.*

25. Chicago *Tribune,* Nov. 20, 1903; H. C. White, "The Warfare Against Unionism, How Shall It Be Met?" *NCF Review,* June, 1903; p. 16; Gompers to Ralph M. Easley, Feb. 3, 1902, *GLB.*

26. Easley to Gompers, Aug. 19, 1907, *AFL Corr.*

27. *NCF Review,* Aug. 1904, p. 8; Oct. 1904, pp. 8, 9, 14; Feb. 1905, p. 2; March, 1905, p. 3; Feb. 1908, p. 2; *Wall Street Journal,* Nov. 20, 1903.

28. *NCF Review,* Nov. 15, 1904, p. 5; Jan. 1905, p. 5; Ralph M. Easley to Gompers, Nov. 30, 1903, *AFL Corr.;* Ralph M. Easley to Mitchell, Nov. 20, 1907, *JMP;* Ralph M. Easley, "A Historical Sketch of the National Civic Federation," p. 8, unpublished manuscript in *NCFA.*

29. *International Socialist Review,* vol. IV, Oct. 1903, p. 240.

30. Quoted in letter of Easley to Seth Low, March 14, 1913, Seth Low Papers, Columbia University Library.

31. Herman Ridder to Ralph M. Easley, Aug. 1908, *NCFA.*

32. R. M. Easley to M. M. Avery, April 27, 1908; R. M. Easley to Andrew Carnegie, May 5, 1906, *NCFA.*

33. *NCF Review,* Oct. 1904, p. 11; Jensen, *op. cit.,* p. 162.

34. Circular, "To Organized Labor of America," Jan. 1, 1910, *AFL Corr. See* also Green, *op. cit.,* p. 291.

35. Cheslaw, *op. cit.,* p. 29; *New York Times,* Nov. 17, 1912; Ralph M. Easley, April 17 (n.y.) in *NCFA*

36. *NCF Review,* Sept. 1907, pp. 6–7; Easley to Mrs. Lynden Evans, June 14, 1912, *NCFA;* Jensen, *op. cit.,* pp. 209–10.

37. John Mitchell to Seth Low, Feb. 24, 1908, Seth Low Papers, Columbia University Library; Sass, *op. cit.,* pp. 53–54.

38. *NCF Review,* March–April, 1907, p. 2; Jensen, *op. cit.,* p. 211; Green, *op. cit.,* p. 221; Sass, *op. cit.,* pp. 73–79; Jensen, *op. cit.,* pp. 88, 309–11; George W. Smith to C. H. McCullough, Jr., June 12, 1912, in *NCFA.*

39. Seth Low to Gompers, Feb. 21, 1908; C. A. Moore to Easley, Nov. 6, 1908; Easley to Senator Joseph L. Bristow, July 17, 1909; *NCFA;* Seth Low to John Mitchell, June 28, 1908, *JMP;* Jensen, *op. cit.,* pp. 309–10; *NCF Review,* July, 1904, p. 10; May 1908, pp. pp. 18–19; Nov. 1909, p. 10.

40. Lewis Lorwin, *The American Federation of Labor,* Washington, 1932, pp. 83–84.

41. *NCF Review,* May 15, 1905, p. 62.

CHAPTER 4

1. Perlman and Taft, *op. cit.,* p. 97; Report of T. J. Shaffer to 27th Annual Session of the Amalgamated Association of Iron, Steel and Tin Workers, 1902, *Journal of the Session,* pp. 6293–95.

2. New York *Tribune,* July 16–19, Aug. 11, 1901; *Journal of the Knights of Labor,* Aug. 1901; Easley to Gompers, Jan. 2, 1901, *AFL Corr.*

3. Hanna to Mitchell, July 16, 22, 1901, *JMP;* Hanna to Easley, July 24, 1901; Easley to Louis Brandeis, Nov. 4, 1912,

NCFA; New York *Tribune,* Aug. 1, 1901; Lorwin, *op. cit.,* p. 64.

4. *Hearings before the Committee on Investigation of United States Steel Corporation,* Washington, 1911, vol. VIII, pp. 300–01; Easley to Brandeis, Nov. 4, 1912, *NCFA;* New York *Tribune,* Aug. 1, 1901.

5. Green, *op. cit.,* pp. 27–28; Philip Taft, *The A. F. of L. in The Time of Gompers,* New York, 1957, p. 239; Lorwin, *op. cit.,* p. 65; Report of T. J. Shaffer to 27th Annual Session, *op. cit.,* pp. 6293–95.

6. Easley to Brandeis, Oct. 28, 1912, Seth Low Papers, Columbia University Library; Ralph M. Easley, "The National Civic Federation," *Independent,* vol. LIV, Aug. 28, 1902, p. 2066.

7. Quoted in T. L. Lewis to Gompers Sept. 8, 1901, *AFL Corr.*

8. Easley to Mitchell, Oct. 9, 1901, *JMP;* T. J. Shaffer to Members of the Amalgamated Association, Sept. 21, 1901, *American Federationist,* Oct. 1901, pp. 415–17; Ware, *op. cit.,* pp. 322–23.

9. New York *Tribune,* Aug. 24, 1901.

10. *Journal of the Knights of Labor,* Aug. 1901, p. 4; Lorwin, *op. cit.,* p. 64.

11. T. J. Shaffer to Members of the Amalgamated Association, Sept. 21, 1901, *American Federationist,* Oct. 1901, pp. 415–17; Taft, *op. cit.,* p. 240.

12. *Journal of the Proceedings of the Amalgamated Association of Iron, Steel, and Tin Workers,* 1901, Report of President, pp. 6317–18; Gompers and Mitchell to Shaffer, Sept. 25, 1901; Shaffer to Mitchell, Sept. 27, 1901, in *ibid.,* p. 6318.

13. *American Federationist,* Oct. 1901, pp. 415–31; Mitchell to Easley, Oct. 18, 1901; Easley to Mitchell, Oct. 9, 1901, *JMP.*

14. *Proceedings,* A. F. of L. Convention, 1902, pp. 172–74; Perlman and Taft, op. cit., pp. 107–10; Ware, *op. cit.,* p. 323; Lorwin, *op. cit.,* p. 65*n.*

15. Michael F. Tighe, Testimony before Committee on Education and Labor, U.S. Senate, *Investigation of Strike in Steel Industries,* Washington, 1919, pp. 341*ff.*

16. *NCF Review,* April, 1903, p. 10; June, 1904, p. 3.

17. Quoted in Joseph Dorfman, *Thorstein Veblen and His America,* New York, 1934, pp. 301–02.

18. Samuel Yellen, *American Labor Struggles,* New York, 1936, pp. 139–40; Philip S. Foner, *History of the Labor Movement in the United States,* vol. II, New York, 1955, pp. 21–22, 345; Perlman and Taft, *op. cit.,* p. 38.

19. John Mitchell to Mark Hanna, March 20, 1901, *JMP; The Public,* Oct. 27, 1900.

20. Robert J. Cornell, *The Anthracite Coal Strike of 1902,* Washington, 1957, p. 59; John Mitchell to Mark Hanna, March 9, 1901, *JMP.*

21. John Mitchell to Mark Hanna, March 20, 1901; Mitchell to Ralph Easley, March, 1901, *JMP;* Ralph Easley, "Report of the Executive Committee of the National Civic Federation on the Anthracite Strike," (1902), *NCFA;* Cornell, *op. cit.,* p. 62.

22. Easley to Mitchell, (March, 1901), *JMP;* Easley, "Report . . . on the Anthracite Strike," *op. cit., NCFA.*

23. Hanna to John Mitchell, (May 23), 1901; John Mitchell to Hanna, Aug. 29, 1901; John Mitchell to Ralph Easley, Dec. 28, 1901 *JMP.*

24. Ralph Easley to Mitchell, Oct. 1, 1901; John Mitchell to Ralph Easley, Oct. 18, 1901, *JMP;* Easley, "Report . . . on the Anthracite Strike," *NCFA.*

25. John Mitchell to Mark Hanna, Aug. 15, 1902; Ralph Easley to John Mitchell, March 5, 1902, *JMP.*

26. Easley, "Report . . . on the Anthracite Strike," *NCFA.*

27. *Ibid.;* Ralph Easley to Frank Sargent, Aug. 4, 1902, copies in *JMP* and *AFL Corr.;* Easley, "Senator Hanna and the Labor Problem," *op. cit.,* p. 485; Mitchell to Easley, March 13, 1902, *JMP.*

28. Easley, "Report . . . on the Anthracite Strike," *NCFA;* Green, *op. cit.,* p. 47; *Proceedings of the Special Convention of the United Mine Workers of America,* 1902; John Mitchell to Mark Hanna, May 22, 1902, *JMP.*

29. George Korson, *Minstrels of the Mine Patch: Songs and Stories of the Anthracite Industry,* Philadelphia, 1938, p. 233.

30. Mark Hanna to John Mitchell, May 20, 1902; Ralph Easley to John Mitchell, May 21, 1902, *JMP.*

31. John Mitchell to Mark Hanna, May 22, 1902; Mark Hanna to John Mitchell, May 29, 1902, *JMP.*

32. Easley, "Report . . . on the Anthracite Strike," NCFA; Herbert Croly, *Marcus Alonzo Hanna,* New York, 1912, p. 396; Philadelphia *Press,* Aug. 5, 1902; Cheslaw, *op. cit.,* p. 18.

33. *Address of President Mitchell to the Special Convention United Mine Work-*

ers of America and Report of Committee on Resolutions, Indianapolis, July 17th, 1902, copies in AFL Corr.

34. Minneapolis Journal reprinted in Cornell, op. cit., p. 118; Easley to Mitchell, July 29, 1902; Mark Hanna to Mitchell, July 18, 1902, JMP; NCF Review, Aug. 1902, p. 11.

35. Easley, "Report . . . on the Anthracite Strike," NCFA.

36. Yellen, op. cit., p. 159; Cornell, op. cit., pp. 139, 152, 154.

37. Caro Lloyd, Henry Demarest Lloyd, 1847–1903, New York, 1912, vol. II, pp. 190–98; 207, 230; Chicago Tribune, Oct. 11, 1902.

38. The Public, Sept. 27, 1902.

39. Ira Kipnis, The American Socialist Movement, 1897–1912, New York, 1952, p. 139; Chicago Socialist, Sept. 13, 1902; The Worker, Aug, 17, 1902; Elizabeth to Leonora O'Reilly, Milwaukee, Oct. 26, 1902, Leonora O'Reilly Papers, Radcliffe College Library; Easley to Gompers, undated, but probably written on Aug. 7, 1902, AFL Corr.; Easley to George W. Perkins, Aug. 23, 1902. NCFA.

40. Mitchell to Hanna, Sept. 8, 1902; Easley to Frank P. Sargent, Aug. 4, 1902; Mitchell to Easley, Aug. 6, 1902, JMP.

41. Easley, "Report . . . on the Anthracite Strike," NCFA; Easley to Gompers, undated letter, fall, 1902, AFL Corr.

42. H. C. Lodge to Roosevelt, Oct. 11, 1902; Roosevelt to Oswald Garrison Villard, Oct. 9, 1902; Jacob A. Riis to Roosevelt, Oct. 11, 1902; Roosevelt to Guild A. Copeland, Oct. 17, 1902; Roosevelt to William C. LeGendre, Aug. 13, 1902, TRP.

43. Scheinberg, op. cit., p. 11.

44. Henry Cabot Lodge to Theodore Roosevelt, Oct. 6, 1902, TRP.

45. Hanna to Gompers, Oct. 7, 1902; R. M. Easley to Gompers, Oct. 7, 1902, AFL Corr.

46. The Public, Oct. 11, 1902.

47. Hanna to Mitchell, Oct. 14, 1902, JMP; Theodore Roosevelt, An Autobiography, New York, 1913, pp. 468–69, 474.

48. Portland (Oregon) Evening Telegram, Oct. 15, 1902; Cornell, op. cit., p. 199; Edward Krier to Gompers, Oct. 15, 1902, AFL Corr.

49. "Report to the President on the Anthracite Coal Strike of May–October, 1902, By the Anthracite Coal Strike Commission," Senate Doc. No. 6, 58 Cong.,

Special Session, Washington, 1903. See especially pp. 64–65, 76–78.

50. Clarence Darrow to Henry D. Lloyd, April 2, 1903, Henry Demarest Lloyd Papers, Wisconsin State Historical Society, Madison, Wisconsin; (hereinafter referred to as WSHS); Commercial and Financial Chronicle, March 28, 1903, pp. 679–90; Wiebe, op. cit., pp. 177–78.

51. NCF Review, April, 1903; Green, op. cit., p. 55.

52. A. Furuseth to Frank Morrison, April 11, 1903; A. Furuseth to Gompers, Sept. 9, 1903, AFL Corr.

53. Carol L. Thompson, "John Mitchell," Current History, Jan. 1950, p. 34.

54. Glück, op. cit., pp. 131–32.

55. NCF Review, June, 1904, p. 1.

56. John B. Lennon to Gompers, March 28, 1904, AFL Corr.

57. Green, op. cit., p. 63.

58. James J. McGinley, S. J., Labor Relations in the New York Rapid Transit Systems, 1904–1944, New York, 1949, pp. 258–59; The Motorman and Conductor, Jan. 1905, p. 25.

59. New York Tribune, Dec. 12, 1904.

60. Ralph M. Easley to John Mitchell, Feb. 24, 1905, JMP; Rowland Hill Harvey, Samuel Gompers, Palo Alto, California, 1935, p. 138.

61. American Federationist, May, 1905, pp. 294–95; The Motorman and Conductor, March, 1905, pp. 13–14, April, 1905, pp. 5–6; New York American, March 10, 1905.

62. McGinley, op. cit., p. 259; Green, op. cit., pp. 64–65; New York American, March 10, 1905; New York Tribune, March 14, 1905; New York World, Jan. 21, 1915.

63. Green, op. cit., pp. 64–65; Bernard Mandel, "Samuel Gompers," unpublished MS., pp. 475–77; Easley to Gompers, Oct. 13, 1905, AFL Corr.

64. Atlanta Journal of Labor, March 21, 1905.

65. Meeting in Memory of Mr. August Belmont, a former president, (and) Mr. Samuel Gompers, first vice-president . . . held at two thirty o'clock Tuesday the thirtieth of December, nineteen hundred twenty-four at Hotel Astor, New York, 1925, pamphlet. My emphasis, P.S.F.

66. Harvey, op. cit., pp. 147–48; John Mitchell to Ralph M. Easley, Oct. 21, 1907, marked "Confidential," JMP.

67. D. J. Keefe to Gompers, Sept. 29, 30, 1905, AFL Corr.

68. B.C. Federationist, Jan. 20, 1912.

69. The Leather Worker, Sept. 1900, p. 22.

70. Proceedings of Convention of Cigar Makers' International Union, Sept. 17–Oct. 5, 1912, "Discussion of Civic Federation," pp. 10a–15a, Typewritten Copy attached to Gompers to A.F. of L. Executive Council, Nov. 15, 1912, *AFL Corr.*

71. Ray Ginger, *The Bending Cross: A Biography of Eugene Victor Debs,* New Brunswick, N.J., 1949, p. 235; Morris Hillquit to Ralph M. Easley, June 6, 1911, *NCFA;* Ralph M. Easley, *National Civic Federation and its Labor Policy,* New York, 1922, p. 14.

72. *See* speech of Delegate Barnes, Proceedings of Convention of Cigar Makers' International Union, Sept. 17–Oct. 5, 1912, *op. cit.,* p. 38.

73. *Proceedings,* A.F. of L. Convention, 1905, pp. 181–82; 1907, p. 188, 340; New York *Tribune,* March 27, 1905; Gompers to Herman Robinson, March 29, 1905, *AFL Corr.* and *GLB.; New York Times,* June 5, 1905; *Union Labor Advocate,* May, 1908, p. 42.

74. Ware, *op. cit.,* p. 323.

CHAPTER 5

1. *Catholic World,* vol. LXXIV, Jan. 1902, pp. 531–32.

2. David J. Saposs, "The Catholic Church and the Labor Movement," *Modern Monthly,* vol. VII, May–June, 1933, p. 225.

3. Marc Karson, "The Catholic and the Development of American Trade Unionism, 1900–1918," *Industrial and Labor Relations Review,* vol. IV, July, 1951, pp. 527–42; Thomas J. McDonagh, "Some Aspects of the Roman Catholic Attitude Toward the American Labor Movement, 1900–1914," unpublished Ph.D. thesis, University of Wisconsin, 1951; Sister Joan de Lourdes Leonard, "Catholic Attitude towards American Labor, 1884–1919" unpublished M.A. thesis Columbia University, 1940; Reverend Paul Stroh, "The Catholic Clergy and American Labor Disputes, 1900–1937," unpublished Ph.D. thesis, Catholic University of America, 1939; John P. Boyle, "Peter E. Deitz and the American Labor Movement," unpublished M.A. thesis, Catholic University of America, 1948; Sister Mary Brophy, "The Social Thought of the German Catholic Verein," unpublished Ph.D. thesis, Catholic University of America, 1941; Patrick W. Gearty, *The Economic Thought of Monsignor John A. Ryan,* Washington, D.C., 1953; Bernard C. Cronin, *Father Yorke and the Labor Movement in San Francisco, 1900–1910,* Washington, D.C., 1943; Mary Harrita Fox, *Peter E. Dietz, Labor Priest,* Notre Dame, Indiana, 1953; Aaron Abell, "The Reception of Leo XIII's Labor Encyclical in America," *Review of Politics,* vol. VII, Oct. 1945, pp. 488–96.

4. Irwin Marc Karson, "The Political Thought and Practice of American Trade Unionism, 1906–1918," unpublished Ph.D. thesis, University of London, June 1, 1949, pp. 441–43.

5. Pope Leo XIII, *Rerum Novarum (On the Condition of Labor, May 15, 1891),* New York, 1939; William Eyre, editor, *The Pope and the People,* New York, 1895, pp. 2–5, 28, 29, 33, 35, 38, 39, 42, 44, 49.

6. Pius X Pope, *E. Supremi,* Oct. 4th, 1903; Pius X Pope, *Singulari Quadam Caritate,* Sept. 24, 1912.

7. Vincent A. McQuade, *The American Catholic Attitude on Child Labor,* Washington, D.C., 1938, p. 166; Rev. Herman Heuser, D.C., "Catholicizing the United States," *Ecclesiastical Review,* vol. XXXV, March, 1906, p. 120.

8. Karson, *op. cit.,* thesis, p. 470; Abell, *op. cit.,* p. 493; *Catholic World,* vol. VI, 1908, p. 109.

9. Most Rev. John Ireland, *The Church and Modern Society,* Chicago, 1896, p. 190; New York *Tribune,* Oct. 7, Nov. 4, 1901; *New York Times,* Oct. 7, 1901; *Literary Digest,* vol. XXIV, April 2, 1902, p. 508; *Buffalo Catholic Evening News* reprinted in *Daily People,* June 29, 1902; Reverend Thomas Donohue, *History of the Diocese of Buffalo,* Buffalo, 1929, pp. 133–39.

10. Bishop J. L. Spalding, *Socialism and Labor,* Chicago, 1902, p. 57; Bishop William Stang, *Socialism and Christianity,* New York, 1905, p. 141; Milwaukee *Social Democratic Herald,* July 23, 1904.

11. Cardinal James Gibbons, *Organized Labor,* reprinted by American Anti-Boycott Association as part of a pamphlet, *The Morals and Law Involved in Labor Conflicts;* Chicago *Daily Socialist,* Nov. 11, 1906; Cardinal William O'Connell, *Pastoral Letter on the Relations Between Employer and Employees,* Nov. 13, 1912.

12. William Kerby, "Aims in Socialism,"

Catholic World, July, 1907, p. 511; Rev. James Powers, editor, *Addresses of Bishop McFaul*, Trenton, N.J., 1908, p. 375.

13. Stroh, *op. cit.*, pp. 32–36; Brophy, *op. cit.*, p. 132.

14. Rev. William S. Kress, *Questions of Socialists and Their Answers*, Cleveland, 1908, pp. 113–14; Karson, *op. cit.*, article, p. 531.

15. *Central Blatt and Social Justice*, vol. III, Dec. 1910, p. 189.

16. McDonagh, *op. cit.*, pp. 105, 107; Leonard, *op. cit.*, pp. 172, 174; Karson, *op. cit.*, thesis, p. 469; Brophy, *op. cit.*, pp. 72–83.

17. *Central Blatt and Social Justice*, vol. II, Dec. 1909, p. 12; vol. V, May, 1912, pp. 35–36; Abell, *op. cit.*, p. 487.

18. Letter of Father Dietz to Sister Joan de Lourdes, quoted in Karson, *op. cit.*, thesis, pp. 471–73; Boyle, *op. cit.*, pp. 29–30, 64–65; *Social Service*, vol. I, May, 1911, p. 59; *Central Blatt and Social Service*, vol. II, Dec. 1909, pp. 9–10; *The Militia of Christ, Constitution and Charter Laws*, Rev. ed., 1912, pp. 3–4, 10.

19. Karson, *op. cit.*, article, p. 534; Boyle, *op. cit.*, pp. 64–65; Fox, *op. cit.*, pp. 45–52; *The Masses*, July, 1912, p. 3.

20. Peter E. Dietz to John Mitchell, Dec. 30, 1911, *JMP;* Boyle, *op. cit.*, pp. 64–65.

21. Saposs, *op. cit.*, p. 225.

22. Peter W. Collins, *Triplets of Destruction*, New Haven, 1919, preface.

23. David Goldstein, *Autobiography of a Campaigner for Christ*, Boston, 1936, pp. 18–60, 117–21; *The American Catholic Who's Who*, St. Louis, 1911, p. 14; *Weekly People*, Sept. 9, 1900; McDonagh, *op. cit.*, pp. 85–86.

24. Father Dietz to Sister Joan de Lourdes, quoted in Karson, *op. cit.*, thesis, pp. 471–73, 481; Peter W. Collins, "The Labor Movement and Socialism," *Central Blatt and Social Justice*, vol. II, Feb. 1910, pp. 7–10; Peter W. Collins, "Why Socialism is Opposed to Trade Unions," *Social Service*, vol. I, Nov. 1911, p. 131; David Goldstein, "Trade Unions; Their Foundation, Achievements, Dangers and Prospects," *Central Blatt and Social Justice*, vol. III, Dec. 1910, p. 189.

25. David Goldstein, *Socialism: The Nation of Fatherless Children*, Boston, 1912, pp. 368–69.

26. Minutes of Executive Council, Oct. 19,

1909, *AFL Archives;* Rev. J. B. Cenler to John Mitchell, Nov. 5, 1909, *JMP.*

27. John P. Mitchell to James T. Carroll, Dec. 7, 1909, *JMP;* Frank Morrison to A.F. of L. Executive Council, Jan. 17, 1910, *AFL Corr.*

28. Rev. Marshall I. Boarman, *The Comedy of Socialism*, St. Louis, n.d., p. 15.

29. P. 5, Copy in Catholic University of America Library.

30. Abell, *op. cit.*, p. 493.

31. Letter of Father Dietz to Sister Joan de Lourdes, quoted in Karson, *op. cit.*, thesis, pp. 471–73; Leonard, *op. cit.*, p. 184; Gompers to *The Common Cause*, Dec. 14, 1911, *GLB.*

32. *Central Blatt and Social Justice*, vol. IV, Dec. 1911, p. 204.

33. Easley to Gompers, April 16, 1906, *AFL Corr.;* Easley to Nicholas Murray Butler, Jan. 18, 1912, *NCFA;* Easley to John P. Mitchell, Aug. 12, 1912, *JMP;* McDonagh, *op. cit.*, pp. 163–66.

34. Eugene Debs Scrapbooks, Volume labeled "Labor Struggles, 1912–13," p. 19, Tamiment Institute Library, New York City. (Hereinafter cited as TIL.)

35. Leaflet, Rochester, N.Y., Nov. 21, 1912, JMP; *The Congregationist*, Aug. 30, 1902; New York *World*, Oct. 13, 1902.

36. *Presbyterian Church. Annual Report of the Board of Home Missions*, 1903, p. 6.

37. Charles Stelzle, "Presbyterian Department of Church and Labor," *Annals of the American Academy of Political and Social Science*, vol. XXX, 1907, p. 459; Charles Stelzle, *The Church and Labor*, Boston and New York, 1910, pp 28, 75, 76, 81.

38. *Presbyterian Church. Annual Report of the Board of Home Missions*, 1907, pp. 8, 11, 13–14; Executive Committee of the Interchurch Conference on Federation, *Church Federation, First Annual Report*, New York, 1906, p. 477.

39. *Presbyterian Church. Annual Report of the Board of Home Missions*, 1906, pp. 6–7; *Proceedings*, A.F. of L. Convention, 1905, pp. 152–54, 178; Minutes of the A.F. of L. Executive Council, June 21, 1906, *AFL Corr.*

40. *Presbyterian Church. Annual Report of the Board of Home Missions*, 1907, pp. 5–6, 12.

41. *Proceedings*, A.F. of L. Convention, 1908, p. 124; *Presbyterian Church. Annual Report of the Board of Home Missions*, 1907, pp. 57, 60, 67–68.

42. Charles Stelzle, *The Church and Labor*, pp. 11–19; Charles Stelzle, *The Gospel*

of Labor, New York, 1912, *passim*. These books contain reprints of many of Stelzle's weekly articles syndicated in the labor press.

43. *Report of the Commission on the Church and Social Service to the Federal Council of the Churches of Christ in America*, December 9, 1912, Pamphlet, p. 13; Charles Stelzle to John P. Mitchell, Nov. 19, 1903, *JMP;* Green, *op. cit.*, p. 139; *Presbyterian Church. Annual Report of the Board of Home Missions*, 1907, p. 6.

44. Stelzle, *The Church and Labor*, pp. 30–53.

45. Irwin M. Taylor, "Protestantism and the Labor Movement, 1890–1908," unpublished M.A. thesis, Columbia University, 1937, pp. 81–82; *Report of the Commission on the Church and Social Service. . . , op. cit.*, p. 13.

46. The Federal Council of Churches, *The Church and Modern Industry*, New York, 1908, pp. 3–4, 8–12, 15–16.

47. William John Villaume, "The Federal Council of the Churches of Christ in America and Labor Problems in the United States, 1908-1933," unpublished Ph.D. thesis, Hartford Seminary Foundation, Hartford, Conn., May, 1951, pp. 35–36, 100, 106, 133, 382–83.

48. Stelzle, *The Church and Labor*, pp. 11, 23–24.

49. Margaret C. Knights, "Attitudes of Congregational Churches Toward the Labor Movement," unpublished M.A. thesis, Columbia University, 1939, pp. 9–10.

50. Quoted by Morris U. Schappes, *The Jews in the United States: A Pictorial History, 1654-1954*, New York, 1958, p. 234.

51. Leonard J. Mervis, "The Social Justice Movement and the American Reform Rabbi," *American Jewish Archives*, June, 1955, pp. 196–97, 205–07.

52. Henry Sommerville, *Studies in the Catholic Movement*, London, 1933, pp. 5–6.

53. *The Common Cause*, vol. I, Jan. 1912, p. 36.

CHAPTER 6

1. Atlantic City (N.J.) *Union Herald*, Feb. 16, 1901; *Bricklayer and Mason*, Nov. 1909.

2. Bernard Mandel, "Gompers and Business Unionism, 1873–90," *Business History Review*, vol. XXVIII, Sept. 1954, pp. 264–75.

3. Eugene V. Debs to Frank Morrison, June 11, 1900, *AFL Corr.*

4. W. J. Clark to Gompers, Sept. 5, 1903, *AFL Corr.*

5. *Eugene V. Debs, His Life, Writings and Speeches*, New York, 1910, p. 132.

6. Harold Seidman, *Labor Czars*, New York, 1938, pp. 12–33.

7. Ira Wetmer to Chas. E. Nordeck, April 18, 1904, attached to letter of Chas. E. Nordeck to Gompers, May, 23, 1904; N. K. Pritchitt to Gompers, stamped received, Feb. 19, 1901; Albert Topeer to Frank Morrison, Nov. 20, 1899, *AFL Corr.*

8. Michael A. Saracino, "International Hod Carriers and Common Laborers Union of America: A Case Study of Corruption," unpublished M.A. thesis, New York University, 1955, p. 28; *See also* Ray Stannard Baker, "Corner in Labor," *McClure's Magazine*, Nov. 1903, p. 376.

9. John Z. White in *Label Bulletin*, official organ of the Central Federated Union of New York, June, 1904.

10. Gompers, Report to A. F. of L. Convention, 1896, *Proceedings*, p. 19.

11. *New York Times*, Oct. 14, 1905.

12. C. O. Sherman to Morrison, June 27, 1903; C. W. Woodman to Morrison, Jan. 7, 1901; Jason Hodges to Morrison, Jan. 25, 1900; Owen Miller to Morrison, Oct. 13, 1903, March 12, 1904; W. D. Mahon to Morrison, Aug. 22, 1904; M. P. Garrick to Morrison, Dec. 7, 1903, March 25, 1904; Frank Morrison to Gompers, Feb. 9, 1910, *AFL Corr.;* Pittsburgh *Leader*, Dec. 13, 1903; *The Carpenter*, Feb. 1902, pp. 2–3; *Proceedings of the Twelfth Regular Convention of the United Brotherhood of Carpenters and Joiners of America*, 1902, pp. 12, 27, 28–40; Taft, *op. cit.*, pp. 234–36.

13. *Daily Report on the Building Trades of Illinois*, Chicago, 1921, p. 44; Edward Levinson, "Business Prefers Racketeers," *New Republic*, Nov. 27, 1935, p. 69.

14. *Cf.* J. D. Pierce to Frank Morrison, Feb. 24, 1901; Eugene E. Sedgwick to Gompers, May 30, 1903; Samuel Rothwell to Gompers, April 21, 1903; Jacob Tazelaar to Gompers, Sept. 19, 1903; leaflet issued by Ohio Valley Trades and Labor Assembly, entitled "Perfidy Exposed!" *AFL Corr.*; F. Farrington to John Mitchell, June 3, 1914, *JMP*.

15. Samuel Rothwell to Gompers, April 21, 1903, *AFL Corr.*

16. Ray Stannard Baker, *op. cit.*, p. 374; Cleveland *Leader*, April 13, 1906; *Daily People*, Nov. 7, 1901; *Eleventh*

Special Report of the U.S. Commissioner of Labor, 1904, p. 602.

17. R. E. McLean to Frank Morrison, July 22, 1901; leaflet entitled, "Why?" attached to John F. Tobin to Gompers, May 17, 1904, *AFL Corr.*

18. *American Federationist,* Jan. 1901, pp. 27–28, Aug. 1901, pp. 293–94, July, 1902, pp. 365–66, July, 1904, pp. 573–79.

19. J. D. Pierce to Frank Morrison, Nov. 26, 1900; J. C. Skemp to Morrison, June 18, 1903; W. E. Dunn to J. C. Skemp, Aug. 2, 1904, attached to J. C. Skemp to Frank Morrison, Aug. 4, 15, 1904, *AFL Corr.*

20. Henry White to Frank Morrison, June 18, 1903; W. E. Dunn to J. C. Skemp, Aug. 2, 1904, *AFL Corr.*

21. Herman Robinson to Gompers, Aug. 27, 1904; J. C. Skemp to Frank Morrison, Aug. 4, 15, 1904, *AFL Corr.*

22. Frank B. Connor, President, to Frank Morrison, May 21, 1900, *AFL Corr.* My emphasis. P.S.F.

23. Charles E. Zaretz, *The Amalgamated Clothing Workers of America,* New York, 1934, pp. 81–84.

24. Henry White to Gompers, July 2, 1904; Charles Zorn to Gompers, Aug. 4, 1904, *AFL Corr.*

25. Herbert J. Lahne, "The Union Work Permit," *Political Science Quarterly,* vol. LXVI, Sept. 1951, pp. 366–69; Seidman, *op. cit.,* p. 57; New York State, *Joint Legislative Committee on Housing, Transcript of Testimony,* Dec. 1921, Final Report, pp. 24–25; J. D. Pierce to Morrison, Feb. 24, 1901, *AFL Corr.*

26. New York *World,* June 29, 1913.

27. *Ibid.,* June 13–Aug. 12, 1913; *Solidarity,* July 19, 1913; New York *Call,* July 1, 16, 1913; *Hearings Before a Subcommittee of the Committee on the Judiciary,* U.S. Senate, 63d Congress, 1st Session, 1913, III, pp. 2541 *ff;* Philadelphia *North American,* Aug. 25, 1913.

28. Henry M. Hyde, "A New Kind of Organized Labor," *Saturday Evening Post,* Jan. 8, 1910, pp. 14–15; *Solidarity,* Jan. 22, 1910, April 22, 1911; Toledo *Union Leader* reprinted in New York *Call,* Jan. 13, 1910.

29. William Haber, *Industrial Relations in the Building Industry,* Cambridge, Mass., 1930, pp. 318–20; Seidman, *op. cit.,* pp. 26, 28, 53–54.

30. New York *World,* July 12, 1910.

31. New Orleans *Daily Picayune,* July 14, 1910.

32. *Appeal to Reason,* July 16, 1910.

33. Chicago *Examiner,* Aug. 25, 1909.

34. *Industrial Worker,* Sept. 2, 1909, July 23, 1910.

35. *De Leon-Harriman Debate,* pamphlet, 1900, p. 35*n.*

36. New York *Evening Mail,* Dec. 17, 1907.

37. Eugene V. Debs Clippings, No. 8, p. 248, *TIL;* Jay Boardman Harriman, *Pinafore to Politics,* New York, 1923, p. 173.

38. John Mitchell to D. J. Keefe, Sept. 6, 1914; John Mitchell to Edgar L. Marston, Dec. 9, 1911, *JMP;* Jack Burke, "Mr. B.'s Private Union," *March of Labor,* Dec. 1950–Jan. 1951, pp. 24–25; Carol L. Thompson, *op. cit.,* p. 35.

39. "Notes on Trade Unionism," 1914, John P. Frey Papers, Container 10, Library of Congress. (Hereinafter cited as *JFP.*)

40. W. D. Mahon to Gompers, Sept. 5, 1902, *AFL Corr.;* Seidman, *op. cit.,* pp. 57–58; "Notes on Trade Unionism," *JFP,* Container 10.

41. Seidman, *op. cit.,* p. 112; Levinson, *op. cit.,* p. 69; Disbrow, *op. cit.,* pp. 307–08.

42. *The American Banker,* vol. LXV, p. 1520; Albert Topeer to Frank Morrison, Nov. 20, 1899, *AFL Corr.*

43. Chicago *Chronicle,* Jan. 3, 1904; Chicago *Tribune,* Dec. 6, 1906; "Notes on Trade Unionism," *JFP,* Container 10; newspaper clipping attached to John Golden to Gompers, April 13, 1907; Albert Hibbert, Gen. Sec'y, United Textile Workers of America, to Frank Morrison, Jan. 9, 1905, *AFL Corr.*

44. Levinson, *op. cit.,* p. 69.

45. Seidman, *op. cit.,* pp. 24–25; *Economist,* vol. XXX, Aug. 29, 1903, pp. 266–67; *Wall Street Journal,* Oct. 24, 1903.

46. Edgar L. Marston to John Mitchell, Feb. 14, 1906; John P. Mitchell to Edgar L. Marston, marked "Personal," May 24, 1905, *JMP.*

47. L. Kress to Frank Morrison, June 29, 1903, *AFL Corr.*

48. Eli Ginzberg, "American Labor Leaders: Time in Office," *Industrial & Labor Relations Review,* vol. I, Jan. 1948, p. 291; Louis Stark, "Problems of Labor Leadership," *Annals of the American Academy of Political and Social Science,* March, 1936, p. 204.

49. Philip Taft, "Opposition to Union Officers in Elections," *Quarterly Journal of Economics,* vol. LVIII, Feb. 1944, pp. 248–51, 263–64; Ginzberg, *op. cit.,* pp. 283–93.

50. W. D. Ryan to Frank Morrison, July 15, 1903, *AFL Corr.*

51. G. E. Carter, etc. to Gompers, Sept. 6, 1902, *AFL Corr.*

52. Newspaper clipping, dated Newburgh, N.Y., April 14, 1898, in *AFL Corr.;* John F. Tobin to William L. Howard, Dec. 1, 1898, and petition from members of Louisville, Kentucky Central Labor Union, 1899, *AFL Corr.*

53. "Charges of Mismanagement and Malfeasance in the Conduct of the Affairs of the International Brotherhood of Teamsters, Issued by Authority of the Sub-Committee, Representing the Committee of Protest at Philadelphia," Pamphlet, copy in *AFL Corr. See also* Cornelius P. Shea, Gen'l President, Brotherhood of Teamsters, to Gompers, Sept. 18, 1905, *ibid.*, and Chicago *American*, Aug. 6, 1905.

54. "To the Local Unions of the International Union of the United Brewery Workmen of America," leaflet signed by Joint Local Executive Boards of Greater New York and Newark, N.J., copy in *AFL Corr.;* Frank C. Pierson, "The Government of Trade Unions," *Industrial & Labor Relations Review*, vol. I, July, 1948, p. 603; Seidman, *op. cit.*, p. 64; letters to Gompers from North Adams, Mass. local, Aug. 6, 1904, *AFL Corr.*

55. John B. Lennon to Gompers, Sept. 28, 1899, *AFL Corr.;* John P. Troxell, "Machinery and the Cigar Makers," *Quarterly Journal of Economics*, vol. XLVIII, Feb. 1934, pp. 340–41.

56. Statement of Executive Officials of Cigar Makers' International Union, 1902; "To the Local Unions of the International Union of the United Brewery Workmen of America," *op. cit.;* "The Philadelphia Situation," An Answer to the Statement of the Executive Council of the International Typographical Union, Philadelphia, Jan. 16, 1905, leaflet, *AFL Corr.*

57. John B. Lennon to Gompers, Sept. 28, 1899, *AFL Corr.;* Ginzberg, *op. cit.*, pp. 283–93.

58. Seidman, *op. cit.*, p. 28.

59. *Union Herald* (Atlantic City), Feb. 16, 1901.

60. Clyde Summers, "Disciplinary Power of Unions," *Industrial & Labor Relations Review*, vol. III, July, 1950, pp. 483–513; Philip Taft, "Judicial Procedure in Labor Unions," *Quarterly Journal of Economics*, vol. LXIX, May, 1945, p. 385.

61. "Report of the Committee to Investigate the Meat Cutters' & Butchers' Trouble," Syracuse, N.Y., Sept. 20, 1899, attached to Bertram Hanover, etc. to Gompers, Oct. 10, 1899; H. D. Call to Frank Morrison, July 14, 1899; H. D. Call to Gompers, Aug. 9, 14, Sept. 23, Nov. 24, 30, 1899; John F. Tobin to Gompers, Oct. 31, Nov. 3, 1899; Tobin to Frank Morrison, Sept. 19, 1899; H. M. Eaton to Gompers, Oct. 16, 1899; Gompers to P. J. McGuire, Sept. 20, 1899, *AFL Corr.;* Brockton (Mass.) *Times*, Aug. 12, 14, Sept.19, 25, 1899.

62. Printed Circular attached to Thos. H. Schroder to Gompers, Oct. 18, 1900; Jas. P. Reed to Gompers, Oct. 21, 1900, and other letters relating to incident in *AFL Corr.*

63. Jno. J. Clark to Gompers, North Adams, Mass., Sept. 7, '04; "An Appeal From and Against Certain Decisions and Acts by and of Henry Fischer, President T.W.I.U.," Milwaukee, Wisconsin, April 6, 1904, typewritten copy in *AFL Corr.*

64. Summers, *op. cit.*, pp. 483–513; Pierson, *op. cit.*, p. 601; John F. Tobin to Gompers, Nov. 3, 13, 1899, *AFL Corr.;* Edward D. Sullivan, *This Labor Union Racket*, New York, 1936, pp. 99–100.

65. Chicago *Chronicle*, May 31, 1904; Seidman, *op. cit.*, p. 18; Frank Reiff, Sec'y Local 1236, United Brotherhood of Carpenters & Joiners, to A.F. of L. Executive Council, March 13, 1905, *AFL Corr.*

66. W. J. Clark to Frank Morrison, marked "Confidential," April 26, 1903, *AFL Corr.*

67. *The Labor Record*, April 22, 1898.

68. Gompers to J. Louidenslager, Feb. 19, 1887; Gompers to P. J. McGuire, Nov. 14, 1892; Gompers to Dr. Branch Clark, Aug. 6, 1894, *GLB; Proceedings*, A.F. of L. Convention, 1902, pp. 143–45; Seidman, *op. cit.*, pp. 9–10.

69. Chicago *Chronicle*, April 17, 1904; John F. Tobin to Gompers, Dec. 1, 1902; A. Furuseth to Gompers, Sept. 9, 1903, *AFL Corr.;* Gompers to John A. Smith, May 13, 1905, *GLB.*

70. *Leather Workers' Journal*, Sept. 1904, p. 6.

71. *Proceedings*, Hod Carriers' and Building Laborers' Union, 1906, p. 62; *Proceedings*, Hotel and Restaurant Employees' Union, 1905, p. 15.

72. Philadelphia *North American*, Aug. 10, Sept. 15, 1908; Frank Morrison to A.F.

of L. Executive Council, Aug. 14, 1908, *AFL Corr.*
73. Philadelphia *North American,* Aug. 25, 1913.
74. Gompers to W. J. Gibbons, Sept. 16, 1905; W. J. Gibbons to Gompers, Sept. 20, 1905, *AFL Corr.*
75. The discussion of the battle in the International Brotherhood of Electrical Workers is based on a vast body of correspondence in the AFL Correspondence. *See especially* Samuel Gompers, *To All Local Unions of Electrical Workers, State and Central Bodies,* Sec. 24, 1909; Gompers to A.F. of L. Executive Council, March 14, 1910; Frank Morrison to A.F. of L. Executive Council, Sept. 18, Oct. 8, Dec. 15, 1909, April 1, June 18, 1910, March 5, 1913; J. P. Frey to Morrison, Oct. 11, 1910; H. D. Thomas to Morrison, Sept. 23, 1909; F. J. McNulty to A.F. of L. Executive Council, May 23, 1911; F. J. McNulty and Peter W. Collins to Dear Sir & Bro., Feb. 2, 1909; Andrew J. Gallagher, Sec'y, San Francisco Labor Council to Morrison, Sept. 22, 1909; J. H. Streif, Sec'y Iowa State Federation of Labor, to Morrison, Aug. 6, 1909; Morrison to J. H. Streif, Aug. 6, 1909, all in *AFL Corr. See also* Cleveland *Citizen,* Oct. 30, Nov. 6, 1909, March 5, 19, 26, April 23, 1910; *Solidarity,* Nov. 9, 1912; Charles Franklin Marsh, *Trade Unionism in the Electric Light and Power Industry,* Urbana, Illinois, 1928, pp. 33–34, 55–63, 101, 103.
76. Marcy H. Cowan, "Labor Unions and Racketeering," unpublished M.A. thesis, New School for Social Research, 1948, p. 60.
77. Seidman, *op. cit.,* p. 60.
78. New York, 1930, pp. 90–91n.
79. Stone to Easley, May 6, 1919, *NCFA.*
80. Bernard Mandel, "Samuel Gompers," unpublished *MS.,* pp. 189–92; Harvard University Seminar, May 11, 1948, *JFP.*
81. Foner, *op. cit.,* vol. II, pp. 291–92.
82. Haber, *op. cit.,* p. 4; Seidman, *op. cit.,* p. 54.
83. Walter Chambers, *Labor Unions and the Public,* New York, 1936, p. 17. *See also* Harvard University Seminar, May 11, 1948, *JFP.*
84. Miners' *Magazine,* June, 1902, p. 4.
85. *Proceedings,* A.F. of L. Convention, 1906, pp. 4–10.
86. C.P.M. Cambridge to Gompers, Jan. 10, 1906, *AFL Corr.*
87. "Excerpt from Report of Austin Davis,

Secretary-Treasurer, Utah State Federation of Labor to the Convention of the Utah State Branch, March, 1909," typewritten copy, *AFL Corr.*
88. Bernard Mandel, "Samuel Gompers," unpublished *MS.,* pp. 190, 193–94.
89. *The Nation,* Sept. 11, 1935.
90. *The Leather Workers' Journal,* Sept. 1904, p. 6.

CHAPTER 7

1. Bernard Mandel, "Samuel Gompers," unpublished *MS.,* p. 286; *American Federationist,* Sept, 1902, pp. 481–82.
2. *Proceedings,* A.F. of L. Convention, 1899, p. 7.
3. Minutes of the A.F. of L. Executive Council, March 22, 1901; Gompers to "Dear Sirs and Brothers," Nov. 7, 1900, *AFL Corr.;* Gompers to Andrew J. Gallagher, Feb. 25, 1911, *GLB.*
4. Samuel Gompers, *Seventy Years of Life and Labor,* New York, 1924, vol. II, pp. 103–05.
5. *Ibid.,* p. 104; *American Federationist,* June, 1910, p. 503.
6. *Ibid.,* March, 1911, p. 220; July, 1912, p. 312; Gompers to Andrew Furuseth, Sept. 18, 1900, *GLB;* "Notes on Trade Unionism," *JFP.*
7. Homer D. Call to Mary E. McDowell, Feb. 5, 1908, Mary E. McDowell Papers, Chicago Historical Society.
8. T. Berry to Gompers, March 7, 1899; James Kearny to Gompers, April 14, 1904; John Murry to Frank Morrison, Dec. 12, 1907, *AFL Corr.*
9. *American Federationist,* Sept. 1897, pp. 143–44, Jan. 1901, pp. 27–28; July, 1902, pp. 365–66; Aug. 1901, pp. 293–94; *The Union Label: Its History and Aims,* Washington, D.C., 1904, Toledo *Union Leader,* Sept. 20, 1912.
10. Union Label Trades Department, *Official Proceedings,* 1911, pp. 9–10; Helen Marot, *American Labor Unions,* New York, 1914, pp. 131–34; Will Herberg, "Jewish Labor Movement in the United States: Early Years to World War I," *Industrial & Labor Relations Review,* vol. V, July, 1952, pp. 504–08; *Proceedings,* United Textile Workers Convention, 1902, p. 9; 1917, pp. 24–25.
11. *Abstract of the Fourteenth Census of the United States,* p. 1021.
12. Frederick J. Allen, *The Shoe Industry,* New York, 1922, pp. 41, 45, 48–53; United States Census Office, *Twelfth*

Census of the United States, Washington, 1902, vol. IX, p. 756; Arthur H. Cole, *The American Wool Manufacture,* Cambridge, Mass., 1926, vol. II, pp. 82–86, 89–91, 99; Melvin T. Copeland, *The Cotton Manufacturing Industry in the United States,* Cambridge, Mass., 1923, pp. 56, 65, 74, 80–81, 83–89, 94–98.

13. Jacob Loft, *The Printing Trades,* New York, 1944, pp. 43–49; *The Comrade,* vol. I, October, 1901–September, 1902, p. 159. George E. Barnett, "The Introduction of the Linotype," *Yale Review,* vol. XIII, Nov. 1904, pp. 251–72.

14. James Hartman, *Evolution of the Machine Shop,* New York, 1905, p. 4; Howard Monroe Raymond, *Modern Shop Practice: Machine Shop Work,* New York, 1916, pp. 265–80; *American Machinist,* vol. XXIII, 1900, pp. 636–37.

15. Geo. W. Crouse to Gompers, Akron, Ohio, 12/26/1900, *AFL Corr.*

16. Copy of letter attached to J. A. Cable to Gompers, 1/25/1900 and J. A. Cable to Gompers, 1/25/1900, *AFL Corr.*

17. Committee representing employees of the Rock Island Arsenal to Hon. Jacob M. Anderson, Sec'y of War, April 14, 1911, copy in Frederick Winslow Taylor Collection, Stevens Institute of Technology, Hoboken, N.J.; Gompers to James Duncan, March 31, 1911, *GLB.*

18. *International Molders' Journal,* vol. LI, 1915, pp. 197–98.

19. Howard M. Gitleman, "Attempts to Unify the American Labor Movement, 1865–1900," unpublished Ph.D. thesis, University of Wisconsin, 1960, pp. 525–26.

20. Gompers to Maurice Mikol, May 20, 1903, *AFL Corr.* and *GLB;* Gompers, *Seventy Years of Life and Labor,* vol. I, p. 373.

21. Loft, *op. cit.,* pp. 48–49.

22. *Machinists' Journal,* vol. IX, 1897, p. 258; vol. XI, 1899, p. 371; vol. XIII, 1901, pp. 258, 654; vol. XV, 1903, pp. 277, 586–89.

23. Letter from James O'Connell, Aug. 28, 1903, in U.S. Commissioner of Labor, *11th Special Report,* 1904, pp. 104–05.

24. Boston *Herald* reprinted in *Machinists' Journal,* vol. XVII, 1905, pp. 915, 955; International Association of Machinists, *Constitution,* 1905, pp. 25–26; J. J. Ashworth, *The Helper and American Trade Unions,* Baltimore, 1915, pp. 83, 85, 97, 100; George Marshall, "The Machinists' Union: A Study in Institutional Development," unpublished Ph.D. thesis, Robert Brookings Graduate School of Economics and Government, Washington, D.C., 1930, Chapter VII, pp. 22–26.

25. Lorwin, *op. cit.,* p. 503.

26. James A. Cable to Gompers, April 7, 1899, *AFL Corr.*

27. Ashworth, *op. cit.,* pp. 85, 94, 96, 99; *Blacksmiths' Journal,* Jan., Dec., 1903.

28. Norman J. Ware, *The Labor Movement in the United States, 1860–1895,* New York, 1929, p. 191; Denis A. Hayes to Gompers, Dec. 28, 1904, *AFL Corr.;* printed message from Denis A. Hayes, March, 1905, copy in *ibid.; The Fur Worker,* Sept.–Oct., 1923, p. 5; *Solidarity,* Jan. 22, 1910, July 22, 1911, Nov. 20, 1915.

29. "The Passing of the National Window Glass Workers," *Monthly Labor Review,* Oct. 1929, pp. 1–16; Pearce Davis, *op. cit.,* pp. 126, 177–78, 192–93.

30. Leo Wolman, *Ebb and Flow in Trade Unionism,* pp. 184–85; Chicago *Dispatch,* May 18, 1900.

31. Handbook of Labor Statistics, 1936, U.S. Bureau of Labor Statistics, *Bulletin 616,* p. 718.

32. Troxell, *op. cit.,* p. 340; Lorwin, *op. cit.,* p. 525.

33. *Solidarity,* July 2, 1910; Gompers to George W. Perkins, Feb. 6, 1908, *GLB.*

34. New York *Call,* Sept. 18, 28, 29, Oct. 1, 1912; Troxell, *op. cit.,* p. 340.

35. *See* Appendix B, Lorwin, *op. cit.,* pp. 494–95.

36. John A. Fitch, *The Steel Workers,* New York, 1911, p. 27; David Brody, *Steelworkers in America, the Non-Union Era,* Cambridge, Mass., 1960, p. 68.

37. Washington *Star,* Feb. 7, 1905; Michael F. Tighe, testimony before Committee on Education and Labor, U.S. Senate, *Investigation of Strike in Steel Industries,* Washington, 1919, pp. 341–48; Jesse S. Robinson, *The Amalgamated Association of Iron, Steel, and Tin Workers,* Baltimore, 1920, pp. 178–85; Report submitted by T. H. Flynn, Cal Wyatt, C. F. Davis, Pittsburgh, Dec. 15, 1904, typewritten copy, *AFL Corr.*

38. *American Federationist,* Jan. 1910, pp. 35–37; Gompers to the International Unions, Jan. 18, 1910; Gompers to George W. Perkins, Feb. 25, 1910, *AFL Corr.*

39. Jacob Tazelaar to Frank Morrison, Feb. 27, 1910, *AFL Corr.*

40. Toledo *News Bee,* Oct. 16, 1909.

41. *Report on Conditions of Employment in*

the *Iron and Steel Industry in the United States,* vol. III. pp. 113–14.

42. Lewis Corey, *Meat and Man,* New York, 1949, pp. 251–52.

43. John R. Commons, "Labor Conditions in Meat Packing and the Recent Strike," *Quarterly Journal of Economics,* vol. XXXIX, Nov. 1904, pp. 1–4; Chas. A. Baustian to Frank Morrison, Chicago, March 31, 1900, *AFL Corr.*

44. Commons, *op. cit.,* pp. 4–6; Harry Rosenberg, "Packing House and the Stockyards," unpublished paper, Chicago Historical Society, pp. 22–25; *Proceedings,* A. F. of L. Convention, 1911, p. 87; Homer D. Call to Frank Morrison, Oct. 28, 1904, Jan. 16, Feb. 6, 20, 1905, *AFL Corr.*

CHAPTER 8

1. *Proceedings,* A.F. of L. Convention, 1894, pp. 123–28; 1896, pp. 236–42; 1899, pp. 314–28.

2. Foner, *op. cit.,* vol. II, pp. 370–72.

3. Gompers to John Mitchell, May 1, 1901, *GLB;* Jas. O'Connell to Gompers, Aug. 22, 1901; Jas. F. Grimes to Gompers, Jan. 9, 1905; P. J. McGuire to Gompers, Jan. 12, 1900, *AFL Corr.*

4. Herman Schlüter, *The Brewing Industry and the Brewery Workers' Movement,* Cincinnati, Ohio, 1910, p. 219.

5. *Coast Seamen's Journal,* Sept. 9, 1903; letter in *Typographical Journal* quoted in Gompers to P. J. McGuire, May 21, 1898, *GLB.*

6. *Proceedings,* A.F. of L. Convention, 1897, p. 14; 1898, pp. 8–15.

7. Charles A. Madison, *American Labor Leaders: Personalities and Forces in the Labor Movement,* New York, 1950, p. 107. *See also* Lorwin, op. cit., p. 75.

8. Samuel Gompers, *Labor and the Employer,* Washington, 1920, p. 122.

9. Gompers to John Goodhue, Sec'y Federal Labor Union 401, May 5, 1892, GLB.

10. John A. Huebner to Gompers, July 28, Aug. 4, 1900; Wm. Lossie to Frank Morrison, Jan. 28, 1901, *AFL Corr.;* Gompers to Joseph A. Bauer, July 21, 1899, *GLB; Proceedings,* A.F. of L. Convention, 1901, p. 11.

11. Leo Wolman, *Ebb and Flow of Trade Unionism,* pp. 138, 192–93; Hyman Hirsch, "The Emergence of Industrial Unionism," unpublished M.A. thesis,

New York University, 1937, pp. 58–59; Knight, *op. cit.,* p. 63n.

12. Gompers to Officers and Members of Federal Labor Unions and Local Trade Unions, June 25, 1901; Gompers to Z. T. Trumbo, May 9, Oct. 21, 1902; Gompers to C. O. Hill, May 3, 1905, *AFL Corr.* and *GLB; Proceedings,* A.F. of L. Convention, 1902, pp. 10, 49, 105–06.

13. *Proceedings,* A.F. of L. Convention, 1901, p. 240; James O. Morris, *Conflict Within the AFL: A Study of Craft versus Industrial Unionism, 1901–1938,* Ithaca, N.Y., 1938, pp. 333–34.

14. John B. Lennon to Gompers, July 17, 1899, *AFL Corr.*

15. Alice Zipser, "The Attitude of the A.F. of L. toward industrial unionism," unpublished M.A. thesis, New York University, 1936, pp. 21–22; Philip Taft, *The A.F. of L. in the time of Gompers,* pp. 194–97; Schlüter, *op. cit.,* pp. 220–22; Marion Dutton Savage, *Industrial Unionism in America,* New York, 1922, pp. 26–28; T. W. Rowe, president American Flint Glass Workers Union, to Frank Morrison, Oct. 20, 1902, *AFL Corr.; Brauer-Zeitung,* Jan. 23, 1904.

16. New Orleans *Picayune,* Oct. 16–24, 1901.

17. G. W. Perkins to Gompers, Nov. 15, 1900; Pedro Casellas and Herman J. Ross of *La Resistencia* to Gompers, Nov. 10, 16, 1900, *AFL Corr.;* Washington *Post,* Nov. 16, 1900; Tampa *Times,* Nov. 12–18, 1900; *Daily People,* Nov. 18, 1900.

18. Theresa Wolfson and A. Weiss, *Industrial Unionism in the American Labor Movement,* New York, 1937, p. 10; *Solidarity,* Dec. 25, 1909, Feb. 12, March 4, 1910; Wesley Russell, Secretary-Treasurer, to Gompers, Aug. 17, 1904, enclosing resolution, *AFL Corr.*

19. Henry S. Mills to Gompers, New Bedford, Mass., July 22, 1898, *AFL Corr.*

20. John P. Frey to Gompers, Dec. 8, 1903; Julius Zorn to Gompers, Nov. 3, 1899, *AFL Corr.*

21. *Proceedings,* A.F. of L. Convention, 1899, p. 34; John B. Lennon to Frank Morrison, Sept. 4, 1899, *AFL Corr.*

22. *See especially American Federationist,* June, 1904.

23. Gompers to Harry Mason, April 9, 1903, *AFL Corr.* and *GLB.*

24. Thos. I. Kidd to Gompers, March 11, 1903, *AFL Corr.*

25. *Decision of the Umpire in Jurisdiction*

Controversy, Carpenters vs. Wood Workers, March 16, 1903; Gompers to Thomas I. Kidd and Frank Duffy, Sept. 27, 1903; Thos. I. Kidd to Gompers, June 8, 1904, *AFL Corr.*

26. For detailed discussions of jurisdictional disputes in the industry, *see* N. R. Whitney, *Jurisdiction in American Building-Trades Unions,* Baltimore, 1941; William Haber, *Industrial Relations in the Building Industry,* pp. 152–97; Royal E. Montgomery, *Industrial Relations in the Chicago Building Trades,* Chicago, 1927, pp. 119–44.

27. Chas. F. Reilly, United Order of Box Makers & Sawyers of America, to Gompers, Jan. 22, 1901, *AFL Corr.;* William O. Weyforth, *Organizability of Labor,* Baltimore, 1912, pp. 40–41.

28. Frederick Shipp Diebler, *The Amalgamated Wood Workers' International Union of America,* Madison, Wisconsin, 1912, pp. 187–88. My emphasis. P.S.F.

29. Weyforth, *op. cit.,* p. 143.

30. *Proceedings,* A.F. of L. Convention, 1902, pp. 13, 16; Gompers to Brotherhood of Painters and Decorators of America, May 17, 1900; Gompers to Charles F. Bechtold, Aug. 17, 1902; Gompers to John G. Meiler, May 4, 1907; Gompers to J. D. Pierce, Aug. 14, 1899, *AFL Corr.* and *GLB.*

31. John Mulholland to Gompers, Oct. 22, 1903; Gompers to John Mulholland, Oct. 25, 1903; Chas. O. Sherman to Frank Morrison, July 4, 1903; Frank Morrison to Chas. O. Sherman, July 8, 1903; Chas. O. Sherman to Frank Morrison, July 14, 1903, *AFL Corr.*

32. *Proceedings,* A.F. of L. Convention, 1903, pp. 18, 19, 103; Wolfson and Weiss, *op. cit.,* p. 11.

33. *Proceedings,* A.F. of L. Convention, 1904, pp. 27–30; 1907, pp. 56–62; 1912, pp. 243, 309–12; M. P. Garrick to Gompers, Dec. 15, 1902; Jack O'Donnell to Gompers, Nov. 9, 1904, *AFL Corr.*

34. Schlüter, *op. cit.,* pp. 219–23.

35. Julius Zorn to Gompers, Nov. 3, 1899, *AFL Corr.*

36. *Proceedings,* A.F. of L. Convention, 1899, pp. 126–28; P. J. McGuire to Gompers, Jan. 12, 1900; Chas. F. Bechtold to Gompers, Dec. 27, 1900, *AFL Corr.*

37. *American Federationist,* June, 1902, pp. 331–32.

38. *Proceedings,* A.F. of L. Convention, 1900, pp. 147–48; 1902, pp. 16–17, 146–47, 208; 1903, p. 112; 1904, p.

217; Schlüter, *op. cit.,* pp. 220–28; Gompers to the Officers and Members of all Affiliated Organizations, May 16, 1904, *AFL Corr.; Brauer-Zeitung,* Jan. 23, 1904.

39. *Proceedings,* A.F. of L. Convention, 1906, pp. 71–75, 211–13; 1907, pp. 44–45, 77–81, 275–77; Schlüter, *op. cit.,* p. 224.

40. Benjamin C. Roberts, "Jurisdiction Disputes Between the Brewery Workers and Other A.F. of L. Affiliates," unpublished M.A. thesis, University of Chicago, 1936, pp. 93, 158; Frank Morrison to A.F. of L. Executive Council, enclosing editorial in *Miners' Magazine, AFL Corr.; Proceedings,* A.F. of L. Convention, 1909, pp. 300–01; 1910, p. 106.

41. Perlman and Taft, *op. cit.,* p. 302.

42. John P. Frey to Gompers, Dec. 8, 1903, *AFL Corr.*

43. *Proceedings,* A.F. of L. Convention, 1907, p. 20.

44. *Proceedings,* A.F. of L. Convention, 1908, pp. 69–71.

45. Theodore Glocker, "Amalgamation of Related Trades in American Unions," *American Economic Review,* vol. V, Sept. 1915, p. 554; John B. Lennon to Gompers, Feb. 23, 1905, *AFL Corr.;* Morris, *op. cit.,* pp. 47–48.

46. Toledo *Union Leader,* Feb. 10, 1911; Lorwin, *op. cit.,* pp. 374–90; *Machinists' Journal,* vol. XVII, 1903, p. 823; *Solidarity,* July 16, 1910; E. C. Cummins, "Industrial Unionism in the Building Trades," *International Labour Review,* vol. XV, April, 1927, pp. 576–77.

47. Marion D. Savage, *op. cit.,* pp. 37–38.

48. *Ibid.,* pp. 281–84; Morris, *op. cit.,* pp. 22–24.

49. Perlman and Taft, *op. cit.,* p. 362.

CHAPTER 9

1. *American Federationist,* July, 1901, p. 252.

2. *Proceedings,* A.F. of L. Convention, 1900, p. 12; *American Federationist,* Dec. 1901, p. 546; Gompers to Mrs. T. J. Morgan, Sept. 10, 1891; Gompers to A. S. Monck, April 13, 1899; Gompers to Auguste Keufer, Jan. 23, 1900; Gompers to J. L. Sullivan, May 22, 1905; Gompers to Frank K. Foster, July 6, 1905, *AFL Corr.* and *GLB;*

Bernard Mandel, "Gompers and Business Unionism," *op. cit.*, pp. 273–74.

3. *American Federationist*, Dec. 1901, p. 546; Gompers to Frank F. Foster, July 6, 1905, *GLB*.

4. F. E. Wolfe, *Admission to American Trade Unions*, Baltimore, 1912, pp. 25–27, 103–04; *Report of the Industrial Commission on the Relations of Capital and Labor employed in Manufactures and General Business*, Washington, 1901, vol. VII, pp. 155, 183, 202, 257, 260, 283, 402, 408, 548, 596, 929, 936, 937; *Solidarity*, Jan. 22, 1910; J. L. Sullivan to Gompers, May 12, 1905; Albert Hibbert to Frank Morrison, June 21, 1904, *AFL Corr.*

5. Daniel Levine, "Gompers and Racism: A Strategy of Limited Objectives," *Mid-America*, vol. XLIII, April, 1961, p. 109.

6. Weyforth, *op. cit.*, p. 159; *Proceedings, United Textile Workers Convention*, 1905, pp. 1–2, 4–5, 8–9, 18, 47–48; Robert R. R. Brooks, "The United Textile Workers of America," unpublished Ph.D. thesis, Yale University, 1935, p. 135.

7. Wolfe, *op. cit.*, p. 25n.; *Proceedings, A. F. of L. Convention*, 1900, p. 12; John R. Commons and Associates, *History of Labor in the United States*, New York, 1918, vol. II, p. 523.

8. Frank Morrison to O. Mattie Hill, June 6, 1900; O. Mattie Hill to Frank Morrison, June 12, 1900; H. M. Eaton to Frank Morrison, June 20, 1900, *AFL Corr.*

9. Fifteenth United States Census, *Population*, vol. V, p. 37, Leo Wolman, *The Growth of Trade Unions, 1880–1923*, New York, 1924, pp. 98–99.

10. Paul F. Brissenden, *Earnings of Factory Workers, 1899 to 1927*, Washington, D.C., 1929, pp. 29, 30, 85, 94 and table 40, p. 103; F. W. Taussig, "Minimum Wages for Women," *Quarterly Journal of Economics*, vol. XXX, May, 1916, p. 414.

11. P. J. McGuire to Gompers, June 14, 1900, *AFL Corr.;* Gladys Boone, *The Women's Trade Union Leagues in Great Britain and the United States of America*, New York, 1942, p. 169.

12. William Hard; Rheta Childe Dorr, "The Women's Invasion," *Everybody's*, vol. XIX, Dec. 1908, pp. 798–810; Grace Hutchins, *Women Who Work*, New York, 1934, p. 40.

13. J. W. Smiley to Gompers, Feb. 1, 1905, *AFL Corr.; Woman's Home Companion*, Sept. 1905, p. 16, reprinted in *American Federationist*, Jan. 1906, p. 36; Frank G. Carpenter to Agnes Nestor, March 15, 1904, Agnes Nestor Papers, Chicago Historical Society.

14. Ray Ginger, *Altgeld's America: The Lincoln Ideal versus Changing Realities*, New York, 1958, pp. 246–47; *American Federationist*, Nov. 1911, pp. 896–97.

15. Hutchins, *op. cit.*, p. 234.

16. *American Federationist*, Aug. 1905, p. 76.

17. Belva M. Herron, "Labor Organization among Women," *University of Illinois Bulletin*, vol. II, no. 12, July 1, 1905, pp. 7–12; John B. Andrews and W. D. P. Bliss, "History of Women in Trade Unions," *Report on Conditions of Women and Child Wage-Earners in the United States*, Washington, 1911, p. 149; Wolfe, *op. cit.*, p. 94.

18. Walter Charriere to Gompers, Feb. 8, 1904, *AFL Corr.*

19. P. Dolan to Gompers, Oct. 29, 1904, *AFL Corr.*

20. Wolfe, *op. cit.*, pp. 85–86; Sarah Simpson to Gompers, March 13, 1903, *AFL Corr.*

21. Wolfe, *op. cit.*, pp. 88, 92; H. D. Call to Frank Morrison, Feb. 14, 1903, *AFL Corr.*

22. Ginger, *op. cit.*, pp. 242–43; Eleanor Flexner, *Century of Struggle: The Woman's Rights Movement in the United States*, New York, 1959, pp. 211, 261; Mary Anderson, *Woman at Work*, Minneapolis, 1951, p. 32; Lillian Wald, *The House on Henry Street*, New York, 1915, pp. 202–59.

23. Flexner, *op. cit.*, pp. 202, 204, 208–09; Ginger, *op. cit.*, pp. 243–45.

24. *Constitution of the National Women's Trade Union League of America, Adopted in Fanueil Hall, Boston, November 17–19, 1903*, Article III.

25. *Ibid.*, Article II.

26. *Annual Report of the Women's Trade Union League of New York, 1907–1908*, p. 5; Boone, *op. cit.*, pp. 166–68.

27. Boone, *op. cit.*, pp. 166–68.

28. *Woman's Labor Leader: An Autobiography of Agnes Nestor*, Rockford, Illinois, 1954, p. 80.

29. *Union Labor Advocate*, Dec. 1907.

30. *Ibid.*, May, 1908.

31. *Proceedings, A.F. of L. Convention*, 1908, p. 12; 1917, p. 32.

32. Leo Wolman, "The Extent of Labor Organization in the United States in

1910," *Quarterly Journal of Economics,* vol. XXX, 1916, pp. 502–04.

33. *Report of U.S. Industrial Commission,* 1900, vol. VII, p. 168.

34. Wolfe, *op. cit.,* p. 93.

35. *Ibid.,* p. 84.

36. Samuel Gompers, *Labor and the Employer,* New York, 1920, pp. 166–79; Bernard Mandel, "Samuel Gompers," unpublished *MS.,* p. 450.

37. W. E. B. Du Bois, editor, *The Negro Artisan,* Atlanta, Ga., 1902, pp. 158–60; Sterling D. Spero and Abram L. Harris, *The Black Worker,* New York, 1934, pp. 220–22; Wolfe, *op. cit.,* p. 117.

38. John T. Wilson to Gompers, Aug. 1903, AFL Corr.; *American Federationist,* Feb. 1900, pp. 34–35; Du Bois, *op. cit.,* p. 157; Spero and Harris, *op. cit.,* p. 89.

39. Brotherhood of Railway Carmen, *Convention Proceedings,* 1905, p. 9; *Railway Carmen's Journal,* 1907, pp. 189, 211; *Proceedings,* A. F. of L. Convention, 1910, pp. 96–98; 1911, pp. 323–25, 334.

40. Foner, *op. cit.,* vol. II, p. 349; L. V. Curtin to Frank Morrison, March 21, 1900, *AFL Corr.*

41. *Proceedings,* A. F. of L. Convention, 1900, p. 263; Gompers to H. A. Stemburgh, July 20, 1903; Gompers to L. E. Turley, Sept. 20, 1905; Gompers to Frank Duffy, March 2, 1906; R. Lee Guard, Secretary to Gompers, to W. B. Davis, May 19, 1905, *GLB.*

42. Gompers to H. A. Stemburgh, July 20, 1903, *GLB;* New York *Tribune,* Dec. 13, 1901.

43. Gompers to David William, Feb. 16, 1903, *GLB;* Frank Morrison to John T. Wilson, Nov. 6, 1903, *AFL Corr.*

44. Minutes of Executive Council, Sept. 21, 1903, in *American Federationist,* Nov. 1903, p. 1191; Gompers to Calmeze E. Henike, March 19, 1903; Gompers to J. H. Patterson, March 14, 23, 1903; Gompers to L. B. Allen, March 30, May 8, 1903; Gompers to James McNair, Nov. 6, 1905; J. C. Skemp to Frank Morrison, July 9, 1904; Frank Morrison to J. C. Skemp, July 28, 1904, *AFL Corr.;* Minutes of Executive Council, Oct. 16–21, 1911 in *American Federationist,* Dec. 1911, p. 1011; statement of Gompers in Toledo *News-Bee,* Oct. 27, 1905.

45. *Electrical World,* April, 1903, p. 102.

46. Taft, *A. F. of L. in the Time of Gompers,* pp. 311–14.

47. George Sinclair Mitchell, "The Negro in Southern Trade Unionism," *Southern Economic Journal,* vol. II, Jan. 1933, pp. 27–28; Herman D. Bloch, "Craft Unions and the Negro in Historical Perspective," *Journal of Negro History,* vol. XLIII, Jan. 1958, pp. 15–25; Herman D. Bloch, "Craft Unions and a Link in the Circle of Negro Discrimination," *Phylon,* Fourth Quarter, 1958, pp. 360–63.

48. Booker T. Washington, *The Negro Problem,* New York, 1903, pp. 84–85.

49. Jack Abramowitz, "Accommodation and Militancy in Negro Life, 1876–1950," unpublished Ph.D. thesis, Teachers College, Columbia University, 1950, p. 189; George James Stevenson, "Brotherhood of Locomotive Engineers and its Leaders, 1863–1920," unpublished Ph.D. thesis, Vanderbilt University, 1954, p. 233.

50. Mitchell, *op. cit.,* pp. 27–28.

51. Foner, *op. cit.,* vol. II, p. 354.

52. Herbert R. Northrup, *Organized Labor and the Negro,* New York and London, 1944, pp. 103, 110; *Report of the Industrial Commission,* 1900, vol. VII, p. 226; H. D. Witten to Jno. Krachenbuhl, Nov. 24, 1903, attached to Henry Fischer to Gompers, Feb. 16, 1904, *AFL Corr.*

53. *Report of the Industrial Commission,* 1900, vol. VII, pp. 488, 489, 554, 555; Robert H. Wiebe, *Businessmen and Reform: A Study of the Progressive Movement,* Cambridge, Mass., 1962, p. 182; John Graham Brooks, *The Social Unrest,* New York, 1903, p. 102.

54. Gompers to Henry M. Walker, Nov. 8, 1899, *GLB.*

55. Gompers, *Labor and the Employer,* pp. 166–67; *American Federationist,* April, 1901, pp. 118–20; Gompers to J. H. Powell, Feb. 12, 1901, *GLB.*

56. St. Paul Union *Advocate* quoted in *American Federationist,* Sept. 1905, p. 636; Aug. 1906, p. 534; Terre Haute (Indiana) *Post,* Nov. 21, 1910 in Eugene V. Debs Miscellaneous Papers, 1910–1911, *TIL.*

57. E. Franklin Frazier, "A Negro Industrial Group," *Howard Review,* vol. I, June, 1924, p. 222. See also *Daily People,* Feb. 10, 1901.

58. *American Federationist,* Aug. 1906, p. 5; Oscar Ameringer, "To Rise Together," in *Sagas of Struggle, A Labor Anthology,* selected by Samuel Colton, New York, 1951, p. 46.

59. Herbert Aptheker, editor, *A Documentary History of the Negro People*

in the United States, New York, 1951, p. 842; *Charities*, Oct. 7, 1905.

60. Booker T. Washington, "The Negro and the Labor Unions," *Atlantic Monthly*, June, 1913, pp. 756–57; Booker T. Washington, *The Negro in Business*, Boston, 1907, p. 317.

61. Abramowitz, *op. cit.*, pp. 174–76.

62. W. E. B. Du Bois, *op. cit.*, pp. 7–8, 169–70; Aptheker, *op. cit.*, pp. 902, 916–18; Langston Hughes, *Fight for Freedom, The Story of the NAACP*, New York, 1962, pp. 17–25; *The Crisis*, July, 1912, p. 131; May, 1913, pp. 31–33.

63. Du Bois, *op. cit.*, p. 177; Gompers to W. E. B. Du Bois, Jan. 5, 1903, GLB.

64. Samuel Gompers, "Trade Union Attitude Toward Colored Workers," *American Federationist*, April, 1901, pp. 118–20; Gompers, statement for memorial book in honor of Booker T. Washington, Jan. 14, 1916, in A.F. of L. "Special Articles" file.

65. *Proceedings*, A.F. of L. Convention, 1895, p. 38; James Gibbons to Gompers, July 22, 1903, *AFL Corr.*; *Journal of the Knights of Labor*, Aug. 1903; *The Metropolis*, Jacksonville, Florida, May 25, 1907, copy in *AFL Corr.*; New Orleans *Daily Picayune*, Sept. 2, 1902, quoted in *American Federationist*, Oct. 1902, pp. 709–10; *British Columbia Federationist*, April 25, 1913.

66. *Proceedings*, A.F. of L. Convention, 1910, p. 237; Gompers, "The Negro in the A.F. of L.," *American Federationist*, Jan. 1911, pp. 34–36.

67. New York *Evening Post*, Nov. 25, 1910.

68. Bernard Mandel, "Samuel Gompers and the Negro Workers," *Journal of Negro History*, vol. XL, Jan. 1955, pp. 60–61; *American Federationist*, July, 1915, p. 517; Gompers, *Seventy Years of Life and Labor*, vol. I, p. 364.

69. *Charities*, Oct. 7, 1905, reprinted in Aptheker, *op. cit.*, p. 839.

70. Mary E. McDowell, "Woman's Union in Packing House," Folder 15, Mary E. McDowell Papers, Chicago Historical Society.

71. Frazier, *op. cit.*, p. 198.

72. New Orleans *Daily Picayune*, Oct. 22, 1902.

73. *Ibid.*, Nov. 17, 1902; Ameringer, *op. cit.*, p. 49.

74. New Orleans *Daily Picayune*, Oct. 5, 18–19, 1907.

75. New Orleans *Times-Picayune*, Oct. 20,

1907; New Orleans *Daily Picayune*, Oct. 30–Nov. 1, 1907.

76. New Orleans *Daily Picayune*, Nov. 1, 4, 1907.

77. *Ibid.*, Nov. 3, 1907.

78. *Ibid.*, Nov. 1, 2, 9, 1907.

79. *Ibid.*, Nov. 21, 1907; Ameringer, *op. cit.*, pp. 53–54.

80. New York *Age*, July 12, 1906, reprinted in Aptheker, *op. cit.*, p. 843.

81. New York *Age*, Aug. 30, 1906, reprinted in Aptheker, *op. cit.*, pp. 843–44.

82. *Leather Workers' Journal*, Oct. 1904, p. 92.

83. Wolfe, *op. cit.*, pp. 122–24; B. F. Lee, Jr. in Philadelphia *Public Ledger*, April 13, 1913.

84. Richard R. Wright, Jr., *The Negro in Pennsylvania: A Study in Economic History*, Philadelphia, 1911, pp. 94–99.

85. *The New Review*, vol. I, Jan. 11, 1913, p. 55.

CHAPTER 10

1. *Historical Statistics of the United States, 1789–1945*, Washington, 1949, p. 33; Samuel Joseph, *Jewish Immigration to the United States from 1881 to 1910*, New York, 1914, pp. 16–18.

2. Report of the Immigration Commissioner, "Statistical Review of Immigration, 1820–1910," *Senate Doc. No. 756*, 61st Congress, 3rd Session, p. 96.

3. *Ibid.*, pp. 100–05.

4. Melvyn Dubofsky, "Organized Labor and the Immigrant in New York City, 1900–1918," *Labor History*, vol. II, Spring, 1961, p. 184.

5. Edwin Fenton, "Immigrants and Unions: A Case Study, Italians and American Labor, 1870–1920," unpublished Ph.D. thesis, Harvard University, 1957, pp. 70, 85–86, 87.

6. Dubofsky, *op. cit.*, pp. 185–86.

7. *Cf.* Thomas Bailey Aldrich, *Unguarded Gates and Other Poems*, Boston and New York, 1895; Madison Grant, *The Passing of the Great Race*, New York, 1916; John Higham, *Strangers in the Land*, New York, 1956; Barbara Miller Solomon, *Ancestors and Immigrants*, Cambridge, Mass., 1957.

8. *American Federationist*, Jan. 1911, p. 3; *Proceedings*, A.F. of L. Convention, 1907, pp. 207–08.

9. Foner, *op. cit.*, vol. II, pp. 361–62; *Proceedings*, National Association of Manufacturers, 1904, p. 121; Albion G. Taylor, *op. cit.*, pp. 57–58; *Bulletin*

of the National Association of Wool Manufacturers, vol. XLII, 1912, pp. 139–41; *American Industries,* vol. I, Oct. 15, 1902, p. 6; vol. II, April 1, 1904, p. 6; vol. XVI, Feb. 1916, p. 9; New York *Journal of Commerce and Commercial Bulletin,* July 23, 1915.

10. Dubofsky, *op. cit.,* p. 185; David J. Saposs, *Left Wing Unionism,* New York, 1926, p. 114; Philip Zausner, *Unvarnished: The Autobiography of a Union Leader,* New York, 1941, p. 40; Wolfe, *op. cit.,* pp. 25–27, 61–65, 99–102, 103–04; *American Labor Yearbook, 1921–1922,* pp. 182–83; Max Naft, "Jewish Workers in the Building Trades," *United Hebrew Trades 50th Jubilee Book,* pp. 195–98; *Documentary History of the Amalgamated Clothing Workers of America, 1914–1916,* p. viii.

11. New York *Call,* Sept. 25, 1909.

12. H. A. Stemburgh to Frank Morrison, April 11, 1904; Frank Morrison to H. A. Stemburgh, April 13, 1904, *AFL Corr.*

13. *New York Times,* July 1, 1901; *Proceedings,* A.F. of L. Convention, 1907, pp. 290–91; *The Weekly Bulletin of the Clothing Trades,* Aug. 2, 1907, p. 1; Dubofsky, *op. cit.,* pp. 187–88.

14. Joseph H. Taylor, "The Immigration Restriction League," *Midwest Journal,* vol. I, Summer, 1949, pp. 55-56; Joseph H. Taylor, "The Restriction of European Immigration and the Concept of Race," *South Atlantic Quarterly,* vol. L, Jan. 1951, pp. 227-28.

15. Gompers, *Seventy Years of Life and Labor,* vol. II, p. 160; Arthur Mann, "Gompers and the Irony of Racism," *Antioch Review,* Summer, 1953, p. 212.

16. *Abstract of Reports of the Immigration Commission,* vol. I, pp. 520–31.

17. *Ibid.,* p. 8.

18. *American Federationist,* Jan. 1911, pp. 5, 8; copy of petition in *AFL Corr.*

19. Isaac A. Hourwich, *Immigration and Labor,* New York, 1912, pp. 325, 326 334-35, 341-42, 349-50, 381, 446-47. For a more recent critical analysis of the Commission's finding, *see* Oscar Handlin, *Race and Nationality in American Life,* Boston, 1957, pp. 97-138.

20. *Facts About Immigration,* Report of the Proceedings of Conference on Immigration held by the Immigration Department of the National Civic Federation, New York, 1907, pp. 68–69, 98.

21. *Chautauquan,* vol. XXIX, p. 21, Morell Head, "Business Attitudes Towards European Immigration, 1880–1900," *Journal of Economic History,* vol. XIII, Summer, 1953, pp. 296, 301–02.

22. C. O. Sherman to Frank Morrison, June 27, 1903, *AFL Corr.; Leather Workers' Journal,* Oct. 1906, p. 108.

23. Report of T. H. Flynn, Cal Wyatt and C. F. Davis, Pittsburgh, Dec. 15, 1904, *AFL Corr.;* AFL Weekly News Letter, No. 11, 1911, mimeographed copy in *AFL Corr.*

24. *Panhellenic,* Feb. 26, 1909, copy of original and translation in *AFL Corr.;* D. Vensto to Gompers, Feb. 27, 1909, *ibid.*

25. Hays Robbins, editor, *Labor and the Common Welfare,* New York, 1919, p. 83; Mann, *op. cit.,* pp. 208–10; Mary R. Coolidge, *Chinese Immigration,* New York, 1909, pp. 368–70.

26. *Some Reasons for Chinese Exclusion . . . ,* pp. 6–7, 19–30, 34–35.

27. *Proceedings,* A.F. of L. Convention, 1901, pp. 21–22, 154–55.

28. Coolidge, *op. cit.,* pp. 244–51; *Proceedings,* A.F. of L. Convention, 1903, pp. 7–8.

29. Carey McWilliams, *Brothers Under the Skin,* Boston, 1951, p. 143; *Proceedings,* A.F. of L. Convention, 1904, pp. 7–8; *American Federationst,* May, 1905, p. 275; Feb. 1906, p. 93; March, 1906, p. 161.

30. *American Federationist,* May, 1905, p. 284; Feb. 1907, p. 103; Gompers, *Seventy Years of Life and Labor,* vol. II, pp. 165–66.

31. Taft, *A.F. of L. in the Time of Gompers,* p. 318.

32. *American Federationist,* Oct. 1913, pp. 836–37.

33. *Proceedings,* A.F. of L. Convention, 1914, p. 469.

34. Carl Wittke, *We Who Built America,* New York, 1939, pp. 459–60; *Fifteenth Census of the United States,* 1930, Population, vol. II, Washington, D.C., 1931; William S. Bernard, editor, *American Immigration Policy,* New York, 1950, pp. 128–34.

35. Coolidge, *op. cit.,* chapter XIX and p. 399.

36. Fred W. Riggs, *Pressures on Congress: A Study of the Repeal of Chinese Exclusion,* New York, 1930, p. 12.

37. *Some Reasons for Chinese Exclusion, op. cit.,* pp. 35–36.

38. *American Federationist,* May, 1905, p. 275.

39. Edward Rosenberg, "Chinese Workers in China," *ibid.*, Aug. 1903, p. 655.
40. There are twenty-two letters from Takano to Gompers in the *AFL Corr.*, covering the period 1896–1898, each of which describes union activity and strike struggles in Japan.
41. Fred Sackwitz, Recording Secretary, L. U. 745 to Frank Duffy, Honolulu, March 9, 21, 1905; Frank Duffy to Gompers, Mar. 21, 29, 1905; Gompers to Frank Duffy, March 23, April 6, 1905, *AFL Corr.*
42. *Third Biennial Report of California Bureau of Labor Statistics, 1888,* p. 84.
43. Jere L. Sullivan to Gompers, June 20, 1904; Gompers to Jere L. Sullivan, June 24, 1904, *AFL Corr.*
44. Oakland *Tribune*, April 21, 1903; Gompers to J. M. Larraras, May 15, 1903; J. M. Larraras to Gompers, June 8, 1903, *AFL Corr.*
45. *American Labor Union Journal,* June 25, 1903.
46. Oakland *Tribune,* April 21, 1903; Stuart Jamieson, "Labor Unionism in American Agriculture," *Bulletin No. 836,* United States Department of Labor, Bureau of Labor Statistics, Washington, 1945, pp. 56–62.
47. Helena (Montana) *News*, Sept. 9, 1908; *Solidarity,* June 18, 1910.
48. Andrew Furuseth to Frank Morrison, June 12, 1903, *AFL Corr.;* British Columbia *Federationist,* Aug. 8, 1913.
49. Wolman, *op. cit.*, p. 503; G. H. Perry to Gompers, New Castle, Pa., Jan. 19, 1910, *AFL Corr.;* Gordon S. Watkins, *Introduction to Labor Problems,* New York, 1904, p. 165; *Bricklayer and Mason,* Dec. 1909; Wolfe, *op. cit.*, pp. 40, 42–43, 50–52.
50. Typewritten memorandum of questions and answers on manual training, July, 1901, *AFL Corr.;* New York *Call,* Jan. 14, 1912.
51. Lockwood Report, final, p. 26.
52. Morris, *op. cit.,* p. 10.
53. *Ibid.,* pp. 11, 14.
54. Washington *Star,* Feb. 7, 1905; Gompers, *Seventy Years of Life and Labor,* vol. I, pp. 147–48.

CHAPTER 11

1. Gompers to the Officers and Members of Local Unions of the International Union of Carriage & Wagon Workers, Oct. 4, 1900, *AFL Corr.*
2. Gompers to D. Sudowitz, July 17, 1899; Gompers to Wm. Mudge, March 19, 1898, *GLB.*
3. *Report of the U.S. Industrial Commission, 1900,* vol, VII, p. 259; Terre Haute (Indiana) *Gazette,* Nov. 28, 1903, in Eugene V. Debs Scrapbooks, No. 6. p. 130, *TIL.*
4. *American Federationist,* Sept. 1902, p. 116; John B. Lennon to Frank Morrison, Mch. 13, 1903, *AFL Corr.*
5. *American Federationist,* Sept. 1900, p. 284; Harvard University Seminar, May 11, 1948, *JFP,* Container 10.
6. John B. Lennon to Frank Morrison, Mch. 13, 1903, *AFL Corr.*
7. *American Federationist,* Sept. 1900, p. 284.
8. *Ibid.,* Sept. 1902, p. 116; Feb. 1914, p. 114.
9. Harold J. Laski, *The American Democracy,* New York, 1948, pp. 222–23; *Proceedings,* A.F. of L. Convention, 1897, p. 22; Hearings before Committee on Labor, *H.R.50,* 1900, pp. 428–29.
10. Robert Hunter, *Labor in Politics,* Chicago, 1915, pp. 32–85.
11. *Coast Seamen's Journal,* July 24, 1901.
12. Thomas W. Page, "The San Francisco Labor Movement," *Political Science Quarterly,* vol. XVII, Jan. 1902, p. 678; *Coast Seamen's Journal,* Aug. 7, 1901.
13. *Coast Seamen's Journal,* Aug. 7, 21, 28, Sept. 11, 1901.
14. Ira B. Cross, *A History of the Labor Movement in California,* Berkeley, Calif., 1935, p. 243; San Francisco *Examiner,* Sept. 1, 1901; *Coast Seamen's Journal,* Oct. 2, 1901; Knight, *op. cit.,* pp. 87–88.
15. San Francisco *Examiner,* July 21, 29, 1901; Edward Joseph Rowell, "The Union Labor Party of San Francisco, 1901–1911," unpublished Ph.D. thesis, University of California, Berkeley, 1938, p. 15.
16. San Francisco *Bulletin,* Aug. 20, 25, 1901; San Francisco *Examiner,* Sept. 2, 1901.
17. *Coast Seamen's Journal,* June 19, July 10, Sept. 7, Oct. 30, 1901.
18. San Francisco *Chronicle,* Sept. 10, 1901; Rowell, *op. cit.,* pp. 28–33.
19. San Francisco *Bulletin,* Oct. 24, 1901; San Francisco *Star,* Oct. 19, 1901; *Organized Labor* (San Francisco), vol. II, No. 30, Oct. 26, 1901.
20. *Coast Seamen's Journal,* Oct. 30, 1901; San Francisco *Bulletin,* Oct, 21, 1901.
21. San Francisco *Examiner,* Oct. 28, 1901; Hyman Weintraub, *Andrew Furuseth,*

Emancipator of the Seamen, Berkeley and Los Angeles, 1959, p. 71.

22. Rowell, *op. cit.,* p. 43.

23. *Ibid.,* pp. 41–42; *Coast Seamen's Journal,* Nov. 3, 1901; Ray Stannard Baker, "A Corner in Labor," *op. cit.,* p. 368.

24. *Coast Seamen's Journal,* Nov. 13, 1901.

25. Rowell, *op. cit.,* pp. 104–05; *Labor Clarion* (San Francisco), vol. I, No. 7, April 11, 1902; Paul Taylor, *The Sailors' Union of the Pacific,* New York, 1923, pp. 102–08; Cross, *op. cit.,* pp. 258–61.

26. San Francisco *Chronicle,* April 18, 1902.

27. San Francisco *Bulletin,* April 17, 26, 27, 1902; Rowell, *op. cit.,* pp. 129–30; *Labor Clarion* (San Francisco), vol. I, no. 10, May 2, 1902.

28. *Tenth Biennial Report, California Bureau of Labor Statistics, 1901–1902,* pp. 66, 78; Knight, *op. cit.,* p. 100.

29. Cross, *op. cit.,* p. 249.

30. Andrew Furuseth to Gompers, Feb. 2, 1903, *AFL Corr.*

31. San Francisco *Bulletin,* Oct. 4, 1903; San Francisco *Chronicle,* Nov. 4, 1903.

32. *Coast Seamen's Journal,* May 11, 1904.

33. *Labor Clarion* (San Francisco), vol. III, no. 12, May 13, 1904; no. 51, Feb. 10, 1905; San Francisco *Examiner,* Sept. 20, 1904.

34. San Francisco *Evening Post,* July 20, 1905.

35. Reprinted in *Coast Seamen's Journal,* April 26, 1905.

36. *Coast Seamen's Journal,* April 26, 1905; Rowell, *op. cit.,* pp. 98–99.

37. San Francisco *Bulletin,* Aug. 10, 1905; San Francisco *Examiner,* Nov. 10, 1905; Knight, *op. cit.,* pp. 140–64.

38. Cross, *op. cit.,* pp. 280–87; Grace H. Stimson, *Rise of the Labor Movement in Los Angeles,* pp. 232–36; Los Angeles *Times,* July 24, 1902.

39. *Leather Workers' Journal,* May, 1903, p. 454; Jan. 1904, p. 32; May, 1904, p. 125.

40. *Direct Legislation Record,* vol. VIII, June, 1902, p. 29; Ray Stannard Baker to Theodore Roosevelt, Nov. 10, 1903, *TRP.*

41. *Proceedings,* A.F. of L. Convention, 1904, pp. 2–6.

42. *Ibid.,* pp. 132, 164; Stimson, *op. cit.,* pp. 233–35; *International Socialist Review,* vol. III, Jan. 1903, pp. 416–18; Los Angeles *Times,* July 28–30, 1902.

43. W. B. Wilson to Frank Morrison, Aug. 16, 1902; *AFL Corr.*

44. Gompers, *Seventy Years of Life and Labor,* vol. II, p. 195; Truax *v.* Corrigan (1921) 257 United States 312.

45. Edwin E. Witte, *The Government in Labor Disputes,* New York, 1932, p. 120; *International Molders' Journal,* Sept. 12, 1910.

46. *American Federationist,* April, 1900, pp. 101–02; May, 1904, pp. 397–99; May, 1911, pp. 32–35; Gompers to Reuben O. Moon, March 2, *GLB;* Bernard Mandel, "Samuel Gompers," unpublished *MS.,* p. 364.

47. *American Federationist,* Sept. 1897, p. 160.

48. Harwood Lawrence Childs, *Labor and Capital in National Politics,* Columbus, Ohio, 1930, pp. 220–22.

49. Washington *Post,* Aug. 21, 25, 1903; Scheinberg, *op. cit.,* p. 86; Fort Worth (Texas) *Register,* Oct. 10, 1903, in Eugene V. Debs Clipping Books, No. 6, *TIL:* H. C. Lodge, *Selections from the Correspondence of Theodore Roosevelt and Henry Cabot Lodge, 1884–1918,* New York and London, 1921, vol. II, p. 51.

50. Sterling D. Spero, *The Labor Movement in a Government Industry,* New York, 1924, p. 97.

51. *New York Times,* July 22, 1903; J. B. Bishop, *Theodore Roosevelt and His Times,* New York, 1920, vol. I, pp. 250–51; vol. II, pp. 15–16.

52. *Proceedings,* A.F. of L. Convention, 1904, pp. 237–41.

53. *American Federationist,* July 15, 1904 (Extra Number).

54. *Ibid.*

55. Reprinted in *The Comrade,* vol. III, Oct. 1904, p. 294.

56. *Proceedings,* A.F. of L. Convention, 1905, pp. 78, 233.

57. Frank S. Stumpf, Rec. Sec. Local No. 49, to Frank Morrison, Oct. 4, 1904, *AFL Corr.*

58. Reprinted in *The Comrade,* vol. III, Aug. 1904, p. 260.

59. New York *Herald,* July 13, 1913.

60. *Official Proceedings of the Thirtieth Republican National Convention, 1904,* Minneapolis, 1904, p. 136.

61. *The Nation,* vol. LXXXVIII, Jan. 7, 1904; *Democratic National Convention. Official Report of the Proceedings,* New York, 1904, p. 129.

62. New York *Journal,* Feb. 6, 1904; New York *American,* March 18, 1903.

63. John F. Winkler, *William Randolph Hearst,* New York, 1928, pp. 188–91; Chicago *Evening American,* Jan. 7, 1904; Chicago *Socialist,* March 21,

1903; Thomas C. Geary, "The Presidential Campaign and Election of 1904," unpublished Ph.D. thesis, University of Iowa, 1937, p. 161; Ferdinand Lundberg, *Imperial Hearst*, New York, 1936, pp. 101–02; W. A. Swanberg, *Citizen Hearst*, New York, 1961, pp. 217–18.

64. Geary, *op. cit.*, pp. 162–63; Scheinberg, *op. cit.*, pp. 94–95; *Democratic National Convention. Official Report of the Proceedings*, p. 168.

65. New York *Tribune*, April 12, 1904; *The Commoner*, April 15, 22, 1904.

66. K. H. Porter, *National Party Platforms*, New York, 1932, pp. 254–56, 265–70.

67. Herbert Green, "The Presidential Campaign of 1904," unpublished M.A. thesis, New York University, 1937, p. 67.

68. Lancaster (Pa.) *Labor Leader*, April 8, 1905; copy of leaflet, headed "Pennsylvania Program," April, 1905, *AFL Corr.*

69. *Leather Workers' Journal*, March, 1905, p. 382.

70. Frank Morrison to James Busch, March 10, 1905, *AFL Corr.*

CHAPTER 12

1. Berry *vs.* Donovan 1888 Mass. 353 74 N.E. 603, 1905; *American Federationist*, Sept. 1905, p. 610.

2. *American Federationist*, Nov. 1905, p. 835.

3. Lochner *vs.* New York, U.S. 43, 1905; Edward Berman, *Labor and the Sherman Act*, New York, 1930, p. 300.

4. *American Federationist*, March, 1906, pp. 156–57.

5. Loewe *vs.* Lawlor, 142 fed. 216, Dec. 13, 1905; Berman, *op. cit.*, p. 300; Marc Karson, *American Labor Unions & Politics, 1900–1918*, Carbondale, Illinois, 1958, pp. 36–37; Leaflet entitled, "Officers of A.F. of L. and United Hatters of North America Sued for $340,000, Danbury, Conn., Sept. 12, 1903," copy in *AFL Corr.*

6. Karson, *op. cit.*, p. 32.

7. Chicago *Tribune*, May 11, 1905.

8. *Ibid.*, May 11–12, 1905; Scheinberg, *op. cit.*, pp. 23–25; Theodore Roosevelt to Henry Cabot Lodge, May 15, 1905, *TRP.*

9. Chicago *Evening Post*, May 11, 1905; Chicago *Record-Herald*, May 12, 1905; J. M. Dickinson to William Loeb, Jr., May 11, 1905, in *TRP.*

10. Theodore Roosevelt to Kermit Roosevelt, May 14, 1905, *TRP.*

11. *American Federationist*, March, 1906, p. 163; *Cong. Record*, 59th Cong., 1st Session, pp. 1604–06; Theodore Roosevelt to W. H. Taft, July 27, 1906, *TRP;* Scheinberg, *op. cit.*, pp. 95–97.

12. *American Federationist*, June, 1905, pp. 361–64.

13. New York *Tribune*, April 16, 1906; R. H. Tawney, *The British Labor Movement*, New Haven, Conn., 1925, p. 26; Henry Pelling, *America & the British Left: From Bright to Bevan*, London, 1956, pp. 66–68.

14. Labour Representation Committee, *Report*, 1902, p. 12.

15. Gompers to A.F. of L. Executive Council, Feb. 13, 1906, *GLB.*

16. "Minutes of Conference of Labor Committee, March 3, 1906," in Samuel Gompers Scrapbook on the Campaign of 1906, *AFL Archives.*

17. Gompers to Executive Officers of affiliated international unions, March 5, 1906, *AFL Corr.* The letters of Gompers to Roosevelt, Frye, and Cannon and their replies are in Samuel Gompers Scrapbook on the Campaign of 1906, *AFL Archives.*

18. *American Federationist*, May, 1906, pp. 316–17.

19. New York *Tribune*, March 22, 1906; *The Nation*, vol. LXXXII, March 29, 1906, p. 254; Gompers, *Seventy Years of Life and Labor*, vol. II, p. 244; James E. Watson, *As I Knew Them*, New York, 1936, p. 99.

20. New York *Tribune*, March 25, 1906; *American Federationist*, May, 1906, p. 293.

21. "Talks on Labor: Trade Unions and Politics," Address by Samuel Gompers before Cigarmakers' Union No. 144, New York City, April 27, 1906, *American Federationist*, Aug. 1906, pp. 542–44; *Text Book of Labor's Political Demands*, Issued by Authority of the Executive Council, American Federation of Labor, Washington, D. C., 1906, pp. 9–10, 12.

22. *Ibid.*

23. *The Independent*, vol. LXI, May 3, 1906, pp. 1050–51.

24. "A.F. of L. Campaign Programme," July 22, 1906, printed copies in *AFL Corr.*

25. *Ibid.*

26. Dallas *Laborer*, July 21, 1906, copy in *AFL Corr.;* Gompers to Henry Abrahams, Aug. 3, 1906; Gompers to Frank K. Foster, Aug. 8, 1906, *GLB.*

27. *United Mine Workers' Journal*, July 26, 1906.
28. Quoted in Gompers' editorial in *American Federationist*, Aug. 1906, p. 536. The name of the periodical is not given.
29. *Ibid.*, Sept. 1906, pp. 643–48.
30. *Ibid.*, Nov. 1906, p. 880.
31. Gompers, *Seventy Years of Life and Labor*, vol. II, pp. 238, 244; Boston *American*, Aug. 21, 1906.
32. *American Federationist*, Sept. 1906, p. 641; Oct. 1906, p. 795; M. C. Cuniff, "Labor in Politics," *World's Work*, vol. XIII, 1906, p. 8130; New York *Herald*, Aug. 26, 1906.
33. Gompers to A.F. of L. Executive Council, Aug. 15, '06, *AFL Corr.*
34. Lewiston (Maine) *Morning News*, Aug. 20, 1906.
35. *Ibid.*, Aug. 20, 22–26, 1906; Boston *American*, Sept. 1, 1906; leaflets in *AFL Corr.*
36. Lewiston *Morning News*, Aug. 18, 20, 27, 1906; Lewiston *Journal*, Aug. 27, 1906.
37. Boston *American*, Aug. 22, 23, Sept. 1, 1906.
38. *Ibid.*, Aug. 22, 1906; H. S. Hobbs to Gompers, in Lewiston *Sun*, Aug. 18, 1906; *American Federationist*, Oct. 1906, p. 799; Gompers, *Seventy Years of Life and Labor*, vol. II, pp. 245–46.
39. Lewiston *Morning News*, Sept. 10, 1906; Gompers, *Seventy Years of Life and Labor*, vol. II, p. 245; *Current Literature*, vol. XLI, Sept. 1906, p. 248.
40. *Selections from the Correspondence of Theodore Roosevelt and Henry Cabot Lodge*, vol. II, p. 230; W. H. Taft to Charles E. Littlefield, Sept. 11, 1906, William Howard Taft Papers, Library of Congress; W. H. Taft to Theodore Roosevelt, Nov. 4, 1906, *TRP;* Roosevelt to Henry Cabot Lodge, Aug. 9, 1906, *ibid.;* Washington *Post*, Aug. 10, 1906; Boston *American*, Sept. 5, 1906.
41. Circular signed by Harrison Loring, Jr., Sept. 4, 1906, attached to Frank Morrison to A.F. of L. Executive Council, Feb. 4, 1908, *AFL Corr.*
42. Lewiston *Daily Sun*, Sept. 1, 1906; Boston *Herald*, Sept. 7, 1906; Rockland *Daily Star*, Sept. 8, 1906.
43. *Wall Street Journal*, Sept. 12, 1906.
44. Gompers to John Mitchell, Aug. 26, 1906, *AFL Corr.*
45. John Mitchell to Gompers, Aug. 30, 1906, *AFL Corr.*
46. Lewiston *Daily Sun*, Sept. 1, 1906.
47. Leaflet dated Washington, D.C., Sept. 24, 1906, *AFL Corr.;* Cuniff, *op. cit.*,

p. 8131; *American Federationist*, Oct. 1906, pp. 815, 906; New York *Press*, Sept. 12, 1906; New York *Commercial*, Sept. 12, 1906.
48. Printed Letter, "To Organized Labor and Friends in the United States," Sept. 24, 1906, *AFL Corr.*
49. W. B. Wilson, "To the Officers and Members of Local Unions of the United Mine Workers, Sept. 12, 1906," *AFL Corr.*
50. "Financial Report of American Federation of Labor Political Campaign of 1906," *AFL Corr.*
51. *American Federationist*, Oct. 1906, p. 883; Stuart Reid to Gompers, Nov. 3, 1906, *AFL Corr.;* Harold Seidman, *op. cit.*, pp. 22–24; Joel Seidman, "Labor in Political Campaigns," *Public Opinion Quarterly*, vol. III, 1939, p. 650; Gompers to John Fenchal, Oct. 12, 1906, *AFL Corr.;* Gompers to John Mitchell, Oct. 6, 1906, *JMP.*
52. Rockland (Maine) *Star*, Aug. 22, 1906.
53. Letter dated Sept. 11, 1906, attached to Frank Morrison to A.F. of L. Executive Council, Oct. 3, 1906, *AFL Corr.*
54. *American Federationist*, May, 1908, pp. 341–53. The article contains a comparative tabulation of the votes cast for Congressmen in the elections of 1904 and 1906.
55. *Ibid.*, p. 341; *World Almanac*, 1906.
56. Letter of Typographia Union #7, Sept. 11, 1906, *AFL Corr.;* Max Hayes, "World of Labor," *International Socialist Review*, vol. VII, July, 1906, p. 56.
57. *Proceedings*, A.F. of L. Convention, 1906, pp. 34–35.
58. *Ibid.*, pp. 183–84.
59. *Ibid.*, pp. 191, 193, 196, 197, 198, 204.
60. *Ibid.*, pp. 185, 187, 192, 193, 203–04.
61. *Ibid.*, p. 204; Lorwin, *op. cit.*, p. 91.
62. *Proceedings*, A.F. of L. Convention, 1906, pp. 34–35; 204; *American Industries*, May 1, 1907, p. 2; Taylor, *op. cit.*, p. 97.
63. Gompers to John Mitchell, Oct. 2, 1907, *AFL Corr.* and *JMP;* Lorwin, *op. cit.*, p. 90.

CHAPTER 13

1. Walter E. Bean, "Boss Ruef, the Union Labor Party and the Graft Prosecution in San Francisco, 1901–1911," *Pacific Historical Review*, Nov. 1948, pp. 452–53.
2. *World's Work*, vol. XIII, April, 1907, pp. 8749–53; "Philadelphia: Corrupt but Content," *McClure's Magazine*,

July, 1904, pp. 162–87; Philadelphia *Public Ledger*, reprinted in *Coast Seamen's Journal*, Jan. 2, 1907.

3. *The Nation*, Nov. 22, 1906, p. 430.

4. *The Leather Workers' Journal*, May, 1907, pp. 550, 583–84.

5. Printed Circular, Oct. 12, 1907, *AFL Corr.*

6. Printed Circular, Oct. 28, 1907, *AFL Corr.*

7. *American Federationist*, July, 1907, pp. 122–24; *American Industries*, Aug. 1, 1908, p. 5; Taylor, *op. cit.*, p. 97; *Proceedings*, N.A.M. Convention, 1908, pp. 292, 297.

8. *Proceedings*, A.F. of L. Convention, 1907, pp. 260–67.

9. Harry W. Laidler, *Boycotts and the Labor Struggle*, New York, 1913, pp. 137–39; *Washington Star*, Dec. 19, 1907; J. C. Kennedy, "Important Labor Injunction in the Bucks' Stove and Range Company Suit," *Journal of Political Economy*, vol. XVI, 1908, p. 98.

10. *American Federationist*, Jan. 1908, p. 98.

11. Gompers to A.F. of L. Executive Council, Jan. 10, 1908, *AFL Corr.*

12. Copy of leaflet in *AFL Corr.*; John Mitchell to Gompers, Feb. 6, 1908, *JMP*.

13. *American Federationist*, Aug. 1908, pp. 614–15.

14. *Ibid.*, March, 1908, p. 180; *Solidarity*, Oct. 15, 1908, p. 12; Loewe *v.* Lawlor, 208 U.S. 274, Feb. 3, 1908.

15. E. E. Witte, *The Government in Labor Disputes*, New York, 1932, pp. 134–35.

16. *American Industries*, March 1, 1908.

17. Gompers to John Mitchell, March 11, 1908, *AFL Corr.* and *JMP*; *American Federationist*, March, 1908, pp. 190–91.

18. John B. Lennon to Gompers, Feb. 27, 1908; Leather Workers' Local 155, Benton, Illinois, to Gompers, Feb. 26, 1908; Gompers to John Mitchell, March 6, 1908, *AFL Corr.*; Dennis J. Keefe to R. M. Easley, Feb. 12, 1908, *NCFA.*

19. Gompers to A.F. of L. Executive Council, March 3, 1908, *AFL Corr.*

20. *American Federationist*, April, 1908, pp. 270–71.

21. *Ibid.*, pp. 261–69; copies of printed "Address to Workers" in *AFL Corr.*

22. Copy of circular attached to letter from Executive Council "To Secretaries of All Central Bodies, April 11, 1908," *AFL Corr.*; *American Federationist*, June, 1908, p. 450; *Proceedings*, A.F. of L. Convention, 1908, p. 32.

23. *Cf.* H.R. 21454, April 30, 1908 and H.R. 21629, May 6, 1908.

24. Gompers to John Mitchell, March 20, 1908, *AFL Corr.*; *American Federationist*, July, 1908, p. 527; *Proceedings*, A.F. of L. Convention, 1908, pp. 33, 527.

25. Circular letters, signed by J. Harvey Lynch, April 1, 25, 1908; Gompers to J. Harvey Lynch, April 14, 1908; J. Harvey Lynch to Gompers, April 21, 1908; J. Luther Langston to Gompers, April 21, 1908, *AFL Corr.*

26. Gompers to A.F. of L. Executive Council, April 15, 1908, *AFL Corr.*

27. J. Harvey Lynch to the Executive Board Members of the State Federation of Kansas, 4/24/1908; Gompers to A.F. of L. Executive Council, May 2, 1908, *AFL Corr.*

28. *Proceedings*, A.F. of L. Convention, 1908, pp. 88–89; Gompers, *Seventy Years of Life and Labor*, vol. II, p. 261; *Republican Campaign Text-Book*, Philadelphia, 1908, p. 464.

29. *American Federationist*, Aug. 1908, p. 464; *Review of Reviews*, July, 1908, p. 161; *Proceedings*, National Association of Manufacturers Convention, 1911, pp. 82–85.

30. *American Federationist*, Aug. 1908, p. 600.

31. *Ibid.*, pp. 596–606; *Proceedings of the Democratic National Convention in Session at Denver*, 1908, p. 192.

32. Gompers to Norman E. Mack, Aug. 27, 28, 1908, *AFL Corr.*

33. Gompers Collection, "Book 2, Index Card #44, Press Statements and Interviews," New York Public Library.

34. *Washington Post*, July 30, 1908; *Washington Times*, Aug. 22, 1908; *New York Tribune*, Oct. 30, Nov. 1, 1908; telegrams dated Oct. 31, 1908 in *AFL Corr.*; Daniel J. Keefe to H. A. Stemburgh, Oct. 19, 1908, copy in *ibid.*

35. Gompers to John Mitchell, July 31, 1908, *AFL Corr.* and *JMP*.

36. Mitchell to Gompers, Aug. 3, 1908, *AFL Corr.* and *JMP*; Mitchell to *UMW Journal*, Oct. 21, 1908, *JMP*.

37. Letters of the different local unions are in *AFL Corr.*

38. Robert Hunter, "The Socialist Party in the Present Campaign," *American Review of Reviews*, vol. XXXVIII, Sept. 1908, p. 299; International Union of the United Brewery Workmen of America to Frank Morrison, May 14, 1908, *AFL Corr.*

39. *What Help Can Any Workingman Expect From Taft or Bryan?* Chicago, 1908, pp. 22–23; Cabinet Makers'

Union, Norfolk, Va., to Gompers, Sept. 12, 1908, *AFL Corr.*

40. *American Federationist,* Sept. 1908, p. 737; William Jennings Bryan to Gompers, Aug. 1, 1908; Gompers to W. J. Bryan, Aug. 6, 1908, *AFL Corr.*

41. Printed Circular, Oct. 12, 1908, copy in *AFL Corr.*

42. New York *Tribune,* Oct. 22, 1908; Copy of Gompers' reply in *AFL Corr.*

43. W. E. McEwen to Frank Morrison, Oct. 27, 1908; Frank Morrison to A.F. of L. Executive Council, Oct. 28, 1908, *AFL Corr.*

44. Letter dated, Sept. 17, 1908; Frank Morrison to A.F. of L. Executive Council, Oct. 3, 1908, *AFL Corr.*

45. Theodore Roosevelt to William Howard Taft, Aug. 24, Oct. 12, 1908; Theodore Roosevelt to John D. Pringle, Oct. 30, 1908; William Howard Taft to Theodore Roosevelt, Aug. 26, 1908, *TRP;* Elting E. Morrison, *The Letters of Theodore Roosevelt,* Cambridge, Mass., 1952, vol. VI, note 1196; Washington *Star,* Oct. 10, 1908.

46. Circulars issued by N.A.M, and signed by James W. Van Cleave, president, copies in *AFL Corr.;* Washington *Evening Star,* Oct. 23, 1908; Washington *News,* Nov. 3, 1908.

47. *American Industries,* June 1, 1909, p. 11; Taylor, *op. cit.,* p. 98; *Financial Report of the A.F. of L. Political Campaign of 1908,* Washington, 1908.

48. Marc Karson, *American Labor Unions and Politics, 1900–1908,* p. 64.

49. *American Federationist,* Dec. 1908, p. 1065; Gompers Collection, Book 1, Index Card #6, "Press Statements and Interviews," New York Public Library.

50. Graham Taylor, "The Industrial Viewpoint," *Charities and the Commons,* vol. XXI, Dec. 1908, pp. 404–08; Robert F. Hoxie, "Gompers and the Labor Vote," *Journal of Political Economy,* vol. XVI, Dec. 1908, pp. 696–99.

51. New York *World,* Nov. 10, 1908.

52. *New York Times,* Nov. 26, 1908; "The Denver Labor Convention," *The Outlook,* vol. XL, Dec. 5, 1908, pp. 754–57.

53. *Proceedings,* A.F. of L. Convention, 1908, pp. 37, 39, 222–23, 234, 243.

54. "Report of the Delegates to the A.F. of L. Convention," *Bakers' Journal,* Dec. 26, 1908.

55. *Machinery News,* vol. I, June, 1909, p. 3.

56. Washington *Herald,* Dec. 24, 1908; *American Federationist,* Feb. 1909, pp. 129, 151.

57. "A Call for Funds for the Defense of the Appeals in the Pending Injunction Proceedings Against the American Federation of Labor, January 18, 1909," copy in *AFL Corr.;* Eugene V. Debs, "The Gompers' Jail Sentence," *Solidarity,* Feb. 15, 1909, pp. 11–12.

58. J. M. Brown to Gompers, Dec. 23, 1908; Gompers to George Perkins, Dec. 23, 1908; Gompers to Morris Brown, Feb. 10, 1909, *AFL Corr. and GLB;* Bernard Mandel, "Samuel Gompers," unpublished *MS.,* pp. 510–16.

59. *American Federationist,* Jan. 1909, pp. 40–46; *Proceedings,* N.A.M. Convention, 1909, p. 256.

60. Taylor, *op. cit.,* pp. 137–38; *Proceedings,* A.F. of L. Convention, 1909, pp. 32–34.

61. *Proceedings,* A.F. of L. Convention, 1909, pp. 32–34, 202, 233.

62. Max Hayes, "World of Labor," *International Socialist Review,* vol. X, Jan. 1910, p. 649; *Proceedings,* A.F. of L. Convention, 1909, pp. 267–69.

63. *American Federationist,* Nov.–Dec. 1909.

CHAPTER 14

1. *The Socialist Trade and Labor Alliance Versus the 'Pure and Simple' Trade Union. Debate: Daniel De Leon Vs. Job Harriman of the Social Democratic Party, at Grand Opera House, New Haven, Conn., Nov. 25, 1900,* p. 23.

2. *Ibid.,* pp. 10–11, 12, 14, 16n.; *Weekly People,* Dec. 17, 1899, April 8, May 18, Dec. 2, 1900, July 19, 1903; *Daily People,* July 2, 1900.

3. *Proceedings of the Tenth National Convention of the Socialist Labor Party, 1900,* New York, 1901, pp. 211–23.

4. Charles W. White, "The Socialist Labor Party, 1890–1903," unpublished Ph.D. thesis, University of Southern California, 1959, p. 285; Foner, *op. cit.,* vol. II, p. 400; *Weekly People,* Nov. 11, 1905.

5. "Trade Union Resolution," Proceedings of Socialist Unity Convention, 1901, typescript in Harper Library, University of Chicago, pp. 529–30.

6. *Ibid.;* Chicago *Socialist,* Feb. 28, 1903.

7. *The People,* July 31, 1898, Feb. 5, 1899, Sept. 8, 1901.

8. *Social-Democratic Herald,* June 1, Sept. 31, Oct. 12, Nov. 16, Dec. 17, 1901; Jan. 4, 1902; Aug. 8, 1903; April 5,

May 6, 1905; *Wilshire's Magazine,* vol. VI, Nov. 1904, pp. 3–4; Ira Kipnis, *op. cit.,* pp. 107–12, 117–21. Deward J. Muzik, "Victor L. Berger, A Biography," unpublished Ph.D. thesis, Northwestern University, 1960, pp. 130–32.

9. Eugene V. Debs in *Social-Democratic Herald,* June 21, 1902; *The Worker,* April 28, 1901; Kipnis, *op. cit.,* pp. 110–13, 164ff.

10. Victor L. Berger, "Party Politics and the Trade Unions," *Social-Democratic Herald,* Dec. 13, 1902; "The Socialist Party and the Trade Unions," *The Worker,* Dec. 14, 1902; "To the Better End," *Appeal to Reason,* Aug. 6, 1904; Kipnis, *op. cit.,* p. 171.

11. *The People,* May 21, 1899, Dec. 2, 1900.

12. *International Socialist Review,* vol. I, July, 1900, p. 51.

13. Victor L. Berger, "Party Politics and the Trade Unions," *Social Democratic Herald,* Dec. 13, 1902.

14. Chicago *Socialist,* Aug. 30, Sept. 20, 1902; *Writings and Speeches of Eugene V. Debs,* New York, 1948, p. 163.

15. William Mailly, "The Anthracite Coal Strike," *International Socialist Review,* vol. III, Aug. 1902, pp. 83–84; Chicago *Socialist,* July 19, 1902.

16. *Social-Democratic Herald,* Oct. 11, Dec. 5, 1902, Jan. 31, 1903; *The Worker,* April 5, 1903; Kipnis, *op. cit.,* p. 140; Muzik, *op. cit ,* pp. 115–17.

17. H. Gaylord Wilshire, *Why American Workingmen Should Be Socialists,* leaflet published by the State Committee Socialist Party of Ohio, Dayton, Ohio, 1904; *Leather Workers' Journal,* Nov. 1900, p. 61; Dec. 1902, pp. 151, 171; Feb. 1903, p. 27, June, 1903, p. 510, Aug. 1904, p. 795.

18. Eugene V. Debs, *Unionism and Socialism, A Plea for Both,* Terre Haute, Indiana, 1904, pp. 23–24; *The Capitalists' Union or Labor Unions: Which?,* Chicago, 1904, pp. 11–12, 15, 27–28; "Resolution of National Committee of the Socialist Party," adopted unanimously, Jan. 30, 1903, *The Worker,* Feb. 8, 1903; Robert Hunter, *Labor in Politics,* pp. 178–79.

19. *International Socialist Review,* vol. III, Jan. 1903, p. 427.

20. *The Socialist Party Official Bulletin,* May, July, 1905.

21. *The Workers' Call,* Dec. 7, 14, 1901; Chicago *Tribune,* Dec. 8, 1901.

22. *The Worker,* Jan. 31, 1904; Chicago *Socialist,* June 30, 1906.

23. Grace Heilman, *op. cit.,* pp. 231–32, 235; *The Worker,* Feb. 8, 1903; Kipnis, *op. cit.,* pp. 146–47.

24. *Social-Democratic Herald,* Dec. 6, 1902; Frederick J. Olson, "The Socialist Party and the Union in Milwaukee, 1900–1910," *Wisconsin Magazine of History,* Winter, 1960–61, pp. 112–14; Victor L. Berger, *Berger's Broadsides,* Milwaukee, 1912, p. 163.

25. *Proceedings,* A.F. of L. Convention, 1903, pp. 72, 116, 217, 218, 253; Max S. Hayes, "The A.F. of L.," *International Socialist Review,* vol. III, Dec. 1902, pp. 371-73; vol. V, Dec. 1904, p. 126; Kipnis, *op. cit.,* p. 149.

26. *International Socialist Review,* vol. III, Jan. 1903, p. 427.

27. *The Socialist Party Official Bulletin,* April, 1907; Kipnis, *op. cit.,* p. 130.

28. *Social-Democratic Herald,* Sept. 14, 1901; Kipnis, *op. cit.,* p. 130.

29. Ray Ginger, *The Bending Cross,* pp. 259–60; Chicago *Socialist,* May 2, 1903. *See also* issue of July 18, 1903.

30. *The Worker,* April 24, 1904; Kipnis, *op. cit.,* pp. 261–62.

31. Max S. Hayes, "American Federation of Labor Convention," *International Socialist Review,* vol. I, Jan. 1901, pp. 419–22.

32. *Proceedings,* A.F. of L. Convention, 1902, pp. 86, 111, 118, 122, 125, 178, 179–84; *American Federationist,* Feb. 1901, p. 45.

33. May Hayes, "The World of Labor," *International Socialist Review,* vol. III, Dec. 1902, pp. 372–73; Victo Berger, "The American Federation of Labor and Socialism," *Social-Democ atic Herald,* Dec. 6, 1902; Berger, "Party Politics and the Trade Unions," *ibid.,* Dec. 13, 1902.

34. *American Federationist,* July, 1899, p. 106.

35. Bernard Mandel, "Samuel Gompers," unpublished *Ms.,* p. 481.

36. *Proceedings,* A.F. of L. Convention, 1900, p. 167.

37. *Proceedings,* A.F. of L. Convention, 1903, pp. 100, 120, 1~6 ~ 7, 131, 132, 137, 138, 139, 143, 147, 151, 152, 188–89, 212; *International Socialist Review,* vol. IV, Jan. 1904, pp. 434–35.

38. Bernard Mandel, "Samuel Gompers," unpublished *MS.,* p. 481.

39. *National Convention of the Socialist Party Held at Chicago, Illinois,* May 1 to 6, 1904, Stenographic Report, pp. 175–203.

40. *Social-Democratic Herald*, Dec. 31, 1904.
41. Max Hayes, "The World of Labor," *International Socialist Review*, vol. V, Dec. 1904, p. 375; Toledo *Times*, May 2, 1904, quoting W. J. Croke, vice-president of the American Flint Glass Workers' Union; *Proceedings*, A.F. of L. Convention, 1904, pp. 198–202, 215–16; *Social-Democratic Herald*, Dec. 31, 1904, Feb. 25, 1905.
42. G. A. Hoehn, "The American Labor Movement," *International Socialist Review*, vol. VI, Feb. 1906, pp. 592–93.
43. Kipnis, *op. cit.*, pp. 122–23, 162–63; Muzik, *op. cit.*, p. 116.
44. Louis Levine, *The Women's Garment Workers*, New York, 1924, p. 108; *Report and Proceedings of the Fifth Annual Convention, International Ladies' Garment Workers' Union*, p. 23; Max Hayes, "Socialism and Trade Unionism," *Solidarity*, vol. I, No. 9, Dec. 15, 1906, p. 17.
45. *The Socialist* (Seattle), April 26, 1903, April 3, 1904; *The Worker*, July 29, 1905; William Z. Foster, *From Bryan to Stalin*, New York, 1937, pp. 42–46.

CHAPTER 15

1. *Miners' Magazine*, Jan. 1901, p. 9.
2. William D. Haywood, *Bill Haywood's Book—The Autobiography of William D. Haywood*, New York, 1929, p. 80; U.S. Commission on Industrial Relations, *Final Report and Testimony*, Washington, D.C., 1915, vol. IV, p. 3855; U.S. Bureau of Mines, Technical Paper #260, p. 9; *Proceedings*, Western Federation of Miners Convention, 1893, p. 4 (hereinafter cited as W.F. of M.); Leon W. Fuller, "Colorado's Revolt Against Capitalism," *Mississippi Valley Historical Review*, vol. XXI, Dec. 1934, pp. 345–46; George Creel, "Colorado: A Grim and a Grimace," *Everybody's*, vol. XXXII, Feb. 1915, p. 214.
3. Morris Friedman, *The Pinkerton Spy*, New York, 1907, p. 64; Benjamin McKie Rastall, "The Labor History of the Cripple Creek District," *Bulletin of the University of Wisconsin*, No. 198, Madison, Wisconsin, 1908, pp. 33, 104–08.
4. Ratsall, *op. cit.*, p. 116; *Proceedings*, W.F. of M. Convention, 1910, p. 16.
5. Colorado Bureau of Labor Statistics, *Biennial Reports*, 1899–1900, p. 127; "A Report on Labor Disturbances in the State of Colorado from 1880 to 1904, Inclusive," *op. cit.*, pp. 52–55, 68; Ray Stannard Baker, "The Reign of Lawlessness: Anarchy and Despotism in Colorado," *McClure's Magazine*, vol. XXIII, May, 1904, pp. 52–53; *Rocky Mountain News*, May 21, 1903.
6. "A Report on Labor Disturbances in the State of Colorado. . . . ," *op. cit.*, pp. 160–63; Perlman and Taft, *op. cit.*, pp. 197–98; Rastall, *op. cit.*, p. 99.
7. Rastall, *op. cit.*, p. 16.
8. "A Report on Labor Disturbances in Colorado. . . . ," *op. cit.*, pp. 181–93; Emma F. Langdon, *The Cripple Creek Strike*, Denver, 1904–05, pp. 133, 140–43; Rastall, *op. cit.*, pp. 99–101.
9. *The Socialist* (Seattle), Nov. 1, 1903.
10. Edmund Philip Willis, "Colorado Industrial Disturbances, 1903–1904," unpublished M.A. thesis, University of Wisconsin, 1955, pp. 115–23.
11. "A Report on Labor Disturbances in Colorado. . . . ," *op. cit.*, pp. 248–52.
12. Haywood, *op. cit.*, pp. 131–35; Perlman and Taft, *op. cit.*, pp. 200–07.
13. *Proceedings*, W.F. of M. Convention, 1908, p. 263; Rastall, *op. cit.*, p. 138; Willis, *op. cit.*, pp. 66–70.
14. "A Report on Labor Disturbances in Colorado. . . . ," *op. cit.*, pp. 151–59, 167–69, 194–206, 287–92, 294.
15. William Hard, "The Western Federation of Miners," *Outlook*, vol. LXXXV, May 19, 1906, p. 127.
16. *Proceedings*, W.F. of M. Convention, 1893, p. 1; *Miners' Magazine*, Dec. 26, 1907, p. 15; Oct. 6, 1910, p. 15; James Maher to Aug. McCraith, Oct. 4, 1896, *AFL Corr.*; Leo Wolman, *Growth of American Trade Unions*, p. 146; Haywood, *op. cit.*, p. 83.
17. *Miners' Magazine*, Dec. 1900, pp. 60–61; Oct. 6, 1910, p. 15; *Proceedings*, W.F. of M. Convention, 1910, pp. 200–03.
18. *Proceedings*, W.F. of M. Convention, 1906, p. 234; 1910, pp. 26–27; *Miners' Magazine*, June 1, 1905, p. 6; Oct. 6, 1910, p. 15; Missouri Bureau of Labor Statistics, *Annual Report*, 1911, p. 745.
19. *Pueblo Courier*, May 18, 199; Peter Paulson, "The Western Federation of Miners," unpublished M.A. thesis, Columbia University, 1951, pp. 60–68, 98.
20. *Proceedings*, W.F. of M. Convention, 1903, pp. 123, 263; Statement issued by W.F. of M., Ouray, Colorado, July 12, 1908, typewritten document attached to Fred Duquette to Gompers, June 23, 1908, *AFL Corr.*

21. *Proceedings,* W.F. of M. Convention, 1904, p. 176; 1906, p. 83.
22. *Proceedings,* W.F. of M. Convention, 1910, pp. 201–03, 356.
23. *Miners' Magazine,* May 25, 1905, pp. 7–8; *Proceedings,* W.F. of M. Convention, 1908, p. 377.
24. *Proceedings,* W.F. of M. Convention, 1906, pp. 270–71; Pueblo *Courier,* May 19, 1899.
25. *Proceedings,* W.F. of M. Convention, 1893, pp. 7–8; 1907, p. 935.
26. *Proceedings,* W.F. of M. Convention, 1893, p. 7; *Miners' Magazine,* June 8, 1905, p. 10.
27. *Proceedings,* W.F. of M. Convention, 1902, p. 9; 1907, p. 203; *Miners' Magazine,* Jan. 1901, p. 16.
28. *Proceedings,* W.F. of M. Convention, 1894, p. 7; Michael Raphael to Gompers, Sept. 2, 1899, *AFL Corr.;* Maria Cahill, *Shorter Hours—A Study of the Movement Since the Civil War,* New York, 1932, pp. 119–24; Montana Bureau of Agriculture, Labor and Industry, *Biennial Report,* 1901–02, pp. 201–03; 1905–06, p. 214; U.S. Bureau of Labor Statistics, *Bulletin #65,* pp. 509–34.
29. *Miners' Magazine,* Jan. 1901, pp. 10, 18; *International Socialist Review,* vol. I, Aug. 1901, p. 141; Nov. 1901, pp. 32–33; *Proceedings,* W.F. of M. Convention, 1902, pp. 94–96.
30. *Proceedings,* W.F. of M. Convention, 1906, pp. 210–45; 1907, p. 421; 1910, p. 310.
31. *American Labor Union Journal,* Dec. 4, 1902; Haywood, *op. cit.,* p. 202; *Proceedings,* W.F. of M. Convention, 1905, p. 101.
32. *Proceedings,* W.F. of M. Convention, 1904, p. 202; *Miners' Magazine,* Jan. 1903, p. 4; June, 1903, p. 54; Aug. 25, 1904, p. 6.
33. U.S. Senate, *Senate Document #122,* 58th Congress, 3d Session, pp. 3, 37–38; *Proceedings,* W.F. of M. Convention, 1904, p. 257.
34. *Miners' Magazine,* July, 1901, p. 19; July 4, 1907, pp. 10–11; *Proceedings,* W.F. of M. Convention, 1906, p. 21.
35. Undated clipping marked 1896 and containing article, entitled, "The Miners' Convention," *AFL Corr.*
36. Edward Boyce to John McBride, Jan. 24, April 1896, *AFL Corr.*
37. Butte *Bystander,* May 15, 1897. I am indebted to Marguerita McDonald, Assistant Librarian of the Historical Society of Montana, for furnishing me with the quotations from Boyce's report to the W.F. of M. convention.
38. Reprinted in "A Statement of the Executive Council of the American Federation of Labor, May, 1897," *AFL Corr.,* and in "Coeur d'Alene Labor Troubles," 56th Congress, 1st Session, *House Report No. 1999.*
39. Chris Evans, W. D. Mahon, R. Cornelius, Max Morris to Gompers, Denver, June 14, 1904; Owen Miller to Frank Morrison, May 30, 1904, reporting conversations with W.F. of M. leaders, *AFL. Corr.*
40. Reprinted in *American Labor Union Journal,* April 14, 1904. (Hereinafter cited as *ALU Journal.*) *See also* "Gompers' Shameful Silence," *The Worker,* May 15, 1904; E. J. Smith to G. W. Perkins, Denver, March 25, 1904, attached to G. W. Perkins to Gompers, Mar. 31, 1904, *AFL Corr.*
41. Jno. B. Lennon to Frank Morrison, July 7, 1904; John Mitchell to Gompers, April 9, 1904, *AFL Corr.*
42. *American Federationist,* Aug. 1904, pp. 671–72.
43. *Miners' Magazine,* Aug., 1904, p. 321; Gompers to A.F. of L. Executive Council, July 20, 1904, containing copy of letter from James Kirwan, Asst. Sec'y Treas. W.F. of M., to E. N. Nockels, Sec'y Chicago Federation of Labor, July 6, 1904, *AFL Corr.*
44. Gompers to A.F. of L. Executive Council, July 20, 1904; Gompers to Chris Evans, July 29, 1904, *AFL Corr.*
45. Bernard Mandel, "Samuel Gompers," unpublished *MS.,* p. 488.
46. *ALU Journal,* April 14, Oct. 1904; *Miners' Magazine,* Oct. 1904, p. 162; *The Worker,* May 15, 1904.

CHAPTER 16

1. *Proceedings,* W.F. of M. Convention, 1906, pp. 15–16.
2. Letter of Gompers, Feb. 10, 1891, *GLB.*
3. Pueblo *Courier,* March 11, 1898.
4. *Ibid.,* May 25, June 3, 1898.
5. *Ibid.;* San Francisco *Voice of Labor,* May 28, 1898.
6. Pueblo *Courier,* June 3, 1898.
7. *The Reveille* (Butte, Montana), Oct. 16, 1899; Daniel McDonald to S. B. Dalton, April 13, 1900, in Daniel De Leon Correspondence, *WSHS.*
8. Michael Raphael to Gompers, Sept. 2, 1899, *AFL Corr.*
9. Harvey Schlamel to Gompers, Oct. 11,

14, 16, Nov. 9, 30, Dec. 1899; leaflet issued by Western Labor Union, Butte, Montana, Feb. 12, 1902, attached to W. D. Mahon to Morrison, Feb. 19, 1902; Gompers to Max Morris, Nov. 1, 1899; Max Morris to Gompers, Nov. 6, 1899; W. G. Armstrong to Frank Morrison, Seattle, Jan. 18, 1900, *AFL Corr.; The Socialist* (Seattle), Jan. 25, Feb. 10, 1900.

10. Leaflet, Butte, Montana, Feb. 12, 1902, attached to W. D. Mahon to Frank Morrison, Feb. 19, 1902; W. D. Mahon to Gompers, May 12, 1902, *AFL Corr.; Miners' Magazine,* Dec. 1901, p. 4; April, 1902, pp. 2, 9, 12.

11. Frank Morrison to F. Stacey Whitney, March 14, 18, 21, 1902; F. Stacey Whitney to Frank Morrison, March 29, 1902, *AFL Corr.*

12. Frank Morrison to A.F. of L. Executive Council, May 2, 1902, *AFL Corr.*

13. Frank Morrison to A.F. of L. Executive Council, June 2, 1902, *AFL Corr.; ALU Journal,* Sept. 3, 1903; *International Socialist Review,* vol. III, Nov. 1902, p. 258.

14. *International Socialist Review,* vol. III, Aug. 1902, pp. 107–08; *ALU Journal,* Dec. 11, 1902.

15. *ALU Journal,* Dec. 11, 1902.

16. Frank Morrison to A.F. of L. Executive Council, June 2, 1902, *AFL Corr.*

17. *Miners' Magazine,* June, 1902, pp. 14–16.

18. "Origins of American Labor Union," *ALU Journal,* Sept. 3, 1903; *Miners' Magazine,* Sept. 1902, p. 27.

19. Frank Morrison to A.F. of L. Executive Council, June 2, 1902, *AFL Corr.*

20. *The Comrade,* vol. I, July, 1902, p. 226.

21. *The Worker,* June 15, Aug. 10, 1902; *International Socialist Review,* vol. III, July, 1902, pp. 46–49; Jan. 1903, p. 410.

22. Eugene V. Debs, "The Western Labor Movement," *International Socialist Review,* vol. III, Nov. 1902, pp. 258–63.

23. *The Worker,* Dec. 21, 1902; *Social Democratic Herald,* Feb. 7, 1903.

24. *Social Democratic Herald,* Feb. 14, 1903; *The Worker,* Feb. 8, May 31, 1903; Kipnis, *op. cit.,* pp. 146–47.

25. Frank Morrison to A.F. of L. Executive Council, June 2, 1902; Gompers to A.F. of L. Executive Council, July 9, 1902; C. E. Hawks to Gompers, Sept. 30, 1902; James M. Lynch to Gompers, April 24, May 21, 1903; A. Furuseth to

Gompers, May 9, 1903; James O'Connell to Gompers, May 13, '03; John B. Lennon to Frank Morrison, Feb. 9, 1903, *AFL Corr.*

26. *ALU Journal,* Dec. 11, 1902, Jan. 29, 1903; *Proceedings,* 1903 Convention, American Labor Union, p. 28.

27. J. D. Pierce to Gompers, Dec. 16, 1902; Gompers to J. D. Pierce, Dec. 22, 1902, *AFL Corr.; ALU Journal,* Nov. 27, 1902, Jan. 29, 1903.

28. *ALU Journal,* Nov. 27, 1902; Feb. 12, 1903.

29. *Official Report of the Proceedings of American Labor Union in its Sixth Annual Convention, Denver, Colorado, May 25-June 13, 1903,* Denver, 1903, pp. 27–28.

30. *ALU Journal,* Dec. 18, 1902, Jan. 29, 1903; *International Socialist Review,* vol. III, Feb. 1903, p. 565.

31. *The Lumber Industry and Its Workers,* Chicago, no date or author, third edition, pp. 61–68; Vernon H. Jensen, *Lumber and Labor,* New York, 1945, pp. 117–19; Charlotte Todes, *Labor and Lumber,* New York, 1931, p. 153.

32. *ALU Journal,* Nov. 27, 1902, May 7, 1903; *Proceedings,* American Labor Union Convention, 1903, pp. 27–28. (Hereinafter cited as A.L.U. Convention.)

33. *Proceedings,* A.L.U. Convention, 1903, pp. 5–7, 21–22, 27–29; *ALU Journal,* Nov. 27, 1902, Feb. 19, 1903.

34. John Mulholland to Gompers, March 27, 28, 1903; to Frank Morrison, Mar. 31, 1903, *AFL Corr.; ALU Journal,* Sept. 3, 1903.

35. *Proceedings,* A.L.U. Convention, 1903, pp. 14–16, 27–28.

36. *Ibid.,* pp. 66–68.

37. *ALU Journal,* Jan. 15, 1903; *Proceedings,* A.L.U. Convention, 1903, pp. 85–86.

38. *Preamble, Constitution and By-Laws of the American Labor Union, Adopted by Referendum,* December, 1903, Chicago, n.d., pamphlet.

39. *ALU Journal,* Sept. 3, 1903.

40. *Ibid.*

41. *Proceedings,* A.L.U. Convention, 1903, p. 68; *ALU Journal,* May 5, 1904; *Voice of Labor,* Jan. 1905; A.L.U. leaflet, "Read and Consider," 1904.

42. *ALU Journal,* Dec. 31, 1903.

43. *Ibid.,* Nov. 5, 1903; Owen Miller to Frank Morrison, July 10, 1904, *AFL Corr.*

44. *ALU Journal,* Dec. 31, 1903; J. C.

Skemp to Frank Morrison, Mar. 16, 1905, *AFL Corr.*

45. Leaflets attached to E. J. Lynch to Gompers, Oct. 4, 8, 12, 1904, *AFL Corr.*

46. E. J. Lynch to Gompers, Oct. 12, Dec. 24, 1904; Gompers to E. J. Lynch, Dec. 30, 1904, *AFL Corr.*

47. *ALU Journal,* April 28, 1904.

48. *Ibid.,* April 23, July 2, 23, 1904.

49. *Ibid.,* April 28, May 19, 1904.

50. Walter Charriere, General President, Shirt, Waist and Laundry Workers' International Union, to Gompers, Dec. 14, 1903; Gompers to Charles E. Nordeck, Sec'y, S.W. & W.I.U., enclosing statement by I.L.G.W.U., Dec. 10, 1903, *AFL Corr.*

51. *ALU Journal,* Aug., Oct. 1904.

52. *Ibid.,* Oct. 1904.

53. Israel Solon to Agnes Nestor, Chicago, Aug. 3, 1904, Agnes Nestor Papers, Chicago Historical Society.

54. *ALU Journal,* Jan. 8, 22, March 5, 19, 1903.

55. *Ibid.,* Dec. 31, 1903.

56. *Proceedings of the National Convention of the Socialist Party,* 1904, pp. 206, 212; *ALU Journal,* May 9, 1904; Kipnis, *op. cit.,* p. 158.

57. *ALU Journal,* April 28, May 12, Oct. Nov. 1904.

58. Chicago *Socialist,* Oct. 31, 1903; *ALU Journal,* Nov. Dec. 1904; *Voice of Labor,* Feb. 1905.

59. *ALU Journal,* Sept. 3, 1903, Oct. 1904; A. G. Lawrence, A.L.U. Organizer in St. Louis in leaflet, dated Dec. 6, 1903, attached to John F. Tobin to Gompers, Dec. 24, 1903, *AFL Corr.*

60. *ALU Journal,* Dec. 28, 1904.

61. *ALU Journal,* July 5, 1904; Frank Morrison to A.F. of L. Executive Council, June 15, 1904, *AFL Corr.*

62. *ALU Journal,* Dec. 18, 1902; pamphlet, Chicago, 1904.

63. Jere L. Sullivan to Frank Morrison, Jan. 28, 1905, *AFL Corr.*

INDEX